Praise for
The GREAT
DISSENTER

"Solidly accessible and thoroughly researched, it makes a persuasive case for Harlan's significance and sometimes reads like a mystery."
—*The New York Times*

"[A] superb biography . . . Canellos writes with fluency, sensitivity and clarity about complex legal arguments. . . . June is the traditional month for major supreme court decisions. One hopes for the moral courage, clarity of thought and practical vision of John Marshall Harlan."
—*The Guardian*

"*The Great Dissenter* is a magnificent biography of the righteous legal trailblazer John Marshall Harlan. Drawing upon a wealth of archival and published sources, deep-diving into the American horror-show of systemic racism, Canellos showcases Harlan as the rare Supreme Court justice fighting for a more equitable economic system and civil rights for all people. Highly recommended!"
—Douglas Brinkley, Katherine Tsanoff Brown Chair in Humanities and Professor of History, Rice University, and *New York Times* bestselling author of *Cronkite* and *American Moonshot*

"What a spectacular achievement! Canellos has single-handedly resurrected the memory of a largely forgotten American hero. Far ahead of his time, Justice Harlan denounced corporate power and passionately defended the rights of labor, immigrants, and African Americans. On the Supreme Court he was a bold and lonely dissenter, but as this book shows, history vindicates him and awards him a place of high honor in the pantheon of American freedom fighters."
—Stephen Kinzer, bestselling author of *The Brothers* and *The True Flag*

"Peter Canellos has vividly brought to life an absolutely fascinating story that I'm embarrassed I didn't know: A man raised in a slave-owning family who became one of the greatest champions of civil rights in the history of the Supreme Court, his lone-dissenter opinions cited decades after his death. John Marshall Harlan needs to be added to our pantheon of American heroes."

—Adam Hochschild, bestselling author of
King Leopold's Ghost and *Bury the Chains*

"John Marshall Harlan is one of the most fascinating and important figures of modern America, and this book does him justice. Carefully researched and rewarding even informed readers with rich insight into Harlan's life and work, *The Great Dissenter* is a must-read, both for students of the Supreme Court and for those concerned about the past, present, and future of racial equality in the United States."

—Gabriel J. Chin, Martin Luther King Jr.
Professor of Law, University of California, Davis

"Peter Canellos is a brilliant researcher and writer who takes us on an enlightening tour through history made new in retrospect. His focus on Justice John Harlan's African American half brother, Robert Harlan, a former slave whose storied career, financial success, and political and race activism were truly remarkable for the day, adds significance and complexity to his storytelling. Both Harlan men taunted and challenged the governmental powers that be, demanding that America tilt toward realizing its best self. This work is a tour de force and every individual interested in the history of our country's political and societal steps, both forward and back, should consider it must-reading."

—Elizabeth Dowling Taylor, *New York Times*
bestselling author of *A Slave in the White
House* and *The Original Black Elite*

"The riveting story of a courageous Kentucky lawyer who initiated significant challenges to anti–civil rights measures during an era of ubiquitous bigotry . . . An impressive work of deep research that moves smoothly along biographical as well as legal lines.

—*Kirkus Reviews* (starred review)

"A meticulously researched and acutely analytical biography . . . Canellos offers a nuanced portrait."

—*Booklist*

The GREAT DISSENTER

The Story of
John Marshall Harlan,
America's Judicial Hero

PETER S. CANELLOS

Simon & Schuster Paperbacks
NEW YORK · LONDON · TORONTO · SYDNEY · NEW DELHI

Simon & Schuster Paperbacks
An Imprint of Simon & Schuster, Inc.
1230 Avenue of the Americas
New York, NY 10020

First Simon & Schuster trade paperback edition June 2022

SIMON & SCHUSTER PAPERBACKS and colophon are registered
trademarks of Simon & Schuster, Inc.

For information about special discounts for bulk purchases, please contact Simon &
Schuster Special Sales at 1-866-506-1949 or business@simonandschuster.com.

The Simon & Schuster Speakers Bureau can bring authors to your live event. For
more information or to book an event, contact the Simon & Schuster Speakers
Bureau at 1-866-248-3049 or visit our website at www.simonspeakers.com.

Interior design by Paul Dippolito

Manufactured in Italy

1   3   5   7   9   10   8   6   4   2

The Library of Congress has cataloged the hardcover edition as follows:

Names: Canellos, Peter S., author.
Title: The great dissenter : the story of John Marshall Harlan,
America's judicial hero / Peter S. Canellos.
Description: New York : Simon & Schuster, [2021] |
Includes bibliographical references and index.
Identifiers: LCCN 2021003146 | ISBN 9781501188206 (hardcover) |
ISBN 9781501188220 (ebook)
Subjects: LCSH: Harlan, John Marshall, 1833–1911. | United States.
Supreme Court—Biography. | Judges—United States.—Biography.
Classification: LCC KF8745.H3 C36 2021 | DDC 347.73/2634 [B]—dc23
LC record available at https://lccn.loc.gov/2021003146

ISBN 978-1-5011-8820-6
ISBN 978-1-5011-8821-3 (pbk)
ISBN 978-1-5011-8822-0 (ebook)

For my mother and father

Contents

Introduction

"A Moral Hero"

There are silences in American history. The suppression of the US Constitution to impose legally enforced segregation, from the 1880s to the 1910s, is one of those hushed intervals. The decades of the Gilded Age were rigorously chronicled as a kind of rolling carnival, with the breathtaking excitement of industrial progress clashing with the grim reality of social regression, all to the tinkling tune of a player piano. But there was, between the notes, an untold story.

In this hidden narrative, millions of American families fulfilled Abraham Lincoln's promise of a new birth of freedom after the Civil War, obtaining skills, starting businesses, exalting in a liberty unimaginable during slavery, and flexing some powerful political muscles. Then, as the narrative turned, those actions were ruthlessly extinguished, not all at once but through a slow, menacing starvation. The ingredients for success—education, access to public accommodations, voting rights, and, ultimately, money—were gradually withdrawn, each deprivation, in turn, receiving the legal imprimatur of the United States Supreme Court. Outside the walls of segregation, there was no recognition of their struggles, their accomplishments, or the tragedy of their lost hopes. There was only silence.

Among powerful white officials, one person's voice rang out. He reminded the nation that the post–Civil War amendments to the Constitution promised equal protection under the law. He advocated

eloquently for Black rights, along with the health and safety of immigrant industrial workers and the rights of people in places such
as Puerto Rico, Hawaii, and the Philippines, which were ruled by the
United States in a time of imperialism.

One can see him now: John Marshall Harlan, a proud, portly,
good-humored gentleman, a father of six, adorned scrupulously in
the pressed black suit and robe of a justice of the US Supreme Court,
even if within his cheek he balances a wad of tobacco and beneath
his velvet chair rests a brass spittoon. No rebellious outsider was
he: a lifelong leader in his Presbyterian church, an arch-believer in
the American system, a Civil War veteran, and even a onetime slave
owner in his native Kentucky. Yet there was within him a striking
difference with the dozens of justices with whom he served over his
thirty-four years on the court from 1877 to 1911. He saw things that
they did not. He acted on impulses that they didn't share.

Three Supreme Court rulings during his long tenure are usually
accorded places among the very worst in court history—decisions
that, after a century or more, are measured both by their flawed reasoning and the staggering numbers of people who suffered with their
consequences. Even today they are remembered in legal shorthand:
Plessy. Lochner. The Civil Rights Cases. Harlan dissented in all three.
In two of them, he was the only justice to disagree with the majority. Before Harlan, dissenting opinions in Supreme Court cases were
few and far between—strange and often unnoticed footnotes. Harlan turned the act of dissenting into something more significant: an
appeal to the next generation of jurists. He spent thousands of hours
holed up under gas lamps creating doctrines that would find their
true light in the electric future. They were beacons to escape from the
maze of tainted opinions laid down by the court's majority.

When, in 1947, a conservative Supreme Court brushed aside a
murder defendant's claim that a California prosecutor had violated
his privilege against self-incrimination, forcing him to testify against
himself, the court's majority breezily noted that such a privilege did
not apply to state courts, despite the Fourteenth Amendment's promise of "due process" of law. One justice pointed out that since the in-

ception of the Fourteenth Amendment—roughly seventy years—"the scope of that amendment was passed upon by forty-three judges. Of all those judges, only one, who may be respectfully called an eccentric exception, ever indicated" that the amendment extended the Bill of Rights to state courts and governments.

Within another twenty years, the court's position would change. The "eccentric" exception would become something like the rule. The one judge, Harlan, would be seen as more right in his interpretation of the law than his forty-two colleagues had been. It would become the greatest expansion of constitutional liberty since the ratification of the Fourteenth Amendment itself.

Harlan's prescience—his ability to look over the horizon and envision the stresses on the superstructure of American life a hundred years in the future—was extraordinary. It reached its greatest altitude in cases involving the men and women freed from slavery. When almost all of white society determined, in the face of bitter disputes over Reconstruction measures, that reconciliation between North and South was more important than enforcing constitutional rights for Black Americans, the Supreme Court was almost entirely complicit in the deal. Harlan was not. In case after case, he laid out a framework for what would become the twentieth-century civil rights movement. Among jurists, he alone expressed the view that when rights are denied to one group, it endangers the protections of all. He alone believed that sowing "the seeds of race hate" in the law would cripple the nation for generations to come.

"The white race deems itself to be the dominant race in this country," he wrote in opposing the court's decision in the seminal 1896 case of *Plessy v. Ferguson*, ". . . but in the view of the Constitution, in the eye of the law, there is in this country no superior, dominant, ruling class of citizens. There is no caste here. Our Constitution is color blind and neither knows nor tolerates classes among citizens. In respect of civil rights, all citizens are equal before the law. The humblest is the peer of the most powerful. The law regards man as man and takes no account of his surroundings or his color when his civil rights as guaranteed by the supreme law of the land are involved. . . .

"Sixty million of whites are in no danger from the presence here of 8 million blacks. The destinies of the two races in this country are indissolubly linked together, and the interests of both require that the common government of all shall not permit the seeds of race hate to be planted under the sanction of the law. What can more certainly arouse race hate, what more certainly create and perpetuate a feeling of distrust between these races than state enactments, which, in fact, proceed on the ground that Black citizens are so inferior and degraded that they cannot be allowed to sit in public coaches occupied by white citizens? That, as all will admit, is the real meaning of such legislation as was enacted in Louisiana."

Thus, Harlan ripped away the fig leaf of "separate but equal," the doctrine embraced by all his brethren that would be the law of the land for sixty years, and exposed its racist underpinnings. At the time, though, neither the majority opinion nor Harlan's dissent aroused much attention in the white community. Like parties to a conspiracy open and obvious to all, most white Americans understood that the outcome of *Plessy v. Ferguson* was foreordained. By 1896, most Black Americans had come to this sad realization as well, including those among the elites who, just a few decades earlier, were eager to embrace the American system and strive to win the respect of the white majority.

One of those early Black leaders was, to all appearances, John Marshall Harlan's brother. Robert Harlan grew up alongside John Marshall Harlan and went on to an extraordinary career. His stunning success as a horse-racing impresario, gold rush entrepreneur, financier of Black-owned businesses, world traveler, state representative, and leading Black citizen in Ohio made an obvious impression on the Supreme Court justice. Robert was also the justice's secret defender, helping him wiggle out of a politically embarrassing situation that threatened to derail his career before he joined the court, and then using his own contacts to push for John's appointment. Robert liked to joke that he received a half day of schooling—which he did, before the teacher in Danville, Kentucky, informed the man who raised him, John's father, that no Black children could be taught at the school, no matter how light their skin. Robert was thereafter taught at home.

Throughout his life, Robert Harlan's parentage would be a matter of hushed discussion, except in the Black press and a few racing publications, where he was sometimes openly noted to have been the son of John's father, James Harlan, and an enslaved woman. In the world to which he was born, the presence of a light-skinned Black child on a farm with slaves wouldn't have been unusual, and some would have speculated that he was John Marshall Harlan's brother. What was unusual was that Robert was raised that way, as a member of the family. James Harlan brought up Robert to take advantage of every opportunity accorded him, and as his opportunities expanded, so too did the scope of success.

The boldness of Robert's exploits—from crossing the ocean to bring Kentucky-style horse racing to the jockey clubs of England, to making an unannounced visit to President Ulysses Grant at his seaside retreat, to debating French politics with the erudite Massachusetts senator Charles Sumner (an exchange that one newspaper report suggested was conducted in French)—made a mockery of the notions of racial inferiority that so often laced the opinions of the Supreme Court majority. Even in the face of stiff resistance by less affluent Black people, who saw the shifting winds of their race's fortunes far earlier than he did, Robert urged them to keep their faith in American institutions. He fought for legislation to allow Black people access to inns and restaurants and public transportation, while founding schools and leading Ohio's first Black state militia unit, arguing that men who are newly free ought to be first in line to defend American freedoms.

Celebrating the passage of the Fifteenth Amendment to the Constitution in 1870, which granted Black people the right to vote, Robert spoke before an audience of Black and white people at a Cincinnati jubilee and offered his prophecy, his creed: "Knowledge is power; and those who know the most, and not those who have the most, will govern this country. Let us combine and associate and organize for this end. In the pulpit, in the press, in the street, everywhere let our theme be education, education; until there cannot be found anywhere a child of us that is not at the school. With this endeavor carried out, who can measure the progress that may be made in a single generation of freedom by a poor, despised, and enslaved race? Then, indeed, would vanish prejudice; then would the noble martyrs of our cause not have died in vain, and human slavery would evermore be an impossibility."

It was an impressive vision, dazzling in its idealism, but one that ran afoul of the seeming immutability of racism. For as John fought to preserve the gains of the Reconstruction era in the Supreme Court, Robert and his family provided a real-life illustration of how those changes in the law choked off hope and ambition.

Under segregation, the many triumphs of Robert's life would fade into the vast silence enforced by the walls placed around those of his race. In 1917 his son Robert James Harlan—raised and educated as a tuxedoed prince of the Black aristocracy—saw his federal salary as a clerk in the Register of the Treasury chopped by the administration of Woodrow Wilson as part of an effort to cleanse the federal workforce of Black people.

"You can understand how hurtful it is to me to be reduced when on every side, salaries are being increased," he wrote to his friend and high school classmate William Howard Taft, the former president. "And having a clean record, and a high rating for efficiency, makes it more humiliating . . . because of a moral lapse made by my grandfather—why should I pay a vicarious atonement?"

As a white man, John Marshall Harlan and his heirs were untouched by discrimination. His reputation was not. As a justice of the Supreme Court, his life's work in revealing what he considered the almost religious providence of the Constitution was largely ignored by white jurists and legal historians as long as his opinions were shrouded in dissent. In the Black community, however, he was "a moral hero," in the words of Frederick Douglass.

"There is no man in this country to whom the colored race is more indebted," the *Washington Bee*, the dominant Black newspaper in the nation's capital, declared when Harlan died in 1911. Bells tolled in Black churches across the country, and thousands of mourners gathered for services, with no expectation that a single white person would attend, so total was the separation between Black and white America. In the years to come, books would be written about the Supreme Court of Harlan's era that didn't even mention the race cases that sparked many of his dissents.

Then, slowly but inexorably, Harlan began to be regarded not only as prescient but right on the law—and not only on racial matters. First came the Sixteenth Amendment, ratified in 1913 codifying Harlan's view, expressed in a furious dissent, that real estate rents and stock dividends, the prime source of wealth for the richest Americans, should be subject to the federal income tax. Then a New Deal-era Supreme Court reversed a thirty-year precedent, angrily refuted by Harlan, that blocked health and safety laws designed to protect children and other exploited workers in factory sweatshops.

Finally, a young Black lawyer named Thurgood Marshall began traveling the back roads of the South, trying to persuade victims of segregation to step forward as plaintiffs in a fresh appeal for equal rights—a step that could jeopardize their homes and their lives, making them targets of the Ku Klux Klan. He was armed only with Harlan's dissenting opinion in *Plessy v. Ferguson*—Marshall's bible, as his close colleague Constance Baker Motley, a pioneering African American lawyer and judge in her own right, put it later. The fact that even a single jurist in the half century of segregation had stood apart from the others, declaring that the Constitution meant what it said about equal protection under the law, was a powerful incentive, Motley explained. The difference between one and none was that between hope and no hope, light and darkness. It suggested that, against all evidence to the contrary, some white people were able to look beyond the prejudices of the moment.

Few Americans outside the legal academy know the name of John Marshall Harlan. All too often, even his admirers cast him as an oddity, a man out of his time, the enigmatic prophet who foresaw the liberal Constitution to come. But Harlan didn't merely predict the rights revolution of the twentieth century—the system of equal protection and due process of the laws that Americans rely upon today—he helped to inspire it. His philosophy, vision, and writings were the seeds from which the modern Constitution grew.

While the source of his wisdom wasn't visible to his contemporaries, it wasn't all that mysterious, either. Born in the heartland and raised on a steady diet of writings by the Founding Fathers, Harlan was the perfect embodiment of the American idea. As his border state was torn asunder by slavery, he found few answers in the documents he revered or the political traditions he admired; like Lincoln, he came to see slavery as more than just the moral wrong that abolitionists preached about, but rather a direct challenge to the American freedom and ideals he cherished. This he believed all the more fiercely for his own injured pride, the way his own actions were tarnished by slavery. He was late to the abolitionist cause, a Unionist who was slow to regard slavery as anything other than a conflict to be avoided.

Unlike most of his contemporaries, however, Harlan didn't lower his guard after the failure of Reconstruction. While most Americans saw the compromise that North and South eventually submitted to—peace in exchange for segregation and the systematic repression of Black lives—as the only hope for restoring the nation, he saw it as a recurrence of the old cancer. Inequality under the law was an existential threat that would always be present, whether through the "Jim Crow" laws that subverted Black people in the South or the callous ambitions of American imperialism, which served to repress native Hawaiians, Filipinos, Cubans, and Puerto Ricans. The bulwark against it was the Reconstruction-era amendments to the Constitution, and the powers they extended to the federal government to crack down on state-supported injustices.

Harlan was more than just a legal theorist. He was a man who suffered through war and peace, victory and defeat, shame and redemption. He acted on what he saw before him. He understood the power of ideas, but also the power of individuals. He learned firsthand, from his family, that those born into slavery could drink just as deeply of freedom as white men could. If the origins of today's system of justice are visible in Harlan's dissents, so too are they visible in his life. The story of the Constitution isn't set in a courtroom. It's an American saga, but also a family saga—many family sagas. That of John and Robert Harlan is one of them. Out of the Salt River of Kentucky flowed a tale that, silent in its time, now resounds in the laws of the land.

Prologue

"One Man with God Is a Majority."

New York's Grand Opera-house was in the midst of a triumphant four-week run of performances by Edwin Booth, the greatest Hamlet of his generation, that Saturday in 1879 when twenty-six-year-old William R. Davis Jr. and his companion approached the huge doors of the heavily marbled theater. An enormous palace-like creation on Twenty-Third Street and Eighth Avenue, the Grand Opera-house was a symbol of New York's post–Civil War economic boom. It had been built, amid much jittery expectation, just three years after the fighting ceased, to present world-class entertainment to an affluent audience. Davis, who had been born enslaved in South Carolina, was no less a symbol of the changes wrought by the Civil War.[1]

The bright-eyed young man and the light-skinned woman who accompanied him strode purposefully toward the theater and were met by the doorkeeper, Samuel Singleton.

"These tickets are no good," he said, instructing them to get a refund at the box office.

They did, and then persuaded a young white customer to go to the window and buy them two other seats. This time Davis's lighter-skinned guest strode into the theater several steps in front of him, encountering no obstacles, while he was told his ticket was invalid. Protesting that he needed to reach his partner, Davis was held back by ushers. Police rushed to the scene and told him he could not enter because he was Black.[2]

Davis wasn't shocked by this turn of events. He may even have expected it. An agent of the *Progressive American*, a plucky Brooklyn-based weekly newspaper edited by the aptly named John J. Freeman, Davis and his boss had made it their mission to expose racial double standards. The *Progressive American* fought aggressively for New York's Black community, taking on such causes as integration of the city's public schools.[3] In fact, four years earlier, Davis had been turned away from another of New York's leading arts venues, Booth's Theatre, on account of his race. Booth's had been owned by the very same Edwin Booth who was preparing to perform at the Grand Opera-house that Saturday. Davis's attempt to make a federal case of that earlier incident had fizzled, and many New Yorkers couldn't help but wonder if, as he approached the doorkeeper at the Grand Opera that Saturday, he was secretly aiming to get kicked out again.[4]

The fact that both of his challenges to the racial prejudices of the city's theaters occurred at performances by Edwin Booth—whose younger brother, actor John Wilkes Booth, had assassinated Abraham Lincoln—only added to the conjecture.

Davis's ejection from the Grand Opera caused an immediate dilemma for New York authorities because of a federal law passed four years earlier. After years of delay, the Republican-led Congress had finally mustered the votes in a lame-duck session to pass a sweeping civil rights law that made it a crime to bar people from stores, inns, or transportation on account of their race. It further required federal officials to step in to enforce the law if the state refused to do so.[5]

The law was Congress's most far-reaching attempt to put teeth into the postwar amendments to the Constitution, which the Southern states had ratified as conditions of their reentry into the Union. The Thirteenth Amendment, ratified in 1865, banned slavery and all "involuntary servitude." The Fourteenth Amendment, ratified in 1868, barred states from violating equal protection and due process under the law, or from depriving citizens of the "privileges and immunities" of their status; it also gave the federal government the power to pass laws to enforce the rights granted under the amendment. The Civil Rights Act of 1875 was Congress's most extensive use of that power.[6]

The act was the crowning achievement of a generation of Black politicians and their allies, though it came at a moment when whites were fast abandoning the cause of freed men and women. For all its political significance, its actual requirements were a matter of dispute. To millions of Black people, it represented access to the bare rudiments of economic life: stores, inns, restaurants, trains, and streetcars. To millions of whites in the South and the North, it represented the unacceptable and long-dreaded "social equality" between Black and white people that many politicians had promised would never occur.

Robert Harlan, the leading Black Republican in Ohio, the most politically important of all the states for its role in both producing and choosing presidents, had been one of the leaders crusading for the act. For years before the passage of the civil rights law, he goaded the white leadership of his party to back it, even traveling to Long Branch, New Jersey, unannounced, to speak to President Ulysses S. Grant in person at his seaside retreat. But he had every reason to fear it might never happen.[7]

Light skinned and immaculately attired, Robert Harlan was an emblem of the "mulatto," or mixed-race, aristocracy that came to power in the Black community after the war. Though every inch a man of action—staging horse races in frontier towns, betting on cockfights in Cuba with the legendary Mexican general Antonio López de Santa Anna—he affected the look and manner of a Victorian gentleman of high order. It was no more than what many white grandees did: the men who bragged about their log cabin upbringings while smoothing their silk cravats. But in a member of the Black aristocracy, the same affectations provoked a different reaction. The *Cincinnati Enquirer*, a Democratic paper unfriendly to Harlan's politics, described him in

1870 with a mixture of ridicule and grudging admiration: "the noble and majestic Robert Harlan, the Colonel of the Black Battalion and the Moses of a Despised Race."[8]

Harlan's gentlemanly bearing, along with his gambler's air of opportunism, were cast in a different light when, in August 1873, a political rival named Peter Clark called a statewide convention of Black people to protest the lack of racial progress under Republican leadership. A surprisingly large crowd answered Clark's call, filling the pillared city hall and courthouse in the former state capital of Chillicothe, Ohio.

"I have no doubt that the office seeker among colored men will be like white office seekers, actuated by a selfish motive, mainly," Clark, who had been born free into a mixed-race family and later became a pioneering Black educator, intoned, in a veiled reference to Harlan and his ilk. "But to the mass of us, who can never be officeholders, the value of the thing is found in the recognition of our equal citizenship. It is the assurance that the last stronghold of slavery has failed. It is the guarantee of future peace and unmolested liberty." Clark was talking about the long-hoped-for civil rights bill, which had yet to materialize eight years after the end of the war. He accused the Black aristocracy of accepting spoils from "a party which favors us as a class only in proportion as it is driven by its own necessities."[9]

Hearing of Clark's attacks, Harlan hustled the ninety miles from Cincinnati and made a dramatic appearance on the convention floor. Dressed in his usual sartorial splendor, he didn't try to answer Clark's accusation of self-interest; instead, he preached fidelity to the character of President Grant, the former Union commander who was still sainted in the Black community. Grant, he insisted, would deliver on the promised civil rights bill.

"We will hopefully and confidently await the assembling and action of the government in the forthcoming session of Congress for the realization of our just expectations," Harlan explained, soothing the crowd.

The patience proved to be justified—but barely so. The Civil Rights Act did indeed pass in the next Congress, but it took a bizarre series of coincidences to make it happen.

Senator Charles Sumner, the Massachusetts abolitionist who, in

1856, had paid for his antislavery stance with a vicious beating at the hands of a South Carolina congressman, died in March 1874 at the age of sixty-three. For the last four years of his life, Sumner had focused his exertions on the passage of the Civil Rights Act, only to be thwarted in every attempt. At a joint House-Senate memorial service, eulogists spoke so movingly of Sumner's commitment to equal rights that, to the surprise of many, his grieving Senate colleagues approved the bill as a final tribute. Meanwhile, in the House, Republicans suffered a staggering defeat at the polls in 1874, going from a 199-to-89 majority to a 183-to-106 deficit—losing almost half their seats. The results proved that the country was turning firmly against hardline Reconstruction policies toward the South, but the Republicans' rejection was so sweeping it removed any incentive to hold back. With literally nothing to lose, the outgoing majority approved the Civil Rights Act during the lame-duck session in early 1875. President Grant honored his promise to sign it but was so fearful of a backlash that he declined to stage a public signing ceremony.[10]

Relieved by the eleventh-hour fulfillment of his party's promise to Black Americans, Robert Harlan wrote a letter of thanks to the congressman who did the most to get the bill through, Benjamin Butler, a former Union general who was so hated in the South for his punitive occupation of New Orleans that he carried the nickname "the Beast."

"Dear Sir," Robert began. "Allow me in the name of the colored people of Cincinnati and of the whole country to thank you for your noble effort in pushing the Civil Rights Bill through Congress." Robert then offered a humble question, asking if Butler "would be kind enough to inform me if colored men are entitled to the privileges of saloons and barber shops under its provinces."[11]

The Beast wasn't so gracious in response. Butler sent a copy of his letter to Harlan to the *New York Daily Herald* and had it republished around the country. After mocking Robert for seeking equal access to sinful drinking establishments, to which, in Butler's opinion, neither Black nor white people should aspire, he turned to the question of barber shops.

"The trade of a barber is like any other trade, to be carried on by the man who is engaged in it at his own will and pleasure, and the civil rights bill has nothing to do, and was intended to have nothing to do, with its exercise," wrote Butler.

So, it wasn't so clear, in the end, what equal access to public accommodations would mean in real terms, on the ground, where many white waiters and innkeepers and ticket takers had no intention of serving freed men and women.[12]

Whatever his goal in making his letter public, Butler's move served to complicate attempts by well-meaning public officials to enforce the act. Just months after its enactment in 1875, prosecutors tried to persuade a federal grand jury to indict the man who refused to sell William R. Davis Jr. tickets to Booth's Theatre, in the Black journalist's initial attempt to test the law. But defense attorneys pointed to Butler's letter to Robert Harlan to argue that the law wasn't meant to give Black people equal access to theaters. The grand jury declined to issue the indictment.[13]

Four years later, when Davis was blocked from entering the Grand Opera-house, he finally found success: a grand jury indicted Samuel Singleton, the man who forcibly denied him entrance to the theater, for violating the Civil Rights Act of 1875.

Nonetheless, the questions about the proper scope of the act were anything but resolved. Cases were piling up around the country. Black Americans demanded justice and, even more importantly, access to public accommodations, while the white defendants claimed they wanted nothing more than to run their businesses as they saw fit.

In San Francisco, a Black man named George M. Tyler was forcibly prevented from taking the seat he'd purchased in the orchestra section of Maguire's New Theatre, after allegedly being told by the ticket taker, "We don't admit no Negroes."[14]

In Jefferson City, Missouri, delegates to the state Republican convention crowded into Nichols House, one of the most comfortable inns in the city. When a Black Delegate, W. H. R. Agee, applied for a bed, the proprietor, Samuel Nichols, refused to accommodate him because, he argued, white guests would leave rather than be served alongside him.[15]

In Grand·Junction, Tennessee, a well-to-do formerly enslaved woman named Sallie Robinson purchased two first-class tickets for a train to Lynchburg, Virginia. When she and her light-skinned, blue-eyed nephew tried to enter the car designated for "ladies and first-class passengers," they were refused, and a conductor forcibly blocked her way, pushing her and calling her "girl." He claimed later that he thought the finely dressed, dark-skinned woman was a prostitute traveling with a younger john. Robinson insisted she was denied entry because of her race.[16]

In Hiawatha, Kansas, on what was still the western frontier, a formerly enslaved man named Bird Gee was ejected from the City Hotel after a confrontation with a white boarder who claimed that Gee had taken his chair at the dinner table. Gee, a forceful figure who had served in the Union army, was accustomed to asserting his rights. He had been one of the few Black veterans to apply for a pension, taking his case all the way to the US Supreme Court. When he lost, he vowed to abandon white society altogether and live in Indian territory. He made good on his promise and ended up earning a fortune as a land speculator in Oklahoma.[17]

All these cases raised a common question about the Civil Rights Act of 1875—and it wasn't as simple as the one posed by Robert Harlan to Benjamin Butler. Rather, the lawyers defending the hotel clerks and railroad conductors and theater ushers claimed that the law was unconstitutional because the Fourteenth Amendment should restrict the actions only of state governments, not individuals. All agreed that a state could not explicitly ban Black people from public accommodations. But the owners and operators of private businesses, the lawyers insisted, should be free to make their own decisions about whom to serve.

The question wasn't easily answered by legal precedent, since the postwar amendments were meant to change the Constitution, to protect the rights of the freed men and women. There was only one body that could decide whether the changes were significant enough to give the federal government the power to enforce civil rights: the Supreme Court.

The Supreme Court of the early 1880s was an unusual group of justices compared to those who came before and after. They had more in common with one another than their fondness for facial hair, the flowing beards and muttonchop whiskers that covered their faces like masks of virtue. For one thing, the justices represented only a little more than half the country. Eight of the nine were northerners or westerners, along with just one nominal southerner, from the border state of Kentucky; the rebellion, followed by twenty-three years of Republican control, had kept any Confederates off the court. The justices were united in having supported the union, creating a presumption of concern for the freed men and women. They were also, however, far more business friendly than many other courts before and since. Almost all the justices had made their fortunes in private law, representing the corporate interests that were starting to put the gilt into the Gilded Age.

Some followed the standard nineteenth-century path of rags to riches; others were born rich but became much richer. Joseph Philo Bradley came from poor wheat farmers in upstate Catskill, New York, hauling homemade charcoal to market, but amassed a fortune as counsel for the Camden & Amboy Railroad monopoly.[18] Stephen Field came from an intellectually ambitious family in western Massachusetts, but he, too, earned his fortune handling business transactions, representing gold-rush speculators in California.[19] Another justice, Samuel Blatchford, was even richer, having founded what would become New York's most powerful law firm. His appointment was a reward from President Chester Arthur, his fellow New Yorker.[20]

The one southerner stood apart. He was John Marshall Harlan, whose background differed in more than geography. Though he came from one of his state's best-known families, he was far less wealthy than his judicial colleagues. Named for his father's hero the great Chief Justice John Marshall, the longest-serving chief justice in

US history, from 1801 to 1835, Harlan was raised from birth to take a seat on the Supreme Court. His conception of justice wasn't sullied by money or corporate interests, but his background was hardly pristine. As a very young man, he had owned slaves and supported slavery right up through the Civil War. He was also on the record as having initially opposed the postwar amendments to the Constitution, maintaining that his state of Kentucky—which had painfully resisted the Confederacy—should be rewarded by getting to make its own decision on whether to free its slaves based on a popular vote.[21]

All these differences made Harlan a figure of suspicion among northern Republicans when he was nominated for the court in 1877, as a kind of human olive branch to the South extended by President Rutherford Hayes. Amid the tense negotiations over the disputed presidential election of 1876, in which competing fraud claims led three southern states to send dueling teams of electors in Washington, Hayes tried to soothe the fury of the Democratic South by promising to put a southerner on the court. Harlan, a Union loyalist and Republican convert from Kentucky, was as close as Hayes could come to finding a southerner who was at least marginally acceptable to northern Republicans. Still, many Republican senators were skeptical that Harlan would ever be able to transcend his slave-owning past and embrace the spirit of the postwar amendments.

"As sure as you and I live, we will both see the hour when he will be the sycophantic friend and supplicant tool of the Democratic Party," wrote one Republican loyalist to the chairman of the Senate Judiciary Committee after Harlan's nomination. "He was that when he thought it was in his interest to be so. He will be so again when he believes his interests require it."[22]

Not everyone doubted Harlan's conversion to Republicanism. Abraham Lincoln's second attorney general, James Speed, a fellow Kentuckian, marveled at how forcefully the former slave owner had turned on the institution. Speed telegraphed the Judiciary Committee that Harlan had "sloughed off his old pro-slavery skin and has since then been an earnest, open, and able advocate of what he had thought wrong or inexpedient." Even in the prewar days, when the very young John Harlan had backed compromises on slavery, Speed wrote, "the idea that ruled his course was the integrity of the country. For that he was ready to sacrifice everything."[23]

Five years after his confirmation, it still wasn't clear which John Harlan had arrived on the bench: the renowned backer of compromises or the man who had thoroughly committed himself to equal protection and due process of the law.

At forty-nine, still the youngest member of the Supreme Court, he had yet to reach a defining moment. Affable and eager to be liked, Harlan often deferred to his more senior brethren. Though he lacked the money to meet the social obligations of his position in a grand style, he and his wife, Malvina, eagerly followed Washington protocol, delighting in the myriad entertainments available to a couple of their station. They had no desire to offend the Washington crowd.[24]

But there was something about the upcoming civil rights cases on the court's docket that struck a different chord with him than with his colleagues—and, really, almost every other white official in the nation's capital. He had made a unique journey from Kentucky to Washington. Unlike all but two of his older colleagues, Harlan had served in the Union army, seeing war firsthand. He'd also experienced something that other Union veterans on the court hadn't: he'd seen his state shattered like an eggshell by slavery, the cracks running through the living rooms of families whose sons chose different sides. Officers from Massachusetts or New York had headed off to war in plumed uniforms to the sounds of marching bands and a rainbow of confetti; young John Harlan had faced the unforgiving enmity of former friends, while taking up arms against his neighbors. In Frankfort, Kentucky, he ordered the shelling of his own neighborhood to root out insurgents. His horror wasn't just war itself, but division: the way he had seen the politics and social fabric of Kentucky shredded over slavery for years even before the fighting commenced.

There were other, more intensely personal reasons why he was prepared to approach these cases with more than the usual amount of diligence. Few in the white community either knew or paid much attention to the fact that the new justice had grown up in the same home as Robert Harlan, watching the formerly enslaved man, who was often treated more like a brother, rise to prominence by dint of his extraordinary talents. And just a few months before the court had convened, John had experienced what he considered the most shattering experience of a life full of upheavals: the death, by typhoid fever, of his beloved eldest daughter, Edith, the joyful heart and guiding light of his family. Of all his six children, the twenty-three-year-old Edith had especially bonded with Washington, DC, helping her mother with her social engagements while volunteering to teach the children of freed men and women in a local industrial school. In his moment of anguish, John wrote to his son James, then a student at Princeton University: "Wherever I go & whatever I may be doing, her presence will be recognized in its influence upon me."[25]

Now Harlan had a unique opportunity to pour all that he had learned into his work on the court. The decisions that he and the other justices made would establish the legal framework for postwar America and the nation's path to civic peace and prosperity. But it wasn't yet clear which path that would be.

To increasingly large numbers of Americans, having lived through the painful and at times violent occupation of the South, the road to peace was clear: reconciliation, allowing for a fair measure of autonomy for the states of the defeated Confederacy, whose views, especially on race, were unlikely to change.

The Civil Rights Act of 1875 remained an irritating itch for white business owners in both the South and the North. By the time that five individual cases—including William R. Davis Jr.'s expulsion from New York's Grand Opera, Bird Gee's rejection by the frontier hotel, and Sallie Robinson's refused entry to the ladies' car on the train—were bound up into one challenge to the constitutionality of the Civil Rights Act, it was 1883. In the eight years since the act had passed, federal troops had been withdrawn from the South, where they had protected Black people, and former Confederates were back on the voting rolls. As a result, almost all Black people elected to political office had been swept from power, and the shift from Republican to Democratic governments left the freed men and women effectively shut out from vast numbers of patronage jobs. Racial violence, which had been rampant in Louisiana, Mississippi, Alabama, and other pockets of the Deep South even before the removal of troops, had become a form of systemic oppression. Between 1875 and 1883, nineteen Black men were lynched in Kentucky alone, part of an escalating epidemic. Local authorities looked the other way. The *Chicago Tribune*, a bastion of northern Republicanism, became alarmed enough that it began running a national tally of lynchings in 1882. It recorded forty-eight such murders of Black people across the United States that year and fifty-five more in 1883.[26]

The Supreme Court, meanwhile, was struggling to come to grips with the changes to the Constitution. There could be little doubt that the three new amendments were meant to elevate the freed men and women to full citizenship, but what exactly constituted the rights of a US citizen was unclear. In giving the federal government the power to pass legislation to enforce the Fourteenth Amendment, the framers intended to reorder the relationship between the nation and the states, giving the national government more clout. But how far did that power go? Did Congress have the right to insist that businesses serve all citizens?

The court's first decisions on the force of the new amendments sent mixed signals. When an all-white jury in West Virginia convicted a man of mixed race named Taylor Strauder of murdering his wife, he appealed the decision on the grounds that the state had banned Black people from the jury pool. The Supreme Court said it was wrong to do so. But the presumptions in the opinion by Justice William Strong—who described how slavery had left the Black race "abject and ignorant," similar to "mere children," and "unfitted to command the respect of those who had superior intelligence"— portended a different outcome. On the very same day, the court came down with another decision that dramatically restricted remedies for Black defendants convicted by all-white juries. That ruling held that unless a state had an actual law banning Black people from jury service, as West Virginia did, there was little that federal officials could do to intervene. If a state judge, on his own accord, kept Black people out of the jury pool, the proper remedy was through the state courts, not the federal ones. In states of the former Confederacy, that meant no remedy at all.[27]

Now Black leaders felt a sense of slowly building panic as the court prepared to rule on whether Congress had the power to order businesses to serve them. Unlike other high-profile cases, when the justices convened in the former Capitol Senate chamber—the very room where the Civil Rights Act's prime author, Charles Sumner, had been beaten nearly to death for his abolitionist views—there would be no verbal fireworks, no passionate assertions of any sort. By agreement, the parties submitted their arguments in writing, and the justices then retired to consider them in light of "the weight of authority which always invests a law that Congress deems itself competent to pass," as Justice Bradley put it in the court's opinion.[28]

The argument of the defendants—the various innkeepers and ticket takers who had rejected Black customers—was straightforward. They asserted that the Constitution had always existed solely as a check on government, not individuals. The fact that the Fourteenth Amendment expanded the Constitution to cover the actions of states didn't change that basic fact. Therefore, Congress could act only to correct injustices by state governments, not business owners and employees like themselves.

The solicitor general of the United States, Samuel Field Phillips, argued in favor of the prosecution. A holdover from the Grant administration, he was widely respected as a supporter of civil rights. There was, he noted, substantial reason to believe that the framers of the Fourteenth Amendment meant to allow just such a law as the Civil Rights Act of 1875. After all, part of the impetus for the amendment itself was concerns about the constitutionality of a similar statute, the Civil Rights Act of 1866. How could anyone argue that the amendment wasn't meant to cover the conduct of private businesses, when it was enacted with just such a purpose in mind?[29]

Moreover, the government pointed out, the types of businesses covered by the act were already recognized as interests of the state. "The relationship of innkeepers to the State differs from that of a man engaged in the more common avocations of life," Field's assistants wrote in the government's brief. "The former is required to furnish the accommodations of his inn to all well-behaved customers who are prepared to pay the customary price." As such, inns are "essential instruments of commerce," as are railroads. Theaters, he added, with somewhat less conviction, are also "under a license from the state."[30]

This expansive view of what constitutes the actions of state governments had roots in the common law long before the advent of the Fourteenth Amendment, when judges sometimes took notice of the public interest in supposedly "private" railroads and inns—they had an obligation to serve all customers. But using such cases as a justification for sweeping federal legislation hit the wrong note with justices who had spent their careers defending railroad-led monopolies from threats of government regulation.

Justice Bradley issued a decision that paid immediate tribute to the rights of private businesses to operate as they see fit. "In this connection, it is proper to state that civil rights, such as are guaranteed by the Constitution against State aggression, cannot be impaired by the wrongful acts of individuals, unsupported by State authority in the shape of laws, customs, or judicial or executive proceedings," he declared. Phillips, in arguing for the law, had maintained that the framers of the Fourteenth Amendment had intended to change that presumption of deference to states' rights. The nation had just learned through "bitter, costly experience" of the need for a stronger federal role in enforcing civil rights; that was the whole idea behind the Fourteenth Amendment. But Bradley's opinion, an otherwise diligent parsing of legal theories and constitutional history, showed no recognition of the plain fact—obvious to all but the most obtuse observers—that the new Democratic-led state governments in the South were not about to enforce the rights of freed men and women, and that their refusal to do so was the act of defiance that had activated the federal law.

Bradley's deeper feelings, and those of his colleagues, may have been revealed in two telling passages. In one, he expresses a fear of a stronger federal hand in cases beyond those involving race. "If this legislation is appropriate for enforcing the prohibitions of the amendment, it is difficult to see where it is to stop," the justice wrote. "Why may not Congress with equal show of authority enact a code of laws for the enforcement and vindication of all rights of life, liberty, and property?" Thus, the economic fears of the Gilded Age conspired with its racial insecurities to leave Black people unprotected.

In a passage that seems quite extraordinary at a time when the *Chicago Tribune* was counting lynchings by the dozen, Bradley avers, "When a man has emerged from slavery, and by the aid of beneficent legislation has shaken off the inseparable concomitants of that state, there must be some stage in the progress of his elevation when he takes the rank of mere citizen and ceases to be the special favorite of the laws, and when his rights as a citizen, or a man, are to be protected in the ordinary modes by which other men's rights are protected."

The court's decision was announced on October 15 to headlines across the country, sending an electric shock of fear through Black men and women everywhere.

It was noted that Justice Harlan, alone, did not agree with the decision.

Dissent. It trembled in the veins of maverick jurists throughout human history but rarely found expression. In America, it was given an actual role in the law. The idea of a dissenting opinion emerged almost by accident when the chief justice for whom Harlan was named, John Marshall, ended the convoluted practice of each court member offering his own opinion, in order to produce a more forceful majority ruling. Thereafter, justices were free to register their equally forceful disagreements, though only one, the avowed Jeffersonian William Johnson, availed himself of the option with any regularity.[31]

As Harlan pondered his response to the court's opinion in the *Civil Rights Cases of 1883*, he could look for inspiration to at least one famous expression of disagreement in the relatively recent past: Justice Benjamin Curtis's dissent in the infamous Dred Scott case of 1857. In declaring that no one whose ancestors came on slave ships could be a citizen, and that the federal government had no power to prevent slavery in the territories, the court's sweeping decision in the Dred Scott case helped bring on the Civil War. Curtis's dissent, admirable as it was, was a one-off; he promptly resigned in frustration. Harlan, by contrast, was counting on having several more decades in his tenure.[32]

Yet he was about to veer away from his fellow justices in a fundamental way, with his interpretation of the postwar amendments at perilous odds to theirs. He had foreshadowed this rupture ten months earlier, when his colleagues stepped in on their own accord to overturn the federal prosecution of a Tennessee sheriff and nineteen other armed white men who'd seized four Black men from a jail, beating them and killing one. The gang was prosecuted under a federal law, championed by President Grant, that aimed to curb the growing power of the Ku Klux Klan. Though neither the prosecution nor the defense had asked the Supreme Court to consider the constitutionality of the law, the justices intervened anyway, declaring that the Fourteenth Amendment did not give the federal government the power to police ordinary crimes. This meant that Black people would have to rely on state governments led by former Confederates to protect them from the Klan—which would be no protection at all, as Harlan understood well from his days in Kentucky. He claimed the court's assumption of jurisdiction was improper, and that alone should invalidate the decision, so he offered no opinion on the merits. His objections were so lightly noted that the ruling was often wrongly reported as unanimous. But the other justices' eagerness to weigh in—the zeal that led them to order the sheriff and his accomplices to go free—clearly made an impression on Harlan. He had seen firsthand the havoc wreaked by the Ku Klux Klan. Now here was the Supreme Court refusing to allow the federal government to do anything about it.[33]

As Harlan holed up in his study at his Washington row house on

Massachusetts Avenue—a home his family would soon vacate because they felt it was haunted by memories of young Edith[34]—he could catalogue numerous ways in which he believed his colleagues had erred in the *Civil Rights Cases of 1883*. For one thing, their assessment of the original intent of the Fourteenth Amendment glossed over its link to the Civil Rights Act of 1866, which covered some of the same types of discrimination as confronted William R. Davis Jr., Bird Gee, or any of the other victims in the case. He also felt the justices gave short shrift to the Thirteenth Amendment, which banned not only slavery but also, as the Supreme Court had previously acknowledged, "badges of servitude": What would such a badge look like if not being prevented from joining other citizens at railroads, inns, or theaters? And then there was the matter that inns, railroads, and theaters were regulated by states; even accepting Bradley's argument that the Fourteenth Amendment applied only to state governments, weren't such institutions licensees of the state government and therefore extensions of its power?

But as days went by, Harlan grew dispirited. Any of these arguments alone could have been a reason to decide the case the other way, but none captured the larger sense of injustice—the betrayal of the most vulnerable of all Americans, the freed men and women—that drove Harlan to break with the rest of the court.

As he agonized, sleepless night after sleepless night, his wife of twenty-eight years, Malvina, tried to soothe him. Finally, she had an idea. John had long made a hobby of collecting items relevant to American history. At one point, he had saved for posterity the very inkstand that the late chief justice Roger Taney had used to write the Dred Scott decision. Then, in a rash act of generosity, he promised to give it to Taney's niece as a family keepsake. When the time came to turn it over, however, he couldn't find it. Unbeknownst to him, Malvina had hidden it, knowing its significance to both her husband and the country.

As the frustrated justice sat hunched over his desk, with no words forthcoming from his pen, Malvina crept to his side. Quietly, she

put the inkstand on his desk. Later, she would insist it was almost
an act of magic: the ink from Taney's well began flowing in Harlan's
script. The connection was more logical than supernatural. To John
Marshall Harlan, the words "Dred Scott" meant many things. They
symbolized the daunting power of the court to strangle the hopes of
millions. They also represented the immutability of the court's decisions; barring a reversal by the court itself, there was no way for the
country to escape the shackles of its opinions. As a twenty-four-year-
old lawyer in Frankfort, John had sensed in his bones that the civil
war he had long worked to avoid, that had shadowed every act of his
nascent political career, would be unavoidable after the Dred Scott
decision. The Supreme Court had put the country on a path to war.[35]

Now, less than two decades after the end of that war, in which at
least 620,000 Americans had died, the court was nullifying its most
important outcome. He couldn't stop it, but at least he could register
his dissent in a way that would inspire future cases.

"The opinion in these cases proceeds, it seems to me, upon
grounds entirely too narrow and artificial," he began. "I cannot resist
the conclusion that the substance and spirit of the recent amendments
to the Constitution have been sacrificed by a subtle and ingenious
verbal criticism. 'It is not the words of the law but the internal sense
of it that makes the law; the letter of the law is the body; the sense and
reason of the law are the soul.' Constitutional provisions, adopted in
the interest of liberty, and for the purpose of securing, through national legislation, if need be, rights inhering a state of freedom, and
belonging to American citizenship, have been so construed as to defeat the ends the people desired to accomplish, which they attempted
to accomplish, and which they supposed they had accomplished by
changes in their fundamental law."[36]

John went on to outline his legal case; why he felt the majority was
ignoring the plain meaning and intent of the Thirteenth and Fourteenth Amendments, and how inns and railroads should be considered more like public services than purely private endeavors. At the
end of his long discourse, however, he returned to the larger themes
evoked at the start: the betrayal of promises made and delivered—

and the racial double standards inherent in the court's actions. After all, in the 1850s, when Northerners questioned Congress's power to approve the highly punitive Fugitive Slave Act on the grounds that slavery was a state matter, the court brushed aside the challenge, even though there was no constitutional language whatsoever to guide the decision; now, with the postwar amendments having been enacted specifically to strengthen federal power to enforce civil rights, the court eagerly stepped in to limit that power.

"It is, I submit, scarcely just to say that the colored race has been a special favorite of the laws," Harlan wrote. "The statute of 1875, now adjudged to be unconstitutional, is for the benefit of citizens of every race and color. What the nation, through Congress, has sought to accomplish in reference to that race is—what has already been done in every State of the Union for the white race—to secure and protect rights belonging to them as freemen and citizens; nothing more. . . .

"The supreme law of the land has decreed that no authority shall be exercised in this country upon the basis of discrimination, in respect of civil rights, against freemen and citizens because of their race, color, or previous condition of servitude. To that decree—for the due enforcement of which, by appropriate legislation, Congress has invested express power—everyone must bow, whatever may have been, or whatever are now, his individual views as to the wisdom of policy, either of the recent changes in the fundamental law, or the legislation which has been enacted to give them effect.

"For the reasons stated, I feel constrained to withhold my assent to the opinion of the court."[37]

Three decades later, Malvina Harlan wrote: "It was, I think, a bit of 'poetic justice' that the small inkstand in which Taney's pen had dipped" when he stripped away Black rights would be the same pool of ink from which John Marshall Harlan issued the stoutest defense of Black civil rights in the nation's history up to that time.

The inkstand had done more than inspire a memorable judicial opinion. It unleashed a new passion in its author. No longer would

John Marshall Harlan be the compliant junior justice. For three decades hence, he would be the court's troubadour for the rights of African Americans and oppressed workers of all races, relentlessly calling out what he saw as the willful prejudices of his colleagues.[38]

The force of Harlan's opinion was widely noted in the Black community. Virtually every Black newspaper, dozens of them around the country, sang the praises of the opinion and its author. "It is refreshing to find a man upright and righteous where so many appear to run after false Gods," declared the *New York Globe*. The *Washington Bee* stated, "Justice Harlan, of the Supreme Court, a Kentuckian, will ever be held in high regard by our race."

The praise for Harlan was balanced, in full proportion, by the devastation felt by Black people who realized that the legal path to freedom would be foreclosed to them for a generation or more. These views were of no consequence to most whites in the country, who were now secure in knowing that eight out of nine justices—if not, annoyingly, all of them—were protective of their right to discriminate. Almost immediately, the doors of white America began to close to people of color. The impact of the decision became visible in Whites Only signs pasted on the doors and windows of businesses—emblems of discrimination that would endure for eight decades or more and block the paths of more Americans than just the descendants of enslaved men and women.

In the South, where the court's consideration of the Civil Rights Act of 1875 was intently watched, there was jubilation at its defeat. The *Atlanta Constitution* ran a headline declaring "A Triumph of Law and Sense," while echoing Bradley's sentiment that the decision prevented Black people from getting special favors under the law.

The *Constitution* also reported the scene at Atlanta's DeGive's Opera House, whose manager had been facing federal prosecution under the act. On October 15, as word of the court's ruling rattled around the country by telegraph, the theater was in the midst of its evening performance. The leader of the acting troupe interrupted the final act of the play to announce the news.

"The audience instantly grasped the full purport of the announcement and burst into such thunderous applause as was never before
heard within the walls of the operahouse," the newspaper reported.
"The people smiled at each other with beaming faces and congratulations were exchanged all through the audience. It was welcome news
to everyone, excepting only the dusky occupants of the colored galleries. These were silent and evidently smitten with dumbfounded
consternation. Not a note of applause came from those solemn rows
of benches, and their occupants evidently believed that the decision
meant the total abrogation of the chief blessings that are involved in
the facts of their emancipation and citizenship."[39]

Frederick Douglass, the abolitionist leader who had been born enslaved and did more than any man to promote the cause of freedom,
despaired at the outcome of the *Civil Rights Cases of 1883*, calling the
court's decision "an act of surrender, almost akin to treachery." Harlan's opinion was the only saving grace. Douglass wrote a letter to Harlan declaring that his opinion was not only the greatest legal treatise
in decades but also that "it should be scattered like the leaves of autumn over the whole country, and be seen, read, and pondered upon
by every citizen of the country, and if I had means, I would cause it to
be published in every newspaper and magazine in the land."[40]

Taking to the pages of the national journal the *American Reformer*,
Douglass urged all believers in justice to drink in Harlan's words, not
Bradley's. Compared to Harlan's "broad and generous" rendering of
the issue, "the decision of the eight judges was like an egg shell to a
cannon ball."

And the prophet-like Douglass wrote movingly of the difference
between one and none, of having at least one map to guide the way
forward. He sought to comfort his followers by calling on them to envision the day when the country would see the light like Harlan did.

"In the early days of the Anti-Slavery conflict, when Anti-Slavery
men were few and were often ridiculed for their numerical insignificance, I was wont to console myself with what seemed to many a

transcendental idea, that one man with God is a majority; that if such a man does not represent what is, he does represent what ought to be, and what ultimately will be," Douglass wrote. "The colored people and their friends may well enough avail themselves of this sublime consolation in their present situation, and in view of the righteous and heroic stand taken in defense of liberty and justice by Justice John M. Harlan." [41]

Book One

Chapter 1

A Father's Prophecy

John Marshall Harlan was born on the precipice; on the very hinge of a society splitting in half.

To the north of his hometown of Danville, Kentucky, an abolitionist wind was blowing after shocking reports of dozens of men, women, and children hacked and bludgeoned to death in the infamous Nat Turner slave rebellion less than two summers before Harlan's birth on June 1, 1833.[1] To the south, feelings were hardening in the opposite direction. Overseers wielded whips and chains to keep enslaved men and women in line, while statesmen moved to preserve and expand their states' legal rights to handle their property in any way they deemed fit.

In Kentucky, all these views were stirring uneasily, making the state a crucible of the nation's growing divide over slavery. All sides had stakes in Kentucky. It had large plantations surrounded by log slave cabins, but also many smaller farms with just a handful of enslaved men and women living in close contact with their masters. It had farms with no slaves, just hardworking families, and also, at the bottom of its social strata, a growing population of free Black laborers.[2]

Kentucky's most admired political leader, Henry Clay, was silky of dress and smooth of voice. He was a wealthy slave owner who nonetheless supported clear limits on an institution he disliked but never disavowed.[3] Clay's views fit his state, if not his country. Ever since Kentucky had broken off from its aristocratic parent, Virginia, four decades earlier, the new state had cultivated its own distinct sense of pride and gentry, with original families like the Clays and the Harlans building a nirvana in the bluegrass that they called "the Athens of the West."[4] A dispute over slavery wouldn't just put Kentucky at odds with its neighbors but also with itself, casting its economic and social differences in a sharp and deadly relief. A national furor over slavery was poison to Kentucky's marrow. That's why Henry Clay dedicated his formidable political talent—the best of his generation, everyone agreed—to forging the compromises necessary to tamp down tensions within the state and across the nation.

In the year of Harlan's birth, all of Kentucky's factions were, almost miraculously, finding agreement in an unlikely place: a ban on the importation of slaves. The bill appealed to plantation owners as a way of protecting their human investments, to moderates as a step toward the "gradual" emancipation they thought would salve tensions, to abolitionists as a push in the right direction, and to poor whites as a way of removing enslaved competitors and, for that matter, keeping Black people out of Kentucky. The new law, called the Nonimportation Act, went through, but the common ground on which it stood began to crumble almost immediately. When it came to slavery, Kentuckians already seemed locked into their own positions. Self-interest ruled, and the interests of Black people usually fell by the wayside.[5]

Above the sea of self-interest, however, there were high clouds of statesmanship. Aristocrat-politicians from the Bluegrass State named Breckinridge, Crittenden and even Henry Clay's abolitionist cousin Cassius M. Clay took turns playing leading roles in the national drama over slavery.[6] They were each impressive enough, but for five decades, the state's ardor for national leadership was most personified by Henry Clay himself, a bantam rooster with a dramatic voice and an urgent cause: the preservation of the Union. No one doubted the sincerity of his commitment to the United States or the validity of his fears for its future. Nonetheless, he was playing a weak hand. Millions of Americans shared his moderate instincts, but there was frustratingly little they could do, in terms of policy, to bridge the gap between the abolitionists and states'-rights conservatives in the South.

That didn't stop Clay from trying. Most of his exertions went into a long-simmering idea that he felt might just garner support across the slavery divide: colonization. Over years and even decades, masters could free their enslaved men and women, perhaps for compensation, and generous-spirited abolitionists would pay their way "back" to Africa, though most enslaved Americans had been born in the United States. Nonetheless, to its proponents, the colonization scheme offered the hope for a just outcome, a rewinding of the clock, letting the descendants of those who were ripped from their homes return to their ancestral continent. Meanwhile, America would be cleansed of its sins and free to develop under the principle of human equality— without having to extend that equality to an unwanted race.

Clay, who had helped found the American Colonization Society in 1817 and later became its president, believed that by the 1830s, the colonization movement was finally starting to gain steam.[7] It had established a settlement in Liberia, on the West African coast, and raised money to send freed men and women there. Despite an alarmingly high mortality rate for the Black colonists, due to the high prevalence of disease in the swampy climate, Clay retained a belief that moving formerly enslaved people to Africa would avoid the pain of abolition in America, while slowly decreasing the number of slaves.[8] And in the colonization movement, as in others of his initiatives, the "Great Compromiser" had a friend and ally in James Harlan, father of John Marshall Harlan.[9]

Tall and bespectacled, with the quizzical expression of a man just looking up from a book, James Harlan was a generation younger than Clay and something of a protégé. He was one of his state's rising aristocrat-politicians, with mounting fame as a prosecutor. He had spent four years as Commonwealth Attorney, the Danville area's leading crime-fighter.[10] Law was more than a profession for him—it was a passion. Amid the nation's roiling politics, he believed the rule of law should be an anchor, a source of firm boundaries, so that disputes couldn't get out of hand. At thirty-three, he was already well along toward achieving his goal of collecting the best private law library in Kentucky. His trove would eventually tally between 600 and 750 volumes, including 200 to 225 law books, at a time when this sort of knowledge represented real power—he could cite legal precedents unknown to other Kentucky lawyers.[11] With the arrival of another son—John Marshall Harlan was the sixth child and fifth boy born to him and his wife, Eliza—he was adding another desk to the family law firm that was his fondest ambition.

"Another big, red-haired boy." That was how Aunt Betty, one of the family's dozen enslaved men and women, announced the birth.[12] James was in the habit of naming his sons after his friends and his heroes. Three years before John's birth, he named a son Henry Clay Harlan. Two years later, when a fourth son was born to him and Eliza, he availed himself of his father's privilege of naming the boy after himself. Now, with another boy in the cradle, he dusted off a name with almost mystical significance: that of the most famous of American jurists, Chief Justice John Marshall. It was Marshall who had asserted the power, left unclear in the Constitution, that the Supreme Court would be the final arbiter of constitutional questions—that if the court declared a law to be unconstitutional, the president and Congress must comply. Marshall's role was unique in American history. He single-handedly invoked the rule of law over politics. To James Harlan, names were prophecies, and he attached to his and Eliza's fifth son that of the greatest American jurist who ever lived.[13]

Growing up amid intensifying strife, John wouldn't have to look further than his own name to remember that law transcended politics, that the US Constitution was the guarantor of liberty, and that the primacy of that document was what separated the United States from all the kingdoms abroad. Those were the heartfelt views of John Marshall and of James Harlan. For the newly christened John Marshall Harlan, American history would be as much a religion as the family's Presbyterian faith. Both would be applied with rigor, with the scholarly James as the family's setter of standards.

The Harlans' belief in America—in the special destiny of the land that they loved—was rooted in their own stake at Harlan's Station, near Danville, Kentucky. The very names given to their family home—the Old Stone House—and the water that flowed to it—the Salt River—suggested strength and permanence. In fact, the roots of this society, carved out of the wilderness, were shallow. The land was just a few decades removed from the control of the Shawnee, and many of the white inhabitants still lived as in the pioneer days, wearing animal skin coats and carrying flintlock rifles.[14] To the Harlans and other old families, however, their two generations in Kentucky might as well have been ten or twelve: they raised their children to be gentlemen and ladies of an enlightened, refined civilization.

That civilization was largely the product of an expedition conducted in the last days of British rule in Virginia, commissioned by a much-despised royal governor from his palace in Williamsburg, in 1774.[15] An adventurer named James Harrod was called upon to pull together a team to explore the western reaches of the colony. Two Virginian brothers, James and Silas Harlan, eagerly signed up, seizing an opportunity to make their fortunes in the West.[16] Harrod's expedition bush-whacked its way to the soft grassy valleys of central Kentucky, where Harrod built a fortification around what is now Harrodsburg, and the Harlan brothers constructed their own stockade a few miles away at Harlan's Station.[17]

For the settlers, Indian attacks were an abiding threat, and the colonists feared for their lives. During the American Revolution, loyalists and British commanders joined forces with Shawnee warriors to roust the settlers from their homes. The land, however, was fertile enough to give the Harlans hope for the future; Silas, the elder of the two brothers, became engaged to a woman from a prominent southern Virginia family, whose robust health and strong limbs seemed well suited to the pioneer life. Before he could marry her, he answered an urgent call to join Daniel Boone and other Kentucky militiamen to defend their settlements against attacks by Indians spurred on by British loyalists.

It was 1782. Lord Cornwallis had already surrendered to General

George Washington at Yorktown ten months earlier, effectively ending the American Revolution, but battles still raged on the frontier.
Silas Harlan and Daniel Boone were among roughly 180 irregulars
who massed together in northeastern Kentucky to pursue the Indians and their Tory-American allies who had raided a stockade about
six miles from Lexington. True to his reputation as the shrewdest of
frontiersmen, Boone sensed that the Indians were using overly conspicuous trail markings to lead the Americans into an ambush near
the Licking River in Fayette County, about eighty miles from Harlan's
Station. But discipline wasn't a strength of the frontier militia. When
a hotheaded frontiersman rejected Boone's advice and galloped into
the trap, hollering, "Them that ain't cowards follow me!" many of his
comrades obliged.[18] The Indians opened fire, killing dozens of Kentuckians, including Boone's twenty-three-year-old son, Israel. Silas
Harlan was among those who lost their lives at the Battle of Blue
Licks, in the dying gasp of British rule.[19]

Silas's bride-to-be, Sarah Caldwell, shifted her affections to his
brother James and produced seven sons, including James Jr. It was the
robust Sarah, who died two years before John Marshall Harlan was
born, who gave the Harlan men their strength. Family legend divided
their offspring into two tribes: the Big Reds and the Little Blacks.
Sarah was the progenitor of the Big Reds, and her little grandson John
was merely the latest prototype.[20]

By 1833, it was a placid world in that sylvan corner of Kentucky, the
frontier having moved westward and the Indian Wars becoming
memories for old men in coonskin caps. A dirt road lined with a low
stone wall trailed the Salt River leading onto the Harlan property, six
and a half miles from Danville center. Along the trickling river, there
was no obvious bank: tufts of grass and weeds rolled down the little
eroded incline and disappeared beneath the surface. The Salt River
provided only a brief, reflective interruption to the undulating tall
grasses. Bright neon algae spotted the surface, but where the algae
wasn't, the water was clear and bright, and the young Harlan chil-

dren, idling over the bridge over the Salt River, could look down in the shadow and count fish and turtles and frogs, and see the moss and stones on the river bottom as clear as on dry ground.[21]

The Old Stone House, with its weathered solidity, attached itself to the hill above. Made of limestone in the style favored by the Pennsylvania Quakers, with twin chimneys bookending a red triangular roof and four rectangular windows on the face of the home, the house had been built around 1785 by James and Sarah for their large family. In time, James Jr. filled it with his own growing family, while some of his brothers built houses of their own nearby.[22] For a small boy looking down from the house, the rolls of hills dotted with hay bales and barns, the mists that hung over the farmland on cold mornings, and the clouds backing up to the blue sky gave the illusion that the bluegrasses of Kentucky might just stretch on forever.

In reality, there were dangers over those hills. The troubled politics of Kentucky and the nation were one. So, too, was a persistent sense of lawlessness. "Human life in Kentucky is not worth the snapping of a man's fingers," bemoaned one local judge.[23] In the year of John's birth, there was another vivid reminder of the proximity of mortality. In a single stroke, a cholera epidemic wiped out about onetwelfth of the population of Lexington, about thirty miles from where John was born. Many famous Kentuckians, including Henry Clay, Mary Todd Lincoln, and even the Kentucky-born Jefferson Davis, the latter back to recruit soldiers for the US Army, were in the city at the time, bearing witness to the tragedy while fearing for themselves and their own. Many others took refuge in the countryside.[24]

For the wealthiest Kentuckians, the most desirable place to retreat from the plague was about ten miles down the road from Harlan's Station. Graham Springs, where wealthy plantation owners, businessmen, and their kin could luxuriate in hot medicinal baths while waiting out the pestilence of the city, was built by one of the state's most colorful entrepreneurs, Christopher Columbus Graham. A medical-doctor-turned-innkeeper-and-developer—and an ex-Indian fighter, to boot—Graham promised his clientele a restorative cure combined with distinctive Kentucky hobbies such as drinking, card playing, and horse racing. In his "Saratoga of the West," the troubles of the city were drowned in a sea of pleasure.[25]

James didn't approve of such amusements. But the mere presence of Graham Springs, and a showman like Christopher Columbus Graham, signaled to aristocratic-minded families like the Harlans that a different Kentucky was emerging on the edge of their secluded paradise.

This new Kentucky, built around the animal pleasures of horse racing and cock fighting, excited the imagination of the one family member whose precise status must have been confusing to the young John. At seventeen, Robert Harlan was a strapping young man with a golden smile. He was also a smooth, persuasive talker. Living by his wits, he confidently sallied forth into the world around Harlan's Station, with its mix of Black and white, frontiersman and aristocrat. Though technically enslaved, the handsome, light-skinned Robert took advantage of his master's indulgence to roam far from home, following his gambler's eye for fresh opportunities. His outsized ambitions came about largely because he was a special favorite of his master, James Harlan, who educated him and gave him a position of trust within the family.

Throughout the slaveholding states, there were, in certain homes, light-skinned family members like Robert, who hovered in an odd status. Neither servant nor master, they seemed to enjoy special privileges and education. Aware of their good fortune relative to the others held in slavery, their attitudes were more optimistic as well; they enjoyed just enough favor within the household to imagine their lives as something other than the product of unremitting toil but harbored no fanciful illusions about their place in the world outside their homes.[26]

Robert had moved into the Old Stone House when he was eight, in 1824, a few years after James's marriage to Eliza. He came to Harlan's Station from Mecklenburg County, Virginia, a rural expanse of giant plantations with scores of field hands ruled by whippings. Robert's mother was light skinned and literate; she took her precocious son on a journey almost as harrowing as that of the Harrod expedition, across hundreds of miles of wilderness. She wanted her talented boy to meet his father, believing that a reunion would lead to better opportunities. Several accounts published during Robert's lifetime said that, upon arriving in Kentucky, the mother and son learned that the father was dead, and that James Harlan, for unknown reasons, stepped in to raise the boy. Other accounts reported that James himself was his father.[27]

In the odd etiquette that surrounded the slave culture, outsiders would have assumed that Robert was the progeny of a Harlan man and an enslaved woman; many would have believed that man was James.[28] But neither they nor other family members would have been likely to say much about it; no explanation would have been demanded or proffered. It was a form of ritual denial, the product of an institution that defied moral boundaries and expectations. The offspring of such liaisons were left in an unspoken limbo, grateful for favors but left at the door of opportunities routinely given to whites.

James was only sixteen when Robert was born, but his mother Sarah's extended family owned plantations in the vicinity of Mecklenburg County. A youthful sexual encounter with an enslaved woman could have made him Robert's father, but no one except Robert's mother would have known the truth.[29] For reasons that were mysterious even to those close to him, James took an intensely personal interest in Robert, acquiring him in slavery but not his mother, who ended up being sold down South. Though oftentimes it was the women of the home who determined whether to educate an enslaved child, James himself made the decision to teach Robert.[30] James's attachment to Robert may have confounded other members of the household, but they dared not question it: James ruled his roost with an iron hand, and even Eliza did not feel empowered to question his decisions. Later, after Robert had grown into a man of wealth and prominence, he would give his own son the name of Robert James Harlan, a tribute to the man whom he considered his father in thought, word, and deed.[31]

James's friends and family admired him for his restraint, not aggression, but that belied his unusual force of character. His daughter-in-law noted that he was "such a shy and reserved man that his family, while holding him in affectionate reverence, stood rather in awe of him."[32] His sons' interactions with him were formal and lacking in demonstrable emotions, but there was never any question whose approval they sought or whose political views they emulated.

James knew where he stood on the great questions of the day. He also knew which political leader he revered—Henry Clay—and which he detested: Andrew Jackson.[33] The hero of the Battle of New Orleans, "Old Hickory" rose to the presidency as the nation's first populist hero. Jackson cast himself as the man of action determined to roust the educated elites, personified by Clay and John Quincy Adams, his predecessor in the White House. He sowed fears of the meddling hand of the federal government and sought to shift power back to states—closer to the small farmers and laborers who provided the bulk of his support. His advocacy for stronger state governments and less federal intrusion was initially welcomed by rich Southern whites, who feared any interference with slavery.[34] The South's reigning political visionary, South Carolina's John C. Calhoun, served as Jackson's vice president.[35]

Thin and wiry, with sunken eyes and flaring brows, the zealous Calhoun was busy perfecting the states'-rights ideology that would eventually lead to secession. But when, in the early 1830s, he and other southerners test-marketed their theory of nullification—that a state could reject a federal law and, if an accommodation were not reached, quit the Union—even Jackson rose up in opposition. In protest, Calhoun quit the vice presidency and returned to the Senate to fight for the right to nullification. Like a railroad worker laying down track, he was setting the legal groundwork for the Southern states to leave the Union, though his stated goal was merely to reduce the high tariffs that hurt the Southern economy. Under Henry Clay's leadership, Congress eventually relented on the tariffs, and Calhoun's dream of nullification receded for a while.[36]

The South, however, seemed emboldened by Congress's capitulation, while Northerners fumed at a tariff policy that they deemed insufficiently supportive of the growing industrial economy. All were aware that an underlying motivation for Calhoun's manipulations was preserving slavery, and here it was dragging down policies that many Northerners considered important to the development of interstate commerce. For landlocked Kentucky, that meant giving up on improvements in transportation and building up cities, steps that would lead away from a slavery-based economy and toward a stronger industrial base like that of its neighbor to the north, Ohio.

Jackson and Calhoun were such formidable forces that competing politicians like Clay and Massachusetts senator Daniel Webster, who often differed on slavery, found common ground in opposing them. James Harlan joined Clay and Webster in recognizing the need for a new party to bring together opponents of Jacksonian policies.[37] They dubbed it the Whigs, adopting a name used by patriots during the Revolutionary War. In policy terms, the Whig Party often meant different things to different people, especially along sectional lines. But its underlying philosophy was what kept its members in line. If Jackson's Democrats represented the rule of the people, the Whigs represented the rule of law.[38]

James found the Whig Party to be a comfortable home. He was enamored enough to run for Congress himself on the Whig ticket. He won and headed off to Washington for what turned out to be two terms in office. Thus, for four crucial years of John's upbringing, from 1835 to 1839, his father was only a part-time resident of Kentucky.

In the distant capital, James did battle with Jacksonians as a deathless ally of Clay, who represented Kentucky in the Senate.[39] The last two years of Jackson's presidency and the first two of Jackson's handpicked successor, Vice President Martin Van Buren, were marked by tensions over Jackson's efforts to destroy the Second Bank of the United States, which Jacksonians saw as a tool of the elites, but which Whigs like Harlan and Clay envisioned as a vehicle for taming the boom-and-bust cycles that plagued the nineteenth-century economy.[40]

James threw himself wholeheartedly into partisan battles, even volunteering to manage the Whig campaign against the Democratic

candidate for governor of Kentucky, who happened to be a personal
favorite of Jackson's. Holed up in a Danville hotel one evening, he was
awakened by a knock on the door. It was a message from his Jacksonian rival, demanding a duel. James was more comfortable going into
a fight with a law book than with a gun, but he did not intend to let
a challenge go unanswered. He quickly accepted. Given the choice of
weapons, he deliberately chose unorthodox terms: rifles, pressed to
the chest.

The response came back: James's terms were "too barbarous" to
accept.[41]

Harlan relatives told the story to attest to James's physical courage,
steely resolve, and instinct for politics—especially since he followed
up by distributing pamphlets denouncing the Jacksonian candidate,
Thomas Moore, for his cowardice and hounding him from politics.[42]

James applied a similar intensity to his attempts to enforce compromises on slavery, but with less success. That was because his
moderate impulses often pulled against each other. He made no secret of his disdain for slave drivers. In the state capital of Frankfort,
he once encountered a man leading a parade of chained people to
market, including elderly men and children, while wielding a leather
whip. James bolted into the middle of the street to challenge the man.
"You are a damned scoundrel," he intoned for all to hear. He then proceeded to church, dragging a wide-eyed young John in tow.[43]

But when rumors began floating that James was an abolitionist
who used questionable legal techniques to free a mother and child
from their master, he denounced the charge. Alerted by a friend to the
rumors, he wrote back that the claims were "as palpable falsehoods as
ever were concocted or uttered by mortal man." Whoever called him
an abolitionist "lied in his throat." In a scratched-out portion of the
letter, he declared that he held abolitionists and those threatening secession in equal contempt: "Each deserves the gallows."[44]

The scratch-out reflected the extent to which slavery gnawed at
James's conscience. He went on in the same letter to say he wouldn't
hesitate to represent a slave seeking freedom if there were good legal
cause.[45] But his moral objections to slavery weren't strong enough

to risk splitting apart the Union. Plainly, he would accept slavery if the Union could be preserved. In letters with Clay, the two friends despaired over the way the slavery issue was tormenting the nation, believing there were troublemakers on both sides.[46] James started attending meetings of the American Colonization Society, which Clay headed, hoping to ship formerly enslaved men and women to Africa.[47]

At the same time, his daughter-in-law recalled, he was quick to see the human potential in his own property. That was her somewhat oblique—and inadequate—explanation for his unusual interest in Robert. But there was little doubt that James believed that African ancestry was not an absolute bar to achievement. Robert, James believed, was destined for bigger things. Shortly after purchasing the boy, James made the unusual gesture of personally escorting him to the schoolhouse near Harlan's Station to enroll him in class and was angered when the schoolmaster later sent him home with the explanation that Black students weren't allowed to receive lessons.

For the rest of his life, Robert would joke about having received "half a day's schooling."[48]

To James, it was no joke.

Barred from school, Robert spent much of John's early years barnstorming the state in search of work and money. His daily life was different from those of John's four older brothers among James and Eliza's brood, Richard, William, Clay, and James Jr. Each of those boys was being groomed in the same manner: to follow an almost cloistered regimen of legal study. Robert, whose obvious intelligence was denied an outlet in academics, was, paradoxically, liberated by prejudice. Having done all he could to educate Robert, James recognized that the young man's race barred him from any of the elite positions to which James aspired for his sons with Eliza; thus, he gave his approval to less high-minded pursuits available to the young man, such as raising and racing horses.

This Robert was quick to embrace. In his midteens, Robert collected cash by "gunning and selling coonskins," according to a later

newspaper account, and then used his earnings to learn to be a barber, one of the few trades available to Black men, opening his own
shop near Harlan's Station. But he saw an even greater opportunity in
the Kentucky turf—the world of horsemanship that Kentuckians saw
as their special distinction and birthright.[49]

Kentucky was already staking its claim to being the Yorkshire of
America. The thirty-mile radius around Lexington was known as the
Bluegrass region, where the topsoil hid a base of Ordovician limestone, producing a type of grass that was said to nourish horses into
the leanest and fastest the world over.[50] In true American style, some
of those fast horses were the progeny of workhorses, while others
were born of steeds brought over by British soldiers.[51] In some Kentucky towns, horses outnumbered people, and racing "meets" drew
villagers from their homes like a town fair, the way that team sports
would in later eras.[52]

The purveyors of racing—horse owners, trainers, jockeys—were
eager entrepreneurs, and Black men, for once, weren't excluded. The
wealthy horse owners who belonged to the Kentucky Jockey Club
used their enslaved men to train and ride their horses, opening the
sport to people who otherwise would be pushed to the sidelines.[53]
One turfman of the era compared the scene at races to a backgam-
mon board, with Black and white people dotting the landscape in almost equal numbers.[54]

In smaller towns, racing was even more democratic, with meets
encompassing no longer than two to four days, from Wednesday
through Saturday, and open fields substituting for a well-groomed
track.[55] Heats typically began at noon. Horses would advance to the
starting line at the summoning of a drum roll, and another roll of the
drum or flare of a bugle would signal for riders to mount up. A final,
single tap of the drum would launch the horses into the race.[56]

Figures of scant means like Robert could, through sheer cunning,
identify potential winners and take home leather pouches stuffed
with winnings. There weren't any set odds on horses; all betting was
informal, usually conducted in a saloon to the accompaniment of liquor and billiards (hence the term "betting pool").[57] Robert sought to

make his mark in this throbbing world. No one was going to give any betting tips to a teenaged slave, so he had to learn to size up an animal by sight. As a bettor, he had to be able to pry his winnings from the most drunken, two-pistol rabble-rouser.

He needed both courage and wits to traverse Kentucky as an enslaved man, even one whose master granted him unusual latitude. All slaves that were away from their homes for more than four hours were required to carry a pass,[58] and even though the law was only spottily enforced, gangs of vigilantes prowled the countryside in search of runaways. "Negro hunting, Negro catching, Negro watching, and Negro whipping . . . constituted the favorite sport for many youthful whites at the time," offered Kentucky historian J. Winston Coleman.[59] Robert's light skin and literacy provided a buffer of sorts—he didn't look or act like a runaway—but he risked trouble every time he left Harlan's Station.

He didn't have to go far, though, to learn more about horses than most men could glean in a lifetime. At Harlan's Station, he was already on the edge of the Bluegrass region, the epicenter of American racing. Nearby Harrodsburg, where he kept his barber shop, and where the Harlans maintained a home and office during much of the 1830s, had a popular racetrack.[60] And a steady stream of high-stakes gamblers—including some of the nation's first millionaires—spent summers behind the Doric columns and on the rolling lawns of Graham Springs, where racing was a popular pastime.[61]

In the eyes of young John, Robert loomed as a man of action, intrepid where his other brothers were bookish, unafraid of the sometimes violent world outside Harlan's Station, and eager to participate in the rough-hewn rituals of frontier life.

John could look at Robert like an adventuresome uncle, cousin, or family retainer from a very different mold. The mold that John came from was cast for James and Eliza's firstborn, Richard Davenport Harlan, and refitted for William, Clay, and James Jr. ahead of him. John wasn't lost in that crowd, however: the mold seemed to have yielded something closer to perfection in its fifth iteration. Naturally bright and studious, with the ease of manner befitting a fifth son and sixth child who had to navigate his own way through a family that eventually reached eleven, John was a willing adherent to the strict regimen of faith and scholarship laid out by his father. His older brothers and older sister, Elizabeth, were his closest companions. Two more sisters, Laura and Sally, followed him, as did a brother, George, who died in infancy.[62]

Of them all, John seemed most eager to emulate Clay. While all of James and Eliza's sons were destined for legal careers, Clay and John stood out for their interest in the world of politics. Clay—as Henry Clay Harlan was known in the family—was the most instinctively attuned to issues outside Harlan's Station, an essayist and budding politician from his grade school years. John, three years younger, followed in Clay's footsteps: a journal from their boyhood features literary and philosophical writings by the precocious Clay, while young John—perhaps already envisioning an important career—practiced signing his name.[63]

Then and always, politics would take a backseat to God. The family's spiritual anchor was the First Presbyterian Church in Danville. Its simple dignity reflected the traditionalism of its theology: a red-brick church with a tall bell tower, it had austere wooden pews and a nave adorned with stained glass windows. Each Sunday morning, the Harlans piled into a carriage and made the journey to Danville. Other than the monthly court day—a Monday when families would trek into town for what had, by the mid-nineteenth century, become a sort of social holiday—attending church on Sunday was the best opportunity to meet up with friends and extended family scattered around the region.[64]

Even by the standards of a deeply religious state like Kentucky, Danville was a devout town.[65] Its many churches—all Protestant, with Presbyterians and Methodists leading the way—knotted together the community, including enslaved people and freed men and women. Even the First Presbyterian, which would later be known as the "Old First," in recognition of its buttoned-down, upper-class image, had Black worshippers lining the rear pews. Presbyterians weren't neces-

sarily believers in racial equality, but their faith had a leavening effect
on their views of slavery. It regarded men as souls and thus obliged its
followers to acknowledge the humanity of all.[66]

However, traditional churches like the Harlans' frowned on social crusades such as abolitionism, believing that such movements reflected too much human agency and too little faith in God.[67] Thus,
slavery could be both morally objectionable and part of God's mysterious plan. Like their politics, the Harlans' faith both tolerated and
objected to slavery. In church, John heard few echoes of the cries of
abolitionism from Northern pastors, but plenty of warnings about
the difficult moral currents of slavery. His pastor was one of the
most respected theologians in the state, John C. Young, an educator
who also served as president of Centre College, Danville's esteemed
place of higher learning. Like James Harlan, Young had a distaste for
bondage—freeing his own slaves at two different points in his life—
but the only absolute in his sermons was the notion that a master,
having undertaken responsibility for a slave, must act with fairness
and justice.[68]

"Our dealings with our servants comprehend a very large part of
that conduct for which we are to be responsible at the bar of God; is
it not, then, of the utmost consequence to ourselves that these dealings should be all regulated by principles of religion?" Young declared
in "The Scriptural Duty of Masters," a widely published sermon he
delivered in 1846. "The Bible lays down precepts for the master and
for the servant, because each has the happiness and well-being of the
other in his power. There is, however, more need for the authority of
religion to enforce the duties of the master, especially the master who
holds the servant in involuntary bondage; for while he has power to
coerce the servant to yield him in some good degree what is his due,
the servant has no reciprocal power to coerce the master."[69]

As a child, John was a diligent reader of the Bible, already im-
mersing himself in Presbyterian theology, a lodestar that would guide
every turn of his life and career. Reverend Young was a trusted mentor, one who would later play a crucial role in his education.[70] But
when John was just seven years old, in 1840, the Harlan family parted

ways with the Old First. James Harlan was about to advance his political destiny, joining the Whig administration as Kentucky's secretary
of state.[71] This meant that the family had to move to the state capital
of Frankfort, where James would take his place at the center of Bluegrass State politics, in all its glaring contradictions.

Chapter 2

Journey into the Heart of Slavery

Robert Harlan didn't make the move to Frankfort. James and Eliza's departure for the capital opened a new chapter in his independence. At twenty-four, he had been racing his own horses for five years.[1] His barber shop in Harrodsburg provided regular income, and though he was still technically enslaved, he acted like a free man, traveling the state in search of racing meets.[2]

But questions about his past weren't far from the surface of the smoothly self-sufficient life he had built for himself. He had no parents to speak of; his only identity was as the ward of James Harlan, whom he saw as a mentor and savior from the shackles of slavery. At Harlan's Station, perhaps while cleaning out his desk for the move, James showed Robert a letter that his mother had written to James fourteen years earlier, two years after he had bought the eight-year-old Robert and she had been sold down South. It was sent from Pointe Coupee, Louisiana, a place whose ignominious history hung over it like Spanish moss. Four decades earlier, twenty-three enslaved men and women had been hanged, with their decapitated heads displayed on posts, and another thirty-one flogged as punishment for one of the most famous uprisings in history.[3]

The news that his mother was living in bondage in such a place had a frightening and sobering impact. If Robert was now old enough to take control of his own life, he was also ready to navigate the tor-

turous byways of the South to find the woman who meant more to
him than any other. He would use his own survival skills to locate her
and free her from her plantation hell. James, who must have known
the feelings he would engender by showing Robert the letter, may
even have approved of the idea. Robert decided on the spot to embark on a rescue mission to Louisiana.

The easiest way to begin the nearly eight-hundred-mile journey
to Pointe Coupee was by steamboat, a languid and glamorous form
of travel that was in its heyday. Ever-larger ships with white-washed
sides and decks layered like wedding cakes plied the waters from
Ohio to the cusp of the Gulf of Mexico. Their slowly turning paddle
wheels and belching smokestacks were part of the iconic imagery of
the Mississippi River. The frequent trips back and forth along the inland waterways turned ports like St. Louis and New Orleans into bustling centers of commerce. The ships, meanwhile, acquired an allure
of their own. Towns along the Mississippi, in the hands of fundamen-
talist preachers, had banned gambling, sending all their cardsharps
and bettors offshore, to the river, beyond the reach of the law. Professional gamblers spent weeks on the steamboats, booking passage
up and down the river, for the chance to challenge wealthy travelers to poker, faro, and other betting games. With their ruffled shirts
and freshly pressed black suits, they made up in style for what they
lacked in respectability. They were a rakish, opportunistic lot. Cultivating an image of boundless wealth helped them win the confidence
of their marks. Free Black people also found solace on the river, away
from the slave hunters and vigilantes who roamed the forests along
the shore. Gambling was one of their few means to make money. For
a young man eager to achieve his fortune, the trip itself would be a
chance to learn the gambling trade by observing some of the best con
artists of the era.[4]

Robert would have drunk in every detail of the gamblers' dress
and manner, not to mention their card playing, because he himself
was already cultivating such an image on the racing circuit. But his
journey was, at heart, a voyage of love and hope for the woman who
cared enough about him to bring him to Harlan's Station, seeking a

better life for him even if she could not share it. Now she was mired in a virtual slave swamp, and he was going to find her.

Arriving in Pointe Coupee, after what would have been days of traversing mosquito-infested wetlands, Robert discovered that his mother had been sold farther south to the Attakapas, a remote planting region worked with enslaved labor. Journeying deeper into the fetid heart of Louisiana, he reached his mother at last. What he discovered in the Attakapas may have surprised him: she had a husband who may have heard little about him or his life in the North. By one account later in his life, Robert bought his mother her freedom and begged her to return with him to Kentucky. She, however, made the understandable decision to stay in Attakapas with her husband.

He departed wistfully, with the satisfaction of having been reunited with the woman who gave him the gift of a better life. But he made the long trip back up north by himself.[5]

With the Harlans having decamped from the Harrodsburg area, Robert gave up his barber shop and moved to Lexington, a city in the midst of its own halcyon days as the "Athens of the West." Known for its educational institutions and lush horse-breeding farms, it was, by Kentucky standards, open minded and progressive in feeling.[6] The hometown of Henry Clay counted roughly seven thousand inhabitants, including immigrants from Germany, Wales, Ireland, and Scotland.[7] But behind its gentrified façade, Lexington still had traces of Kentucky's wild frontier edge, with its threat of violence and lawlessness.[8]

A disproportionate share of Kentucky's free Black people were clustered in Louisville and Lexington, but they represented only a few hundred people at most; enough to be a presence, but also to remain a distinct minority within a minority.[9] There were far more enslaved people, living in shacks or cottages behind their masters' homes, creating tiny, back-alley Black communities.[10] While a third of free Black people were economically successful enough to own homes of their own, they were still subject to race-based regulations aimed at preventing slave revolts; there were, for example, strict limits on the numbers of Black people who could gather on the streets, and police would crack down on any grouping that was large enough to seem threatening.[11]

Despite the evident tensions, Robert saw Lexington as a place to put down roots. He opened a grocery store and began earning a steady income. The stability put him in the mind-set to find a wife of his own, falling quickly in love with a Lexington woman named Margaret Sproul. The two were married on November 19, 1840, with Fayette County records attesting that they were both "free." This wasn't quite true in Robert's case, and the fact that the clerk saw the need to make the same assertion about Margaret suggested that she, too, was of mixed race.[12]

Happy in his home life, Robert poured his energy into his grocery business and rapidly expanding family. He and Margaret would welcome five daughters in the next eight years, though their lives would be tinged with grief: two of their girls died in early childhood. Living as a Black family in a slave state wouldn't prove to be as hospitable as he'd hoped, either. As he strived to provide for his family, Robert's ambition helped to sustain him; his dreams were always bigger than Kentucky.[13]

John's political initiation came in 1844 when, as an alert eleven-year-old, he witnessed the slow-motion collapse of Henry Clay's all-but-certain victory in that year's presidential campaign against Tennessee Democrat James Polk, a former congressman and governor. It was the third time that his and his father's political hero had gone down to defeat in a national election. John made the plebiscite a subject of intense study, the focus of his interest in politics and statesmanship. As a result, Clay's failure hit him with the bitter force of boyhood disappointment. It felt like the death of a dream. John had charted Clay's campaign with the meticulous and intense curiosity with which other boys mapped out historic battles. Politics was no game for the Harlan men or for many other Kentuckians of their era. Every election posed an existential threat. The prospect of another Democrat winning the presidency was terrifying to any son of James Harlan, and the horror was all the greater for being so unexpected. James and other devotees of Clay, the Whig Party's nominee, had been especially confident of their man's chances because of the unraveling of the Jacksonian coalition in the Democratic Party. But Clay's campaign foundered again on the horns of sectionalism.[14]

"I remember that many of Mr. Clay's friends talked of his defeat . . . as meaning the ruin of the country," John would later write, still unable to stanch the pain of the loss, relating the "widespread grief among [Clay's] political and personal friends," including, of course, the man whose opinion mattered more to him than anyone else's, his father.[15]

The most contested issue in the election was the proposed annexation of Texas, for eight years an independent republic on the southwestern flank of the United States. Despite its independent spirit, Texas was too weak to perpetually defend itself against Mexican land claims and incursions. From the US point of view, annexation would remove Texas as an obstacle to future expansion to the Pacific, which many Americans considered their destiny. In the delicate politics of slavery, however, annexing Texas would be a profoundly disturbing event. It would likely enter the Union as a slave state, upsetting the fragile balance of power that Clay himself had engineered in the Missouri Compromise twenty-four years earlier, as a youthful Speaker of the House. Many northerners strongly opposed annexation, fearing that slave states would achieve a permanent majority; southerners, including Polk, embraced it.[16]

As John monitored the returns from Frankfort, the election unfolded slowly, with states choosing their presidential electors at different times. All looked promising for Clay until the results from New York came through. Once considered strongly in the Whig camp, the Empire State ended up tilting to Polk because of a forceful third-party challenge by newspaper editor James G. Birney. A fellow Kentuckian once based in Danville, Birney had been among the Bluegrass State's leading abolitionists and a thorn in Clay's side before shifting his operations to Ohio. Like many unyielding opponents of slavery, Birney had been infuriated by Clay's seeming equivocation on the Texas question. True to his moderate instincts and openness to compromise, the Whig nominee had declared in a series of letters that he might consider annexing Texas if he could do so without destabilizing the Union. The letters were a sop to moderates in the South, and few expected Clay to support annexation. But Birney wasn't appeased, and his candidacy siphoned off enough support to give the state of New York to Polk. New York alone provided enough electoral votes to swing the election to Polk and the Democrats.[17]

For John, the experience offered two important lessons. One was the extent to which slavery represented a profoundly destabilizing force, infecting all corners of political life. The other, he felt, was the danger of extremism, as represented by Birney, whom he believed had deliberately aided Polk in hopes that a Democratic victory would so enrage the North as to push the slavery debate to a crisis point.[18] Against those powerful currents, young John came to believe that the decent, patriotic Clay—the one man willing to put the nation's interest above sectional concerns—was no match.

The implications of the Polk victory hit home for the Harlans in more than just bruised feelings. Polk did indeed annex Texas, triggering a crisis with Mexico. When disarray in Mexican leadership made it difficult to negotiate a peace deal, vast numbers of Americans rose up in anger, inflamed with war fever.[19] The Clays and Harlans, despite being in the opposition party, quickly found themselves swept up in the furor. Henry Clay himself made a widely quoted quip about wanting to "capture or to slay a Mexican." His own son, thirty-five-year-old Henry Jr., a West Point graduate, eagerly signed up to fight, despite being the father of five young children who had recently lost their mother.[20] Richard Davenport Harlan, at twenty-three the eldest of James and Eliza's brood, joined the Kentucky volunteers, who filled their enlistment goal in five days.[21] Clay Harlan—the most idealistic of John's brothers—started recruiting a company of his own, even though he was barely on the cusp of seventeen at the time. At thirteen, John tried to sign up alongside his elder brother. The company was never called upon, probably because of the boys' ages, but their lust for patriotism and adventure was unabated.[22]

Polk sent troops to the disputed lands, prompting an attack by the Mexican army. The president obtained a congressional declaration of war, though many Whigs remained skeptical, if not outright opposed. General Antonio López de Santa Anna, the attacker of the Alamo, once again commanded the Mexican forces.[23] Richard Harlan, Henry Clay Jr., and many other Kentuckians—including Cassius M. Clay and three of John's uncles and cousins—were mustered under the command of the erratic General Zachary Taylor, known more for his fearlessness in pursuing the enemy than his strategic cunning.[24]

In February 1847 Taylor established a position in the hills above a Mexican village called Buena Vista, essentially daring Santa Anna, whose loosely trained army consisted of three times as many men, to attack. Taylor's troops bravely held off Santa Anna's forces over two days of brutal combat, with heavy losses on both sides. John's brother and other relatives survived. His cousin, "Big Jim" Harlan, even went down in Kentucky lore for bucking his musket to rout sixteen Mexicans using only a "bean pole."[25] But among the 267 Americans who died was Henry Clay Jr., leaving his elderly parents awash in grief and concerned for the fate of their five orphaned grandchildren.[26] Taylor, it turned out, had defied orders by venturing so far into Mexico, and lost much of his command. He had been a foolhardy leader in many ways, but his victory was cheered throughout the United States, and the little-known Taylor was suddenly a name on the tongue of every American.[27]

Henry Clay received the news of his son's death at his plantation in Lexington, to which he had retired after his 1844 defeat.[28] By 1847, he was just past his seventieth birthday and presumed to be done with politics. But he quickly apprehended how excitement over the war was creating an ever-greater lust for expansion, which would, in turn, create irresolvable conflicts over slavery. While Polk and other war supporters grandly envisioned a larger union, they were, Clay believed, planting the seeds of its dissolution. That was enough to lure the old warrior back into the public square.

"The day is dark and gloomy, unsettled and uncertain, like the condition of our country," Clay declared on November 13, 1847, speaking before a huge crowd in the Lexington marketplace, which may have included a young Illinois congressman named Abraham Lincoln. "The public mind is agitated and anxious and is filled with serious apprehensions as to its indefinite continuance, and especially as to the consequences which its termination may bring forth, menacing the harmony, if not the existence, of our union."[29]

In the front of the audience, seated beside his father, fourteen-year-old John Marshall Harlan was in awe. Here was one of the truly great men of the century holding forth with eloquence on the fate of the Union and of the war that held its grip on so many families, including the Harlans. "I remember that during the whole time of Clay's speech, I sat at his feet, and was charmed with his magnificent, bugle voice," John would later write to his own son.[30]

Clay's Mexican War speech would reverberate around the nation, planting fresh doubts about the war and the future of slavery. For John, the speech provided indelible lessons in what it meant to be a statesman, a Whig, a Kentuckian. Clay's willingness to stand against the wind and point the way to a better future thrilled him. For James and many other Clay admirers, it signified something more immediate and, to them, exhilarating: the old man still had some political life left in him.[31]

As he entered his thirties, as a husband, father and breadwinner, Robert Harlan faced a painful reality: families of mixed race like his own were increasingly under siege as anger surrounding the national debate over slavery spilled over into the communities of the South. In Robert's home environs of Lexington, a vigilante gang began targeting the homes and businesses of prosperous Black men like himself, as well as those of white abolitionists. The gang members hid their racism and violence behind war paint, and called themselves the Black Indians. They were neither Black nor Native American. Underneath the dark paint, their faces were white, and the hatchets they carried weren't tomahawks. In 1845, in an explosion of violence, the gang broke into the Lexington offices of the *True American*, an abolitionist newspaper published by Cassius M. Clay. After wreaking havoc inside, they spilled out into a Black neighborhood and began beating men randomly, leaving one free Black man tarred and feathered in the public square. Stunned by the attack, the abolitionist cousin of Henry Clay moved his newspaper north to the free state of Ohio. Black families like Robert's weren't able to pick up and leave as quickly or easily.[32]

After each spasm of violence, the gang members melted back into the population of Lexington, their faces blending into the white crowd, and the authorities would do no more than throw up their hands.[33] Every few months, the Black Indians would pop up again. The more successful the Black family, the more likely they'd be a target—especially Black businessmen, whom the Black Indians dubbed "sassy n----rs." Robert was constantly on guard, aware that all that he and Margaret had built could crumble in seconds.[34]

He found his means of escape after a man named James Marshall discovered gold in Coloma, California, on January 24, 1848. It didn't take long for word of the miraculous find to make its way eastward.[35] By that summer, it reached Kentucky.[36] The news was explosive, life changing. For Robert, who was lightning quick to spot opportunities where a Black man could be given a chance—from selling coonskins to barbering, from horse racing to opening a grocery store—the mass exodus to California seemed a moment to seize. Instinctively, he understood that prejudice would be slow to take hold in unmapped corners of the little-known coast. The gold rush would be a colorblind scramble. The first in line would take home the greatest rewards.

With his innate self-confidence, Robert could envision making a fortune in the West, then returning to share it with Margaret and the girls. He would earn enough for his family to leave the Black Indians behind and build a new life in a free state. He had little time to waste. Already thousands of prospectors were flocking westward with nothing but the shirts on their backs. Robert was prepared to join them. First, he had some business to attend to: securing his own freedom. James Harlan was more like a father than a master, but as the nation's disputes over slavery became more severe, so too did the types of retribution meted out against men and women who were deemed runaways. Robert could no longer risk a long journey without proof of his freedom.

In September 1848 James Harlan petitioned the Franklin County, Kentucky, court for a deed of emancipation for Robert Harlan. The court soon declared that Robert—who, the clerk scrawled in splintered English, "is ascertained to be of the following description vis thirty two years 12th decr next six feet high yellow big straight black hair blue eyes a Scar on his right wrist the Size of a dime"—was now officially a free man. Robert insisted on paying $500 to James, in the form of a promissory note.[37]

Robert knew exactly where he planned to earn that $500: A dusty little place called Coloma, California.

Robert's emancipation came at the end of a brutal summer for James. The fraying of the nation's politics weighed heavily on him. For three months after Henry Clay's speech against the Mexican War, James had helped to lay the groundwork for yet another Clay presidential campaign. Then, in February, came the signing of the Treaty of Guadalupe Hidalgo, ending the war and extending the southern edge of the United States to the Rio Grande River. The successful conclusion of the war seemed to obliterate the entire rationale for another Clay candidacy, but the enthusiasm generated by his speech in Lexington kept him in contention; many even considered him, at seventy-one, the front-runner for what would be his fourth presidential nomination. The challenge to Clay for primacy among the Whigs came not from within the party but from an upstart outsider who rejected almost all its precepts: Zachary Taylor.[38]

Ever since the stunning electoral success of Old Hickory, Andrew Jackson, parties had been eager to nominate generals—as the Whigs had successfully done eight years earlier with "Old Tippecanoe" William Henry Harrison. Often, these generals lacked any discernible ideology or record on the issues of the day, but their battlefield heroism was enough to win the trust of many Americans. Now "Old Rough and Ready," as Taylor was called, let it be known that he was prepared to lead the Whig ticket, as long as it wasn't encumbered with too much Whig baggage.

The Taylor challenge enraged the Harlans and other Clay supporters because of its sheer cynicism. The ironies were stacked high. Henry Clay was going up against the man whose rash actions had led his son to his death. And that man was refusing to endorse any of the defining positions that Clay and Webster and James and other Whig leaders had established in creating their party.[39]

Young John, who monitored the contest as scrupulously as he did four years earlier, but with perhaps fewer expectations, later put it ruefully, "The Mexican War occurred, and out of that contest came Zachary Taylor."

Nonetheless, Clay's political weakness, as much as Taylor's strength, would be a factor at the cacophonous nominating convention in Philadelphia. The Mexican War speech, while initially hailed as a triumph, had wiped out much of Clay's Southern support. Even his longtime admirer Abraham Lincoln was ready to throw in his lot with Taylor. Clay just didn't seem electable.[40]

But James Harlan didn't see fit to choose a man for president just because he seemed electable. He traveled the better part of seven hundred miles to the City of Brotherly Love to woo undecided Whig delegates to back Clay. The opulence of its setting belied the convention's eagerness for a candidate who could appeal to the common man. The Whigs installed themselves in the famed upper saloon of the Chinese Museum in Philadelphia, a gathering place that was noted for its Grecian columns, lavish balls, and annual Philadelphia Horticultural Society flower show.[41] But it soon became clear that the only candidacy in bloom that season would be Taylor's, not Clay's.

James and other Clay loyalists, including the famed newspaper editor Horace Greeley, strategized in their makeshift headquarters in the office of Philadelphia mayor John Swift to make Clay, not Taylor, the last man standing.[42] The Whigs had announced that they would hold four ballots, and the Clay forces envisioned winning the plurality of votes on the first ballot, then picking up the backing of various native-son candidates in succeeding ballots. But the softness of Clay's support became apparent almost immediately. There were persistent reports—some accurate, some erroneous—of mutinies in Clay's Kentucky delegation. The notion that even Whigs in his own state doubted his viability may have led wavering delegates to side with Taylor. When the results of the first ballot were announced, it was Taylor, not Clay, who had a plurality. And Clay's support dwindled further from there.[43]

By the fourth ballot, there was only one vote left for Clay in the Kentucky delegation: that of James Harlan.[44]

James, one Kentucky newspaper wrote, "voted first and last the truth."[45] It was a display of loyalty that Clay and his family would never forget.

Fifteen-year-old John did not make the trip with his father to Philadelphia, instead tracking the convention debacle from home. Despite the outcome, the bruised and battered Clay remained John's hero. In an atmosphere in which both abolitionists and states'-rights conservatives seemed willing to destroy the Union to get their way, only Clay was speaking up for the national interests that the Harlans considered sacred.

It would turn out that the Great Compromiser had yet another act in him. Returning to Washington as a senator from Kentucky, Clay would push through the Compromise of 1850, a series of measures that included admitting California as a free state; letting the Utah and New Mexico territories decide by popular sovereignty whether to be slave or free; banning slavery in the District of Columbia; and, most significantly, enacting a highly punitive Fugitive Slave Act.[46]

There was much for both sides to like and dislike in the compromise, but most agreed that Clay's exertions on its behalf, coming while his health was collapsing due to tuberculosis, were a poignant act of political will.[47] That November, the ailing Clay spoke before the Kentucky Legislature in Frankfort for one last time, putting an emotional exclamation point on his love of the Union. More than a half century later, John would recount every detail of Clay's final address, remembering, "He was in full dress on that occasion, except that his cravat was black. Standing on the aisle of the House, as he spoke, he strode backwards or forwards, traversing the whole aisle, and looked as if he felt himself to be master of the situation. His manner was that of a great general, ready to join issue with any one who was opposed to the Compromise Measures . . . or who questioned his motives."

Disconcerted by the Whig Party's nomination of Taylor and his subsequent victory, Clay now recognized that he occupied a political island of his own. He seemed to welcome the freedom, after all the years of trying to forge compromises with others. He could muse, as an old man, that there was dignity and integrity in such a position. Clay's bitterness about partisan politics informed the most memorable line of his speech, the one that implanted itself in the memory of the teenaged John: "If there be any man on this broad earth who feels himself perfectly independent, I am that man."[48]

That Clay's lifelong crusade had turned into a lonely one only ennobled it in John's eyes. That Clay would die fearing, perhaps even knowing, that the civil war he had long sought to prevent was just around the corner didn't diminish the righteousness of his cause or the courage of its bearer.

Robert's race against time, and against hordes of like-minded adventurers from the East Coast, would take him on one of the more treacherous journeys in the mapped-out world. He would have to make his way through a rain forest, disease-infested swamp, and famously deadly shipping narrows. His goal was to make it to San Francisco before the end of 1848, knowing that there were hundreds of thousands of greedy and anxious men in his wake. For companionship and protection, he linked up with several other Kentuckians. The first leg of this journey—from Lexington to Panama—would follow the same path that once had led him to his mother.[49]

Robert would have taken a steamboat down the Mississippi again, this time staying aboard to the end of the line in New Orleans. There he would have booked passage on a sailing ship to Panama. Docking at the Panamanian port of Colón, he and his mates commenced to travel by mule, canoe, and foot across the forested expanse of the territory.[50]

A neck of land just sixty miles wide, the isthmus of Panama was the shortest route to the Pacific, but it was deceptively dangerous. There was no well-trod path from sea to sea. Robert and his party had to hack their way through poisonous jungles, climb over and around the jagged mountains that formed the Continental Divide, and paddle through tangled wetlands. Yellow fever and malaria were constant companions. Some of the men in Robert's party took sick and died, never making it to Panama's Pacific coast.[51] Reaching Panama City, he discovered that the large steamers that North American newspapers had promised would transport men on the perilous three-thousand-mile journey northward to San Francisco simply didn't exist; instead, he joined a crowd of hundreds on the rickety docks in hopes of buying passage on old, overcrowded, and often filthy vessels.[52] The coastal voyage to San Francisco consumed the better part of two weeks, buffeted by powerful tides, fog, and winds before threading through the narrow and rocky strait known as the Golden Gate.[53]

Upon arrival, the crew probably ditched the ship in the harbor. At the height of the gold rush, as many as forty-five boats arrived in San Francisco Harbor every day, with too few piers to handle them. Captains realized they could make more money in the desert panning for gold than on the ocean returning to Panama. They left their ships to rot, but not before ransacking them as fodder for the tent cities rimming the harbor.[54] There was a voracious hunger for all types of supplies: a thousand feet of lumber, worth $1,000 in New York City, was going for $14,000.[55]

Fires blew through this makeshift metropolis on an almost monthly basis, only to have more tents and ramshackle structures spring up again within days.[56] Saloons and hotels were popping up everywhere, while merchants set up shop on street corners to peddle overpriced shovels and pickaxes. Amid all the bustle and lawlessness, there was little appetite for the racial tension Robert faced in Kentucky. "The streets were full of people hurrying to and fro," reported the eminent travel writer Bayard Taylor in 1850. "It is by chance . . . that the New Yorker is distinguished from the Kentuckian, the Carolinian from the Down-Easter, the Virginian from the Texan. The German and Frenchman are more easily recognized. Peruvians and Chileans go by in their brown ponchos, and the sober Chinese [are] cool and impassive in the midst of the excitement."[58]

Robert, whose Kentucky upbringing imbued him with the conviction that gambling was a demonstration of a gentleman's panache, was very much at home. With few women on hand, drinking and card playing consumed men's evenings. Visitors counted as many as a thousand gaming parlors, or one for every twenty-five people: "Gambling was the amusement, the grand occupation of many classes . . . the life and soul of the place," wrote the three authors of the 1855 book *The Annals of San Francisco*.[57] The larger gambling houses, called hells, clustered around the center of town. Hastily hung glass chandeliers dangled precariously from the ceilings; gilt mirrors and plush furniture added to the air of soiled glamour. As if to remind the men of what they couldn't have, many of the hells were decorated with hastily drawn paintings of naked women. The city's original hell, aptly named El Dorado, vibrated beneath a giant tent that later gave way to a shed that cost $40,000 per year in rent, a testament to the riches being exchanged within.[59]

Robert readily partook of the gaming houses, though he would later deny that his fortune came from gambling. Rather, as an experienced store owner, he opened his own establishment in gold rush–era California and took advantage of the massive inflation on even the most basic goods—a process that would have mimicked gambling in the trading of cash or gold for products and then selling them at a spectacular markup. Most likely, he collected money any way that he could—perhaps even by taking out a pan and prospecting for golden nuggets in the California riverbeds.[60]

One way or the other, he returned to Kentucky with a fortune that was the envy of most of his contemporaries; news reports counted his wealth at between $45,000 and $90,000—or between $1.4 million and $2.8 million in 2021 dollars, though the money would have gone even further in the booming western frontier of his era.[61] Robert was now, by all estimates, rich beyond the imagination of all but a hand- ful of his Lexington neighbors. By the age of thirty-two, a man who had been born enslaved in a county full of field hands had traveled the world, opened businesses, immersed himself in the sport of horse racing, joined in the gold rush, and come away with serious means.

Robert made the long journey home with the satisfaction of hav- ing defied the greatest odds known to man—passing from slavery to wealth, the kind of story that entranced readers of nineteenth-century fiction and won applause for traveling theater companies. Robert's mind would have been overflowing with plans. He would leave Lex- ington. Quit Kentucky. Be a man of the world. The free states beck- oned. There he could help other freedmen find their own footing. And he could provide a new life for Margaret and the girls.

With his eyes on those horizons, Robert would have backtracked his way through the Panamanian jungle, dragging his chest full of gold. On the Atlantic coast, he boarded a ship for New York. After docking in Manhattan, he contracted with a bank to secure his for- tune.[62] When he finally made it to back to Lexington, however, he found not joy but tragedy. A grim message awaited him: Margaret had died while he was out west.

He was now a widower with three surviving daughters. He had no wife and no home.[63]

In all his years to come, Robert would seek to repay the family that raised him, to show that he was there as a brother, willing to share his money and influence with those he considered kin.

A few years after Robert returned from California, when James and Eliza's family gathered to celebrate the wedding of their eldest daughter, Lizzie, to a fine young doctor from Indiana named James G. Hatchitt, the polished and sparkling wedding gifts were displayed for all to admire. Most impressive of all was the beautiful handmade piano for the music-loving Lizzie, sent with full compliments on the joyful occasion by her now wealthiest of relations, Robert Harlan.[64]

Chapter 3

Faith and the Founding Fathers

John's sense of patriotism found even greater expression at Centre College in his old hometown of Danville. John's childhood minister John C. Young presided over the college as a stern but kindly father figure. Reverend Young shared most of James Harlan's nationalistic political views along with his Presbyterian faith. He invested the United States with a special providence and suggested its democratic institutions carried an almost religious mandate.[1]

John followed in the footsteps of his brother Clay, who had just completed his own academic career at Centre. Moving in with one of his father's brothers, John took up residence near the Danville campus where, despite a strict Presbyterian ethos that marked bars, theaters, and horse races as off-limits, he was able to engage in the occasional collegiate hijinks.[2] He joined Beta Theta Pi fraternity, which had just organized on campus, its founders having transferred from Miami University in Ohio.[3] Colleges of any type were few and far between on the frontier. Established in 1819 by the Kentucky General Assembly and named for its central position in the state, Centre had an illustrious reputation.[4] It offered more than just rigorous instruction in religion and classics: there were classes on subjects as varied as moral philosophy, economics, physiology, international law, the US Constitution, civil architecture, and zoology.[5]

It also emphasized rhetoric, forcing students to hone their skills in public speaking by composing original speeches every week.[6] In the nineteenth century, public speaking was a source of entertainment and improvisation, as well as political suasion. In developing his own voice, John drew on his outsized sense of national pride. Whether or not his speeches addressed the feud over slavery directly, the great issue of the time echoed within his every syllable. It was as if John wanted to grab his listeners by the lapels and remind them of the greatness of the Constitution precisely so that they would join him in protecting and preserving the Union at any cost.

John liked to contrast the genius of the American system, with the people as sovereign, with the despotic reigns of monarchs abroad; he begged his countrymen to appreciate the novel virtues of the American rule of law over men.

"The name, the fame, the achievements of our heroes, were sounded abroad, and served as a watchword to the lovers of liberty all over the world," the teenaged John declared during his first year at Centre, quoting an unattributed piece of rhetoric of the swooning style popular in the nineteenth century. "Our country was the birthplace of modern freedom; but no sooner had her opinions acquired strength and maturity, than she flew forth in other climes, to establish her temples on the ruins of baronial castles and feudal prison-houses."[7]

For John, the "baronial castles and feudal prison-houses" were emblems of Europe's despotic class system, which stifled people's natural yearnings for freedom. The mere example set by the United States of a different model of governing was enough to incite revolutions and inspire reform movements around the world. He probably meant to imply that it would be unthinkable for Americans, who gained so much from this system, to squander it either by attempting to force the abolition of slavery on unwilling neighbors or by defiantly tethering themselves to the outmoded slave economy.

While John was extolling the greatness of the American system, Robert was escaping its despotism by moving his daughters and Margaret's mother to the free state of Ohio. From the time he had been a child at the Old Stone House, Robert had felt the lure of the Ohio River, the border between Kentucky and freedom.[8] Cincinnati, the city on the other side of the border, had all the pulsating energy of a thriving port, a gateway for thousands of people arriving each year by steamboat from as far south as New Orleans and as far north as Pittsburgh.[9]

To white travelers from the gentler precincts of the East Coast and Europe, Cincinnati was "Porkopolis," a giant hog pen. Fanny Trollope, the English novelist, visited in 1832 and took note of its dozens of meat-packing plants and the smells that emanated from them. "If I determined to walk up Main-street, the chances were five hundred to one against my reaching the shady side without brushing by a snout fresh dripping from the kennel," sniffed Trollope in her widely read book *Domestic Manners of the Americans*. For decades afterward, European writers seemed determined to outdo Trollope with ever-richer evocations of the city's appalling pig effluence.[10]

Meanwhile, the stench of Porkopolis fell hardest on its Black neighborhoods, the East and West End areas along the Ohio River, dubbed Bucktown and Little Bucktown, with Little Africa between them. Bucktown abutted Deer Creek, the primary dumping ground for the meat-packing district.[11]

For many Black people, however, Cincinnati was more than a ghetto plagued by pig odors: it was a beacon of hope; the first glimpse of freedom for enslaved men and women traveling on the Underground Railroad and for free Black people coming north by steamboat.[12] For Robert Harlan, who spent most of his childhood 120 miles from Cincinnati, the city was synonymous with the dream of a free life. "Even in boyhood, Cincinnati had been a promised land to him, and when in trouble, he always threatened to run off to Cincinnati," the *Cincinnati Commercial* would later report in a profile of Robert.[13] Upon returning from the gold rush, Robert immediately laid plans to move to the metropolis to the north. He wasn't alone: by the late 1840s, Cincinnati's population had swelled to well over a hundred thousand, making it the largest city in the West, more than ten times the size of Lexington.[14]

Robert would have crossed paths with plenty of Ohioans in his years in Kentucky, through his grocery business and horse racing meets. He knew that opportunities for Black people were greater in a free state, even if Ohio fell dramatically short of anything like racial equality. In fact, Cincinnati was a cauldron of racial strife. The chains that held Black people in the South were loosened here, but only enough to produce more furious pulling and tugging, which, in turn, prompted greater pushback from itinerant whites. Life in the Queen City was brutal enough that some Black people claimed to find it little better than slavery. "I thought upon coming to a free state like Ohio, that I would find every door thrown open to receive me, but from the treatment I received by the people generally, I found it little better than Virginia," wrote the African American memoirist John Malvin in the 1820s. "I found every door closed against a colored man in a free state, excepting jails and penitentiaries, the doors of which were thrown wide open to receive him."[15]

In 1829, two decades before Robert's arrival, Cincinnati was upended by some of the nation's first race riots, as mobs of between 200 and 300 white men ransacked the city's Black Fourth Ward, destroying homes and shops. The rioters were trying to force about 1,500 Black laborers out of their jobs, presumably to free up more work and higher wages for whites.[16] The tactic seemed to succeed: between 1,100 and 1,500 Black Cincinnatians fled north, many of them to start a colony in Canada.[17] At least an equal number stayed to rebuild their homes and stores, but life became even harder in the 1830s. Barred from skilled professions, Black men found work instead at the docks, as boatmen, freight workers, stewards, and porters.[18]

In 1841 violence broke out again. This time, when seven hundred lawless whites descended on the Black wards, Black people fought back. The battles on the streets were furious enough that white vigilantes even took to firing a cannon into the Black part of town. The bloodshed shocked the consciences of many wealthier whites.[19] By the end of the 1840s, life in Cincinnati was a little brighter for Black people, who demanded and received more legal protections. Ohio courts, in 1842, granted full voting rights to people of mixed race, as long as they were less than 50 percent Black. To some people, this was a sign of progress—an advancement over the "one drop" rule that was applied in the South and deemed any person of mixed ancestry to be Black—but it stoked fresh tensions in the Black community, dividing people by their skin tone.[20]

Robert may have known that a "mulatto" like himself would get a better shake in Cincinnati than other freed men and women. He also would have known of the city's violent racial past. But he had a plan. He saw potential in the growing Black community, about half of whom were former slaves like himself.[21] Some of them had first glimpsed Cincinnati as passengers on the Underground Railroad, for which it was the first stop in the free states.[22] These people needed access to capital to create the kinds of businesses that he himself had operated in Kentucky. His first step was to purchase property. He bought a big house on the corner of Fifth and Broadway, on the edge of Bucktown, with a large retail space on the first floor, which he rented to a Black grocer named Samuel Wilcox.[23]

Robert was striving to advance his people. He was also trying to make more money for himself.

Clay Harlan, at twenty, was a recent college graduate taking his first steps to a legal career when he wrote to a family friend about a terrible cholera epidemic that was sweeping through Frankfort. A month later, he was dead. "Time and a patient resignation and submission to the Will of Him who, having given us our children, has the right to take them from us when he pleases, can heal the wounds inflicted," wrote the elderly Henry Clay to James, lamenting the loss of his namesake.[24]

John would have felt the loss of the brother who was most like him as keenly as anyone in the family. He didn't speak of it later in life, however, though he expressed the fond hope and expectation that he would be reunited in heaven with all the loved ones he had lost.[25] Large families in the nineteenth century found grief a constant companion. For John, the plague of infectious disease, with its shocking potential to claim early deaths, would serve to elevate the fifth son in the family order. Friends and family had at least tacitly regarded Clay and John as the Harlan sons with the most potential. Now John himself was, more than ever, the vehicle for his father's fondest hopes.

A year later, John once again followed in his brother's footsteps in graduating from Centre College with honors. The colorful commencement ceremonies began with a prayer and music, then featured no fewer than twelve speeches interspersed with musical interludes. Many of the addresses had to do with the perennial theme of growing up, while others ranged further afield, from "Ireland—Her Hopes," to "Tragedy—Its Moral Influence." The penultimate speech of the day, before the valedictory address and presentation of diplomas by Reverend Young, was by John Marshall Harlan. His speech, entitled simply "The Foreigner," gave him a chance to wax on his budding theories of American exceptionalism.[26]

Despite his evident interest in national politics, John was surprised to discover that his own mother had come up with a different plan for his future. A strong-willed woman who commanded the domestic sphere of the house, Eliza took it upon herself to write to her relatives who were prominent business leaders in Philadelphia. After watching four of her sons follow their father into the law, she wondered if her fifth might try something else, perhaps going into business in the East. She failed, however, to take sufficient note of her son's name and the special destiny accorded to him in his father's mind. James quickly overruled his wife's plans: "Without hesitation, he said that it would never do. . . . He had not named him 'John Marshall,' after the great chief justice, only to have him spend his life in the counting room of a mercantile pursuit," John's wife recalled in later years. John would prepare to enter the law and, at a time when most lawyers learned by apprenticeship alone, would test his academic abilities at the state's leading law school: Transylvania University in Lexington.[27]

The Robert Harlan who bought up properties in Cincinnati was a very different man from the one who strove for money in Kentucky. He was free. He was hardened by the loss of a beloved wife. The journey to the gold rush had done more than burnish his bank account; it made him a man of the world. His eyes were keen for new vistas. If he could thrive amid the chaos of San Francisco and withstand the rain forest of Panama, there was seemingly no climate he could not endure, no expanse he could not navigate.

Wealthy Americans in the East sent their children on grand tours of Europe to give them an extra dose of sophistication. By the 1850s, the trip was easier than in earlier eras. The steam engines that had proved themselves on the churning waters of the Mississippi River had cut the sailing time from New York to Liverpool, England, from more than a month to two weeks, give or take a few days. With his own bank account, Robert endeavored to do for himself, a thirty-five-year-old formerly enslaved man, what Boston Brahmins did for their sons: he would take the grand tour. There was a deeper hunger in Robert than in the sons of rich Bostonians. He wanted to learn about the Old World, but also whether a man of color, born into slavery, could succeed in that world.

In 1851, dense, foggy, proliferate London was suddenly the epicenter of global civilization. The Great Exhibition, opened that spring by Queen Victoria and her visionary consort, Prince Albert, was a showcase of innovation and design—a dazzling attempt to capture the spirit of the future under a single roof. Indeed, by the time Robert booked his passage to England, there was some debate as to whether the roof was more impressive than all the spectacular innovation underneath.[28]

Dubbed the Crystal Palace, the exhibition hall was itself a credit to the industrial revolution. Two decades earlier, a pair of brothers had invented a method of producing giant sheets of glass strong enough to withstand the winds and rains of an English winter; that had led to a boom in greenhouse construction, allowing wealthy Victorians to enjoy exotic fruits and plants all year round. When the building committee for the Great Exhibition fumbled its task, resulting in a design too cumbersome to erect on a tight deadline, planners seized on a proposal from a little-known architect who had just produced a greenhouse for the Duke of Devonshire. Rarely has a mistake yielded such a spectacular success. The Crystal Palace quickly became the symbol of the exhibition and its most breathtaking attraction. Essentially a giant greenhouse of roughly a million square feet, it housed ten miles of corridors displaying the latest machinery and technology from around the world.[29]

The normally taciturn Victoria was moved to a high pitch of excitement, calling the day of the opening ceremony "one of the greatest and most glorious of our lives. . . . It is a day which makes my heart swell with thankfulness."[30] British writers chimed in to mark the occasion. William Makepeace Thackeray put his bursting national pride into poetry: "A palace as for a fairy prince / A rare pavilion, such as man / Saw never since mankind began /And built and glazed."[31]

Robert, in walking the corridors of the exhibition, took special interest in the cutting-edge industries on display, perhaps sensing that new technology wasn't yet corrupted by old prejudices; a Black man would have a decent chance to succeed in these emerging industries. Among the products from around the world was one that Robert would have instantly recognized: a daguerreotype panorama of Cincinnati. The image, taken in 1848 from a rooftop across the river in Newport, Kentucky, by Charles Fontayne and William S. Porter, was the first known photograph of any city in the world.[32]

Robert had traveled four thousand miles to discover that some of the most sublimely impressive advancements were being made back home.

Transylvania Law School was dominated by a large, rotund professor named George Robertson, who as a young man had served three terms in the US House only to return to politics three decades later as a devout Whig in the Kentucky legislature.[33] At sixty, the imposing Robertson, with his shock of graying hair and copious jowls, played a leading role in providing Kentucky Unionists with a legal and intellectual justification for their positions on slavery and secession.[34] In his introductory lecture to John's class at Transylvania, Robertson took aim at the Kentucky and Virginia Resolutions of 1798, which Southerners were citing as justification for states' rights to nullify federal law.[35] The resolutions, secretly written by Thomas Jefferson and James Madison in opposition to the Alien and Sedition Acts passed by the rival John Adams administration, were deeply controversial in their time, prompting a rebuke from none other than George Washington. But they popped up again a half century later as a theoretical justification for secession. They suggested that state governments, rather than courts, could make their own interpretations of what was unconstitutional.[36]

Robertson found little justification for the resolutions and spent much of the address berating those who would even contemplate dismantling the Union. But at the end of the long, stem-winding speech, he injected a curious note of nativism. "Our organic institutions have survived many trials of their purity and their strength," he intoned. "They have been saved by the patriotism of such men as Washington, and Clay, and Webster. . . . But the signs of the times portend an approaching crisis more decisive of their fate than any through which they yet have passed. Foreign influence and foreign politics are taking root in the virgin soil of American Republics. The old world, repressed with the incubus of a restless and starving population, intent to empty itself on the new."[37]

The allusion to foreign influence was an emerging trope of conservative Unionists such as Robertson. With so many people willing to tear apart the nation for their personal causes, Kentucky Unionists believed that the great decisions looming in the 1850s would separate the true patriots from those aligned with sectional interests. In their clarion call for patriotism, many Unionists were skeptical of the huge numbers of immigrants emerging every day from the bowels of the fast steamers from Europe. Between 1845 and 1854, almost three million immigrants had poured into the country, more than in the entire rest of the nation's history to that point. A large proportion of these huddled masses were victims of the Irish potato famine, which killed a million people and sent another million fleeing the shores. They, presumably, were less schooled in the American Constitution, concerned mostly with escaping the wretched conditions in their native land. Not incidentally, Catholic immigrants in the North had become a main-

stay of the Democratic Party—the party of would-be Southern seces-
sionists, as well. In Kentucky, a thousand miles from the docks of New
York, many people doubted these immigrants' commitment to the
Union, and many abolitionists regarded them as pro-slavery, to boot.[38]

Robertson's intolerance of the influx of "restless and starving" Europeans gnawed at the edges of the unionist ideology, but it gave the
high gloss of a major thinker to what was, in other precincts, a base
prejudice. At nineteen, John was enough of a believer in American
exceptionalism—and in the wisdom of his Kentucky mentors—to applaud Robertson's views, including the tacked-on warning about foreign influence. He joined with two other classmates to implore the
professor to allow them to publish and promote his address as widely
as possible.[39]

Law in Kentucky—real law enforcement, in the county courtrooms
that still bore the mud prints and tobacco stains of the frontier—
hardly resembled the high-minded constitutional debate going on
in Robertson's classroom. John learned this the hard way when one
of his first cousins—also named John—got into a fight with a violent man and, fearing for his life, pulled out a pistol and shot the man
dead. John's cousin was indicted for murder, but the victim had a gang
of friends in the Danville area, not far from Harlan's Station, who
wanted to take justice into their own hands. Harlan men from far and
wide were called in to help protect their cousin as he went up for trial.

Family honor required that they defend their kin, right or wrong.
And John, by now a striking young man of more than six feet, joined
a posse of Harlans led by the famous Big Jim Harlan, hero of the Battle of Buena Vista, who once took on sixteen Mexicans alone and
without his weapon. The cousins were all armed to their teeth, with
Big Jim wielding his bowie knife to ward off any attackers. They surrounded the defendant in the courtroom and escorted him back to
the jailhouse. When John's cousin was finally acquitted, John and
James brought him back with them to Frankfort, keeping him safely
in their home for several months until the gang lost interest.[40]

The trial came with a lesson: behind the laws are real people, sometimes involved in life-and-death disputes, and courts are the only bulwarks against vigilante justice. But to preserve the strength of these vital institutions, the call of justice requires the support of right-thinking people from the community.

Robert returned to Cincinnati from his grand tour by the beginning of 1852, brimming with ideas for new businesses and adventures in the United States and abroad. As he spoke about his journey before groups of Black and white people, he was held up as a figure of admiration—a credit to his race. As a rich, handsome young widower, he got his share of social attention as well. There, in Cincinnati, he met a fellow member of the Black elite as glamorous and attractive as himself and reputed to be of similarly illustrious lineage. Josephine Floyd was said to be the daughter of John Buchanan Floyd, the outgoing governor of Virginia who would go on to serve as US secretary of war and lead Confederate forces as a general in the Civil War, and an enslaved woman.[41]

Josephine's reputed parentage, like Robert's, gave her a whispered cachet in social circles both Black and white. Robert was smitten. When she accepted his proposal of marriage, he quickly purchased two giant rowhouses on Harrison Street on the edge of Bucktown, near his other properties.[42] His three surviving daughters and their grandmother would reside in one of them, and in the other, he and his new bride would enjoy space of their own, in a setting befitting two of the city's mixed-race elites.

On June 10, 1853, Robert Harlan donned his perfectly pressed clothes and tipped his cap to the many spectators in their own finery arriving at Louisville's Oakland Racetrack. He passed by the stately white-columned clubhouse, with its intentional resemblance to the neoclassical plantation mansions of the Deep South. All the trappings of the Southern gentry were on display here, at the very citadel of the favored pastime of the state's upper class. On the balcony and behind the green-shuttered windows, wealthy, white thoroughbred owners clinked glasses of bourbon to their chances in the day's races.[43]

Robert's goal was to beat them on their own turf. His trip to England had kindled a fascination with British racing, which only served to amplify his interest in the American sport. He had made a keen assessment of the ways in which the two countries could learn from each other in breeding and training horses. On this day, Robert was racing a colt with the auspicious name of Black Warrior. He was a foal of a famed British thoroughbred named Glencoe, one of the first racehorses to make the trip across the Atlantic. The four-year-old Black Warrior was a valuable horse, and Robert hoped to offset his purchase price by taking the $200 purse, a sum impressive enough to attract some of the state's most famous owners. Alexander Pope Churchill, known as A.P., was a racing pioneer whose family would go on to found Louisville's fabled Churchill Downs racetrack, home to the Kentucky Derby. He entered his colt Star Davis. John Harper, perhaps the state's leading breeder of horses, entered a filly called Jenny Lind, after the Swedish opera sensation who was just making a triumphant tour of the United States. R. P. Fields's colt rounded out the field.[44]

That some of Kentucky's richest owners, including two legends such as Churchill and Harper, would be racing against Robert Harlan, a formerly enslaved man, was the kind of irony that followed Robert like the well-pressed tail of a tuxedo.[45] The horses would run as many as five heats, with points accorded for their finish in each one. This was to test not only the colts' ability to sprint but also their stamina.[46]

The drum rolled, and the sleek animals trotted to the starting line, their jockeys decked in brightly colored jackets to help spectators distinguish among the animals. While Churchill, Harper, and their ilk likely retired to the segregated clubhouse, Robert would likely have followed the races from the bleachers. At the sound of another drum roll, the jockeys mounted their horses. A final drumbeat sent off the racers.[47] The brown-coated Black Warrior bolted from the starting line, but when the animals pounded their way to the finish line, he was in third place behind Star Davis.

This only increased the pressure on Robert's horse, who couldn't afford to finish behind Star Davis in two more heats, or the day of racing would be over. In the second heat, Black Warrior advanced to second place, giving Robert a moment of hope even though he again finished behind Star Davis. But when Black Warrior came in third yet again in the third heat, the day was over: Star Davis had swept the first three heats, claiming the purse that was strung across the finish line.[48]

For Robert, it was a disappointment of a type that racehorse owners learned to take in stride, with sporting good humor. Smiles and congratulations and thanks for the honor of competing were marks of etiquette that masked the intense competition that underlay the sport, the way that so many bettors cloaked their desperation under top hats and ruffled shirts.

Robert knew this world from the ground up; it was the one point of connection in every chapter of his life. That gave him an edge over other owners. Unlike most of them, he had been a trainer himself and learned to size up a horse by sight. His expertise was honed on the back trails of a state that held him in bondage. And through all the travails of his life—from stunning accomplishments to shocking snubs—the racetrack was the one arena that treated him generously, even respectfully.

"His luck was proverbial," the *Baltimore Sun* would later enthuse about Robert, in late middle age. "One day he bet $5 against $100 that a certain horse would fall down. The horse did fall down."

"No well-regulated race can be without him," the *Louisville Courier-Journal* wrote with evident affection long after Robert had moved to Ohio. "He is one of the ever-lasting racing figures."

On that June day in 1853, Robert was just starting out. His mind was full of plans. Black Warrior's defeat in the elite matchup at Oakland did not deter him. Nor did it quell his fascination with British racehorses, the progeny of the "sport of kings." On that score, he had bigger goals in mind.

The year 1853 also marked a watershed in Robert's personal life: Josephine gave birth to his son. Robert's joy went beyond the usual paternal pride. For a man born into slavery, destined to have his own parenthood discussed only in hushed tones, the arrival of a son to share his name conveyed a sense of legitimacy. It also extended the scope of his life into a future that carried more promise for Americans of color. This boy, unlike his father, was born free. He would have the best schooling in the land. He would have gentle manners—no "gunning and coon skinning" in his upbringing. He would occupy a strange but exalted place as a gentleman of color. He would, perhaps, prove to skeptical whites that a Black man could be just as cultivated as any white son of the finest families.

Robert determined that his son would share not only his own name but also that of James Harlan—a prophecy as powerful as the one James bestowed on his son John when he named him after America's greatest jurist. There is no record of Robert's letter to James announcing the arrival of Robert James Harlan. Perhaps this naming gesture, made in fondness and respect, was also shrouded by the conspiracy of silence surrounding the culture of slavery: it suggested an intimacy that could never be acknowledged. But Robert was in touch with members of James's family, who would at least incidentally spread the word of the new arrival. Robert could only hope that James took note of the boy's name and felt a pang of connection.[49]

Six months later, little Robert James Harlan was large and strong, well on the way to the life his father envisioned for him. With an heir under his roof, and a dazzlingly beautiful wife, life in Cincinnati was more satisfying than Robert could have imagined. But less than a year after the baby's birth, Josephine was dead.[50] Whether she failed to recover from the delivery—her complications lingering before taking their final toll—or succumbed to infectious disease, she suffered the same fate as Margaret: an early death at a moment brimming with promise. Once again, Robert faced an incalculable loss.

Josephine's beauty and mystique had added a dose of glamour to the life Robert was building; she was poised to become a leader in the city's emerging Black society. Even as he fought to advance himself and his family against the odds, fate bestowed new challenges to his fabled resiliency, and grief cast its veil upon him: for the second time in four years, he was mourning the death of a woman with whom he had planned to share his life.

The Whig Party, which had for so long avoided taking definitive stances on the future of slavery, collapsed over it.[51] The roots of its destruction dated back to the Philadelphia convention of 1848, when James made his lonely stand for Henry Clay over Zachary Taylor. As president, Taylor regarded himself as an independent figure and did little to advance the party or clarify its principles.[52] On July 4, 1850, after sixteen months in office, the sixty-five-year-old Taylor ate raw fruit and frozen milk at a fund-raising event for the Washington Monument. He came down with acute gastrointestinal distress and died after being blistered and bled by his doctors.[53] His passing gave the presidency to Millard Fillmore, a Clay ally who satisfied the demands of many conservative Unionist Whigs by signing the Compromise of 1850, Clay's great valedictory gesture.[54] Stricken with tuberculosis, the wizened Clay would leave his loving family in Lexington and make a painful journey to Washington, to pass away in the nation's capital.[55] The former senator, House Speaker, secretary of state, and three-time presidential nominee chose to die on the battlefield of the fight for the nation's survival. Back home at Ashland, the family plantation, Clay's son sent the old man's cane to James Harlan as a memento of their undying friendship.[56]

Clay's final compromise succeeded in quieting the drive toward secession in the South for four long years but wreaked havoc in the North. The most toxic aspect of the compromise was the Fugitive Slave Act, which imposed penalties on officials in free states who did not seek out and return runaway slaves. This had the perverse effect of making the slavery debate a directly pressing matter in every town in the North, even to people who had disdained it as a Southern problem.

Even worse, in a sop to the South, the law denied recourse to courts for Black people who were being unfairly targeted. This meant that even men and women with entirely legitimate cases for freedom were re-enslaved—or, in some cases, enslaved for the first time—on the mere say-so of a purported owner. The fear and pain of these victims inflamed antislavery sentiment. Northern Whigs blamed Fillmore.[57]

Since the incumbent president was too unpopular to be nominated for another term, the Whig Party once again tried its luck with a general at the top of the ticket, Winfield Scott. But the lightning that struck with William Henry Harrison and Zachary Taylor did not do so a third time. "Old Fuss and Feathers," as Scott was known, went down in flames. Democrat Franklin Pierce, a former senator and representative from New Hampshire, won twenty-seven states to Scott's four, clobbering him by 254 to 42 in the electoral college.[58]

Northern Unionists shifted their allegiances to a new party, the Republicans, dedicated to curbing the extension of slavery while pointedly rejecting the Fugitive Slave law. They also stood against the Kansas-Nebraska Act, the latest proxy for the slavery debate.[59] The law, championed by Illinois senator Stephen Douglas and signed by President Pierce in 1854, allowed the territories of Kansas and Nebraska to decide for themselves, by popular sovereignty, whether to legalize slavery. This not only set off violent clashes in the territories but also created the very real possibility of reimplanting slavery in the North.[60]

Republicans, in opposing the law, seemed to walk right up to the line of abolition, inflaming the South. That was going too far for conservative Unionists in Kentucky, whose fear of a war on their own soil grew stronger every day. "If one ideal characterized late antebellum border state life more than any other, it was the desire for order—social, economic, racial, and ultimately political order," wrote border-state historian Aaron Astor.[61]

Order was the one element missing in the national debate. That left the Harlans and most of their Kentucky allies without a national party to call their own.

On a gray morning in June 1855, two sons of Kentucky's leading families—Thomas Crittenden and John Harlan—rode out from Frankfort to the nearby hamlet of Bridgeport, Kentucky, for a political event in a small schoolhouse. The crowd of fewer than a hundred people was coming together as part of a new movement, rising quickly in Kentucky.[62] It was known as the American Party, or the Know-Nothings, because it arose out of a once-secret society whose members weren't allowed to acknowledge its existence. Now the new party was quickly filling the void left by the Whigs among conservative Unionists such as the Harlans and Crittendens in Kentucky, just as the Republicans were suddenly emerging up North.[63]

John's father had embraced the American Party, with its moderate position on slavery that mirrored that of the Whigs. But the Know-Nothings had another, sharper edge: they hoped to stem the tide of immigration, particularly from Catholic countries. In their view, Catholics, with their adherence to the Pope—the religious equivalent of absolute monarchy—weren't suited to enjoy and, more pointedly, defend American freedoms.

In later years, John would express reservations about his time in the American Party and suggest that he had uncritically accepted his father's guidance when he headed out to their meeting with his friend Tom Crittenden that June morning. John wrote later to his son Richard that he was so reluctant to recite the Know-Nothing oath, a vestige of the secret society, that he considered running from the room where it was administered. "While I was intense, as I still am, in my Protestantism, I did not relish the idea of proscribing anyone on account of his religion," John insisted in the letter.[64]

But that resistance wasn't anywhere in evidence that cloudy day in 1855. John understood well that Catholics were a growing share of the Democratic Party—which he saw as the primary threat to the Union—and had evinced no objections to his mentor George Robertson's carefully articulated reservations about immigrants. He could easily have envisioned how the American Party's antiforeign views would have a red-meat appeal to nativists in immigrant-filled cities, including Louisville. At the same time, it was plain that the Harlans and their aristocratic allies weren't primarily concerned with stopping the influx of foreigners. Saving the union was their overwhelming priority. In their view, the American Party was the only national alternative to the Republicans, whose views were entirely unacceptable to the South, and the Democrats, many of whom supported states' rights and opened the door to secession. By contrast, the Know-Nothings were vaguely antislavery, in the same gradualist manner as the Whigs, even if their nationalism was less high minded and more exclusive—exclusive, in fact, to Protestants.[65]

At twenty-two, the lean John Harlan already carried the fresh-scrubbed air of a dashing political tyro—one whose charisma and erudition exceeded his experience and wisdom—when he and Tom Crittenden dismounted their horses that cloudy morning in Bridgeport, Kentucky. Crittenden, the son of Kentucky's US senator John J. Crittenden, was the day's featured speaker, hoping to promote the American Party's candidate for governor. He went on for about forty-five minutes, leaving the crowd twisting in the chairs. Outside, rain began beating down hard, coating the classroom's windows and flooding the ruts in the road; no one would be going home for a while. "Let's hear from John Harlan," came one voice in the crowd.

John was surprised to be called upon and hadn't prepared a speech. When other voices joined in, he responded, "If I must, I must, seeing that the rain keeps you fast in the house." His wit, combined with his Centre College training, kicked in. For at least as long as Crittenden had spoken, John held forth on the great challenges of the day—weaving together his high-toned patriotic principles with his support for middle-ground compromises. When it was over, the audience roared its approval, and John's confidence soared.

He would later recall, "It seemed to me that a new career was then opened up before me, and I felt that I had some gifts for talking to a miscellaneous crowd."[66]

Public speaking wasn't a family trait. James was a clomping speaker, so notoriously dull that political opponents would ridicule him while supporters quietly shifted their attention to more articulate leaders. His campaign-trail speech endorsing Taylor in 1848, after having been a lone holdout for Clay, was a famous flop. "My friends, I have already detained you too long," he concluded. "I have done so in a rambling way." Democratic newspapers chortled that the Whigs should trot out James to speak on behalf of all their candidates.[67]

John, however, was a natural performer. He was invariably described as handsome and funny, courtly and charming, capable of connecting easily with his audience. He had a faith in his own abilities that attested more to his exuberance than arrogance.

Returning home after his speech in Bridgeport, John related the whole story of his success to James. The family patriarch was pleased and proud, while John was almost bursting with adrenaline-fueled excitement. "Turning the matter over in my mind, the next day, I concluded that as my profession required me to talk, I must go farther, and speak in the city," John recalled. By the next morning, he was on his way to the printing office, and plastered Frankfort with advertisements for a speech that very evening at the Frankfort courthouse.

He arrived there to find every seat full. Years later, Harlan recalled having some jitters—which are hard to credit, given the confidence he displayed. "I was able to talk for an hour and a half without notes, and never halted for a word. . . ." he wrote. "When the meeting closed, I was congratulated on all hands, and I went to bed that night feeling that a 'big thing' had been accomplished."[68]

His audience agreed. The *Kentucky Tribune*, in Danville, validated John's account of the large turnout in Frankfort, writing that despite John's youth, "his fame had preceded him, and the expectation that he would make an eloquent and effective defense of American [Party] principles." That he did. "We do not think that a speech better calculated to increase the true American sentiment, more abundant in sound argument, or better supported by sound proof, has been delivered during the present canvass," the paper enthused. Reports of the speech described it as "high toned" and focused on national patriotism; that suggested he may have glossed over the American Party's less high-minded scapegoating of immigrants and Catholics. John, the *Tribune* wrote, won hearts with "none of that violent abuse or disgusting slang, which have become striking characteristics of those opposition orators."[69]

The morning after John's debut in Frankfort, he asked his father for two favors to furnish a statewide speaking tour: a horse and a silver watch. His father agreed, and John set to work preparing handbills to advertise his tour through mountainous eastern Kentucky. Just ten days later, he set off alone and on horseback, his clothes stuffed into two saddle bags.[70] Notices in local papers showed him hitting eleven towns in twelve days, from Danville on Friday, July 6, to Bradfordsville on July 18.[71] The turnouts were so large that Democratic politicians raced to debate him, wary of a grass-roots explosion and eager to glom on to his crowds. John seems to have gotten the best of them.

"Last night we had one of the most delightful speeches from Mr. John M. Harlan of Frankfort," one observer wrote in the *Louisville Daily Courier* about an event in Lawrenceburg, Kentucky. "I say delightful, for it is a pleasant thing to sit under the sound of such a voice, modulated as it is to please the most cultivated ear, and still more cheering to listen to words fraught with sound reasoning, strong argument, and manly eloquence.

"Mr. Harlan bids fair to become one of America's best orators."[72]

On Election Day, August 6, 1855, gangs of Protestants in Louisville descended on German wards east of downtown and Irish neighborhoods to the west, blocking immigrants from getting to the polls.[73] In Kentucky's largest city, about a third of the white population was now Catholic, a sharp increase from just a few years earlier. White Protestant militants, inflamed by the rhetoric of the Know-Nothing Party, felt themselves to be defending the purity of the United States.

The mob pillaged three German coffeehouses; in the Irish areas, Catholics fought back. Men with rifles took to their rooftops to pick off the Protestant invaders. By the afternoon, it was a scene of horror, with men armed with shotguns, muskets, and rifles converging on the Catholic church. The Protestant mayor, John Barbee—himself a member of the Know-Nothings—heroically blocked their way, and they moved on to other targets. A large brewery exploded into flames. By the end of the day, twenty-two men lay dead in a miasma of smoke and fire.[74]

John and his father weren't in Louisville on what came to be known as Bloody Monday, a day of infamy in the history of the city, but James's name had been quite visible in the news that morning. The Democratic paper, the *Louisville Daily Courier*, had claimed that James, as the state's attorney general, was conspiring with Louisville City Council members to limit the number of voting places in fast-growing immigrant neighborhoods. "Are We to Have a Dictator?" was the headline of an article on the very morning of the riots, accusing James of misusing his office.[75]

In another story that day, the paper suggested James was doing the bidding of both the "Frankfort clique"—its sarcastic nickname for the old families who dominated the state's high offices—and the Know-Nothings: "High as has been our opinion of the legal abilities of Mr. Harlan, we can place no confidence in his decision on any subject where the interests of the Frankfort clique or the Know-Nothing order are involved. He is chief of the former, and the latter he is sworn to serve in any and every capacity, no matter how much against his conscience."[76]

Across the country, the Know-Nothings were in the midst of an unprecedented boom, destined to elect a hundred members of Congress between 1854 and 1856.[77] In Kentucky, the Know-Nothing candidate for governor prevailed on the very day of the riots.[78] The disintegration of the Whigs opened the door to the Know-Nothing ascendency, as men such as John and James Harlan, whose primary concern was preserving the Union, joined forces with those who trafficked in anti-foreigner sentiment. Much as the Harlans were willing to tolerate the continuation of slavery, despite their moral reservations, to spare the Union, so too were they willing to ally themselves with anti-immigrant forces to help create a political firewall against secession.

At the end of his life, John would write ruefully that, in his early twenties, he "did not have the boldness to repudiate the organization," especially at that first moment of oath taking, surrounded as he was by James and other mentors. His contrition was apparently deep enough that he would point the finger at his usually sainted father, explaining that James's resistance to the Democratic Party was so fierce that he would accept even unpalatable allegiances to keep it from power. This, John would explain to his own son just three months before his death, "was the kind of political meat upon which my father fed me as I grew up."

"He hated democracy and all its leaders, Jefferson, Jackson, and Van Buren," John would write. "Often I heard him say that John C. Calhoun ought to have been hung for treason. I quite agree, even now, that a man may say, if he can do so honestly, that notwithstanding the errors or misdoings of his party in reference to particular political questions, it is safest, on the whole, for the country, that his party should remain in power than that the other party should control."[79]

The enemy of my enemy is my friend, James reasoned. In the slavery debate, the Harlans saw themselves as voices of calm and moderation. But the party they were supporting left its own bloody handprint on a decade of hatred and division.

Chapter 4

Dread and Dred Scott

John Harlan was a man out of his time, preaching the virtues of a system that was collapsing under the weight of its contradictions. A party man, his first two political allegiances dissolved before he was past his midtwenties. A picture of youthful dignity, he strode purposefully through a landscape polluted by nativism and slavery. Only later would he realize that he had been stained along the way and that the same taint had been pressed into the fabric of the nation he uncritically embraced.

John saw himself as a disciple of the Founding Fathers, carrying forward their great truth in a time of peril and bastardized ideologies. He wouldn't see, until later, that the system he was extolling wasn't the spotless rendering of the documents he revered, the Declaration of Independence and the Constitution. It was, instead, the unfortunate expression of what the Founding Fathers had gotten wrong, the compromise over slavery that even some of them feared would one day cause their whole experiment in self-government to come crashing down.

Despite the moral confusions of the era and his own conflicted conscience, the youthful John still managed to make an enduring mark. He diligently cultivated a reputation for strength, reason, and integrity that would outlast the calamitous 1850s. Even as his long blond hair thinned and his body thickened, people would remember the brilliant orator who charmed them in his twenties, rousing the packed schoolhouses and town halls of small-town Kentucky with uplifting appeals to patriotism amid expressions of good humor, before saddling up his horse and moving on.[1]

Six decades later, the former Malvina Shanklin would remember how, as a fifteen-year-old precariously poised between girlhood and womanhood, she peered between two window slats of her home in Evansville, Indiana, and saw a dazzling stranger five years older than she, "his magnificent figure, his head erect, his broad shoulders well thrown back—walking as if the whole world belonged to him."

She knew even then, six months before actually meeting him, that this was the man she wanted to marry. John was in Evansville, a fast-growing town on the Ohio River, thriving with the type of slavery-free commerce that was enriching the northern frontier, to visit his older sister, Lizzie Hatchitt, and her husband and young son.

The lovestruck Malvina remembered every detail of his clothing, the way his dark-blue frock coat was decorated with large brass buttons on both sides of the front and back, and along the waistline. She recalled how he parted his "beautiful sandy hair" on the right instead of the left, defying convention in a way that attested to his confidence and individuality. When she finally met John, he was romping boyishly around the living room with his nephew. Behind the puffed-out chest, she could sense a playful spirit.[2]

She saw, too, that he was a man of promise. At the time, a Whig governor who was indebted to his father had appointed John to the largely ceremonial post of adjutant general of the Kentucky militia; the state didn't have an active militia, only a few chartered military academies, but the official position gave John an air of regimental gravitas.[3]

Malvina knew she was too young to marry, but quickly reached an understanding with John. Their relationship survived three years of separation, punctuated by his periodic visits to stay with Lizzie and her family. Then, without warning, amid the festive Christmas season of 1856, Malvina's parents let their friends know that they'd "be at home" on December 23, and enclosed two cards tied together with a white ribbon. One bore the name "John Marshall Harlan," and the other

"Malvina French Shanklin." The families who eagerly gathered were treated to a wedding ceremony in the back parlor and a reception in the front parlor. The eighteen-year-old bride, known for her ability to play and sing popular ballads, provided the finest entertainment. Beaming, John escorted his new wife to the piano. The couple spent their honeymoon under her father's roof. Much of the holiday week that followed was spent hopping joyously from party to party hosted by friends.

Even though he'd been practicing law for two years, the penniless groom borrowed $500 from his father to see himself and his bride through the wedding.[4]

Malvina's family was unalterably opposed to slavery. Her favorite uncle was an unabashed abolitionist, using dinner table conversations to fill his niece's and nephews' minds with tales of the mistreatment of enslaved men and women. To the Shanklins of Indiana, Kentucky was simply "the South." Malvina felt tremors of trepidation at the idea of moving to Frankfort to live with John's parents in a house maintained by enslaved people.[5]

The men and women enslaved by the Harlans worked mostly within the home, a somewhat gentler life than the vast majority who tilled the fields from dawn until dusk. But despite their avowed benevolence, the Harlans didn't deviate far from the norms of other slaveholding families in similar situations. Their enslaved workers lived in cabins behind their home in Frankfort. There were maids for each of the women in the family, while the men tended garden and handled home repairs.[6] The Harlans had a second house on a mountain overlooking Frankfort, to which they retreated in the summer. It was managed by an Irish-born overseer who made sure the enslaved people kept up the property and ferried the family's belongings up and down the mountain with all due haste.[7]

In the humid Kentucky summers, the family members enjoying the mountain breezes included James and Eliza's surviving sons and their two younger daughters, with some spouses as well. The lives of the enslaved men and women, their births and deaths and illnesses, were also a part of the vicissitudes of family life. While the Harlan kids enjoyed a bantering relationship with their servants, exchanging the occasional salty opinion, they and their young spouses were always addressed as "Missus" and "Marse."[8]

Malvina grew fond of the people held in slavery, starting with a ninety-year-old man named Uncle Joel, who lived with his wife in a state of semiretirement in one of the cabins out back. She was enthralled by the singing and the earthy cadences of the enslaved people, and the natural poetry of their illiterate minister. "There were almost as many slaves as there were members of 'the Family,' and they were all carefully looked after, not only physically but morally," she wrote reassuringly, in an almost certainly sugarcoated account long after abolition.[9]

John, too, felt a sense of loyalty and warmth toward the people his family held in slavery. Like many men and women born to large families with house slaves, John had deep feelings for his childhood nursemaid, from whom he may literally have nursed. In his young adulthood, he nearly died trying to save the life of his nursemaid's daughter. The young woman was mending clothes late at night in the sitting room of the Harlans' summer home when she drifted asleep. Her drowsy motions tipped the candle she was using, which set her skirt on fire.

Smelling smoke, John and Malvina bolted up from bed. They found the young woman thrashing about and looking like "a veritable pillar of fire." John reached out with his bare hands to yank off her burning clothes. By the time he could put out the flames, the young woman was severely burned over much of her motionless body. She succumbed soon afterward and was laid to rest with a hymn-laden funeral service that brought together white and Black. John himself suffered serious burns along his own arm and hands and was ordered to bedrest. A few days later, he was struck with fever, became delirious and started having convulsions. Enslaved people and family members alike scrambled down the path to Frankfort in search of doctors. Those who made the panting trek up the mountain found a young man fighting for his life. Tormented by pain, John required round-the-clock care before slowly climbing back to health.[10]

The trauma of having seen the flames, struggled to save the dying woman, and then coming near to death himself left a lasting mark. Whether it was fear of his own death, horror at the idea of a fatigued enslaved woman working deep into the night to the point of collapse, or some mingled physical and moral trauma is unclear. But Malvina attested that for decades to come, he would still awaken in sweat, thinking about that day.[11]

Outside of the Harlan home, America engaged in a twisted debate: Were enslaved men and women like children, fated to require the patronage of whites for the entirety of their lives, or could they be trusted to live as free men and women? On May 15, 1856, the *Independent Democrat*, a nationally known abolitionist newspaper based in New Hampshire, weighed in with an article with the facetious title of "Can't Take Care of Themselves."

The story declared, "Who has not heard the argument of pro-slavery hunkerism that negroes are rightfully held in Slavery because they 'can't take care of themselves.' Can't take care of themselves. Just as though a beneficent Creator had made a race with all the wants incident to humanity without endowing them with the capacity of satisfying those wants! The man who thinks so is an Atheist, or worse." The article then proudly offered up a list of formerly enslaved men who "have been able to prove the falsehood of the charge often made by Slaveocrats that negroes can't take care of themselves and therefore dark-skinned laborers should not be paid the value of their services, but have masters to rule and feed them." Some of those men born into slavery amassed wealth and professional success that far exceeded those of most whites.

Among the men listed as having thrived beyond all expectation, in a way that might shame whites who demeaned the intelligence of Black people, was Mr. Robert Harlan of Cincinnati.[12]

John and his family kept abreast of Robert's successes. Their mere awareness of Robert's kinetic personality, his ability to find his way through whatever doors were open to him, while always striving to reach a higher level of refinement, shaped their own perceptions of what Black people could achieve in freedom. As the *Independent*

Democrat noted, Robert's life story represented a thorough refutation of the notions of Black inferiority.

James maintained his great sense of confidence in Robert's abilities, as Malvina attested.[13] The family patriarch would have been surprised by Robert's success only in light of the prejudices he overcame. Robert kept in contact with other Harlan family members, including John, with letters. They were carefully wrought and serious in tone but carried an air of common understanding. There was less sense of an emotional connection; none of the Harlan men expressed emotion in letters.

Rather, Robert's actions—offering political advice and assistance to John, gifting the piano to Lizzie, extending credit to brother James Jr. to help him through a tough financial patch—revealed his desire to play the role of an intimate family member. His sense of equality wasn't asserted but quietly implied. John, for his part, seemed respectful of Robert's position and appreciative of his offers of help. If all men had been equal under the law, Robert's accomplishments would have been merely impressive; in the 1850s, when inequality was the state of the law, they had extra significance. Robert was exposing not only the wrongs of slavery but also the wrongness of all prejudices based on race.

In 1856 the pulse of the nation's debate over slavery quickened; blood was flowing, and now, suddenly, blood was spilling.

In the territory known as "Bleeding Kansas," passions aroused by the Kansas-Nebraska Act pushed the populace to the brink of civil war. The free elections to choose between slavery and abolition became farcical, as outsiders on both sides, including the violent abolitionist John Brown, poured into the largely ungoverned territory.[14] A mob of pro-slavery vigilantes sacked the city of Lawrence, burning the Free State Hotel, destroying two newspaper offices and ransacking stores.[15]

On the floor of the US Senate, the abolitionist senator Charles Sumner passionately decried the "crime against Kansas." He blamed two of his Democratic colleagues, Stephen Douglas of Illinois and Andrew Butler of South Carolina, for the carnage: Douglas for putting humanity and morality up for votes in the territories, and Butler for his bullying defense of the prerogatives of slave owners. In a florid allusion, Sumner cast slavery—or the "Slave Power," as abolitionists dubbed the distorting influence of slavery on the workings of society—as a tawdry mistress. Butler, Sumner declared, had taken a lover "who, though ugly to others is always lovely to him; though polluted in the sight of the world is chaste in his sight—I mean, the harlot slavery."

The references to whores and adultery humiliated the courtly Butler, mocking his Southern manners and dignity. Butler's younger cousin, thirty-six-year-old Representative Preston Brooks, raced across the Capitol to defend his family honor against the forty-five-year-old Sumner. He found the strapping senator sitting with his knees under the tiny wooden desk assigned to him on the floor of the Senate chamber. Believing that Sumner was not a man of honor and therefore unworthy of a duel, Brooks vowed to treat him like a rabid dog. Rushing up behind the unsuspecting senator, Brooks brought down the metal tip of a cane upon Sumner's head.

Trying to rise in order to ward off the attack, Sumner's legs became pinned under the desk, paralyzing him like a man tied to a chair. Brooks rained down blows until the senator collapsed, unconscious, in a pool of blood. Afterward, while Sumner fought for his life, Southerners cheered the attack. They feted Brooks at picnics and rallies. Some community leaders presented him with replicas of the bloody cane. But they seemed unaware that, for many Northerners, they were proving the truth of Sumner's arguments about the Slave Power. Brooks's attack and the South's celebration of it stripped away any veneer of gentility among the planter class. Northerners could only wonder aloud at all the ways in which slavery had unleashed Southern brutality.[16]

Meanwhile, in Robert's own Cincinnati, the human cost of slavery hit home in a fresh and devastating way. Mass exoduses across the Kentucky-Ohio border had become more common, as runaways made increasingly desperate thrusts for freedom. To enforce the Fugitive Slave Law, US marshals recruited vigilante "slave catchers" to keep up with the flow. When a group of seventeen enslaved men and women from Kentucky made what the *Cincinnati Enquirer* called "a stampede" across the frozen river, the slave catchers scrambled into action. Eight of the freedom seekers were from one family. Margaret Garner, her husband, and their four children, along with her husband's father and his wife, made it as far as the home of Margaret's uncle along the Mill River. The other nine men and women slipped the posse and escaped to Canada through safe houses on the Underground Railroad. As the slave catchers and marshals encircled the house of Margaret's uncle, the trapped family tried to ward them off with a rifle.

With the lawmen closing in, a pregnant and terrified Margaret used a butcher knife to kill her infant daughter and then frantically attacked her other children with a shovel, intending to kill them and herself rather than return to bondage. The shocking tale, with its echoes of Greek tragedy, gained even more attention when Ohio's governor, the abolitionist Salmon Chase, sought to try her for murder in order to prevent her from being sent back to a Kentucky plantation. He failed, and she received the one punishment she dreaded the most: a return to slavery.[17]

The horror story of a mother's desperate, fatal lunge for freedom reverberated from the slave cabins of the South to the parlors of Boston and New York. Lucy Stone, the pioneering feminist and abolitionist, rushed to Cincinnati from Massachusetts to visit Margaret Garner in jail. "I told her a thousand hearts were aching for her, and they were glad one child of hers was safe with the angels," Stone declared. "Her only reply was a look of deep despair—of anguish such as no words could speak."[18]

Northerners sensed a changing mood in the land. Now they could smell the blood of the Slave Power on their hands as well.

The horror of Bloody Monday was still fresh in the minds of Kentuckians the following April when a group of old-line Whigs met in

Lexington to talk about quitting the Know-Nothing movement and reviving the more high-minded Whig Party. Conservative unionists like the Harlans were eager to distance themselves from nativist extremism, proclaiming that "every right protected by the Constitution should be faithfully accorded to every class of men to whom its provisions extended, without regard to section, without regard to birth or religion of the parties entitled to such rights."[19] That was just one sign that the American Party was fracturing within a year of its greatest triumphs. Meanwhile, the party was under pressure from its Southern wing to erase any antislavery sentiment, while Northerners were demanding a tough stance against the Kansas-Nebraska Act. The results, a series of pitifully vague statements about promising to "maintain the existing laws upon the subject of slavery, as the final and conclusive settlement of that subject," reflected the party's desire for the whole controversy to just go away.[20] "That cursed question of 'slavery' is at the bottom of all our troubles," groused Kenneth Raynor, another Whig-turned-Know-Nothing, in 1856.[21]

The Whig revival fizzled. There was no hope of mounting a national campaign in 1856. Instead, the Know-Nothings turned to a former Whig president, Millard Fillmore, as their standard-bearer: on campaign posters across the states, Fillmore's picture appeared over the slogan "I know nothing but my Country, my whole Country, and nothing but my Country."[22]

Meanwhile, Franklin Pierce joined his predecessor, Fillmore, to become the second straight president to lose his job over an unpopular slavery compromise. Whereas Fillmore was felled by the Fugitive Slave Act, Pierce went down over the Kansas-Nebraska Act. His Democratic Party declined to renominate him, opting for James "Buck" Buchanan, one of the few national figures untainted by the slavery debate, in his case by dint of having spent the past term overseas as ambassador to Great Britain. Buchanan and Fillmore were both being challenged by a relative newcomer, California senator John C. Fremont, representing the nascent Republican Party. A hero of the Mexican War who had made a fortune in the gold rush, Fremont was an appealing personality, but while his party's antislavery message was hailed in the North, it lacked any meaningful support south of the Mason-Dixon Line, including in Kentucky.

John took to the hustings on behalf of Fillmore and even had the honor of being introduced by the former president himself in Malvina's hometown of Evansville, Indiana. His speech, at a theater called the Apollo Hall, was hailed as a triumph of rhetoric, "full of vigor and interest, while at times he was truly eloquent," according to the *Evansville Daily Journal.* "The close of his speech was one of the most eloquent perorations we think we have ever listened to."

John laid into the Democrats for favoring policies that put the nation on the path to disunion. He expressed strong opposition to the "unnecessary and unwise" Kansas-Nebraska Act, which had violated the Missouri Compromise. Clay's brainchild, he went on, had "saved the country—yet now it is denounced by the Democratic Party in Kentucky, whose entire delegation went for it." He also sought to defend, but at the same time soften, the nativist reputation of the American Party. This brand of Know-Nothings, he declared, "had no intention of interfering with any man's religion, but it did insist upon our Constitution and government being considered by Catholic Americans as by all other citizens, the highest temporal power on earth," the *Daily Journal* reported. Harlan also defended a plan for a six-month waiting period for naturalized citizens, declaring that it would protect the interests of both naturalized and native-born citizens.[23]

His efforts were for naught. Buchanan's Democrats surged to victory in both Kentucky and Indiana, part of a national landslide that routed Fremont as well as Fillmore. The American Party fared especially poorly, winning only the state of Maryland and a 22 percent share of the national vote. It would never be a force again.[24]

Buck Buchanan, whose political career had been spent stepping around the question of slavery, knew the fate of his two predecessors and didn't intend to repeat it: from the moment of his election, he began expressing hope that the Supreme Court would settle, once and for all, the slavery question. His comments were a dog whistle to an institution that had been in a two-decade slumber under Chief Justice Roger Taney, the Jacksonian who succeeded John Marshall.

The wizened Taney (pronounced *tawny*, like a cat of many colors) represented everything that James and John Harlan disdained. Not only was he an appointee of Andrew Jackson, whose populism had emboldened the secessionists, but he had been one of Old Hickory's key lieutenants. A former attorney general of Maryland, Taney served as Jackson's Treasury secretary during the piqued battles over the Second Bank of the United States. As chief justice, Taney adhered closely to Jacksonian principles favoring the states over a strong federal government, while the profile of the court, which had risen under Marshall, receded. To those enamored of a robust Constitution and a forceful national government, it was an extra slap in the face that Taney was occupying the seat of the sainted Marshall, the man who simultaneously advanced the powers of the court and the federal government.[25]

The vehicle for a court decision on slavery was waiting in Taney's docket: the case of the long-suffering Dred Scott. Scott was an enslaved man who had traveled the country in the service of two masters. The first was a man named Peter Blow, who owned only six slaves. He deployed Scott to help run his farm in Alabama and then, when it failed, to help operate a family boardinghouse in St. Louis. When Blow died, Scott was sold to an army surgeon, Dr. John Emerson. Scott so disliked the doctor that he tried to run away but was caught. Thereafter, Scott traveled with Emerson from posting to posting, eventually spending four years in the free state of Illinois and the free territory of Wisconsin, where he met his wife, Harriet, who was also acquired by Emerson. When the doctor died in 1843, the Scotts tried to buy their freedom from his widow, Irene, for $300. She refused and chose instead to lease them out as hired hands, with the proceeds of their labor filling her own coffers.[26]

It was then that the Scotts began a legal odyssey that exposed all the cruel inconsistencies of a system beholden to slavery. In those days prior to the Fugitive Slave Act, the Scotts had a good case that their time spent in Illinois and Wisconsin, which banned slavery, should have accorded them freedom. After years of procedural wrangling, a Missouri jury agreed, granting them their freedom in 1850. But that joyous event was short lived: two years later, the state supreme court, under intense political pressure, reversed twenty-eight years of precedent by declaring that the state was not bound to respect the laws of free states. Thus began a pattern of wins and losses that eventually brought their case to the ultimate arbiter: the US Supreme Court.

When the court heard final arguments in the case in December 1856, it suddenly became apparent that the justices were prepared to engage the slavery question in a fundamental way, determining whether a Black man could receive justice in the United States. Behind the scenes, President-elect Buchanan was lobbying the justices to do the country a favor, using its unique power of finality to put African Americans in their place. In his inaugural address in March 1857, a secretly confident Buchanan expressed the hope that the nation's agony over slavery would be "speedily and finally settled"—by the Supreme Court.[27]

The decision that was announced later that month was so sweeping that it shocked most of the country, prompting joy among Southern whites and fury in much of the North. Taney wrote the opinion for a 7-to-2 majority that included six Southerners and Justice Robert Cooper Grier, who was secretly lobbied by President Buchanan, his fellow Pennsylvania Democrat. The ruling was so decisive that Taney not only ended the slavery question, but also he effectively ended the Union. Taney declared that Dred Scott had no claim to citizenship, because the framers of the Constitution envisioned no rights for Black people. Not only slaves but also free Black men and women would forever be denied the "privileges and immunities" of US citizenship.

The question is simply this: Can a Negro, whose ancestors were imported to this country, and sold as slaves, become a member of the political community formed and brought into existence by the Constitution of the United States, and as such become entitled to all the rights, and privileges, and immunities, guaranteed by that instrument to the citizen? One of which rights is the priv-

ilege of suing in a court of the United States in the cases speci-
fied in the Constitution. . . . We think [Black people] are not, and
that they are not included, and were not intended to be included,
under the word "citizens" in the Constitution, and can therefore
claim none of the rights and privileges which that instrument
provides for and secures to citizens of the United States.[28]

Taney and the rest of the court's majority had shockingly extended
their ruling beyond slavery to the question of race, and based a broad-
brush decision on a largely improvised conclusion about the racist
intentions of the nation's founders. The flagrantly racist opinion went
on for pages about the inferiority of Black people, in a knowing tone
that suggested the truth of the assertion could not be denied.

"They had for more than a century before [the advent of the Con-
stitution] been regarded as beings of an inferior order, and altogether
unfit to associate with the white race, either in social or political relations; and so far inferior, that they had no rights which the white man
was bound to respect," Taney wrote.[29] The chief justice was wrong on
the facts: at the time the Constitution was ratified in 1790, citizenship was not based on race in five of the Union's thirteen states, and
Black people enjoyed legal protections there. There were many framers in northern states who had no intention of enshrining racial discrimination in the Constitution, even as they labored to appease their
southern brethren that the document would not interfere with slavery where it existed.[30]

Taney, however, asserted that the Constitution intended to protect slavery throughout the land—that Congress therefore had no authority to commit to treaties or impose rules on territories banning
slavery; he explicitly declared the Missouri Compromise—which
had kept slavery out of the northern territories for decades—to be
unconstitutional.[31]

Two justices dissented from the opinion. Seventy-two-year-old
Justice John McLean of Ohio had served in the cabinets of James
Monroe and John Quincy Adams at a time when many framers of the
Constitution were still alive; he rejected the idea that they intended

to deprive Black people of rights under any circumstances, pointing to the states where Black civil rights were protected. He declared Taney's opinion "more a matter of taste than of law." Justice Benjamin Curtis of Massachusetts went further, producing an opinion that exceeded Taney's in length and detail. This was something rare: a full-scale rebuttal spelling out all mistakes he believed the court's majority was making.

Curtis noted at the start that the court's only holding related to Dred Scott himself was that federal courts had no jurisdiction to hear his case; under normal practice, the court's inquiry should have stopped there.[32] Why, then, did Taney go on and on in invalidating the various compromises on slavery? Plainly, the chief justice was venturing beyond the confines of the law. The act of writing the dissent, and the bad feelings it engendered with his colleagues, were such a shattering experience that Curtis quit the court in disgust.[33] Other northerners were in a more fiery mood, as northern newspapers condemned the court and Taney as agents of the Slave Power who had hijacked the Constitution; now the United States seemed destined to be a permanent slave nation, even in places where abolitionist feeling was overwhelming. "Wherever our flag floats, it is the flag of slavery," bemoaned the influential poet and *New York Evening Post* editor William Cullen Bryant.[34]

Indeed, reaction to the Dred Scott ruling split broadly along sectional lines—precisely the result most likely to further the path to war. Based almost entirely on his own assertion of the framers' intentions, Taney had declared the Constitution to be a white supremacist document, removed legal bars to slavery in the North, and consigned all descendants of enslaved men and women—even those living in freedom with as much wealth as Robert Harlan—to the permanent purgatory of second-class status in the nation to which they were born.[35]

The Dred Scott decision was a body blow to Robert's dreams not only for himself but also for his young son Robert James—often called Robert Jr.—and others of his race. Since making his fortune in California,

Robert had taken to handing out loans to young Black men of promise, urging them to start businesses with him as their lead investor.[36] He believed in them, regarding the mass of humanity emerging from the pits of slavery as an untapped resource; almost an industry in itself. A legal blow to their status was thus a double blow to himself. And while Robert lived the life of a well-groomed gentleman, creating an aspirational ideal for others who had been born into slavery, he was also holding the lease of the hotel that was the beating heart of the Cincinnati Black community, honeycombed with hiding places for runaway slaves.[37]

Dumas House, as the hotel was known, was the kind of brashly fashionable meet-up place that only a port city could host. Black people of every stripe of life would stop before its august brick exterior, with its two-story iron veranda, and gawk at what was lauded as the most elegant Black establishment in the country. In 1900 the *Cincinnati Enquirer*, looking back at the Dumas House's 1850s heyday, proclaimed that its barroom featured "the best of liquors, the finest of cigars . . . furnished with the most lavish splendors." Robert held court there, often joining rich visitors in a regular card game in which "thousands of dollars changed hands nightly on the turn of a card," as the *Enquirer* put it.[38]

The hotel manager was Sandy Shumate, a finely attired, smiling bachelor who personified the hotel's reputation for "high living, sport, and gambling." Late at night, with liquor flowing, punches sometimes flew, and pistols were drawn from the gamblers' satin coat pockets.[39] But behind all the conspicuous consumption and fancy fisticuffs was the real business of the Dumas: hiding runaway slaves. Underground Railroad passengers found safety in the bowels of the hotel, with its dense web of corridors and secret rooms.[40] The Dumas House was station number one on the road to freedom, and no fugitive slaves were ever apprehended there; they could slip out through a network of passages.[41]

Other freedmen, those lacking the resources to join the elites in the barroom, found the Dumas to be a place to gain work experience in an atmosphere rich with mentors. A teenager named P. B. S. Pinchback—described by the *Enquirer* as "a bright, handsome, saddle-colored lad"—was a porter there, finding a role model in the confident, savvy Robert Harlan, two decades his senior. Pinchback would go on to become the Reconstruction-era governor of Louisiana, the first African American to reach such a position, and one of Robert's closest friends.[42]

Even as the city's racial mood was darkening, Robert's wealth grew through his various businesses and real estate investments—plus, perhaps, the cash being exchanged on the felt tables of the Dumas. He traveled widely and was a regular visitor to Europe, where he closely scrutinized British and French horse racing, while remaining alert to the latest technologies. After witnessing the sensation that the daguerreotype of Cincinnati made at the Great Exposition in London, Robert purchased what was hailed as the largest photography gallery in the West, working with numerous Black photo pioneers to make portraits of wealthy Cincinnatians. In 1857 he went into business with a legendary daguerreotype pioneer, James Presley Ball, known as J.P., in a photography studio called Ball & Harlan.[43]

With his bald head and long, flowing beard, the mixed-race Ball was a distinctive presence, soon to achieve fame for journeying to England to photograph Queen Victoria and author Charles Dickens. Even more ambitious and influential was his 1855 opus, a panoramic painting that purported to document the lives of men and women living under slavery, based on photos of cotton and sugar plantations. The tableau covered a 2,400-square-foot canvas and was exhibited as far away as Boston, where it helped inflame the city's abolitionist sentiment; a pamphlet Ball wrote to accompany the panorama appealed to northerners to recognize the brutality of slavery.[44]

Shortly after Robert joined forces with Ball, the partnership collapsed in acrimony. Not hesitating to take the dispute public, Robert purchased an advertisement in the *Enquirer* to condemn his partner. "I wish the public to know that J. P. Ball, now doing business under the protection of A. Thomas' name, at 120 West 4th-street, was obliged to leave the firm Ball & Harlan, on account of dishonest principles unbecoming a gentleman. Harlan may be found at the old stand, 28 and 30 West 4th-street, where he is still successful in taking pictures of every description, and also involved in liquidating the debts of this unworthy man. I am obliged to make this statement on account of petty annoyances, too mean in their nature to warrant further notice."[45]

The Harlan-Ball feud was a harbinger of other spats among Cincinnati's mixed-race elites, who would repeatedly take to attacking one another for alleged financial and sometimes sexual peccadillos, condemning their rivals for behavior unworthy of a gentleman. In competing for the patronage of white leaders, they found the easiest way to vanquish a competitor was to play on white prejudices of Black men as lacking honor and trustworthiness. Robert's charges against Ball would be echoed in later years in attacks on himself—in some cases, by some of the same Black aristocrats whose businesses he sponsored and with whom he played cards at the Dumas House. Thus, the cutthroat racism of white society repeatedly pitted Black elites against one another.[46]

Even as he feuded with some of his Black business partners, Robert knew that anything that advanced the cause of Black people would benefit him as well. He became determined to help build up the community, finding capital wherever he could. That led to one of his more unusual partnerships, with the city's richest man and most enigmatic mogul.

Nicholas Longworth was a lawyer-turned-investor who made a fortune in wine making; as such, he earned the odd sobriquet Father of the American Grape Culture.[47] He was the progenitor of a proud line of Longworths who enriched the city's political and philanthropic communities. But like many self-made men, he disdained pretension and preached a gospel of self-reliance. In 1858 he was seventy-five years old and well along in cultivating a reputation for kindness and eccentricity in equal measure. Once, while paying his respects at the Longworth mansion, Abraham Lincoln mistook the shabbily dressed plutocrat for a gardener.[48] Lincoln's error was understandable, since Longworth was known for prowling the streets of Cincinnati in such slovenly garb that he was sometimes mistaken for a beggar. But he was generous with his vast fortune, especially to those he considered deserving of advancement.

Robert Harlan was the kind of man Nicholas Longworth liked: a capitalist who looked beyond the obstacles in life and stood on his own two feet. Robert reciprocated with admiration for the city's richest citizen, who was also, perhaps not incidentally, a supporter of Black photographic pioneers. Nonetheless, it was education, not photography, that was behind Robert's dealings with Longworth. Robert's memories still burned with his rejection from grade school when James tried to enroll him, a loss for which he spent his entire life trying to make up. Now he saw that Cincinnati's fast-growing Black community lacked schools. With access to education, he believed, the sons of freed men and women like his own Robert Jr. would earn their equal positions alongside whites.[49]

Longworth agreed. At Robert's urging, they both invested in the East Side Seventh Street Schoolhouse, the first public school for Black citizens sanctioned by the local school board. It opened in late 1858 to local fanfare, with Robert proclaiming it a brick-and-mortar symbol of the advancement of Black people—even if it was founded more than a year after the Supreme Court had put a permanent lid on Black aspirations.[50]

John Harlan had every reason to detest the Dred Scott decision. First there was the central role of Taney, the human vestige of a political movement so objectionable that James Harlan considered it treasonous.[51] Then there was the fact that the decision violated everything that Henry Clay, James Harlan, and John himself had endorsed in the Missouri Compromise and other federal efforts to limit the spread of slavery.[52] John had openly defended the compromise—which Taney declared unconstitutional—in the recent presidential campaign, saying in his speech at Malvina's hometown that "Nothing but this com-

promise saved the country." And, in later years, John would condemn
Taney and the Dred Scott decision in the harshest possible terms.[53]

But on the campaign trail in Kentucky, where fear of war was
growing by the minute, along with the conviction that Kentucky
would bear the harshest fighting, John refrained from criticizing the
opinion. Instead, he urged Kentuckians to abide by the ruling as a
means of settling the issue. The setting for his comments was the 1859
congressional election, in which John was unexpectedly thrust into
the position of candidate. The relative lack of coverage of his comments on Dred Scott suggested that he didn't dwell on the issue and
may have been harboring private disagreement. His focus, as always,
was on avoiding war.[54] He was also the progressive in the race, running against a Democrat who was determined to win the seat by dint
of his greater love for slavery. None of this prevented John from later
regretting the positions he took during the campaign.

Despite his vast ambition, John wasn't eager to run for Congress
that year. At twenty-six, he was enjoying a new job as an elected
county judge.[55] This brought him to some of the same buildings
where he had spoken as a politician, but this time as the arbiter for
a range of offenses: from family disputes, to serious criminal charges
of the type that his cousin John had faced just a few years earlier. For
an intellectual like John, the judgeship was a chance to see how the
struggles of average Kentuckians intersected with the law. After three
years of debating the slavery question, he was now confronting disputes he could actually resolve, helping to protect the peace and keep
families safe.

But his party called, and, as usual, he answered. The party wasn't
the Know-Nothings. James Harlan and a large number of former
Whigs had finally succeeded in extricating themselves from the
American Party, loyalty oath be damned. The new venture, called the
Opposition Party, was defined by what it was against: it didn't endorse
the states'-rights arguments of the Democrats, the free-soil demands
of the Republicans, or the noxious nativism of the American Party.[56]

John attended the Opposition Party's convention in the spring of
1859 with no intention of becoming a candidate. When a fellow del-

egate declared that the party needed a young, fresh face and put his name in nomination, he tried to refuse the honor. "I started to jump up and say that I was not a candidate and couldn't think of being one," he wrote later, but a fellow member of the Franklin County delegation yanked him back, pulling "the skirt of my alpaca frock coat so strong as to nearly tear it off."

He narrowly won the nomination and plunged into the campaign with his usual intensity. Representing what was jokingly referred to as "the no party," John was popular enough to consign the Know-Nothing nominee to the sidelines. That gave him a clean shot at the Democrat in the race: a much older Mexican War veteran named William E. Simms, who agreed to a series of debates with slavery the main issue.[57]

The Northern fury that had been unleashed by the Dred Scott decision had scared many Kentuckians. They saw that the northern states were swinging powerfully to the Republicans; adding up the electoral math, they found enough votes in the North alone to elect a Republican abolitionist as president in 1860. In the eyes of many southerners, that would be the trigger for secession—the end to all the compromises. John sought to reassure slave owners that their interests would be protected regardless of the outcome of the following election. There was, he pointed out, the precedent of the Dred Scott decision. So, too, would John support a federal law to prevent "Negro stealing," the southern term for helping a slave escape his or her masters.[58]

The Supreme Court, he reminded his audiences, had declared that "Congress had the power, and it was its bounded duty, to pass such laws as might be necessary for the full protection of the rights of slave owners in the territories, whenever the local legislatures shall either attempt to destroy his right by unfriendly legislation or shall fail to pass such laws as are necessary for his protection."[59]

Simms went much further, vowing to "hang the n----r stealer as high as Haman." While John beseeched voters to embrace reason, moderation, and the rule of law, Simms played on their emotions.[60] John's debating skills, however, quickly began to make a mess of

Simms's chances. The young orator with the charismatic aura didn't give an inch, insisting that Simms's provocative policies, as much as the Republicans', would bring about a crisis.

Then came a charge that jolted his reputation for moderation. A local slave owner named R. B. Logan declared that John Harlan had, six years earlier, helped his slave named Nathan Williams to sue for his freedom. Another lawyer, a Harlan family friend, stepped forward to say that he and John's brother William Lowndes Harlan had represented the man, not John. The slave owner was appeased, but the Simms campaign quickly spread the rumor.[61]

Like his father in an earlier campaign, John was obliged to deny any abolitionist tendencies, even though he believed, like James before him, that some Black people had legitimate claims to freedom and that they deserved representation.[62] For a high-minded young man like John, the twists and turns required to navigate the slavery issue were becoming degrading, if not demeaning.

To cap it off, John lost the race to Simms by just 67 votes out of almost 13,797 that were cast. The Opposition Party cried fraud. By his own investigation, John declared that he had found 300 people on the voter rolls "of persons whom no one knew and of whom no one in the county had heard." But Democrats also alleged that there had been irregularities in pro-Harlan precincts and threatened a political donnybrook if John challenged the returns. In the end, he backed off, preferring to return to his judgeship and family life in Frankfort.[63]

Years later, he professed relief that he had been spared an agonizing turn in the increasingly partisan Capitol, trying to promote moderation in a frenzied time of extremism. "If I had gone to Washington at twenty-six, I might have lost all the character I had," he conceded.[64]

Even before the Supreme Court declared he could never be a full citizen, Robert had his eyes on other horizons. Outwardly, he was a success beyond all imagining. He had freed himself from slavery. He had moved to the great free-state mecca of Cincinnati and left a powerful mark, from the businesses he financed, to the Dumas House, to win-

ning the support of the city's richest man for his charitable work. But
racism dogged him at every turn; he lived in a community hounded
by slave catchers. Freedom in America, as the Supreme Court decided, would never be complete. There were fewer strictures across
the Atlantic Ocean.

Robert began making regular trips to England to survey the racing
scene.[65] He compared his Kentucky-bred skills as a horseman with
those of owners and trainers in bucolic Newmarket, the green-grass
capital of the British turf, about fifteen miles from the storied university town of Cambridge. For more than a hundred years, the titled grandees of British racing had been gathering there in the halls of
the members-only Jockey Club to buy and sell horses. For hundreds
of years before that, horse lovers such as King Charles II, who built
a palace and stables in the town, had gathered to race horses on the
Newmarket Heath.[66]

It was audacious for any American to believe he could make a
mark in that world. It was that much more audacious for a man born
into slavery to believe he could do so. But Robert could see that in
distant England, with its small Black population, there was less prejudice to greet him, excepting that which would naturally attend to an
American. Robert would be carrying the flag of American racing into
battle in Europe, even as he was trying to shake free of America's racial discrimination.

In 1858 he began pouring money into expanding his stable. On
November 18 the *Louisville Daily Courier* announced that Mr. Robert Harlan of Cincinnati had purchased an unnamed three-year-old
filly from Mr. James L. Bradley of Fayette County for $3,500 (about
$110,000 in 2021) and a two-year-old filly for $2,300 (about $72,000
in 2020) from Dr. L. Herr.[67] These were two of America's most promising horses, the first the winner of the Produce Stake at the Kentucky
Association track in Lexington that fall, and the second coming off a
win in a fall stakes for two-year-olds. The news circulated in papers
throughout the region.[68]

"Robert Harlan, a colored man, an excellent judge of horses, and a
first-rate trainer, has purchased two of the best horses going in Ken-

tucky, at high prices, and will take them to England in the Spring to contend for honors of the turf," the *Liberator*, the nation's leading abolitionist newspaper, announced breathlessly in January 1859.[69]

But it wasn't just the Black press that was hailing Robert. With his mission to take on the British, all of the American turf was taking notice.

"Shrewd, energetic, and sagacious, his match races were always successful," boasted the *Memphis Daily Avalanche*, noting that Robert had "visited England on three years in succession, timed their horses, and made himself familiar with their sporting men and sporting manners."[70]

Soon after, Robert purchased another top thoroughbred from the famed stables of John Harper.[71] Perhaps coincidentally, it bore the name of Lincoln, the man who had attained national attention the previous year in a series of debates against Senator Stephen Douglas of Illinois and who was already being whispered about as a presidential candidate the following year.[72]

"The three horses purchased by Mr. Robert Harlan, in Kentucky, last summer—'Des Chiles,' 'Cincinnati,' and 'Lincoln'—are in this city," the *Cincinnati Commercial Tribune* reported eagerly. "Mr. Harlan intends to resort to the turf and will soon sail to Europe, in order to match his stud against the best English horses. He is said to possess a heap of 'horsesense,' and will enter his horses 'judgmentally.'"[73] With his huge outlay of funds and his boundless ambition, Robert was taking his place among the kings of American racing.

The attention given to Robert aroused the interest of a highly regarded competitor, Richard Ten Broeck. The scion of a military family who left West Point under mysterious circumstances—later challenging one of his instructors to a duel—the New York–born Ten Broeck moved south as a young man, riding the steamboats of the Mississippi and amassing a fortune in gambling. In New Orleans, he became part-owner of the Metairie Race Track, one of the most popular gathering places for the elites of Louisiana society.[74] He also produced a champion colt named Lexington, later to become the most famous stud in American racing.[75] Ten Broeck was in many ways Robert's northern-born doppelganger. He was a sharp dresser, a shrewd asses-sor of horses, and an entirely self-made man who was unafraid to take risks. He also had the advantage of being white.[76]

Ten Broeck had made a run at the British turf himself three years earlier but had flopped in a manner so disastrous and embarrass-ing that he was said to have been down to his last ten pounds before betting it on his filly Prioress as a 100-to-1 shot.[77] Prioress's victory was cold comfort, however, and he was eager to make amends for his earlier disappointments. The *Cincinnati Enquirer* reported on Feb-ruary 22, 1859, that Ten Broeck was in town, staying at the famed Burnet House hotel at the corner of Third and Vine Streets. He had brought with him a stable of horses. He was there to confer with Robert, apparently to lay down an agreement to collaborate, rather than compete, against the British owners. "Between the two," wrote the *Enquirer*, "the American turf will be well represented abroad the ensuing season, and we cannot doubt that they will be successful in bearing off at least a share of the honors and profits."[78]

Robert and Ten Broeck each sent some of their teams of jockeys and stable workers ahead to Europe on a steamship called the *City of Baltimore*.[79] Then, in April, the two horsemen themselves headed across the ocean on one of the most glamorous ships afloat, the Inman Line's *City of Manchester*.[80] At 265 feet long and 35 feet tall, with a saloon that spanned the center of the ship, the *City of Man-chester* carried 350 passengers in three classes. First-class passage was $30 each way, or roughly $1,000 in 2021 dollars.[81]

Robert wasn't planning to return home anytime soon. He brought along three of his children—Mary and Laura Harlan, two of his three surviving daughters with Margaret, and his six-year-old son, Robert Jr.[82] Together the Harlan family would be leaving the racial chaos of the fast-imploding United States to seek its fortune in the Old World.

As racing enthusiasts intently followed reports of Robert's and Ten Broeck's exploits overseas, the nation's leading racing paper, the New York–based *Spirit of the Times*, wrote a story in response to a flood of letters demanding more information about the mysterious Mr. Harlan. It reported what the southern papers hadn't: that Robert was the son of James Harlan, though it alluded only to Robert's race, referencing unspecified feelings of prejudice against him.

"In response to a great many inquiries about this person, we will only say that he, is a native of Kentucky and the son of old Judge Harlan of that State," the *Spirit* reported. "He is somewhere in the turn of fifty years of age [actually forty-two], is a man of wealth and a citizen of Cincinnati, in which city he has business carried on in his absence. . . . He is to be regarded in the South and West as certainly the equal, to say no more, of Mr. Ten Broeck, as a turfman, though there exists an extensive prejudice against him."[83]

The news circulated widely in Kentucky, though it's not known whether John or James, with no particular connection to horse racing and increasingly consumed with the national political crisis, ever saw it.

Chapter 5

The Soul of Kentucky

On November 6, 1860, John's fears came true. The North elected a president with no southern support. Divisions became chasms. Abraham Lincoln won all the northern states and enough votes in the electoral college to become president. In Kentucky, Lincoln's native state, he didn't compete seriously. John and his father pushed the cause of the moderate Constitutional Union Party candidate, John Bell, and were successful enough that Bell beat native Kentuckian John C. Breckinridge, the Southern Democratic nominee (the party having split into Northern and Southern halves), to claim the Bluegrass State's twelve electoral votes. Across the country, it was a complicated election with a very simple outcome: an antislavery president who was reviled throughout the South.[1]

This was enough of an affront that seven states, led by South Carolina, declared their intention to secede before Lincoln even took office on March 4, 1861. John wrote to Joseph Holt, President Buchanan's secretary of war, asking him to pull federal troops from the South, suggesting such a move would be "a display [of] magnanimity to a misguided people which [could] but be followed by the happiest results." His view, from the cauldron of Kentucky, was that any aggressive action by the federal government would merely inflame secessionist sentiment in states like his own. In the letter to Holt, he added that "whenever it becomes a settled fact that the people of the seceding states are unalterably opposed to the Federal Government . . . they should be allowed to go in peace."[2]

He didn't really mean it. Preserving the Union was the overriding concern of John's political career and its essential proposition; he wasn't about to let the nation break in two without a fight. But he estimated shrewdly that wavering Kentuckians would lash out at whichever side appeared to be the aggressor. With his friend Orlando Brown, the son of a pioneering Bluegrass State politician, John helped to convene, in late 1860, a special convention of the Constitutional Unionists and pro-Union Democrats to reassert their unalterable commitment to the Union. He was named secretary of the convention and played a role in quashing a plank in which delegates vowed to use force, if necessary, to preserve the Union. He considered it too provocative. But the prospect of violence was so palpable it was on everyone's lips: "As she was the first in the great family of Western states to be admitted into the Union, so she will be the last to leave it," Brown told the crowd, speaking of their beloved Kentucky. "She will never unfurl any other flag than the Stars and Stripes under which she has so often marched to battle and to victory, and if all others desert it and she too must fall, she will wrap the flag around her and fall with the dignity that becomes her great name and deeds."[3]

The state reeled with a sense of impending doom. The *Frankfort Commonwealth* reported that church attendance was rising. "The nation stands upon dread abyss," began a poem that the paper published. It ended, "Though death has still his God like eloquence / Is there no magic in the name of Clay?"[4]

The corridors of power in Frankfort and the street corners of Louisville teemed with Confederate spies. With secession in the air, the merest utterance could be considered treason. In the capitol and other government offices in Frankfort, John stealthily endeavored to root out secessionist plots. He was so intent on hearing every whisper of rebellion that he slept nights on the floors of the offices of friendly officials.[5]

Beriah Magoffin, the state's governor, was suspect number one. A pro-slavery Democrat, Magoffin condemned Lincoln and the Republicans, before they took office, for their outrageous disrespect of the South. Confederate sympathizers implored Magoffin to secede. "Shall we wait until our enemies shall possess themselves of all powers of the Government?" wrote an emissary from the governor of Alabama. "Until Abolition judges are on the Supreme Court bench. Abolition collectors in every port, and Abolition postmasters in every town; secret mail agents traversing the whole land, and subsidized press established in our midst to demoralize our people?"[6]

Magoffin held out, trying to chart a path around secession. He proposed a convention of all the state governments to discuss rewriting the federal Constitution to provide ironclad protection for slavery, now and forever, as a means of preserving the Union. Even if that effort failed, he said, the slave states could, "after calm deliberation," present their own petition to the incoming administration seeking other guarantees to protect Southern rights and autonomy.[7]

Despite the restrained tone of these proposals, John distrusted Magoffin. To some eyes, he might have been playing the traditional Clay-like role of brokering a compromise, even in the darkest hours. John had a different view. He thought Magoffin was scheming, step by carefully orchestrated step, to maneuver Kentuckians into joining the Confederacy.[8]

So, when Magoffin pushed for the state to send representatives of his choosing to a conference of border states, John and his father pressured the legislature to reject the governor's plan in a demonstration of Unionist political muscle. That kicked off weeks of gamesmanship between the Confederate sympathizer Magoffin and the pro-Union legislature, with the fate of Kentucky—and the nation— in the balance. At some moments, it seemed certain that Southern sympathies would prevail; at others, it seemed like the Unionists were holding sway.[9]

When he felt he could safely trust his Unionist allies to keep Magoffin in check, John decided to take his case to the people. He rushed to Louisville—the state's one real metropolis, where the allegiance of Kentucky was being debated on every corner—grabbed a bullhorn, and took to the streets.[10]

On March 4 Abraham Lincoln took the oath of office before the half-finished Capitol dome in Washington. His inaugural address was an open letter to the South, promising fair treatment, extolling the virtue of constitutional checks and balances, and, finally, seething with emotion: "I am loath to close. We are not enemies, but friends. We must not be enemies. Though passion may have strained, it must not break our bonds of affection. The mystic chords of memory, stretching from every battlefield and patriot grave to every living heart and hearthstone all over this broad land, will yet swell the chorus of the union, when again touched, as surely they will be, by the better angels of our nature."[11]

Lincoln was more wistful than hopeful about the chances of quelling the rebellion peacefully. He described his task as more difficult than that confronting any president, including Washington. He recognized instantly the strategic importance of Kentucky, both geographically and as a model for the other border states of Missouri and Maryland, and shared John's view of the necessity of winning the hearts and minds of the Bluegrass State, where he, Lincoln, had been born.

Rumors ricocheted around Frankfort that the new president had said, "I hope to have God on my side, but I must have Kentucky." That may have been an embellishment spread by his opponents, hoping to impute impiety to the hated leader of the "Black Republicans." But Lincoln did write an even more pointed line to a US senator from Illinois: "I think to lose Kentucky is nearly the same as to lose the whole game."[12]

In moss-draped Charleston, the proud South Carolina port where Black stevedores loaded bales of cotton and tobacco onto freighters bound for Europe, and white planters built pillared city mansions along flower-covered streets, people got tired of staring out at their beautiful harbor, only to see the Stars and Stripes flying from an island fortress.

On April 12 Confederate general P. G. T. Beauregard ordered a massive bombardment of the Union encampment at Fort Sumter. There were fewer than a hundred federal troops hunkered down on the island, while Beauregard commanded six thousand men and dozens of the most powerful artillery yet invented. When Confederate fire rained down, turning the nighttime harbor into a blaze of light, the federal commander was forced to surrender.[13]

Robert Augustus Toombs, the florid and emotional Georgia senator who had just been appointed secretary of state to the new Confederate president, former Mississippi Senator Jefferson Davis, had warned against the attack. Resorting to violence, Toombs insisted, "will lose us every friend in the North," and "It is unnecessary. It puts us in the wrong. It is fatal."[14]

Davis ignored him, and, by July, Toombs was out of his post.[15] Thousands of South Carolinians proudly lined the battery of Charleston Harbor to witness the spectacular attack, the culmination of decades of frustration with antislavery policies in the North and a carefully crafted theory of secession dating back to John C. Calhoun's nullification battles with Henry Clay and Andrew Jackson.

But Toombs's verbal bombs proved more spot-on than Davis's artillery. Suddenly Kentuckians and others whose support the Confederacy desperately needed saw wisdom and moderation in President Lincoln's policy of calmly appealing to peace-loving citizens throughout the country. It was the first data point in a dynamic that would stretch to the end of the war: Lincoln's political instincts were shrewder than those of Davis. Even when succeeding militarily, the Confederacy would be hampered by Davis's missteps.

Just as both John Harlan and Abraham Lincoln predicted, sympathy for the Union in strategically vital Kentucky surged in the wake of the attack on Fort Sumter.[16]

John didn't need Lincoln, a man he considered too beholden to the antislavery cause, to remind him of his loyalty to the nation and the Constitution. But he recognized that in this endeavor, he and the new president were on the same side.

Lincoln's most trusted representatives in Kentucky were the brothers Joshua and James Speed. The handsome, charismatic Joshua Fry Speed was the melancholy sixteenth president's closest friend, former housemate, and confidant in difficult times. The Speeds—from an aristocratic family whose 550-acre hemp plantation was run by sixty slaves—were far from ardent Republicans, their political views closer to those of the Harlans than to Lincoln's.[17] But in Kentucky's season of betrayal, their personal relationships with Lincoln were fixed points in an atmosphere of conflicting loyalties. Back in the 1830s, Joshua Speed had comforted the disconsolate Lincoln through months of depression during his tumultuous courtship of Mary Todd; the two lawyers had been close enough that they climbed into the same bed each night, a common practice among bachelors at the time.[18]

Now John Harlan was coordinating his pro-Union message with President Lincoln's best friend. John and the Speed brothers took turns mounting grocery boxes on the recently paved street corners of Louisville, standing under tall, elegant gas streetlights and amid the rising brownstones of a bustling city of seventy thousand people.[19] To draw crowds and create a festive spirit, they hired musical bands to play patriotic tunes; the scene was reminiscent of July 4 celebrations. Thousands of passersby witnessed the Speeds and the much younger John—only twenty-eight but among the state's best-known orators—extol the virtues of the Union. "There was hardly an afternoon I did not, while standing on a store box, on the pavement, address a public audience," John wrote.[20]

At night, he and the Speeds conspired to save the Union in a different way. They feared that while the governor and legislature wrangled over secession, Confederate troops would invade Kentucky and settle the issue.[21] The Confederacy added a star to its flag, claiming Kentucky in spirit if not in possession.[22]

In response, John and the Speeds launched a stealth mission to help the president. The brothers had secretly negotiated with the Lincoln administration to send five thousand muskets to arm its supporters in the Bluegrass State. In Frankfort, James Harlan helped to devise a strategy to get the guns to the right people. Unmarked crates of muskets would be smuggled into Kentucky through Ohio and then distributed to Union supporters in strategic places; James, with his intimate knowledge of the state's political class, knew who could be trusted and who might waver. The first shipment of "Lincoln guns" made it to Louisville's Unionist mayor, who hid them at a nearby military camp. But when the engineer driving the train carrying weapons bound for Lexington spotted a group of rebel sympathizers, he turned around in fear and backtracked to Cincinnati. Then John stepped in.

John Harlan had been nurtured as a man of words, not physical action. His weapon of choice was persuasion. The times, however, demanded more, and he discovered that he was prepared to go further than merely argue for the cause: he would willingly put his life on the line. The shift to action provoked tremors of fear in his marriage but generated no second thoughts of his own. He seemed to have envisioned such a patriotic moment of decision—putting his ideals to the ultimate test—and even prepared for it. The man who, at thirteen, had tried to join the Mexican War alongside his similarly underaged brother now had a fight to call his own.

With little hesitation, John secretly arranged for the muskets to be shipped down the Ohio River by boat to his own address in Louisville. He and a fellow Union supporter then hid among the shadowy dock buildings to meet the boat and personally carried the weapons to the train depot, where they were sent off by freight car to Lexington.

John had played many roles in his short life. This was a new one: spy.[23]

In Frankfort, the legislature and Governor Magoffin hammered out a policy they called "armed neutrality," in which the state would recruit and provide weapons for a militia under the control of a committee of six prominent Kentuckians—not the governor. Its purpose would be to defend the state against Confederate or Union troops, should either try to violate its boundaries. John signed on quickly to be a captain in one of the militia units, dubbed the Crittenden Zouaves, after his close family friends the Crittendens and the legendary North African–inspired French soldiers whose drilling tactics the unit followed.[24]

Meanwhile, special elections would be held for each of Kentucky's US House seats, followed by a new election for the entire state legislature, which would help establish the true sentiments of the population. The political battles were more important than military might. These plebiscites would go a long way toward determining whether Kentucky would cast its lot with the North, South, or neither. Wealthy Confederate sympathizers, having utilized stealth political tactics to rig the Bleeding Kansas referendums, were at work in Kentucky.[25]

John took the lead in countering one of their most promising plots. George D. Prentice was the legendary editor of the *Louisville Journal* and a longtime ally of James and John Harlan, known for his elegant but sometimes viciously critical editorials. Like the Harlans, the Connecticut-born Prentice was a Union loyalist in spirit and temperament who nonetheless had little patience for the urgent demands of the abolitionists.[26] In the spring and early summer of 1861, having witnessed the Republican ascendency in Washington, the great editor was wavering; his Kentucky-born wife was, in John's words, an "intense rebel," and his two sons were preparing to join the Confederate army. They wanted to see the *Journal* show more sympathy for the secessionist cause.[27] John learned from a friendly editor on the paper of an even greater threat to Prentice's support for the Union: a former Know-Nothing governor of Kentucky, Charles S. Morehead, whose own fortunes were tied up in a Mississippi plantation and therefore dependent on the success of the Confederacy, was proffering an astoundingly high $100,000 bribe to the famous editor to switch sides. With Prentice in the fold, the pro-Southern candidates would have a significant edge in the special elections.[28]

John believed the *Journal* to be an absolutely crucial voice for the

Unionist cause, and he sprang into action to keep Prentice on the side of the Stars and Stripes. John's first weapon was his own father. At sixty-one, James Harlan was a figure of wisdom and integrity, softer of voice than his son but even more highly principled. James had known Prentice for decades; they were fellow warriors in political battles going back to the 1830s. Prentice had been as devout in his support of Henry Clay as James had been, authoring an acclaimed biography of the great statesman and providing journalistic grist for Clay's various compromises; then, less successfully, he'd helped shepherd former Clay supporters such as James and John in the Know-Nothing direction. His sharply anti-Catholic editorials were incitements that contributed to Bloody Monday, though he, too, had mellowed in his thinking about immigrants in the intervening years.[29]

John arranged for James and two other senior former Whigs, longtime allies, to visit the fifty-eight-year-old editor under ostensibly friendly circumstances. Under John's plan, James would go to Prentice and, without betraying his knowledge of the bribe, tell the editor that he had learned of Morehead's plots on behalf of the Confederacy. James told Prentice that he considered such acts akin to treason and punishable by hanging. This was no idle comment: Morehead would later be charged with treason by the federal government and spend much of the war imprisoned at Fort Warren in Boston Harbor. Prentice absorbed the news without any discernible reaction.

Meanwhile, John reached out directly to the *Journal's* owner, a businessman named Isham Henderson, and warned him of Prentice's wavering allegiances. The owner, a staunch Union man, vowed that he'd rather see the paper "sunk to hell" than on the side of the rebels. Henderson backed up his vitriol with some skullduggery of his own: he arranged for John Harlan himself to write unsigned editorials for the paper, handing them directly to the pressmen with an order to publish them unaltered. Thus, readers expecting the wisdom of George D. Prentice got the secret voice of John Harlan instead.

This went on for two weeks, while the ostensibly ill Prentice stayed away from the office. Finally, John wrote, "the skies cleared," and "Prentice's natural love of the Union and the Union cause came up again, and he commenced to write editorials against the rebellion and the rebels of Kentucky."[30]

With the *Louisville Journal* leading the charge, pro-Union candidates took nine of the ten House seats in a special election on May 27, and Unionists won 103 of 138 seats in a special legislative election that August.[31] The votes dealt a serious blow to the state's avowed secessionists but left open the question of what would happen if Kentucky's neutrality was violated by force. Families on both sides stockpiled their weapons. Housewives and young boys began taking target practice, preparing to defend their homes and loved ones in a battle that all hoped would never come, but many expected anyway.

After two weeks on the frothing North Atlantic, the passengers on the SS *City of Manchester* climbed to the decks to witness the first glimpses of land appear through the mist.[32] Ahead lay the cliffs of Ireland, still a wintery brown in the March chill. Teenagers Mary and Laura Harlan and six-year-old Robert James Harlan braced for an experience that few children their ages could even contemplate. Their father girded for an adventure of his own; another great leap in a lifetime of them. This one required so many moving pieces—trainers, jockeys, horses, stables, racing colors—that his mind could only spin along with the ship's propeller at all the decisions ahead. Below deck, stirring in their stalls, were Robert's treasure: the horses he'd purchased with a sizable portion of his fortune. The pedigreed animals were housed in a forward section of the ship that steerage-class immigrants would occupy on the return trip to America. Robert brought along a rooster to remind the animals, in the dark of their quarters below sea level, to awaken at sunrise.[33]

There was no news of the deteriorating situation back home for passengers in the pre-telegraph days. But Robert knew he was moving his children from a country where they were a despised minority, facing an ever-tightening noose of restrictions, to a place where they were merely exotic. England had relatively few dark-skinned people, of various races. This led to more expressions of curiosity than prejudice. But it didn't mean the people of England would be entirely welcoming. Breeding, that mysterious alchemy, definer of destiny for racehorses and humans, was as much on the minds of the British as the Americans. Class, and not necessarily race, defined the pecking order in Queen Victoria's Britain. While the upper classes weren't about to consider any Americans as full equals, nor were they to consign them to the permanent substrata of their own lower classes. For Robert, this was a friendlier climate than the one he left behind in Cincinnati; another crevice of opportunity to slide through.

The noise and vibration increased, and black smoke poured out of the chimney, as the single-screw steam engine of the *City of Manchester* turned down the coast. When the vessel entered Liverpool Harbor, Robert's first sight was the familiar spire of the Church of Our Lady and Saint Nicholas, near the River Mersey. Soon the red walls of the shipping warehouses came into view.[34] Disembarking into the dockside clamor, the four Harlans quickly made their way to an opulent oasis: the Adelphi Hotel, a handsome Georgian edifice, with a façade resembling the executive mansion in Washington. This was the most popular resting place of upper-class travelers, replete with a generous-sized stable to accommodate Robert's horses—the racers Lincoln, Cincinnati, and Des Chiles, along with a famed trotting horse named Jack Rossiter—before they could be sent to permanent stalls in the racing capital of Newmarket.[35] For once, Robert was able to entertain his children in a station reflective of their economic well-being. There was no embarrassed rush to find a Black establishment like the Dumas House, or a Black family willing to rent rooms: Britain was letting Robert in through the front door.

There was even a friendly write-up in the *Liverpool Daily Post*: "Judging from an importation by the *City of Manchester*, on her last trip from New York, our transatlantic cousins are beginning to turn the tables on us . . . and they are now sending over racers, trotters of admirable symmetry and evident power, as well as of good pedigree, to try conclusions on the British turf. The American trotting horses have long been known, and celebrated in English sporting circles, but race-horses from 'Yankeeland' are somewhat of a novelty, and, as such, deserve attention."[36]

An Irish paper, the *Waterford Mail*, picked up a story from a New York paper offering inside information on the Americans heading to England. Robert read with pride that his stable consisted of "exceedingly fine animals, and the very fact of their being selected by so experienced a race-man as Mr. Harlan is a guarantee that they are considerably above average in their points and promise."[37]

Around the mahogany tables of the redbrick Jockey Club in Newmarket, amid the crystal and chandeliers, dinner conversation turned to the mysterious Americans who were now stabling their racehorses in town. Could American animals really compete with their Old World cousins on equal footing? For generations, the British had documented the breeding of their best racers, registering them in a stud book, while the Americans had yet to verify the lineage of their horses. How would these suspiciously sired animals stand up to the best of the British Isles? Some members insisted they couldn't; that much was clear. But others suggested that they just might—though that would be attributable to the fact that some of the best American horses had British bloodlines. It fell to Admiral Henry John Rous, the veteran of the Napoleonic Wars who was the seminal figure in British racing, to sum it up:

"Our American friends have improved their horses in an equal degree to our own by sticking to the same blood," he commented in 1859, in what must have been a direct reference to Robert and Ten Broeck. "For the last fifty years, we have been breeding from our stoutest horses, but principally from large, powerful horses with extraordinary speed. The Americans have bred for stoutness; both parties have succeeded. . . . The comparative stoutness of the American and English racehorse is not yet decided. The odds favor out to be three to one, estimating our numerical superiority. If we best them, we should have no reason to crow."[38]

Robert was a regular visitor to Newmarket, where he could only gaze at the palace-like Jockey Club, built of red brick along a classically British garden and lawn suitable for bowling. Everyone understood that Queen Victoria was the rare monarch who disliked horses, leaving her eldest son, Albert Edward, known as Bertie, as the royal ambassador to the racing world. In later years, the Jockey Club would add a private entrance, giving the Prince of Wales, who adored the racetrack, exclusive access to a towerlike suite where he could visit his many lady friends.[39] For other members, there was the main club, where the highborn could conduct business over fine wines and whiskey. There was also a lesser membership for the Jockey Club "rooms," a status assigned to horse owners of middle-class backgrounds who had grown rich in the industrial revolution; these captains of industry were wanted more for their money than for their company.[40] Finally, there was the courtyard, where a newcomer of no discernible status, such as Robert, could negotiate to buy or sell a horse, or make a bet.[41]

He knew that his mere presence, along with that of Richard Ten Broeck, was causing a stir.[42] He also knew that his moment for fame would pass quickly if his horses didn't prove themselves on the track.

The Newmarket course wasn't anything like the Oakland Racetrack in Louisville or any of the other large racing venues back home, with their flat ovular, dirt tracks. Like many British courses, it was grassy with gentle hills, the kind of place that, to foreign eyes, appeared more suited to a foxhunt than a horse race. The races were held in a sprawling field just outside town, with the starting and finish lines shifting around between heats. There was no grandstand, only a few bleachers, and crowds milled around the edges of the track.[43]

The spectators were the elites of Newmarket racing, usually including Sir Joseph Hawley, a four-time winner of the Derby, England's premier race, and the outspoken William Day, a former jockey who frequently drew raised eyebrows for his cheeky remarks. To his fellow owners, Day was a rotter who could not be ignored, because he happened to own one of the best racers of the day, a horse named The Promised Land. In his usual ungentlemanly manner, he made it known that Americans were foolish even to try to compete with the superior British horses. "There is one thing pretty clear: the American horses, in spite of all the long work they do, have never stayed better than our own," he wrote.[44]

The transatlantic battle was thus engaged. On May 13, less than eight weeks after his arrival in England, Robert made his Newmarket debut with his horse Cincinnati. This first contest of British and American horsepower went to the home team. Cincinnati finished "a bad third" out of four horses, as the British racing calendar reported ungenerously.[45]

The British press believed that the Americans had more of an advantage with their trotters—horses who engaged in the far longer heats involved in harness racing, a sport as old as the Assyrians and made famous by Roman charioteers.[46] Despite its long and heroic lineage, and its popularity in America and France, harness racing was relatively unfamiliar in England. As such, it carried some of the sheen of the new, and British owners were eager to test their horses against Robert's finest, Jack Rossiter.[47]

With his showman's instinct, Robert raised the ante by offering 500 pounds sterling—about $90,000 in 2021 dollars—to any horse that could beat Jack Rossiter. A well-known bettor named Marshall took him up on the offer and agreed to square off their horses on a field outside of Cambridge. But when five thousand spectators showed up, eager to witness the battle of continents, they quickly grew restless and angry. No horses appeared. After a short while, Robert called off the race. He explained later, in a letter to the London sporting paper *Bell's Life*, that Marshall and his horse hadn't made it to Cambridge by the proper time. At the train station heading back to London, he ran into Marshall, just arriving, who agreed to pay a forfeit fee.

"I am at this moment," he concluded his letter, "ready to match my horse for £500 to trot a greater distance, within the space of an hour, than any other horse, mare, or gelding in the universe. Upon those terms, I will make a match to trot either in two days or two months."[48]

The cancellation of the Cambridge race, the *Belfast News-Letter* and other papers reported, only whet the public appetite for a late-summer meeting between the American trotters and their British counterparts: "The eagerly anticipated trotting match has not come off after all, the affair terminating in a dispute of some sort or another; so that, until the 25th of August, the sporting public's taste for trotting will not be gratified," the *News-Letter* reported.[49] The race would be held at the famed Aintree course in Liverpool, in the first running of a special international contest, the Sefton Stakes. It attracted not only Robert's horse but also another American trotter named Mountain Boy, entered by an agent representing Richard Ten Broeck. Five other horses joined the race, but the favorite—at 2-to-1 odds—was Mountain Boy.[50]

"Aintree racecourse yesterday presented such a scene of excitement as has rarely, if ever, been witnessed or recorded in the annals of racing," gushed the *Liverpool Mercury*. "A glorious summer's sun shone upon some 20,000 spectators, assembled to watch the great contest between the American trotting horses."[51]

The prospect of a showdown between Jack Rossiter and Mountain Boy, the two American legends, drew most of the attention. In the first heat, Mountain Boy appeared to fulfill those expectations by jumping out to an early lead, only to be eclipsed at the end by a surprise contender, a British horse named Daw, to the shrieking delight of the spectators. In the second heat, Robert's horse, Jack Rossiter, seized the lead, but Daw slowly began to close the distance. The two horses rumbled down the stretch in close fashion, as the grandstand rocked. The British horse finished ahead by several lengths, a close result in trotting. Nonetheless, the two first-place finishes carried the day for Daw. The delirious crowd began singing in unison, "Old England forever!"[52]

"The excitement now appeared to know no bounds," the *Mercury* reported breathlessly. "A perfect cloud of hats hurled aloft darkened the air for a time. The horse was surrounded, and it and its rider were heartily cheered to the weighing room. The rider was subsequently carried on the shoulders of the delighted crowd."[53]

The race left Robert worried. His other American horses had yet to make a splash, losing all the races they entered, so he cut his losses by selling some of them and buying British racers instead.[54] One of his purchases, a horse named Ochiltree, actually won a few races, a testament to Robert's acumen as an owner and trainer, perhaps, but not to the talent of American mounts.[55] It didn't lessen Robert's disappointment to realize that his fellow displayer of the Stars and Stripes, Ten Broeck, was in much the same position.[56]

The British had carried the day and, so far, the season; the excitement generated by Robert's and Ten Broeck's Yankee challenge had buoyed the fame and fortune of British racers far more than their own.

Despite his struggles on the turf, Robert could find solace in the fact that his family was together, ensconced in the upper-middle-class north London neighborhood of Islington, popular among the newly wealthy industrialists who were propelling the British economy to new heights. The redbrick Canonbury Villas, where the Harlans lived, were handsome and within walking distance of pubs and stores; like all buildings in Dickensian London, the new homes and businesses in Islington bore some of the stains of London's relentless growth, shaded a darker hue by the linger of coal smoke. But it was no small compensation that here in the British capital, the agonies of American slavery and discord were four thousand miles away, in the backwash of a steamer.[57]

John had a family to look after, too, and suddenly it was in danger. He and Malvina were at the National Hotel in Louisville with their two toddlers, Edith and Richard—the latter named for John's deceased brother—when Confederate troops under General Leonidas Polk, a cousin of the former president, poured over the Tennessee border. In response, Yankee soldiers stormed in from the north and mustered at Paducah, on the state's western edge. The long-feared invasion, with Kentucky as the fought-over middle ground, was happening. A group of rebel home guards moved toward Louisville, aiming to seize the state's largest city before the Unionists could organize a defense. John and his fellow loyalists in the home guard scrambled to join a company of Yankees under the command of General William T. Sherman to intercept the Confederates and save the city from attack.[58]

Malvina, who was pregnant again, feared for her children. The National Hotel, where the family had been staying while John and the Speed brothers whipped up public sentiment for the Union, presented a fetching target for the invading forces. In a mad rush, John swept her and the toddlers off in search of the safest private home he could think of: that of Judge William Bullock, an older ally and law partner.[59] Troops massed on every corner, making it difficult for the huddled family to navigate the city. A fifteen-minute walk under normal conditions stretched into hours. Night had descended by the time they arrived, veiling the house in darkness. John and Malvina could only pray that the family would be in bed. Their insistent knocking finally brought the Bullocks to the door. Pain etched itself on the faces of the older couple; though they were Union supporters, their only son had run off to join the Confederate troops. John deposited his wife and children in the Bullocks' care and rushed off into the darkness. All night, Malvina sat up in fear for John's life with the Union forces, listening to the prayers and tears of Mrs. Bullock for her son with the Confederates.[60]

By the time that Sherman's forces, with John among them, reached the spot where the rebels had been massing, they found the secessionists had abandoned their ground. Two days later, John made his way back to Louisville and the Bullock house. He deemed it safe enough to return to the National Hotel—but only for a few days.[61] That night, John paced endlessly, his mind torn over whether his proper place was with General Sherman or with his own vulnerable family. Finally, at dawn, he sat on the bed beside Malvina and told her the decision was hers.

"I knew what his spirit was, and that to feel himself a shirker in the hour of his country's need would make him most unhappy," she recalled later. "Therefore, summoning all the courage I could muster, I said, 'You must do as you would do if you had neither wife nor children. I could not stand between you and your duty to the country and be happy.'"[62]

With rebels in every corner of Kentucky, Malvina decided to take her babies to her parents' home in Indiana, 150 miles down the Ohio

River. Boarding a steamboat with little Edith and Richard, she ran into a female cousin of John's who practically spat in her face, declaring herself embarrassed that any of her kin would be fighting for the Union. She then spotted two women her own age, one of them the wife of John's groomsman from their wedding. They were hoping to make it to Bowling Green, Kentucky, to visit their husbands, who were in the Confederate army. For the first time, she encountered friends as enemies, and resentment stirred in her breast. Soon, however, the ship's captain received word that both women's husbands had been killed in fierce fighting near Bowling Green, the news trickling down among the shocked passengers who were just coming to grips with the reality of war. As she comforted the stunned young women, newly minted widows in their traveling finery, it occurred to Malvina that their roles could easily be reversed. "We were all in the same frame of mind in those bitter days," she recounted later.[63]

Kentucky was neutral, but her citizens were choosing sides. John saw fit to make a formal announcement of his decision to join the Union army, publishing it in Prentice's still-loyal *Louisville Journal*. The violent takeover of Fort Sumter and General Polk's invasion had convinced him that the South was now in the control of dangerous extremists. Sounding notes closer to those of the Republicans than of his fellow conservative Unionists, he cast the war not only as a fight for the Constitution but for freedom itself. He stated his intention to raise an infantry regiment: "I appeal to my fellow Kentuckians to come forward and enroll themselves for service. Their invaded state appeals to them. The cause of human liberty and of republican institutions everywhere appeals to them. All that is most glorious in human government is now at stake, and every true man should come to the rescue."[64]

The reference to human liberty—an indistinct echo of the antislavery movement—may have jarred those who just two years earlier had heard John talk of protecting the rights of slave owners. But the rebellion had obviated the need for appeasement or consolation of those in the throes of the Slave Power, even though the situation in Kentucky remained precarious.

All around the North, other leaders were making similar outreaches for troops. But they addressed populations that were almost entirely in line with the Union, with the only debates being over how aggressively to fight the secessionists. John raised a regiment under the very noses of the enemy, with pro-Confederate newspapers mocking his every move. When he succeeded—persuading nine hundred men to rally behind him, in a testament to his charisma and ability to inspire the confidence of others—even some Confederate sympathizers were impressed. The *Louisville Daily Courier* accused John and other Unionists of attempting to "coax, persuade, bully, bribe, or buy" soldiers; the pro-Confederate paper declared that the Unionists had falsely promised men a $100 bonus and lifetime pension if they signed up. "And yet," the paper conceded, "the most popular of them [John Harlan] has probably succeeded better than any of the other new fledged colonels created by the administration in the state, in raising troops."[65] Farther south, the Confederate *Nashville Tennessean* similarly ridiculed the appeals made by Kentucky Unionists but acknowledged that John's recruitment efforts were "going forward briskly," and his regiment was "filling with uncommon rapidity."[66]

The role of military leader quickened John's blood; at twenty-eight, with his flowing blond hair and fast-emerging beard, he looked the part of a dashing young soldier.[67] Moreover, he relished the chance to prove himself based on strength and stamina, not to mention manly courage, to an audience of men who had little awareness of the acuteness of his constitutional arguments or the depth of his knowledge of American history. As colonel, he was the regiment's role model and inspiration, which gave him a direct connection to every private in every muddy tent in the sea of canvas surrounding their parade grounds. Many of those privates were Catholics, and they taught him a lesson about patriotism. Witnessing their life-and-death devotion to the Union, John realized that his concerns about their fidelity to the Papacy may have been overblown.

"It was magnificent to see how the boys struggled through mud and rain to reach the field of battle," he recalled later. "The ground was so wet and muddy under them that their feet slipped at every step. I see now with great distinctness old Father Nash posing along on foot with the boys. Equally earnest with him was a Catholic priest from Washington County who had come with Catholic soldiers from that county."[68]

In leading his men, John shed any hints of campaign-trail pomposity; he was no longer a politician, an aristocrat, a golden boy. He punctuated his injunctions to the men with swear words, including from the Bible; one captain in the regiment, a Baptist minister in civilian life, refused to swear himself but exhorted the troops by yelling, "Boys, give them hell, as Colonel Harlan says!" John wanted to speak the language of the men as he showed himself to be their equal—or more—in all the physical trials of soldiering. "He could outrun, outjump, outwrestle any man in the regiment," boasted Champ Clark, a future Speaker of the US House who, as a boy, knew the soldiers in John's regiment. All of them, Clark attested, loved him, both because of his courage and his willingness to acknowledge their fears—and even to suggest that he sometimes shared them.[69]

The regiment bivouacked in Lebanon Junction, the same small town where their home guard predecessor, the Crittenden Zouaves, had mustered with General Sherman, a bonding process so close that John had ended up sleeping on the floor of Sherman's quarters.[70] The new regiment called its home Camp Crittenden.[71] John had a feel for the terrain, close enough to the Tennessee border that his soldiers could pounce on encroaching Confederates. Winter arrived, with rain and mud accompanied by chilling winds; temperatures dipped below freezing on many nights.[72] Soon enough, John's Tenth Kentucky Volunteers were on the move, slogging through desiccated forests with packs of thirty pounds or more of provisions on their backs. General George H. Thomas ordered them to join with other Yankee forces massing against a large Confederate encampment near the town of Logan's Crossroads. While other troops would be engaging the Confederates directly, John's unit was ordered to wait along the railroad tracks, blocking any trains that tried to pass into the Confederate-controlled area, thus choking off supply routes from the South.

The men established their positions, muskets ready, in the woods beside the track, but no train came. Soon a cavalryman arrived with the frantic news that Thomas's troops were engaged in fierce fighting and that John's unit should rush to the Logan's Crossroads area as reinforcements. By the time the regiment reached the battlefield, the Confederates were hightailing back to the South. John led his men in pursuit as far as the Cumberland River.[73]

Northern newspapers hailed the Battle of Mill Springs, as the confrontation came to be known, as the first decisive victory of the war. About ten thousand men participated on both sides, with two hundred of them, mostly Confederates, losing their lives.[74] John made a lonely inspection of the battlefield, his eyes struck by the corpses rotting in the open air. The remains of the Confederate commander, General Felix Zollicoffer, lay splayed on a slab of wood.[75] Zollicoffer was a former Whig congressman from Tennessee who, like John and his father, turned to the American Party after the Whigs dissolved. Zollicoffer's politics were similar to John's. They were from neighboring states, and both loved the Union. Even though Zollicoffer opposed secession, he had refused to turn his back on his native Tennessee. That pitted him, face-to-face, against men with whom he actually agreed, each armed and prepared to kill the other.[76]

John was staring at the death mask of a man very much like himself.

General Thomas's troops, the Tenth Kentucky Volunteers among them, marched quickly from Kentucky to Tennessee, shifting from defense to offense. A Union general named Ulysses S. Grant commanded a massive force in the western part of the state, preparing to challenge the Confederate army of Mississippi for control of the rivers and railroads of the West. March turned into April as Thomas's men slogged their way across the Volunteer State to join Grant's burgeoning forces. The speed of the march, combined with the weather, rendered their tents and sleeping bags sodden, their clothes and mess kits teeming with vermin.[77] Then, with Thomas's men still several days away, the Confederates launched a surprise attack on Grant's encampment near a Mississippi River dock known as Pittsburg Landing. Tens of thousands of men in gray under the command of the famed tactician Albert Sidney Johnston spilled out of the woods, raining fire on the unsuspecting Union army. The following day, when the rebels assumed the Yankees were regrouping, Grant turned the tables, launching a vicious and unexpected counterassault. The Battle of Shiloh was by far the most monstrous of the war so far, and all of American history up to that time, engaging more than 110,000 men. There were four times as many casualties as in the First Battle of Manassas, the raw carnage of which had shaken the consciousness of the North just ten months earlier.[78]

John's regiment arrived after the fighting ended, with more than thirteen thousand casualties on the Northern side and only slightly fewer for the South. The Union army had held firm; the Confederate gambit failed, partly because its architect, Johnston, had been killed early in the fighting—a blow that some in the South considered far worse than merely losing the battle. Though they hadn't fought, John's men suffered from disease and fatigue after marching all day and night. When they came upon a giant Mississippi River steamboat, its boilers growling in the cold of night, John told them to board it and sleep in the engine room; it would be their only chance for a few hours in a dry, warm setting. When they approached the gangplank, however, a Union army guard refused them entry, saying the boat was under the control of "headquarters." Impatient with army bureaucracy, Harlan ordered his men to force their way on board. If any guards tried to stop them, he told a captain, "pitch them in the river." The men complied eagerly and enjoyed a peaceful night beside the thrumming engines.

Only in the morning did John realize that the boat was, in fact,

General Grant's headquarters, with the commander himself asleep in a stateroom upstairs. Fearful of recriminations, John ordered his men to leave the boat.[79] He then made his way to the ravaged battlefield. For some acres, he couldn't pass a few feet without stepping around a dead soldier. Union troops had positioned themselves along a road in an area nicknamed the "Hornet's Nest" and somehow withstood the initial Confederate attack; now saturated with blood and littered with the refuse of battle, the road exuded the solemn calmness of a mass gravesite.[80] Amid the wreckage, John spotted General Sherman, his old friend from Lebanon Junction. Sherman, whose reputation as a man of action had only been enhanced by his heroic actions at Shiloh, impulsively offered to take John under his wing to visit General Grant.[81]

Grant couldn't talk for long, because he was under siege. Northern newspapers, hearing of his reputation for heavy drinking, declared that the Union commander had gotten drunk and left his men vulnerable to Confederate attack. Members of Congress demanded his dismissal. The Northern victory at Shiloh seemed likely to be the final defeat for an enigmatic general who lacked the charm and grandeur of his Southern counterparts, allowing rumors of his alcoholism and depression to grow to worrisome extremes. President Lincoln, however, chose to pay greater attention to Grant's courage in launching the counterattack, a willingness to take on the South that he found lacking in others of his commanders. He expressed his full confidence in the man.[82]

The Union army was struggling badly in the East even if it was merely holding its own in the West. It would need more from General Grant, along with Sherman and many others, including the eager young colonel in charge of the Tenth Kentucky Volunteers.[83]

Robert's fame in England exceeded his success on the track. With his immaculate dress, ready smile, and talent for self-promotion, he made himself a fixture at famed British racecourses. This was true at Epsom, as well, the crown jewel of British racing, where a series of contests staged around the greatest of them all—the Derby—was cause for a national celebration every June.[84] Londoners of all classes packed themselves into special Derby rail carriages to venture to the otherwise sleepy town just twenty miles from the city; the journey was a mixture of drunken revelry and frustration. Cars would often be so overcrowded that the engine couldn't pull the train, and an attendant would have to uncouple the rear coaches, leaving them stuffed with confused and angry fans, helpless on the tracks. More revelers would travel by horse and buggy, and on foot. On a clear day, from a bend in the road outside the Downs, arrivals could look back over their shoulders and see the smokestacks of London in the distance.[85]

During Derby week in 1859, Robert entered two races, only to see his horses Des Chiles and Lincoln finish near the back of the pack.[86] But at Epsom, like Newmarket and other legendary courses, Robert remained a figure of interest, both to the transatlantic press and his fellow owners, who accepted his presence with equanimity if not full embrace. In the United States, the courtly manners he picked up on the riverboats of the Mississippi distinguished him from less cultivated men freed from slavery, but at the cost of labeling him as a certain type of confidence man; he was often treated with ridicule, like a man in a costume. By contrast, when he acted the part of Kentucky colonel in Queen Victoria's court, he was regarded as an American eccentric; a flower from a different greenhouse. There was less suspicion and fewer knowing glances.[87]

Thus did Robert take his place beside the elites of the sport at Doncaster, a South Yorkshire County city whose ivy-covered ruins attested to its medieval roots. Every September, the Doncaster track was the scene of one of Britain's most celebrated racing festivals. Robert entered the horses he'd brought from America in several heats that day, without success. His fortune dwindled with every loss, but the day's flagship race—the St. Leger, one of five "English Classics," first established in 1776—offered an opportunity to recoup.[88] The fabled colt known as The Promised Land, whose strutting owner, William Day, was so contemptuous of Americans, would be taking on a lackluster field of challengers.[89] Robert didn't enter a horse, believing that The Promised Land—a horse so popular he was known simply as "the Land"—was unbeatable. This was the unanimous view of the racing press as well. "We think that if ever there was a certainty of picking a winner, this of Promised Land is the one," proclaimed *Sporting Life*, while *Bell's Life* declared that The Promised Land "could lay claim to the distinction of being the best horse of the year."[90] All his life, Robert had prided himself on sizing up horses in person, like a doctor examining a patient, and making his own judgment of their racing ability. The Promised Land, his eagle eye discerned, was a champion for the ages.[91]

On the day of the big race, with brilliant sunlight bursting through the clouds, The Promised Land made a grand entrance.[92] He was the last horse to be saddled and led onto the track by William Day and his brother, the horse's jockey, Alfred Day, to a great swell of applause.[93] Within seconds of the start, The Promised Land sprinted up the first hill in stunning time, outpacing all the other horses by three lengths. He was so far ahead by the middle of the run that some spectators turned away. Then suddenly the gap began to close. The Promised Land fell behind, then vaulted up front again, only to fall back badly, as if stricken. By the end, the *Sporting Life* reported, "Promised Land seemed to stand still . . . without power for a final struggle."[94] A Yorkshire-bred horse named Gamester finished first, followed by three more contenders. The Promised Land was a distant fifth.[95]

"For some moments, the air was rent by the most vehement cheering" at the upset of the nation's most famous horse by a local favorite.[96] There was little sorrow for the losing horse's unpopular owner or his jockey-brother. The Promised Land's defeat was a blow to the Day brothers, but also to many of the sport's biggest bettors, who had risked their fortunes on the horse's victory. Even those without significant means, made richer by "the early harvest and the prosperous state of manufacturing," in the opinion of the *Illustrated London News*, chose to wager their earnings and—most of them—lost.

Robert was among them. In his desperation over the failures of his own horses, he had borrowed money from other people to put ever-larger sums on The Promised Land. The cold rain that poured down after the race mirrored his spirits.

"I admit that if I did not get broke, I was pretty badly bent," he confessed grimly in a letter back home to the *Spirit of the Times*. It was an unusual confession of defeat.[97]

Robert's financial reversals had an immediate impact, leading him on a fantastic and—in the eyes of a suddenly mocking American press—farcical journey. At some point before Robert's debacle in betting on The Promised Land, an American bettor traveling in England named James Bevins had lent him money. The two had exchanged cash before, sometimes resolving the debts by promising to pay each other's creditors, and Robert considered his debt to Bevins to have been covered in this manner to all but a fraction of the full amount. The peripatetic Robert then headed off on a trip to Scotland. While Robert was enjoying the autumn scenery on the Scottish moors, Bevins, after paying off some of Robert's staff, took his horse Jack Rossiter from its stables in Newmarket and promptly disappeared.[98]

Robert returned to England to find his most famous trotter—the one he had hyped with all his showman's zeal, turning him into a transatlantic celebrity—missing from his empty stable. Bevins, far from hiding his theft, registered the horse under his own name for transport purposes at the Newmarket train station; he wished it to be known that he considered the beloved racer to be collateral for Robert's debt.[99] In a panic, Robert traversed England to inspect places where Bevins might have hidden Jack Rossiter, before taking his quest across the English Channel. Bevins, Robert knew, was a frequent visitor to Paris. Harness racing—Jack Rossiter's specialty—was far more popular in France than in England, and Bevins might reasonably have assumed that Robert wouldn't venture so far as to track him down there.[100]

But to the fascination and amusement of racing fans, he did. Spying on racetracks and stables around the city, Robert commenced to search nearly every arrondissement of the French capital. Finally, he spotted Jack Rossiter being walked by a Black stable hand whom he recognized as working for Bevins.[101] Robert followed the horse and the young man back to the stable, establishing both the identity of the horse and the fact that Bevins had taken possession of it; he then returned to England to gather up his documentation to back up his case. That proved to be a mistake. Learning that Robert had been sniffing around, Bevins moved the horse to a different Parisian stable and then sold him to a friend.[102]

Undaunted, Robert returned to Paris, renewed his stakeouts, and spotted Jack Rossiter once again, this time cantering down the street under the reins of a stable owner with ties to both Bevins and the man to whom Bevins had sold the horse. Alleging a conspiracy between the three of them, Robert hired two French attorneys to bring the case to trial, to the avid fascination of the racing press.[103]

This tale of international intrigue captured the interest of none other than the *New-York Times*, which in a sprawling account presented it as both a comical adventure and a love story between a man and his horse. "Harlan is the master, Jack is the horse; but he is no vulgar beast, the latter, without genealogy," the *Times* wrote, in what was quite likely a mocking allusion to Robert's slave ancestry and the whispers about James being his father.[104] The racing publication *Spirit of the Times* weighed in on behalf of Bevins, claiming in an editorial: "We have known Mr. James J. Bevins ever since he was little Jim, half an hour high." It went on to give Bevins a free opportunity to answer the "scurrilous" attacks on his reputation by Robert and his friends. Bevins claimed that Robert had promised Jack Rossiter as consideration for a loan, and, with the backing of Robert's staff, took possession of the horse while Robert was away. He did not address why, if all this was part of an up-and-up agreement, he went so far as to stash the horse in Paris.[105]

The Parisian court ruled in Robert's favor, but all the talk of debts and creditors and deals damaged his reputation.[106] The derisive tone of the *Times* article and other reports in the American press was especially painful in light of the heroic treatment he received when he first launched his journey to England, waving the American flag in the face of the skeptical British. Despair, however, was not in Robert's emotional repertoire. A man born into slavery didn't suffer much for merely financial reversals. His reputation alone had never earned him a penny.

A far more bitter blow awaited him, though. While at home in

Canonbury Villas, Robert's fourteen-year-old daughter Laura Frances Harlan died—a victim of the consumption that was rampant in the country that year.[107] The grieving father effectively conceded that his dream of dominating the racing world of Europe was over. Just three months earlier, Tattersalls, the auction house that handled almost all transactions involving racehorses, had reported the sale of the aging Jack Rossiter. At a temple-like building in London's Hyde Park, beside a decorative water trough known to all turf denizens as "the Fox," for the painted statue in its domed room, Robert's beloved trotting horse had been sold for just 90 guineas—no more than $20,000 in 2021 dollars.[108]

Robert's brief, glorious, soul-expanding foray into ownership of racers at England's most iconic tracks was over—but he decided to stay in the country and use his horse sense to figure out ways to recoup his fortune.

Chapter 6

John vs. John

John put the blood and death of Shiloh behind him, only to confront fresh and categorically different horrors of war. At a quick march, he led his men on an odyssey through the clinging branches of the backwoods of the rebellion, dodging sharpshooters while contending with the duplicities of people in one-horse towns along the way. Danger and disease were the soldiers' constant companions. So, too, was sadness and bitterness. Everywhere, John found evidence of how completely the country was torn apart, the national fabric ripped into banners of Stars and Stripes, and Stars and Bars.

The men alighted in Corinth, Mississippi, just south of the Tennessee border, where a large force of Confederates was massing. The Tenth Kentucky Volunteers joined up with thousands of seasoned Union troops under the command of General Henry Halleck. They pitched their tents so close to the Confederate encampment that they could "hear the rebel yell."[1] But Old Brains, as the scholarly Halleck was known, was one of the Union commanders who had what Lincoln derisively called "the slows."[2] John couldn't hide his exasperation. When the Tenth Kentucky Volunteers finally took action against the Confederates, they found a deserted camp. The rebels had sussed out the attack and moved their troops and artillery. "Not even a barrel of crackers was found for the use of our soldiers," John complained.[3]

Following a stop at the deserted Tennessee River hamlet of East-port, Mississippi, John and his men marched southward through the blossoming trees of an Alabama springtime to the town of Florence.[4] That Sunday morning, John proudly led a group of soldiers into the First Presbyterian Church near the center of town. It was a rare chance to attend services, the weekly ritual he had adhered to since childhood. He fretted about entering the house of the Lord with a long, sandy beard but strived to present as respectful an appearance as possible. The rhythms of the service were an abiding comfort. The minister, an older man named William Henry Mitchell, launched into a brief prayer and hymn, followed by a reading from the New Testament. But then he veered menacingly off course. His eyes washing over the Union troops lining the pews, Mitchell improvised a special prayer for the Confederacy. He loudly decried the Yankee oppressors who violated the rights of a devout and humble citizenry. May God smite these vicious invaders, Mitchell intoned, his voice rising.

The Union soldiers leaped up in their pews, huffing and stomping their boots to the unblinking stares of the other worshippers. John maintained a respectful silence, then joined his men in the vestibule while Mitchell continued to rain hellfire on their souls. Some wanted to shut him up by force. Hoping to prevent a confrontation, John promised instead to report Mitchell's impudence to General Thomas. But when John described to Thomas how the minister had deliberately altered the service to condemn the Union men in the flock, the general ordered him to arrest the seething preacher.

Walking down the aisle alone and looking up at the pulpit, John condemned Mitchell for having called down God's wrath on men who had humbly and in good faith come to worship. The minister bristled with dignity. "Very well, sir, I submit to your authority," he announced, as John led him down from the altar to the arms of a military police unit and off to a Union prison.[5]

In John's angry opinion, the war had claimed another victim: the sanctity of his Presbyterian Church.

In the first months of the war, John's troops had, by bitter coincidence, found themselves arriving at battles too late to make a difference, after the bayonets were sheathed and the fields strewn with corpses. The march northward to Decherd, Tennessee, where the Tenth Kentucky Volunteers were to join General Don Carlos Buell, marked a change. All along the route, John and his men confronted Confederate raiders, finally engaging the enemy in a fight at Courtland, Alabama, in late July, 1862. The Tenth Kentucky Volunteers killed eleven Confederates and wounded twenty more, while incurring just one loss and four injuries of their own.[6] Dysentery proved to be more of a threat than bullets. By the time John's regiment reached Shelbyville, Tennessee, about thirty miles from Decherd, seventy-five of his men were too weak to carry their rifles.[7]

As the sick and weary troops trudged toward town, they confronted a gruesome sight: two Black men in Union uniforms were swinging from a tree outside town, their eyes bulging and necks broken under tight nooses. Believing that the killers had dressed the corpses in Union garb for a reason, John took the lynchings to be a threat to him and his men. He felt the good townspeople of Shelbyville were so united in their brutality that they intended to launch more guerrilla attacks upon anyone in a Union uniform.

Fueled with "horror," as he put it later, John ordered his healthy soldiers to march into town and capture six of the best-dressed young men on the streets—all leading citizens of Shelbyville—and hold them as prisoners. After the men were rounded up, John approached on his horse and told them and other townspeople about the lynchings and why he saw them as a promise of more guerrilla activity to come. "Now, I warn you that for every soldier absent from my camp this evening, two of these arrested citizens will be shot by my orders," he declared.

There were no attacks that night, and John let the innocent men go home. He repeated the tactic, rounding up the leading young men of all the Tennessee towns in which his men camped, until the Tenth Kentucky Volunteers were able to meet up with General Buell's troops, arrayed outside Decherd.[8]

The rendezvous with Buell was a homecoming for John. The Union forces knew how much the Confederates coveted Kentucky and how they considered it a proud slaveholding part of their cultural diaspora. Confederate generals Braxton Bragg and E. Kirby Smith planned an aggressive "heartland offensive" in the summer of 1862 to bring Kentucky into the Confederate fold by force. Part of their strategy was to awaken a "slumbering majority" of Confederate sympathizers in the Bluegrass State—the types of people whose voices presumably had been quelled by James and John Harlan, among others of the state's Unionist elites.[9] Buell's Union forces numbered roughly eighty thousand, and he led them on a long, slow march along a key railroad line from Nashville to Louisville, intended to showcase his side's commitment to defending Kentucky.[10]

John felt a surge of excitement at the prospect of returning to Louisville. He rushed to persuade Malvina to make the trip from Evansville for a visit; she came by steamboat bearing their new son, James, named for his grandfather, and shared a few precious days with her husband. The reunion buoyed the spirits of both husband and wife but soon gave way to John's frustrating return to the army.[11]

As proud as John was to be defending his home state, he chafed under Buell's command. Here was yet another Union general afraid to commit to battle, terminally afflicted by the slows. Buell's Union forces tagged along behind the Confederates under Bragg and Smith all summer and into the fall, repeatedly failing to engage in large-scale fighting. In early October several columns of Union troops finally clashed with Bragg's forces at Perryville, Kentucky, near Harlan's Station. When the Confederates launched a counterattack, the Yankees fell back into a defensive line. Buell, as it happened, was several miles from the fast-developing battle in the rear of the long line of troops; when John and his men joined in the desperate fighting, they were taking the field without a commander. As the second day of fighting dragged on, more Union troops arrived, Buell among them, strengthening the Yankee position. Despite the Union army's vast numerical advantage of fifty-five thousand to sixteen thousand, the Confederates held their own in the fighting and inflicted greater casualties. However, they soon realized the futility of their push against a much larger force, ending their heartland offensive in frustration, if not defeat.[12]

Buell's failure to pursue the Southerners reinforced a distressing pattern of Union defensive victories that nonetheless did little to quell the rebellion or damage the confidence of the South. Worse, some of those serving under Buell accused their commander of hiding behind his men, a charge that John considered unfair. Gathered in a schoolhouse, a group of angry Union officers debated whether to accuse the Ohio-born Buell of being a Confederate sympathizer. Despite his own frustrations, John defended Buell's honor; he had been near enough to Buell's position to know that a howling wind had blocked any sound of the battle up ahead. The wind, and nothing else, had prevented the general from joining the battle any sooner. Nonetheless, John had no reluctance to adding his name to a long list of officers making a formal request to Washington for a new commander—a request that never got made. The morning after the meeting in the schoolhouse, the Union army announced that William S. Rosecrans was replacing Buell as commander of the forces massed in Tennessee and Kentucky.[13]

Under Rosecrans, John became a folk hero—the man who fought back against an even more charismatic hero on the other side. The Confederate cavalry raider John Hunt Morgan, whose leather cowboy hat tilted raffishly to the left, was the bane of Rosecrans's command. The scion of one of Kentucky's wealthiest families, Morgan was like John Harlan without any sense of gravity or responsibility. He attended Transylvania University for two years before getting expelled for dueling. He fought in the Mexican War but was something of a ne'er-do-well in his late thirties, when, like many of his ilk, he found his calling as a fighting man in the Civil War. Morgan's ancestry leaned to the South, and so while John was recruiting a Kentucky regiment for the Union, Morgan was rounding up the best Kentucky horsemen he could find for his crackerjack Confederate unit. His Second Kentucky Cavalry fought bravely at Shiloh but proved to be even more valuable to Southern commanders for its quick and daring raids behind enemy lines, keeping the Yankees perpetually fearful and on edge.[14]

John encountered Morgan for the first time while the Tenth Kentucky Volunteers were camped with other Union soldiers northeast of Nashville. The Yankees were scattered in the woods one December morning, huddled over their breakfast fires, when some of the men heard a rustling of dead leaves and crackling of limbs. Morgan's horsemen loomed through the trees. John heard an explosion of musket fire and ran toward the noise. He arrived in time to witness a scene out of medieval tales: Morgan's men galloped over nearby hills with Union soldiers on their backs as human shields, having seized prisoners from under the noses of their commanders.[15]

Soon afterward, General Thomas gave John the orders he craved: he and his men were to pursue the reckless Morgan as he continued to rain destruction on the Union lines. John knew that Morgan had more of a purpose than just terrorizing the enemy: he wanted to destroy the railroad tracks that provided crucial supplies to the Union troops. Already Morgan had succeeded in damaging the rails outside of Chattanooga, disrupting the supply route to Rosecrans's headquarters. Realizing that Morgan had a larger and more seasoned force, John tracked him stealthily, using the railroads to carry his infantry troops to defensive positions along the line. The train moved slowly enough that John suspected the engineer of being a Southern sympathizer. The Tenth Kentucky Volunteers snaked their way from Gallatin, Tennessee, to Bowling Green, to a smaller Kentucky town called Munfordville, where they first spotted and dispersed one of Morgan's raiding parties. Then, in a place called Elizabethville, John gleaned crucial intelligence from townspeople about the whereabouts of Morgan's forces.

After calling for reinforcements—a cavalry unit plus artillery and more infantry—John led his men at a quick march toward a scenic bend in the Salt River, about forty miles from where he was born. When the Union cavalry spotted Morgan's men encamped at the spot known as the Rolling Fork of the Salt River, John and the rest of the

Union forces sprang into action. They caught the Confederate raiders almost as unawares as the Union had been in Tennessee. Bullets flew by John's ears as he raced after Morgan on horseback. The Confederates scrambled to their mounts and galloped off into the horizon. Left untouched was a crucial bridge on the Louisville and Nashville (L & N) Railroad that the raiders had hoped to destroy. The Union supply lines were saved.[16]

John's heroism won him a battlefield commendation. His superiors quickly recommended him for promotion from colonel to brigadier general. President Lincoln went so far as to submit the promotion papers. But the Battle of Rolling Fork marked the premature end of John's US Army career. Soon afterward, he received devastating news from Frankfort: his father was dead.[17]

John blamed the war for the "unspeakable calamity" of James Harlan's death.[18] At sixty-two, James was still John's lodestar, his financial backer and his most respected political adviser. More than father and son, they were mentor and student. James's term as attorney general had ended early in the war, and President Lincoln appointed him as the state's US attorney. From that post, he delicately handled the responsibility of building treason cases against Kentuckians who manifestly aided the Confederacy; despite this awkward public role, his clout in the state was significant enough, with his stature undimmed, that he continued to draw high-paying law clients.[19]

When the Confederates invaded Frankfort briefly in the summer of 1862, James moved to Union-controlled Louisville, leaving Eliza behind to manage their affairs. By fall, however, the rebels had left the state capital and James was yearning to return. The countryside between the cities teemed with raiding parties, so he took a circuitous route, traveling by river to Cincinnati and then by rail to Lexington. Under the cover of night, he rode in an open carriage from Lexington to Frankfort, a distance of twenty-five miles, his trusted Henry rifle by his side. He neglected to bring an overcoat. As the chill of the late-autumn night deepened, a stiff wind blew. By the time he got home, he was wracked with congestion. Still, there was no sense of immediate danger. John stopped by for a visit while roaming Kentucky in pursuit of Morgan's raiders. He found his father feeling unwell but fully expecting to recover. Soon afterward, however, the infection in his chest deepened. James was dead by February 23, a few months shy of his sixty-third birthday. The family blamed the unprotected carriage ride, in the fog of war, for his loss.[20]

John grieved for his father more than anyone else in his life and recognized that James's death presented an immediate family crisis.[21] James had maintained the lifestyle of a wealthy man while living hand to mouth. His stature as a lawyer guaranteed a steady flow of high-paying clients, but there was no underlying asset—no investment portfolio or plantation—to keep income flowing in his absence.[22] Clearly, the only hope for the Harlans was for John to step in and try to keep James's legal practice alive.

James's great dream of uniting his and Eliza's five sons in a family law firm had crumbled. Richard, the eldest and a Mexican War hero, had followed his younger brother Clay into an early grave in 1854. James Jr. got married and lived for a while in Indiana; he was already on a path that would lead to severe alcoholism and destitution. William Lowndes Harlan was the only one of John's brothers to continue working with James, but he was always considered a lesser light—nothing close to the rising star that John had become. William, Eliza, and the rest of the extended family would be facing hard times without James to provide for them; Malvina, John, and their three children drew from the same bucket of funds.

John knew what he had to do but nonetheless felt guilt about leaving the army. More than just disappointing his men, he feared that other people would read into his decision a lack of confidence in the progress of the war. He also had a political career to think about. It wouldn't help to be seen as abandoning the Union cause. He decided to lay out his situation in frank detail in a resignation letter to Rosecrans's chief of staff, General James Garfield, and then to release it to Kentucky newspapers:

The recent sudden death of my father has devolved upon me duties of a private nature which the exigencies of the public service do not require that I shall neglect. Those duties relate to his unsettled business which demands my immediate personal attention. I deeply regret that I am compelled, at this time, to return to civil life. It was my fixed purpose to remain in the Federal army until it had effectually suppressed the existing armed rebellion, and restored the authority of the National Government over every part of the Union. No ordinary considerations would have induced me to depart from this purpose. Even the private interests to which I have alluded would be regarded as nothing, in my estimation, if I felt that my continuance in or retirement from the service would, to any material extent, affect the great struggle through which the country is now passing. If, therefore, I am permitted to retire from the army, I beg the Commanding General to feel assured that it is from no want of confidence either in the justice or ultimate triumph of the Union cause. That cause will always have the warmest sympathies of my heart, for there are no conditions upon which I will consent to a dissolution of the Union. Nor are there any concessions, consistent with a republican form of government, which I am not prepared to make in order to maintain and perpetuate that Union.[23]

John's letter conveyed more than a hint of his future ambitions. In ending his military foray, he was preparing to reopen his political career. He envisioned peace talks with the South at some point in the near future, after which supporters of the Union would have to decide which concessions to grant the Confederacy in exchange for reunification. On this great question, John had only one unbreakable demand: a republican form of government. The ultimate fate of slavery, he believed, should remain on the bargaining table.

Robert tracked the progress of the Civil War from a large, comfortable rowhouse in a bucolic suburb of London, where he lived with Mary and Robert Jr. British newspapers recorded the exploits of Colonel John M. Harlan, but there was no one with whom Robert could share his feelings about John's heroism or, for that matter, the death of James; all of Kentucky seemed, for the moment, a ghost from the distant past. Much had happened in the intervening years, most of it vexing. His career as an owner of thoroughbreds had ended with the sale of his mounts by auction at Tattersall's; losses on the turf, combined with the toll the war was taking on his investments in Cincinnati, cut deeply.[24] He avoided creditors by declaring bankruptcy, but then moved aggressively to recoup his fortune by training and betting on horses, both in England and across the Continent.[25]

Bankruptcy did not require a descent into poverty. After the death of his daughter Laura, Robert moved from Canonbury Villas to a much larger home in the Thames River town of Richmond.[26] He and Mary and Robert Jr. settled into a four-story brick rowhouse with bay windows, decorative tiling, and a walled garden in back, along with ample space for servants; the handsome property was only a few steps from the gently winding river.[27] In earlier centuries, King Henry VIII and his entourage would travel past this spot in pillowed comfort aboard a cavalcade of barges moving between London and Hampton Court Palace. Just steps from Robert's house was Richmond Palace, the chosen retreat of Henry VIII's daughter Queen Elizabeth I. The Virgin Queen had endured her final courtship, by the handsome Duke of Alençon, twenty-one years her junior, within its friendly walls. After her death in her Richmond Palace bedroom in 1603, the town was largely appropriated by writers and artists.[28]

By the 1860s, the verdant landscape of Richmond represented an appealing contrast to the coal-fired density of central London. Laura's death at Canonbury Villas may have given Robert a permanent impression of the city as a breeding ground for disease—one reinforced by the many Victorian-era Londoners who lost children to consumption.[29] It also took Robert further from the tempest of the political debate over the war in America. Angry British merchants, deprived of Southern cotton by a Union blockade, demanded that their government recognize the Confederacy—a move that would open up the possibility, much dreaded in the North, of foreign aid for the rebellion.

Inflamed by shocking reports of the brutality of American plantation owners, British reformers pushed strongly in the other direction—casting the Confederacy as a danger to human dignity. Caught in the middle was a wavering Parliament.

In that intense atmosphere, escaped former slaves journeyed from America to tell their stories to rapt audiences. A few streets away from Robert's home at Canonbury Villas, a formerly enslaved man named Howell related tales of floggings before a gathering in a schoolroom, organized by a local reverend. "If you said to master, who was about to flog you, 'Pray, mass,' he would say 'I'll make you pray!' and after a flogging, he would make you return thanks," said Howell, an escapee whose wife remained enslaved, according to the *North London Record*. Howell told the entranced audience that he "thanked the Lord for his escape." Another formerly enslaved man named Washington Dove informed Londoners that the reality of slavery was actually worse than the atrocities that they had read about in the 1852 novel *Uncle Tom's Cabin* by Harriet Beecher Stowe.[30]

Robert supported the Union cause passionately and yearned for emancipation, yet he didn't choose to lecture about his experiences. His story wasn't typical. It was laced with plenty of horrors—likely having been the product of a non-consensual relationship between a white man and an enslaved woman, and having seen his mother sold down South—but there were none of the whippings and floggings that sparked outrage among Londoners. The fact that he was grateful to his master, regarding him as a father figure, was a complication that might do the cause more harm than good. He was, in fact, grieving for that master-father at the very moment. The London Emancipation Committee, which was fixated on the living conditions of people in bondage on American plantations, wasn't looking for a story about how slavery ensnarls the most basic of human relationships. That was the twist from which Robert was struggling to disentangle himself, concentrating, as always, on moving forward—finding his way through whatever doors were open to him.[31]

Despite John's insistence that he had no problems with the Union cause, he had serious issues with the Union's commander in chief. On January 1, 1863, just seven weeks before James's death, President Lincoln's Emancipation Proclamation had taken effect; in every state under rebellion, men and women in slavery were freed by the president, utilizing his absolute military authority. Lincoln insisted it was a wartime necessity: enslaved men and women needed to know they'd be protected if they turned on their masters.[32] Moreover, Black soldiers joining the Union army required the extra motivation of knowing that they were fighting for the freedom of their people. The proclamation didn't liberate any enslaved people in Kentucky, which was not in rebellion, but it nonetheless upset a fragile political balance.[33] The conservative Unionists who'd answered John's call to strike down the Confederacy, on the grounds that Southerners were the aggressors, now had reason to question which side was trying to remake the country.[34]

John the lawyer and ardent constitutionalist believed Lincoln was stretching his power. The president had already used his authority as commander in chief to suspend habeas corpus: the right of people to challenge their unjust imprisonment in court. Now Lincoln was freeing slaves in the South, on the grounds of military necessity. But was it really necessary? If so, why hadn't he done it sooner? And why so much agonizing? Obviously, it wasn't the military pushing Lincoln to free the slaves, but Lincoln pushing the military.

John the politician saw this as a betrayal. He, personally, had rallied support for the Union based on Lincoln's promise that the war was to preserve the nation, not free the slaves. The president had been disingenuous. Worse, all the detested Kentucky Democrats— the secessionists that John had spent his life opposing—now looked prescient in their insistence that Lincoln was a secret abolitionist, using the language of unity to push through a deeply divisive change in the national order.

John was prepared to see the end of slavery. But he felt that Kentucky's loyalty to the Union entitled the state to make its own choice of whether to abolish slavery. Then, when Kentuckians made their decision, it would be accepted as the will of the commonwealth. There was no logic in repelling an invasion from one side only to submit to the dictatorial powers of the other.[35]

Within two weeks of John's departure from the military, while he and his brother James Jr. sorted through the family's threadbare finances as coexecutors of their father's estate, he accepted the Union party's nomination for attorney general. This sudden reemergence into politics didn't violate his promise that family would always come first; as Kentucky's attorney general, he would have the prominence to attract the kind of high-paying law clients James had relied upon. His political success would provide the legal fees to restore the Harlan family fortunes.[36]

Moreover, it was a rare chance for an easy victory. The Emancipation Proclamation was so unpopular in Kentucky that the Republicans didn't even field a slate of candidates. That effectively threw most of the pro-Union support to John's party. Success against the Democrats, who were fractured by Confederate sympathies, seemed inevitable.[37]

The race also gave John a chance to return to the campaign trail with a new, battle-tested gravitas; like many of his generation, he'd grown up quickly. The very young Champ Clark, future House Speaker, recalled watching John speak alongside the Union party candidate for governor, Thomas Bramlette. At thirty, and fresh from the rigors of the battlefield, John "was as magnificent a specimen of a physical man as one would have found in a month's journey—standing six foot three in stockings, weighing 200 [pounds] without an ounce of surplus flesh, red-headed, blond as any lily, graceful as a panther. . . . Governor Bramlette was a large, handsome man and made a good speech, but Harlan easily overtopped him mentally, physically, and oratorically. Mere chunk of a boy as I was, I could see that Harlan was the greater man, and I thought that therefore he ought to have been running for the greater office."[38] John cruised to victory by more than fifty thousand votes.[39]

Leaving the military didn't keep John from the battlefield. The war, in the person of his old antagonist John Hunt Morgan, found him.

In June 1864 Governor Bramlette passed on reports that Morgan's raiders were again targeting the Capitol. John grabbed his father's old Henry rifle and raced up a hill behind the government buildings, which was fortified with two small cannons. Other Union-supporting members of the home guard joined him. From their vantage point, they spotted the Confederate raiding party across the Kentucky River. The raiders were massing in a field just below the Harlan summer home, where John's mother was staying. John ordered the men to fire the cannon in the direction of his mother's house, rousting the Confederates. The home was not damaged, but a legend grew up about John's actions: here was a man who would fire on his mother in order to prevent the rebels from taking the Capitol.[40]

John had been attorney general for less than a half year when the Union army took away a large part of his job: responding to the flood of guerrilla attacks by Confederate sympathizers, President Lincoln placed Kentucky under martial law. This meant that the orders of the top Union commander in the state, the notoriously brutal General Stephen Burbridge, overrode the laws that John was entrusted to enforce. John always favored a robust national authority, but the tension between his responsibilities as the state's chief law enforcement officer and the dictates of "Butcher Burbridge" presented a conflict between his Union sympathies and his legal duties.[41] As a former senior officer in the Union army, John had at least a passing sympathy for Burbridge's efforts to crack down on Confederate collaborators. But the Kentucky-born-and-bred Burbridge, who had entered the war by pulling together an infantry unit like John's, took some already extraordinary military tactics to dangerous extremes. When Union troops were attacked by guerrilla Confederates, Burbridge ordered four guerrilla prisoners executed for every Union man who was killed. While John had threatened something similar in Shelbyville, Tennessee, Burbridge saw to it that his orders were carried out. He seemed to revel in his ability to decide life and death, and to punish traitors.[42]

The extra pain inflicted by martial law on a torn and ravaged Kentucky shook John to his marrow. While he refused to yield his support for the Union army, he faulted the Lincoln administration for pursuing its aims too ruthlessly.

With the 1864 presidential election on the horizon, John turned his own affections to General George McClellan, the Democratic nominee. An able organizer and tactician, McClellan had won the respect of his men as the Union's commanding general in the early years of the war; he believed the Union would prevail by utilizing its numerical advantages to overwhelm the South. In practice, that translated into a reluctance to fight. The thirty-four-year-old McClellan wouldn't take the field without having the clear upper hand, a posture made even less tenable when he consistently overestimated the strength of Southern armies. It was because of McClellan that Lincoln first complained of "the slows."[43] The angry and preening McClellan—many people believed the diminutive general modeled himself on the young Napoléon I—dismissed the awkward-looking president as "nothing more than a well-meaning baboon."[44] Lincoln fired him and, after a brief reinstatement, fired him again.[45] Seeking vindication, McClellan ran against Lincoln as a "war Democrat" who nonetheless sought to appease the party's antiwar wing by envisioning a gentler path to peace talks.[46]

John's views dovetailed with McClellan's. He believed that the general, as a military man, would bring the war to an honorable close, preserving the union but making an enduring peace with the South. Lincoln's support for emancipation was a dominant issue in the election; John, like many McClellan supporters, believed the president was prolonging the war by alienating Union sympathizers in the South with his insistence on freeing the slaves. Taking to the hustings on McClellan's behalf, he charged that Lincoln had changed the aims of the war, from preserving the union to freeing Negroes. Lincoln, John argued on the campaign trail in Indiana, was "warring chiefly for the African race."[47]

Most of John's speeches echoed with his characteristic moderation, proclaiming his faith that McClellan would take the fight to the Confederates while resisting the demands of Northern radicals who yearned to punish the South.[48] On one occasion in Kentucky, John added a racist exclamation point. He told a story about a French-man who had a comical and excessive love for his "little black cow," which he compared to the radical Republicans' love for "ze little black n----r."[49]

Some former allies expressed surprise that John would back a Democrat, let alone oppose a president who had gone to such lengths to preserve the union. But John was channeling the views of most Kentucky unionists. When the votes were counted, McClellan lost almost everywhere. Among the three states that supported him, he won narrow victories in tiny Delaware and next-door New Jersey.[50] Kentucky, however, showered him with 70 percent of its votes.[51]

The Bluegrass State disliked Lincoln more than it liked McClellan. And Lincoln could thank Butcher Burbridge for that.

Both Attorney General Harlan and Governor Bramlette tried to curb Burbridge's power under martial law but succeeded only in getting him fired. Mincing no words, Bramlette sent a telegram to Lincoln's secre-tary of war, Edwin Stanton, declaring that the "imbecile commander" had driven a wedge between Kentucky and the Union. Burbridge's replacement was the Kentucky-born General John M. Palmer.[52] He was less brutal and more idealistic but managed to enrage white Kentuckians almost as much as Burbridge had. An Illinois farmer-turned-lawyer-turned-politician, Palmer epitomized the nineteenth-century ideal of personal transformation.[53] Like his friend Lincoln, he was a shrewd politician who hated slavery and believed the time was ripe to eradicate it.[54] After nearly four years of war, Palmer made no secret of his feeling that "all that was left of slavery was its mischiefs."[55] He resolved to use all the levers of his position as Union commander in Kentucky to defeat the detested institution.[56]

On March 3, 1865, Congress passed a law declaring that the wives and children of Black Union soldiers were free. Instantly, Palmer began enlisting enslaved men in the army in order to free them and their families—up to a hundred families per day. He also seized on a complaint by Louisville's mayor of the dangers presented by high concentrations of runaway slaves in Black neighborhoods to grant them special travel passes for railcars and steamboats. These "Palmer passes" sent many thousands of enslaved Kentuckians heading to freedom in Ohio and Indiana. Slave owners erupted in fury. Officially, they still owned their property, but their slaves were running free.[57] "Slavery is such a condition that neither masters nor Negroes know whether it exists or not, lawlessness of every shade," bemoaned Kentuckian Lizzie Hardin, who later gained fame for the insights recorded in her diary, "and in the midst of it all, between Southerners and the Union people, a hatred, bitter, unrelenting, and that promises to be eternal."[58]

In early April the Union army seized the Confederate capital of Richmond, Virginia. President Davis and other leaders fled southward. Two days later, Lincoln visited the defeated city. Arriving by boat, the president stood in his top hat among the smoke-stained ruins. Suddenly the enormity of this accomplishment became visible when freed men and women rushed to him from every corner of the wreckage, tears flowing, praying at his feet, and welcoming him as a messiah.[59] The following Sunday, April 9, Confederate general Robert E. Lee surrendered to General Grant at Appomattox, Virginia.[60] And, just five days later, John Wilkes Booth shot President Lincoln to death in the balcony at Washington's Ford's Theatre, where he and his wife were watching the comedy *Our American Cousin*. "Sic semper tyrannis!" the actor declared, leaping from the president's box and onto the stage—"Thus always to tyrants!" the words attributed to Brutus upon killing Julius Caesar that also happened to be the Virginia state motto.[61]

The shocking events left John, as Kentucky's chief law enforcement officer, with a seemingly endless number of quandaries. The war was effectively over, and yet Kentucky remained under military occupation. In the waning days of the fighting, Lincoln had pushed through Congress the Thirteenth Amendment, freeing enslaved men and women across the nation, which was now in the process of being ratified by the states. The amendment would leave Kentucky with little to show for its loyalty, forcing it to give up slavery by means of the same strong arm as had been applied to its rebellious neighbors.[62] Even though Lincoln's successor, Andrew Johnson of Tennessee, was unaccountably eager to bring about reconciliation, a Congress increasingly dominated by Republicans had no truck for slave owners anywhere; Kentucky could expect little sympathy for its unique plight.[63]

John insisted that abolition of slavery should not be imposed on Kentucky from the outside. This was the cornerstone of his youthful political career, as he stood firmly between the poles of secession and abolition. He cast it as a matter of principle: He would oppose the Thirteenth Amendment even "if there were not a dozen slaves in Kentucky." But his posture was outmoded. Even some allies like Bramlette, realizing that the Thirteenth Amendment would pass the requisite three-quarters of states even without Kentucky's concurrence, proposed that the Bluegrass State should ratify the amendment as of way of gaining leverage for federal compensation for slave owners.[64]

John didn't budge. He also felt obliged to sue Palmer for going beyond his authority in helping enslaved men and women flee their masters. What military necessity existed now that the war was over? The Kentucky Court of Appeals, in an opinion by John's Transylvania University mentor, George Robertson, endorsed his view. But there was little the state could do to lift itself from under the iron thumb of martial law.[65]

Loyal Kentucky was effectively a conquered territory.

Henry Clay's premonition came true. For decades before the Civil War, Kentucky's foremost statesman warned that, if war came, his state would suffer the brunt of the destruction.[66] In terms of fighting, he wasn't entirely correct. While Kentucky was the scene of some memorable battles, Virginia, among other states, emerged with more visible scars. But in other respects, Clay's foreboding was born out more completely than he could have imagined. At the start of the war, Kentucky was among the eight largest states and known for its progressive attitudes. Its higher education was the best in the West and had produced renowned statesmen. There were vestiges of frontier justice, but also frontier optimism and entrepreneurship. A can-do spirit reigned. Compared to the conservatism of the Deep South, with its feudal economic system, and the rawness of the Far West, Kentucky was an oasis of enlightenment.[67]

The war lowered the veil on Kentucky's horizons, opening up divisions that didn't heal. The Confederate guerrillas who terrorized the Union army quickly turned to vigilantism after the war, fueling a lawlessness that far exceeded that of the frontier days. This time their targets were Black people.[68]

On October 19, 1866, a gang of more than two dozen whites galloped on horseback into the Black areas of Lebanon Junction, not far from where John's Tenth Kentucky Volunteers had mustered at their hastily assembled Camp Crittenden. The gang ransacked the homes of Black families, beating down doors, tearing off roofs and chimneys, and kidnapping some of the men. The attackers boasted that they had an "army" of 120 men and would wreak havoc among the freed men and women. When federal officials investigated, they found that white law-enforcement officials knew in advance about the raid and did nothing; no one was ever indicted. A month later, in the same county, a mob of about 100 white men broke into a jail, made off with three Black prisoners, and lynched them. A US Army investigator found that the same local authorities had learned of the break-in beforehand and simply stood aside; the prisoners, explained one official, "deserved hanging."[69]

The previous December, six former Confederate officers in Pulaski, Tennessee, had founded a mysterious social club that they dubbed the Ku Klux Klan.[70] As its rituals and costumes and cross burnings began to gain attention, it added a sense of menace and mystique to the nighttime raids by white gangs in next-door Kentucky. In fact, there were fewer bars to racial violence in Kentucky than in the states of the former Confederacy. Those states were under the control of much larger Union forces. Nearly all of the white men who had supported the rebellion were barred from voting. That, by default, handed local offices, including law enforcement, to supporters of the local Black populations; it was a brief leg up for a beleaguered race.

But there were no similar assertions of power for the comparatively small Black population in Kentucky, where the numbers of whites banned from voting was smaller.[71]

Even though he was attorney general, John had no control over the murderous gangs or the complicit local officials. He watched the state's descent into carnage in powerless frustration. At first, he tried to forge a political consensus for moderation by encouraging his fellow conservative unionists to cooperate with Democrats; some of the conservatives, including his brother James Jr., who was elected to the Kentucky legislature in 1865, joined with Democrats in voting to allow former Confederates back on the voter rolls.[72] The strategy backfired. With a fresh influx of support from ex-Confederates, Democrats played to the political extremes and stopped cooperating with moderates. Most Democratic leaders offered at least tacit support to the Klan, downplaying and even denying the violence.[73]

The sense of denial extended to the state's major newspapers, the *Louisville Journal* and the *Louisville Courier*, which would merge just six months later.[74] The centrist *Journal*, still under the editorship of the aging George Prentice, made light fun of the Klan, as if it were a band of pranksters. The only beneficiaries of the Klan, the paper wrote in April 1868, were Black gunsmiths, who were getting plenty of business from paranoid Black people. "Several jokes have already been played upon them by fools shrouded in white sheets, who approach unawares, and frighten the negroe out of whatever little wit he might possess," the *Journal* declared.[75] The Democratic *Courier*, however, was a full-throated cheerleader, writing that same month that "We wish some member of the organization would tell us when, where, and how to join the mysterious order, as from one to three hundred applications are made to us each day." It even published a poetic tribute to the Klan, titled "Death's Brigade," that included the ominous lines "A river black is running / To a blacker sea afar / And by its banks is waving / A flag without a star."[76]

Even John's childhood hometown of Danville—where he swam as a boy in the Salt River, worshipped in the First Presbyterian Church under the pulpit of Reverend John C. Young, and studied the classics at Centre College—fell under mob rule. Once a part of the genteel center of the state, where civic-minded families founded churches and universities, Boyle County became a staging ground for lynchings.

"Jails are forced [open] by them . . . and their victims ruthlessly torn from legal custody and murdered," wrote an exasperated Governor Bramlette, referring to the frightful mobs who began taking over Kentucky towns in 1866. "Those standing on bail, who are obnoxious to their murderous wrath, are dragged from their homes and executed. . . . Within the last few days, during the session of Boyle Circuit Court, these murderers took from the jail of the county a man there confined, to answer on indictment, and hung him to death within the limits of the town."[77]

The state's descent into lawlessness would have a profound impact on John. In the past, he hadn't so much switched parties as the parties switched on him: he remained true to his support for the union and his antipathy for the secessionists and abolitionists, even as old alliances crumbled around him and new ones beckoned. But in early 1868 he made a change that even he acknowledged was more fundamental, passionate, emotionally driven.

In March of that year, the *Frankfort Commonwealth* announced that Harlan would support a Republican named R. T. Baker for governor and the Republican former Union army commander Ulysses S. Grant for president. The Unionist paper was enthusiastic: "This patriotic determination on the part of this able and distinguished lawyer and former Union officer will be hailed throughout the State with satisfaction and pleasure by the friends of the Republic."[78]

The paper neglected to mention that "friends of the Republic" were a distinct minority in Kentucky at that freighted moment. Anger over martial law, broken federal promises, and the precipitous end of slavery was driving Democratic support as much as it was fertilizing the culture of mob violence.[79] In the immediate aftermath of the war, John had professed to understand the anger. The imposition of martial law and forced emancipation, no matter how nobly intended, damaged Kentucky's democracy. Political choices were imposed, not forged in the heat of debate. Could anyone be surprised that there was no institutional support, no cushion, to help freed Black people and no robust authority to prevent violence? A certain amount of resistance was inevitable, if not justified. But when that resistance took the form of abuse of innocents and embrace of hatred, he could see only a dark path ahead.

In 1867 John made a last-gasp attempt to create a third party. For its brief lifespan known by the unwieldy title of Union Democratic Party of Kentucky, it condemned the now-dead Confederacy but also "any party that proposes to reduce any State or States to the condition of territories, or compel them to adopt negro suffrage, or place them as subjugated provinces under military government."[80] John ran for reelection as attorney general under the Union Democratic colors, and the party fielded a slate of congressional candidates. All of them, including John, were swept away by large margins.[81] The Democrats ruled Kentucky. And the Republicans suddenly looked like the only vehicle for progress and improvement.

When John took to the hustings for Grant and the entire Republican ticket in 1868, one old friend and supporter wrote that he was "powerful glad when I heard you had opened on the Ku Klux Democracy. . . . I see the future as you do, for dear Kentucky. Just now she is in the hands of a stupid . . . leadership; but not for long. In an age when great events are born every day, this leadership does nothing but say no, to the yes of 40 millions."

The writer, a Kentucky politician named W. H. Wadsworth, accurately depicted John's feelings.[82] He saw now that his efforts to acknowledge the wrongs done to Kentucky had done little to lance the wound; instead, they became rallying cries for Confederate dead-enders and fuel for crimes that made a mockery of civilized democracy. John came to see the Republicans as the party of high ideals—that what he once ridiculed as excessive concern for slavery was, in fact, an affirmation of the constitutional values of freedom and equality that he revered as a boy. But his optimism, like that expressed in Wadsworth's letter, was misplaced: Kentucky was destined to enter into decades of saying "no" to the yes of millions, to its undying detriment.

Chapter 7

"Knowledge Is Power"

Robert eased into his fifties from the comfort of his riverside haven in Richmond, England, but he was already gearing up for the most meaningful chapters of his life. He had been a house slave, barber, store owner, real estate investor, photographic pioneer, horse trainer, gambler, and owner of thoroughbreds. Despite the vastness of those transformations, he could envision an even bigger one. Living in Europe had enabled him to step out from under the weight of his ancestry. Now he was ready to reassume the burdens of being a Black man in America. He would return to Cincinnati and an utterly changed racial landscape. Four million Black people were undertaking the same passage to freedom that he had made. He had role models; they did not. Perhaps he could be their guide, their leader, their inspiration.[1]

But before that could happen, he faced a rude awakening. If he believed that whites in America were prepared to accept Black people on more equal terms, the response to his decision to return to Ohio alerted him otherwise. Despite the reversals in his British racing career, the London press gave him a respectful send-off: "Most of our readers have known, either by sight or repute, the tall, dark American who was formerly associated with Mr. Ten Broeck," wrote the *London Sporting Life* in January 1868. "He was to be seen at nearly all our race meetings; betting upon every race, and was, in fact, one of the most persistent backers of horses ever known."[2]

In America, Texas-based *Flake's Bulletin* picked up the *London Sporting Life* report, but added its own gratuitous commentary, focusing on his race: "Robert Harlan, thus alluded to, is the son of one of the most distinguished men in Kentucky, now deceased. His mother was a mulatto woman, and a slave. . . . About ten years ago, a number of wealthy men in Cincinnati purchased several race-horses, the most prominent of which were Babylon, Des Chiles, and Cincinnati, and sent them to England in charge of Harlan. The venture proved a disastrous one. . . . Harlan has returned to the United States, we presume, a ruined man."[3]

In fact, racing records showed that Robert himself was the owner of Des Chiles and Cincinnati; Babylon was owned by Richard Ten Broeck. And Robert was far from a ruined man. While his racing career in Europe hadn't enhanced his fortune, it had helped to establish a noteworthy precedent: never again would the lords of British racing dismiss the fitness of American horses.[4] Now, he was coming home to Cincinnati with a fresh sense of purpose.

The war years had changed Cincinnati as much as the time in Europe had changed Robert. The metropolis on the Ohio River hosted, at one point or another, many of the Union forces in the West. It was the crossroads for all transportation to and from the South and the East. Union troops flowed through the portals of Cincinnati by river and rail; so, too, did masses of white Union loyalists from the South and formerly enslaved men and women pouring northward.[5] Despite the tumult of the intervening years, Robert returned to the same large house at 39 Harrison Street that he bought when he married Josephine Floyd; about a year after he moved back from England, he gave the house a new mistress. Robert's bride was a much younger woman of mixed race named Mary Ann Graham.[6] In celebrating the marriage, the *Cleveland Leader*, one of Ohio's leading Republican newspapers, described Mary Ann as "young, beautiful, and wealthy in her own right."[7] Soon after getting married, the couple gained a financial cushion by selling two pieces of property for a total of $6,125—about $110,000 in 2021 dollars.[8]

Robert's courtly manners, refined even further after nearly a decade touring Europe, gained him attention among admiring Black people and some whites as well. After meeting up with Robert in Chicago and hearing of his European adventures, O. S. Poston, a close Harlan family friend, dashed off a letter to John: "I saw Robert Harlan, late of England, here this week. He seems to have improved by eating English beef and breathing British air."[9]

Indeed, in this new era of his life, Robert plunged into writing and delivering speeches with as much zeal as John. He joined literary societies and wrote poetry.[10] He regaled parlors full of guests with stories of life across the Atlantic Ocean but felt an even stronger desire to comment on the unique racial situation in the United States. He also delivered inspirational messages to his fellow Black Americans. His talents as an intellectual, which were rarely visible in his previous endeavors, brought him renewed acclaim. His carefully scripted addresses captured the spirit of a moment when Black equality seemed not only inevitable but also perhaps less than a lifetime away.[11]

On April 14, 1870, at a parade celebrating the ratification of the Fifteenth Amendment, which granted voting rights to Black people, he delivered his paean to education before thousands of people, white and Black. "Knowledge is power; and those who know the most, and not those who have the most, will govern this country," he declared. "Let us combine and associate and organize for this end. In the pulpit, in the press, in the street, everywhere let our theme be education, education; until there can not be found anywhere a child of us that is not at school."[12]

The enthusiastic praise from both Black and white people that greeted his remarks would be repeated nine months later when he dazzled an all-Black crowd at Cincinnati's Allen Temple, the foremost gathering place for Black citizens.[13] At a time when many orators either adopted a debating posture, as John did, or clothed their remarks in classical allusions, Robert was earthy and inspirational; from his vantage point as a formerly enslaved man of mixed race, he captured the full scope of the nation's transformation. Dressed in a formal military uniform—white pants and a black frock coat—and accompanied by members of Cincinnati's Second Battalion, the all-Black state militia unit that he cofounded and commanded, Robert proclaimed in thundering tones the significance of the Emancipation Proclamation and how it spurred Black people to great deeds.[14]

"It is not my purpose, on this occasion, to present anything original, but to give in my imperfect way expression to current sentiment," Robert began, following the rhetorical rule of beginning with an expression of modesty. "The people of the North were afraid to proclaim that they were fighting for the great doctrine of the equality of man. They fought for it, but dared not announce it to the world, and so the world thought they were simply fighting to save the union with slavery. This was their great and costly mistake. God frowned on them. . . .

"At length, God moved Abraham Lincoln to declare this great and glorious principle, the Proclamation of Emancipation. Happy Lincoln. Who would not die a thousand deaths to have lived one such life? And who would not have endured the cares and griefs and struggles of a thousand such lives to be permitted to ascend the highest heavens with four million broken fetters in his hand? The chariot of fire in which Elijah ascended was a grand affair, but it dwindles into insignificance as the triumphal car of Abraham Lincoln approaches, and the everlasting gates of heaven lift up their treads to let him in."

The Emancipation Proclamation, he declared, "was not the creation of political rights, but the acknowledgment of them. . . . Even when we were slaves, we were equal before heaven, at least. . . . [But] when this was proclaimed on the part of government, when this became its public policy, the enfranchisement of our race, then the tide of victory after victory set in, great generals sprang up, the ranks were filled, the colored man seized the musket and went boldly to the front. It was then he felt he had a country and would fight for it. His acts and deeds are well known to you. We have made a record in the army rolls of the Republic that will stand as long as the American flag waves over the land of the free and the home of the brave."

The *Cincinnati Commercial Tribune* proclaimed it a "Grand Jubilee of the Colored People." Allen Temple erupted with cheers as the knell of Robert's voice faded away.[15]

Robert's message reminded Black people of the role that powerful whites played in their emancipation, while crediting themselves
with having propelled the final push to freedom. He also envisioned
a dawning era of self-improvement, as Black men and women strived
to prove themselves the equals to whites in achievements as well as
rights. Leaders of the Ohio Republican Party saw the growing numbers of freedmen as a powerful Republican-voting constituency in
need of leaders. Here, in the person of Robert Harlan, was an inspiring speaker who gave credit to Republican heroes such as Lincoln and
Grant. Here, too, was a man who understood that the Black community faced a struggle to win the approval of whites. He also happened
to believe the struggle was winnable—and wasn't afraid to encourage Black people to put their faith in the idea that their advancement
would continue for years, if not generations.

"We may do much for our own improvement, but many of us
are too far advanced in life to change our occupation and habits bequeathed to us by slavery, much as we may desire to do so," he told a
crowd gathered a year later at a picnic to benefit the Colored Orphan
Asylum in Cincinnati. "Far different is the case with our children: and
here is the supreme duty of our generation. Let us resolve that come
what may, though it be biting poverty, coarse garments, plain food,
and humble shelter, our children shall receive the full measure of education that our capacity can admit of."[16]

Robert made the Second Battalion—known to many in Cincinnati
as the Black Battalion—the expression of his hopes for how Black men
could win the approval of whites and integrate themselves into white
society. Sharing in the defense of the state was an important assertion
of Black people's willingness to assume the responsibilities of the full
citizenship granted to them under the Fourteenth Amendment: equal
rights implied equal burdens. Plus, a colored unit in the state militia would be a force for stability in a city in which poor whites were
hardly willing to acknowledge the newfound equality of Black people.
Colored men would carry rifles and have a mandate from the governor to keep the peace in times of trouble.

Robert helped pull together a group of leading Black Cincinnatians, including Civil War veterans, to meet in May 1870 to discuss the formation of a Black battalion. The group initially gave command of the force to William Travis, a foot doctor who was one of the city's best-known Black leaders and, at various times, Robert's friend and rival. Reports in white-led newspapers noted that Travis had darker skin and more African-looking features than Robert, who by contrast was portrayed as "a very fine-looking man, who could easily be mistaken for a thorough-bred white."[17] Travis's appointment met with opposition from within the battalion itself, culminating in a meeting at which charges were raised that Travis had tried to take $50 from the battalion's coffers under the very eyes of Robert and another man, who persuaded him to return the money.[18] Cincinnati newspapers—clearly uncomfortable with the idea of a Black battalion—fanned the flames of the dispute with headlines such as "Stormy Time Among the Colored Warriors."[19] And yet the underlying charge of attempted thievery was also typical of the way Black elites sought to undermine one another by leveling charges of corruption or immorality, only to become friends again at later dates.[20]

Whatever the truth of the thievery allegation, the city's Black leaders preferred Robert as the face of the battalion, despite his lack of military experience. After initially refusing the command, Robert agreed to lead the battalion after entreaties from the men themselves. His credibility among whites played a role in winning official endorsement for a fighting unit the *Enquirer* dismissed as "black braves."[21] In October 1870 the Second Cincinnati Battalion was officially recognized by the state. Robert himself received a commission as colonel from Governor Rutherford B. Hayes.[22]

He would thereafter be addressed as Colonel Robert Harlan, a respectful designation at a time when large numbers of men were using their military titles from the Civil War. The title also conferred a formal role in public life—a seat at the table of power.

With his large house, sartorial splendor, and mixed-race ancestry, Robert quickly became an emblem of a distinct culture: that of the aristocrat of color. A relatively small number of men and women came together after the Civil War to form this unique community. Born of both the need for leadership in the Black community and whites' unwillingness to accept anyone of mixed race into their own society, the aristocrats of color developed their own values and social habits. The fact that they were, in many cases, light of skin and "blue of vein," as some Black people put it, provoked troubling responses on both sides of their ancestry.[23] Some whites regarded them as phonies—Black people dressing up as white—and tried harder to put them in their place. Black people, on the other hand, veered between admiration and suspicion, especially for those like Robert who seemed to reap personal benefits from his status as a leader of the Black community.[24]

Politics squeezed the aristocrats of color from both sides. Their status as Black leaders was partly conferred by whites. Mixed-race aristocrats who were also literate and savvy in business could negotiate with whites on fairly equal terms. Thus, they gained power as representatives of Black people through their contacts in the white world. Political rivals would sometimes seek to discredit them by leveling charges likely to damage their standing among whites, suggesting that they were liars, swindlers, or libertines—in other words, Black men unworthy of trust. To the freed men and women, however, the aristocrats of color presented themselves as role models on pedestals—examples of all that could be accomplished through erudition and hard work. Many freed men and women accepted them on this basis; others regarded them as a breed apart.[25]

Socially, aristocrats of color encompassed a universe of their own. Excluded from white living rooms, they gave special attention to their own abodes and entertainments. When traveling, Robert and his powerful Black friends such as P. B. S. Pinchback, Frederick Douglass, and the Black intellectual John Mercer Langston would stay in one another's homes and host lavish parties to introduce one another to the cream of the local Black society. Gourmet cuisine, expensive fashions, worldly sophistication, and appreciation of the arts—even more than skin tone—separated Black elites from the masses of freedmen.[26]

Robert embodied the self-proclaimed virtues of the Black elite. He had a large house, entertained frequently, and cut a glamorous image. He sent his son, Robert Jr., to the city's acclaimed Woodward High, a predominantly white school where Robert Jr. became a lifelong associate of a classmate named William Howard Taft.[27] Robert was also among a handful of leading figures of color in a very large and politically important city, in a state controlled by Republicans who relied on Black votes, and which played a disproportionate role in national politics. The *New York World* went so far as to state that Robert's "influence over his race was second only to that of Fred Douglass."[28]

Racism, however, threatened to make a mockery of his accomplishments. At a local Republican convention in 1870, a white delegate challenged his credentials, asking angrily why "naygurs" were allowed in the room.[29] The following year, in a terrifying incident that conjured up memories of the Black Indians of his Lexington years, the *New-York Tribune* reported that Robert had been "Ku-Kluxed" outside his Cincinnati home, beaten in the streets by a white gang as punishment for casting a vote.[30] Beyond the physical threats, the dismissiveness of the white press was enough to sink a less resourceful man. The Republican-leaning *Commercial*, for instance, labeled him "De Big Kunnel," while the *New York Herald*, reporting on one of his speeches, called him "His Duskiness."[31] Robert swallowed his pride and fought back against such reporters, especially the Democratic-leaning *Enquirer*, a perennial foe. At times, he seemed even to enjoy the verbal combat.

When the *Enquirer* failed to make sufficient note of his triumphant Fifteenth Amendment Jubilee speech extolling the importance of education, Robert was quick to register his complaints. The result was an extraordinary piece of journalism in which the writer wrestled with the uneasiness of a postwar moment when whites couldn't decide whether aristocrats of color were entitled to respect or ridicule.

"We regret very much that our remarks concerning Mr. Harlan and his participation in the jubilee exercises last Thursday should have caused that gentleman the biting pain of annoyance," the *Enquirer* wrote, adding that the paper bore "no malice or ill will. . . . Of all the colored men in this city, we know none who are entitled to more respect than Mr. Harlan." The paper praised him as a pioneer in establishing Cincinnati's colored schools and credited his Kentucky upbringing for imbuing him with "principles of honor, fair dealing, and gentlemanly bearing."

Robert's jubilee speech, the article continued, was "the finest, most sensible, most logical, and, above all, the most statesmanlike of any that day delivered, by either white or black. We said so at the time, and we say so now after calm reflection and mature deliberation, he is a man of great natural force and is destined to become a leader in the new political element which has just sprung up in the land."[32]

The *Enquirer*'s praise for Robert was nonetheless laced with irony and backhanded compliments; seven months after hailing his jubilee speech, the newspaper produced a profile of Robert with the subheadline "A Horse Racer and Cock Fighter Who Prays Every Night." It recounted that *Enquirer* reporters were lounging at their desks when a knock on the door announced the arrival of "the noble and majestic Robert Harlan, the Colonel of the Black Battalion and the Moses of a Despised Race." Robert removed his hat with an air of "Parisian politeness" and crossed his legs, scanning the bookshelves. "We had abundant time to examine his *physique* and note his *tout ensemble*," the article continued, referring to his "shining black dickey, embellished with a delightful 'spark-prop'; the upright projecting collar, surmounted with heavy mastiff jaws, the ponderous mustachio, the olive complexion, and furtive eye."

Robert complained about a report that he had bet on a dogfight, which had played into white impressions of him as a seedy character immersed in the gambling world. He denied any interest in dogfighting, which he considered an inhumane sport forced on a "noble animal." Arriving at the city's Haymarket Saloon, he explained, he hadn't realized, in the jumble of a large crowd, that there was a dogfight in progress, but "of course I couldn't resist betting, because I always wager."

"I never play cards, drink liquor, or swear," he insisted. "I have no vices. . . . I was brought up in Kentucky, where every gentleman is expected to keep either a racehorse or a game chicken, and I was educated to believe there was no harm in it." He went on to describe participating in cockfights in Panama and Havana, Cuba, where he competed against the exiled General Santa Anna, the Mexican commander whose troops had ransacked the Alamo. In England, he explained, he attended the 1860 prizefight between American John C. Heenan and Britain's Tom Sayers—a legendary, underground two-and-a-half-hour bare-knuckled brawl that ranks among the most famous in the sport's history—and mingled with all classes of people, "from the Queen to the peasant."

"I profess to be a Christian, I subscribe to the church, go to church myself, and never go to bed at night without saying my prayers. . . ." he said. "There are gentlemen in this office who have known me for thirty years and know nothing harmful of me further than I *will* go to cockfights and *will* attend horse racing."

The *Enquirer* concluded its article by reporting, "He paused at the door and begged to remind us that the statement to the effect that he had lost ninety dollars at the dog fight was entirely erroneous. It was not more than half that sum, and the loss was in a measure due to his unfamiliarity with the quality of the canines."[33]

As the opposition newspaper—journal to an avowedly racist readership—the *Enquirer* couldn't give Robert credit without dunning him for his race; but its rounded portrayal nonetheless revealed the extent to which Robert had captured the imagination of his adopted hometown.

In the summer of 1871 Robert journeyed to the nation's foremost warm-weather destination: the spa-retreat-cum-gambling-mecca of Saratoga Springs, New York, in a lush mountainous setting. Home to the most famous racecourse in the Northeast, Saratoga Springs was the August gathering place for the elites of the racing world and, by happy coincidence for Robert, many of the Black aristocrats of New York City.[34] They found accommodations by renting rooms among the city's relatively large Black community, based just two blocks behind the enormous, white-pillared hotels on Broadway.[35]

Once a place of rest for white gentlemen and their ladies, the town took on a more raffish profile when the famed Irish boxer John Morrissey brought casino gambling in the early 1860s; in 1870 Morrissey cut the ribbon on the ultraexclusive Saratoga Club House that became a plush hideaway for some of the richest New Yorkers of the era—men such as Cornelius Vanderbilt, J. P. Morgan, and the barbed wire mogul John "Bet a Million" Gates—where they could gamble and consort with ladies of ill repute into the wee hours of the night.[36] Meanwhile, their families spent the summer quartered in luxury at hostelries such as the famed Grand Union and United States Hotels, which combined an almost southern ambiance of pastoral comfort with the latest telegraph connections to Wall Street.[37]

The distinguished writer Henry James, visiting the previous year, noted approvingly that the summer community in Saratoga Springs had grown more diverse and had developed a "dense, democratic, vulgar" charm all its own: "You behold an interesting, indeed, quite momentous spectacle: the democratization of elegance." The figures of all backgrounds who congregated in Saratoga Springs shared only one attribute, James noted: "They are men who have positively, actually lived."[38]

Robert certainly fit that description, and, from his customary quarters in the most luxurious Black boarding establishment, the Gilbert House, he drank in the energy of a town devoted to healthfulness and sinful pleasures, often in the same twenty-four hours.[39] By day, Robert would scour the racetrack, with its broad wooden grandstand and maze of stables, sizing up the horses and placing bets.[40] At night, politics was on the agenda, as Black intellectuals debated the shifting prospects for their race. Fellow aristocrats of color eagerly devoured his perspectives on the status of Black people in the Midwest.[41]

Departing Saratoga Springs that August, Robert made a two-hundred-mile detour that he hoped might avail his blossoming political career. His destination was the seashore community of Long Branch, New Jersey, where wooden hotels and large clapboard homes were set amid green lawns running down to a wide beach. Here, during the summer months, President Grant governed the country

from a three-story "cottage," surrounded by verandas, on a bluff overlooking the ocean. Rich friends had bought the large home for Grant,
and he used it during his summer retreats from Washington.[42] Robert had sought an introduction to Grant from two Ohio congressmen
and one senator but, when none was forthcoming, decided to show
up at the presidential cottage unannounced. Robert felt confident
that he could bond with Grant, whose fondness for cigars and horse
racing was well known. Indeed, the president welcomed him at once
but, to Robert's surprise, was more eager to talk politics than horses.[43]

"Mr. President, I don't know if you observed it, but I think it
proper to say to you that I am a colored man, and I would rather you
would not misunderstand that fact," Robert began, establishing the
parameters for their conversation.

Grant observed calmly that he would not have made that assumption but then turned his chair closer to Robert's, in a gesture of
approval.[44]

The two men talked about a recent treaty with England, with Robert offering his perspective from his many years in London. Grant
then complained that Cincinnati's Republican newspaper, the *Commercial*, was giving him an unfair hard time about having appointed
family members to federal positions. Grant insisted that the list of relatives gaining favors was inflated. "Why, they named no less than six
or ten of my family who hold office whose names I never even heard
of in my whole life," the president fumed.

Robert replied soothingly, "The Good Book, you know, tells us
that he who does not provide for his household is worse than an
infidel."[45]

At some point, the conversation turned to the racial situation.
Robert and the president became so engrossed in conversation that
Grant kept putting off entreaties from his wife, Julia, and their youngest son, thirteen-year-old Jesse, to go riding together. "Presently, my
son," the president said, waving off his child's request.

"It is not every day that I have the pleasure of talking with someone of your race who can speak for them so well," he told Robert—as
Robert would later relate to the *Commercial* and other papers.

Robert came away from the conversation as one of the president's most prominent confidants in the Black community—and one of his most aggressive defenders.[46]

Seven years after delivering her previous child, Malvina Harlan was expecting again, at age thirty-three, in 1871. Both parents rejoiced at the prospect of adding to their family after a half decade of profound losses. They named the baby Laura Cleveland Harlan, after John's sister Laura, who had died the previous year at age thirty-five. That same year, John's mother, Eliza, succumbed at age sixty-five, joining his beloved father in the family plot. John's brother William had passed away at forty-three in 1868. James Jr. was the only other one of James and Eliza's sons who remained, and he was fast disappearing into a cloud of addiction.[47]

Thankfully, there was no hand of fate pressing on the shoulders of John's immediate family. His and Malvina's eldest child, fourteen-year-old Edith, was a source of pride and companionship to both her parents, a high-spirited replica of Malvina, with a beautiful singing voice and appreciation of music.[48] Then came three boys born over five years: Richard, James, and John Maynard. Richard was quiet and scholarly; James and John Maynard were more rambunctious and, even in boyhood, eager to challenge their father's views. John didn't bristle at his sons' curiosity—he saw it as a sign of an original intelligence, and cultivated more of a give and take with his own boys than the fearsome James had ever attempted with him and his brothers.

In truth, John worried far more about the world his children were inheriting than any of their individual challenges or imperfections. The enlightened Kentucky of his youth had been swept away by the winds of war and, he now realized, was as much a relic of history as the hand-carved mausoleum in Lexington Cemetery that housed the remains of Henry Clay. The state that nurtured the Clays and Breckinridges and Crittendens was an increasingly brutal backwater. In fifteen counties in central Kentucky, the Ku Klux Klan had overwhelmed the local governments, establishing mob rule.[49] When, in

1870, Black men tried to vote in Harrodsburg, near Harlan's Station, white mobsters confronted them with guns, stones, and clubs.[50] Most distressing to John was that so many whites regarded Klan suprem- acy as a justified political response to the forced emancipation of the Thirteenth Amendment.[51]

If the breakdown of law and order wasn't enough, the Civil War left behind a crisis in the other abiding faith in John's life: the Presby- terian Church. And he was as much at the center of the disorder in the church as he was in the politics of the Bluegrass State. The elders of the national Presbyterian General Assembly had taken a strong stance in favor of the union and against slavery, which prompted a wartime split of the denomination into Northern and Southern fac- tions. After the fighting ceased, the elders hired John to represent them in securing church property in Louisville. Thus began a legal odyssey that would end up in the Supreme Court—the most intricate endeavor of his private legal career. John won the case after years of reversals. Even though he did not argue before the high tribunal, it endorsed his reasoning, in one of the more satisfying moments of his legal career. But the entire episode showed him, yet again, the intrac- tability of the wartime divide, and how racial violence and separation had replaced slavery as the battle cry of rebellious Southerners.[52]

John's passionate advocacy for the Presbyterian elders carried over into his support for the Republican Party. In the past, when con- fronted with a deeply polarizing conflict, he gravitated to the center, seeking to bridge divisions by offering a half loaf to each side. Now, in the wake of war, those disputes were no longer understandable or tol- erable to him. No longer was the Constitution ambiguous. Law and wisdom and enlightenment were all on one side.

That side despaired over its lack of clout in Kentucky. But Repub- licans controlled the federal government. As Congress passed federal laws against the Klan, US attorneys used the new tools to try to bring mobsters to justice. One of the most spirited of these prosecutors was Benjamin Helm Bristow, who became chief US prosecutor in Louis- ville in 1866. He secured twenty-nine convictions of whites for com- mitting racially motivated violence, including one murder, over three and a half years in office.[53] Despite having received his education in the East, which may have influenced his early embrace of Republicanism, Bristow's background was similar enough to John's—being the son of a Kentucky Whig politician and then a staunch unionist himself—that the two felt a natural affinity. Twinned in age, politics, and ambition, they entered into an almost fraternal alliance.

During his time in the US attorney's office, Bristow reached out to John for legal and political help, nudging him further toward the Republican Party.[54] Confident and at times brash, Bristow was comfortable swimming against the tide. He approached the challenges of the postwar years with more pragmatic energy than John, if less passion for the fate of American ideals.

In 1870 Bristow resigned his federal post to become a law partner in Louisville with John and a former Republican-appointed federal judge named John E. Newman. It was a brief partnership. President Grant soon chose Bristow to assume the newly created position of solicitor general, arguing the Grant administration's positions before the Supreme Court.[55] Left behind in Louisville, John worked hard to earn enough money to support Malvina and the children. This included taking on cases defending whites accused of race-related crimes; the fact that John was increasingly associated with the Republican Party and known to be an archcritic of the Ku Klux Klan made him especially desirable to such clients.[56] "I once thought I would have nothing to do with cases of this kind, but, upon reflection, I find that I must play lawyer in those as in other cases [or] abandon good fees, which I am not able to do," he wrote ruefully to Bristow in Washington.[57]

But his commitment to Republican ideals was affirmed when, in 1871, he received by acclamation the party's nomination for governor of Kentucky. Bristow delivered a soaring address endorsing his candidacy. John, in turn, pledged to uphold a party platform that included many positions he had formerly opposed or avoided, from encouraging an influx of immigrants to enhance the state's "agricultural, mineral, and manufacturing" capacity, to endorsing the post–Civil War amendments that granted Black people freedom, citizenship, and voting rights.[58]

John's opponent, the incumbent Democratic governor Preston Leslie, was something of an accidental figure, having gained the position by dint of being the president of the state senate when his predecessor resigned to join the US Senate. Despite displaying a flowing beard and scowling countenance, Leslie was less of a fanatic than some rivals within his party were. A former Confederate sympathizer, he would eventually speak out against Klan violence and reverse a policy barring the testimony of Black people against whites—which had made it almost impossible to prosecute racial crimes in state court. Still, he had no hesitation about running an almost entirely race-based campaign against Harlan.[59] John's policies, Leslie charged, would lead to miscegenation and force white boys and girls to contend with the "scent of a n----r" in their classroom.[60]

John insisted the state was shirking its responsibility to provide for the education of Black children, though, in the face of Leslie's virulent rhetoric, he conceded that it need not be in the same school as whites. But when the governor ridiculed the notion of equality between Black people and whites, John declared that Black people were made in the image of their creator, the same creator of whites. Instead of balancing the prejudices of whites against the rights of Black people, as he did before the war, John declared that racial division was a poison that would eat away at the foundation of the state. Whites needed to get beyond such hatreds. He declared that there could be no conceivable justification for the Klan, "a band of murderers and assassins."[61] Such actions not only inflict a moral wrong on individuals, they impose a moral taint on the state.

"What is to be made toward the peace and happiness of this state by arousing the feeling of bitterness which the gentleman would desire to arouse between the white and colored people of this commonwealth?" he proclaimed in a debate with Leslie, suggesting the governor would seek to drive Black people out of the state rather than recognize their civil rights. "Here they are, mortal beings, with immortal souls like ours, fashioned in the image of their Maker. I would feel myself a dishonored man if, for the sake of obtaining votes in this or any other part of the state, I would be willing to foster a sentiment which every noble and generous man would spurn. . . . This land would roll in blood before [such a] great wrong would be tolerated, and this I say to you as a southern man. They have sympathies, love their wives and children and the spot of nativity as we do; and I put it to you, does it accord with your feelings of justice that politicians should try to keep up in this commonwealth of Kentucky a feeling of bitterness and hate for all time to come?"[62]

Kentucky newspapers weren't sure what to make of this new Harlan. A fraud? An extremist? An opportunist? The *Louisville Courier-Journal* saw elements of all three. George Prentice had died, and the merged *Journal* and *Courier* was now under the leadership of Henry Watterson, a Confederate veteran. Though he would later gain a reputation as a progressive on racial issues, the young Watterson wasn't buying what John was selling.[63]

On July 28 the *Courier-Journal* published two lengthy and dismissive accounts of John's stump speech, zeroing in on the fact that he was condemning people, in harsh terms, for holding positions that he himself had once endorsed. One article declared: "The beacon light of Black Republicanism, Gen. John M. Harlan, whose clarion notes, in the estimation of his adherents and admirers, forever silence his ablest opponents, gave us yesterday one of his longest tirades, which, while utterly devoid of one single sentence worthy of rank as a manly and honest argument, has no parallel in the annals of political warfare for unblushing egotism and shameless effrontery, considering the record of that horrible martyr at the shrine of principle."[64]

John took the charge head-on, admitting that his views were different because the times and the conditions of the state were different. Besides, he declared, echoing his hero Henry Clay: "Let it be said that I am right rather than consistent."[65]

On the very day of the articles in the *Courier-Journal*, John delivered one of his most passionate addresses of the campaign in Livermore, Kentucky. The articles seemed to be on his mind, and he wanted to make clear that his repudiation of slavery and embrace of racial equality extended to the deepest core of his being. Running for governor allowed him to proclaim—and explain—his changes of heart in every corner of the state. It enabled him to purge any vestiges of his prewar and early postwar self, while absolving him of the charge that his conversion to Republicanism was a matter of convenience, and that his private sentiments rested elsewhere.

In his own view, the changes in his politics weren't an unfathomable mystery but rather the logical progression of a man whose top priority had always been the preservation of American ideals. Before the war, he never saw, in the fevered atmosphere of Kentucky, a quick path out of slavery that didn't involve destruction of the nation. After the war, John came to see that the damage had been immense, but that as the nation rebuilt, it must never allow such a poisonous institution—the very contradiction of its high ideals—to take root again. He held individuals responsible for the crimes of the Ku Klux Klan. But he blamed the larger forces that had embraced and perpetuated slavery, making even gradual emancipation a distant dream, for the underlying divisions in Kentucky society.

"It is true, my fellow citizens that almost the entire people of Kentucky, at one period in their history, were opposed to freedom, citizenship, and suffrage [for] the colored race," he told the crowd at Livermore. "It is true that I was at one time in my life opposed to conferring those privileges upon them, but I have lived long enough to feel and declare, as I do this night, that the most perfect despotism that ever existed on earth was the institution of African slavery. It was an enemy of free speech; it was an enemy of good government; it was an enemy to a free press.

"The time was, and not long ago in Kentucky, when any declaration, such as I now make, against the institution of slavery, would have imperiled my life in many portions of the state. With slavery, it was death or tribute. It knew no compromise, it tolerated no middle course. I rejoice that it is gone; I rejoice that the Sun of Liberty does not this day shine upon a single human slave upon this continent; I rejoice that these human beings are now in possession of freedom, and that that freedom is secured to them in the fundamental law of the land, beyond the control of any state."[66]

Four years earlier, the Republican Party had been swamped in state elections, and few saw a chance for anything better than a marginal improvement in 1871. Over time, however, with John bringing prestige and a forceful campaign presence to the ticket, Republican hopes began to rise. Leslie and his fellow Democrats fought back harder.

Making a surprise appearance on the campaign trail on behalf of Leslie was none other than Reverend William Henry Mitchell, the Confederate minister whom John had arrested for raining damnation on the Union army. He journeyed from Florence, Alabama, to wreak havoc on the man he blamed for his several months of incarceration by the Union army. Mitchell warned the people of Kentucky that their self-righteous candidate for governor wasn't beneath hauling an elderly man of God out of his pulpit for opposing the Yankee army. Mitchell injected yet another blast of Confederate resentment into the campaign, but John defended his actions.[67]

In the end, Leslie beat John by the solid margin of 59 percent to 41 percent, though John polled twice as many votes as the previous Republican candidate. In addition, with Democrats controlling the election apparatus, Republicans felt certain that Leslie's margin was inflated by fraud. In any case, it was a strong enough showing by the Republican nominee that John Marshall Harlan, at age thirty-eight, earned a reputation in Washington as a figure of unusual abilities, who had yet to reach his full potential.[68]

After John's defeat for governor, he turned his attention to an equally difficult challenge: helping President Grant win the state of Kentucky in his reelection battle.[69] However, Kentucky remained resistant enough to the "radical" Republican agenda that the president's team had largely written it off; a victory in the Bluegrass State would be a nice bonus, but hardly essential to the president's chances. Not so with Ohio. This meant that the Harlan man with the greatest importance to Grant wasn't John at all, but Robert.[70]

Accusations of corruption surrounding the president were serious enough that some prominent Republicans ditched him altogether in his 1872 reelection campaign. The Democrats, despairing of ever regaining power after their flirtation with the Confederacy, turned to a surprise candidate: Horace Greeley, the abolitionist newspaper editor who had actually prodded Lincoln to be more aggressive in freeing the slaves. Greeley declared himself to be running under the banner of the newly created Liberal Republican Party but was endorsed by the Democratic National Convention as its standard-bearer as well. No less of a Republican hero than Massachusetts Senator Charles Sumner broke with Grant to endorse Greeley.[71]

The Black vote was a wild card that threatened to throw several large states, including Ohio, to Greeley. That summer, at Saratoga Springs, Black leaders openly debated whether to abandon a president who, despite his willingness to keep federal troops in the South to protect the rights of freedmen, had failed to produce a civil rights bill. Greeley's record on race, by contrast, was stellar; he claimed to be a better friend to the Black man than the general who had won the Civil War.[72]

Fortified by his meeting in Long Branch the previous summer, Robert was firmly in the Grant camp. In August he helped lead a torchlight parade from the local Republican headquarters in Saratoga Springs to the heart of the Black neighborhood, where hundreds of people were gathered. At his side were O. C. Gilbert, the proprietor of the Gilbert House, and John Mercer Langston, who just four years earlier had founded the Howard University Law School. Robert, however, held the position of honor as the final speaker. As the flickering orange of the torches cast shadows on his face, he reminded the crowd of all it had to fear in a Democratic government.

"Colored people are asked to vote for Mr. Greeley upon the ground that he is their best friend," Robert proclaimed to the all-Black crowd. "He might have been, but he has deserted us and gone over to the enemies, and we cannot follow him outside the Republican ranks. All we can do is thank him with hearts full of gratitude for the noble efforts in the past to elevate our race; but we cannot approve of Mr. Greeley's recent course, looking to the destruction of the Republican organization and the restoration to power of Democratic leaders who have persistently opposed every effort to protect us in our rights. Any Republican who allows himself to be elected by Democratic votes will be Democratic in policy. . . . As you are more prosperous than you ever were, I appeal to you to hold on to that which you have, rather than fly to evils you know not of. Seek no change that will bring disaster."

Robert then grew passionate in denouncing the racism that was spreading throughout the land. He blamed unscrupulous Democrats for cynically sowing the seeds of racial hatred, especially among Irish immigrants, who competed with freed men and women for jobs in many states. As proof, he pointed to his own travels in the Emerald Isle, where he never encountered a hint of prejudice.

"At home, who ever heard of a disciple of the great O'Connell being a Negro hater?" Robert offered, referring to the famed Irish nationalist. "Whether at Donnybrook fair or basking in the cool breeze from the beautiful lake of Killarney, I never heard from Irish lips that color made the man, but there the soul was his measure. But let those kind-hearted gentlemen I met in Ireland but be one day under the teachings of the great American Democracy, and I would be hissed from the sidewalk. . . . This is one of the brutalizing effects of these fellows. But what is it done for? Simply that the high, generous nature of a true Irishman may be reduced to the moral degradation that will submit itself to the demagogues who will command their votes."[73]

Robert's speech resonated among Black voters well beyond Saratoga Springs. White Republicans, as well, praised his loyalty and eloquence.[74]

Politics in the nineteenth century was a strange mixture of high rhetoric and low tactics. Part of any campaign was the moral and intellectual suasion of great ideas, articulated in a grand manner. Another was a brutal street fight for votes in the machine-dominated wards of urban America.

After having his speeches lauded as part of the intellectual debate, Robert confronted the other reality on the night of October 7, 1872.

Ohioans would cast their votes for president the following day. Greeley's supporters in Cincinnati felt confident of victory.

Tying cloths to wooden poles and dipping them in kerosene, they made torches to lead a loud parade through the center of Cincinnati. The noisy crowd of Democrats, shouting Greeley slogans, barreled its way up Broadway toward Allen Temple, where Robert was rallying several hundred Black voters on behalf of Grant. There some of the Democratic marchers left their lines and began hurling insults in the direction of the temple. People inside feared that they were about to be attacked.[75] Before Robert could stop them, some of the men vaulted out of the pews and ran to the converted church on New Street that served as the armory for Second Cincinnati—the Black Battalion.[76] Returning to the temple with loaded rifles, they turned the place of worship into a fortress, with about fifteen or twenty men taking positions along its upper balcony windows. Others scrambled onto the roofs of adjacent buildings. When the white Greeley supporters refused to budge, someone in the temple yelled "Fire!" and a line of rifles discharged into the Democratic crowd. Two or three men dropped at once.[77]

Bells rang out, and a phalanx of firetrucks pulled by horses pounded onto the scene. Realizing they weren't what was needed, the firetrucks then turned around and were replaced by about sixty policemen, who "after a good deal of clubbing, drove the negroes back to their quarters, and kept the crowd of whites, who had by this time gathered around, from going near," the *Enquirer* reported. The writer said he saw Robert pushing through the crowds on New Street waving a seven-shooter pistol, but he didn't fire it.[78]

Soon after, Mayor Simon Stevens Davis arrived on the scene. Robert met him and led him into the temple, where the still-armed Black men had taken refuge.

"Now gentlemen," a clearly nervous Davis began. "We've had an affair that's a very unfortunate affair here tonight. It is an affair that, as an affair, injures the city and gives us a bad reputation aroundabouts. I would like you to stack your arms, gentlemen."

The men refused to yield, and Davis, a Republican who counted Robert as an ally, tried a different tack. "I did not expect you would be abused as you were tonight, or I would have had the police force and the military, and all the means I had to protect you," Davis pleaded. "I am not here talking politics. As you can plainly see, I am the mayor of the city, and I want to have peace."

The crowd cheered, and Robert spoke up.

"Mr. Davis, these boys are perfectly harmless, but you can see that they don't want to be murdered in their beds," he insisted. "I do not think that they ought to stack their guns and leave here, because there is danger. I do not want to see any trouble and would have prevented it if they had not overpowered me and broken into the armory to get the guns."

Davis offered reassuringly that there were enough police officers to keep the peace, but Robert disagreed: "I don't believe that's so. I don't believe two hundred policemen can stop a crowd of a thousand rowdies. Here, right now, a man tells me they are on Broadway, coming up here with a cannon."

The mayor pleaded further, and Robert added, "So far as you can protect us, Mr. Davis, you will do so, I know, because you like us. But I don't believe, though, you can do it, and I am opposed to the boys laying down their guns. We don't want no Georgia customs here."

The men cheered Robert's words. For two more hours, they sat with their rifles at the ready, until the Democrats dispersed, and the tension eased. They then relinquished their weapons to the police and headed home.

In the morning, the Democratic-aligned *Enquirer* headlined its coverage "Riot—War of the Races Inaugurated," with a subhead of "Drunken Negroes Parading the Street with State Arms." The paper blamed Robert for inflaming tensions.[79]

In the wake of the chaos, there was good news for Robert: Grant beat Greeley in Ohio by a healthy 7 points on the way to a landslide reelection. Across the river, Kentucky refused to join the parade, despite John's best efforts.[80] The Bluegrass State went for Greeley by a comfortable margin.[81]

On November 25 Robert convened the Second Cincinnati Battalion at the New Street Armory, where just six weeks earlier men had ripped open the doors and seized the rifles without his permission. Robert deplored the riot but was pleased to announce that the battalion would retain its weapons: "The adjutant general came to Cincinnati and investigated the whole affair, and finding that neither the officers nor the men of the battalion were engaged in breaking open the armory and using the guns unlawfully, he allowed us to retain them, but advised me to remove them to a place of safety, which I did, and they have never been out of my possession."

The men applauded. Once again, Robert's diplomatic skills and the confidence he engendered in whites had saved the day, sparing the battalion.[82]

After delivering the good news to the men gathered at the armory, Robert journeyed to Washington to share in the excitement over Grant's victory—and to make sure no one forgot his role in rallying the Black vote behind the Republican ticket. Many people considered him a strong candidate for minister to Haiti, the top federal position available to a Black man. As it happened, the job didn't come open. Ebenezer Bassett, a close ally of Frederick Douglass's who had held the post in Grant's first term, stayed on.[83]

Nonetheless, Robert rejoiced in his growing clout within the Republican Party. In the capital, newspapers rushed to cover an impromptu debate between him and Senator Sumner, the former head of the US Senate Foreign Relations Committee, about French politics. Sumner felt the Third Republic, which had followed the overthrow of Emperor Napoleon III, was there to stay, while Robert, who had traveled in France, worried that another monarchy would assert itself. One paper suggested that the erudite Robert and Sumner may have conducted the debate in French.[84]

Later, he put on his fanciest clothes and attended Grant's inaugural ball, a truly extraordinary event at which politically powerful

Black people drank and danced alongside whites. The ball was otherwise best remembered for the unfortunate fact of being held in an unheated temporary structure on one of the coldest days of the year. The temperature dropped so precipitously that hundreds of canaries who were part of the elaborate décor froze to death.[85] But the star-crossed event did, however, symbolize the moment when aristocrats of color took their place among the ruling elites of Reconstruction-era Washington. For Robert and his brethren, it was a moment of deep satisfaction, when even more progress seemed just around the corner.

As his personal reward, Robert came away with one of the more important and sought-after posts in Ohio: special agent for the United States Postal Service in Cincinnati.[86]

Robert enjoyed the fruits of his far-flung travels and burgeoning political fame alone. After just three years, his marriage to Mary Ann had ended in an embarrassingly public spat. As their union faltered, Robert moved out of the house on Harrison Street and took up temporary residence at the home of Elliot and Mary Clark, two friends among Cincinnati's Black aristocracy. Mary Ann, however, filed suit against the couple, alleging they "seduced her husband into bad habits, late hours, and undue absence from the family bed and board," according to the *Cleveland Leader*. While she "asks no alimony nor wishes for her truant husband to return, she considers herself abused and wishes to know whether there is any protection in the law for the family hearthstone."[87]

Indeed, suits for alienation of affection were common in the nineteenth century, but they were usually aimed at a spouse's new romantic partner. Mary Ann Harlan stopped short of claiming her husband had an affair, and the Clarks won the lawsuit.[88] Nonetheless, Mary Ann may have been on to something. Three years later, after Elliot Clark's death, Robert made Mary Clark the fourth Mrs. Harlan.[89]

Chapter 8

John, Robert, and Benjamin

When Republican leaders in Ohio's Hamilton County needed a galvanizing speaker to fire up their supporters, propelling Cincinnatians to the polls for the otherwise dull local elections in 1873, their minds turned toward John Marshall Harlan. His forceful showing in the Kentucky governor's race rendered him a hot commodity across the country, and next-door Ohio was no exception. He produced excitement.[1] But with only a week to go, there wasn't time to send a formal invitation. Casting aside the etiquette of past decades that left unspoken the mysterious bonds between white families and their light-skinned former slaves, the party leaders asked their own Colonel Robert Harlan to make a personal appeal.

On October 4, 1873, Robert hurried off a letter to John, explaining, "The Campaign Committee requested me to write you thinking I might have more influence with you than they had." He added his personal endorsement—"I believe that you will draw better than any other speaker we can get"—and stressed the political significance of the invitation as well: "Please do not say no, as they are anxious to carry this county, and the people want to hear you."

He signed the letter, "Yours sincerely, Robt."[2]

With sixteen and a half years between them in age, and, for nine long years, the vast expanse of the Atlantic Ocean separating their households, John and Robert had gotten used to measuring each other's progress from a certain distance. When Robert rose to fame in the horse-racing world, collecting a fortune in the gold rush before making his triumphant departure for England, John could only take vicarious note of how Robert had fulfilled James's faith in his abilities. But when Robert returned from England and assumed an entirely different persona—that of political leader and nationally noted orator—John's and Robert's lives converged in a powerful new way. Now they were on the same trajectory, fighting for the same causes. They held close to some of the same friends, and their shared history—still a subject on which to tread gently—was acknowledged by both, even as its precise dimensions remained unclear.[3]

John took the full measure of Robert's ascendance in the Republican Party at precisely the moment that many of his fellow Kentuckians were asserting a doctrine of racial superiority. The presumption of Black inferiority had been implicit and, at many points, explicit in the debate over slavery, despite all the language about states' rights and property rights. But when slavery ceased to exist, the supposed inferiority of Black people became the prime justification for suppressing them. Such a policy made no economic sense—indeed, it would deprive the South of qualified workers and consumers, stifling the regional economy for generations, as John quickly comprehended—but it became an ideology unto itself, spreading to the highest reaches of politics, business, and academia.

Robert was the living refutation of Black inferiority. And John, as he strived to make the case that Black people loved their families and places of their birth just like whites, and deserved an equal shot at education and success, knew from his own observation that Black blood was no curse. Robert, he had to recognize, had already become vastly more successful than any of his white brothers.

Indeed, Robert's clout had rescued John from a potentially devastating political mistake just two years earlier. It started with a sensational shooting. Seemingly inexplicably, John's cousin on his mother's side of the family, a Union army veteran with a wooden leg and a raging drinking problem, busted into the office of a Washington, DC, justice of the peace named Orindatus Simon Bolivar Wall and fired two shots with his Smith & Wesson six-shooter in the direction of the unarmed justice. One flew wide. The other lodged in Wall's abdomen. The injured Wall staggered to his feet and tried to subdue the shooter, James L. Davenport. Coworkers, alarmed by the gunshots, rushed into the room and wrestled the man to the floor. Wall collapsed in a pool of blood.[4]

The son of a white slave owner and an enslaved woman, Wall was a hero to many Black people. His father had granted him freedom as a teenager and sent him to be educated among Quaker abolitionists. Before the war, he risked his life to help escapees on the Underground Railroad, to the point of facing arrest and prosecution under the Fugitive Slave Act. During the war, he fought heroically in the Union army and recruited scores of other Black soldiers. Afterward, he volunteered to go down South to work with the Freedmen's Bureau, to assist the men and women liberated from slavery, and then moved to Washington, where he graduated from Howard Law School, which was founded by his brother-in-law, the famed academic John Mercer Langston.[5]

As Justice Wall fought for his life in the face of an unprovoked attack, much of Washington's Black community reacted in shock and grief. The *Daily Morning Chronicle*, a DC newspaper, reported that Wall "lies suffering in excruciating pain" with only "slight hopes" for recovery. Davenport was hauled off to jail, where the *Chronicle* reporter attested to his high state of drunkenness.[6] The federal government controlled the DC court system.[7] The Grant administration, which was counting on overwhelming Black support for its upcoming reelection campaign, was well aware of the symbolic importance of a case in which a drunken white man attacked a Black man of significant social standing.

When he sobered up, Davenport realized he was in trouble. His lawyer, Thomas F. Miller, declared his chances of conviction to be overwhelming. A long jail term loomed, and possibly worse if Wall were to die. In desperation, Davenport reached out to the one man who could help him, his cousin John, whose standing in the Republican Party might be his only hope.[8]

The one thing John cared about more than his political career was his family, and Kentucky's code of honor held fast to the rule that a gentleman must help a kinsman in need. John had lived up to that code many times in his life, going back to when, as a teenager, he and other family members stood protectively beside his Harlan cousin at his murder trial in Danville.[9] James Davenport had claim to his sympathies. John rarely imbibed himself, but he knew his cousin to be a drinker and despaired about the toll alcohol had taken on his family members. His brother, James Jr., was another victim.[10]

Miller, the attorney, wrote to John that he was the only hope for saving his cousin. Outwardly, the attorney was requesting legal assistance, but his real hope was to use John's political connections to "relax what we have reason to believe will be a very vigorous prosecution," as Miller delicately put it.[11] Within days, a Washington newspaper reported that the esteemed John Marshall Harlan was joining Davenport's defense team.[12]

The announcement was devastating to John's future political prospects. Unlikely to gain elected office as a Republican in Kentucky, no matter how vigorously he campaigned, John's best hope for advancement was at the national level, as a cabinet appointee or—in a fulfillment of his lifelong dream—a Supreme Court justice. But as a Kentuckian who had once owned slaves, campaigned for McClellan over Lincoln, and initially opposed the Thirteenth Amendment, John's credibility on the core Republican issues of the day was wafer thin, no matter how spirited his conversion. National Republicans might give him some leeway for the exigencies of politics in Kentucky, but only for past deeds. Even then, he could expect a lot of skepticism if he were ever to be considered for a high-level appointment. Defending a man who was clearly responsible for shooting a politically connected Black leader—a Republican-appointed justice of the peace, of all things—was beyond the pale in 1871, when defense of Black rights was central to the Republican platform.

As the precariousness of his position began to dawn on him, John reached out to his close friend and confidant Benjamin Bristow. As Grant's solicitor general, Bristow had enormous clout in the US Justice Department and Washington's court system; if any man could fix the case for Davenport, Bristow was the one. Bristow, however, wasn't buying it. He was characteristically blunt in response to John's letter: Davenport was a drunkard who had engaged in a "wanton and reckless" shooting and was hardly deserving of John's support. The law should take its course. Nonetheless, Bristow was a good enough friend to agree to meet with Davenport and help the unfortunate Harlan cousin pull together his bail money. "Of course, I wish not [to] be known as taking any part of the case," Bristow added delicately. In a later letter, he brainstormed with John about the possibility of having President Grant pardon Davenport, should he be found guilty.[13]

Such an act was highly unlikely, since the Black community would presumably erupt in outrage. Already Wall's family—including his wife, Amanda, and brother-in-law John Mercer Langston—fumed openly at the idea that John would pull strings in the case. They had the clout to turn it into a public spectacle, if necessary. Among the Wall and Langston families, and within the larger Black community, there was a persistent feeling that the shooting was a shocking act of racism—a white southerner taking aim at a symbol of Black ascendancy.[14] However, the truth may have been slightly more nuanced. Newspapers reported that the penniless Davenport had sold a faulty stove to a Black Howard University employee, who had sought Wall's advice in bringing a claim against him. Davenport knew Wall, and felt him to be plotting against him. Furious over the situation, Davenport sought revenge.[15]

Gradually, the justice of the peace recovered, sparing Davenport the charge of murder.[16] But he was still facing many years in prison—with the eyes of the Black community upon him—when Robert made a hasty journey to Washington "to see what I could do for Mr. Davenport," as he reported to John in a letter.

Robert's avowed concern may have been for Davenport, whom he knew from his upbringing in the Harlan home, but his real mission was preserving John's reputation. Robert called on Langston, his friend from Black leadership circles, and listened to the esteemed law professor air his grievances against John. Langston believed, based on Davenport's own assertions, that "you had written to the president and other governmental officials in behalf of Mr. Davenport and that you had also authorized other parties to draw on you for large amounts of money for the purpose of clearing Mr. Davenport," Robert reported to John.

Amanda Wall was also a longtime friend of Robert's, but he was distressed by how unyielding she was in her determination to make Davenport pay for shooting her husband. She believed that "Mr. Davenport shot her husband because he was a colored man and held an office," Robert wrote to John. But when Robert approached Wall himself, he found a different kind of understanding: His feelings were "not so hostile" as his wife's.[17]

If ever there were a man to understand Robert's desire to help John by making such a visit, it was O. S. B. Wall. Like Robert, he had grown up in a benevolent household with a white family who treated him more as a relative than as a slave.[18] Wall had one deeper conviction, though: John Marshall Harlan's money wasn't going to buy him off.

Robert sensed as much, and thus contoured an appeal to Wall that was more political than financial. He stressed the way that John had taken up the cause of Black people, becoming such an important voice for Black rights in Kentucky, of all places. He urged Wall to think of John's contributions to their race and their party. Subtly, Robert was pleading that, should Davenport somehow escape punishment, the Walls and Langstons should try to be understanding of John's motives. Seeing a kinsman go to prison under such circumstances would be a terrible embarrassment to the Harlans. Davenport, Robert argued, was born into "a very respectable family" but had been laid low by the war. Robert assured Wall that he himself had known Davenport "almost from childhood." If Davenport were to go free, Robert assured Wall, he would guarantee that the troubled man would never set foot in the District of Columbia again.[19]

Eventually all sides agreed to a deal along those lines. Davenport pleaded guilty to "assault with intent to kill" but was quickly pardoned by Grant.[20] According to a write-up in the *Daily Milwaukee News*, the president explained that Davenport wasn't "in full possession of his faculties at the time of the shooting." The Walls and Langstons kept quiet.[21] Later, when John was under consideration for top appointments, no one, Black or white, raised the strange case of his cousin and the Black war hero.[22]

John put the news about his cousin behind him long enough to join a cadre of Republican stars, some of them longtime celebrities and some up-and-comers, to enjoy the summer breezes on the rocky coast of Maine. The invitation to John, several Grant cabinet members, former Union generals Ambrose Burnside and Benjamin Butler, and the rest of the group came from the Speaker of the House, Maine representative James G. Blaine. Ostensibly, the purpose was to barnstorm the state to promote Grant's reelection. Actually, the center of attention was Blaine himself, who was already gearing up for his own presidential race in 1876 and eager to boost his standing among the party grandees who would determine the nomination. The invitation attested to the growing perception of John as a kingmaker capable of swaying the entire Kentucky delegation. It also put John on the same dais as Frederick Douglass, the nation's preeminent Black leader and moral voice for abolitionism. With his vast head of hair gone gray and his eyes focused intently on the horizon, Douglass spoke with the authority of an Old Testament prophet. John discovered that he and Douglass shared the same preoccupation: combatting the growing sense of nostalgia for the Confederacy, which both considered a dangerous sentiment that was plaguing the national conversation long after the smoke of battle had cleared.[23]

In Portland, the state's largest city, the dignitaries joined a torchlight parade and fired up audiences of thousands with tributes to Grant, Blaine, and the Republican Party. Douglass received a loud ovation and was in a bouyant enough mood to quip that he was there to "give color to the affair."[24]

John used his remarks to remind the Mainers, along with hundreds of Union veterans visiting for a convention, that he had been born in a slaveholding state, and that he was there to celebrate with "the free men of the North that the sun of American liberty does not shine upon a single slave." He went on to attest to the totality of his embrace of Republican values.[25]

"We do not keep one set of principles for the North and another for the South," he said, in a swipe at Democrats. "Our party rests on the broad foundation of truth, justice, equality, and freedom."

Later, at a celebratory dinner at Blaine's sprawling clapboard mansion in Augusta, John was seated directly beside Douglass, and the two new friends talked earnestly of the future of the nation.[26]

Robert's job as special agent for the United States Post Office raised his profile throughout the city, but it also made him a target. While traveling on official business in Kentucky, he needed an escort of soldiers to protect him from vigilantes "who declared that no 'n----r' official of Uncle Sam should ride the trains in that state," according to a news report.[27] Within the Black community, Robert's federal post added to the perception that fidelity to the Republican Party yielded rewards for the Black aristocracy, but not, perhaps, for the average freedman.

Giving voice to the Black community's frustrations with the Republican Party was one of Robert's rivals among Cincinnati's aristocrats of color: Peter H. Clark, a teacher and political activist. The two men had traveled starkly different paths. Clark was born free in Cincinnati in 1829; Robert was born enslaved in Virginia thirteen years earlier. Clark's father, a barber, was Black; Robert's father was white. Clark earned a college degree and later a master's; Robert had no formal schooling. Clark's life was spent largely within the confines of Cincinnati's Black community; Robert had roamed the world, and earned his money in mixed-race settings, dealing with whites. Still, in the tiny world of Cincinnati's Black aristocrats, they were sociable, at times even friendly; they were members of some of the same clubs.[28]

When Clark, in 1872, began signaling his displeasure with the Republicans, claiming that President Grant and his followers in Ohio had taken Black votes for granted, Robert sensed danger for both the cause and the party he had embraced. If Black people were to start re-treating from the Republican camp, they would lose their only lever-age to win federal protection of their civil rights. Clark didn't see it that way. In an audacious gamble, he sought to lay bare the community's grievances by inviting all the "colored citizens of Ohio" to a conven-tion in the former state capital of Chillicothe on August 22, 1873.[29] He declared in the local *Scioto Gazette* that the event would "take into consideration our political situation and the cause of the dissatisfac-tion among us."[30] His timing was shrewd: a local Republican conclave had finished the night before, and a Democratic one was scheduled for the following day. The town was full of politically minded visitors. Plus, the circus was in town.[31]

Clark's convention, the *Gazette* reported, drew a far larger crowd than anyone had expected.[32] After initially snubbing the event, Rob-ert raced the ninety miles to Chillicothe to defend Republican honor and prevent Clark from steering Black support away from the party.[33] In doing so, Robert knew he would have to defend himself against a hostile crowd that was deeply suspicious, and perhaps also jealous, of his federal appointment.

Clark, who would later become known as the nation's first Black socialist, saw himself as a truly independent thinker whose views tilted more toward Black nationalism than allegiance to either major party. He envisioned a growing network of publicly funded Black schools, educating a future class of consumers for Black-owned busi-nesses. Clark explained that he "didn't care about social mingling" with whites, but still insisted that Congress pass the bottled-up civil rights bill because "we demand the opportunity to make ourselves the social equal of any man in this land and derive whatever benefit we can from concerts, theaters, and schools."[34] Robert, however, had a different vision: he foresaw an integrated future in which Black peo-ple interacted freely with white friends and colleagues.

Making a dramatic entrance on the convention floor, Robert pre-sented himself as an avenger of President Grant—his own friend and patron, yes, but also the hero of Appomattox and the man who had done more than anyone alive to win freedom for slaves. Clark wasn't impressed. He retorted dryly that "a Congress containing a two-thirds majority of Republicans, while it can find a two-thirds vote of amnesty to rebels, cannot find a majority in favor of a satisfactory civil rights bill." Based on that sorry record, "we will at least not be deceived by the idea that we are voting for and with our friends."[35]

In what quickly became a seesawing debate—on subjects that would generate heat in Black America for decades to come—Robert forcefully defended the need to strive for progress through the party system, while Clark called for prodding the system from the outside: presenting demands as a unified Black community against a monolithic white establishment.

Robert, however, pleaded that "I want us to be true to the Republican Party, as that party has been true to us." He put his reputation on the line by declaring that he had personally visited Grant and some of the president's cabinet members and received their assurances of a new civil rights bill as "realization of our just expectations."[36]

Clark questioned Robert's motives, suggesting he was merely "earning his day's wages in behalf of the Republican Party."

Robert tried to steal Clark's thunder by putting forward two resolutions expressing support for Grant and the Republican Party as they pursued a civil rights bill. Surely no right-thinking freedman could disagree. But Clark swiftly sidetracked the resolutions by referring them to a special committee.

Robert erupted in protest. "I want to be heard. I came here expecting to be a quiet looker-on. I came here more as a peacemaker than otherwise, but I must say that you have done that for which the colored people will never forgive or forget. I sent up a resolution to the effect that the colored people of Ohio were satisfied with the splendid results of General Grant's administration, and the colored men assembled in Chillicothe have voted down such a resolution as that. Oh, on what meat hath these Caesars fed that they hath grown so fat?"

That rhetorical flourish prompted another withering retort from Clark: "Colonel Harlan has been appointed a special mail agent, and he can afford to apologize for the Republican Party."

Robert tried to turn the tables on Clark and his fellow organizers: "I want to show that this convention is composed of soreheaded office seekers. There is not a colored man in Cincinnati who has not been seeking office and who has been disappointed, hence his sore-headedness. I can prove it. I only want to state the facts."

As the crowd roared in protest, he repeated, "They are all sore-heads. They want office. I helped them. I signed their papers for them."

Then, as the chairman moved to silence him, Robert asked, "Are you going to put me down because I tell the truth? I tell you, General Grant's administration is going to do justice to the colored people. . . . Why, just see what has been done already. A few years ago, Mr. Clark was teaching school in a mean little alley in Cincinnati, and now they have colored schools that have cost between seventy thousand and eighty thousand dollars. The colored people are unjust. Why, if the Republican Party were to give the colored people all they ask for, it would be swamped in twenty-four hours. I asked for an office, and they would not give me one. I came home and worked for the party another year and a half, and then I went to Washington, and General Grant, when I went to see him, said, 'Oh, come tomorrow, and I will assign you to a position.' I went, and got my office, and I think it is not for us to be ungrateful. Six months ago, General Grant's name could not be mentioned without its calling forth a shout. Now when I introduce a resolution showing how splendid has been his administration—"[37]

With that, the chairman gaveled the proceedings to a close. Clark's condemnations of the Republican Party had carried the day among the friendly crowd, though Robert staged an effective counterconvention the very next week at Allen Temple in Cincinnati.[38]

The two men had lit a fire in the Black community. Embers from the Chillicothe debate kept flaring up in Ohio and beyond. National luminaries including John Mercer Langston[39] and Frederick Douglass journeyed to Chillicothe within a month to second Robert's positions. Douglass urged Black people in the Buckeye State to be true to their Republican friends and not be fooled by the false face of the Democrats.[40]

In Cincinnati, the debate drove a wedge through the small community of Black elites, dividing families into pro-Clark and pro-

Harlan cliques. The social snubbing sometimes reached comical extremes: the Clark Literary Circle, a book club named for Peter H. Clark, voted to oust Robert as a member. The following February, Robert persuaded enough members to vote to readmit him; others then quit in protest, claiming Robert had been obnoxious to them since the conflagration in Chillicothe. Unable to reach a consensus, the club disbanded. Clark's friends started a new circle under a new name but released a statement of their continued veneration of Peter H. Clark: "While we part with the name of Peter H. Clark, we still have the same esteem and regard for him which led us in the past to adopt his name as our beacon light."[41]

But such a small community couldn't stay at war with itself forever. A year later, Robert married Clark's in-law, Mary, and the two families resumed their friendship.[42] By 1879, Robert would be hosting a gala engagement party for Peter Clark's daughter Ernestine, with two hundred guests and a live band. The *Enquirer* social page, noting the extravagance of the affair, declared admiringly, "No man in Cincinnati has had a better opportunity to know how to entertain better than the genial colonel."[43]

John didn't want to run for governor in 1875, dogged by fears of lost income and, perhaps, a dawning awareness that his political future was outside of the Bluegrass State. But he was the overwhelming choice of the Kentucky Republican Party, anyway, and he felt a responsibility to lead his team into battle.[44] At forty-two, he carried more political weight along with his rapidly thickening frame.[45] His fame as a politician who could deliver the party's message, while also exercising sway in the backrooms of power, had spread in the four years since his previous run. Expectations were higher. Important eyes were on him. His closest confidant, Ben Bristow, was the toast of the capital with his recent appointment as Grant's Treasury secretary, taking on the messy but politically advantageous assignment of cleaning up the bribery and favoritism scandals involving Republican appointees that were sucking the life out of the president's second term.[46]

On the campaign trail, John was every bit as imposing as in his youth, with his larger body and hair rapidly thinning and turning gray.[47] He and Malvina had just celebrated the birth of what would be their final child, another daughter, Ruth. His eldest, Edith, was already eighteen, the age her mother had been at her marriage. The three boys were growing in height and intellectual attainments as well. Kentucky, however, had not advanced much. A painful sense of nostalgia for the prewar days hung in the air like a fever; John felt a need to address it from the stump, speaking of the war as a great wrong done to the South, though he placed the blame entirely with the secessionists.[48]

John's Democratic opponent, James B. McCreary, was five years younger, but boyish enough that people seemed to think of the two of them as coming from different generations. As if to underscore their rivalry, McCreary had served in the Confederate army under none other than John's old antagonist John Hunt Morgan. Nonetheless, there was little animosity between them. McCreary was far wittier and more likable than John's 1871 opponent, Governor Preston Leslie. John so enjoyed barnstorming the state with McCreary that they amiably shared a bed in small towns. But after all their sparring over economic issues—the Panic of 1873, spurred in part by railroad speculation, had led to bank failures that decimated Kentucky's small farmers—the contest showed every sign of coming down, once again, to race.[49]

With the civil rights act pending in Congress, Republicans wrestled with a tension that would extend into later generations—that is, how to enforce equality while allowing space for people to decide with whom they wish to associate. The logical separation was between purely personal conduct and business; people could choose their friends but not their customers. In the small towns of Kentucky, though, such lines were blurry enough that McCreary and his party eagerly fanned the fears of unwanted contact between freed men and women—still a menacing presence in many white minds— and white women and children. The civil rights law, McCreary contended, would give a Black man the right to "take a seat by the side of your wife and sister." The proposed law, the Democrat insisted, invoking the standard line of his party, would give Black people superior rights to whites, making them the special favorites of the law.[50]

The argument, absurd in a state where lynchings were rampant, nonetheless set white heads nodding at debates. John pushed back, maintaining that the "manifest purpose of the act was to secure equal, not superior, privileges to the colored race." He did, however, express disagreement with the idea that the federal government could order innkeepers and theater managers to serve Black customers.[51]

That hardly satisfied the vast majority of voters who favored racial separation. A man interrupted one of John's speeches to ask if it were true that he had "sat by the side of a Negro at a dinner table in Maine a few years ago?"

John replied that he had—Frederick Douglass. The meal, he pointed out, was at the home of Speaker Blaine, and no one would expect him to "rise from my seat and lecture Mr. Blaine at his own table."

But then, as if remembering his fine conversations with Douglass, John rose up in a righteous defense of his friend: "I not only ate by the side of Douglass at Blaine's house, but during the campaign sat at the same table with him at public hotels and spoke from the same platform with him. And here let me say that there is no man of any party in Kentucky who can make an abler address before a public audience than Frederick Douglass. And now, fellow citizens, you know all the facts. I not only do not apologize for what I did, but frankly say that I would rather eat dinner any day by the side of Douglass than to eat with the fellow across the way who sought to entrap me by a question that had nothing to do with this contest."

In John's later recounting of the event, the crowd lustily cheered.[52] But on Election Day, he fared no better than four years previously. McCreary rolled into office with a solid majority, leaving John to wonder if he would ever again be elected to any office in Kentucky.[53] In fact, he had already set his sights on Washington. His next mission, if successful, would put him in line for the cabinet or the Supreme Court. To achieve it, he planned to be the man who made Benjamin Bristow president of the United States.

John's belief that Bristow was the man to lead the Republicans was hardly fanciful. Voters hated the scandals dogging the Grant administration. Many would naturally welcome a change of parties in power after sixteen years, if only to cleanse the air. Bristow, however, would provide a breath of fresh air without a switch of parties. He was perhaps the country's leading reformer, targeting corruption within and outside the administration, while remaining a Republican Party loyalist. He could help his party overcome voters' fatigue with the Grant administration.[54]

A man of law, a man of action, assertive in some areas where John was equivocal, practical in areas where John was idealistic, Bristow was an entirely plausible president. He took over a corrupt Treasury Department and quickly broomed out seven hundred political cronies while ushering in civil service protections to prevent future abuses. He pushed Grant to restore the gold standard, which helped to end the Panic of 1873, and then he took on the Holy Grail of public corruption: the so-called Whiskey Ring.[55] A group of the nation's leading distillers, based in the beer capital of St. Louis, the ring had allegedly bribed officials for generations to cheat on alcohol taxes. Cracking down on the Whiskey Ring, more than any other action, made Bristow a hero.[56]

Looking ahead to 1876, Bristow's vulnerability was less with the voters than with the party leaders who remained protective of the spoils system. When they gathered on the horsehair couches of the smoke-filled saloons, Bristow's wasn't the first name mentioned. John's challenge was to persuade them, after they snuffed out their cigars, that Bristow, and Bristow alone, could beat the Democrats. As Bristow's closest friend in politics, at a time when it was still considered unseemly for candidates to negotiate on their own, John would have to take the lead in dealing on his behalf.

Much was at stake for John, too. His close friend's presidency would place him tantalizingly close to realizing the dream, bequeathed by his father, of appointment to the Supreme Court. And, in a synergy that might also have been dreamed up by James Harlan, John found a true friend and partner in Robert. Having already drawn on his personal contacts to spare John the political price of freeing his cousin—while also cutting the deal that ensured the cousin would go free—Robert had invested heavily in John's future. Now he could do so much more to bring John's dreams to fruition. In the states of the Deep South, Republican delegations would be composed partly of Black men as well as white carpetbaggers—out-of-state opportunists who took state jobs and contracts that otherwise would go to ex-Confederates. Robert counted scores of friends among America's aristocrats of color, including influential figures such as P. B. S. Pinchback who, as a teenager, had admired Robert's style in the front salon of the Dumas House in Cincinnati. That was before he moved to Louisiana and became a power in local politics, where a strange combination of circumstances led to him becoming the nation's first Black governor, albeit for only thirty-five days.[57] Pinchback had been acting lieutenant governor and took over the top job at the very end of the term when the incumbent stepped aside amid an election scandal.

In a flurry of letters, John and Robert plotted strategy. Robert, whose letters to John are the only ones to survive, offered insider advice on how to court various delegations. His letters were familiar, though not effusive, in tone, occasionally sharing family information. Robert wrote as though his support for John, and agreement with John's views, could be taken for granted. For his part, John would have been well aware of the myriad ways in which Robert could help tip the scales for Bristow in the presidential race—and he would have been touched by the solidity of Robert's friendship. To Robert, this blossoming partnership may have meant even more: by taking him into his confidence, John was acknowledging their familial bond, the unspoken connection of their shared history, and the trust it engendered.

On March 28 Robert wrote to assure John that he was cultivating

support for Bristow within the giant Ohio delegation, having journeyed the hundred miles to the state capital of Columbus to extol the
Treasury secretary's attributes before leading politicians. By custom,
the Ohio delegation would be expected to throw its support on the
first ballot to its "favorite son," former governor Rutherford B. Hayes.
Robert himself owed a debt to Hayes, having received his commission as a state-militia colonel from him. But the most important votes
would come after the first ballot. By then, Hayes would, presumably, be trailing badly, and the candidates with the broadest national
appeal—Bristow and Blaine—would be battling for the nomination.
At that point, Robert's work would pay off, as delegates who'd chosen
Hayes on the first ballot shifted their support to Bristow.

"General Bristow has many friends here who pretend to be for
Hayes," Robert, with quiet confidence, assured John.[58]

The support of the Ohio delegation would be crucial for Bristow.
If a Kentuckian were to grab the nomination, he would need as many
votes from next-door Ohio as possible.

But there was one more reason John would need Robert's help:
the convention was being held in Cincinnati.

Republican power brokers arrived from every corner of the country by steamboat and train, filling every one of the Queen City's hotels and spare bedrooms starting in early June. From dawn until the
wee hours on sultry nights, the sounds of brass bands reverberated
through the city blocks. Marchers paraded down Broadway carrying banners touting the various candidates; every theater, restaurant,
and arena was the scene of festive parties. Revelers would drink and
sup together, then disappear into dark corners to strategize about the
next day's events at Exposition Hall, the cathedral-like Gothic arena
that was housing the convention.[59]

As the city's leading Black Republican, Robert served as host to
the nation's Black elites. To his disappointment, he was not granted a
coveted seat among the Ohio delegation—the *Cleveland Plain Dealer*
reported that racist sentiment alone denied him the honor—but he

was a full participant in the politicking nonetheless.[60] His mansion on Harrison Street was a second home for Black leaders from around the country; news reports buzzed about how Robert entertained Pinchback, Frederick Douglass, US House representative C. E. Nash of Louisiana, and other Black leaders in his living room.[61] Many of those visiting dignitaries probably stayed over at Robert's house as well. Fine hotels were reluctant to serve Black people, yielding an unwritten rule among aristocrats of color to open their homes to one another.[62] They also had a lot to discuss. Though Grant and the Republican-led Congress had finally, in January, enacted the civil rights law, Black leaders sensed that white Republicans were beginning to look for ways to reconcile with the South, at the cost of abandoning Black people. If anything, lawlessness in the states of the former Confederacy was increasing. Just a week before the convention, Nash had decried the actions of murderous night riders in a speech before the US House of Representatives, stating that "a government which cannot protect its humblest citizens from outrage and injury is unworthy of the name and ought not to command the support of free people."[63]

While Robert caucused with black leaders, strategizing for the future of their race, John settled into the Burnet House, Cincinnati's most prestigious hotel, to begin cultivating support for Bristow. A domed structure with the look of a state capitol, the internationally celebrated 340-room Burnet House was where celebrities such as Britain's Prince of Wales, "Swedish nightingale" singer Jenny Lind, and the waspish Irish playwright Oscar Wilde moved in for long stays. Abraham Lincoln had been a guest on the way to his first inauguration; Grant and Sherman had huddled over maps in the Burnet House, devising the strategies that led to the Confederate surrender.[64] Now its luxurious rooms would host nightly strategy sessions for the Bristow campaign. With the Treasury secretary remaining at his post in Washington, John would be a de facto leader of the Bristow forces.

He was widely viewed as one of Bristow's finest assets. In a profile of John entitled "The Man of Impressive Manners," the *Enquirer* wrote a few days before the convention that John would, "in all probability, place Benjamin H. Bristow in nomination in Cincinnati, and he will do it superbly."[65]

John was also viewed as the most influential person among Kentucky's twenty-four-member delegation, along with the hundreds of other Kentucky Republicans who flooded the city.[66] They set up their state headquarters at Pike's Opera House, a glamorous, five-story structure of blue sandstone with an ornate façade.[67] John had chosen the site on Robert's recommendation. He had written to John two weeks before the convention to alert him that "the hall will hold all the Kentuckians you can bring here."

That wasn't the only way in which Robert had been John's eyes and ears on the ground. He also proffered advice on choosing bands and manufacturing campaign materials. "Of course you will bring with you one of the finest bands that can be procured in Louisville and have large and copious Bristow badges printed," he wrote to John. The badges, he continued, "can be done here so much cheaper than in Louisville [that] perhaps it would be best for you to have your badges printed here in order that they may all be alike."

Robert was also still talking up Bristow among prominent Ohio Republicans and eager to apprise John of his progress.

"I have no doubt you will be pleased on seeing the eleven hundred and thirty names in the *Commercial* this morning comprising the Bristow Club," the letter began. It ended with a family reference. Proudly, Robert informed John that the beautiful penmanship in the letter belonged to Robert Jr., now a college graduate on his way to law school, who was serving as his father's clerk.[68]

The snubbing of Robert's bid to become a delegate was just one of many signs that political power was seeping out of the Black community—offenses that must have fired up the late-night discussions at Harrison Street—but Frederick Douglass was still famous enough to score a speaking slot on the convention's first day. Despite his prestige, party loyalty, and the importance of Black support to Republican candidates, Douglass had to withstand a racist challenge before taking the podium. A Michigan delegate moved to adjourn for the day before Douglass could speak; the motion was defeated, and the great Black sage, with his flowing gray beard, mounted the stage.

True to his reputation as a brilliant orator, he quickly got to the heart of the party's greatest dilemma of the moment: whether to keep striving to give meaning to the hard-won advances of the Civil War or retreat into a state of denial about the atrocities being perpetrated in the South.

He was there, he told the thousands of spectators, to talk about principles—"the principles involved in the contest which carried your sons to the battlefield, which draped our Northern churches with the weeds of mourning, and filled our towns and cities with mere stumps of men—armless, legless, maimed, and mutilated." While some would say the war was over, "I say those principles, those principles involved in that tremendous contest, are to be dearer to the American people in the great political struggle now upon them than any other principles we have."

The rights secured for Black people after the abolition of slavery— the cause for which millions of people lay dead or injured—are meaningless, he said, if not enforced by the law. The cause was being eroded every day, in every corner of America.

"You have emancipated us," he declared. "I thank you for it. You have enfranchised us. I thank you for it. But what is your emancipation? What does it amount to if the black man, by the letter of the law, is unable to exercise that freedom; and, after having been freed from the slaveholder's lash, he is to be subject to the slaveholder's shotgun? Oh, you freed us! You emancipated us! I thank you for it. Under what circumstances have we obtained our freedom? Sir, our case is the most extraordinary circumstance of any people ever emancipated on the globe. I sometimes wonder that we still exist as people in the country; that we have not all been swept out of existence, and nothing left to show that we had ever existed. . . . But when you turned us loose, you gave us no acres; you turned us loose to the sky, to the storm, to the whirlwind, and, worst of all, you turned us loose to the wrath of our infuriated masters."

Even as Douglass scolded the white man in seemingly personal terms, the Cincinnati *Gazette* reported, there was applause on the floor.[69]

Well into the afternoon of the second day, after numerous procedural resolutions were passed, John mounted the podium to deliver his much-anticipated nominating speech for Bristow. He presented few of the rhetorical fireworks typical of such a moment, but offered instead a shrewd argument for electability, suggesting that Bristow's clean reputation was all that stood between the convention and Democratic rule. John knew that among defenders of the spoils system, Bristow was viewed as insufficiently protective of the perks that some party men regarded as their due. He had targeted fellow Republicans! But John sought to turn this apostasy to his favor. Who better to give the voters the fresh start they craved, after four consecutive Republican victories, than one who would uphold the ideals they cherished, while sweeping away any taint of corruption?

"It is his proud record . . . that no man has been able to say that Colonel Bristow, in the administration of the duties of that office [of Treasury secretary] has favored his own party. His mode has been to execute the law; and, if the Republican Party contained offenders who betrayed their trust, or who were thieves, he let them be punished as well as anybody else," John declared. In choosing Bristow, he concluded, "you can combine with enthusiasm all elements of opposition in this country to the Democratic Party, and thereby secure not only honest government but the perpetuation of Republican principles; and therefore we express the earnest hope that this convention will not adjourn in its deliberations till they have made him our leader in this contest in the war for Republican principles against corruption and fraud."[70]

John's speech led to a protracted demonstration on the convention floor, but it wasn't nearly the match—at least in rhetorical excess—to orator Robert J. Ingersoll's florid nomination of Blaine. The former House Speaker's reputation had been soiled by an accusation that he had received $64,000 in bribes from the Union Pacific Railroad and then engaged in skullduggery to hide the evidence. Blaine had taken to the House floor to deliver an emotional defense that partly quieted his critics. Ingersoll sought to cast Blaine's performance as heroic and legendary: "Like an armed warrior, like a plumed knight, James G. Blaine from the state of Maine marched down the halls of the American Congress and threw his shining lance full and fair against the brazen foreheads of the defamers of his country and maligners of his honor."[71]

Forever after, Blaine would be known as "the plumed knight."

Blaine's supporters knew their man had been damaged by the bribery charges and that Bristow might well benefit. But in the weeks before the convention, Bristow also had to slough off reports of bribery planted by his opponents. So, too, was a third candidate, Indiana senator Oliver P. Morton, sullied, for allegedly knowing of the railroad bribe to Blaine and having done nothing to prevent it. As the delegates prepared to choose a nominee, the lines were clear: Blaine and Morton were favorites of the party establishment, while Bristow was the reformer—the real "plumed knight."[72]

Of the three, Blaine was by far the most enthusiastic campaigner, having navigated the party's backrooms for decades in plotting to become president.[73] That hard work seemed to pay off on the morning of the convention's third day, as balloting began. There were 378 votes required to win the nomination, and Blaine tallied 285. He was already almost three-quarters of the way to the nomination. Morton clocked in at 124, and Bristow lagged with 113, with several delegations having reserved their influence by voting for their own governors or senators—as Ohio did for its former chief, Rutherford B. Hayes.[74]

John had his work cut out for him. He needed to consolidate all of the Blaine opposition behind Bristow, which meant persuading even the Morton backers to go with the reformer over the party boss.

Conventions were known to go on for dozens of ballots, covering days of intense politicking. In 1876, however, all of the sweat came on one day, June 16. John knew that as the convention moved to a second ballot, and then a third, the states that supported favorite sons would begin to show their true colors. Blaine's lead was substantial, but he was such a prominent figure and had fought for so long behind the scenes, that John could reasonably assume that delegates who opposed him on the first ballot were doing so for deep-seated reasons, and that most would be reluctant to jump on his bandwagon. John could also assume that Morton, who had survived a paralytic stroke a decade earlier and whose commitment to a presidential campaign was questionable, might not be formidable enough to rally the anti-Blaine forces. Bristow's hopes were alive.[75]

Indiana, which was Malvina's home state and where John had spoken frequently, would be key. If John could pry the Hoosier State delegates from Morton to Bristow, it could start a stampede that would swamp Blaine in his tracks. But as hard as he tried, John couldn't persuade the Hoosiers to accept Bristow. As the balloting went on—for the second, third, fourth, fifth, and sixth time—Blaine's totals inched up to 308; the section of the room housing his multitudes erupted in cheers. Michigan, another state that might have embraced Bristow, surprised the convention by switching its votes to Hayes, whose support suddenly seemed much broader than his own Ohio delegation. Any Buckeye State delegate who, under suasion from Robert or anyone else, might have shifted to Bristow now had an incentive to stick with his own former governor. This was a strong signal that the party establishment, if unable to push Blaine over the hump, wanted to make sure the main alternative wasn't Bristow. Hayes wasn't a crusader like Bristow, a man willing to shake things up; but nor was he dragging a chain of Washington bribery and scandal like Blaine's.[76]

As he watched the leaders of each state's delegation rise to declare their votes, John performed mathematical calisthenics in his head. He could try to hold together the Bristow forces for a seventh ballot, but only at the risk that enough votes would tip to Blaine to give the plumed knight the nomination. When, in the midst of the seventh ballot, Indiana unexpectedly joined Michigan in moving strongly for Hayes, John's calculations told him that adding Bristow's support to the growing tally for Hayes might well be enough to ensure that, at the very least, the Republican flag would be carried by a man untainted by corruption.

When John walked to the stand to cast Kentucky's votes, he wore a new expression on his face. He looked like a man in pain. Delegates stirred in their seats. Waves of cheers cascaded around the room. John's lips trembled. He waited a long time for the noise to clear before speaking in a deep, powerful voice. He thanked those who had supported Bristow for having the courage to overcome the prejudice that a man of the South could never be loyal to Republican principles. As proof, he pointed to the delegates in Massachusetts and Vermont who had backed the Kentuckian over a fellow northerner like Blaine. But then he delivered the words that changed history—the nation's and his own.

"Without detaining you further, Kentucky unanimously instructs me to withdraw the name of Benjamin H. Bristow from this convention and, in withdrawing his name, to cast her entire vote for Rutherford B. Hayes of Ohio."[77]

A reporter for an Akron, Ohio, newspaper, tried to capture the import of John's fateful shift to Hayes, declaring: "Never did a man facing such an audience say so much in so few words."[78]

Chapter 9

"Do-Do Take Care"

John's decision to transfer Bristow's supporters to Hayes brought the Ohio governor the nomination and earned John a giant chit to be redeemed in the event of a Hayes presidency.[1] Within minutes of the end of balloting, Hayes's nephew pumped John's hand and said as much.[2] With a sense that his honor was at stake, John immediately set out to write a defense of his actions to Bristow, who learned of his withdrawal by telegraph. John painstakingly laid out the math. By the time the voting on the seventh ballot had reached Kentucky, Blaine had gained thirty-two votes from the previous tally, which put him just thirty-eight shy of the nomination. With New York and Pennsylvania still to vote, along with several unpredictable southern delegations, John felt that Blaine might pick up enough votes from Morton and other candidates to win the nomination unless drastic action was taken. Creating a bandwagon for Hayes might sway some of those later voters in a different direction. Figuring that "we were gone," John explained, he felt obliged to do what he could to produce a good, clean nominee. The loss, coming as an unseen blow from afar, stung Bristow, but he seemed to accept John's logic, understanding that he, too, would be owed a debt by Hayes.[3]

Neither John nor Bristow could count on cashing in those chits. Voters were hungry for change. New York governor Samuel Tilden, the Democratic nominee, was poised to carry the Empire State for his party.[4] Meanwhile, Republicans could no longer count on Reconstruction laws barring enough ex-Confederates from the voting rolls in the South to put those states in the Republican column. More significantly, the Ku Klux Klan and other marauders were vowing to wreak havoc by forcibly keeping Black voters away from the polls.[5]

All of those factors clicked into place, with an astounding result: Tilden won the popular vote by 3 percentage points and the big prize of New York along with three other northern states and all the border states. Hayes carried New England, the West, and upper Midwest. The former Confederacy went for Tilden, except for three states—South Carolina, Louisiana, and Florida—where dueling teams of electors claimed victory for both parties. In Louisiana and South Carolina, where racial anger and nostalgia for the Confederacy were especially strong, the election produced a total breakdown of order. Republicans and Democrats set up rival governments. Without Louisiana, South Carolina, or Florida in Tilden's column, he was still one electoral vote shy of victory; if all three went for Hayes, the Republican would assume power.[6]

Democrats pointed to chicanery by Republican boards of electors. Republicans pointed to the unfettered Klan violence that had kept so many freedmen from the polls. Once again, the South's determination to subjugate Black people was tearing at the fabric of the country. Violence stood ready to trump democracy.[7]

Many northern whites believed that civil war was about to break out again; many southern whites, especially in South Carolina and Louisiana, welcomed the prospect.[8] Some Black people literally feared re-enslavement. In Washington, President Grant received reports that eight thousand ex-Confederate militiamen were plotting to storm the state capitol in South Carolina; in Louisiana, the Republican who claimed victory in the disputed governor's race was a virtual prisoner of white mobs.[9] More than a thousand members of the White League, a Klan affiliate, surrounded the makeshift statehouse in New Orleans, forcing the sheriff to flee his post. Alarmed, Grant nonetheless rejected calls for troops to guard the capital in case southern mobs tried to install Tilden by force.[10]

Amid the growing sense of emergency, the administration and congressional leaders came up with an intriguing plan to sort out the disputed election: a special commission would be established, composed of equal numbers of Democrats and Republicans, and with one independent, Supreme Court Justice David Davis, as the deciding vote.[11]

Solomonic in its wisdom, this delicately balanced commission loomed, against the odds, as a solution that all could respect. Despite having been a close friend of Lincoln's, Davis had no visible party allegiance. His preference between Tilden and Hayes was unknown. At sixty-one, he was a mountain of a man, with a belly that preceded him into a room by several feet. He was, to both Republicans and Democrats, the personification of judicial strength and independence.[12]

And then suddenly he wasn't: the legislature in Davis's home state of Illinois elected him to the US Senate, with strong Democratic support. Some Republicans claimed that Democrats were buying Davis's assistance in settling the presidential election. Discomfited by the accusation of impropriety, Davis withdrew from the commission. There was no other independent justice to replace him, so the parties uneasily drafted Justice Joseph P. Bradley, considered to be the least partisan of the Republicans on the Supreme Court, to be the deciding vote.[13]

Much of the evidence set out before the commission was gruesome. In the white-hot fury of their desire to take back power, southern "redeemers" had turned a blind eye to the river of blood stemming from Klan violence. According to a later US Senate investigation, as many as sixty Black men were butchered in one Louisiana parish to prevent them from voting.[14] On the other side, there was an element of cobbled-together fraudulence to the electoral results submitted by Republican officials; canvassing boards appeared to have found pretexts to invalidate just enough votes to give Hayes the nod.[15]

Justice Bradley backed the Republicans, and the Electoral Commission voted 8-to-7 to accept the Hayes slates and give the presidency to the Ohioan by one electoral vote. Tilden's forces cried fraud, but there was little they could do, short of starting a war; Republicans controlled the relevant levers of government. Still, northerners of both parties were eager for some sort of deal, written or unwritten, that would unite the country and prevent the crisis from exploding. For sixteen years, the fortitude of white America had been challenged by slavery and its aftermath. In the Republican Party, the dominance of Civil War–era radicals had given way to the ascendency of the Gilded Age elites, as evidenced by the Grant scandals. Their willingness to enforce the gains of the war yielded to fatigue over the "southern question," and a businessman's desire for stability.[16]

After Bradley's vote, Democrats and Republicans staged informal, behind-the-scenes negotiations. The subject, invariably, was the fate of the southern states. Even before the electoral crisis, Hayes had indicated a willingness to withdraw federal troops, fully aware that it would mean that ex-Confederates would seize power. Grant, formerly a stalwart in defense of Black rights, wavered as well. Gathering at Wormley's Hotel on Washington's H Street—a fancy hostelry that happened to be owned by an aristocrat of color who was also a voice for civil rights—the two parties hammered out a deal that set back civil rights for decades. In exchange for vague Democratic promises to be attentive to Black rights, Republicans agreed in principle to withdraw troops and allow Democrats to take control in South Carolina and Louisiana.[17]

When Hayes arrived at the executive mansion to embrace a distressed and chastened Grant, whose only pleasure came at the prospect of handing the nation's problems to another man, the precise contours of the agreement that led to Hayes's peaceful assumption of power weren't known, perhaps even to the two of them. Nonetheless, nearly everyone grasped the fact that Reconstruction, as defined by the "radical" Republican policies to protect the rights of freedmen, was about to come to a bruising halt.[18]

The presidential election wasn't fully resolved until two days before Hayes's inauguration on March 4. For John and his fellow Republican leaders, it was a moment for celebration, though the precarious nature of the victory and Hayes's avowed temperance put a damper on the revelry.[19] However, John had every reason to expect that deeper satisfactions were in the offing. The chit he had earned at the convention burned a hole in his pocket. If ever he were to play a starring role on the national stage, this was the time. Hayes publicly floated his name for attorney general, only to run into objections at having a Kentuckian in such a politically important post.[20] Senator Morton, for one, tartly reminded Hayes that Kentucky had never cast an electoral vote for a Republican and was unlikely to do so in the future.[21] Hayes then suggested John for a top diplomatic post, but he was, as Malvina put it, "such an intense American that he could not bear the thought of being out of his native land for four years."[22]

The appointment that John finally received from Hayes was more of an albatross than a plum. The new president desperately needed John for a delicate task for which his southern heritage made him an ideal candidate: settling the disputed governorship of Louisiana. John and four other men would serve as Hayes's personal representatives in New Orleans. This would thrust John directly into the maw of the nation's tortured politics, the "southern question" and the tragic plight of freed men and women. Even worse, he would be entering the den of iniquity with his hands tied behind his back.[23]

Though Hayes, through his secretary of state, solemnly instructed the commission to find facts and seek solutions, the president had already decided to withdraw troops. He and other Republican leaders believed that their party's alliance of Black people and carpetbaggers had run its course; without support among white southerners, the Republicans would be consigned to oblivion in those states. Perhaps an honorable retreat by a Republican president would provide the impetus for conservative southern Democrats to embrace a pro-business Republican Party in the future.[24]

That left little hope for the besieged carpetbagger governor, Stephen B. Packard, a Union veteran from Auburn, Maine, who was clinging to power in the Crescent City. He longed for help from federal troops, but there was little that the presidential commission would be able to say or do that could change the verdict rendered at

Wormley's. The commission was traveling to hostile territory to en-force law and order but had no ammunition in its holster.[25]

Sensing a memorable turning point in the nation's history, John in-vited his eldest son, Richard, an eighteen-year-old Princeton Univer-sity student, to accompany him to New Orleans.[26] As the two Harlan men made their way from Louisville through the Mississippi Delta, they bore witness to the vestiges of war in a scarred and ravaged land. Bands of ex-Confederates patrolled the moss-encrusted delta, terrify-ing the freed men and women as they tried to scythe a living from the loamy soil. The warmth of a southern April couldn't hide the ruins of war or the injustice of a brutal peace.

Part wishful and part determined, John was already reconciling himself to the idea that tough but fair law enforcement could replace brute force in protecting the rights of Black people. Hayes's conclu-sion that southern states couldn't be governed by Black people and carpetbaggers forever was rooted in practical reality; the Republicans of the South had failed utterly in winning over moderate white south-erners. Only a revival of faith in the Constitution could unite them behind a Republican banner and defeat the Confederate dead-enders. This was, at best, a long-term strategy, but it seemed to represent the only hope to cling to, as national Republicans rigorously cast their eyes away from the pain and suffering of freed men and women.

Arriving in New Orleans, a port so geographically southern and isolated that it felt like a separate land, John and Richard settled into the comfort of the Boston Club, a white mansion on Canal Street on the edge of the French Quarter. True to the city's raffish spirit, the club, a headquarters for wealthy Louisianans, was named not for the Massachusetts city but a card game.[27] From that central vantage point, John could see clearly that Governor Packard had control over nothing more than a few blocks surrounding the St. Louis Hotel, in which he was a virtual prisoner. Those blocks included the statehouse and courthouse, though both were under federal guard and so com-pletely surrounded by White League ruffians that little business could be transacted there. The real leader of the state was Francis T. Nicholls, the Democrat who had set up a rump government nearby.[28]

The five commissioners—of whom only Harlan and former governor John C. Brown of Tennessee, a Confederate veteran and moderate Democrat, were southerners—quickly began hearing from local officials on both sides of the divide.[29] Some of this testimony was heartrending. One Black legislator in the Packard government reported that his brother, a local tax collector, had been murdered "at noon-day in the heart of a populous town."[30]

Nonetheless, John's thoughts were pointing in another direction. Writing to his friend Bristow, John admitted to having seen and heard things "which stir my blood as a Union man & a Republican," but he seemed to find a plague on both houses. "Of all the states I've visited, this beats all," John wrote. "Its politics are in utter confusion, and it will puzzle anyone to get at the exact truth." But he credited the Democrats with having "advanced" and accepted the need to deal more fairly with freed men and women, and "they talk more liberally than they would have dared to do 8 years ago upon such matters."[31]

Indeed, Nicholls, a former Confederate who had lost his arm in the Shenandoah campaign, had shrewdly assessed the situation: the federal government was on the verge of pulling out troops, after which he would be able to govern as he pleased. All the president and his representatives needed were some assurances that he wouldn't immediately oppress Black people. Those he offered rather freely—perhaps too freely to be credible, in light of all that had happened in the name of the White League. Nonetheless, the commissioners were pleased to hear that Nicholls would support all the postwar amendments to the Constitution and accept the election of 240 Black men to state and local offices, while keeping twenty-one others in appointed positions.[32]

While the commission was in New Orleans, many of the Republican legislators who had been backing Packard read the writing on the wall and shifted to the Nicholls government. Soon enough, Nicholls was commanding a quorum of the duly elected legislature. Then, just two weeks after the commission arrived, Hayes gave the order to recall the troops. On April 24, five companies of soldiers solemnly marched down St. Louis Street, from where they had been protecting Packard, to the levee and out of the city for good. As they trailed away, the *New Orleans Democrat* reported, someone whooped the rebel yell.[33]

Nicholls took over the statehouse. He found graffiti on the walls making clear the Packard supporters' feelings about Hayes's decision to withdraw the troops. "R. B. Hayes, the Traitor of 1877," read one scrawl; "Rutherford Bastard Hayes," read another. In the House chamber, according to Philip D. Uzee, author of "The Beginnings of the Louisiana Republican Party," there was "a damp unpleasant smell" awaiting the victorious Democrats.[34]

John and his son were only too happy to head home to Kentucky. "The Louisiana crisis therefore settled itself, without any action whatsoever, or even advice, on the part of 'the Louisiana Commission,'" Richard wrote, showing his eagerness to absolve his father of any responsibility.[35] In fact, none of Nicholls's assurances brought about any long-term benefits for Black people, who were destined to be shoved into the virtual imprisonment of segregation. And despite his willingness to mouth the justifications of the Hayes administration, John walked away with an abject lesson in the pervasiveness of racial discrimination, and the hatred it engenders.

John returned to Louisville and the welcome news that his name was in contention for the Supreme Court seat vacated by David Davis. With all the problems facing the country, Hayes had put off his court selection until the fall.[36] The delay produced an avalanche of letters offering conflicting advice, and intense behind-the-scenes politicking. From the start, the president leaned toward choosing a southerner. With the troops leaving the region, and the carpetbaggers soon to follow, the president dreamed of rebuilding the Republican Party along the lines of the Whig Party, appealing to southerners with a national perspective and faith in the Constitution. Harlan's roots in the Whig Party made him a model for the new-type Republican that Hayes envisioned. There were numerous obstacles to putting him on the court, however. Some were practical: the high court already had two justices from the circuit that included Kentucky. Some were political: many northern Republicans, including a fair number of disgruntled radicals, hated the idea of a southerner on the court and doubted John's commitment to the postwar amendments.

There was another, more immediate obstacle: Ben Bristow was sending out signals that he wanted the job himself.

Bristow was coy. Perhaps sensing the intensity of his friend's interest in the post, he reassured John early on that he wouldn't be a candidate for the Supreme Court. Later, when three of John's friends cornered Bristow in a hotel room and persuaded him to make a more public disavowal of interest, he wrote the president's secretary that he "did not desire" the appointment and recommended John instead. Bristow's choice of language—saying he wouldn't be a candidate and didn't desire the job—seemed couched in a way to suggest he was open to persuasion. In the political semaphore of the era, he may have been saying the opposite of what his telegram, at first glance, suggested. Bristow felt strongly that protocol required that he, Bristow, by dint of his service in Grant's cabinet and status as a former presidential contender, was the senior Republican in Kentucky and thus would have first dibs at any appointment.[37]

The growing distrust between Bristow and Harlan burst into the open after Hayes, apparently seeking to soothe Bristow's feelings, told John to reassure the former Treasury secretary that he would be consulted on any Kentucky appointments. Bristow was, at the time, fuming over Hayes's lack of attention. But John failed to convey Hayes's message. When Bristow learned later what Hayes had said, he suspected that John had withheld the news so that Bristow would continue snubbing the president, reducing the chance that Hayes would choose him for the court. John took umbrage at Bristow's suggestion that he had acted inappropriately, penning a furious rebuttal. He claimed he had indeed passed the news to Bristow when they crossed paths at the Louisville railroad depot, and accused Bristow of trying to undermine his chances for the court.[38] In a cocky aside, he predicted confidently that Hayes would pick him, in any case.[39]

While Bristow was sending smoke signals, John was calling in every favor he had ever amassed. Letters extolling his brilliant legal mind streamed in to Hayes from John's Louisiana Commission colleagues, Kentucky's Democratic governor, James McCreary, and numerous Republican allies. Despite their distrust of John's commitment to Black civil rights, northern Republicans saw him as a better intellectual fit for the court than the more ambitious and impulsive Bristow.[40] John's pressure campaign worked: one of Hayes's closest advisers later revealed a private letter from that September in which the president wrote, "Confidentially and on the whole, is not Harlan the man? Of the right age, able, of noble character, industrious, fine manners, temper, and appearance. Who beats him?"[41]

Robert took his new closeness to John, forged through their joint endeavors surrounding the Cincinnati convention, as a cue to further action. He made it his personal priority to help elevate John to the Supreme bench. He, more than anyone, knew of James Harlan's ambitions for the boy and most likely saw their fulfillment as vindication of the father through the son.

Robert also believed in John himself. Their speeches embodied the same principles: a faith in equality under the law, tempered by a recognition that equal social status would have to be achieved through education and commitment to American ideals. To many Republicans, John's speeches may have seemed like standard recitations of party dogma. Robert knew better: he would have heard echoes of John's upbringing in the Harlan home, and James's deathless admiration of the nation's founding principles. John may have struggled to reconcile those truths with the strictures of Kentucky politics in the years surrounding the war, but his subsequent embrace of Republicanism didn't ring hollow or expedient to Robert—he understood the depth of John's commitment to the Founding Fathers. He understood it because he, Robert, had the same faith now that the aims of the Declaration of Independence had, at least in theory, been applied to people like himself.

As early as March 7, 1877, before the advent of the Louisiana Commission, Robert wrote to John, passing on a tidbit of gossip from a person close to Hayes that the president was considering him for the Supreme Court.[42] Then, a month later, Robert wrote to warn John of the political risks in accepting the assignment in New Orleans; plainly, he was worried that John would be blamed for surrendering the state to the ex-Confederates. Robert fondly invoked their shared past, reminding John of the wisdom offered by an elderly enslaved man in the Harlan home: "I beg to repeat to you the words of an old Colored man that formerly belonged to your father—they were do-do-take-care." He underlined the words: "Do-do-take-care." He meant for John to be careful, to avoid any unnecessary political missteps. [43]

On June 1, five weeks after Hayes had withdrawn the troops from the South, Robert wrote to John in despair. He composed the letter "with tears in my eyes" over the state of the Republican Party. Four years after he had put his reputation on the line to defend Republican honor at Chillicothe, here was proof of Peter Clark's dire assertions about how the party takes Black people for granted.

"There is not one Republican here out of ten but who is [not] displeased with the president," Robert reported from Ohio. Unless "something is done before the fall election, the Democrats will carry the state by a large margin. The colored people will vote the Democratic ticket or not vote at all. I write these lines with tears in my eyes—that the good Republican Party, hero of many battles and author of national sovereignty, American freedom, Civil and Political rights is being slayed here in the home of its friends."

Robert put a formal salutation on the letter. In the past, he'd signed his letters to John casually as "Rob't." This time he wrote, "Yours very gratefully, Robt. Harlan."[44] It may have been a sign he wanted John to share the letter with other party leaders.

On October 10, as speculation about the Supreme Court heated up, Robert assured John that he was pressing the case for him in Washington with Hayes's friends, while reporting on other people who had spoken "to the president while here in your favor" and conveying the message that a key Hayes intimate "had no doubt that you will be appointed."[45]

The flurry of communications came amid other letters in which Robert pressed John for relatively small amounts of money—which seem to have been repayments for political tasks or other errands. Some may have dated from the Bristow campaign, but others appeared to be ongoing.

"I have to again ask you a favor which I trust you will not refuse, as I have always kept my word with you," Robert wrote to John on November 10, 1877. "General Buford being a little pressed for money, I paid the note enclosed before it was due. Which compelled me to borrow. If you will kindly endorse the enclosed note by writing your name across the back of it, I will feel greatly obliged to you."

The letter, like others in a similar vein, attested to a bond of trust that was rooted in their personal history, but also to the fact that their collaboration was ongoing. Robert ended his November 10 letter with a mysterious vow: "I will never ask you for anything in this line that will hurt you. Please return note as soon as possible."[46]

Just six days after Robert assured John that he would get the Supreme Court appointment, President Hayes submitted his nomination to the Senate Judiciary Committee.[47] John could sense all the strands of his life coming together. His earnest studies, the great events he'd witnessed, from the Clay era, to the Civil War, to the tragedy of Reconstruction, the mentorship of his demanding father, the fond hopes of his ever-admiring wife, had evolved into a kind of destiny. He would be applying the lessons of his life on the greatest tribunal in the land; and never before had recent experience been so intricately connected to the law, injected into the Constitution through its postwar amendments.

There was just one more hurdle, and that would prove to be a surprisingly high one.

The Senate Judiciary Committee embodied the roiling angst of the Republican Party. Its chairman, George Edmunds of Vermont, was a passionate defender of civil rights who doubled as a lawyer representing railroad interests. Though elements of the party's journey from abolitionism to industrialism were written into his own life story, Edmunds was troubled by Hayes's abandonment of Reconstruction. He didn't share the president's confidence that conservative Democrats would soften their stance on race and join with Republicans once the provocation of having federal troops on every corner was ended; rather, southerners must be compelled, by the force of law if not the force of the army, to respect the rights of freedmen.[48] John Marshall Harlan, a southerner with an imperfect record on civil rights, was hardly the man to apply the full force of the law on the South. He was a disappointing choice for Edmunds and some others on the committee, such as New York's famed power broker Roscoe Conkling.[49]

They weren't alone. Senators received a steady flow of letters opposing the nomination, including reminders of how Harlan had owned slaves, disavowed the abolition movement, and even spoken out against the Thirteenth Amendment in the years immediately after the war.[50] A fellow Kentucky unionist named Speed Fry, who served with John in the Civil War but later became angered by John's failure to help him get a patronage appointment, claimed that, as late as 1866, Harlan had compared buying a slave to "buying and selling a horse, [suggesting] that the right of property in a negro was identical with that of the property in a horse."[51] Other Kentuckians, including James Speed, who had briefly served as Lincoln's attorney general, rushed in to attest that Harlan's rejection of slavery and support for the postwar amendments was not only sincere but also carried the extra faith of the converted.[52]

That wasn't enough for Edmunds, so John sent a flotilla of friends to Washington to work the lobbies.[53] He also sat down to address the committee's concerns in writing. He shot down rumors, spread by radical opponents of his nomination, that he had left the Union army in protest of the Emancipation Proclamation and that the Louisiana Commission had been bribed into backing Nicholls over Packard. His support for the postwar amendments, he wrote, was sincere and unyielding. The force of his own words, along with the constant pressure of his friends, began to satisfy the doubters. Soon John's friends were writing to him that his confirmation would be certain if only the nomination could make it out of Edmunds's committee. Unfortunately, the Vermont senator was in no hurry to have a vote, leaving John's fate hanging in the balance.[54]

The *Argus and Patriot*, a Vermont newspaper, reported that Edmunds was deliberately blocking the nomination because Harlan had "voted for Gen. McClellan and opposed the constitutional amendments."[55] In late November, however, a break occurred: John's nomination was voted out of committee with one missing senator—Edmunds himself.

The *Morning Herald*, an Iowa newspaper, purported to have the scoop. Edmunds, it explained, had continued to oppose Harlan, but when he was away from a committee hearing, his fellow Republicans brought up the nomination and "confirmed their man." Edmunds could have demanded reconsideration, the paper stated, but his objections weren't serious enough.[56]

More likely, Edmunds was in on the subterfuge. A flinty northerner, he had little compunction about saying no. He wanted to register his displeasure but not go so far as to prevent the nomination from moving forward. Edmunds would never regret allowing John Harlan to join the court. The two men, George and John, would become close friends and trusted allies in many of the fights to come.

On Thanksgiving morning, John, Malvina, and their children attended services at the College Street Presbyterian Church in Louisville. John was troubled about the machinations in Washington, and so he decided to relieve his nervous energy by playing in a foot-ball (later soccer) game on the outskirts of town, joined by his three teenaged sons. Tired after a long afternoon at fullback, racing back and forth to protect the area around the goal, John slowly made his way home to partake of his wife's holiday feast. There he found a telegram announcing the surprise that his nomination had been voted out of committee. Confirmation was assured.

Malvina later recalled the "mingled happiness and pride" of the family as it sat down to dinner. "The unconscious prophecy embodied in my husband's baptismal name, 'John Marshall,' was to be ful-filled, for he was to sit on the august tribunal whose far-reaching opening chapter had been mainly written by the great Chief Justice of that name," Malvina wrote.[57]

Once again, John's highest ideals had been challenged by the great question of race. Thanks to the exertions of many friends and sup-porters, including Robert, he had escaped its ferocious undertow. His judicial career represented a new beginning. The conflicts of poli-tics, which could tangle the mightiest of intellects, would give way to the more orderly conflicts of law. Fate had conspired to put him ex-actly where he wanted to be, where he needed to be. As he opened the docket on his Supreme Court career, he would be writing on a clean slate.

Book Two

Chapter 10

Destiny

John Marshall Harlan stood under a brass chandelier[1] in the ornate home of the United States Supreme Court,[2] in what had been the Senate chamber before the recent Capitol expansion, and received the oath of office. The words were given to John to repeat by Chief Justice Morrison Waite, a bearded Ohioan who was himself a relative newcomer, with only three years on the high court.[3] The First Lady of the United States, the esteemed Lucy Webb Hayes, a behind-the-scenes adviser to her husband and the first presidential spouse to have a college degree, escorted a beaming Malvina to the ceremony in her carriage, igniting a fast friendship.[4]

It was December 10, 1877, and the new president, who delighted in taking guests for brisk rides over the snowy pastures surrounding Washington in his sleigh,[5] had every reason to pray for a peaceful holiday season. The first eight months of the Hayes administration had been a time of pain and discord, even by the standards of a nation bearing the wounds of a civil war.

While an excited John and Malvina accepted congratulations from the chief justice and the first lady in the holly-bedecked Capitol, the embers of disputes that would eventually mark his tenure on the court smoldered in many corners of the country.

Louisiana, South Carolina, and other states of the former Confederacy welcomed the return of rebel leaders to positions of authority in Democratic-led state governments. Almost coincidentally, the Ku Klux Klan strengthened its grip on rural communities, sending fresh waves of terror into formerly enslaved men and women and shaking the landscape with hoof-pounding, torch-lit raids.

Even as the nation grew weary of the old sectional disputes and resigned to the restoration of ex-Confederates in the South, it confronted a wholly unexpected explosion of violence in the North and Midwest. The engine of strife was the nation's railroads, which relentlessly cut workers' wages in the middle of an economic downturn while rewarding wealthy investors. In July the president of the Baltimore and Ohio Railroad approved a 10 percent dividend for shareholders on the same day that he cut wages for workers by 10 percent. Laborers in Maryland responded by walking off the job. At the B & O switching yard in Martinsburg, West Virginia, strikers blocked the departure of freight trains, stranding rural communities without the manufactured goods they needed. Nonetheless, in town after town, factory workers, frustrated by their own job losses and wage cuts, flooded to the rail yards to show their support for the strike.[6]

What followed was almost a spontaneous revolution. The work stoppage along freight lines extended from Maryland, to West Virginia, to Pennsylvania, Ohio, and Illinois; managers across the country vowed never to give in to such mob rule. In New York, Washington, and Boston, financiers and intellectuals alike wondered in whispers whether the spirit of the bloody Paris Commune uprising of six years earlier, in which radical socialists held the French capital under siege, had risen up across the Atlantic.[7] Certainly, some of the same class-based tensions were on display. But anger toward the railroads was fueled by more than just economic frustration: low-income neighborhoods of cities and towns in the industrial North, many of them proud ethnic enclaves built by immigrants, had been cut in pieces by hastily laid tracks and choked by coal smoke. Without proper fencing, children, elderly people, and animals were often struck by locomotives or stampeded by horses spooked by train noise—hundreds per year in the state of New York alone.[8] The gleaming rails that connected East and West were symbols of more than just progress; exploitation and inequality followed the path of industry.

In Pittsburgh, where local officials and state militia largely supported the workers over management, railroad executives prevailed upon the governor of Pennsylvania to send troops from rival Philadelphia to protect company property. The result was a confrontation that left between ten and twenty people dead, forty buildings destroyed, and two thousand railcars burned in their tracks.[9] In Chicago, where socialists and other labor groups had already been organizing in German, Irish, and other immigrant neighborhoods, activists implored factory workers to walk off their jobs in a general strike. Many complied. President Hayes ordered federal troops to leave their posts in the Indian Wars of the Wild West to keep the peace in civilized, urbane Chicago. There the resulting conflagration was even more extensive than in Pittsburgh; the death toll reached thirty, with two hundred people injured.[10]

By fall, all was largely quiet; a combination of management concessions and a crackdown by law enforcement had reduced the worker uprising to a simmering froth. But the class-based lines that were established in the Great Railroad Strike of 1877 seemed destined to exist for decades. So too did the centrality of the railroads in the violent clashes of the age; the iron rails were the physical manifestation of corporate penetration into every corner of American society, the curled tentacles of the industrial revolution. The railroads enabled the industrial combinations that suppressed local manufacturing, while the closely cultivated monetary ties between railroad owners and political leaders left workers stranded without a government they could trust to resolve disputes fairly.

This was the world John would be addressing from the pinnacle of the Supreme Court, the tribunal of last resort for people in a society that burgeoned with promise at one moment and trembled on the verge of disintegration at the next.

The problems of the average worker could seem distant in Washington. The village-like capital marched to its own syncopated rhythms, and neither wars nor economic depressions disturbed its time-honored social rituals. Thus, as John and Malvina ascended to positions of prominence—in government and Washington society, respectively—they inherited a set of expectations that would prove difficult to manage. One afternoon per week, the wives of Supreme Court justices arranged to be "at home" to receive guests—mainly the wives of other officials. These seemingly frivolous get-togethers carried grave political consequences—Andrew Jackson's presidential administration almost fell apart because of social tensions between his cabinet members' wives—and thus put intense pressure on the various participants.

The Harlans were seemingly well prepared to meet these challenges: both Malvina and twenty-year-old Edith were charming and outgoing, able to entertain guests with their cultivated musical talents and gracious manners. Indeed, Malvina's keen intelligence, which was immediately noticed by Lucy Hayes, quickly elevated her and her husband to the top of the White House guest list. The couple was less well fortified for the demands of Washington in another respect, however: they had notably less money than most of John's court colleagues and the other government officials whose wives came to call.

John's $10,000 annual salary as a Supreme Court justice was generous by ordinary standards—about $250,000 in 2021 dollars—but still not enough to cover the social demands of his exalted station.[11] While other justices made their journeys to Washington carrying fortunes in payments from the nation's leading railroads and other corporate clients, John could count on little from his own small firm to replenish his perpetually empty coffers. His surviving brother, James Jr., and young protégé Augustus "Gus" Willson tried to keep the Louisville practice alive. Having John's name on the door was enough to impress potential clients, but they would soon learn that the thirty-one-year-old Willson was inexperienced and James Jr. increasingly befogged by alcoholism; realistically, John and Malvina could count on little money from back home except what they might borrow from her relatives in Indiana, who were already embarrassingly frequent targets of loans.[12]

Demands on their pocketbook were destined to grow. Their second son, James, was soon to join Richard at Princeton, while third son John Maynard entered a private high school in Washington.[13] Edith was approaching marriageable age, and a Supreme Court justice would be expected to foot the cost of a society wedding for his daughter. Those and other financial pressures necessitated a constant juggling of loans and expenditures. Wisely, John and Malvina chose to "board" for their first few years in Washington, a common, socially acceptable practice at a time when House members often served only a single two-year term and spent months at a time back in their home states. The Harlans moved into a series of rooms at a boarding house on Twelfth Street run by a Mrs. Rines.[14] In later years, Malvina expressed relief at the break from housekeeping and noted that "boarders," unlike families whose main residence was in Washington, weren't expected to serve on fine china or show off their elegant possessions.[15]

Nonetheless, every Monday afternoon at two, Malvina and Edith prepared a table spread with "all kinds of dainties"—salads, cakes, finger foods, and teas[16]—and greeted a rolling carnival of between two hundred and three hundred guests; John and other men of the city sometimes joined the festivities, if they were not detained on business. Edith would excite the crowd with her singing voice, which might lead to dancing.[17] While alcohol was sometimes served at such receptions, in the form of a sugary punch spiked with rum, Malvina chose to honor the preferences of her friends the president and Mrs. Hayes, who supported the temperance movement.

Though Mrs. Hayes gained the somewhat derisive nickname "Lemonade Lucy," it soon came to be understood that the president was the member of the first couple with the greater commitment to temperance.[18] As Malvina became an ever more frequent guest—and intimate friend—of the First Lady's, she noted how Lucy got around her husband's edict by serving a frozen "Roman punch" as a palate cleanser between courses of White House dinners. "Dear Mrs. Hayes always partook," Malvina recalled approvingly, "and some good-natured comment was occasionally made as to the distinction which she seemed to draw between 'eating' intoxicants and 'drinking' them."[19]

Pretty soon, Malvina and John had drop-in privileges at the Hayes White House, stopping to visit the first couple informally after services at the New York Avenue Presbyterian Church, which was a few blocks away. In the comfort of the Green Room, they and their children and other guests would sing hymns and enjoy light Sunday suppers. The familial intimacy came in handy at formal receptions, where Malvina helped Lucy receive her guests, who included foreign luminaries and, as the Gilded Age took hold, increasing numbers of breathtakingly rich industrialists.

On every such occasion, there were reminders of the accumulation of wealth going on in the country and the Harlans' considerably less affluent circumstances. At one White House reception, Malvina recalled seeing the wife of John Jacob Astor III, the New York financier, "being fairly ablaze with diamonds," her décolletage reputedly worth $800,000[20]—or $20 million in 2021 dollars.

There was no time for frivolity at the court itself. Once relegated to the bowels of the Capitol, the justices had in recent decades emerged into the skylights and damask of the Old Senate Chamber, where Clay and Webster and Calhoun had sparred in the decades before the Civil War. The move, which took place in 1860, when the Senate assumed larger quarters in a newly completed wing, seemed to signal the arrival of the court after the Dred Scott case as a pivotal institution, the third pillar of American government, touching on all aspects of everyday life.

Compared to previous eras, the nine justices were awash with work, with few clerks to assist them. Seeking to prevent state courts from favoring their own citizens in disputes with parties outside their borders, Congress had recently expanded access to the federal court system for plaintiffs and defendants who hailed from different states. This added an enormous number of mundane business cases to the federal docket, many of them requiring at least a cursory review by a Supreme Court justice. By custom, the justices divided themselves among the federal circuits, in order to more efficiently oversee the workings of the federal system. John's home circuit was already covered by the seventy-three-year-old Lincoln appointee Noah Swayne, so he got assigned to the Seventh Circuit, which covered Indiana, Illinois, and Wisconsin.[21]

Swayne, who wrote relatively few opinions, was among three justices over seventy, each of whom was politely regarded as being past either his physical or intellectual prime.[22] A fourth member of the court, sixty-eight-year-old Ward Hunt, soon suffered a paralyzing stroke but refused to resign for nearly four years until Congress granted him a pension. The infirmities of these colleagues combined to put pressure on the remaining justices, of whom only three—the physician-turned-lawyer Samuel Miller, corporate-law specialist Joseph Bradley, and ideologically adventurous conservative Stephen Field—were intellectual leaders, the kinds of judges from whom Harlan, by far the youngest member of the court, could draw inspiration.

The confident, assertive Field came closest to John in his view of a judge's responsibilities. Field recognized that the court's precedents had broad consequences for people's lives, and often adjudicated cases with an eye on their larger implications for society. But the experiences that helped to mold Field's judicial philosophy could hardly have been more different from John's.

Born to a prominent New England family and raised in western Massachusetts, Field was the sixth of nine children of Congregationalist minister David Dudley Field. The eldest son in the family, David Dudley Field II, was eleven years older than Stephen and already reputed to be one of the great legal minds of his generation when Stephen, who had followed his brother's path to Williams College, became his apprentice. He practiced with David until he was in his early thirties and, yearning to be his own man, took off for California in the gold rush.

There, in the far reaches of California, so pregnant with possibilities but also fraught with danger, Stephen shook off the dust of the

East Coast and the burdens of following a famous father and brother. Like other forty-niners, he claimed to have discovered his manhood in a place where fortunes were made in a day and lives ended in a second. His own cache wasn't to come from prospecting for gold but rather from establishing legal order in a nearly lawless wilderness. Being elected "alcalde," a combination of mayor and justice of the peace, just three days after arriving in Marysville, one of the Mexican-flavored towns exploding under the gold rush, Field asserted himself by instituting a whipping post to punish lawbreakers. Hounding criminals with one hand, he drafted contracts for newly wealthy businessmen with the other, watching his bank account and his political clout increase by the day.

In 1857 he was elected to the California Supreme Court, where it was feared that litigants might try to resolve cases with firearms rather than briefs. Field devised a special coat with pockets big enough to hold two pistols, which he could fire through the coat. Two years later, he became chief justice after his predecessor killed a US senator in a duel and fled the state.

Intellectually agile and enlivened by the rough-and-tumble of gold rush–era California, Field brought a swashbuckling certitude to the staid offices of the Supreme Court after being appointed, at age forty-six, by President Lincoln in the midst of the Civil War. Fifteen years later, when Harlan joined the court, Field was just beginning to develop the libertarian, business-friendly judicial philosophy that would eventually clash with John's belief, cultivated in the run-up to the Civil War, in the need for a strong national government.

In 1878, however, Field and Harlan were exceptions to the rule of somewhat colorless, dutiful justices who, like their chief, accounted for the Waite Court's middling reputation—neither especially distinguished nor especially weak in the annals of Supreme Court history.[23]

The Waite Court's lesser place in the judicial constellation masked the fact that its mandate was as great as any since the days of John's namesake. The court and its immediate predecessor, helmed by

Salmon P. Chase, were tasked with charting the dimensions of the postwar amendments to the Constitution—a fundamental reordering of the relationship between the federal government and the states, and the states and the individual.

The Thirteenth, Fourteenth, and Fifteenth Amendments were the "new birth of freedom" that Abraham Lincoln prophesied in the Gettysburg Address. No longer would slavery or "badges of servitude" be permitted in the United States of America. No longer would states, with their narrower sectional interests, be able to deprive people of "due process" or "equal protection" under the law. Every citizen would enjoy the "privileges and immunities" of being a part of the federal union, which no state or federal government could take away. The right to vote would not be "denied or abridged" based on race or color.

These sweeping amendments were the price of reentry for the states of the former Confederacy. They were the tangible fruits of the great contest, the righting of the wrongs that had led to war. They were the plugs to the holes and gaps in the Constitution through which the union fell into crisis. They were the rights guaranteed to all Americans that were purchased with the lives of 620,000 of their countrymen.

They were also only words. It fell to the Supreme Court to decide just what constituted a "badge of servitude," and whether such a badge could be applied by a state legislature, a gang of hooded Klansmen, or a small-town baker refusing to serve a client of a different race. It fell to the court to determine whether "due process" of laws meant a set of procedures or a set of rights, and whether the legal requirement of "equal protection" could be satisfied with separate accommodations.

The last of the postwar amendments was ratified in 1870. Seven years later, when John joined the court, there was still surprisingly little clarity to what they meant—to just how much of a legal revolution had been won on the battlefields of Shiloh, Antietam, Gettysburg, and Manassas. No one could confidently declare how much protection these amendments would provide to newly freed African Americans, let alone the millions of immigrants seeking the very freedoms that John and Justice Field and the rest of his brethren were bound to uphold.

Finding the right answers to those questions would be the mission of John's life on the court.

As the newcomer on the nation's most storied panel, John sought to win the confidence of his colleagues by deferring to them. "I incline to think that, in view of the importance of the questions in the Oregon case, the opinion should come from one of the older members of the Court," John wrote to Chief Justice Waite on his very first week in office.[24]

At forty-four, John was intensely aware of his relative youth. In later years, Malvina recalled John's desire to please his elders: "It was not long before his brothers of the Court (many of whom had been on the bench for years and were looked up to and revered by the whole country) came to think of him as their equal in every way, although, in the intimacy of the Conference Room, they called him 'The Boy of the Court.'"

Age might not have been John's only cause for reticence. While several of his colleagues, including Bradley, came from far less auspicious upbringings than his, almost all had come to the court with more experience in Washington and New York, working for or alongside the business elites of the North. As a child of the South and the West, John was of an entirely different place and mind-set.

Chief Justice Waite, whose main claim to fame before selection to the court was having won damages from the United Kingdom for the destruction of Union vessels by Confederate warships built in England, put a high priority on achieving broad consensus among the justices. He was a peacemaker and administrator, not an ideologue, and quickly came to like and respect the young Kentuckian who was so evidently eager to fit in.[25] John joined in many unanimous votes, and willingly deferred to his senior justices when the chief justice decided who would write the court's opinion.

In his first big case, John sided with his unanimous colleagues in

a sensational 1879 decision that upheld Congress's power to ban big-
amy in the Utah Territory—a policy aimed at criminalizing the common Mormon practice of plural marriage. In addition to attracting
wide popular attention, the case was a rare test of the extent of the
First Amendment's grant of freedom of religion. Mormons claimed
that polygamy was a religious practice, but the court drew a sharp line
between beliefs and actions, ruling, in an opinion authored by Waite,
that the First Amendment protects religious views but not necessarily
religious practices.

"Our crime has been: We married women instead of seducing
them; we reared children instead of destroying them; we desired to
exclude from the land prostitution, bastardy, and infanticide," bemoaned an unrepentant Mormon apostle named George Q. Cannon,
who had six wives of his own and instantly became a fugitive from
justice. Nonetheless, the court's decision was widely applauded and
endorsed by legal scholars.[26]

More divisive cases loomed on the court's docket, challenging
Waite's desire for unanimity and John's determination to win the respect of his senior colleagues.

The scene in the bedroom of the small house on Market Street
in Wheeling, West Virginia, was horrifying: The body of a young
woman, Anna Strauder, sat perched in a rocking chair in her bloody
night clothes. Huge gashes shredded the flesh of her temple and behind her ear, bearing the imprints of a bloody hatchet near her lifeless
body. In another room, her nine-year-old daughter lay terrified in her
bed. The girl explained that her stepfather, a carpenter named Taylor
Strauder, had warned that "If I made any noise or get out of bed, he
would kill me, too."[27]

The thirty-two-year-old Taylor, who had been married only a year,
was known to relatives and neighbors as a wife beater; after one especially vicious attack, Anna had summoned the police and had him arrested. The murder evidence against him was overwhelming. He fled
Wheeling by train but was soon apprehended. A West Virginia jury

had no hesitation about convicting him. However, Taylor Strauder was of mixed race, and from the moment of his arrest had complained that he couldn't get a fair trial because West Virginia barred Black people from juries. When state courts rejected his claims, Strauder's lawyer appealed to the Supreme Court.[28]

Meanwhile, in rural Patrick County, Virginia, along the North Carolina border, two Black teenaged brothers, Burwell and Lee Reynolds, got into a fight with two white brothers, Green and Aaron Shelton, after the Shelton boys reputedly made fun of a nearby school for freed men and women. When Aaron Shelton sent the younger Reynolds boy, seventeen-year-old Lee, tumbling over a log, his older brother, Burwell, nineteen, pulled out a knife and stabbed the white boy. Aaron Shelton died of the wound, but the Reynolds brothers insisted they had not meant to kill him. Virginia prosecutors disagreed, and an all-white jury convicted Burwell Reynolds of first-degree murder and Lee Reynolds of second-degree murder. Those verdicts were set aside on appeal for lack of evidence. In the retrial, the jury deadlocked on Burwell's culpability but again convicted Lee of second-degree murder, imposing a sentence of eighteen years.

The brothers' lawyer complained from the start about the lack of any Black people in the jury pool for either trial, insisting that the Fourteenth Amendment entitled the Reynolds brothers to a jury that was at least one-third Black.[29] The judge dismissed the request and didn't make any changes to the all-white jury pool, even though the rural county, which had been home to numerous antebellum plantations, contained hundreds of formerly enslaved men and women.

After that rejection, the Reynoldses' lawyer requested that their cases be transferred to federal court under the provisions of the Civil Rights Act, on the grounds that Patrick County was denying them their Fourteenth Amendment rights. The plea caught the attention of the local federal judge, Alexander Rives.

A wealthy former planter and slave owner, and a descendant of the exalted First Families of Virginia, Judge Rives was a gentleman of the Old Dominion to his core. He was also a firm believer in the law and a bit of an iconoclast. During the furious rush to war in 1860, Rives made a lonely stand against secession; but when his beloved Virginia withdrew from the Union, he dutifully supported the Confederacy, for which his brother served as a state senator. After the war, Rives became the sixth rector of the University of Virginia and was elected a judge on the Virginia Supreme Court of Appeals. In 1869, however, the commander of the occupying Union forces ousted him from the court for his loyalty to the Confederacy. Rives went on to lose a race for Congress in the district that included Thomas Jefferson's hometown of Charlottesville. His decision to run as a Republican earned him the moniker of "scalawag" from his shocked ex-Confederate neighbors, but also the gratitude of President Grant, who appointed him to a federal judgeship. Rives swore to do his duty without fear or favor and then proceeded to shock his neighbors once again with his willingness to do just that.

The seventy-two-year-old Rives determined that, based both on the Fourteenth Amendment and the federal Civil Rights Act, Lee Reynolds was entitled to have his case removed from the Virginia court system and tried in federal court. To the fury of local officials and many other whites in Patrick County, US marshals removed the boy from the local jail and placed him in federal custody for his own safety.

Rives then proceeded to make his own inquiry into whether state judges in his Danville jurisdiction excluded Black people from the jury pool in violation of the Fourteenth Amendment and the Civil Rights Act. "If [Rives's] instructions shall be literally construed and carried out by the grand jury, it is thought nearly every State judge in Judge Rives's district will be indicted," reported the shocked *Alexandria Gazette*.[30]

That pretty much proved to be true. The Danville grand jury issued indictments against five of the seven state judges in Rives's district, including Samuel G. Staples of Patrick County, who had presided over the trials of the Reynolds brothers. Virginia residents strongly backed the state judges and condemned Rives in harsh terms.[31] When one of the state judges, James D. Coles of Pittsylvania County, was arrested, he promptly petitioned the Supreme Court, claiming that the Fourteenth Amendment did not give the federal government the

power to impose criminal penalties on state officials simply for excluding Black people from the jury pool.

"Great excitement exists and knots of excited persons are standing
on every street corner eagerly discussing the developments," the *Gazette* reported.[32] "Judge Rives is pretty freely condemned, and his conduct is characterized as a feeble attempt to awaken race prejudices,
make political capital, and save the waning fortunes of a dying party."

From the iron mills of Wheeling, considered the buckle of West Virginia's industrial belt along the Ohio River, to the desiccated plantations of Patrick County, where formerly enslaved men and women
tried to till a living as sharecroppers, local officials fumed while Black
people eagerly awaited word from the Supreme Court. The court's
decisions on the cases springing from the gruesome murder of Anna
Strauder and the far murkier case of the Reynolds brothers would determine just how much the postwar amendments to the Constitution
had enhanced fairness and equality in courtrooms across America.

The Fourteenth Amendment seemed to have been intended for
precisely these situations. When the US Senate had debated the need
for a Civil Rights Act to enforce the Fourteenth Amendment, Henry
Smith Lane of Indiana had succinctly argued that Congress had "reason to fear that the emancipated slaves would not have their rights in
the courts of the slave states."[33]

John was still the Supreme Court's junior member, hoping to in-
gratiate himself by showing deference to his senior colleagues, and
Chief Justice Waite was earnestly trying to cajole the court into
speaking with one voice. What resulted was a series of unanimous
decisions (or nearly unanimous, with Field and Justice Nathan Clifford concurring in most aspects but dissenting on some issues) that,
taken together, seemed almost contradictory, even though the majority opinions in all of them were written by the same justice, seventy-
one-year-old William Strong, who was in his last year on the court.

The decision in the case of Taylor Strauder appeared to be a major
victory for African Americans, asserting that the Fourteenth Amend-

ment was "designed to assure to the colored race the enjoyment of all the civil rights that under the law are enjoyed by white persons"[34] and "is to be construed liberally, to carry out the purposes of its framers."[35]

The court overturned Taylor Strauder's murder conviction and insisted he be retried by a jury chosen from a pool that did not purposely exclude Black people. The sweeping language in the opinion written by Strong—to which other justices, including Harlan, may have contributed—seemed to portend an aggressive posture in enforcing Black rights in the future; Strong was merciless in condemning West Virginia's exclusion of Black jurors as "practically a brand upon them, affixed by the law, an assertion of their inferiority, and a stimulant to that race prejudice which is an impediment to securing to individuals of the race that equal justice which the law aims to secure to all others."[36]

Alas, the *Strauder* ruling actually rested on much narrower grounds than all the impassioned verbiage suggested: the court was simply saying that if a state overtly, as its official policy, excluded jurors on the basis of race, it ran afoul of the Fourteenth Amendment and the Civil Rights Act. The *Strauder* decision needed to be viewed in the context of the two other cases, *Virginia v. Rives*, in which the state court challenged Judge Rives's decision to "remove" Lee Reynolds to federal court, and *Ex Parte Virginia*, in which the state judge, James Coles, challenged his arrest for preventing Black people from becoming jurors. And those decisions, released several months earlier, painted a very different picture of the Supreme Court's willingness to defend Black Americans' rights under the Fourteenth Amendment.

First, the court rejected Lee Reynolds's claim that he and his brother had the right to a jury with one-third Black members; the Fourteenth Amendment, the justices declared, only mandated that Black people couldn't be systematically excluded from the jury pool, not that every jury had to include Black people. It was an important distinction. Of course, Black people had indeed been excluded from the jury pool in Patrick County—according to Reynolds's plea, there had never been a single Black candidate for a jury—but the court ruled that the exclusion wasn't systematic.

The justices found that the failure to include Black people in the jury pool was the fault of the county judges, not state law. Virginia's jury law, unlike that of its neighbor West Virginia, did not make any explicit exclusion of Black people. If judges or court administrators failed to follow state law, the Supreme Court reasoned, that was a problem for Virginia's court system to address. It was not a reason for federal courts to step in and take over a case like the murder trial of Lee Reynolds; thus, the Reynolds boy had to be returned to state prison and his eighteen-year murder sentence.[37]

The justices must have understood that the distinction between a state policy excluding Black people and a broad pattern of exclusion of Black people by local officials was meaningless to a defendant such as Lee Reynolds. They also knew that the authors of the Civil Rights Act, like Senator Lane, had clearly anticipated that officials would try to discriminate against Black people. So why did the Supreme Court take such a blindered view of the rights granted by the Fourteenth Amendment? It's possible that the justices thought they were sending a strong signal to states to crack down on discriminatory judges. If they wished to send such a message, however, it would have had more impact if they had allowed Lee Reynolds to be retried by the federal court.

The justices' decision in *Rives v. Virginia*, with John Marshall Harlan in agreement, was an early signal that they were willing to accept legal fictions and fig leaves while ignoring the plainest evidence of racial discrimination—such as the fact that Patrick County had never had a Black juror.

Why would John go along with this? After only a little more than a year on the court, he may have lacked the confidence to break with his colleagues. Most likely, he agreed with the rejection of Reynolds's demand for one-third Black representation on the jury—an extreme interpretation of the Fourteenth Amendment—and may have been blinded to the implications of the rest of the ruling by none other than Judge Rives's courageous willingness to bring charges against five state judges for excluding Black people from juries.

Rives offered an unexpected—and ultimately unrealistic—glimmer of hope for those who thought the state courts could be fixed, and the Supreme Court, in the decision known as *Ex Parte Virginia*, backed Rives's power to bring charges against the state judges. Only Field and Clifford disagreed. Judge Coles and his racist brethren would have to face the consequences of their actions.

But even at that moment, Harlan and the other justices should have understood that Rives was an outlier—a man with an unusual willingness to stand up to his neighbors, even at the pain of being labeled a scalawag. And the state judges would feel little pressure from within their own court system to stand up for Black rights. The popular winds were blowing in entirely the opposite direction.

In the end, John may have decided to pin his hopes on the powerful language of the court's opinion in *Strauder v. West Virginia* rather than the parsing of words in *Virginia v. Rives*. He may even have contributed some of that language. Certainly, the forceful assertions of the *Strauder* opinion sounded more like Harlan than Strong, an impression that would only strengthen over time.

The country's failure to fulfill the promises of emancipation changed Robert Harlan, as he gazed at the shifting political landscape in Cincinnati and the rest of the country. The removal of federal troops from the South challenged his fundamental optimism. The man who had found ways to thrive even in the most adverse climates began to fear for the future—his own and the country's. President Hayes's actions dismayed him. The Republican Party had strayed horribly from the path set by the esteemed Grant, as Robert indicated in his cry-of-pain letter to John, in the middle of 1877.[38] Though still active in the Republican Party, Robert had to acknowledge that the party of Lincoln was no more—and that Black people had no true refuge in the political system.

Back in 1876, before the end of Grant's second term and the withdrawal of troops under Hayes, Robert had been as willing as ever to challenge Peter Clark and even erstwhile allies such as P.B.S. Pinchback and Mississippi senator Blanche K. Bruce when they, at a Nashville convention of Black people, suggested that the Black comunity would be better served by dividing its support among Republicans and Democrats. Taking the podium, Robert derisively suggested that some "soreheads, disappointed aspirants for office, were there trying to make use of the colored people to avenge their own private injuries"— a surprisingly caustic insult to friends like Pinchback, Bruce, and others who were losing their platforms as former Confederates returned to rule the southern states. Even the *Cincinnati Commercial* reported that Robert's remarks received lackluster applause.[39]

Robert soon shifted gears. He changed his tune dramatically at the next National Colored Convention, also in Nashville, in 1879. No longer did he urge the audience, filled with some of the leading Black voices of the day, to trust the Republicans to come to the rescue of their race. Rather, he endorsed an old solution to the nation's race problem, the same one that had long entranced Henry Clay, James Harlan, and, at times, Abraham Lincoln: colonization. Robert wasn't keen on a return to Africa, but he began to muse on whether Black people would be better off heading west and starting their own towns and businesses, free of the white world entirely. In his own life, he had never hesitated to pick up stakes in search of more hospitable racial environments, be they in San Francisco, Cincinnati, or London. Now he began to wonder whether some sort of "exodus movement" might be to the advantage of freed men and women. John Mercer Langston had similar views.

Mounting the dais of the Tennessee House of Representatives, which had loaned its chambers for the convention, Robert delivered one of the most widely discussed speeches of his career. He began by speaking of how Black people had earned the right to go anywhere and do anything in the United States. "The blood of the colored man fertilized the land and has cemented the union," he thundered, insisting that Black people deserve nothing less than full equality. But where once he advised that, by committing themselves to education and economic advancement, people of color could overcome white racism, he now urged more direct action. "The Republic owes to every citizen protection for his home and security for his rights," he declared. "Let this security be given, and until that be done, let us cry aloud against those who refuse it, whether in the North or in the South."[40]

But, he added, "If the leading men of the South will make another Egypt of these bright and sunny valleys, then must the oppressed go forth into the promised land of liberty, in the western states and territories, where the people are at peace and the soil is free, and where every man can secure a home for himself and family with none to molest him or make him afraid."

Despite Robert's idealized depiction of life in the Far West, he correctly anticipated the migration of Black people in future decades from the Jim Crow South to the North and West. At the conclusion of his speech, Robert clarified that this was not what he wanted for Black people, but it might be the best course left for them when caught between the betrayal of the national Republican Party and the utter disregard of the Democrats.

"The reaction [against Reconstruction] has robbed southern Republicans, both white and colored, of their votes and of their voices, and this has thrown the nation into the hands of our opponents, who are determined to strip us of the last measure of protection," he declared.

Robert's speech was widely reprinted.[41] It made waves among Black people across the country and prompted a retort from Frederick Douglass.[42] Having fought much of his life for emancipation, Douglass took issue with those like Robert who, in his comparison between the South and Egypt, suggested that Black people were scarcely better off than in slavery. However unfortunate the recent turnabout in national politics, Douglass declared, Black people must embrace the promise of emancipation and not make an "untimely concession" to white racism. The exodus movement, he believed, would give the racists exactly what they wanted.[43]

Pinchback, Robert's former protégé, seems not to have been swayed by Robert's arguments, either. His newspaper, the *Louisianian*, reprinted an interview with Robert by the *Cincinnati Commercial* in which he explained his support for Black migration, citing the deteriorating conditions for formerly enslaved men and women in the South.

"Our big, good-natured friend, Col. Bob Harlan, of the 'Paris of America,' commonly called Cincinnati, has been interviewed by the *Commercial* of that city about the exodus and matters generally in the

South," the *Louisianian* wrote in introducing Harlan's interview. "In some parts of his statement, he mixed up places, names, and persons with a freedom which entitles his interview to be declared a first-class jumbolaya [*sic*]. Colonel, be a little more careful, or we'll be compelled to invest in a small map of Louisiana for your special benefit."[44]

Ridicule aside, Robert's views struck a chord among disheartened formerly enslaved men and women, who would only grow more desperate as they came to realize that their abandonment extended to the Supreme Court as well.

After nearly three years at Mrs. Rines's boarding house, John and Malvina moved into a large rowhouse on Massachusetts Avenue. A quarter mile away, at the White House, their friends Rutherford and Lucy Hayes were in the process of moving their possessions, en route to retirement in Fremont, Ohio.

Hayes had promised early in his term not to run for reelection, and, by 1880, his hold on the Republican Party was tenuous enough that he wouldn't have been likely to get renominated, anyway. James A. Garfield, a former Civil War general and minority leader of the House of Representatives, emerged from a large group of Republican luminaries who contested for Hayes's empty seat.

John remained politically neutral in his new role as Supreme Court justice. Robert, however, staged a rally at the Allen Temple in Cincinnati to demand that he be made a delegate to the convention—a demonstration of his new, more aggressive posture. He succeeded in getting himself elected as one of four alternates in the Ohio delegation. He attended the Chicago convention, and joined in behind-the-scenes maneuverings as Ohio came to embrace Garfield as a favorite son. After the convention, Robert and fellow delegate P. B. S. Pinchback—having renewed their friendship, with Robert's criticism of Pinchback's attacks on Republicans having been balanced by Pinchback's criticism of Robert's support of the exodus movement—traveled together as far as St. Louis. There the two Black leaders were interviewed by the *St. Louis Post-Dispatch* while touting the Garfield–Chester Arthur ticket over breakfast at the Hoskins House hotel. Asked if he felt the Republicans were destined for victory, Pinchback demurred.

"It is too early to express an opinion on that point," he replied.

That fall, Garfield won a close race against a Democratic nominee with a very similar platform and profile—former general Winfield Scott Hancock, a Union hero of the Battle of Gettysburg—in a sign of how the nation's politics had aligned since the first decade of Reconstruction. Garfield, however, made some gestures to restore the confidence of Black Americans, including appointing Frederick Douglass, John Mercer Langston, and Blanche Bruce to federal posts. He also prodded the Supreme Court to enforce Black rights, declaring in his inaugural address that "Freedom can never yield its fullness of blessings so long as the law or its administration places the smallest obstacle in the pathway of any virtuous citizen."

The fact that Garfield, a skilled lawyer who had argued before the Supreme Court, included a reference to fairness in the "administration" of laws rather than just the laws themselves, could be seen as a backhanded rebuke to the court's willingness to tolerate racial double standards as long as they were by state officials, and not state law.

Four months after taking office, the forty-nine-year-old Garfield was shot in the back while waiting to board a train at Washington's Gothic B & O station by a disgruntled office seeker named Charles Guiteau, who proclaimed his intention to make Arthur president. Aides carried the injured president back to the White House, where doctors poked and prodded in search of the bullet, often inserting their unwashed fingers and instruments into his bleeding wound.

A short distance away, John and Malvina spent that whole summer in Washington, forgoing a vacation, in order to acclimate themselves to their new home and prepare for a joyous event: Edith's marriage to a young lawyer from Worcester, Massachusetts, named Linus Child.[45] While the Harlans shuttled between their home and the New York Avenue Presbyterian Church, the site of the wedding, they passed the White House, where a still-conscious Garfield wasted away under a primitive air conditioner that was rigged to blow air off blocks of ice to protect him from the capital's humid weather.

In September 1881 Garfield, now a skeletal 130 pounds, traveled by specially cushioned railroad car to a seaside mansion near Grant's old haunt of Long Branch, New Jersey. There, amid the sound of the crashing waves, he struggled to overcome a rampaging infection that may have been exacerbated by the unsanitary practices of his physicians. He survived a scant two weeks, with Arthur taking the oath of office amid an atmosphere of grief and mistrust.

"No one deplores the calamity more than Senator Conkling and myself," said Arthur, who received death threats of his own amid gossip that he, Conkling, and other Stalwarts—opponents of civil service reforms advocated by Hayes and Garfield—had conspired with Guiteau. "These reports are so base and unfounded that I cannot believe they will be credited."[46]

John and Malvina shared in the nation's grief for Garfield, exacerbated by the long, twilight feeling of having him ebb away for two months behind the stoic columns of the White House.[47] John had crossed paths with Garfield in the Civil War and respected his love of the law. But even his concern over the death of the president couldn't diminish his happiness at Edith's wedding. She was the favorite of both her parents. An accomplished musician, she also taught Black children at a school for the poor.[48] Malvina noted how Edith's preparations for the wedding reflected her personal modesty, devotion to her church, and love of family. She refused to have the sanctuary be decorated, considering such ornamentation disrespectful, and relented only to allow a few flowers to be placed at the pulpit. For attendants, she insisted that only family members be included, with each of her parents flanking her and the groom, and her three brothers and Linus Child's three brothers grouped on either side.[49]

After the wedding, the young couple headed off to Chicago, where Linus was starting his law practice. Ten months later, John and Malvina were grandparents, as Edith gave birth to a girl who shared her name. Baby Edith was strong and healthy, but at some point over the following three months, the joyful new mother contracted typhoid fever.

As reports of Edith's deteriorating condition filtered back to Washington, an alarmed John left the court, determined to be at his daughter's side. He and Malvina journeyed for two days to Chicago, in terror of what they might find. There, in an eerie repetition of the vigil that had attended the president, the two parents sat by their twenty-five-year-old daughter, watching for signs of hope while praying for recovery. John sent regular dispatches to his sons and other family members. On November 12 he sent a telegram to Richard saying she had taken a turn for the worse. Later that day, in a terse, anguished message, he informed his son that his beloved sister had passed away.[50]

Two days later, on what would have been her twenty-sixth birthday, John and Malvina brought Edith's body back in Washington for a funeral in the church where she had been married thirteen months earlier. This time her three brothers and brothers-in-law flanked her casket as pallbearers, along with two of her cousins. Her devastated parents held close to their now motherless granddaughter, gaining permission from Linus to keep her in Washington and raise her as their own child.[51]

"I find it difficult to realize that we are to see Edith no more in this life," John wrote to his son James. "The blow was so sudden & unexpected that I can scarcely recognize that she is gone. I do not expect to be able ever to feel that she is away from us. Wherever I go & whatever I may be doing, her presence will be recognized in its influence upon me. She was to me not simply a child, but companion. I am quite sure no character more noble & elevated ever appeared on this earth."[52]

Chapter 11

Standing Alone

The average person couldn't afford to go to a theater like the New York Grand Opera, where the young newspaper agent William R. Davis Jr. and his light-skinned date got turned away from Edwin Booth's performance. Nor could the average person treat herself to a first-class railroad ticket the way that Sallie Robinson and her nephew, traveling from Grand Junction, Tennessee, to Lynchburg, Virginia, did. The average person lacked the wealth of Bird Gee, who fought his ejection from the frontier rooming house in Hiawatha, Kansas, or the political clout of W. H. R. Agee, the delegate to the Missouri Republican Convention, who was expelled from the Nichols House inn in Jefferson City because white guests didn't want to share quarters with him. But the mistreatment of Davis, Robinson, Gee, Agee, and George M. Tyler, the San Francisco theatergoer who was ousted from his orchestra seats, struck a major chord. It amplified the everyday experiences of the average Black person.[1]

Those cases evoked the frustrations of farmers and sharecroppers and laborers and small-business operators who sensed, through their own daily slights and exclusions, that whites were shutting their doors and closing their eyes to them. Their pain was the backdrop for all the anguish expressed by Robert Harlan and the other speakers at the 1879 National Conference of Colored Men in Nashville and their willingness to entertain the notion of a mass exodus.[2] For all Black people, elites and laborers alike, the reality of discrimination—the quiet conspiracy of whites in their communities to serve only their own kind—made the importance of the Thirteenth, Fourteenth, and Fifteenth Amendments to the Constitution and the Civil Rights Act of 1875 vivid in a way that tortured arguments over the inclusion of Black people in jury pools did not.

"Few Blacks were involved with grand juries," noted the civil rights lawyer and historian John R. Howard.[3] "On the other hand, any black traveler, tired at the end of a long day's journey into night, might wish to rest at the nearest wayside inn; any black laborer, spent at the end of the day's work, might wish to drop into the nearest tavern; any black family might wish to take their children to the theater or the circus. The Civil Rights Cases spoke to the issue of caste and an evolving etiquette of social degradation."

The five cases, bundled together for the Supreme Court, carried an urgent sense of importance in the white world as well. The fact that white innkeepers and theater managers could be punished for refusing to serve Black people was tangible evidence of the reordering of society in the wake of the Civil War, a slap in the face of the South that kept stinging. The cases gave rise to the argument, seemingly foolish on its face but surprisingly resonant, that the Civil Rights Act had made Black people the special favorites of the law: after all, a theater owner couldn't be hassled for throwing out undesirable white people.

Beneath all the professed outrage over government interference in private businesses was a more fundamental conflict: the Fourteenth Amendment and the Civil Rights Act—regarded by critics as a last-gasp relic of the old, misguided Radical Republican Congresses of the Reconstruction era, determined to protect the rights of freed men and women—got in the way of the southern states' efforts to reintegrate themselves into the Union. But by drawing a distinction between state laws and the discriminatory practices of individuals in the jury cases, the Supreme Court had opened a loophole through which much of the former Confederacy was driving toward segregation. As long as acts of discrimination were committed by individuals—business owners, professionals, banks, clubs—rather than state governments, they were beyond the scope of the Constitution. That was the claim being driven home by lawyers for the white conductors, theater managers, and innkeepers who were accused of excluding Black customers.[4]

Even though anger toward the Civil Rights Act reverberated through the North as well, whites in southern states were particularly quick to grasp the idea that the Civil Rights Cases, now being considered by the Supreme Court, represented a unique opportunity to extinguish protections for Black consumers once and for all, freeing white-owned businesses to serve only those they pleased.

"The cases were argued by the United States solicitor general in support of the social pretensions and claims of the negroes," scoffed the *Times-Picayune* of New Orleans in January 1883. "It is obvious that the decision of these cases is of immense importance to hotel keepers and many other proprietors throughout the country, as well as the general public."[5]

Three months later, the *Weekly Advertiser* in Montgomery, Alabama, chimed in with a prediction: "Although the wish to stir up strife and ill-will prevailed in the passage of this bill [the Civil Rights Act of 1875], yet the judicial authorities are not so blinded as to set all law and decency at defiance."[6]

John turned fifty in the months before the *Civil Rights Cases of 1883* were heard before the Supreme Court. He was not at peace. Edith's death the previous fall had plunged him into depths of grief that he once considered unimaginable. Like almost every person in a large family in the nineteenth century, he had faced sudden losses of loved ones who were seized with infections and dwindled away in mere days and even hours; but the death of his dearest child, the one closest to his family circle, invested him with a new sense of purpose. Edith's benevolent spirit would be his moral guidepost, just as caring for her daughter would be his practical concern.[7]

In truth, all the experiences of his life were pressing in on him. After five decades, he was old enough to see over the horizon. Life was nothing if not a series of lessons, and he was ready to apply them to his work; to build a legacy that would reflect the values of Edith and others who shaped his character and now shone in the afterlife. He knew that the Supreme Court afforded him a unique vantage point and a voice in the future of the nation. He was ready to use it.

Despite his advancing years, he was still the youngest justice on the court, but now far from the lowest in seniority. No fewer than four new justices had been confirmed in the early years of the decade.[8] No longer did John feel like a junior partner in a well-oiled enterprise. He had no need to defer to his elders, to prove himself as part of a team.

Earlier, as the court sought fitfully to discern the meaning of the postwar amendments, John had stepped in to write the majority opinion in a case in which the chief justice of Delaware acknowledged that no Black people served on juries in the state because "the great body of black men residing in this state are utterly unqualified by want of intelligence, experience, or moral integrity, to sit on juries."[9] John called that a "violent presumption," and ruled that a Black man accused of raping a white woman be given a new trial.[10] The case nudged the law a little closer to protecting Black rights, though it would apply only in instances where state officials admitted to having excluded Black people by reason of prejudice. Nonetheless, both Chief Justice Waite and Justice Field objected even to that narrow ruling, with Field declaring that the federal government had no power to require states to consider Black people for juries.

Then John joined with a unanimous court in an opinion written by Field that rejected a claim by an interracial couple that the state of Alabama violated their Fourteenth Amendment rights by imposing tougher penalties on couples of different races engaging in "adultery and fornication." Tony Pace and Mary Jane Cox acknowledged being a couple, but challenged their conviction for fornication by noting that "an ordinary misdemeanor is made a felony because one of the offending parties happened to be a Negro."[11] Field wasn't impressed, reasoning that, since the law imposed the same sentences on both the Black and white members of the offending couple, it did not run afoul of the Fourteenth Amendment's prohibition on disparate penalties.[12] Pace and Cox chose not to contest the case on the grounds that they were denied the right to marry; rather, in a show of deference to the morals of the times, they acknowledged the state's power to limit marriage to couples of the same race. Marriage, they argued, was a privilege; adultery and fornication were crimes that were unaffected by the races of the offenders.[13]

Justice Field's majority opinion reflected the type of reasoning that John, in later years, would reject: the equal application of an entirely unequal law. But at that time, few people, even in the Black community, were eager to make a strong stand in support of interracial relationships, and John, the devout Presbyterian, may have been disinclined to break sharply with his brethren over a case involving adultery and fornication.

The same would not be true in the so-called *Civil Rights Cases of 1883*, involving access to railroads, inns, and theaters, which clearly inflamed John's sense of injustice more than the plight of an adulterous couple. Here was a rejection of equal rights so obvious that it violated his sense of the world brought forth by the Civil War, the society envisioned by the framers of the postwar amendments. Racial double standards under the law caused the collapse of the Union; the postwar amendments to the Constitution were intended to correct that flaw. Eliminating legal discrimination was, as John wrote, "the ends the people desired to accomplish, which they attempted to accomplish, and which they supposed they had accomplished by changes to their fundamental law."[14] Now John's fellow justices seemed intent on thwarting the framers' intentions, thereby joining the rest of post-Reconstruction white America in sweeping the problem of racial inequality further under the rug.

Though John viewed inequality as an existential threat to the American ideals embodied by the Declaration of Independence and Constitution, he also felt it to be an injustice to individuals. While other justices were swayed by assertions like that of the Delaware chief justice—that Black people were unqualified by "want of intelligence"[15]—and by the lawyers for innkeepers and theater managers who claimed that excluding Black people was necessary to avoid offending white customers, John saw the grievous unfairness of surrendering to prejudice. He grew up around Robert Harlan and plotted with him politically; they shared a last name and a family background. He had watched Robert soar to wealth and prominence, and heard the eloquence in his speeches. John also sat next to Frederick Douglass and praised him as the greatest orator of his generation. With these men among his family and acquaintances, how could he embrace the notions of Black inferiority that underlay the views of other justices? If sitting beside a Black person at a theater might spark momentary discomfort, so too could it yield to greater acceptance and understanding.

Justice Joseph Philo Bradley, who wrote the court's majority opinion, grew up poor on a farm in the North, but during his long and lucrative career as a patent and railroad attorney he'd had little, if any, exposure to Black people.[16] His opinion avoided any serious discussion of the racial situation in favor of ice-cold logic, overturning the Civil Rights Act without really accounting for the injustices it was meant to correct.

The Fourteenth Amendment, Bradley noted, had five sections, of which only the first and the fifth bore on the case. The first section declared: "All persons born or naturalized in the United States, and subject to the jurisdiction thereof, are citizens of the United States and of the State wherein they reside. No State shall make or enforce any law which shall abridge the privileges or immunities of citizens of the United States; nor shall any State deprive any person of life, liberty, or property, without due process of law; nor deny to any person within its jurisdiction the equal protection of the laws."

The fifth section read: "The Congress shall have power to enforce, by appropriate legislation, the provisions of this article."

Bradley zeroed in on the language in the last sentence of the first section, beginning, "No State shall make or enforce . . ." By dint of this construction, Bradley judged, the Fourteenth Amendment pertains only to state governments. Thus, the "appropriate legislation" referred to in the fifth section must apply only to states, not individuals. The Civil Rights Act, in restricting the actions of railroad conductors, innkeepers, and theater managers, clearly overstepped those bounds.

What, then, of the Thirteenth Amendment? It declared: "Neither slavery nor involuntary servitude, except as a punishment for crime whereof the party shall have been duly convicted, shall exist within the United States, or any place subject to their jurisdiction," and "Congress shall have the power to enforce this article by appropriate legislation."

Bradley conceded that the Thirteenth Amendment seems to contemplate action by Congress beyond simply correcting state laws; but, he argued, the crimes established in the Civil Rights Act have nothing to do with slavery or involuntary servitude. "The only question under the present head," Bradley wrote, "is whether the refusal to any persons of the accommodations of an inn or a public conveyance or a place of public amusement by an individual, and without any sanction or support from any State law or regulation, does inflict upon such persons any manner of servitude or form of slavery as those terms are understood in this country? Many wrongs may be obnoxious . . . which are not, in any just sense, incidents or elements of slavery."[17]

Thus, Bradley and seven other justices concluded, the Civil Rights Act was an unconstitutional overreach by Congress, and must be struck down.

The court convened under the ionic columns of the Old Senate Chamber, designed to reflect the proportions of an ancient Greek temple, to announce its decision on October 15, 1883. The justices sat beneath a canopy of red fabric and a bright gold statue of an eagle in flight, the symbol of national power.[18] It was only days after the second of two Saturdays when the court met in private to discuss the case, at which time John made amply clear to his colleagues that any hopes for unanimity in this decision would be unfulfilled. The vote was 8-to-1 and would stay that way unless anyone cared to join his dissenting opinion.[19]

Feelings around the cases were so strong that many leading figures of the day crowded into the very same galleries where people had once lined up for hours to hear Senator Daniel Webster denounce slavery, defending the legal right of Congress to ban the dreaded institution in the territories under its control.[20] Now the Supreme Court was about to remove many of the legal protections designed to wipe away the vestiges of that same institution.

Bradley announced the majority opinion first, explaining why he and his colleagues believed that neither the Thirteenth nor Fourteenth Amendment could justify the Civil Rights Act: The Thirteenth only allowed laws to prevent slavery, while the Fourteenth applied only to actions of state governments. Those clean boundaries would restrict federal efforts to protect the rights of Black people for generations, while simultaneously clearing the way for white-dominated institutions to discriminate at will. An entire structure of segregation would be built on such a foundation.

When Bradley finished, Justice Harlan leaned forward to offer his rebuttal. The moment was noteworthy for court watchers because John had been reluctant to turn on his colleagues in the past, internalizing Chief Justice Waite's preference for consensus. This Justice Harlan, however, took on his brethren with a righteous tone and rhetoric that soared as high as the golden eagle overhead. His remarks conveyed both the intensity of his disagreement with his fellow justices and the rigor of his legal analysis; he felt the case to be a shocking injustice and also went to a great effort to forge an alternative legal path, lest anyone would think his objections were based on emotion alone.

"The opinion in these cases proceeds, it seems to me, upon grounds entirely too narrow and artificial," his dissenting opinion began. "I cannot resist the conclusion that the substance and spirit of the recent amendments of the Constitution have been sacrificed by a subtle and verbal criticism."[21]

The court's majority, he believed, was nullifying the efforts of postwar Congresses and statesmen who struggled, through years of the arduous ratification process, to put in place a working system of constitutional protections for freed men and women.

A fair reading of the Fourteenth Amendment, he said, would show that section 5, granting Congress the power to enforce the amendment by appropriate legislation, applied to more than just the sentences that began "No State shall . . ." The amendment included a broad grant of national citizenship, with rights attending it, that transcended state actions. Plus, he argued, it would make little sense for the framers to have given Congress the power to legislate only so far as to crack down on state governments that violated the amendment, since the courts stood ready to do just that. Plainly, the framers intended to provide legal authority for more sweeping protections of civil rights.

This rang true to much of John's audience, since many of the framers of the Fourteenth Amendment were still alive and knew that their purpose had been to validate civil rights protections—including the Civil Rights Act of 1866 that was then in place and went well beyond just policing state governments.

Nonetheless, John declared, the current Civil Rights Act could be justified even under the stricture that it may apply only to state actions, since common law recognized that private transportation providers and innkeepers were performing public functions on behalf of the state. This interpretation would, presumably, allay the concerns of some justices that an overly broad rendering of Congress's powers might upset the balance of federalism; Congress would be limited to protecting equal access only to those private businesses that performed important public functions. And yet the court resisted even this narrower interpretation, based on centuries of common-law cases.

So too did John believe that Justice Bradley was overly quick to dismiss the Thirteenth Amendment and its grant of power to Congress to legislate against practices that degrade minorities, holding them to second-tier status. He insisted that the framers believed that Congress could legislate to prevent "badges" of servitude that excluded people from the stream of everyday life and commerce.[22]

"They are burdens which lay at the very foundation of the institution of slavery as it once existed," he stated, referring to exclusions of Black people from railroads, inns, and theaters. "They are not to be sustained, except upon the assumption that there is, in this land of universal liberty, a class which may still be discriminated against, even in respect of rights so necessary and supreme that, deprived of their enjoyment in common with others, a freeman is not only branded as one inferior and infected, but, in the competitions of life, is robbed of some of the most essential means of existence."[23]

In John's mind, a ghost hovered over the proceedings. It was the legacy of the Dred Scott case and earlier cases involving the Fugitive Slave Act. That a court would grant Congress expansive power to force private individuals to turn over runaway slaves, and then, two and a half decades later, turn around and deny Congress's right to compel private individuals to do business with freed men and women, struck him as evidence of the court's bad faith.

Indeed, when individuals challenged fugitive slave laws on the grounds that the federal government was intruding on state prerogatives, the court insisted Congress had broad power to enforce the Constitution against individuals and states alike: "It would be a strange anomaly and forced construction to suppose that the national government meant to rely for the due fulfillment of its own proper duties, and the rights which it intended to secure, upon State legislation, and not upon that of the Union," the Supreme Court ruled in the 1842 case of *Prigg v. Commonwealth of Pennsylvania.*

Based on that precedent, John declared, Congress would have the right to impose a Civil Rights Act even if neither the Thirteenth nor the Fourteenth Amendment offered any grant of authority for enforcing legislation. So why the double standard?

"With all respect for the opinion of others, I insist that the national legislature may, without transcending the limits of the Constitution, do for human liberty and the fundamental rights of American citizenship, what it did, with the sanction of the court, for the protection of slavery and the rights of the masters of fugitive slaves," he thundered.[24]

Thus did John, in his voluminous and monumental dissent, establish a pattern he would follow as a dissenter to court opinions in the years to come. In future cases, he would again refer to the dark shadow of the Dred Scott decision—which he regarded as a kind of judicial original sin.[25] He would also ruthlessly expose double standards in the law, insist that courts give proper deference to decisions of Congress, and invoke universal concepts of freedom and justice.

All of those points of departure from his colleagues emerged in the *Civil Rights Cases of 1883*.

Among the many double standards in those cases, he noted that the Supreme Court approved the use of municipal bonds to assist the railroad companies under Congress's power to regulate interstate commerce.[26] Now the court was saying Congress lacked the power to compel railroads to serve Black customers. "It may become a pertinent inquiry whether Congress may," under its power to regulate interstate commerce, "enforce among passengers on public conveyances, equality of right, without regard to race, color or previous condition of servitude . . ."[27] Eighty-one years later, the Supreme Court would approve a Civil Rights Bill on just such grounds.[28]

Harlan also blasted the court for substituting its own judgment about what was necessary to enforce the Fourteenth Amendment for Congress's. It would be a constant refrain, that justices must not impose their own political judgments over those of the political branches. "The judiciary may not, with safety to our institutions, enter the domain of legislative discretion, and dictate the means which Congress shall employ in the exercise of its granted powers," he declared.[29]

Finally, John was willing to acknowledge the very issue that the court's majority wished to avoid: The case's implications for African Americans and others who might, in the future, rely on civil rights protections. John's colleagues, in ignoring the vast evidence of discrimination that was unremedied by state governments, seemed to be saying "the law's the law" and throwing up their hands. But John insisted that, far from merely applying the law, the justices in the court's majority, with their parched reading of the powers granted to Congress by the postwar amendments, were distorting the meaning of the Constitution to achieve their own desired ends.

Near the conclusion of Bradley's otherwise straightforward and

legalistic opinion, the justice had betrayed his true feelings about the
Civil Rights Cases when he offered: "When a man has emerged from
slavery, and, by the aid of beneficent legislation, has shaken off the inseparable concomitants of that state, there must be some stage in the
progress of his elevation when he takes the rank of a mere citizen and
ceases to be the special favorite of the laws."[30]

This statement, so glaringly at odds with the painful experiences
of free Black people before and after the war, drew a direct and equally
personal rebuke from Harlan.

"It is, I submit, scarcely just to say that the colored race has been
the special favorite of the laws," he concluded. "The statute of 1875,
now adjudged to be unconstitutional, is for the benefit of citizens of
every race and color. What the nation, through Congress, has sought
to accomplish in reference to that race is—what has already been
done in every state of the union for the white race—to secure and
protect rights belonging to them as freemen and citizens."[31]

The court's decision to strike down the Civil Rights Act of 1875 was a
national sensation, igniting celebrations in many white precincts of
the South and almost funereal convergences in Black neighborhoods
of cities and towns across the country. Denunciations of the court's
ruling by Black speakers were usually paired with reverential praise
for Harlan. His dissent provided the only shred of faith in the system, the only real evidence that America wasn't completely separating along color lines, never to share the same feelings again.

In Washington, more than two thousand people crowded into an
events hall to protest the court's decision, with hundreds more hovering outside.[32] A shaken Frederick Douglass took the stage and pointed
to Harlan's dissenting opinion as the one source of hope.

"I have only a few words to say to you this evening, and in order
that those few words shall be well chosen, and not liable to be mis-
understood, distorted, or misrepresented, I have been at the pains of
writing them out in full," the great orator began in mournful resignation. "It may be, after all, that the hour calls more loudly for silence

than for speech. Later on in this discussion, when we shall have the full text of the recent decision of the Supreme Court before us, and the dissenting opinion of Justice Harlan, who must have weighty reasons for separating from all his associates, and incurring thereby, as he must, an amount of criticism from which even the bravest man must shrink, we may be in a better frame of mind, better supplied with facts, and better prepared to speak calmly, correctly, and wisely than now. The temptation at this time is, of course, to speak more from feeling than reason, more from impulse than reflection."[33]

John's written opinion more than lived up to Douglass's hopes and expectations, prompting one of the most moving tributes John would ever receive. The eminent Black leader hailed John's lonely stand in a letter expressing his conviction that "one man with God is a majority."[34] Amid all the effusions, former New York senator Roscoe Conkling, himself a framer of the Fourteenth Amendment and once a Harlan skeptic, affirmed John's assessment of the amendment's original intent and proclaimed his dissent to be "the noblest opinion in the history of our country."[35]

This heartfelt praise pleased John, but it was more than balanced by the distressingly joyful exultations of many whites over Bradley's majority opinion—an outcome that John, in later years, professed to have expected.[36] Like the other great change in his public posture—when he finally stepped out from the wreckage of the Whig Party, American Party, and various conservative unionist parties to embrace the Republicans—John's break with his colleagues over the postwar amendments was complete. He never looked back or expressed regrets.

His willingness to stake out a dramatically, forcefully different position than all the other justices was surprising because he wasn't instinctively a loner or outsider or contrarian. He lacked the rectitude that sustained many of society's dissenters. Unlike his aloof father, he was unfailingly convivial, eager to like and be liked. He regularly exchanged letters with his judicial colleagues—and expressed warm feelings for their families and great respect for their legal views—among them Bradley, whose *Civil Rights Cases* opinion he so reviled.[37] Harlan was a colorful storyteller and a natural teacher. His lectures at Washington's Columbian University, which later was renamed George Washington University, drew great crowds, as much for his buoyant humor as his perspective on the court.[38] The leaders of the District of Columbia Bar Association proclaimed him their "regular and favorite guest" on their annual excursion up the Potomac River, where the justice joined in baseball, target shooting, and bowling, while leading sing-alongs.[39]

But from the moment he announced his dissent in the *Civil Rights Cases of 1883*, he never shied away from differing with all his colleagues, especially in race-related cases. His confidence in the rightness of his stance never flagged. Perhaps that was because his outlying opinion on the postwar amendments rested on precepts that were deeply embedded in his life story.

Foremost was his religious faith, which conferred a moral obligation and what some theologians call "the right of private judgment."[40] In the liberty of his own conscience, John felt compelled to answer for his opinions. A devout Protestant and weekly Sunday school teacher, he believed his relationship with God to be an enhancement of his own power to discern right and wrong. He could not simply defer to his colleagues or follow the precedents handed down by his judicial forebears without endorsing them in a moral sense.

His reverence for the Constitution and the Founding Fathers was part of the prophecy bestowed by his father. Having tried himself, in his early years in politics, to move beyond disputes over racial double standards, he learned through hard experience that it couldn't be done—that racism was a poison that destroyed American ideals. Having watched as the states surrounding his own went to war over their sectional prerogatives, he was less bothered than his fellow justices by perceived federal intrusions into state matters: a stronger national government was the hard-earned legacy of the Civil War, worth preserving at all costs. John's respect for the basic humanity of Black people was also a product of personal experience. Unlike most of his brethren, he grew up alongside enslaved people and other people of color, developed affection for some of them, and watched one of them—Robert—reach great heights. His immediate family reinforced his views: Malvina and all three of his sons endorsed his feelings about racial equality under the law.[41] Finally, there was also Edith,[42] who had extended herself so generously and enthusiastically to the education of poor Black children. The *Civil Rights Cases* reached the court at a moment when John felt the greatest determination to preserve some part of his late daughter's spiritual legacy.

As much as he wanted to be liked, he also desired to be true to his experiences and to share with posterity a vision of the United States that was forged on the frontier, in war, and in the peace of his own home. The fact that it differed from that of his colleagues was no obstacle.

He dissented.

Chapter 12

"The Colonel Has Indeed Surprised Us"

More than four hundred of Cincinnati's leading Black citizens crowded into the striking, new Zion Baptist Church, with four slender Gothic spires reaching heavenward, to approve a resolution hailing Justice John Marshall Harlan. They voted to honor his "patriotic and unselfish devotion in recognizing one of the safeguards of the negro"[1] by virtue of his courageous stance against the Supreme Court's decision to strike down the Civil Rights Act.

Their own Harlan, Robert, was not present on that late October day in 1883. Perhaps that was because he was already en route to Washington, where he would spend the end of the year attending a subcommittee meeting of the National Colored Convention and visiting with his son, Robert Jr., or, more likely, because one of the lead organizers of the Zion Church meeting was Peter Clark. A decade after their epic encounter at Chillicothe, the two leaders of Cincinnati's Black elites were again at odds over politics. In the intervening years, Clark had gone so far as to become a socialist, running unsuccessfully for school commissioner and US Congress on the ticket of the Workingman's Party of the United States.[2] His dream of a biracial coalition to challenge the inequities of the Gilded Age collapsed in part because of racial tensions, and he became a Democrat. The year before the Supreme Court decision in the *Civil Rights Cases*, Clark helped to engineer Democratic backing for a local civil rights ordinance in Hamilton County.

Thus, when the court struck down the federal law, Clark urged the people gathered at Zion Church to put their faith in their local government. The crowd at the meeting approved a resolution expressing hope that "as the two races grow in wisdom and tolerance, the prejudices which bar our way will be dissipated, and that in the future all American citizens will stand undisputed on a platform of equal political and of equal civil rights."[3]

The resolution reflected an optimism that was not shared by people at other Black gatherings throughout the country.[4] The difference may best be understood in the context of Clark's efforts to pry Black voters away from the Republican Party. Clark was urging Black people to engage with the Democrats, if only to force both parties to compete for Black votes, in the belief that if a hand were extended, it would be accepted with magnanimity. With virtually all Black voters instinctively backing the Republicans, there was little incentive for either party to exert itself on civil rights.

Robert had no such faith in the Democrats, whose southern leadership brimmed with unreconstructed Confederates. Nonetheless, he, too, recognized that the postwar desire for racial reconciliation, a centerpiece of the Radical Republican philosophy, had dissipated along with much of the animus toward the Confederacy. Like Clark, he understood that without greater pressure and clearer political incentives, white leaders would do little or nothing for Black people. But since white Republicans in Cincinnati conceded the mathematical reality that they needed Black votes to win countywide elections, Robert concentrated on leveraging that support to his and his people's advantage. He organized mass meetings to issue demands to party leaders. Foremost among them was the inclusion of Black candidates on the countywide ticket.

In 1879 Robert had sought this end by promoting his own candidacy for county clerk, warning Republicans that Black voters would abandon the party if they weren't given a chance to vote for their own kind. For Robert, making the leap into electoral politics was a natural progression in his long path from slavery, to wealth, to power, a trajectory he believed would catapult him into elected office, representing all the people, Black and white. The patronage-rich post of county clerk seemed to be his best chance for victory. But in this, as in so many of his other goals, he ran into a wall of racial double standards. Republican leaders, who nominated candidates for office at a raucous county convention, made clear that they would tolerate only one Black candidate for a countywide seat. Even that token nomination would have to be gaveled past the objections of some angry white delegates.[5]

Thus, Robert's desire to be county clerk ran headlong into the furious ambitions of George Washington Williams, one of the most aggressive and peripatetic men of color of his day. A full generation younger than Robert, Williams had begun his own rise to prominence in the same manner as his rival: by earning good money in the barber's trade.[6] At fourteen, he assumed a fake identity to join up with the Union army in the waning days of the Civil War, after which he signed on with a band of Mexican Republicans struggling to oust Emperor Maximilian I.[7] Still in his teens, he fought Indians with the US military in the West before moving to Massachusetts to study theology. His next stop was Cincinnati, where he was given an unusual opportunity to learn the law under the tutelage of the city's most prominent citizen, Alphonso Taft, father of the future president.[8] Despite his serious demeanor and impressive military past, the thirty-year-old Williams lacked the sixty-three-year-old Robert's credibility in the community, not to mention in the local Republican Party. Still, the upstart gained traction among Black voters who were upset with the rising backlash against them, and who no doubt hoped that a fresh, unsparing voice might shake up the local establishment.

Both Williams and Robert understood that Republicans would back only one of them, and that would be solely for the strategic purpose of keeping Black voters in the Republican camp. So, the two men competed aggressively to showcase their Black support, expecting that white Republicans would gravitate toward whichever one stirred up more excitement among the Black electorate. The dark-skinned Williams openly suggested that white Republicans would prefer Harlan as a safer choice—a reference to Robert's closeness to the party apparatus but also, perhaps, his lighter skin.[9] In response, Robert staged rallies showcasing his personal ties to Cincinnati's Black community. After one such meeting at Zion Baptist ended with the crowd embracing Robert's candidacy, a probing *Cincinnati Commercial* reporter asked voters if they were bothered by Robert's association with horse racing. "They said no," the reporter wrote, "for even General Grant was fond of racehorses. Grant smoked cigars and looked at races himself."[10] A later *Commercial* article quoted a voter named William Alexander as saying that Cincinnati's Black community would never turn its back on Harlan.

"I never knew Harlan, and I have known him fifty years, to turn his back on a colored man," said Alexander.[11]

Still, Robert sought to leave nothing to chance. A month later, on a steamy July evening, he drew seven hundred voters to a torch-lit rally featuring a fife and drum band. The procession ended at Fountain Square on Fifth Street, an esplanade decorated with the city's most famous piece of art: a thirty-eight-foot bronze structure topped by a woman in robes, called *The Genius of Water*, with liquid raining down from her outstretched hands.[12] Amid a sea of campaign signs, all of which, the *Commercial* reported, "boomed for the Colonel," Robert staked his claim to be county clerk with a rousing speech.[13]

Williams, however, proved to be a clever and equally relentless campaigner. At another mass meeting organized by Robert, Williams arranged for his supporters to deliver a letter to the stage. Sensing a trap, Robert refused to read it, but Williams's supporters demanded he do so, claiming it was not "in the least prejudicial to the interests of Colonel Harlan."[14] After others at the meeting asked to hear the letter, Robert obliged.

"The Williams letter was cordial and gracious, pledging to support Harlan for the county clerkship, and solicit Harlan's support for his legislative race," wrote Williams's biographer, the legendary John Hope Franklin. "If he was defeated for the nomination, Williams promised to 'stump the county' for Harlan and the entire ticket." In response, a Williams supporter asked that everyone at the meeting endorse Robert for county clerk and Williams for the legislature, a disingenuous move given that only one was likely to prevail, but a gesture that succeeded in disguising the meeting's preference for Harlan.[15]

The Hamilton County Republican convention on July 30 proved to be a disaster for Robert. Party leaders asked him to withdraw his candidacy for county clerk, claiming that he couldn't win, but run for the legislature instead, promising him full support. Though he only tallied 144 votes on the first ballot, the party chiefs promised to deliver the nomination on the second ballot. However, in all the hubbub, a delegate moved to increase the threshold for candidates to remain on the second ballot from 100 to 150. Robert believed the motion was out of order and rose to issue his objections, but no one could hear him in the commotion.

In the end, Williams ended up with the legislative nomination, and Robert was left off the slate entirely.

In an angry letter to the *Commercial*, Robert claimed that several wards that had pledged to back a Black candidate had not realized he was in the race, a mistake he later "ascertained was a result of the industry of Williams's workers."

"That there was deception and manifest unfairness must be apparent to every right-minded citizen," Robert concluded.[16]

In the general election that October, the nine-member Republican legislative slate swept the county. Williams received the fewest votes of the nine but still topped the highest Democrat, thus making him the first Black person elected to the Ohio legislature.[17] The following night, Black Cincinnatians celebrated the breakthrough by marching through the city to Williams's house on Linn Street. There were two bands and, at the head of the parade, the city's two most prominent Black leaders, Robert and Peter Clark, each hailing Williams's accomplishment in a spirit of unity.

When the crowd of five hundred people arrived at Williams's house, they found him and his wife celebrating quietly with "several white personal friends."[18] The crowd massed around the entry, and the first speech of congratulations was delivered by none other than Robert Harlan.[19]

Robert swallowed his disappointment by journeying for the holidays to Washington, a place that had become a refuge for him. He and his fourth wife, Mary Clark, were leading somewhat separate lives, while Robert Jr., to his joy, had made an advantageous marriage and given him two grandchildren, a boy named Robert Dorsey Harlan, after him, and a daughter named Louise. (Another daughter would arrive a few years later.) Their happy home on N Street in Washington[20] was the fulfillment of Robert's highest hopes for his only son. Robert had endured a political backlash over his decision to send Robert Jr. to the best school in Cincinnati—the nearly all-white Woodward High—but would tolerate no less than the best for his namesake. Robert Jr. went on to Cincinnati Law School, clerked in a law office, and then, in his midtwenties, received a federal appointment as deputy internal revenue collector.[21]

That appointment, in the middle of the Hayes administration, was almost certainly the product of Robert's connections to Hayes, dating from his governorship. It helped catapult Robert Jr. to the pinnacle of Black society in the nation's capital. Even more enhancing of his status among the nation's Black elites was his marriage to the former Mamie Dorsey. Her father, Thomas, had bought his freedom in the years before the Civil War and launched a successful catering business, Dorsey's Dinners, in Philadelphia.[22] There he became active in the abolition movement, hosting William Lloyd Garrison, Charles Sumner, John Brown, and other important figures in his art-filled home. By the time Mamie married Robert Jr., both Thomas and his wife had passed away, leaving his daughter as heir to his fortune and his gallery of portraits and mementoes.

Mamie decorated her and Robert Jr.'s large home with oil paintings of Sumner, Brown, Frederick Douglass, Wendell Phillips, Thaddeus Stevens, and other heroes of the antislavery fight, along with framed letters from those figures to Thomas Dorsey. An article in a leading Black newspaper about the glamorous couple declared that an important conversation piece in their home was a "bed-stead upon which old John Brown frequently slept at Mr. Dorsey's home."[23]

In this museum-like setting, Mamie and Robert Jr. cohosted, along with the visiting P. B. S. Pinchback, one of the social events of the year in Washington's Black community just months after Robert's disappointment at the Cincinnati convention.[24] On January 2, 1880, Robert, Pinchback, and Douglass, along with many other Black elites, including Daniel and Anna Murray, among the city's leading Black socialites, gathered at Robert Jr.'s house to celebrate the new year. The eggnog was so heavily spiked that one guest insisted on "pouring in milk afterwards and bringing it back down to average,"[25] while Anna Murray entertained the guests by singing along with Miss Mattie Lawrence, one of the acclaimed Fisk Jubilee Singers.[26]

Robert's pride in his son was evident. While the self-made father had portaged canoes across a rain forest and finagled a fortune through betting games, Robert Jr.—known for being "jolly" and "big hearted"[27]—was every inch the aristocrat, with the placid air of the gently born. He would don a tuxedo and escort an exquisitely dressed Mamie to the Murrays' lavish parties, dancing to Strauss waltzes performed by Anna on the piano. At one garden party held at a Black elite resort, Robert Jr. sang several roles in a presentation of Gilbert and Sullivan's operetta *HMS Pinafore*.[28]

The fact that Robert Jr. and Mamie had to do none of the scraping and clawing of their parents served as validation of Robert's success: in one generation, his son and daughter-in-law and grandchildren were living lives almost as rich with privilege as those that James and Eliza's children had enjoyed at Harlan's Station and in the hills overlooking Frankfort.

George Washington Williams failed to thrive as an Ohio legislator, alienating many Black people in Hamilton County by pushing a bill aimed at closing off new burials in the cemetery of an African Methodist church in a gentrifying suburb of Cincinnati.[29] Williams declined to run for reelection in favor of an academic career that led to a groundbreaking role in exposing Belgian atrocities in the Congo in the late 1880s and early 1890s.[30] Williams's shift in focus worked to Robert's advantage, as he finally secured a place on the Republican legislative slate for 1881, the culmination of thirteen years of party loyalty.

Thus, he was dismayed when, on Election Day, all of the Republican candidates except himself were elected—a defeat he openly attributed to racial prejudice.

"You can imagine how far this prejudice extends when I tell you that of the ten Republican candidates for the legislature, nine were elected by majorities ranging from 1,400 to 3,500," he told the *Commercial* in an emotional interview. "I am very thankful to the 25,000 men who voted for me, but it would seem to a casual observer that if our Republican friends in Hamilton County were all consistent party men, they would have supported the whole ticket and not scratched anybody."

"The colored men of Cincinnati feel justly indignant," he added. "One of them said to me just before I left home that the Republican Party was always glad to have us as privates in the rear ranks, but when it comes to running for office, they sit right down on us and give us to understand that we were only freed for one purpose, and that was to play second fiddle at all times to our white Republican friends."[31]

Less than a year later, Robert sounded the same despairing theme in a story in the *Washington Post*, declaring, "White Republican votes defeated me . . . and I stand today as a living witness that race prejudice still has a strong foothold in the proud state of Ohio. . . . We are tired of acting as pack mules to the white Republicans." The *Post* reporter endorsed Robert's frustrations and affirmed his fitness for office, writing that had he been elected, he would have been the natural leader of the ten-member Hamilton County delegation.[32]

Robert was again in Washington for the holiday season of 1883, where he attended a meeting of the executive committee of the National Colored Committee, with two representatives for every state.[33] The entire organization was reeling from the blow of the Supreme Court's decision to strike down the Civil Rights Act. The committee convened at Carson's Hotel on December 19 and began discussing how best to respond to the disastrous news. Halfway through, Frederick Douglass arrived and proposed that they make a unanimous endorsement of Justice Harlan's dissent as a powerful riposte to the court's majority; the following day, the Subcommittee on Civil Rights formally adopted Douglass's proposal, making John's dissent the official position of the National Colored Convention.[34]

Robert's proximity to John during this period and other holiday season visits to the nation's capital raises the question of whether they spent time together. Even though society was trending toward entirely separate engagements for Black and white figures, Robert's close dealings with John over the James Davenport shooting and the 1876 Republican convention, along with their strategizing over the Supreme Court nomination in 1877, suggested they remained on good terms and would normally have sought each other out. Nothing indicates otherwise.

None of Robert's letters from John are collected, and only a selected number of John's from Robert or anyone else among his family members and colleagues has survived the decades. Nonetheless, given Robert's intense interest in the Civil Rights Act—from the days of the Chillicothe convention to his famous letter to Benjamin Butler[35]—he would not have missed a chance to express his gratitude to John in person for the stirring dissent that inspired the leaders of the National Colored Convention. John's emergence as the nation's leading white defender of Black equality would have been an enormous source of satisfaction for Robert, who had toiled so long to help make John's appointment a reality. Robert's role in helping to preserve John's political viability for the Supreme Court by clearing his name of the Davenport stigma would have resonated in Robert's mind, along with his lobbying in Washington among Republicans who opposed John because they believed he was insufficiently supportive of Black people. John's vindication on that count was also a credit to Robert's judgment and wisdom in vouching for him.

The year 1885 marked a tumultuous turn in Robert's life. In April his wife, Mary, died unexpectedly while visiting her mother in New Orleans. She and Robert had been wedded for ten years, and though each had separate finances and were often apart, he was shaken by her sudden death. She was his third wife to pass away, after Margaret and Josephine. Following a funeral at their home on Harrison Street,[36] he eventually interred her body in Union Baptist Cemetery, choosing to designate his own future resting place beside her.

A few months later, he once again became a Republican nominee for the state legislature, a sign that Black votes still tipped the scales in Cincinnati. Once again, Election Day ended in frustration, but this time the whole Republican ticket shared Robert's dismay. The 1885 Hamilton County elections were among the most corrupt in history, with each party claiming a sweeping victory. Democrats set off fireworks from their Cincinnati headquarters to celebrate the big win, while Republicans shot a cannon. By the Republican count, all their legislative candidates prevailed by between four hundred and eight hundred votes except for Robert, who trailed a Democrat named A. P. Butterfield. The Democrats proclaimed a clean sweep. But allegations of rampant fraud cast all those numbers into doubt. Suddenly the battle for control of Hamilton County was national news and a cautionary tale for urban machines.

The *New-York Times* reported credible claims of fraud, including "switching of ballots, the stuffing of ballot boxes, the stealing of Republican ballots after the boxes were opened for count in the evening, and the falsifying of returns."[37] For example, the *Times* reported, in one precinct there were 200 more votes cast than registered voters, and while 111 Republicans were known to have voted, only 48 were tallied. At first, reporters accepted the idea that Robert had lost his race in yet another instance of Republican voters refusing to back a Negro, with the *Philadelphia Bulletin* reporting that he was only on the ballot to "catch the colored vote for his companions" and was "mercilessly slaughtered in the house of his white friends."[38] But as evidence of Democratic fraud mounted, with a Republican majority in Columbus controlling the investigative apparatus, Robert's fate, too, came under scrutiny.

On January 12, 1886, the House was called to order at ten in the morning, and a minister offered a prayer: "His entire tune was that he hoped no blood would be shed," reported the *Cleveland Plain Dealer*. "In fact, he made this request at least half a dozen times."[39] Ten Democrats arrived to take the oath of office, after which Republicans moved to unseat nine of them—all but Butterfield, whose race with Robert was still undecided. Though Democrats cried fraud, they knew they were outvoted. Nine Republicans filed down the aisle to be sworn in, met by a deafening cheer from the Republican side and hisses of "Rats, Rats," on the Democratic side. In the galleries, "hats went flying into the air, handkerchiefs waved from the hands of hundreds of ladies, and the scene was one of animated rejoicing and reckless confusion, lasting for several minutes."[40]

When the celebration ended, Robert was once again "out in the cold," in the words of the *Stark County Democrat*.[41] However, Republicans quickly came to his rescue, using his race as a vehicle to prolong the investigation into Democratic fraud. The House probe went on for two more months. When it was over, Democrats still refused to acknowledge having corrupted the election, but saw the writing on the wall clearly enough that Butterfield was seen packing his belongings before any vote was taken on whether to accept the results of the investigation.[42]

On March 26, ten weeks after his colleagues had taken their seats, Robert Harlan was at last declared the winner of a seat in the Ohio House of Representatives. It was the culmination of nearly two decades of political maneuvering, and an accomplishment he had every reason to believe would always elude him. Validation came in the least triumphant manner but nonetheless attested to his endless perseverance against a rising tide of prejudice. Even in his joy, Robert saw signs of the disintegrating platform for people of color. While Republicans applauded the vote to grant him his seat, "no officer or member of the House would disgrace himself by walking down the aisle to the clerk's desk where the oath was administered to him," in the words of the Democratic-leaning *Cleveland Plain Dealer*.[43]

The *Plain Dealer* probably exaggerated the extent of the Republicans' contempt for Robert. At least three of his white legislative colleagues joined a larger group of revelers at his Harrison Street mansion on April 12, 1886. The house throbbed with celebration, as scores of friends and allies enjoyed sandwiches and beer and listened to marching band music. A long list of speakers paid tribute to the tenacious new state representative, and Robert offered his thanks in return.[44]

Robert's legislative career was less memorable than the circumstances surrounding his election. His first bill was a resolution honoring Alphonso Taft's long career in public service that had ended with his return to Cincinnati in 1885 after having served as US ambassador to Imperial Russia. Robert stood before the chamber alongside Taft himself, no doubt recalling how Robert Jr. and Alphonso's son William Howard had been classmates at Woodward High.

In February 1887, he offered a passionate speech before a state convention of Black men calling for a memorial to the radical abolitionist John Brown, whose deadly raid on the US arsenal at Harpers Ferry, West Virginia, presaged the Civil War. "He was a fit leader of that mighty host of men who died for a cause a few years later, Lincoln, Grant, John Brown," Robert declared. "The nation guards the memory of the first two. Let those for whom he lived and died rear a noble monument for the last in that Trinity of American Greatness." The *Cleveland Gazette* noted that the crowd was especially attentive to Robert's speech because he had actually known Brown, who had been hung for his role in the Harper's Ferry attack in 1859, three decades earlier. The convention adopted a resolution to push for a statue of Brown,[45] though it appears not to have been erected.

Like George Washington Williams before him, Robert also ran afoul of powerful Black constituents. His sin was to draw attention to some possible consequences of a bill that would repeal the state's Black Laws, a vestige of prewar America that enforced some forms of segregation in public life. Though Robert expressed his support for repealing the Black Laws, he raised questions about whether the portion of the bill desegregating schools would become a pretext for firing Black teachers in Cincinnati, warning that a new certification process would be skewed toward white applicants.

"Knowing that the wiping out of colored schools would necessarily throw a majority of colored teachers out of employment," he explained, "I did not desire to see those who are as well educated and have as much experience as any teacher in this city compelled to pass another examination for appointment under the new order of things." The state's leading Black newspaper, the *Cleveland Gazette*, strongly supported the repeal, which was sponsored by one of Robert's two Black colleagues, Benjamin W. Arnett of Xenia, Ohio.[46]

"The Colonel has indeed surprised us," the *Gazette* wrote, forcing Robert to backtrack with a letter proclaiming his unyielding support for Arnett's bill. But that wasn't enough to quiet the fury. The paper ran a story about a Black Cincinnati teacher who rebuked Harlan for his misguided concern that the Arnett bill would harm Black teachers[47] and, in an editorial, decried Robert's "depth of ignorance that would discredit the intellect of a wild hottentot."

The *Gazette*'s furious crusade damaged Robert's political standing in the Black community enough that Hamilton County Republicans left him off the ballot that fall, replacing him with a Black man named William Copeland. The *Gazette* described Copeland, apparently approvingly, as an "assistant market master and well-known hustler in our community. . . . The fact that he beat the Colonel for the nomination is sufficient to show his hustling qualities."[48]

At the same time as Black people in Cincinnati were suffering from a racial backlash, a Chinese man named Lee Yick was caught up in an even more sudden shift in feelings in California. During the state's rampant growth after the gold rush, the United States had encouraged Chinese workers to come to the West Coast, even promising in a treaty to protect their safety and promote their well-being. By agreement between the United States and the Imperial Chinese Government, the workers would remain Chinese citizens and would not have the right to become naturalized in the United States. The result was a flood of much-needed Chinese workers who helped build the West, especially the railroads that connected the coasts. But when the boom ended, emblemized by the Panic of 1873, Chinese workers kept arriving in the Port of San Francisco while both white Americans and Chinese of longer residency struggled to find work. "There were one Chinese and two whites for every job in San Francisco," lamented journalist Iris Chang in her book *The Chinese in America: A Narrative History.*[49]

"The gold disappeared, and with it all those businesses that supported mining and prospecting," Chang explained. "The railroad was complete, and the men who built it found themselves out of work. Thousands of ex-miners and discharged track laborers, white and Chinese, roamed the region in search of jobs."[50]

As a result, what had been, in good times, an uneasy, arms-length relationship between whites and the Chinese, became a state of roiling prejudice and hostility as whites blamed the Chinese for their misfortunes. This brought about a series of anti-Chinese actions and events that amounted to one of the most repugnant explosions of racial prejudice in American history. Over the next two decades, numerous cases stemming from injustices toward the Chinese would make their way to the Supreme Court.

Lee Yick was one of the first to have his day in court. He had come to the United States in 1861, in the relatively palmy days when Chinese immigration was encouraged. For more than two decades, he built a laundry business, a line of work that disproportionately attracted Chinese men and women. But as the backlash hit in the 1870s and intensified in the '80s, white San Franciscans took aim at Chinese businesses with an ordinance requiring all laundries in wooden buildings to apply for special permits to continue their operations. Ostensibly enacted under the local government's power to legislate for health and safety, the city's true aim became clearer when none of the two hundred Chinese applicants was granted the permit, while only one white person was rejected.[51] Lee Yick felt he had no other choice but to keep running his business and refused to pay the $10 fine for violating the ordinance. When he was arrested along with 150 other Chinese launderers, most of them businessmen of long-standing reputations, he appealed to federal courts, claiming that San Francisco was violating the Fourteenth Amendment's guarantee of equal protection under the law.

Thus, nearly a decade after it first sought to discern the scope of the Fourteenth Amendment as applied to Black jurors, the Supreme Court confronted another instance of a law that seemed neutral on its face—banning laundries in wooden buildings—but was applied in a manner to exclude all people of one race. This time, unlike in the jury cases, the court did not ascribe the discrimination to the actions of a few individuals; it felt obliged to acknowledge what "must be apparent to every citizen of San Francisco"[52]—that the ordinance was aimed at excluding Chinese.

One of John's more recent colleagues, Stanley Matthews, wrote the decision for a unanimous court: "The effect of the execution of this ordinance in the manner indicated in the record would seem to be necessarily to close up the many Chinese laundries now existing, or compel them to pull down their present buildings and reconstruct of brick or stone . . . either of which would be little short of absolute confiscation of the large amount of property shown to be now, and to have been for a long time, invested in these occupations."

As Matthews's wording suggests, the court seemed moved by the fact that business interests and properties were involved, and may have recoiled at the thought of a city government interfering in a capitalist enterprise; then, too, the fact that so many hardworking businessmen ended up being arrested and criminally charged after being put in such an impossible position couldn't have helped but sway some of the justices.

John joined the majority and had every reason to applaud the expansion of Fourteenth Amendment protections after having argued so passionately against the court's decision in the *Civil Rights Cases of 1883*. The expansion of liberties in the case of *Yick Wo v. Hopkins* were limited in scope, but significant in two respects: it established that the Fourteenth Amendment applied to everyone legally doing business in the United States; the fact that Lee Yick remained a subject of the Chinese emperor didn't alter his protections. And, secondly, it marked a step away from the court's head-in-the-sand refusal to acknowledge obvious patterns of discrimination.

While the court was debating the fate of Chinese launderers, anti-Chinese hysteria in California reached its apotheosis. In the northern river town of Nicolaus, a stopping point during the gold rush and, for decades, the home of Chinese workers, a gang of white men invaded the homes of the Chinese, forcing them all to crowd into a barge on the Feather River, and drove them out of the county. When local prosecutors looked the other way, the federal government seized on language in pre-1875 civil rights laws to prosecute ringleader Thomas Baldwin and other members of the gang for depriving the Chinese of their civil rights.

The members of the gang appealed their arrests, claiming that the specific language of the statutes referred to "citizens," and the Chinese victims were, of course, subjects of their emperor. Federal officials countered that the Burlingame Treaty, which carried the force of the US law, guaranteed that all Chinese workers would share the privileges and immunities of US citizens. The Supreme Court, which had already shown its skepticism of civil rights laws in previous cases, sided with the gang: in an opinion written by Chief Justice Waite and joined by six other justices, the court decreed that the civil rights statute didn't apply to aliens. Justice Field concurred in that judgment but disagreed with other aspects of Waite's analysis. John, however, took exception.

"By the treaty of 1880–1881 with China, the government of the United States agreed to exert all its power to devise measures for the protection, against ill treatment at the hands of other persons, of Chinese laborers or Chinese of any other class. . . . " he began. "It would seem from the decision in this case that if Chinamen, having a right under the treaty to remain in our country, are forcibly driven from their places of business, the government of the United States is without power in its own courts to protect them against such violence or to punish those who in this way subject them to ill treatment. . . . I do not think that such is the present state of the law, and must dissent from the opinion and judgment of the court."[53]

While conceding that the civil rights law used the term *citizen*, he pointed to the fact that it explicitly intended to punish anyone who deprived people of their "rights secured by the Constitution or laws of the United States."[54] Four years after his ringing dissent in the *Civil Rights Cases of 1883*, John was once again standing apart from all his colleagues in calling for greater civil rights protections for all Americans.

John's willingness to advocate for Chinese workers was the product of his more expansive reading of the powers granted to Congress in the Fourteenth Amendment and his firm belief that the court should give wide latitude to the opinions of Congress. The following year, 1888, those same beliefs conspired to put him on the opposite side of his colleagues in the case of a Chinese worker who left the country but, while on his way back to San Francisco, was aboard a vessel that was attacked by pirates. The worker, Jung Ah Lung, declared that the certificate authorizing his reentry was part of the booty stolen from the ship. Upon his arrival in San Francisco, he related his dramatic tale and asked if other documents showing him to have been a US resident would suffice to get him readmitted. An immigration clerk refused to accept anything but the proper certificate. The refusal left Jung stranded on a steamship in the harbor. He sued for unjust imprisonment.

Six of the nine justices reasoned that, since the theft was beyond Jung's control, and his other documents appeared to demonstrate his legitimacy, the immigration clerk was wrong to refuse reentry. John, writing for himself and Field and Justice Lucius Lamar, maintained that the clerk was merely following the expressed will of Congress.

"We have been unable to reach any other conclusion [than] that the Congress intended, by the act of 1882, to prohibit the return to this country of any Chinese laborer . . . unless he produced such certificate at the time he sought to reenter," John wrote. "If the appellee's certificate was forcibly taken from him by a band of pirates, that is his misfortune. That fact ought not to defeat what was manifestly the intention of the Legislative branch of the Government."

Jung's dilemma was shared by other laborers who left the United States and returned, only to find changed laws and unyielding officials. In its eagerness to choke off the flow of Chinese workers—138,941 of whom had come between 1870 and 1880[55]—Congress adopted ever more stringent restrictions in the early and mid-1880s. Those laws often were challenged by Chinese workers who were denied reentry into the United States. The most legally significant of the challenges was brought by a man named Chae Chan Ping, who came to the United States under the protection of the Burlingame Treaty in 1875, only to witness a dramatic tightening of the laws.

The so-called Chinese Exclusion Act, which banned new workers arriving from China, was signed by President Arthur in 1882. Though it didn't alter the status of Chinese people already in the country, a revision in 1884 required workers to obtain a permit for return before leaving the country. Chae obtained the permit before heading back to China in 1885; after a yearlong stay, he boarded the steamer *Belgic* for the weeks-long voyage from Hong Kong to San Francisco. Unbeknownst to him, a few days after his departure, the United States tightened the rules yet again—this time banning the return of all Chinese workers who had left the country, whether or not they had obtained a permit under previous laws. That left him stranded at the docks of the city he had called home for a full decade.

Backed by a network of well-funded Chinese advocacy organizations, Chae obtained the support of some of the leading lawyers of the day, including former Ohio governor George Hoadly and Thomas S. Riordan, who specialized in challenges to the Chinese Exclusion Act. They argued that the protections Chae had received from the Burlingame Treaty and earlier laws amounted to an implied contract—or at least a promise that the government was bound to honor—to allow him to return to the country.

The court unanimously disagreed, asserting that Congress's power to establish immigration laws was absolute, and that subsequent laws would naturally overrule earlier statutes and treaties. The court's opinion, by Justice Field, declared that, as an expression of national sovereignty, the United States had the power to control its own borders.

Field, the former gold rush entrepreneur and California judge, didn't stop there. He went beyond the holding to offer reasons why excluding the Chinese was a sound policy.

"It seemed impossible for them to assimilate with our people, or to make any change in their habits or modes of living," Field wrote disparagingly of the Chinese. "As they grew in numbers each year, the people of the [West] coast saw, or believed they saw, in the facility of immigration, and in the crowded millions of China, where population presses upon the means of subsistence, great danger that at no distant day that portion of our country would be overrun by them, unless prompt action was taken to restrict their immigration."[56]

Field's hysterical language marred the court's decision in the more enlightened eyes of later generations, though the holding has never been overruled. While few people would argue with the idea that an act of Congress would overrule earlier laws, including treaties,[57] advocates had hoped that the court would recognize the essential unfairness of Chae's situation and find a way to credit his reliance on past laws.

So why would John Marshall Harlan, who just six years earlier had invoked basic fairness as a consideration deciding whether civil rights legislation was enabled by the Constitution, go along with the decision? For one thing, there were significant differences in the cases. No one on Chae's team argued that the Chinese Exclusion Act was racially discriminatory. There was no claim raised under the Fourteenth Amendment's equal protection clause. All agreed that the underlying legal issue in the case was whether a subsequent act of Congress could nullify a treaty, and Harlan—the champion of a strong national government—had no doubts on that score.

Still, the court's handling of cases like *Chae Chan Ping v. United States* became a coda to a sad chapter in American history, in which prejudiced Californians succeeded in prodding Congress to curtail

Chinese immigration as a way of appeasing white economic frustrations. Even though the court—and Harlan himself—did, on some occasions, advocate for Chinese victims, it did not disrupt the flow of progressively more punitive laws.

Four years after its decision in the case of Chae Chan Ping, the court went further in supporting Congress's right to demand that even long-tenured Chinese workers register with the government or face deportation.[58] In that decision, however, John played no part. He was in Paris on a special mission, serving as one of two arbitrators appointed by President Benjamin Harrison in an international dispute over control of the Bering Sea, in which major powers battled over fur trading and the need to protect seals.

The chance to go abroad for the months-long Bering Sea arbitration came after a much-needed expansion of the federal court system had reduced some of the workload of the Supreme Court, minimizing the number of mundane appeals and allowing the justices to concentrate on the most important disputes.[59] This would give John, in the latter half of his tenure on the court, a greater opportunity to place his own mark on the law for generations.

In the meantime, he welcomed the break that President Harrison's request permitted. He and Malvina had long ago given up any hopes of seeing what she called the "Old World."[60] They encouraged their children to make ambitious travels in their stead.[61] Now, much of the family—son Richard and his wife, daughters Laura and Ruth, and granddaughter Edith—had an opportunity to spend the better part of fifteen months overseas, with the esteemed justice and his wife feted by some of the aristocratic heads of Europe.[62]

The trip also presented a break from domestic challenges. Finances were bleak. After Edith's death, John came to believe that the family's home on Massachusetts Avenue would always be painfully marked by her presence. He and Malvina made the decision to move to the faraway suburb of Rockville, Maryland, more than an hour's commute from the court. Malvina acknowledged that the move was partly a way to reduce spending,[63] and that living so far from John's workplace wasn't feasible for the longer term. Since their parents were tapped out, John's three sons agreed to borrow money to buy a suitable home for the justice on Washington's Euclid Place.[64] Predictably, the new residence became both a source of happiness and another drag on all their finances.

There were also family pressures emanating from Kentucky, where both John's brother, James, and his nephew, James's son, Henry, were in ruinous alcoholic and drug-addicted declines.[65] Close in age to John, James had fallen into such a state that he sometimes spent nights on the street, partially clothed, drenched by rain and infested with vermin.[66] Warned by a friendly postmaster that James would use any money that John sent to buy opium, John chose instead to wire cash with instructions that it be used to provide James with necessities.[67] Gus Willson, John's young protégé who had practiced law with James, helped to look after him at John's behest for the better part of a decade, sending bulletins back to Washington on James's faltering attempts at sobriety. "As he is now going, he will be in the gutter and penniless before the summer is over unless he is taken charge of at once and held in," Willson reported in one grim dispatch early in James's struggles.[68]

John accepted responsibility for his brother but also often expressed exasperation. When Henry Harlan, James's son, was fired from his government job for drinking, and appealed for help, John shot back with an avuncular warning about the dangers of alcohol. "Frankness compels me to say that your case is a hopeless one, if you touch strong drink at all," John wrote. "One drop is evidence to me that you are destined to a drunkard's grave at an early day, and, supposing that you now and then drank, I had concluded that it was a waste of time for me to follow after you as I have often others, and try to save you from ruin."[69]

John's frustration stemmed not just from James's and Henry's battles but also those of additional relatives in his and Malvina's extended families; in a letter warning his son John Maynard of the dangers of addiction, John keyed his own success to limiting the use of alcohol and tobacco.[70] But what seemed like good, hard advice and common sense to John felt like the back of his hand to James, who railed in letters against his more successful younger brother.

"You have done your best to degrade me," James wrote to John in an undated letter that may have been in response to John's decision to use the postmaster as an intermediary for sending money. "It's cruel and mean to treat me in this way. . . . You can't do worse than you have done if you were my enemy. God knows I don't deserve such treatment."[71]

Though they lived in different cities, James Harlan maintained a steady contact with Robert as well as John. At many points, James seems to have confided his problems in Robert, who extended a no-strings-attached offer of assistance. It's unclear whether James actually drew on Robert for funds, but he was not only grateful for what he considered Robert's kindness but also contrasted it with John's displays of what would later be called tough love.[72]

"It is well settled beyond change that I can't stay here," James once wrote in seeming desperation to John. "I am afraid to do so. Bob Harlan has often offered to assist me, but I do not wish to be driven to the necessity of appealing to him—my position is as deplorable and contemptible as it can be, and few have been so utterly abandoned by fate as I have."[73]

In an even more groveling appeal to John, James wrote, "If you can't help me, I can try others—Bob Harlan will let me have the money if he has it."[74]

James doesn't say whether Robert gave him a loan, but soon after making that suggestion to John, he seemed to take a turn for the better. He was able to make a new start in uncharted territory, now Oklahoma. The change of scenery did him an initial bit of good. His letters to John were far less hostile and more fraternal, and he again expressed appreciation for Robert's kindness.[75] Given Robert's own willingness to venture forth on the road to self-improvement, it's easy to envision him encouraging James to put his disappointments behind him. "Bob Harlan has for two years been unusually kind to me, not, however, putting me under any obligation," James wrote to John.[76]

For Robert, James's willingness to take him into his confidence and seek comfort, even for the purpose of securing a loan, served to affirm his place in the Harlan family; simply put, James treated Robert as a brother. The fact that James was contrasting Robert's generosity with John's tough love most likely annoyed John. But there is no record that John ever gave James the satisfaction of a response.

With no illusions about James's condition, John was only too willing to embark on a mission in Europe. There he would have the pleasure of taking his place among respected fellow judges at the Bering Sea tribunal in Paris, sharing with Malvina the vast beauty of the Rhine River Valley,[77] and comparing legal perspectives with the leading lawyers of London at a party hosted in his honor by the US ambassador, Robert Todd Lincoln, son of the Great Emancipator.[78]

Though more than a year in duration, the trip went by like a whirlwind. "After our fifteen months of stay in Europe . . . it was most interesting to see my husband's joy at being again in his own country and with his own people," Malvina wrote later. ". . . We returned to our land just in time to see the wonderful Chicago Exposition, after which my husband resumed his work on the Bench with new vigor and interest."[79]

Indeed, John would add a new pitch to his voice, speaking for the average worker and taxpayer against the corporate amalgamations that were strangling the economy. And, just like in the years before his European journey, his voice would be heard the loudest when ringing in dissent.

Chapter 13

In Trusts We Trust

On March 23, 1888, a blue-eyed, slightly rotund man of medium height[1] took the witness seat before the US House Committee on Manufacturers and made himself a national hero.[2] Claus Spreckels was no stranger to the "vertical integration" that enabled Gilded Age businessmen to amass fortunes by controlling means of transport and production. A sugar baron, he also managed to own the largest shipping line between Hawaii and California, and thus was able to procure the entire Hawaiian sugar crop to refine at his plant in San Francisco.[3] Dominance was his goal, and wealth was his creed.[4] But Spreckels also purported to understand the dangers of monopoly, the mysterious tipping point when acts that seem like mere efficiencies, streamlining production and distribution, become constraints on trade. A German immigrant who rose from store clerk, to beer brewer, to one of the richest Americans of his era, Spreckels was no liberal reformer.[5] He was nothing if not a believer in free enterprise. But he was firmly against the trusts that strangled American businesses and consumers alike.

On that day, he explained to Congress how the Sugar Trust, created by the Havemeyer family, owners of American Sugar Refining Company, pressured him to join with them to eliminate competition. Spreckels claimed to know little of the inner workings of the New York–based conglomerate that was his main competitor, but offered a story about how he was approached by an agent for the Havemeyers.

"I asked what inducement there was to go into the trust, and all I could get was 'when you are in the trust, you are in the trust and can't get out,'" he testified. "I came here from Germany for liberty, gentlemen, and that liberty I will maintain."[6]

For that he received an ovation.[7]

Thus began the sugar wars of the late nineteenth century, with the public cheering for the multimillionaire David taking on the Goliath of the Sugar Trust. Hoping to establish a foothold in the trust's East Coast domain, Spreckels built the world's largest and most modern refinery in Philadelphia. "The trust has trampled on my toes, and I won't stand it," he said shortly after his testimony before Congress.[8] A year later, he proclaimed, to the delight of his fans, "I am my one and only trust."[9]

In 1891 Spreckels reduced the price of granulated sugar produced at his Philadelphia plant to one-sixteenth per pound below the price charged by American Sugar.[10] Shortly thereafter, the Havemeyers cut their price to one-sixteenth per pound below Spreckels.[11] American consumers, whose love of sugar was so great that they were on their way to each consuming a whopping seventy pounds of it per year,[12] rejoiced. Then, just as suddenly as it began, the sugar war was over. Spreckels's company, along with three other Philadelphia refiners, including the E. C. Knight Co., quietly entered into deals with American Sugar. Virtually overnight, the trust controlled 98 percent of the refining capacity in the United States. Only the tiny Revere company in Boston—so small that it almost didn't register on the national market—remained a holdout.

The Havemeyers won. So did Claus Spreckels. The losers were the everyday Americans who cheered on Spreckels in the belief that he alone was powerful enough to stand against the wave of monopolization that was repressing factory wages and commodity prices paid to farmers, while removing the competition that kept costs low for consumers.

Those who applauded Spreckels shifted their hopes to the only institution powerful enough to take on the trusts: the federal government. That force had thus far been sheathed. Even while acknowledging that national conglomerates were swallowing local manufacturers at a record clip, cutting exclusive deals with railroads to drive out any remaining competitors and then setting prices in a way that often hurt both farmers and consumers, the federal government raised its hands in surrender. Corporations were creatures of the states, not the federal government. That translated into a belief that states alone could solve this problem, at least in the eyes of federal lawmakers, some of whom were themselves awash in campaign cash from the trusts.[13]

The states weren't prepared to handle such a fundamental shift in the American economy, either. Between 1865 and 1873, the United States laid thirty-five thousand miles of railroad tracks,[14] at a cost and pace that required enormous ongoing investment backed, at various points, by government entities. Railroad loans bloated the coffers of northeastern banks while railroad profits boosted Wall Street to unseen heights; but most of the tracks pointed West, where states quickly became dependent on the rail lines and investors for everything from consumer goods to carrying farm products to market. State officials who catered to the railroad barons often found themselves rewarded with Pullman passes for free travel and sometimes even private cars (Pullman was the manufacturer of railroad cars, a name that soon became synonymous with the railroads themselves).[15]

"The *State Journal* is to-day able to give its readers the first plausible reason for the reduction of the Pullman taxes in Kansas, which was made this year by the state board of railway assessors," proclaimed the *Winona Clipper*. "It now appears that the men, who only a few months ago were trying to make political capital . . . by pretending to be enemies of the corporation . . . had Pullman passes in their pockets all the time." The Kansas state attorney general, state treasurer, and state auditor all blithely acknowledged getting unlimited free transportation from the railroads.[16]

When, under intense pressure from farmers and consumers, states began reining in the size of the conglomerates that conspired with railroads to drive competitors out of business, the trusts simply shifted their incorporation papers to friendlier venues. New Jersey, which struggled under a heavy bond debt from the Civil War, turned around its finances virtually overnight by making itself the most trust-friendly state in the country—gladly willing to enable the largest combinations.[17]

That only increased the heat on the federal government. In response, both Democrats and Republicans began paying lip service to the need to "bust" the largest trusts, even as each party remained under pressure from its pro-business northeastern wings to do nothing of the kind.

In the 1884 presidential election, a Democrat prevailed for the first time in twenty-four years—a system-cleansing event at a time when most government jobs were partisan appointments. But this breakthrough was accomplished at some cost to the party's core principles; in seeking a nominee, the Democrats pragmatically turned to the governor of New York, Grover Cleveland, who was more conservative than the party's agrarian base. Nonetheless, in a race against James G. Blaine—who finally scored the Republican nomination for which he had toiled much of his life—Cleveland represented the voice of the people against the giant industrial combinations. Blaine's ties to railroads and other corrupting influences was a major issue in the campaign, and Cleveland countered with a plan to lower tariffs, which would allow more foreign-made goods into the market, as a way of countering the growing power of corporations.

Dogged by a weak economy, however, Cleveland narrowly lost the White House four years later to Benjamin Harrison, a scion of the legendary Virginia family of military leaders and statesmen who had made his career in Indiana. In a nomination battle against the better-known Ohio senator John Sherman, Harrison gained the support of the party's northeastern wing as the lesser of two evils. Nonetheless, even such devout Republicans as Harrison and Sherman were increasingly worried about monopolies throttling the economy. In an early echo of what would become "national greatness" conservatism under Teddy Roosevelt, Harrison favored an aggressive foreign policy and stronger federal government. His support for American business interests was leavened by his conviction that the federal government must assert the power to control industrial combinations.

At this odd moment, when both major parties teetered between support for business and concern about monopolization, the government produced one of its most significant pieces of legislation: the Sherman Antitrust Act. Even more mysteriously, the act passed with near-unanimous backing in Congress: 242 to 0 in the House, and 51 to 1 in the Senate. The sweeping support, after very little debate, suggested the measure was embraced both by true reformers and pro-business conservatives, the latter of whom may have been looking for political cover to pass the notorious tariff increase known as the McKinley Tariff.[18]

Sweeping in its language—"Every contract, combination in the form of trust or otherwise, or conspiracy, in restraint of trade or commerce among the several States, or with foreign nations, is declared to be illegal"—the Sherman Act was nonetheless hampered by the vagueness of concepts such as "restraint of trade." Plainly, Congress wanted to make a strong statement of its willingness to address the problem of trusts, but, just as plainly, it was counting on presidential administrations and the Supreme Court to separate the truly problematic trusts from corporate business as usual.

At first, nothing happened. The Sherman Act was signed into law by President Harrison in 1890, but the administration took no steps to enforce it, while corporate lawyers started a debate about whether it was enforceable at all. Of the two major bills of 1890, the McKinley Tariff proved to be the more consequential in the short term, as the economy began to sputter. Harrison paid the price. The campaign of 1892 was a rematch between Cleveland and Harrison, neither of whom campaigned aggressively, partly in consideration of the failing health of Harrison's wife, Caroline.[19] Much of the energy was supplied by the insurgent candidacy of People's Party nominee James B. Weaver, who won five western states and garnered 8.5 percent of the national vote on an ardently antitrust platform. Nonetheless, Cleveland prevailed over Harrison, 46 percent to 43 percent in the popular vote, with a slightly larger margin in the electoral college.[20]

The return to power was a great vindication for Cleveland. Four years earlier, his young wife, Frances, had cheekily told the ushers to keep the White House ready for when they moved back in.[21] But within months of the family's triumphant return, Cleveland confronted the Panic of 1893, an economic freefall that led to rampant voter anger and demands for action against the trusts. Spurred by the collapse of overextended railroads such as the Philadelphia and Reading, which led to a banking crisis, the panic deepened into a four-year national depression—among the worst in American history. With the People's Party organizing with renewed vigor across the West, much of the public clamored for Cleveland to dust off the Sherman Antitrust Act to take on the business elites who were responsible for the downturn. That decision, however, fell to his taciturn attorney general, Richard Olney. The son of a New England mill owner and banker, the fifty-seven-year-old Olney had risen to prominence as the favorite attorney of Boston's upper classes and, when the railroad boom took hold, as New England's premier railroad attorney.[22] In choosing Olney, Cleveland had respected the Bostonian's probity and welcomed a "competent" New Englander to provide geographic diversity in his cabinet.[23]

Olney, however, radiated skepticism about the Sherman Act, expressing in his first Justice Department annual report that the public must not assume a broad interpretation of the government's powers under the act. Caution was his byword. His "estimate of the meaning of the law corresponded to the [narrow] opinion of the Bar; but not with public demand," a biographer conceded in 1923.[24] The Boston Bar Association, Olney's professional home turf, felt that rampant prosecutions under the act would destabilize the economy. Later, the association editorialized in appreciation of Olney that "clearly he would have been guilty of demagogic and irresponsible extravagance had he launched the Government on a wide campaign of prosecution . . . in disregard of his own well-grounded misgivings about the law, and in the face of the business panic of 1893."[25]

There remained, however, the well-documented saga of the Sugar Trust—of how the public had cheered on Claus Spreckels as he railed against the morbid power of American Sugar, trying to suck every competitor into its maw, only to watch the feckless Spreckels capitulate and join the trust. This seemed, in the public eye, to be a vivid demonstration of how monopolization cost the nation jobs, economic growth, and innovation, while harming farmers and consumers. The ever-greater disparities of wealth seemed to grow inevitably out of this foul equation. Even Spreckels had alluded to the trust's determination to control both the purchase of sugar cane from farmers and the price of products on the open market.

The *New Orleans Times-Picayune* noted that the trust paid less for Louisiana sugar than that produced elsewhere even though it had a nearby refinery and could save on transportation costs. "It would appear that common prudence would dictate that a monopoly protected by the laws from foreign competition should not risk arousing popular resentment by taking undue advantage of the fact that it has practically the power to dictate prices," the paper opined shrewdly in the fall of 1893.[26]

Finally, with some evident reluctance, Olney decided to file suit against American Sugar, Spreckels, E. C. Knight Co., and two other Philadelphia refiners who had sold out to the trust, declaring them all in violation of the Sherman Antitrust Act. His case called for American Sugar to return the stock and property to the four Philadelphia-area manufacturers, thereby holding the trust below 70 percent of the nation's refining capacity.[27]

It seemed modest enough, but the mere decision to pump life into the Sherman Act set off alarms at the highest reaches of the business world. For the leading moguls of the age, the Supreme Court loomed as the best, and perhaps the last, recourse for the giant trusts that dominated the economic landscape.

The same forces that had remade the business world, creating a small class of national leaders with astounding wealth, also transformed the practice of law. Storefront practices and small partnerships, in which even the best-connected lawyers collected modest fees, gave way to far larger firms anchored by superlawyers whose negotiating skills and ability to navigate their way around regulatory schemes rendered them invaluable to the moguls of the age. Their stake in the trust-based economy was as great as that of the men who paid them. Far more than hired hands, they were power brokers who stood on equal footing with their corporate clients. Olney had been such a lawyer in Boston. In Chicago, his opposite number was the man to whom he would now address his arguments against trusts: Chief Justice Melville Fuller.

The colorful, avuncular Fuller, with a haystack of gray hair and drooping, broom-like mustache, looked so much like the humorist Mark Twain that he was often mistaken for his man-of-the-people doppelganger. But while Fuller shared some of Twain's twinkle-eyed persona, he differed considerably in his political sensibilities. The child of a couple who divorced when he was one year old, in an era when few families split up, Fuller was raised by his maternal grandfather, a judge in Augusta, Maine.[28] Like John Harlan, who was born the very same year, young Fuller carried a childhood destiny to excel in the law. Unlike John, who went on to fight in the Civil War and toil with mixed success in the politics of a war-ravaged state, Fuller fled Maine as a young man, avoided military service, and made a fortune representing banks and railroads.[29]

Fuller watched Chicago boom from a destination of about a hundred thousand inhabitants when he arrived in the late 1850s to a metropolis of more than a million when he left to take his post as chief justice, following the death of Morrison Waite in 1888.[30] Elegant, stone-fronted office buildings designed by famous architects would go up along Michigan Avenue only to be torn down a few years later and larger ones erected in their place; the 1871 Chicago Fire helped clear the way for the development of the skyscraper and the most distinctively American architectural vernacular, the prairie house. Behind all this opulence was teeming poverty in immigrant enclaves on the South Side and West Side, a fact underscored by repeated labor convulsions: from the 1877 strikes to the bloody Haymarket riots of 1886, in which a peaceful rally for an eight-hour workday descended into violence when someone threw a stick of dynamite at police.[31] In 1894, just as the Cleveland administration was deciding to take on the Sugar Trust, Chicago exploded again with the Pullman strike, triggered when the company that made railroad cars slashed wages by up to 50 percent in response to the Panic of 1893, with no reductions in rents and utilities in the company-owned town where workers lived.[32]

Nonetheless, as he grew from youth to middle age, Fuller watched the creation of entire industries in his beloved Chicago, the frontier town that grew overnight into one of the world's leading cities. Cosseted in his own wealth and called upon repeatedly to represent private businesses against government regulators, he emerged an arch-believer in capitalism, the system that spun gold out of the Illinois prairie grass.

As it happened, Fuller's ascension to the court's leadership, in the last days of the first Cleveland administration, was followed by the appointment of two more justices who grew wealthy representing corporations: Henry Billings Brown, another northeasterner who found his pot of gold in the Midwest—in his case, in Detroit[33]—and George Shiras Jr., one of the richest corporate attorneys in Pittsburgh, who also happened to be the cousin of James G. Blaine.[34]

They joined a court that still included Stephen Field, joined recently by his nephew David Brewer, on a bench that had grown markedly more conservative in the seventeen years since Harlan's appointment. This was the lineup that, in 1894, prepared to hear the Sugar Trust's challenge to the charges brought by the Cleveland administration, with the trust's defense led by John G. Johnson, another titan of corporate law who was renowned for his representation of J. P. Morgan, the world's leading financier.

The Cleveland administration appeared to believe the case was cut and dried: it aimed to show that the Sugar Trust was, indeed, a monopoly with the power to set prices, and therefore in violation of the Sherman Act. But the lower courts seemed unwilling to accept the government's assertions, and it soon became clear that Olney's team had skimped on its fact-finding.[35] A court-appointed federal examiner established that the trust did, indeed, control more than 90 percent of the US refining capacity, and got John E. Searles, the agent for American Sugar who engineered the purchases of the Philadelphia refineries, to acknowledge that the industry had been in an "unsatisfactory condition" because of overproduction before the mergers, though he disclaimed any intent to set higher prices. Searles agreed that sugar prices had since gone up, but not by so much as to reach a record high.[36] A wholesale grocer testified that the trust fixed prices but also noted that there were limits on how high it could go before foreign sugar became a viable alternative.[37]

Based on this mixed bag of evidence, lower courts declared that the government had failed to demonstrate that the trust had fixed prices in restraint of interstate commerce and threw out the case. In its petition to the Supreme Court, the government sought to clean up its case with some simple arithmetic: the trust refined almost all the sugar in the country; the states where the trust had plants constituted only about half the national population; sugar, however, was "consumed throughout the United States in proportion to the population." Therefore, it was a mathematical certainty that the sugar was sold across state borders at prices established by the trust.[38]

The fact that sugar was transported across state lines was important because the Constitution gives Congress the power to regulate interstate commerce; any transaction that occurs purely within a state is beyond the legal reach of the federal government.

Even though American Sugar sold its product across the country, Johnson argued that it was a monopoly in manufacturing alone; when it came to interstate commerce, it was beholden to the market. Johnson's theory was hardly foolproof: it would have been no leap at all for courts to assume that a manufacturing trust that sets prices was seeking to restrain interstate commerce. But Johnson found a highly credulous audience on a Supreme Court of wealthy, pro-business conservatives who seemed only too eager to limit the scope of the Sherman Act.

As the justices prepared to hear the arguments, people across the country began to take notice, realizing, in the words of the *Boston Journal*, that the decision would be "of the greatest importance, as upon it depends not only the results of similar suits instituted against other corporations alleged to exist in violation of the law, but also the law itself."[39]

The decision came three months later, on January 21, 1895. Fuller wrote for the entire court except for a lone dissenter. The only hint of the chief justice's avowed affability was in the occasionally sorrowful tone of his opinion, as if he understood the popular desire behind the Sherman Act but acceded to the cooler wisdom of the law.[40] Otherwise, he offered a dry treatise laying out the differences between manufacturing and commerce, and then striking down the case on the grounds that Congress lacked the power to regulate a manufacturing monopoly, only a commercial monopoly, and the government had failed to prove that the Sugar Trust restrained commerce.

Concluded Fuller, "There was nothing in the proofs to indicate any intention to put a restraint upon trade or commerce."[41]

Why did Fuller not believe that having just a single seller was a restraint on trade? Perhaps he felt that the trust, even as a monopoly supplier, had to accede to consumer demand. Or perhaps he felt that foreign sugar, even if blocked by tariffs, represented more than the whiff of competition that statistics suggested it was. But the chief justice didn't feel the need to explain himself any further.

Once again, John Harlan asserted himself as the lone dissenter. This case, designated as *United States v. E. C. Knight Co.*, bore some of the emblems of his earlier bucking of the court's majority in the *Civil Rights Cases*. He accused the court's majority of construing Congress's power so narrowly as to deprive the democratically elected representatives of the tools to address a pressing national concern. In the *Civil Rights Cases*, it was racial discrimination; in this case, it was protecting a free and fair market for farmers, consumers, and businesses alike.

"The Constitution, which enumerates the powers committed to the nation for objects of interest to the people of all the states, should not therefore be subjected to an interpretation so rigid, technical, and narrow that those objects cannot be accomplished," he declared, invoking his namesake and hero, Chief Justice John Marshall, who said the Constitution must be construed to give Congress powers commensurate with its status as a legislature capable of addressing national issues.[42]

Even accepting the court's distinction between manufacture and commerce, Harlan suggested, the majority strained credulity in giving credence to the idea that a monopoly manufacturer who buys out all competitors doesn't necessarily interfere with interstate commerce.

"A general restraint of trade has often resulted from combinations formed for the purpose of controlling prices by destroying the opportunity of buyers and sellers to deal with each other upon the basis of fair, open, free competition," he stated. "Combinations of this character have frequently been the subject of judicial scrutiny, and have always been condemned as illegal because of their necessary tendency to restrain trade." [43] He painstakingly cited numerous state cases as examples.

"It is said that there are no proofs in the record which indicate an intention upon the part of the American Sugar Refining Company and its associates to put a restraint upon trade or commerce," he continued. "Was it necessary that formal proof be made that the persons engaged in this combination admitted in words that they intended to restrain trade or commerce? Did anyone expect to find in the written agreements which resulted in the formation of this combination a distinct expression of purpose to restrain interstate trade or commerce? Men who form and control these combinations are too cautious and wary to make such admissions orally or in writing." [44]

As in the *Civil Rights Cases*, Harlan chided his brethren for obtuseness—for willfully ignoring the problem at hand in their eagerness to guard against congressional overreach and thereby treading on legislative turf. Rather than focus on the prices obtained through interstate sales, he maintained, the justices should look at a trust's overall effect on the stream of commerce: how it quashes competitors and alters the market before the first products are sold. "Any combination . . . that disturbs or unreasonably obstructs freedom in buying and selling articles manufactured to be sold to persons in other states, or to be carried to other states—a freedom that cannot exist if the right to buy and sell is fettered by unlawful restraints that crush out competition—affects not incidentally but directly, the people of all the states," he declared.

Finally, as in many of his dissents, Harlan implored his fellow justices to adopt a realistic view of the facts at hand: "It is conceded that the object of this combination was to obtain control of the business of making and selling refined sugar throughout the entire country. Those interested in its operations will be satisfied with nothing less than to have the whole population of America pay tribute to them. That object is disclosed upon the very face of the transactions described in the bill. And it is proved—indeed, is conceded—that that object has been accomplished to the extent that the American Sugar Refining Company now controls ninety-eight percent of all the sugar refining business in the country, and therefore controls the price of that article everywhere."

Despite all those stipulations, Harlan bemoaned, the court somehow found its way to believing that the Sugar Trust was not an unlawful combination, even under the sweeping language of the Sherman Act.

As a result, he warned, the flow of goods necessary for the "well-being of the people" might soon find itself "under the absolute control of overshadowing combinations having financial resources without limits and an audacity that recognizes none of the restraints of moral obligations controlling the actions of individuals; combinations governed entirely by the law of greed and selfishness—so powerful that no single State is able to overthrow them."[45]

Harlan's eye-opening rebuke, like the court decision itself, only added to the tumult of the moment, especially among farmers feeling the pinch of lower prices for their crops and laid-off factory workers with nowhere to turn but settlement houses, the charitable living option for people without money. In between the court's hearing of arguments and its decision, Republicans had borne the benefit of the Panic of 1893 and made huge gains in the congressional elections;[46] even though progressives were also making inroads into the Democratic Party, the beneficiaries of the economic collapse, for the moment, were conservatives.

Protests followed the court's decision in the *Knight* case, demanding that the Cleveland administration undertake more prosecutions under the Sherman Act.[47] Olney, however, seized on the court's decision to pull back. "The government has been defeated on the trust question," he said. "I always supposed it would be and have taken the responsibility of not prosecuting under a law I believe to be no good."[48] What followed was a drought in antitrust actions that would last until Theodore Roosevelt's presidency, seven years later.

States tried, with fitful success, to fill the void. In 1897 Henry O. Havemeyer, the president of American Sugar Refining Company, was called to testify before a special committee of the New York State Legislature investigating trusts. "The tendency of the testimony was to show that the American Sugar Refining Company does control the price and output of refined sugar in the country, which Mr. H. O. Havemeyer admitted," the *New-York Tribune* reported. "He insisted this was not the object of the company."[49]

Trust consolidation and combination accelerated. By 1901, J. P. Morgan had combined three of the nation's largest steel companies into U.S. Steel, with a market valuation of $1.4 billion[50]—almost three times the entire federal budget.[51] It controlled about 70 percent of the steel market in the United States.[52]

That same year, John wrote a letter to his protégé and law partner, Gus Willson, warning that "The greatest injury to the integrity of our social organization comes from the enormous power of corporations."[53]

But John wouldn't have to wait long for another chance to weigh in on the Sherman Act and Congress's power to regulate interstate commerce. Alone among his greatest and most passionate dissents, his opinion in *United States v. E. C. Knight Co.* would essentially become the law of the land in his own lifetime.[54]

Chapter 14

Requiem for the Gilded Age

On January 30, 1894, a thirty-three-year-old congressman, swept into office in a populist wave that covered the South and the West, took to the floor of the United States House of Representatives to respond to claims that he was fomenting anger against the upper classes. With his black hair slicked back and his large body standing in robust defiance, he challenged his colleagues to question their own assumptions about taxation. Why, he asked, were tariffs on basic goods considered a sound economic method of financing the government, while taxes on higher incomes were stigmatized as class warfare?

"They tell us that it is wise to limit the use of the necessaries of life by heavy indirect taxation, but that it is vicious to lessen the enjoyment of the luxuries of life by a light tax upon large incomes," he declared. "They tell us that those who make the load heaviest upon persons least able to bear it are distributing the burdens of government with an impartial hand, but that those who insist that each citizen should contribute to government in proportion as God has prospered him are blinded by prejudice against the rich. They call that man a statesman whose ear is tuned to catch the slightest pulsations of a pocketbook and denounce as demagogue anyone who dares to listen to the heartbeat of humanity."[1]

By the end of his long, extemporaneous peroration, the young congressman had established himself as a hero to progressive reformers. Outside of the House chamber, in the vast spaces of the nation, an economic crisis of unfathomable dimensions was unfolding. Millions of lower-wage workers had lost their jobs in the past year, with no safety net to cushion their fall. And the depression of the 1890s had yet to bottom out.[2]

Suddenly people inside and outside of government were listening to this young Nebraskan, with his gift for soaring oratory and passionate connection to farmers and mill workers angered by a government that paid greater attention to the financiers of the Northeast.

Whether in hope or fear, William Jennings Bryan was a name to remember.

If trust-busting was a frontal attack on giant industrial combines, the creation of a federal income tax was a rearguard action against the accumulation of wealth among Gilded Age moguls. While never as much of a populist rallying cry as antitrust actions or expansion of the money supply through silver-backed currency, the income tax nonetheless struck an even greater terror in the monied elites. Many could foresee a permanent shift from tariffs on goods to taxes on income; in that atmosphere, the newly agitated masses would be constantly tempted, like wide-eyed children before a candy jar, to eat away at the great fortunes. Defenders of the status quo believed that great wealth and great achievements went hand in hand; without the incentive to earn a fortune, who would develop the industries of tomorrow and the powerful transportation networks to carry those products to market?

As the Panic of 1893 took hold, progressives set their sights on the "bourbon" Democratic administration of President Grover Cleveland. Though he was a president of their own party, Democratic progressives felt that the New Yorker was hardly their leader. Not only had Cleveland stood steadfastly behind the gold standard, even as financiers rushed to cash in their greenbacks for gold bars, but his administration would go on to borrow $60 million from the nation's richest financier, J. P. Morgan, to buy back his own gold reserves.[3] To pacify the progressives, Cleveland sought a sharp reduction in tariffs. This would anger northern industrialists, whose purchase of raw materials might become more expensive, but help rural communities by loosening restrictions on agricultural exports. There remained the question of how to make up the lost revenue. Bryan had battled unsuccessfully in the House and within the administration for a silver-backed currency; but the young congressman had better success in rallying southern and western lawmakers behind an income tax. More importantly, President Cleveland was receptive.

Thus, in 1894, the winds of populist change in American politics ran into a hurricane of the monied interests in Congress, producing a strange and unsatisfying economic package known as the Wilson-Gorman Tariff Act. Initially intended as a free-trade measure, cutting tariffs dramatically while filling the revenue void with an income tax, the bill was heavily altered in the Senate. Business-friendly senators inserted protections for numerous industries, including the always-aggressive Sugar Trust. This frustrated both Cleveland and Bryan, who could only take cold comfort in knowing that the income tax had made it through the gauntlet.[4]

On the surface, the measure seemed benign enough—just a 2 percent levy on incomes over $4,000 (or about $90,000 in 2021 dollars). But it marked the first peacetime income tax in history. Abraham Lincoln had helped finance the Civil War with an income tax, but that was easily dismissed as a one-off—an emergency measure that was discarded in the postwar boom. The new income tax of 1894, by contrast, portended a shift toward a permanent income tax, and the opening of a can of worms that would permanently infest the pocketbooks of the wealthy.

Despite the fury of many rich Americans, there appeared, at first, to be no grounds for a legal challenge. True enough, the Constitution imposed some restrictions on federal taxes, but they had been ironed out over a century of Supreme Court jurisprudence that clearly supported the right of Congress to impose an income tax. In seeking to

John Marshall Harlan was born in the Old Stone House that his grandfather built (shown here shortly before its demolition), set above a verdant pasture and the bucolic Salt River in Kentucky's famed Bluegrass Country.

2

3

John was the sixth child, and fifth son, born to James Harlan, known for amassing the best private law library in the state, and his wife, Eliza Davenport Harlan.

The great Chief Justice John Marshall, who asserted the Supreme Court's power to review the constitutional basis of laws passed by Congress, was James Harlan's hero. In naming his son after Marshall, James created the prophecy that put young John on a path to the Supreme Court.

Tall, rugged, and handsome, Robert Harlan (seen here in middle age) was an enslaved man for whom James Harlan had a special regard—and who was widely believed to be James's son.

Malvina Shanklin was fifteen when she saw twenty-year-old John "walking as though the whole world belonged to him." They were married three years later.

The famed Kentucky senator and presidential candidate Henry Clay was a close friend of the Harlan family. John, like Abraham Lincoln, grew up revering Clay's willingness to put national loyalty ahead of states' interests.

Desperate to preserve the union, John—by now a renowned politician in his late twenties—spent days and nights in Kentucky's Old State Capitol Building, successfully preventing Governor Beriah Magoffin, a Confederate sympathizer, from having Kentucky join the rebellion.

Shown here in his colonel's uniform, John raised his own regiment to the support the North, seeing considerable action throughout the long western campaign.

The daring Confederate raider John Hunt Morgan was the bane of the Union forces in Kentucky and Tennessee, but Harlan's men defeated him at Rolling Fork near the Salt River, preserving a crucial railroad bridge.

While John built a precocious political career, Robert Harlan bought his freedom, undertook a perilous journey across the continent, and made a fortune in San Francisco during the gold rush.

Robert took his newfound wealth across the Ohio River to booming Cincinnati, the first stop of freedom for enslaved men and women coming north on the Underground Railroad. The riverfront, filled with steamboats, is shown here in 1840, about a decade before Robert made his move.

14

Robert used his money to invest in Black-owned businesses, including the famed Black hostelry known as the Dumas House (*left*). Elegantly dressed cardsharps matched wits in the ornate front room while runaways from slavery were hidden in secret chambers. Robert was one of the nation's first Black owners of racehorses, famed for his ability to size up an animal's racing potential based on a visual examination. He competed against white owners at plush venues such as Louisville's Oakland House and Racecourse (*right*).

In a daring move, Robert took his horses to England in a highly publicized challenge to British supremacy. He kept his mounts in Newmarket, where the British gentry ruled the "sport of kings" from the exclusive Jockey Club, shown here.

Though his racing fortunes waned, Robert spent the Civil War years in Europe, including a stint in the Thames River town of Richmond, where he lived in this handsome rowhouse.

CAPT. O. S. B. WALL, U. S. A.

After serving as Kentucky's wartime attorney general—from which post he fought federal efforts to force abolition of slavery in the state—John turned strongly against slavery and its legacy. He befriended the great abolitionist Frederick Douglass (shown here), sparking a backlash at home.

When a drunken cousin of John's shot the respected Black leader Orindatus Simon Bolivar Wall, John's reputation was tarnished. Robert stepped in to smooth the waters with the Black community, thus preserving John's image in the Republican Party.

When Republicans gathered in Cincinnati for their 1876 national convention, both John and Robert were major players: while John led the forces for his friend Ben Bristow—and helped settle the nomination by directing Bristow's delegates to support Rutherford B. Hayes—Robert entertained the nation's top Black leaders.

Rutherford B. and Lucy Hayes: John's decision to transfer Bristow's support to Rutherford B. Hayes earned him considerable political clout. Later, Malvina Harlan would become close to Hayes's spirited wife, Lucy Webb Hayes

A prophecy fulfilled: Hayes rewarded John with appointment to the Supreme Court. After overcoming the skepticism of northern Republicans who doubted his commitment to civil rights, John was sworn in on December 10, 1877.

When an usher at New York's plushest theater—the Grand Opera-house—was indicted for refusing to seat a Black customer, it set in motion a challenge to the Civil Rights Act of 1875. The Supreme Court ruled 8 to 1 that the law was unconstitutional. Harlan's wide-ranging dissent signaled his break with his colleagues in fundamental ways.

A vivid intellect and colorful personality, Justice Stephen Field crafted laissez-faire economic doctrines that blocked government from addressing social and economic ills, and became a Harlan foe.

Peter H. Clark, Robert Harlan's friend and rival among Cincinnati Black leaders, argued forcefully that the Republican Party was betraying its colored supporters.

4

Sugar baron Claus Spreckels blasted the Sugar Trust for price-fixing, then joined it and benefited from the Supreme Court's decision against the Sherman Anti-Trust Act, over Harlan's passionate—and prescient—objection.

Amiable and often mistaken for his look-alike Mark Twain, Chief Justice Melville Fuller oversaw the court for most of Harlan's tenure. They got along personally but clashed over civil rights and economic justice.

6

Harlan joined his colleagues in striking down a biased law designed to shutter Chinese laundries in San Francisco (above). But Harlan's failure to speak up for Chinese rights in some other cases led to subsequent criticism.

When Homer Plessy was arrested for refusing to sit in a separate car for Black people on the East Louisiana Railroad, it led to the case in which the Supreme Court endorsed the notorious separate-but-equal doctrine. Harlan stood alone in opposition. His passionate dissent became an enduring statement of moral purpose and intent in the law.

"We, a jury composed of men who know cigar values, find that the plaintiff, the Judge Harlan Cigar, is entitled to recover 10 cents from every smoker"

Judge Harlan 5¢ Cigar

HART & MURPHY, MAKERS, *ST. PAUL, MINN.*

Behind the veil of segregation, Harlan was a deeply revered figure and a household name in America's Black communities, as evidenced by this attempt to market "Judge Harlan Cigars" in Black newspapers.

On major cases, Henry Billings Brown, the author of the court's opinion in *Plessy v. Ferguson*, frequently took the opposite side from Harlan. The two would clash again in the famed Insular Cases, in which Harlan was the court's leading exponent of granting full constitutional rights to people in Hawaii, the Philippines, Puerto Rico, and other US protectorates.

Joseph Lochner, an immigrant baker, ran afoul of state laws restricting the number of hours employees could work in a week. His challenge resulted in one of the most notorious Supreme Court rulings against labor protections, despite Harlan's vigorous dissent.

Known as Robert Jr., Robert James Harlan, the son of Robert Harlan, was a distinguished, erudite figure. But segregation ended his and his father's dream of Black people achieving equality through education and accomplishment.

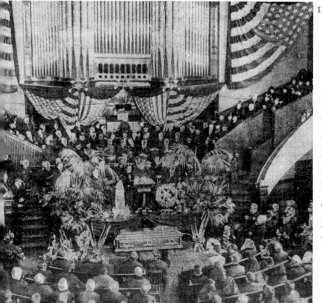

In a sign of how much had changed between 1865 and 1895, America's white leadership shunned the massive funeral of abolition leader Frederick Douglass; only Harlan and Ohio's senator John Sherman deigned to join the largely Black mourners.

Ed Johnson Who Was Lynched.

the jail office. Then a few more came in, and after awhile there were about 75. About one-third of them were actively engaged in what followed.

While some of them argued with Gibson, two heavy doors were laboriously battered down. Just two and one-half hours were consumed at the jail by the mob, and in the course of that time Sheriff Shipp was summoned to the jail by telephone. He endeavored to argue with the mob but was locked up in a bath-room.

After securing him the mob dragged the negro through the street, vetoing the suggestion of several men "to kill him now."

On the bridge, all demands for a confession were met with the words from Johnson, "I'm ready to die, but I never done it." He was promptly hoisted off his feet by a rope round

Door Where Lynchers Entered Chattanooga Jail.

A laborer from Chattanooga, Ed Johnson was convicted in 1906 of raping a white woman despite substantial evidence of his innocence. Harlan stepped in to order a review of the trial, in a landmark attempt to assert federal oversight of deeply biased procedures in southern states.

14

Outraged by Harlan's order, a white mob seized Ed Johnson from a lightly guarded jail and hung him from Chattanooga's Walnut Street Bridge. Harlan then persuaded the court to prosecute the sheriff and others for contempt of court, marking the first and only time the Supreme Court stood as a trial court.

In his last years on the court, Harlan embraced his role as its leading advocate of civil rights. "God bless our country," he said at a testimonial banquet. "God bless every effort to sustain and strengthen it in the hearts of the people of every race subject to its jurisdiction and authority!"

Malvina Harlan (shown in her later years) was a shrewd observer of the Washington scene whose autobiographical recollections attest to her love for her husband and her constant role in supporting and advising him in his work on the court.

Harlan's Presbyterian faith guided him throughout his life, and he spent decades on the board of Washington's New York Avenue Presbyterian Church. His final mission—unfulfilled—was to build a new Presbyterian cathedral in the nation's capital.

The first Black woman appointed to
the federal bench, Constance Baker
Motley, had been a leader in the fight to
end segregation. She extolled Harlan's
dissent in *Plessy v. Ferguson* as the prime
legal source of inspiration and guidance
in the fight for civil rights.

Future Supreme Court justice Thurgood
Marshall, who as a litigator succeeded
in overturning the separate-but-equal
doctrine through *Brown v. Board of
Education of Topeka*, was a deep Harlan
admirer, insisting that Harlan's views, not
those of the *Plessy* court, represented the
true spirit of the Constitution.

John Marshall Harlan II, Harlan's
namesake grandson, joined the Supreme
Court shortly after *Brown v. Board of
Education*. Harlan remains the only
Supreme Court justice to have a direct
descendant serve on the court.

A powerful symbol of the importance of an independent spirit and adherence to principle in judging, a portrait of the aged John Marshall Harlan adorns the justices' conference room in the US Supreme Court Building.

prevent the federal government from unfairly targeting one state over another, Article I, Section 9, clause 4 of the Constitution declared that "no capitation, or other direct, tax shall be laid unless in proportion to the census." The focus on "capitation"—a flat fee applied per head—seemed to underscore the framers' intentions: each head had to be treated equally, whether in New York or South Carolina.

The reference to "other direct" taxes, however, proved more difficult to adjudicate. Some economists envisioned a clear line between "indirect" taxes on economic activity and "direct" taxes on people and property. But the line wasn't so clear in the furious litigation that inevitably attended the imposition of any sort of tax. When, in 1796, President George Washington imposed a levy on horse-drawn carriages, seeking to make the wealthy pay a greater share of the nation's debts, opponents tried to get it overturned as a direct tax.[5]

The carriage dispute underscored the fact that even the framers of the Constitution didn't have a common definition of direct taxes. One delegate to the Constitutional Convention, Rufus King of Massachusetts, had asked for clarification of the term's meaning while the document was being debated; he didn't get an answer, and the faulty language remained.[6] When the carriage tax passed, no less a constitutional father than James Madison opined that it was, indeed, a direct tax and thus impermissible. His fellow author of the Federalist Papers, Alexander Hamilton, took the opposite view. Hamilton traveled to Philadelphia to personally defend the tax before the Supreme Court. His three-hour argument, which was attended by "the most crowded audience I ever saw there," in the recollection of one justice, carried the day: every justice agreed that a carriage tax was "indirect," largely because it applied to consumption rather than "capitation."[7]

Thus began a long string of cases in which justices whittled down the definition of "direct" taxes to only two types: per-head levies and taxes on land holdings. When, in 1881, the high court addressed the case of a man who had refused to pay the Lincoln-imposed income tax, believing it to be unconstitutional, the justices ruled against him unanimously, declaring that "direct taxes, within the meaning of the

Constitution, are only capitation taxes, as expressed in that instrument, and taxes on real estate."[8]

In the eyes of the entire nine-member court, including Justice Harlan, the Civil War income tax was an entirely permissible form of federal taxation. But a lot had changed in the thirteen years since the court's ruling. Even if the new income tax was nearly identical to its Civil War–era cousin, the politics behind it were not. Fears of rising populist sentiment and an assault on free enterprise dominated the nation's news coverage. Conservative newspapers in the North portrayed the income tax as "class legislation," in which the poor soaked the rich, "an invasion of private rights," "discriminatory," and "communistic."[9] And in the eyes of many of its backers, the tax was, indeed, a way to get the rich to carry an appropriately greater share of the nation's burdens.

No one was more outraged—and sensed a keener opportunity to make a mark on the law—than a rising young attorney named William Dameron Guthrie. At thirty-five, Guthrie was already one of the true wunderkinds of the bar, with a reputation for brilliance and cockiness in equal measure. Born in California, he had made his way to New York as a teenager and worked as a messenger boy at the blue-chip firm of Blatchford, Seward, Griswold and Decosta. He dropped out of Columbia Law School to enter the bar at age twenty-one. Within a few years, he was so sought after as a corporate attorney that the firm changed its name to Seward, Decosta, and Guthrie.[10] He spent much of his twenties obtaining financing for railroads and defending them against financial claims. This put him in direct contact with many of the wealthiest men in the country—the very men who were apoplectic over the advent of the income tax.

He shared their concerns. Guthrie, too, saw a giant wave of populist anger rising in the nation and wondered if it would come crashing down on American business. Congress—even the Senate, with its aristocratic airs—could no longer be trusted. Only the courts could protect the corporate elites. The Constitution made no mention of capitalism, but Guthrie believed fervently that corporate protections were embedded in that document, and that justices—so many of them corporate attorneys like himself—just needed to be given a plausible argument to believe it, too.[11]

With his head of bushy, brown hair, narrow eyes burning with intensity, and toothbrush-sized mustache, Guthrie looked less like a corporate titan than a door-to-door salesman—which, in some sense, he was.[12] To defeat the income tax, he'd have to make the sale of a lifetime—persuading the Supreme Court that for a hundred years, in case after case, it had been entirely wrong about what constituted a direct tax.

That wasn't the only hurdle Guthrie faced. First and foremost, the court had a strict policy of refusing to review federal policies before they took effect; in other words, people would have to pay the tax first, and then sue to have it declared unconstitutional. Guthrie knew, however, that to wait until millions of dollars had been collected would put too much pressure on the courts to approve the tax. A difficult argument would become an impossible argument.

This put Guthrie's brain into overdrive. He devised an end-run around the court's rule: he recruited a minor stockholder named Charles Pollock to sue the giant Farmers' Loan & Trust Company of New York (later known as Citibank) to enjoin it from paying the income tax.[13] The case was entirely concocted by Guthrie, to the point that he even recruited the lawyer to defend Farmers' Loan & Trust.[14] After a trial court dismissed the case on the grounds that it was premature, Guthrie appealed. Worried that the case would be delayed— or, worse, that the Supreme Court would choose a different case on which to judge the constitutionality of the income tax—Guthrie then urged the US solicitor general, Lawrence Maxwell Jr., to intervene in his case. This provided an expedited route to the Supreme Court and had the further effect of causing chaos in the Cleveland administration. Spurred by Guthrie, Maxwell had acted without the approval of the president or the attorney general, and was forced to resign after what was reported to be a "violent quarrel" over his insubordination. That left the overburdened attorney general, Richard Olney, to defend the income tax himself.

As the case proceeded, Guthrie sent letters to his firms' clients and other wealthy Americans, likely including John D. Rockefeller and the Astor family, to help cover the costs of the case.[15] The case may have borne the name of humble Charles Pollock, a near-anonymous Massachusetts man who happened to own ten shares of Farmers' Loan & Trust, but the real plaintiffs were the monied elite of the entire country.

Guthrie's youthful brashness—his refusal to follow any rules but those he made up himself—was what propelled the case forward, but even he seemed to realize that such qualities might be a liability in arguing before the much grayer and more procedure-bound Supreme Court. This problem was solved by using the money Guthrie collected from his clients to bring aboard the nation's most prominent litigator, Joseph Hodges Choate. At sixty-three, Choate was a confidant of presidents, negotiator of international treaties, and seemingly permanent fixture on the national scene. Though renowned for his relentless cross-examinations, he was also an avuncular presence who would go on to a successful diplomatic career.[16] He exuded stability and spoke in portentous terms about the stakes of the case. "If this law is upheld," Choate offered about the income tax, "the first parapet would be carried, and then it would be easy to overcome the whole fortress on which the rights of people depend."[17]

If Guthrie provided the audacity necessary to overturn a hundred years of Supreme Court precedents, Choate was the kind of man who could soothingly nudge skeptical justices into line. He shared their class and their manners; even if Choate was, effectively, representing the richest of the rich, he seemed to convey a concern for the national interest in his every thought, word, and gesture.

On March 7, 1895, Guthrie and Choate led an unprecedented dream team of nationally prominent lawyers into the Supreme Court chamber of the Capitol. Two of these titans were especially familiar to John Harlan; his longtime Kentucky friend and ally, Benjamin Bristow, with whom he'd fallen out over Bristow's presidential race and John's subsequent court nomination, and George F. Edmunds, the

civil-rights-oriented former senator who had opposed John's nomination before becoming his friend. Attorney General Olney headed
the Justice Department team that would argue for the government,
and James C. Carter, the lawyer recruited by Guthrie to represent
Farmers', would stand in for the banking defendants.[18]

Perhaps out of respect for all the legal eminences—or perhaps signaling his desire to give the plaintiffs every opportunity to challenge
the court's previous rulings—Chief Justice Fuller allotted an almost
unprecedented five days for arguments. Nonetheless, his own court
was hampered in its ability to hear the case. Justice Howell Jackson
had contracted tuberculosis shortly after his appointment to the
court in 1893; rather than resign, he went home to Tennessee in an
attempt to recuperate, but rarely was able to make it to Washington.
With Jackson's empty chair, there were only eight justices to hear the
case.[19]

The assault on the income tax was major news and as much a
topic of everyday conversation as any other case in Supreme Court
history. Congressmen lined the back of the court chamber; lawyers
traveled by train from every corner of the land to witness the greatest minds of their generation sparring over the future of the country.
Those who stayed home could not only follow the news reports but
also read large excerpts of the written arguments, thoughtfully reproduced in newspapers everywhere.[20]

In those written arguments, the plaintiffs shrewdly chose not to
make a direct attack on *Springer v. United States*, the unanimous ruling in favor of the Lincoln-era income tax. Rather, they sought to
tear it apart in a piecemeal fashion. First, they claimed to accept the
case's core holding that a tax on earned income was indirect and thus
permissible; but they zoomed in on the part of the tax that applied
to earnings derived from rents on real estate properties. Since the
Springer decision had declared that real estate taxes were direct taxes,
shouldn't a tax on rental income, which diminishes the economic
value of the real estate, also count as a direct tax? Moreover, Congress
included income from stocks and bonds, but carved out exemptions
for certain types of bonds; such picking and choosing meant that the

tax was not applied evenly. Each head was not treated the same. Further, the plaintiffs argued that the court had rightly given Congress broad powers to impose an income tax to fund the Civil War, which was necessary in a time of emergency, but in peacetime, there were other, less intrusive means of funding the government.[21]

In the courtroom, Guthrie sought to reassure the justices that the rich men paying his bills were patriots committed to funding the government, declaring, "We are not instructed to present any argument which shall abridge the taxing power of Congress or embarrass the government in any emergency that may now exist or hereafter arise. Let Congress remodel the act, apportioning direct taxes and equalizing indirect taxes, within the limitations of the Constitution, and none more willingly that our clients will contribute their share of the burden to maintain, defend, and preserve the national government even if it should take all their property."[22] (Guthrie seemed to have abandoned the fiction that poor Charles Pollock was his client, not the nation's wealthiest titans.)

He continued in his high-flown tone: "Recognizing that authority to tax in its nature must be without limitations except equality of burden, and that it involves the power to destroy, we are here to plead that the destruction must result from some necessity or peril of the union, and must be equal and uniform and not of selected individuals or classes: we are here to plead that Congress cannot sacrifice one—the lowliest or the richest—for the benefit of the others."[23]

Thus, in earnestly flowering language, did the youthful Guthrie present a 2 percent income tax as a "destruction" of wealth and property, aimed in discriminatory fashion at the very wealthiest of Americans. His esteemed partner, Clarence A. Seward, nephew of Abraham Lincoln's secretary of state, William H. Seward, followed him to the dais and further sought to ease any discomfort the justices may have had of stepping away from the *Springer* precedent so soon after it was issued.

"There is a tradition in the legal profession that once when a suggestion was made to Mr. Lincoln that a judicial decision settled a question, he responded with some firmness that in this country nothing was settled until it was settled right," Seward declared, with no one escaping the reference to his uncle's old friend and comrade, the slain president. "Upon that basis, we are here, Your Honors, to ask for a modification of the decision in the *Springer* case."[24]

While Guthrie's and Seward's arguments were lawyerly and intended to massage the justices, Edmunds, the former senator, was bombastic. He went straight at what he saw as the nakedly class-based politics of the measure. Known for his steadfast support for Black rights, on which he found common ground with John Harlan, Edmunds was also a defender of the capitalist system and a former railroad attorney.[25]

"It would be interesting to know how many of those who voted for the tax expected to pay a part of it," Edmunds quipped sarcastically in a courtroom speech likened by one newspaper to "a tirade." The former senator wondered openly "how long the government can last under a system which allows those who pay nothing to tax their fellow citizens. One evil step will lead to another, as one vice follows another, until by and by we will have revolution, then anarchy, and then a tyrant to rule us."[26]

The Justice Department lawyers, led by Olney, sought to turn down the temperature. Their core argument was that the court need only to follow its own precedent—a clearly marked path—to uphold the income tax. But they also sought to defang some of the claims made by Guthrie and Edmunds.[27]

Edward Whitney, an assistant attorney general, argued that the term "direct tax" applies only to a tax on a fixed item, not something as variable in nature as an income. And he rejected Guthrie's notion that a tax on some but not all forms of income wasn't applied uniformly under the Constitution. The requirement of uniformity, he argued, was geographic in character, and "means that the tax must be the same in each State that it is in every other State"—not that it must affect each person equally.[28]

Both Olney and Carter, the lawyer for Farmers' Loan & Trust, de-

cried the emotional overload of Edmunds's arguments and, by extension, the fears of the wealthy and the warnings of a coming revolution,
calling them "mere clamor."[29] More to the point, Carter suggested that
the court should not try to substitute its political judgment for that of
Congress, saying, "Nothing could be more unwise and dangerous—
nothing more foreign to the spirit of the Constitution—than an attempt to baffle and defeat a popular determination by a judgment in
a lawsuit."[30]

That prompted a sharp response by Joseph Choate, who finally
showed his worth in rising with rhetorical thunder to present the
closing argument for the plaintiffs. After a long anecdote referencing Jupiter and Mercury and "the inhabitants of Olympus," the famed
attorney declared, "I thought that this court was created for the purpose of maintaining the Constitution as against unlawful conduct on
the part of Congress. It is news to me that Congress is the sole judge
of the measure of the powers conferred to it by the Constitution, and
it is also news to me that the great fundamental principle that un-
derlies the Constitution—namely, the equality of all men before the
law—has ceased to exist."[31]

". . . I have felt the responsibility of this case as I have never felt
one before and never expect to again," Choate continued solemnly.
"I do not believe any member of this court ever has sat or ever will
sit to hear and decide a case the consequences of which will be so
far-reaching as this—not even your venerable associate who survives
from the early days of the Civil War, and has sat on every question of
reconstruction, of national destiny, or state destiny, that has come up
in court during the last thirty years."[32]

After such epic thunder—and epic flattery, in Choate's tribute to "venerable" Justice Field, whose tenure stretched back to the Civil War—
the court's decision came surprisingly quickly, just a month after the
start of the arguments. It was as if Chief Justice Fuller were disinclined
to allow a single dollar to be collected without the court's approval.
Unfortunately, the court failed to resolve most of the issues; the eight

justices split 4 to 4 on three of the most important legal questions. However, a five-justice majority agreed that a tax on rental income was the same as a property tax—or, at least, not "intrinsically" different enough to merit separate treatment. "We are unable to perceive any ground for the alleged distinction," the chief justice declared.[33]

Field, the seventy-seven-year-old prophet of free enterprise, went further, suggesting in a concurring opinion that any graduated tax would be unconstitutional on the grounds that it was lacking in uniformity. Channeling the deep emotions that infected all aspects of the case, Field launched into a wistful lecture on economics and good citizenship: "Under wise and constitutional legislation, every citizen should contribute his proportion, however small the sum, to the support of the government, and it is no kindness to urge any of our citizens to escape from their obligation. If he contributes the smallest mite of his earnings to that purpose, he will have a greater regard for the government, and more self-respect for himself, feeling that, though he is poor, in fact, he is not a pauper of the government. And it is to be hoped that, whatever woes and embarrassments may betide our people, they may never lose their manliness and self-respect. Those qualities preserved, they will ultimately triumph over all reversals of fortune."[34]

The Louisianan Edward White, who had just joined the court as a Cleveland appointee that year, wrote a dissent challenging Fuller's contention that taxes on rents were equivalent to taxes on real estate; the first Confederate veteran to be appointed to the court and—by one account, at least—a former Ku Klux Klan member, White was no moderate on the social issues of his time, but he was a deep skeptic of the power of northeastern business elites.[35]

White proceeded to eviscerate Fuller's claim of little "intrinsic" difference between a rental tax and a property tax, pointing out that the rental tax is collected only if the property yields income; its application is entirely different from a direct tax on the property itself. "If land yields no rental, it contributes nothing to the income," White stated. "If it is vacant, the law does not force the owner to add rental value to his taxable income. And so it is if he occupies it himself."[36]

Harlan joined White's dissent and added his view that the court should never have heard the case, because the tax hadn't been collected yet, and the central issue—whether an income tax was direct or indirect—was already resolved by precedent. "Upon the several questions about which the members of this court are equally divided in opinion, I deem it appropriate to withhold any expression of my views, because the opinion of the chief justice is silent in regard to those questions," Harlan wrote, in a broad hint at violent disagreements to come.[37]

Those remaining questions loomed large. First was the issue of whether the tax on stocks and bonds was permissible under the Constitution. Then there was the matter that so concerned Justice Field: whether a tax that does not apply to everyone is unequal and therefore unconstitutional. Finally, there was the question of whether the entire tax law should be invalidated if only portions of it were found to be inconsistent with the Constitution.

Choate, as the senior plaintiffs' counsel, applied for a rehearing, which was promptly granted. Then, in a series of cajoling letters, Chief Justice Fuller suggested that the absent Justice Jackson should resign if he weren't able to hear the case, prompting the terminally ill Tennessean to jeopardize his life in making the journey to Washington for the rehearing. Now there would be a full complement of nine justices to hear the case.[38]

The arguments in the rehearing were sufficiently boiled down that most of the plaintiffs' legendary team of lawyers remained on the sidelines; only Guthrie and Choate reprised their arguments, receiving praise from the press for their forceful lucidity. They were answered by Olney and Whitney, whose performances were widely panned. At one point, Whitney acknowledged that he was "not so carefully prepared" as he had been for the first hearing—a shocking admission from a lawyer arguing before the highest tribunal in the land. Olney appeared so disengaged that he ended up using only half the time apportioned to him.[39]

The drama in the courtroom was nothing, however, compared to the drama behind the scenes, as the justices engaged in arm-twisting

and other machinations that were only hinted at in public. Those maneuvers apparently prompted one justice who had been in favor of the
tax in the first vote to change his position in the second round. That
proved decisive, because, in the end, the ailing Justice Jackson came
down in favor of the tax, along with White, Harlan, and Henry Billings Brown. The fact that the formerly absent judge voted to uphold
the tax should have settled the matter decisively in favor of Cleveland
and Bryan and the progressives who had fought so long for the income tax. But that didn't happen. One of the justices who supported
the tax in the first vote shifted his position to strike it down; since
Fuller hadn't revealed the names behind the 4-to-4 split, observers
could only speculate on which justice changed his position and why.[40]

The sense that Fuller had engaged in backstage manipulations
was enhanced by the haste with which the chief justice rushed to announce the results, before opinions were completed. In this, he was
prodded by Justice Field, who claimed to have suffered a botched
injection of carbolic acid into his injured knee that left him in such
pain that he feared he would die before the case could be resolved. In
a conspiratorial-sounding letter to the chief justice, he warned that
should he lose his fragile "hold on life," then "our action in reference
to the Income Tax cases would be entirely defeated."[41]

Field would live another four years, but Fuller acted as though
every minute were critical. On Monday, May 20, just a month after
the rehearing and three days after Field's letter, Fuller gaveled the
court into session to announce a stunning 5-to-4 vote, invalidating
the tax on income from stocks and bonds, along with rental income,
and declaring that because of those deficiencies, the entire tax must
be struck down.[42]

After the chief justice expounded on the matter for nearly an
hour, the forces of dissent had their say. This time it was Harlan, not
White, who rose to counter Fuller, and he did so with an explosive
passion that etched itself into the memories of almost everyone in the
crowded chamber.

Socialism in action. Assault on American values. Destruction of property through taxation. The poor storming the castles of the rich. All of the accelerants thrown on the pyre of the income tax of 1894 left a strange residue in the air of the Supreme Court chamber. At times it seemed like the court had ceased to exist as a judicial tribunal, and a ghostly parliament of philosophers had taken over the red-velvet seats at the front of the room. There was Joseph Hodges Choate—who lived in baronial splendor in Lenox Hill, Manhattan, and Stockbridge, Massachusetts—declaring that the nation was more imperiled by this 2 percent tax than any other threat in his memory. Stephen Field, fearing that the end was near, vowed to destroy the income tax as a valedictory expression of his life's values. There were also the behind-the-scenes maneuvers, the shifting of votes, and Fuller's unseemly haste to deliver the decision.

It was a time when everyone seemed to lose his mind and reach into his soul; however, while Edmunds and Choate sketched out an apocalyptic vision for the nation if the tax were allowed to go forward, there had been no corresponding reach for the heavens on the pro-tax side. The government lawyers were businesslike in their duties; Carter, the defense lawyer recruited by the plaintiffs, got good reviews, but mostly for sticking to the facts and trying to tamp down the drama.[43] There was no Bryanite defender to counter the existential passions stirred up by the plaintiffs.

John Marshall Harlan filled that gap. As always in his most stirring moments, one could see how his teachings and life experiences played on his jurisprudence—how his rural Kentucky upbringing gave him a detached perspective on the issues stirred up by the industrial revolution; how his faith in the wisdom of a strong national government, harkening back to his Whig childhood, overrode any concerns about overreach in taxation; and how his intense focus on equal protection under the law, the best curative for the strife that caused the Civil War, led him to believe that the rich were using their powers to thwart the normal processes of democracy.

That theme—that the court was taking extraordinary action in redefining what constituted a direct tax, based on no new evidence at all—saturated the lengthy dissent; clearly, Harlan implied, the mandate for change came not from any fresh insights on the law but rather the justices' antipathy for the income tax, and their sensitivity to the class-based fears it aroused. They were acting less as independent arbiters and more as rich people eager to preserve their privileges. The dubiousness of the legal argument against the tax was clear to see. Fuller, in his majority opinion, claimed to base the decision on the "plain and obvious" language in the Constitution, but how could a truth that eluded even the Founding Fathers be so suddenly obvious and easy to discern?

"A question so difficult to be answered by able statesmen and lawyers directly concerned in the organization of the present government can now, it seems, be easily answered, after a reexamination of documents, writings, and treatises on political economy, all of which without any exception worth noting, have been several times directly brought to the attention of this court," Harlan declared. "And whenever that has been done, the result always, until now, has been that a duty on incomes, derived from taxable subjects, of whatever nature, was held not to be a direct tax."[44]

By contrast, Harlan offered, justices for a hundred years believed that, if a tax were applied directly—that is, per head or per acre—it should be apportioned equally among the states. The mere fact that an income tax cannot be apportioned based on the census confirms that it is indirect and thus permissible under the Constitution. He proceeded to review the findings of numerous cases that supported this logic.

Now, he argued, the court's strange turnabout on its own past decisions served to strand the federal government without the capacity to raise large amounts of revenue, except through tariffs on trade, which would quickly diminish in wartime.

"In my judgment—to say nothing of the disregard of the former adjudications of this court, and of the settled practice of the government—this decision may well excite the gravest apprehensions," Harlan declared. "It strikes at the very foundations of national authority, in that it denies to the general government a power which is or may become vital to the very existence and preservation of the union in a national emergency, such as that of war with a great commercial nation, during which the collection of all duties upon imports will cease or be materially diminished. It tends to reestablish that condition of helplessness in which Congress found itself during the Articles of Confederation."[45]

Finally, and most powerfully, he aimed at the moral core of the decision, its reordering of the burdens of citizenship: in the wake of the *Pollock* decision, he contended, the prime instruments of wealth will now be beyond taxation, while the more meager incomes of working classes remained subject to levies. The concepts of fairness and equality had been turned on their heads.

"Let me illustrate this," he went on. "In the large cities or financial centers of the country, there are persons deriving enormous incomes from the renting of houses that have been erected, not to be occupied by the owner, but for the sole purpose of being rented. Nearby are other persons, trusts, combinations, and corporations, possessing vast quantities of personal property, including bonds and stocks of railroad, telegraph, mining, telephone, banking, coal, oil, gas, and sugar-refining corporations, from which millions upon millions of income are regularly derived. In the same neighborhood are others who own neither real estate, nor invested personal property, nor bonds, nor stocks of any kind, and whose entire income arises from the skill and industry displayed by them in particular callings, trades, or professions; from the labor of their hands, or the use of their brains.

"And it is now the law, as this day declared, that . . . Congress cannot tax the personal property of the country, nor the income arising either from real estate or from invested personal property . . . while it may compel the merchant, the artisan, the workman, the artist, the author, the lawyer, the physician, even the minister of the Gospel, no one of whom happens to own real estate, invested personal property, stocks, or bonds, to contribute directly from their respective earnings."[46]

Harlan's turning the class argument on its head—his implication that this was, after all, the rich asserting their privileges over the poor, rather than vice versa—caused immediate waves of praise and criticism, rippling outward across the country; but critics seized on more than just his words, attacking the supposedly disrespectful manner in which he asserted his points.

The conservative *New York Sun* reported that Harlan "pounded the desk, shook his finger under the noses of the Chief Justice and Mr. Justice Field, turned more than once almost angrily upon his colleagues of the majority, and expressed his dissent from their conclusions in a tone and language more appropriate to a stump speech at a Populist barbecue than to an opinion on a question of law before the Supreme Court of the United States."[47]

Even the less conservative *New-York Times* suggested that Harlan "turned deliberately to the Chief Justice, who sits next to him, and gesticulated almost in his very face."[48] The *New-York Tribune* also found Harlan intemperate, noting that "Old lawyers who had practiced at that tribunal for more than a quarter of a century sat aghast as sentence followed sentence."[49]

Did Harlan go too far? The determination to seize on the practical consequences of a decision was, by then, a Harlan trademark that rankled some lawyers but wasn't more of a digression than, say, Justice Field's expounding on his own economic principles and sense of "manliness and self-respect." Harlan's willingness to address directly the elephant in the room—the class-based sentiments that were behind both the legislation and the legal challenge—provoked predictably angry responses, given the deep conviction among corporate businessmen that the rich were the victims in the case. But the presentations by Guthrie, Choate, and Edmunds had all been saturated with class-based arguments; Harlan wasn't crossing any line that hadn't been violated routinely in the case for months.

Unlike his dissent in the *Civil Rights Cases*, whose enormous impact in the Black community was largely hidden from whites by the rising walls of segregation, Harlan's dissent in *Pollock* was a sensation across the nation. Letters of praise and criticism poured in. Some wanted the justice to run for president; others decried his dissent as grandstanding calculated to achieve just that purpose.

Harlan was unbothered by the accusations, except in two respects. He did not wish to be president, and debated whether a public declaration on that point would extinguish the talk or further it.[50] He also didn't want his sons to be embarrassed by their father, crediting what they read in the "lying" newspapers, which he believed were speaking on behalf of their wealthy owners who feared the income tax.

"Dear James and John," he wrote to his two younger boys. ". . . Do not be at all alarmed by the reports sent out by lying newspaper correspondents as to what occurred in court last Monday, or as to the views expressed by the minority about the decision. The statement that I gestured in the face of the Chief Justice has not the slightest foundation in truth. The Chief is always courteous and would never give anyone occasion to be rude towards him, and he knows that I was not rude to him on Monday."

Rather, the justice explained, "The fact is that Justice Field, who has acted often like a mad man during the whole of this contest about the income tax, bothered the Chief Justice on his left and [Justice Horace] Gray on his right, with sharp running comments on my opinion as it was being read. Offended by his unseemly conduct and discourtesy, I turned sharply towards him and read a part of my opinion directly at him."

It was Field, not Fuller, to whom Harlan directed his wrath, he wrote, acknowledging, "My voice and manner undoubtedly indicated a good deal of earnestness, and I am quite willing that it should have been so interpreted. I felt deeply about this case, and naturally the extent of my feeling was shown by my voice and manner."

He went on to excoriate some of the newspaper owners and level a prediction about the legacy of the *Pollock* decision: "Just as certain as anything can be, this recent decision will become as hateful with the American people as the Dred Scott case when it was decided."[51]

The fight over the income tax was a turning point for more than just the personal relationship between Justices Harlan and Field.

William Jennings Bryan emerged with his reputation as the "boy orator of the Platte" enhanced by his eloquent advocacy for the tax in the House of Representatives. Two years later, he electrified the Democratic convention with a speech calling for silver-backed currency. His "Cross of Gold" speech so successfully rousted the Cleveland faction that Bryan, at thirty-six, won his party's presidential nomination that year. He would go on to win it in two of the following three presidential elections but would never prevail over the Republicans. His brand of populism couldn't attract quite enough supporters to overcome its conservative critics, though its impact would extend well into the New Deal of the 1930s.[52]

As for the other boy wonder named William—William Dameron Guthrie—his prestige, along with that of his firm, which eventually became the mighty Cravath, Swaine & Moore, soared on Wall Street. In a 1948 history of the firm, partner Robert T. Swaine wrote that speculation was rampant that the firm had earned between $500,000 and $1,000,000—or between $15 million and $30 million in 2021 dollars—for its work on the *Pollock* case. In fact, Swaine claimed, it received only a comparatively paltry $26,000.[53]

But money poured into Guthrie's pockets from somewhere. Within four years, the young lawyer began construction on what was to be the largest house in Locust Valley, Long Island, a marble palace that looked somewhat like a scale replica of the White House, but with enormous wings that more than doubled its size. There was a Louis XV hall, an Italian garden, and a Chinese room; terraced gardens unfolded for acres to the ocean, where a two-story bathing pavilion welcomed guests. Guthrie himself commuted back and forth to Manhattan on his personal 111-foot yacht.[54]

The giant house presided like a monument over the lesser mansions that grew up around it. In 1913, however, the United States ratified the Sixteenth Amendment, which explicitly overruled the *Pollock* decision. Thereafter, the tax burden on the wealthy began to soar.

The Guthrie mansion, like many of its brethren, became difficult to maintain on a reduced income.

In 1935, when Guthrie died, the highest income-tax brackets reached 63 percent, heading up to 94 percent within a decade,[55] a testament, perhaps, to his prescience in sensing that the 2 percent tax was only a foot in the door to far more onerous levies.

In the 1940s, Guthrie's lush acres of land were subdivided into smaller lots for more modest homes. Parke-Bernet Galleries auctioned off his possessions in 1956, and the ghostly Long Island mansion fell prey to the wrecking ball soon after. Only some columns and the ornate bathing pavilion, which was reconstructed after a fire in 1994, linger as reminders of the man who, against all odds, persuaded the Supreme Court to forestall the advent of the income tax, and thereby extend the Gilded Age, for nineteen wealth-saturated years.[56]

Chapter 15

The Humblest and Most Powerful

On a cold day in January 1891, a tall, well-dressed, distinguished-looking Cincinnati lawyer took a party of excited children to Harris' Family Theater—one of the city's most popular sources of entertainment—to see the rollicking adventure story of *Daniel Boone*. The children were looking forward to seeing how the coon-skinned frontiersman blazed the path of modern civilization through their own part of the country. But when the proud father led his three kids and their friends to the orchestra seats he had purchased in advance, the managers stopped them: the party would have to relocate to the balcony.[1]

After a pointed but polite exchange, the lawyer summoned all his pride to escort the children out of the theater; there would be no *Daniel Boone* on this day. Instead, the children would be filing racial discrimination suits.[2]

The lawyer was Robert James Harlan—Robert Jr.—who had moved with his family from Washington to Cincinnati to attend law school and be closer to his father. The group of kids included three of Robert's grandchildren: Robert Dorsey Harlan, Louise Josephine Harlan, and the youngest, Carrie Langston Harlan, who shared a name with the wife of John Mercer Langston and sister of O. S. B. Wall—all close friends of Robert Jr. and Sr.[3]

Robert Jr.'s humiliation at the hands of the three managers of Har-

ris' Theater drew immediate attention because it seemed to mark a
change in the city's unwritten racial code. This was no setup or test
case. Like most well-off Cincinnatians, the Harlans had surely attended many performances at Harris' and its host venue, the ornate,
1,800-seat Robinson's Opera House, which had been attracting Queen
City audiences since 1872.[4] They fully expected to take their orchestra seats and enjoy the show. The fact that a party of children was involved only added to the sting of rejection and the pain of racism.

An article from the predominantly Black *Chicago Conservator*, reprinted in the *New York Age*, reported that the Harlans, on their own,
"would have passed alright," but that "two or three" of the other children in the party were of a darker hue. The *Cleveland Gazette* quoted
one of the three managers of Harris' Theater as saying, "Any respectable colored person can always be accommodated in our balcony."
The *Gazette* responded in a mocking tone: "*Rats!* Think of it: the *balcony!* Then the disreputable colored people must 'be accommodated'
downstairs, where the white trash are seated? We hope Harlan and
the others win their suits; and they will too."[5]

Despite the *Gazette's* show of bravado, the law wasn't nearly so
friendly. There were a dwindling number of statutes and doctrines to
assist Robert Jr.'s lawsuit. Eight years previously, the Supreme Court
had overturned the federal Civil Rights Act. Local laws had filled the
gap in many places in the North, but now, in the 1890s, those protections were eroding as segregation crept northward. The three lawsuits brought by Robert Jr. on behalf of his minor children languished
in the courts for almost twenty-five years without resolution, finally
being dismissed in an apparent purging of the docket in 1915.[6]

The rejection of Robert's family from the theater was indeed a harbinger of change: the Black aristocracy, which had somewhat been
spared the pain of segregation, was starting to feel the walls closing in
in the 1890s. The barriers of race admitted fewer exceptions.[7]

That was particularly shocking to Black elites in New Orleans, the
city with more people of mixed-race backgrounds than any other. Even

in the antebellum years, Louisiana held fast to its own distinctive racial history and attitudes. While enslaved people like Robert's mother toiled in conditions every bit as dire—if not more so—than elsewhere in the South, mixed-race Creoles, of a lineage that combined French and Spanish colonial ancestry with that of Africans and Native Americans, lived a life of freedom and, in many cases, privilege in the Crescent City. They traced their bloodlines back for two centuries and occupied a settled place in Louisiana society. After the Civil War and the turmoil of federal occupation, Louisiana politics veered closer to that of other states of the former Confederacy. In seeking to repress the hundreds of thousands of freed men and women the state government enacted laws that increasingly placed the population into two racial categories: Black and white. While some mixed-race Creoles quickly identified as white, others, by dint of their skin color, could not. Still others, in an act of defiance, chose not to deny their heritage.[8]

In 1890, just one year before Robert Jr.'s ejection from the Cincinnati theater, the Louisiana State Legislature heeded political pressure to enforce legal segregation by approving the Separate Car Act, which required railroad companies to maintain separate compartments for Black and white customers. The law was signed by Governor Francis Nicholls—the same chief executive who, thirteen years earlier, had prevailed in the violent election dispute that drew John Marshall Harlan and other federal commissioners to New Orleans. At the time, Nicholls had sworn to protect the equal rights of the Black population; returning to power in 1889, with no federal troops on the ground or aggressive federal law enforcement to contend with, Nicholls had no such compunctions. The Separate Car Law stigmatized both the descendants of people held in slavery and mixed-race Creole elites, keeping them out of view of whites unless they were servants.[9]

Nicholls's decision to codify under the law a wall of separation that had been built through private acts of discrimination alarmed the many Creoles who occupied positions of wealth and leadership. Louis A. Martinet, a Creole doctor and lawyer who published a civil rights–oriented newspaper, the *Crusader*, and his editor, Rodolphe Desdunes, immediately called for a legal assault on the new law, declaring in an editorial, "We'll make a case, a test case, and bring it before the Federal Courts on the ground of the invasion of the right of a person to travel through the State unmolested. No such case has been fairly made or presented."[10]

Most of Louisiana's Creole elites rallied around Martinet and Desdunes. At the suggestion of Aristide Mary, the richest person of color in the state, a group of prominent Creoles came together to form a Citizens' Committee "to give a dignified appearance to the resistance" and raise money for the legal fees.[11] "Cost what it may!" Mary declared in a show of confidence.[12] The committee promised to take its challenge as far as the US Supreme Court, if necessary. Three years later, while the case was still wending its way through the legal system, Mary shot himself three times in the chest in his mansion on Canal Street, killing himself within seconds.[13]

"It is a singular coincidence that many of the very wealthy colored men of this city have taken their own lives," the *New-York Times* mused in its report on Mary's death. "Always neatly dressed, gloved, and wearing a wide standing collar, wide-brimmed silk hat, his mustache waxed, and swinging a natty cane, Mary was a conspicuous figure on the street."[14]

The "singular coincidence" may have been less of a mystery than the *Times* suggested. Mary had been educated in Paris, inherited a real estate fortune, and lived the life of a French Quarter grandee, boasting that he had never worked a day in his life.[15] Reconstruction altered his world. Yankee general Philip Sheridan appointed him a city alderman, and he went on to serve as treasurer of the Louisiana Republican Party, a testament to his wealth. But like other Creole elites, he went from a position of prominence to one of suspicion and even derision when Democratic redeemers took power. The Separate Car Act was a particularly degrading blow.

Nonetheless, an affront that was a life-and-death matter for some wealthy Creoles aroused somewhat less spirited opposition among the descendants of freedmen; for them, lynchings and Ku Klux Klan attacks were a more urgent threat than being ejected from a first-class railroad carriage. While Martinet and the Citizens' Committee were trying to build momentum to take on the Separate Car Act, they confronted a somewhat ambivalent Black community. Following a pattern that would continue into a new century, the ever-tightening grip of segregation served to crush Black hopes and limit horizons; with more pressing concerns such as Klan violence, voter intimidation, and lack of access to money or property, some Black leaders were wary of a high-profile fight for equality in transportation, even knowing the potential significance of a victory in the Supreme Court. When a committee member wrote to Frederick Douglass about the plans to challenge the Separate Car Act, he received a disappointing response: Douglass would not support the effort. He felt no good would come of it.[16]

There was some sad wisdom behind Douglass's otherwise perplexing rebuff, which infuriated Martinet.[17] Many Black leaders, including Douglass and Robert Harlan, had come to the conclusion that "social equality" was a stumbling block in racial relations; a large swath of the moderate white population appeared receptive to Black appeals for political or economic rights, but drew the line at racial mixing. To Douglass and Harlan, the assumption that Black people were conspiring to gain access to white clubs and invitations to white parties was an insult to Black dignity: as long as a man was given voting rights and economic liberties, he could choose his own friends.[18] And while almost all Black leaders recognized the deep wrong of segregation, the barriers to overturning it could seem insurmountable, especially given the current makeup of the Supreme Court. Douglass had despaired over the court's decision in the *Civil Rights Cases of 1883*, regarding it as almost a mortal blow to Black aspirations.[19] He wasn't about to put his faith in the wisdom of the justices again.

Meanwhile, a new Black leader, Booker T. Washington, was pursuing what he saw as a pragmatic agenda of providing basic education to the descendants of those held in slavery, including instruction in morals and proper deportment. He took as his starting point the inferior position of Black people in society, which he sometimes seemed to suggest was warranted by their lack of attainments. "Our greatest danger is that in the great leap from slavery to freedom, we may overlook the fact that the masses of us are to live by the productions of our hands," Washington declared in Atlanta in 1895, in what came to be known as his "Atlanta Compromise" speech. Black people, he argued, "shall prosper in proportion as we learn to draw the line between the superficial and the substantial, the ornamental gewgaws of life and the useful. No race can prosper till it learns that there is as much dignity in tilling a field as writing a poem. It is at the bottom of life that we must begin, and not at the top. Nor should we permit our grievances to overshadow our opportunities."[20]

Washington was girding for a long, slow march to respectability; Louis Martinet and his fellow Louisianans were hoping for a transformative legal victory that would produce something like true equality—at the very least, for Creoles like themselves. The two approaches were at odds and aimed at very different populations. Nonetheless, Washington's seeming acceptance of inequality and Douglass's sense of looming defeat cast a pall over the work of the Citizens' Committee in Louisiana.

"The fight we are making is an uphill one under the best circumstances, and yet those for whom we fight make it still harder," Martinet wrote in frustration.[21]

Against such long odds and pervasive doubts, even among the supposed victims of the Separate Car Act, Martinet needed a lead attorney who was not only skilled in the law but also a righteous idealist who understood the transformative potential of a favorable Supreme Court decision.

He found such a person in Albion W. Tourgée, a lawyer, former judge, and best-selling novelist who had dedicated much of his life to promoting racial equality. Tourgée had a strikingly different personality than John Marshall Harlan—he was a loner who wrestled with depression[22]—but nonetheless shared John's belief that the Civil War stood for far more than putting down a rebellion: It represented a fundamental reordering of the relationship between the states and the federal government and, especially, between the races.

Five years younger than John, Tourgée was an only child of

middle-class white parents who grew up in abolitionist strongholds in Ohio and western Massachusetts. After starting college at the University of Rochester in upstate New York, he gave up his studies to join the Union army. In the first major battle of the war, at Manassas, he suffered a freak injury when he was hit with a piece of equipment by Union troops scrambling in retreat; the wound to his spine left him temporarily paralyzed, but he eventually returned to the field only to be captured and put in a Confederate camp. After a prisoner exchange, he saw further action at Chickamauga and Perryville before resigning his commission because of his persistent back pain, which would continue throughout his life.[23]

After the war, Tourgée made the bold decision to move to North Carolina during the period of federal occupation, when the Confederates were still barred from positions of leadership. Part of the impetus was his health: doctors believed his back would respond better in a warmer climate.[24] But he was also eager to shape the postwar landscape. Many of his fellow carpetbaggers headed south for money; Tourgée had humanitarian goals in mind. He wanted to remake the South along the principles of democracy and equality. After briefly editing a Republican newspaper in Greensboro, he became a fierce legal advocate for equal political and civil rights, free public education, and criminal justice reform.[25] At a time when most ex-Confederates were still banned from voting, Tourgée was elected a North Carolina judge, a post from which he put many of his principles into action. After six years, when the return of white Democrats to the voting rolls made his reelection impossible, he found a new way to articulate his beliefs: fiction. In 1879, two years after the Hayes administration withdrew troops from the South, he wrote a novel, *A Fool's Errand*, that depicted the betrayal of Black rights during Reconstruction. By that point, he was so accustomed to the life of the South that he portrayed the Southern resistance to change as an entirely predictable attempt to overturn the verdict of the war; he viewed the lack of northern willingness to enforce the postwar amendments to the Constitution as a potentially greater tragedy— an abdication of national principles. Like some other progressives, he traced the northern surrender to the growing accumulations of wealth as the Gilded Age took hold; in his view, the industrialists and slave owners shared a common mind-set.[26] *A Fool's Errand* was a huge best seller.

By the time a member of the Louisiana Citizens' Committee recommended him to Louis Martinet as a possible lead counsel to challenge the Separate Car Act, Tourgée had lived in upstate New York for more than a decade, where his fortunes had waned. He wrote a Sunday column for a newspaper called the *Chicago Inter Ocean*, under the pen name the Bystander, which advocated aggressively for the principles of the long-gone Radical Republicans.[27] Tourgée's radicalism provoked strong reactions, including death threats. But his passion for the cause of racial equality impressed the Citizens' Committee. Martinet believed he had found his man—a decision made even easier when Tourgée, casting aside his financial struggles, agreed to work on the case without a fee.[28]

Even as Tourgée began planning with Martinet and Desdunes on legal strategy, he remained up north, leaving the ground work to a local attorney, James C. Walker, who was better schooled in the mossy legal byways of the Crescent State.[29] Together the group confronted a series of strategic decisions before it could proceed with its test case.

Above all, the members resolved to avoid unnecessary confrontations; the heart of their case was the illogic of the Separate Car Act— the fact that it proceeded from no actual problem on the rail lines but rather an unjustified political motive. Therefore, they were determined to show that Black and white people could comfortably and respectfully share a rail carriage. Noisy protests would undermine the case—as would any scuffles or, God forbid, violence when their test plaintiff got himself arrested. (And the plaintiff would be a man: conductors would be less certain to take action against a woman.)

Most significantly, Tourgée, Martinet, and the rest decided that, to best illustrate the absurdity of the law, they wanted a plaintiff who looked entirely white but would then correctly identify himself as part Black, earning a dismissal to the colored car.[30] It happened that they had just such a person in their inner circle: Daniel Desdunes, the son of Rodolphe Desdunes, who was only one-eighth Black. The young man clambered aboard a whites-only car headed to Alabama, identified himself as colored, and then refused to leave. At the next stop, two detectives who had been hired and briefed by the Citizens' Committee took him into custody. A police captain swore out an affidavit against him for refusing to leave the whites-only car. A member of the Citizens' Committee then paid the bond to secure his release. All of these actors, from the L & N Railroad, to the police captain, were aware that they were playing roles in a scripted drama, intended to create a scenario in which a mixed-race plaintiff could challenge the Separate Car Act.[31]

The defense of Daniel Desdunes turned out to be easier than anyone expected. Tourgée and Walker argued that the Separate Car Act violated both the US Constitution and the federal Interstate Commerce Act of 1887, which governed interstate railways and had no requirement of racially segregated cars. Because federal law superseded state law, the lawyers reasoned, the Commerce Act should supersede the Separate Car Act on trains traveling between the states. Desdunes's train was, after all, bound for Alabama.

Before Desdunes's fate could be determined, the Texas Supreme Court handed down a ruling in a similar case, declaring that the federal law superseded Texas's own version of the Separate Car Act for interstate travel. Louisiana's Supreme Court agreed with its next-door neighbor. Even though Tourgée, Walker, and the Citizens' Committee didn't have the satisfaction of winning the case on their own, Louisiana's acceptance of the Texas ruling meant that the charges against Desdunes would be dismissed—a victory, if not quite a complete one.

"The Jim Crow car is ditched and will remain in the ditch," enthused the *Crusader* in an editorial, which went on to commend the courage of the young plaintiff Desdunes, who happened to be the musician-son of the paper's editor: "The young professor Desdunes is to be congratulated on the manly assertion of his right, and his refusal to ride in the Jim Crow coach. The people should cherish the performance of such patriotic acts and honor the patriots."[32]

There remained, however, the matter of railroad trips entirely within the state of Louisiana. On each of those journeys, the Separate Car Act was still in effect, and the state wasn't backing down.

On the cusp of thirty, Homer Plessy was a shoemaker from the colorful, middle-class New Orleans neighborhood of Faubourg Treme. He identified strongly with his diverse community and fellow New Orleans Creoles, helping to start a French language newspaper[33] and joining the board of a charity that advocated for education of Black children, among many other civic endeavors.[34] Like some other New Orleans Creoles, Plessy's grandfather had been born in France—in Bordeaux—and sought to make his fortune in the French colony of Haiti. But when Haiti was overrun by a slave rebellion, Germain Plessy, like many other French men and women, decamped for New Orleans—the French-flavored jewel of a port where the Mississippi Delta meets the Gulf of Mexico. Amid the palms and balmy breezes, he met and married a local free woman of color and had eight children. One of them, Joseph Adolphe Plessy, a carpenter, married a seamstress of mixed race named Rosa Debergue. Homer, their son, was only seven when his father died; later, he became a maker of fancy shoes like his stepfather.[35]

Despite his relative youth, Homer Plessy's work in starting the French-language newspaper and on many other Creole organizations put him in direct contact with the Martinet and Desdunes families in the years before the Separate Car Act took effect. Even though he lacked the wealth and attainments of the older members of the Citizens' Committee, Homer's youth and light skin made him an ideal plaintiff for a new test case.

Like Daniel Desdunes, Homer rehearsed his moves and followed a carefully plotted path to being arrested. This time the target would be the East Louisiana Railroad for a trip entirely within the state: a roughly sixty-mile journey from New Orleans to Covington, a city on the other side of Lake Pontchartrain, the giant estuary that separated the Crescent City from inland Louisiana. On June 7, 1892, Homer walked up to the window at New Orleans's Press Street Station and purchased a first-class ticket for the four fifteen train. Most of his fellow passengers were making late-spring excursions to the popular picnic areas around the lake. He aroused little attention when he boarded the whites-only carriage, but, when questioned by the conductor, acknowledged that he was a person of color. Then, just like Daniel Desdunes before him, he refused to leave and was arrested by detectives who had been briefed in advance by the Citizens' Committee.[36]

While New Orleans newspapers reported Homer Plessy's arrest, the case drew little notice outside of bayou country—a reflection, perhaps, of the fact that few people, if any, expected Plessy to prevail on constitutional grounds, while much of the nation's racial concern was focused on the shocking numbers of lynchings that year, not the rising tide of segregation.[37]

Nonetheless, Tourgée, Walker, Martinet, and other backers of the case were girding for a long process, already envisioning a trip to the Supreme Court. Their first stop, however, was the courtroom of a newly appointed judge, John Howard Ferguson, who happened to be a carpetbagger who had been born on the Massachusetts island of Martha's Vineyard and studied law under an abolitionist attorney in Boston.

Unlike Albion Tourgée, however, John Howard Ferguson was no radical. While other carpetbaggers enraged locals by serving in Reconstruction governments, Ferguson married a local woman, put down roots, and became a Democratic ally of Francis Nicholls. After a long and successful practice in criminal law, Ferguson was appointed to a judgeship by Nicholls's successor, Governor Murphy Foster, around the same time Foster elevated none other than Nicholls himself to the post of chief justice of the Louisiana Supreme Court.[38]

Despite his brief tenure, Ferguson was seasoned in the courtroom and gracious from the bench. Nonetheless, few expected that he would have the temerity to rule against a law that was, after all, quite popular among Louisiana Democrats. Homer Plessy arrived at the historic courthouse, known as St. Patrick's Hall, with James Walker at his side to serve as defense lawyer, on October 11, 1892; Louis Martinet and Rodolphe Desdunes sat expectantly in the audience. Following a strategy determined by himself and Tourgée, Walker called for the charges to be dropped on the grounds that the state should not have the power to determine someone's race—especially based on the spurious opinion of a railroad conductor. Moreover, under the Constitution, the state had no power to establish separate rights and privileges based on race.[39]

The only surprise in the case came when the proceedings were delayed by a sweeping labor strike that almost paralyzed New Orleans. After three weeks, however, Ferguson conformed to expectations by ruling in favor of the law. He declared that the state was well within its powers to regulate railroads for the comfort and safety of passengers, including by seeking to avoid messy racial confrontations. Meanwhile, Ferguson averred, the separate-car policy provided fully equal accommodations to Homer Plessy, depriving him of any claim of unequal protection under the law. The case against him would go forward. The Citizens' Committee had lost.

The next stop was Nicholls's Louisiana Supreme Court, where the outcome was, if anything, more foreordained. With an eye toward the US Supreme Court, Tourgée and Walker unveiled some of their core arguments, claiming that the law—whose purpose, they declared, was to appease racist whites at the expense of colored people—was an illegal "badge of servitude" under the Thirteenth Amendment and also violated various provisions of the Fourteenth Amendment. Moreover, because the law failed to provide a workable definition of who was Black and who was white, it violated the due-process rights of people of mixed race who identified as white, exposing them to criminal penalties for a crime they had no intention of committing.

The Nicholls court was unmoved. It upheld the law, 5 to 0.

There was a trap built into the newly named case of *Plessy v. Ferguson* as it wended its way to the US Supreme Court. That was the separate-but-equal doctrine itself. In equal parts ridiculous and ingenious, it was designed to provide a legal fig leaf for segregation. The states of the South, which had been hiding behind this fig leaf for years, essentially dared the rest of the country to rip it off—and, in so doing, reignite the hostilities of the Reconstruction era. Few people in the North were willing to take the dare; many quite approved of segregation, but even those who did not were wary of reviving sectional disputes and racial animus. All the Supreme Court justices had to do was squeeze their eyes, push aside the obvious doubts, and make the decision that seemed likely to please the greater number of white Americans.

Even Albion Tourgée, who had failed to heed the warnings of Black leaders outside the Louisiana Creole community that bringing such a case would damage their interests, realized that, absent a change in public sentiment, the court was likely to endorse the separate-but-equal doctrine. He also recognized that a loss in *Plessy v. Ferguson* could make the situation for people of color worse, putting a legal stamp of approval on what had been an ad hoc, if relentless, process of separation. So, he froze. In a letter to Martinet, he explained his strategy of delay: "If we can wipe out the indifference of the white people of the North upon this subject, there is a chance that the Supreme Court . . . when moved by the awakened and potent conscience of the people, may grant its edict against caste."[40]

It's not clear what Tourgée believed was likely to change in a few years, except perhaps a growing revulsion of lynchings, which were garnering significant attention in the northern press. Unsurprisingly, when Tourgée realized he could wait no longer, he found that public sentiment had hardly shifted an inch.

On April 13, 1896, Tourgée made his way to the Capitol to argue Plessy's case before the justices; a Louisiana attorney working in Washington, Alexander Morse, defended the state and Judge Ferguson. No demonstrations or shows of support greeted these legal gladiators; the case received almost no press attention, and aroused little interest, even in the Black community. The contrast with the national cacophony that had surrounded the Supreme Court's consideration of the *Civil Rights Cases* thirteen years earlier spoke more loudly about the suppression of Black rights than anything Tourgée could argue.

Morse's strategy was to present the case as unexceptional: a routine exercise of Louisiana's so-called police power to enact regulations for the well-being of its citizens. The Separate Car Act, he pointed out, removed any danger of racial strife within the cars, and secured the safety and comfort of both races. Meanwhile, the provision of entirely equal accommodations satisfied any constitutional questions, he said, noting that neither Homer Plessy nor anyone else had questioned the quality of the service for Black customers.[41]

For Tourgée, however, this was a moment to assert, with the passion of a true believer, that this was most certainly not an unexceptional piece of legislation—it not only shredded the Constitution but arbitrarily changed the race of "octoroons" like Plessy from white to Black.

His written brief, which formed the basis of his argument, was, in places, almost operatic in its intensity, replete with dozens of rhetorical questions, exclamation points, sarcasm (saying the law turned a railroad conductor into "the autocrat of Caste"),[42] and slippery-slope arguments such as: "But if the state has the right to distinguish between citizens according to race . . . may it not require all red-headed people to ride in a separate car?"

Tourgée displayed the full range of his intellect, calling the Separate Car Act "obnoxious to the spirit of republican institutions, because it is the legalization of caste."[43] He also quoted, among other sources, Justice Harlan's dissent in the *Civil Rights Cases of 1883*.[44] He defended the principle of equality under the law, declaring that "Justice is pictured blind, and her daughter, the Law, ought at least to be color blind."[45]

But he also kept reverting to the particular injustice done to people of mixed race—in this case, the Creoles—who believed themselves to be white but were deemed by the law—or, worse, by the arbitrary determination of a railway conductor—to be Black.[46] This argument was, in itself, an affront to most freedmen. It gave the court the option of striking down the law only because it lacked a workable definition of "colored," which would merely invite Louisiana to approve a new Separate Car Act with clearer standards. Under that scenario, the Creoles might escape the stigma of the "Jim Crow" car, but darker-skinned people would not.

Tourgée's insistence on attacking the law as an offense against people with small, barely discernible portions of African blood was probably one reason that Black leaders like Douglass shied away from *Plessy v. Ferguson*: fairly or not, they distrusted wealthy Creoles to represent any interests beyond their own. That wasn't entirely the case with Plessy, Martinet, and Tourgée, but the *cri de coeur* of innocent people of mixed race who were designated under the law to be Black pervaded their arguments.

"Where on earth should he have gone?" Tourgée exploded in reference to Homer Plessy's ejection from the white carriage. "Will the court hold that a single drop of African blood is sufficient to color a whole ocean of whiteness?"[47]

Tourgée's entreaties, as dramatic and at times theatrical as they were, didn't change a single vote.[48] Douglass, it turned out, had been right: the justices weren't willing to issue a transformative decision on race—not in 1896, not with relations between the North and South on the road to recovery and the lion's share of white opinion unbothered by racial segregation.

The court announced its ruling five weeks after the hearing, with a comparatively short opinion by Justice Henry Billings Brown befitting the lack of fanfare surrounding the case. Brown essentially accepted the no-big-deal-here attitude of Louisiana, casting the Separate Car Act as a "reasonable" exercise of the state's police powers—that is, its power to impose regulations for public health and safety.[49] The dishonorable truth of the decision was embedded in its determination of "reasonableness." Brown accepted that the very state of nature required that the two races would compete, disagree, and sometimes dislike each other, thereby justifying Louisiana's decision to keep them separate. Rather than invoke the Constitution to quell racism, Brown invoked racism to quell the Constitution.

Without offering much in the way of analysis, Brown similarly brushed aside the idea that separate facilities violated the "equal protection" of the laws: "A statute which implies merely a legal distinction between the white and colored races—a distinction which is founded in the color of the two races and which must always exist so long as white men are distinguished from the other race by color— has no tendency to destroy the legal equality of the two races or reestablish a state of involuntary servitude."[50]

Why? Brown didn't say. His tone was that of a trial judge handing down a verdict, not a legal thinker wrestling with constitutional issues. Born three years after John Harlan, Henry Billings Brown had followed the arc of many well-heeled northerners of his era. He spent his youth in abolitionist-friendly Massachusetts and Connecticut, matriculating at Yale College and studying law at Yale and Harvard Law School.[51] Despite his opposition to the Confederacy and reservations about slavery, he chose not to fight in the Civil War, hiring a replacement soldier instead.[52] Moving to Detroit and marrying the daughter of a wealthy man, he built a corporate practice and reputation as an expert on Great Lakes admiralty law; activism in Michigan Republican politics and a federal judgeship followed. Appointed by President Benjamin Harrison to the Supreme Court, he wasn't the most conservative justice on the bench, but he adopted, with even greater ease and less introspection than others of his colleagues, the blithe assumption of white, male, Anglo-Saxon superiority that defined the era.[53]

"We consider the underlying fallacy of the plaintiff's argument to consist in the assumption that the enforced separation of the two races stamps the colored race with a badge of inferiority," Brown wrote. "If this be so, it is not by reason of anything found in the act, but solely because the colored race chooses to put that construction on it. The argument necessarily assumes that if . . . the colored race should become the dominant power in the state legislature, and should enact a law in precisely similar terms, it would thereby relegate the white race to an inferior position. We imagine that the white race, at least, would not acquiesce in this assumption.

"The argument also assumes that social prejudices may be overcome by legislation, and that equal rights cannot be secured except by an enforced commingling of the two races. We cannot accept this proposition. If the two races are to meet upon terms of social equality, it must be the result of natural affinities, a mutual appreciation of each other's merits, and a voluntary consent of individuals. . . . Legislation is powerless to eradicate racial instincts or to abolish distinctions based upon physical differences, and the attempt to do so can only result in accentuating the difficulties of the present situation."[54]

In this scolding passage, Brown shows his and his brethren's willful obtuseness—claiming with a straight face that any badge of inferiority is imposed by Black people themselves, and then chiding the plaintiff for believing that legislation can overcome social prejudices; in fact, the legislation in question was imposed by whites to prevent racial commingling. It was the Louisiana government that sought to achieve its social ends through legislation. Brown's attempt to turn around the arguments was too obviously unpersuasive to count as trickery; most likely, the justices shared his prejudices and his acceptance of segregation. They knew they were twisting both the facts and the law to reach that judgment.

Seven members of the court, including Chief Justice Fuller, sided with Brown.

One justice, David Brewer, didn't participate because of a family emergency: the death of his daughter.

One—John Marshall Harlan—stood alone against the rest.

If Zeus had hurled a lightning bolt into the Old Senate Chamber that Monday, May 18, he could not have rained more fire on the Supreme Court's majority than John Harlan did.

Whereas his dissent in the *Civil Rights Cases* had been long and methodical, painfully wrought from late nights of the soul in his study on Massachusetts Avenue, his dissent in *Plessy v. Ferguson* was crisp and definitive. In 1883 he had introduced novel legal theories and interpretations, seeking to preserve what he saw as the true intent of the post–Civil War amendments; in 1896 he offered a perfect distillation of those theories, fully thought through and matured. It was the work of a man who knew exactly what he believed and what evils he foresaw, and who had been living those intervening thirteen years with every dire forecast and premonition weighing on his mind and conscience.

Harlan blew past the sense of fatalism, hiding behind Louisiana's claim of business as usual, that surrounded the case. He made it clear that the majority's decision in *Plessy v. Ferguson* was hardly a routine rubber-stamping of Louisiana's police powers; it was an upending of the Constitution, a gutting of the principle of equal protection under the laws, and a violation of the spirit underlying both the Thirteenth and Fourteenth Amendments.

"In respect of civil rights common to all citizens, the Constitution of the United States does not, I think, permit any public authority to know the race of those entitled to be protected in the enjoyment of such rights," he wrote. "Every true man has pride of race, and, under appropriate circumstances, when the rights of others, his equals before the law, are not to be affected, it is his privilege to accept such pride and to take action based upon it as to him seems proper. But I deny that any legislative body or judicial tribunal may have regard to the race of citizens when the civil rights of those citizens are involved. Indeed, such legislation as that here in question is inconsistent not only with that equality of rights which pertains to citizenship, national and state, but with the personal liberty enjoyed by everyone within the United States."[55]

These were the concepts, equality and liberty, that John had been raised on; the inviolable truths that his father had drummed into him, and the edicts that he himself, through hard experience, had come to see were all too conveniently cast aside by moderate unionists like himself in favor of stability and security. He had followed, step by step, the road that led Abraham Lincoln to decry slavery as a sin and a stain on the national honor. Back then, at least, the compromises accepted by Lincoln and Harlan and their mutual hero, Henry Clay, were made in the name of preventing the dissolution of the union. Now, with no such peril in the offing, the Supreme Court was making the same mistake in believing that the nation's founding principles applied to one group only: white Europeans. The victims of this kind of thinking, Harlan believed, were not only Black people but also whites. The divisions that it would inspire would hamper both races, and the denial of personal liberties to one race would create a precedent that could someday be used against others.

The doctrine of separate but equal, John declared, was an obvious fallacy. "The thin disguise of 'equal' accommodations for passengers in railroad coaches will not mislead anyone, nor atone for the wrong this day done," he wrote.[56]

"Everyone knows that the statute in question had its origin in the purpose not so much to exclude white persons from railroad cars occupied by blacks as to exclude colored people from coaches occupied or assigned to white persons. Railroad corporations of Louisiana did not make discrimination among whites in the matter of accommodation for travelers. The thing to accomplish was, under the guise of giving equal accommodation for whites and blacks, to compel the latter to keep to themselves while traveling in railroad passenger coaches," he added. "No one would be so wanting in candor as to assert the contrary."[57]

The court's acceptance of the separate-but-equal doctrine, John believed, was not simply an unfortunate concession to prejudice or an act of expediency to avoid upsetting the racial equilibrium in the South. It was a rewriting of the Constitution that would haunt American history for decades. "In my opinion, the judgment this day rendered will, in time, prove to be quite as pernicious as the decision made by this tribunal in the Dred Scott case,"[58] he wrote.

There was no news coverage of the reaction of John's colleagues, but they would have been bemused by such a ridiculous notion: the Dred Scott case had been a cataclysmic event that precipitated the Civil War; *Plessy v. Ferguson* was a squabble that even some Black leaders disregarded and that remained unheard of by most Americans.

But John described the way the Dred Scott decision had gone beyond defending the legality of slavery to declare that no Black people, even those granted freedom, would ever enjoy constitutional rights, thereby embedding racism in the nation's foundation. *Plessy v. Ferguson* was doing the same thing.

"The recent [post–Civil War] amendments of the Constitution, it was supposed, had eradicated these principles from our institutions," he declared. "But it seems that we have yet, in some of the states, a dominant race—a superior class of citizens, which assumes to regulate the enjoyment of civil rights, common to all citizens, upon the basis of race. The present decision, it may be apprehended, will not only stimulate aggressions, more or less brutal and irritating, upon the admitted rights of colored citizens, but will encourage the belief that it is possible, by means of state enactments, to defeat the beneficent purposes which the people of the United States had in view when they adopted the recent amendments. . . .

"Sixty millions of whites are in no danger from the presence here of eight millions of blacks. The destinies of the two races in this country are indissolubly linked together, and the interests of both require that the common government of all shall not permit the seeds of race hate to be planted under the sanction of law. What can more certainly arouse race hate, what more certainly create and perpetuate a feeling of distrust between these races, than state enactments which, in fact, proceed on the ground that colored citizens are so inferior and degraded that they cannot be allowed to sit in public coaches occupied by white citizens. . . .

"The sure guarantee of the peace and security of each race is the clear, distinct, unconditional recognition by our governments, national and state, of every right that inheres in civil freedom, and of the equality before the law of all citizens of the United States, without regard to race. State enactments regulating the enjoyment of civil rights upon the basis of race, and cunningly devised to defeat legitimate results of the war under the pretense of recognizing equality of rights, can have no other result than to render permanent peace impossible and to keep alive a conflict of races the continuance of which must do harm to all concerned."[59]

Thus did Harlan predict all the agonies to come—the relentless lynchings, the riots in American cities, the bullhorns and firehoses of the civil rights movement sixty, seventy, and eighty years in the future, the thwarting of Black potential and the seeds of discord it planted—at a time when no one else in a position of authority was willing to entertain such notions.

In doing so, he stayed true to his lifelong faith in the law as the structural foundation of the United States. The court's majority was willing to bend the Constitution to accommodate the views of the South—what Brown, in his majority opinion, called "the established usages, customs, and traditions of the people."[60] But John saw more powerfully how the society follows the law, not vice versa. Justice promotes peace; the legal recognition of prejudice and injustice can only perpetuate those ills.

In defining his own creed—his vision of the Constitution, different from that of the majority—John borrowed a term from Albion Tourgée's written argument. Tourgée, the radical and idealist, wrote in aspirational terms that "Justice is pictured blind and her daughter, the Law, ought at least to be colorblind." John Marshall Harlan, the firm believer in the Constitution, made the sentiment concrete, writing that, "in view of the Constitution, in the eye of the law, there is in this country no superior, dominant, ruling class of citizens. There is no caste here. Our Constitution is color blind and neither knows nor tolerates classes among its citizens. In respect of civil rights, the humblest is the peer of the most powerful. The law regards man as man, and takes no account of his surroundings or of his color when his civil rights as guaranteed by the supreme law of the land are involved."[61]

Despairing of the future under a compromised Constitution; furious over the betrayals of his judicial brethren; seething with compassion over the wrongs done to people of color, Harlan's dissent was a monumental statement. The case of the Louisiana Separate Car Act had yielded a majority opinion that rubber-stamped the views of the racist South and a dissenting opinion that defended the Constitution as a force for equal rights. If the Supreme Court could deprive the nation of its founding principles, now applied to African Americans through the clear verdict of the Civil War, at least its betrayal would not be unanimous. One thread of truth would connect to a brighter future. It would be John's proudest achievement, the culmination of his career on the bench, and his greatest contribution to the future of the nation. But the sheer force of his argument wouldn't be felt for decades.

"Three Louisiana Cases Decided," declared a headline in the *New Orleans Times-Picayune* on May 19, 1896. The case of Homer Plessy didn't even merit its own headline in its own city; in a sign of just how humdrum the decision was seen to be, the paper saw fit to announce that there was no ruling on a highly watched sugar case before reporting the result in *Plessy v. Ferguson*.[62] The news got scant more attention elsewhere in the country. The only sign that something momentous to race relations had occurred was in Black newspapers.

"Beyond the decision of the Supreme Court, there is no redress, and that august body which is supposed to measure out justice to all alike, has decreed that a certain element of this great American people must be set aside and subject to any sort of indignities that may be heaped upon it," lamented the *Enterprise* of Omaha, Nebraska. The paper added that it had "nothing but profound respect and gratitude for Justice Harlan for such an honest opinion and for the courage displayed in speaking his convictions."[63]

A month later, the *Enterprise* saw fit to return to the subject of Harlan's dissent, having found within it a source of renewed hope. "We have read nothing so clear, so manly, so straight forward and uncompromising in many a day as Justice Harlan's dissenting opinion in the Louisiana separate coach law . . . he uttered words that will ever endear him to the hearts of the colored people."[64]

But before Harlan's words could actually help the people of color, Black America would face a crackdown of monstrous dimensions. Unfettered by the Supreme Court, Jim Crow became the law of the South. When the decision in *Plessy v. Ferguson* was announced, there were 130,334 registered Black voters in Louisiana. Eight years later, there were only 1,342.[65]

"Between the two dates the literacy, property, and poll tax qualifications were adopted," wrote historian C. Vann Woodward in his 1955 book *The Strange Career of Jim Crow*. "In 1896, Negro registrants were in a majority in twenty-six parishes—by 1900, in none."[66]

The Supreme Court had effectively removed the Constitution as an obstacle to even the worst excesses of racial discrimination, and the doors of opportunity would be slammed shut to African Americans for generations to come.

Chapter 16

The Walls of Segregation

In the Queen City on the Ohio River, the Supreme Court's decision in *Plessy v. Ferguson* was just a trifle, meriting only a fleeting mention on page 10 of the May 19, 1896, *Cincinnati Enquirer*. "The Jim Crow Car Case," was the unremarkable headline. The one-paragraph news nugget declared: "The Supreme Court of the United States decided to-day what is known as the 'Jim Crow' car case of *Plessy v. Ferguson* that the statute of the State of Louisiana requiring railroad companies to supply separate coaches for white and colored persons is constitutional, affirming the decision of the Court below. Justice Brown delivered the opinion. Justice Harlan dissented."[1]

The item no doubt captured the attention of one of the *Enquirer*'s closest readers and most frequent letter writers. At seventy-nine, Robert Harlan was finally feeling the effects of the struggles he had once overcome with such stunning vigor. Just five years earlier, when he was seventy-four and keeping up the same peripatetic routine as he had all his life, the *New York Age*, a popular Black newspaper of the time, wrote that Robert "continues to grow young." The writer observed, "He looks younger now than when I first saw him eight years ago."[2]

But even as Robert continued to work in a lucrative federal Treasury Department appointment throughout the Harrison administration, make his annual pilgrimage to Saratoga, turn up at horse tracks throughout the country, and remain a regular presence at Colored Conventions, the causes to which he had devoted his life—and the golden future he envisioned for people of color—were fading in a twilight of segregation.

The 1890s were a time of grave risks and relentless turmoil for Black Americans. Their rights to vote and to participate with any semblance of equality in civic life were essentially nullified in all the states of the former Confederacy.[3] Violent repression ruled the Black landscape.[4] After her goddaughter's father was dragged from his jail cell in Memphis and shot dead, the Black journalist Ida B. Wells wrote in 1892 that "[s]omebody must show that the Afro-American race is more sinned against than sinning, and it seems to have fallen upon me to do so."[5] The great migration that Robert endorsed had not yet begun in earnest, but as more Black people moved north, some of the problems they were fleeing followed them into their new homes above the Mason-Dixon Line.

Robert could see the deterioration in the experiences of his own family. The pride of his life was Robert Jr., the son he raised entirely on his own. He wanted Robert Jr. to embody the fulfillment of Black people's potential, to be a gentleman of the first order, a thinker and scholar worthy of his own name and that of James Harlan. Robert Jr. had, to all appearances, lived up to his father's demanding expectations. He and Mamie were socialites and intellectuals. And yet, when he and Robert's three grandchildren went to the theater in the very city that Robert had represented in the state legislature, they were booted out of their orchestra seats on account of their race. The slap in the face was deafening.

Like everyone else in America, Black and white, Robert would have had no illusions about what the Supreme Court would render in *Plessy v. Ferguson*. Nonetheless, the short sentence at the end of the *Enquirer*'s report proclaiming, "Justice Harlan dissented," would have warmed his heart. Of all the loyalties of Robert's life—to Cincinnati society, to American ideals, to the Republican Party—his faith in the Harlan family came the closest to being vindicated. Despite his years of enslavement in the Harlan household, he chose to remember all that James Harlan did to educate him and show faith in his abilities. He also believed that James's virtues had been passed on to John. Robert worked hard to promote John as a potential Supreme Court justice. Now Robert could feel that his faith in John had been well founded.

In the decades since the abolition of slavery, some of the veneer of politesse that forbade discussion of the parentage of mixed-race men and women born into slavery had melted, especially in the North. Some Black newspapers had for years referred to Robert as James Harlan's son, and now white newspapers seemed willing to engage in similar speculation. In April 1889, when Robert was seventy-two, the *Louisville Courier-Journal* ran a story about a rainy day at the Ivy City racetrack in Washington, DC, on which Robert had shown his incredible horse sense by picking the top three finishers in a race based only on his visual inspection of the animals. The endorsement of his credentials as a turf man was flattering, but the *Courier-Journal* went on to report that Robert, "a well-proportioned mulatto . . . is built on the same heroic molds as Associate Justice Harlan, of the United States Supreme Court, and only differs in facial appearance by being more sallow and wearing a jet-black mustache, while the eminent jurist is a clean-shaved, decided type of blond."[6]

Did this kind of mischievous reporting—implying their kinship through snickering details—get in the way of Robert's relationship with John? There's no evidence it did. The flurry of correspondence between the two of them in the years before John's appointment to the court suggest a relationship of trust, but only Robert's letters to John have survived; John's writings to Robert are alluded to but lost to posterity. All available evidence—Malvina's reference to Robert as a "quasi-family member," his close contact with John's brother James during the 1880s—suggests that Robert remained on good terms with John's family. Thus, during the many years when Robert was a regular visitor to Washington, spending holidays with Robert Jr. and Mamie and checking in with Republican officials, he probably visited John as well. The fact that many people, including journalists, believed they were brothers would hardly have been a surprise to either of them, even if they maintained a polite silence on the subject.

Whether Robert talked to John about cases on the court or offered his personal testament to the deteriorating state of racial relations is likewise unknown. But whenever John's judicial colleagues spoke knowingly about the inferiority of people of color, images of Robert would have lingered in his mind—Robert, the Harlan man who had achieved more than any other in the family circle excepting, perhaps, John himself. And Robert had done it in the face of legal deprivations, including slavery, that, John knew, were designed to hold him and every other person of his race in a subordinate position.

So, Robert would have seen much of himself in John's memorable dissent in *Plessy v. Ferguson*, his bracing *j'accuse* against his court brothers and everyone else responsible for violating American laws and ideals in the name of racial segregation. It would have been a small, but meaningful, comfort to an old man.

Robert had vaulted into his seventies as a man on top of his game. As his birthday approached in December 1886, he was still serving in the Ohio legislature. In his honor, Robert Jr. and Mamie organized a formal ball at his Harrison Street home, with a string band for dancing. Two hundred invitations went out to the leading Black aristocrats in the state.[7] The social columns of the *Cleveland Gazette* gushed that his birthday celebration was "one of the grandest entertainments that Cincinnati society has seen in a number of years."[8] Mamie Harlan, it wrote, dazzled in "a canary colored manantiquo silk, hand-painted with Spanish lace and pearls" and was "one of the finest and most graceful dancers in the house." Robert, too, knew how to cut a rug. Despite his seven-plus decades, the paper reported, the colonel "does not look a year over sixty; can dance as sprightly as he did twenty-five years ago." Not until "the wee hours of the day began to dawn" did guests take their leave.[9]

Soon after Robert's term in Columbus expired, the Republicans returned to power in Washington. Grover Cleveland's election in 1884 as the first Democrat in twenty-four years had wreaked havoc among aristocrats of color; senior Republicans such as Robert had been systematically broomed out of their patronage positions. Benjamin Harrison's victory four years later offered a chance to recoup; both Robert and Robert Jr. took up federal posts in Cincinnati, Robert as special inspector of customs at the Treasury Department.[10]

Not everyone in the Black community considered this a big step forward. "Bob Harlan, feeling his importance and the indispensability of his infinite wisdom, goes as a committee of one, representing Harlan, to secure an appointment," wrote a letter writer to the *Cincinnati Enquirer* in October 1889. The writer suggested that Robert's mixed-race status made him unrepresentative of the Black community: "He got the same dues that the committee representing Civil Rights got, notwithstanding the fact that he was the blue-blooded Bob Harlan. He was a negro, and that settled his case."[11]

Indeed, many Black people were furious at the Republican Party and achingly aware of its betrayals; decades of party loyalty had left them in a worse position than in the years immediately after the Civil War. Robert was concerned enough to play elder statesman and re- mind a younger generation of the importance of voting and partici- pating in public life. "Today we fill thousands of positions of trust in the land," he declared in a speech entitled "The Negro in Politics," that he delivered at Zion Baptist Church in March 1891. "Our young men honorably perform duties of public trust. . . . Let them withdraw from politics, renounce their manhood and citizenship, and they must re- nounce and abandon all they have achieved since emancipation day. There can be no middle order in this Republic. Slavery was abolished and, let us hope, can never again be restored. But abandonment of political rights is only a step toward slavery."[12]

The suggestion that Black people had indeed advanced through politics, along with the implication that they could now be held re- sponsible for abdicating their gains, didn't sit well with the younger generation. When Robert repeated some of these arguments in a speech at the East End Republican Club later that year, William H. Parham, who had been the first Black graduate of the University of Cincinnati in 1874, rose to object, claiming Republicans had consis- tently underrepresented Black voters in federal jobs. "I believe that inasmuch as the Republican men poll so many votes in Ohio, they should be given a fairer and better showing in the matter of official position," Parham declared. "At the courthouse, the Democrats, in proportion to the vote they got from colored men, have been more liberal with offices than the Republicans have. . . . Those facts Colonel Harlan and his friends will not bear in mind."[13]

A Kansas-based Black newspaper called the *Historic Times* took note of the increasing criticism of Robert, arguing that he deserves better "at the hands of the young element whose progress he has assisted to make possible." Still, the paper emphasized that "like many men, [Robert] has erred in his judgment at times, and we think he errs now, when he attempts to reconcile the Afro-Americans to the belief that they are fairly treated."[14]

It wasn't quite true that Robert had declared Black people to have been fairly treated by Republicans; he merely saw no avenue for success in the Democratic Party, the organ of southern segregationists. Far from complacent, he sometimes conveyed an element of desperation in his later speeches and writings. The disillusionment of some younger Black people may have been a logical response to the retrenchment of the 1890s, but he felt that their impulse to retreat into their own communities would only compound the injuries of segregation.

Indeed, the reality of segregation put the uncomfortable issue of social equality front and center in the Black community. Like most Black leaders, Robert approached the issue warily. He knew that white racists used the specter of intermarriage and enforced socializing between Black and white people to justify a state of separation. He often insisted that Black people wanted no such thing: equal rights in the voting booth and economic marketplace were far more important.

The issue came to a head in Washington when Ohio's progressive senator John Sherman held a reception that included both Black and white supporters. When Black couples joined whites on the dance floor, many white couples stormed out.[15] Back in Ohio, a Black member of the state Republican Committee demanded that the organization condemn the incident, asserting that "The colored ladies who danced that night were just as elegant ladies as Mrs. Harrison, the wife of the president."[16]

Robert then spoke up, agreeing with his colleague that there should be no "color line" in the Republican association. But, the *Washington Post* reported, he dismissed the idea of social equality between the races. The paper summarized Robert's comments as follows: "Mr. Sumner had truthfully stated years ago that there could never be any such thing as social equality between the races. All he wanted—all any sensible colored man could want—was equal rights under the law. He [Robert] did not believe in social equality. There might be members of the association whom he might object to have visit his wife and family. Each man must be a judge of such things. No colored man of sense would ask for social equality."[17]

Robert's speech was "frequently interrupted with applause," the *Post* reported.[18] A few months later, on July 4, 1892, Robert helped to host a national convention of African Americans at Cincinnati's Zion Baptist Church. As chairman of the resolutions committee, he helped produce a revealing set of demands to the white community, declaring, "We ask nothing of you in behalf of colored people, except to eat the bread our own hands have earned, to dwell safely in our homes, to pursue our vocations in peace, to be granted fair and equal opportunity in the race of life."

The second resolution addressed Black people themselves: "We appeal to colored people in every part of our land, to bear in mind that their prosperity, and advancement of civil rights will be in proportion to their own good conduct and approved good character."[19]

This was not the future Robert imagined at the start of his political career, when he proclaimed that education would lead to full acceptance of Black Americans. That ascension was not forthcoming, even for those, like Robert Jr., who had college and graduate degrees. In its place was an impenetrable wall of separation. And the fact that Robert saw fit to denounce social equality and remind Black people that their civil rights would depend on "good conduct and approved good character" illustrated just how far from his ideal American society had veered.

As he reached his late seventies, Robert began to be drawn more into the past. In 1893, following the defeat of Harrison and the return of Grover Cleveland to the White House, he lost his post as special customs agent. When his name appeared in the press, it was more likely to be in connection with reminiscences of the days before the Civil War than commentary on the current political situation.

When a new generation of American horse owners began taking their racers to Europe, the *Enquirer* offered a flattering reminder of how Robert had been nearly four decades ahead of them in seeking to take on the British. "It will be news to many turf followers that Robert Harlan, the well-known colored politician, once took a string of horses to the other side of the ocean," the paper reported in January 1895.[20]

The following month, Frederick Douglass dropped dead of a heart attack at the age of seventy-seven at his home in Washington. In recent years, Douglass—who, like Robert, often played the role of explaining the Black community to white politicians—had wrestled with some of the same dilemmas as Robert. He had challenged the white community's desire to bury any differences between the North and the South, decrying the neglect of the cause that animated the Civil War, but also urged Black people not to grow so disenchanted as to abandon politics entirely.[21] Despite the vast acclaim for Douglass among abolitionists before the Civil War, the nation's white leadership largely turned its back on him later in life. At his four-hour service at Washington's Metropolitan AME Church, the two most prominent white attendees were Senator John Sherman and Supreme Court Justice John Marshall Harlan.[22] President Cleveland and top congressional leaders didn't show up to honor the greatest Black leader of the century; neither did any of John's court colleagues.

In Cincinnati, Robert headed a committee of illustrious African Americans who planned a memorial service for Douglass in early March at Allen Temple. A bust of Douglass, draped in red, white, and blue, stood at the center of the altar beside a portrait of Abraham Lincoln.[23] But when the day of the service came, Robert was too ill to preside, the *Enquirer* reported.

He rebounded, however, to make a few ventures into the spotlight the following year. In June 1896, after the announcement of the Supreme Court's ruling in *Plessy v. Ferguson*, Robert was well enough to travel to St. Louis for the Republican National Convention, helping to rally support for the presidential nomination of Ohio's just-retired governor, William McKinley. Nearing eighty, Robert acknowledged to the *Piqua Daily Call*, an Ohio newspaper, that he was "all the more enthusiastic because he feels that this may be his last national convention."[24] The *Cleveland Gazette* was blunter. In listing prominent African American attendees, the Black paper parenthetically noted of Robert, "the old veteran seems failing very fast."[25]

He passed his eightieth birthday that December with little fanfare. For much of the next nine months, he seemed to be in a state of decline, due more to the weakness of old age than any specific illness. Eventually he moved in with Robert Jr. and Mamie. On the night of September 20, 1897, sensing that the end might be near, Robert Jr. and Mamie opened their home to scores of friends in the Black community, many of whom had gotten their starts in business with Robert's assistance.[26] After seeing his friends, he passed away quietly the following day.[27]

Both the *Louisville Courier-Journal*[28] and the *Cincinnati Enquirer*, newspapers that had sometimes deprecated him in the past, published long, flattering obituaries that befitted a truly major figure. The *Enquirer*, in particular, portrayed Robert as a model of thrift and enterprise, hailing in its headline the "Remarkable Career of a Poor Colored Boy Who Rose to Fame and Fortune."[29] It recounted the full arc of Robert's life, from his birth in slavery in distant rural Virginia, to his years in the Harlan home, to his fame in the racing world and his national impact as a politician.

The paper then regaled readers with tales of Robert's horse-racing expertise, his rise to wealth in the gold rush, the excellence of his photo studio ("the largest of its kind in the West"), his visit to the Crystal Palace in London, his decision to escape from "American prejudices" and live "in grand style" in Europe, and, finally, his decision to return to Cincinnati and launch his political career. The paper noted that "for years, no great turf event or gathering of his party took place but that the stalwart figure of 'Bob' Harlan was to be noticed in the throng of celebrities." It also declared him to have been a personal confidant of every major Republican, from Sumner, to Grant, to Hayes, to Garfield, to Blaine, and a "warm personal friend of President McKinley." But his greatest legacy in Cincinnati, the *Enquirer* predicted, would be his advocacy for civil rights and his founding of "the first school for colored children that was erected in this city."

The *Enquirer* offered no explanation for how or why Robert was raised as a member of the Harlan family, but recounted his homeschooling by James and noted that "thus 'Bob' Harlan came by the name he honored throughout his long life."[30]

Indeed, Robert did more than just honor the Harlan name. His ability to look beyond the prejudices of the moment, seize opportunities whenever they presented themselves, and put his faith in the long-term vindication of American ideals of liberty and equality represented the practical embodiment of the philosophy of James and John Harlan: he lifted their ideas off the page and put them into action. But at the time of his death, Robert would have been foolish not to wonder if Black people's faith in American ideals would ever be rewarded.

Three days after Robert's death, mourners filled the pews at St. Paul Episcopal Church on the corner of Seventh and Plum Streets. Among them was a large gathering of the state's Black elites.[31] An all-Black choir, St. Andrews Colored Mission, filled the hall with hymns. After his eulogy, Reverend A. G. McGuire broke custom to allow the attendees to file by the open casket to pay their personal respects.[32] Then the crowd headed out to the Cincinnati suburb of Warsaw, where Robert's body was interred in a Black cemetery under a six-foot white marble marker, alongside the remains of his fourth wife, Mary Clark Harlan. The ornate gravestone, with Gothic carvings, contains the words, "Robert Harlan, December 12, 1816 to September 21, 1897."

The last years of the century were good ones for John: his lucrative series of law classes at Columbian University eased some of his financial burdens. He proved to be a popular professor, taking the stage at a large lecture hall for two hours in the evening and on weekends, standing in a formal black suit before a crowd of students. He walked his audience through a real-time discussion of the most pressing legal issues facing the country, covering a litany of cases and citations.[33] He welcomed input from the students and expansively reframed their questions to explore all the contours of a legal dilemma.[34] Whenever he discussed a Supreme Court case in which he dissented, he would outline the majority opinion and then his counterview, adding, to students' laughter, "But of course I was wrong."[35] In the eyes of the Supreme Court, the majority is unerringly correct.

Malvina wasn't pleased to have her already work-focused husband take on a demanding second job but recognized it as a necessity to support their large household and the social obligations of his position.[36] John himself discussed with his students the financial stresses imposed on leading public figures and revealed his own sense of why the allure of public service remained strong despite the sacrifices, according to the extremely detailed shorthand notes of a Columbian student from 1897–98 named George Johannes.[37]

"No senator, except upon the utmost economy, can get along in the city of Washington, make ends meet at the close of the year, upon the salary he gets," John declared, according to Johannes's notes. "Well, you ask, if that is so, why do they remain in public life? I cannot tell, except from the feeling of the ambition that is planted in the breast of every man to live after he is dead and gone in the memory of his fellow citizens."[38]

By those years, 1897 and 1898, John was well along toward achieving that ambition. He was living a comfortable life in the Euclid Place home that his sons had bought for him and, most excitedly, at a summer colony in Quebec, Canada. The summer home was something of a reward for him and Malvina after their sons completed their educations, married, and, in the case of one of them, began raising a large family of his own.

John's eldest son, Richard, the most serious minded of the three boys, graduated at the top of his class at Princeton. Sharing the devout Presbyterianism of his parents and his late sister, Edith, Richard went on to attain master's and divinity degrees at Princeton. He then embarked on a career in the ministry and academia.[39] John's second and third sons, James Shanklin Harlan and John Maynard Harlan, followed Richard to Princeton but then veered off into the law. While neither hit the books with the diligence of Richard, James nonetheless impressed his father with his lawyerly reasoning; John began to envision James as following in his judicial footsteps.[40]

The mercurial John Maynard, the justice's third son, was the least disciplined of them all. When he was expelled by Princeton for a second time for hazing other students, his despairing father questioned his character. John Maynard's actions offended John's sense of fair play. Writing to young James about his brother's plight, the justice used the occasion to lecture both boys on the importance of standing up for the little guy. "He knows my abhorrence of hazing," John wrote about John Maynard. "If a freshman happens to be a weak-spirited fellow, it is mean and cowardly to impose on him. There is an element of brutality in the spectacle of a crowd of boys making one boy a subject of ridicule and indignity. . . . The spirit out of which hazing comes is that kind of low brutality which crops out finally in robbery, burglary, and murder. I cannot think of hazing without abhorrence of its innate wickedness."[41]

John's fears about his son proved to be exaggerated. John Maynard repented and finished Princeton, then followed his brother James to Chicago to practice law. A progressive reformer, John Maynard shared his father's crusading spirit; elected a Chicago alderman, he twice ran for mayor on the Republican ticket, losing to favored Democrats. John Maynard was the only one of John's sons to present his parents with heirs to carry on the family name: a daughter, Lysbeth, in 1891, followed by a much-adored son in 1899, who was named John Marshall Harlan II. Two more daughters would be born in the following decade.

With the boys well launched in their careers and the family burgeoning with in-laws, John and Malvina searched for the perfect place to bring the whole group together for the summers. They eventually found it in a serene village named Pointe-au-Pic on the lower Saint Lawrence River, in Quebec. Known as Murray Bay, the colony included a community of French Canadians joined in the summers by prominent families from Canada and the United States, including the Tafts. After renting one large cottage stuffed to the brim with themselves, their two younger daughters, their granddaughter Edith, all three sons and their wives, plus two of the boys' mothers-in-law, John and Malvina decided to build a home of their own. They chose a site overlooking the mountains and the distant sea and constructed a Victorian-style wooden home that they named Braemead, in a nod to Malvina's Scottish-Irish ancestors. Richard's wife and John Maynard bought and leased separate cottages for their own families.[42] Entranced by the peacefulness of the community, John took up the game of golf—his first regular exercise in two decades on the Supreme Court.

From June through September, with the court in recess, John would reside full-time at Braemead. As Malvina recalled later: "My husband and I passed many hours together on the Braemead verandah, drinking in the beauties of the scene, my husband often saying with a thrill of loving reverence in his voice . . . 'I do not believe there is a more beautiful spot on God's earth.'"[43]

During the years he was discovering the joys of Murray Bay, John participated in two cases that, while of only modest interest at the time, would later prompt scholarly debate over his legacy.

One concerned the still relatively new and emerging concept of public education. Public high schools were somewhat rare around the country, especially in the South. Georgia's Richmond County, which included the city of Augusta, was one of the few local governments in the region to play a significant role in secondary education, whether for Black or white people.[44] A Reconstruction-era legislature passed an education law that included a provision requiring that Richmond

County "shall provide the same facilities for both [white and Negro children], both as regards schoolhouses and fixtures, attainments, and abilities of teachers."[45]

Augusta's Black elites sent their children to all-Black Ware High School, which had been founded in 1872 in a burst of idealism by reformers of both races to provide a classical Latin and Greek education to the most promising children of freed men and women.[46] An exemplary institution for its time, it received public funds, though it also charged tuition. In 1897, however, the school board decided to switch course from subsidizing Ware to providing vocational training for young Black children at free "common schools"; the board reasoned that the same funds that benefitted sixty high school children could help elevate between three hundred and four hundred younger kids. Common schools had been praised by Booker T. Washington, and many Black people outside the circle of Black aristocrats felt that common schools offered a more practical form of education for a greater number of people. At the high school level, the board reasoned, Black students could enroll at any of three church-supported institutions that offered secondary education to students of all races in Augusta, and at a lower tuition than at Ware; while sectarian in nature, those schools did not bar students based on religion, and two of them even received public funds. In addition, the board promised to revive Ware when more money was available.[47]

Dismayed by the all-white board's decision to abandon an important institution in their community, a group of Ware parents filed suit. They demanded an injunction blocking Richmond County from using any funds on the white public high school, arguing that such spending was illegal under Georgia's education law if the county didn't maintain a public high school for Black youths as well. The petition did not reference *Plessy v. Ferguson*. Nor did it argue that Black students should be admitted to the white high school. The parents simply wanted their beloved Ware High School back.

The Ware parents found a sympathetic judge in Enoch Calloway, a former state senator with a reputation as a racial moderate.[48] He granted the petition and blocked the school board from spending money on the white high school until it reopened the Black one. However, the Georgia Supreme Court reversed Calloway's ruling, finding that the law had been satisfied because the Black students continued to have access to comparable high schools at equal cost. The Ware parents appealed to the US Supreme Court.

Their case got a boost when George F. Edmunds—the former senator who had made such an impassioned argument against the income tax in the *Pollock* case—agreed to come out of semiretirement at age seventy-one to argue on behalf of the plaintiffs. Edmunds attempted to raise an argument under the Fourteenth Amendment's equal protection clause that hadn't been stressed in the initial filings. But he, too, focused on the need to enjoin the board from funding the white school until it restored the Black one, and made no argument that the children of the two races should be educated together.[49]

In an unsurprising decision, the US Supreme Court affirmed the ruling of its state counterpart in Georgia, contending that the law did not require the county to maintain a public high school for Black students if a comparable institution was available at equal or lower cost. What was mildly surprising was that Justice Harlan, who had disagreed so thunderously with the separate-but-equal doctrine three years earlier, joined in the unanimous decision and wrote the court's opinion.[50] John made a point of noting that the plaintiffs had not claimed that the school board had acted out of racial discrimination, somewhat tying the court's hands.

"We are not permitted by the evidence in the record to regard that decision as having been made with any desire or purpose on the part of the board to discriminate against any of the colored children of the county on account of their race," John wrote. "But if it be assumed that the board erred in supposing that its duty was to provide educational facilities for three hundred colored children who were without an opportunity in primary schools to learn the alphabet and to read and write, rather than to maintain a school for the benefit of the sixty colored children who wished to attend a high school, that was not an error which a court of equity should attempt to remedy by an injunction that would compel the board to withhold all assistance from the high school maintained for white children."[51]

Why did John decide to join this decision, which, in the eyes of some later critics, came to be seen as an endorsement of segregation? It wasn't because he opposed having Black and white students educated together; indeed, nine years later, he would write a blistering opinion in defense of integrated education.[52] Rather, the answer seems to be in the extremely narrow, technical opinion that he wrote, stressing all the ways in which the pleadings and the record prevented the court from making a judgment on racial discrimination. If John had dissented from the court's decision, another justice—probably Henry Billings Brown—would have been tapped to write the opinion. He then might have used the occasion to strengthen and reinforce the doctrine of separate but equal. By grabbing ahold of the reins, John ensured that the court's ruling was narrow enough to apply only to this specific, and rather peculiar, situation. The fact that the case, *Cumming v. Board of Ed of Richmond County*, would go on to be cited only a paltry six times in future Supreme Court cases suggests John succeeded in minimizing its impact as a legal precedent.[53]

Clearly, he believed that the school board had made a reasonable decision to prioritize one type of education over another. Equally clearly, he made sure that the case could not be used by other courts to promote segregation or discourage integration.

Perhaps more concerning to later generations was John's vote in the case of Wong Kim Ark, the twenty-two-year-old son of Chinese workers who had been born in San Francisco in 1873.[54] When he tried to return to the United States in 1895, after a yearlong sojourn in China, Wong was denied reentry.[55] He claimed that, based on the Fourteenth Amendment, he was entitled to US citizenship even though his parents had been subjects of the Chinese emperor. Indeed, the Fourteenth Amendment, ratified just five years before Wong's birth, stated that "All persons born or naturalized in the United States, and subject to the jurisdiction thereof, are citizens of the United States and of the State wherein they reside."[56]

No one disputed that Wong had been born on US soil. The only question was whether that alone was enough to make him a citizen. When the case made its way to the Supreme Court, the justices debated the plain language of the Fourteenth Amendment and, in particular, the meaning of the term "subject to the jurisdiction thereof." Was that meant to include visitors? Or did it mean that only children born to US citizens or immigrants involved in the naturalization process could be granted such "birthright" citizenship? This called attention to the unnaturalized status of Chinese workers. Under the treaty in force at the time of Wong's birth, his parents were in the United States to work but could not become citizens.

A majority of six justices decided the case in Wong's favor, ruling that both the language of the amendment and the common law that surrounded it did not restrict birthright citizenship to the children of parents who were themselves citizens or in the process of becoming citizens.[57] John dissented from the ruling but did not offer an opinion of his own. Rather, he joined a dissent by Chief Justice Fuller, who insisted that the phrase "subject to the jurisdiction thereof" meant that parents whose children received birthright citizenship had to be more than just visiting the United States; they needed to be subject to its "political jurisdiction"—that is, owing their sole allegiance to the United States.[58]

Given the intense anger and racial discrimination that still simmered in California regarding its Chinese population, Fuller and Harlan were seen by some later critics as having caved in to the prejudices of the time. Harlan's decision to join in Fuller's dissent was especially eye-opening because, more than a decade earlier, he had been one of only two justices insisting that a Native American who left his tribe should be granted birthright citizenship.[59] That case involved a Winnebago Indian named John Elk, who left the reservation and lived in Omaha, Nebraska. The Supreme Court refused to grant him citizenship under the Fourteenth Amendment, arguing that Indians were foreigners under the law. The injustice of that case led to a classic Harlan dissent—an impassioned cry of outrage against racial prejudice and defense of the rights of Native Americans.

"If he did not acquire national citizenship on abandoning his tribe and becoming, by residence in one of the states, subject to the complete jurisdiction of the United States, then the Fourteenth Amendment has wholly failed to accomplish, in respect of the Indian race, what, we think, was intended by it," John thundered, "and there is still in this country a despised and rejected class of persons with no nationality whatsoever, who, born in our territory, owing no allegiance to any foreign power . . . are yet not members of any political community, nor entitled to any of the rights, privileges, or immunities of citizens of the United States."[60]

What, then, was the difference between a Native American like John Elk and a Chinese man like Wong Kim Ark? In John's mind, a lot. Black people and Indians were Americans, born in this country but denied their constitutional rights.[61] Elk left his tribe and expressed his loyalty to the United States. By contrast, Wong's parents—and Wong himself—remained subjects of the Chinese emperor. Such dual loyalties rankled John, offending his sense of American exceptionalism and touching on a deep-rooted skepticism about whether people who lived under monarchies could adapt to American democracy. In his youth, he had expressed worries about Catholic immigrants who maintained a loyalty to a dictatorial Pope—and those families, unlike Wong's parents, were eagerly and wholeheartedly embracing American citizenship.

After the court's decision in *United States v. Wong Kim Ark*, John discussed the case with his students at Columbian University. According to George Johannes's notes, the justice posited the example of an English couple, loyal to the British crown, who "went down to Hot Springs [Arkansas] to get rid of the gout" and had a child before returning to England. "Is this child a citizen of the United States, born to the jurisdiction thereof, by the mere accident of his birth?" Harlan asked rhetorically.[62] In answering no, Harlan was signaling that his objection to Wong's citizenship would apply equally to a white European whose parents remained subjects of a monarch.

"My belief [was that the Fourteenth Amendment] was never intended to embrace everybody in our citizenship if he was the child of parents who cannot under the law become naturalized in the United States," John declared in his lecture to the students, referring to the *Wong* case.[63] But he added, as was his custom, "I was one of the minority, and of course I was wrong."[64]

Chapter 17

The Constitution Follows the Flag

As the nineteenth century drew to a close, the North Shore of Oahu, Hawaii, with its palm-shaded beaches and vast acres of citrus and sugar cane, was ground zero for the dawning of a new age of American imperialism. For two decades, the imperialism had been mostly economic: US business interests fronted the local Kahuku Plantation Company and sugar mill, importing workers from Asian countries to live in ethnic communes while planting, clearing, cutting cane, and operating the mill, all under the heavy hands of western overseers.[1] Then the imperialism became political. American plantation owners and other westerners, backed by the US military, overthrew the Hawaiian monarch, Queen Lili'uokalani, in 1893, during the waning days of the Harrison administration. Though the coup plotters envisioned the creation of an American colony, incoming president Grover Cleveland shocked them by declaring the coup illegal and the US intervention "wholly without justification."[2] Five years later, amid a surge of public support for territorial expansion, a different president, William McKinley, welcomed the nascent Hawaiian Republic into the formal embrace of the United States.

Suddenly the Kahuku plantation and others like it were part of the United States territory of Hawaii, under the control of the US Congress. And so it was on March 26, 1899, when about fifty Japanese workers restlessly gathered amid the palm trees, some carrying sticks, to avenge a wrong done to one of their number by workers at the nearby Chinese encampment.[3] Tension between ethnic groups was an unfortunate byproduct of plantation life; the Japanese and Chinese pickers lived at different camps and knew only their own languages.[4] Mistrust and competition simmered behind such barriers.

On this day, the friction exploded into violence. Japanese men stormed the Chinese camp. A melee ensued. One of the Chinese workers, Chew Foon Wing, dropped to the sand and bled to death. Several of his fellow Chinese purported to identify the attacker who stabbed Chew, along with other Japanese who wielded weapons near the scene of the crime. Hawaiian authorities under the leadership of Attorney General Edmund Pearson Dole—a New Englander who had been recruited by his cousin, Sanford Dole, the territorial governor— brought first-degree murder charges against five of the Japanese men: whether or not any of the defendants had struck the decisive blow, the territorial authorities reasoned, all had precipitated the murder by arming themselves and invoking lethal force.[5]

A jury of twelve men wasn't entirely persuaded by the government's broad-brush theory. Some jurors apparently resisted the idea that the Japanese workers had plotted in advance to use such serious violence;[6] other jurors seemed to have trouble parsing out the culpability among the five individual defendants. Language barriers and conflicting testimony presented frustrating obstacles.[7]

When the verdicts came down, one man was found guilty of first-degree murder for stabbing Chew. Another, named Osaki Mankichi, was acquitted of murder, while the jurors split, 9 to 3, over the lesser offense of manslaughter. Under Hawaiian law, however, defendants could be found guilty if only nine of twelve jurors thought so, even if the others disagreed.[8]

Mankichi appealed his manslaughter conviction to the Hawaiian Supreme Court, claiming that the jury's theory of the case in finding his fellow defendant guilty of first-degree murder was incompatible with its conclusions about his role. The Western-led territorial court acknowledged some of the ambiguities of the jury's findings but deferred to the jurors, concluding, "While it is difficult to reconcile many parts of the testimony, we find that the jury had sufficient evidence before them to justify them in arriving at the conclusions they reached, and we decline to interfere with the verdict."[9]

Under the old system, that would have been the final word. But Osaki Mankichi was being held under the authority of the United States of America, the Constitution of which forbids convictions except by unanimous verdicts. By that standard, Mankichi argued, he should be a free man. And he demanded that the US Supreme Court give him his constitutional rights and his freedom.

Building a global empire wasn't part of the American plan. When colonists rose up against the king of England, their sword and shield was the principle of self-government. The Declaration of Independence condemned the moral wrong of taxation without representation. The US Constitution imposed clear limits on the power of government over individuals. That such a people—proudly protective of their independence, freedom from a monarch, and unalienable rights—would seek to hold other nations under a different set of rules, was ironic, to say the least.[10]

And yet, in the 1890s, Americans were feeling hemmed in. Across the ocean, they saw European nations hungrily gathering colonies from Africa to the Far East to produce raw materials to fuel their own, vaguely threatening, economic and military expansions. Though Spain was a waning power, having lost most of its South American possessions to wars of independence, its colonial fingers nonetheless extended into the United States' own hemisphere. Spanish control of Puerto Rico and Cuba, just a few hundred miles off the US coast, felt like an intrusion to some Americans and a provocation to others, especially since the islands' economies were increasingly tied to US markets.

When, in 1895, a hike in US tariffs precipitated a collapse of the Cuban economy, Cubans rose up against their colonial masters. Spain responded by sending 150,000 troops to repress the rebellion.[11] American newspapers, led by the *New York Journal*, the prime mouthpiece of thirty-five-year-old press baron William Randolph Hearst, campaigned openly for US intervention, proclaiming in screaming headlines every alleged atrocity at the hands of the Spanish commander, General Valeriano "Butcher" Weyler.

"Credible witnesses have testified that all prisoners captured by Weyler's forces are killed on the spot; that even helpless inmates of a hospital have not been spared, and that Weyler's intention seems to be to murder all the pacificos in the country," declared a *Journal* editorial. ". . . The American people will not tolerate in the Western Hemisphere the methods of the Turkish savages in Armenia."[12]

Goaded by Hearst and other imperialists, President McKinley sent the battleship USS *Maine* to Havana to protect American interests, only to have the vessel explode overnight, killing 250 people. While the precise cause of the disaster was never determined, and, to this day, theorists insist it could have been a mechanical explosion, vast numbers of Americans—including those stimulated by sensational reports in the "yellow" press of Hearst and Joseph Pulitzer—pounced on the idea that Spain was responsible. "Now to Avenge the Maine," read a four-inch headline, in capitals letters, in Hearst's *Journal*.[13]

In truth, the Spanish-American War represented the confluence of many forces in American life: the hunger for new customers and raw materials of Gilded Age manufacturers (though many on Wall Street had initially been wary of a disruptive conflict);[14] transportation advances that expanded the range of credible military threats against the United States; the triumph of westward expansion that loosened the limbs of its adherents and left them bright-eyed for new horizons;[15] and a growing popular identification with the Cubans yearning to shake free of their colonial master.[16]

On April 20, 1898, McKinley demanded that Spain relinquish its control of Cuba; declarations of war soon followed. The chance to move forcefully against Spain proved to be a tonic for a nation eager to shake off the stigma of the Civil War and revel in its newfound unity and purpose. The army brought together the sons of North and South, along with a smattering of veterans who had actually worn the

Blue or the Gray; even segregated African American units were to play a patriotic role in yellow-fever-imperiled Cuba.[17]

The navy was the blunt face of American power in the Pacific. Admiral George Dewey electrified the world by rousting the Spanish navy in the Philippines' Manila Bay without losing a man; that military triumph was followed by a political masterstroke when Dewey shipped in an exiled Filipino revolutionary, Emilio Aguinaldo, to foment an indigenous uprising against the Spanish. The rebellion succeeded, after which the United States turned on Aguinaldo and, after the Philippine-American War, seized the archipelago for the red, white, and blue.

The army and the navy amassed enough victories in Cuba and Puerto Rico, as well, that a beleaguered Spain quickly sued for peace. By the end of 1898, with the Treaty of Paris, Spain formally surrendered the Philippines, Guam, and Puerto Rico to the United States; Cuba would be granted self-rule as a US protectorate, and the United States would acquire a permanent military base at Guantanamo Bay. In the midst of the short war, McKinley and Congress hastily completed the annexation process for Hawaii, too.

Suddenly, at the dawn of the new century, the United States not only spanned from coast to coast in North America, but also ruled almost 8 million Filipinos,[18] 953,000 Puerto Ricans,[19] 154,000 Hawaiians,[20] and 12,000 men and women on the sunny sands of the beautiful and strategically important West Pacific island of Guam.[21]

The fact that such a colonial arrangement seemed entirely at odds with the principles of democracy and national self-determination that underscored the American Revolution wasn't lost on many of the thinkers of the day. Not everyone was caught up in the hullabaloo surrounding the Spanish-American War. Indeed, at the very moment that Dewey was in Manila and Congress debated the annexation of Hawaii, a group of Massachusetts civic leaders gathered at one of the storied meeting places of the republic—Faneuil Hall—just blocks

from the scene of the 1770 Boston Massacre, in which American colonists were killed by British soldiers, to express grave concern about
assuming dictatorial control of faraway islands.[22]

"The policy of imperialism threatens to change the temper of our
people," declared Charles Ames, a noted theologian. ". . . Once we
enter the field of international conflict as a great military and naval
power, we shall be one more bully among bullies."[23]

There were less high-minded concerns as well. "Hawaiian religion
is the embodiment of bestiality and malignity that frequently lapses
into crimes of lust and revenge," asserted Kentucky congressman
John Rhea on the floor of the House.[24]

The fact that the natives of both Hawaii and the Spanish colonies that were being acquired as war booty were nonwhite helped
to alleviate guilt about taking their lands: some idealistic imperialists reasoned that the natives would be elevated by the guiding hands
of white Americans, much as Hawaiians were said to have benefited
from the presence of Western missionaries in earlier decades; other,
less idealistic imperialists simply felt unbothered by any notion of repressing a nonwhite population, believing it to be genetically incapa-
ble of American-style order and civilization.[25]

Indeed, the belief that self-government was suitable only for European extracts pervaded the country; whether nonwhite populations
could, in time, mature into societies capable of self-government, or
were forever constrained by their racial inferiority, was a debate for
another day. Almost no one envisioned giving the colonists rights
equal to those of Americans on the continent.

In a lecture in Richmond, Virginia, a decade later, Charles Francis
Adams Jr.—bearer of a hallowed name of the founding generation—
explained that the "scriptural" notions of brotherhood of man that
guided his great-grandfather's generation had been replaced through
time and hard experience by a more "scientific" understanding of the
capacities, or lack thereof, of certain racial groups.[26]

But even if racial prejudices had hardened since the era of Adams
and Jefferson, the language of the Constitution remained the same.
The widespread assumption that overseas territories should be gov-

erned by different standards than those on the continent presented an obvious constitutional issue. Article Four gave Congress the power to regulate territories but did not specify whether the people who lived there had constitutional rights; the Supreme Court under Chief Justice John Marshall had insisted they did. The whole question of territorial growth beyond the nation's continental shoulders challenged Lincoln's notion of government "of the people, by the people, for the people": the people in overseas colonies didn't consent to American oversight and weren't being given a choice in their government.

John Harlan could see the coming clash. He could envision a time, increasingly imminent, when the acquisition of colonies would come into conflict with the rights he had sworn to uphold.

Thus, on February 21, 1900, before the Supreme Court had any chance to weigh in on such questions, John seized on an invitation to dedicate a new law building on the campus of the University of Pennsylvania to publicly declare his belief that constitutional rights should apply to everyone under the jurisdiction of the United States.

After professing that the new building, part of a flowering of legal education at the turn of the century, was a gift to all "lovers of liberty," he offered his Philadelphia audience a pointed explanation of what such liberty entailed.

"When I speak of liberty, I mean such liberty as is enjoyed in our country," he announced. "This fair land is in a peculiar sense the home of freedom—the freedom that takes account of man as man, that tolerates no government which does not rest upon the consent of the governed, and recognizes the right of all persons within its jurisdiction, of whatever race, to the equal protection of the laws in every matter affecting life, liberty, or property."[27]

That majestic sentiment echoed his dissent in *Plessy v. Ferguson*. It also touched on his cherished notions of American exceptionalism—"the home of freedom," a nation governed by collective beliefs rather than mere common interest—with a nod to the Declaration of Independence as well.

But to those in the audience listening carefully, it also portended a coming explosion—a thunderous clash between those founding principles and the headstrong notions of politicians bent on acquisition of territory with little thought or concern about the status of the people who lived there. Once again, Justice Harlan was preparing to stand against the tide of public opinion in the name of constitutional fidelity and national destiny.

The first legal tests of the new territories' status under the Constitution came not from jubilant colonists seeking to assert their rights but from importers seeking to avoid tariffs. Puerto Rico supplied the continental United States with sugar and many of the citrus fruits that were becoming increasingly popular among American consumers, especially during the long northeastern winters. When the Treaty of Paris formally conveyed the Caribbean island to the United States at the end of 1898, many fruit vendors welcomed the news, expecting to pay less for pineapples, oranges, lemons, and other Puerto Rican delicacies.[28] But the Port of New York continued to collect the tariffs as if Puerto Rico were still a foreign country. Then, in 1900, Congress passed the Foraker Act, which purported to be a kind of special constitution for Puerto Rico. The original House version of the bill would have extended to Puerto Ricans the same rights as continental Americans, but the Senate thought better of it. The *New York Times* reported that "the change was made because of the opinion generally expressed by the members of the committee that our Constitution is not suited to the Puerto Rican people."[29]

Among the many differences between the treatment of Puerto Rico and continental territories was special tariffs on goods transported from the island to the mainland, a favor to Floridian citrus barons and others who feared competition with Puerto Rican growers. The legal challenges to the government's handling of Puerto Rican tariffs came fast and furious. The Supreme Court realized that far more was at stake than duties on oranges. But as in the first few years after the ratification of the postwar amendments, the justices seemed to have vastly different, and sometimes idiosyncratic, views on what constituted a fundamental reordering of the American system. Clearly, it wasn't going to be easy to rally the court behind a cohesive theory on when, whether, and under what terms the Constitution applies to colonies.

Once again, the eyes of the country were on the Supreme Court. The legal battle over American Empire dominated the front pages of newspapers, and even made it into the comics. Mr. Dooley, a fictional Irish American bartender from Chicago whose accented witticisms made him the Mike Doonesbury of his day, opined, "No matter whether th' constitution follows h' flag or not, th' Supreme Court follows th' election returns."[30] McKinley's landslide reelection in 1900, with the "Rough Rider" hero of the war in Cuba, Teddy Roosevelt, on board as vice president, gave a boost of popular approval to colonialism just as the court was preparing to hear the cases.

Nonetheless, the administration was taking nothing for granted. It feared that an adverse ruling would tie its hands overseas; granting full constitutional rights to Hispanics and Pacific Islanders would compound the nation's administrative responsibilities in those colonies and create immigration and commercial complications back home. Seeking to put pressure on the court, McKinley signed a resolution directing the publication of the full record of the court's proceedings in the first round of the so-called Insular Cases, thereby putting the justices on the spot for every question or utterance from the bench.[31]

McKinley's attorney general, John W. Griggs, would carry the government's flags into battle. A highly respected corporate attorney who was elected governor of New Jersey, Griggs had resigned his post in Trenton when McKinley persuaded him to join the cabinet in 1898.[32] Griggs replaced Attorney General Joseph McKenna, who had joined the Supreme Court as the replacement for Stephen Field, who had finally heeded his colleagues' entreaties to resign because of increasing dementia.

Now McKenna sat on the bench in front of the eagle statue and damask drapes in the Old Senate Chamber, one of the few justices who were considered solidly behind the government's case for wide latitude in dealing with overseas colonies. As the justices began questioning Griggs, the range of their disagreements with him and one another became more apparent. Harlan was the most deeply skeptical of the idea that Congress and the president could set up an entirely different system of government for people who, after all, lived under the auspices of the US Constitution.

John suggested that the government's theory of its own powers was so open ended that it could appoint kings and queens and dukes and earls to preside over its overseas possessions.

"Do you admit that Congress could establish titles of nobility in the territories of the outlying possessions?" he demanded of Griggs.

The attorney general responded, "We are not dealing with titles of nobility," before adding, coldly, "International law declares that the new sovereign may deal with the inhabitants of conquered or ceded territory, and give them such law as he sees fit. They receive political privileges and benefits at the will of the new government and not by virtue of the automatical [sic] operation of the laws of the new sovereign."[33]

Later, John asked Griggs whether he believed Congress could establish a nonrepublican form of government in the colonies. Griggs said yes. Harlan then repeated his question about titles of nobility, and Griggs, seemingly lacking a good response, declared, "I do not think, if your honors please, that that is a territorial question, any more than is the question as to whether Congress can grant titles of nobility here."[34] (In fact, as Harlan clearly knew, the Constitution specifically prohibits the granting of titles.)[35]

When the solicitor general, John K. Richards, took over the administration's case, he claimed that, while previous treaties such as the Louisiana Purchase had intended "that the civilized inhabitants of the ceded territories should ultimately—not immediately, but *ultimately*—become citizens of the United States and be incorporated in the United States, this treaty [the Treaty of Paris] left the determination of their civil rights and political status to Congress."

Harlan interjected, "What treaty has used the word *civilized*?"

Richards demurred. "I do not assume to quote the precise language of the particular treaties, but simply state the effect of them."[36]

Then Harlan challenged Richards's assertion that "certainly the treaty never intended to make these tropical islands, with their savage and half-civilized and civilized people, a part of the United States in the constitutional sense."[37]

Most problematic for Griggs and Richards was the fact that the Supreme Court, under Chief Justice Marshall, had already rejected the notion that Congress could deny constitutional rights to people in territories.[38] The 1820 case of *Loughborough v. Blake* dealt with the District of Columbia. To distinguish that case from the current matter, Griggs and Richards strived to emphasize the "savage" conditions of these new territories, thereby carving another racial division into the American justice system.

When the justices assembled four months later to announce their rulings in the Puerto Rico cases, it was apparent they'd faced a lot of difficulty reaching any kind of consensus: the court delivered no fewer than five opinions in the most significant of the cases, *Downes v. Bidwell*. However, when all these disparate views were added together, they amounted to a 5-to-4 endorsement of Griggs's position—and a huge win for the government.

Once again, the court relied on the scattershot logic of Henry Billings Brown to render the majority opinion. His basic holding was that the Constitution, while assessing a careful division of powers between the federal government and the states, made no effort to restrain those powers inherent in national sovereignty, which include the right to obtain and govern colonies as Congress sees fit. And where a half decade earlier he had held forth on racial differences in defending segregation in *Plessy v. Ferguson*, now Brown juxtaposed "Anglo-Saxon" values versus those of people in other climes to put a gloss of reason over Congress's efforts to restrict liberties in Puerto Rico.

"Grave apprehensions of danger are felt by many eminent men . . . [that] an unrestrained possession of power on the part of Congress may lead to unjust and oppressive legislation in which the natural rights of territories, or their inhabitants, may be engulfed in a centralized despotism," Brown wrote. "These fears, however, find no justification in the action of Congress in the past century nor in the conduct of the British Parliament towards its outlying possessions since the American Revolution. . . . There are certain principles of natural justice inherent in the Anglo-Saxon character which need no expression in constitutions or statutes to give them effect or to secure dependencies against legislation manifestly hostile to their real interests."

In this extraordinary passage, Brown brushed away every manifest abuse of British colonialism in Africa and Asia for more than a century, suggesting instead that the record shows that the "Anglo-Saxon character"—and not freedom or democracy—would safeguard the "real interests" of people in other lands.

Brown's opinion was endorsed by justices McKenna and Shiras, who also joined a concurring opinion by Justice White, and by Horace Gray, who supplied his own concurrence. Chief Justice Fuller, along with justices Brewer and Rufus W. Peckham, delivered a withering dissent, concluding that the idea that Congress could operate outside the Constitution was refuted by the document itself in language "too plain and unambiguous to permit its meaning to be thus influenced."[39]

Harlan, for his part, declared that Fuller's arguments "meet my entire approval," but added, "In view, however, of the importance of this case, and of the consequences that will follow any conclusion reached by the court, I deem it appropriate . . . to add some observations suggested by certain passages in opinions just delivered in support of the judgment."[40]

He proceeded to issue a blistering rebuttal to Brown's assertions, starting with the idea that the Constitution was a compact among states. "Although the states are constituent parts of the United States, the government rests upon the authority of the people, and not on that of the states," he wrote.[41] This, no doubt, stemmed from John's bitter experiences before the Civil War: No man who grew up amid the all-consuming threat of secession could believe that, even after a momentous conflict over just such a proposition, the states could be regarded as masters of the federal government.

To then extrapolate that, outside of its relations to the states, the

federal government enjoyed far greater powers, would be to twice in-
jure the Constitution, in John's view.

"I will take leave to say that if the principles thus announced
should ever receive the sanction of a majority of this court, a radical
and mischievous change in our system of government will be the result," he declared. "We will in that event pass from the era of constitutional liberty guarded and protected by a written constitution into an
era of legislative absolutism."[42]

Harlan then directly ridiculed Brown's notion of "Anglo-Saxon
character," asserting that: "The wise men who framed the Constitution and the patriotic people who adopted it were unwilling to depend
for their safety upon what, in the opinion referred to, is described as
'certain principles of natural justice inherent in Anglo-Saxon character which need no expression in constitutions or statutes.' They
proceeded upon the theory—the wisdom of which experience has
vindicated—that the only safe guarantee against government oppression was to withhold or restrict the power to oppress. They well
remembered that Anglo-Saxons across the ocean had attempted,
in defiance of law and justice, to trample upon the rights of Anglo-
Saxons on this continent."[43]

Finally, he rejected the assertion, endorsed by Brown, that granting equal rights to "uncivilized" people could provoke grievous
consequences.

"Whether a particular race will or will not assimilate with our
people, and whether they can or cannot with safety to our institutions
be brought within the operation of the Constitution, is a matter to be
thought of when it is proposed to acquire their territory by treaty," he
stated. "A mistake in the acquisition of territory . . . cannot be made
the grounds for violating the Constitution or refusing to give full effect to its provisions. The Constitution is not to be obeyed or dis-
obeyed as the circumstances of a particular crisis in our history may
suggest the one or the other course to be pursued. The People have
decreed that it shall be the supreme law of the land at all times."[44]

Two years later, the court's focus turned to Hawaii, another tropical island chain robustly flying the Stars and Stripes almost six thousand miles away. Osaki Mankichi, who had been convicted of manslaughter by a 9-to-3 jury vote almost four years earlier, finally got to bring his case before the ultimate tribunal. There were two important differences between *Mankichi v. Hawaii* and the Puerto Rican cases that came before it. First, there was an individual plaintiff pleading for his freedom, which would be granted to him if the Constitution were fully in force in his island home. Second—and potentially more significant—the Newlands Resolution, which made Hawaii a US territory, included language that appeared to give Congress's endorsement to full constitutional rights for Hawaiians. The resolution stated that "The municipal legislation of the Hawaiian Islands, not enacted for the fulfillment of treaties so extinguished, and not inconsistent with this joint resolution *nor contrary to the Constitution of the United States* [emphasis added], shall remain in force until the Congress of the United States shall determine otherwise."[45]

Such was the state of the law on the day when Kahuku Plantation erupted in violence, leading to the murder charges against Mankichi and his fellow Japanese defendants. Hawaii had adhered to its municipal legislation, but in allowing a conviction with less than a unanimous jury vote, its procedures were clearly at odds with the US Constitution. The territorial authorities, however, claimed that Congress hadn't really intended to require that Hawaiians be given full constitutional rights—that, despite the plain language of the Newlands Resolution, the government's true intention was to maintain Hawaiian municipal law as it was.

In the Puerto Rican cases, the court's 5-to-4 majority, led by Henry Billings Brown, had declared the will of Congress to be determinative of whether citizens of territories enjoyed full constitutional liberties; now, despite evidence of just such an intent regarding Hawaii, the same five justices ruled that Congress couldn't possibly have meant what it said. Once again, Brown wrote the majority opinion, and White offered a concurrence. This time Brown began by declaring the municipal procedures of Hawaii to have been fair and wise, largely because they were inspired by American and British immigrants.

"Since 1847, [the Hawaiian Islands] had enjoyed the blessings of a civilized government and a system of jurisprudence modeled largely upon the common law of England and the United States," Brown declared. "Though lying in the tropical zone, the salubrity of their climate and the fertility of their soil had attracted thither large numbers of people from Europe and America, who brought with them political ideas and traditions which, about sixty years ago, found expression in the adoption of a code of laws appropriate to their new conditions."[46]

Would Congress wish to upset the "blessings" of such a carefully crafted system? No, answered Brown. Rather than offer legislative history of the Newlands Resolution to support his conclusion, he based it on the larger goal of the resolution, which was to cause as little disruption as possible to life on the islands. "In all probability," he concluded, "the contingency which has actually arisen occurred to no one at the time. If it had and its consequences were foreseen, it is incredible that Congress should not have provided against it."[47]

The outcome of the case was devastating for Osaki Mankichi, but it also served to show just how far the five-justice majority would go to avoid interfering in the administration of the overseas colonies. Once again, Fuller offered a dissenting opinion, shared by Brewer, Peckham, and Harlan. As before, John stepped forward to offer a further rebuttal of his own. He cited historical evidence, including letters from government and diplomatic officials, that suggested there was a common understanding that Hawaii would be incorporated into the United States with full constitutional rights.

The Constitution, John maintained, "clearly forbids a conviction in any criminal prosecution *except upon the unanimous verdict of a petit jury* [emphasis added]. In other words, neither the life nor the liberty of any person can be taken under the authority of the United States except in the mode thus prescribed."[48]

The court's belief that Congress could simply erase that provision "assumes that Congress, which came into existence and exists only by virtue of the Constitution, can withhold fundamental guarantees of life and liberty from people who have come under our complete jurisdiction—who, to use the words of the United States minister, have become our fellow countrymen."[49]

What John saw in the Insular Cases, and no other justice even alluded to, was the potential for exactly the kind of divisions and hypocrisy that had fanned the flames of civil war: the injustice of keeping some people in subservient conditions, coupled with the economic structures that grow up around such deprivations, and the simple tension of two systems existing under one flag, adding up to a threat to the future of the nation.

"Thus," he warned, "will be engrafted upon our republican institutions, controlled by the supreme law of a written Constitution, a colonial system entirely foreign to the genius of our government and abhorrent to the principles that underlie and pervade the Constitution. It will then come about that we will have two governments over the people subject to the jurisdiction of the United States—one, existing under a written Constitution . . . the other, existing outside of the written Constitution, in virtue of an unwritten law, to be declared from time to time by Congress, which is itself only a creature of that instrument."[50]

During his years of wrestling with the Insular Cases, John received—and rejected—advice from an unusual source: his son James. In late 1900, when the court was first preparing to weigh in on the status of Puerto Rico, the McKinley administration appointed thirty-nine-year-old James the island's attorney general. It also named Justice McKenna's son to an army inspector general post in Puerto Rico.

The moves raised eyebrows among anti-imperialists. South Dakota's outgoing senator, Richard F. Pettigrew, seized on the appearance of the administration cultivating Supreme Court justices through their sons to put a hold on James's confirmation.[51] "Harlan's Confirmation Blocked: Mr. Pettigrew Refers to Appointment of Justice's Son as 'Indecent,'" blared a January 1901 headline of the *New York Times*.[52] A war of words between Pettigrew and Ohio's imperialist senator Joseph Foraker ensued. Pettigrew's term expired two months later, and James eventually won his confirmation.

Though the appointment seemed a welcome step toward his and his father's long-cherished goal of getting him a federal judgeship,[53] the effort to build an American-style legal system in the former Spanish colony weighed on James. On June 3, 1902, he wrote to his father, "From a practical standpoint, it is for the present impossible in this island to administer the local government along constitutional lines. It must be much less possible to do so in the Philippines."[54]

As it happened, the Supreme Court was soon to consider the status of the Philippines, but John was hardly swayed by James's experience. Like Hawaii and Puerto Rico, the Philippines maintained a separate judicial system from the mainland United States, and it happened to make libel a criminal offense. When a newspaper editor was brought up on charges for running a news report on a trial involving a prominent member of the Philippine Commission, the islands' governing body, under the headline "Traitor, Seducer, Perjurer—Wife Would Have Killed Him," the editor appealed to the Supreme Court.[55] He challenged both the law itself and the fact that he had requested a jury trial and been denied; a judge had found him guilty on his own fiat.

There were two constitutional problems with this case. The criminal libel law likely violated the First Amendment, and the Constitution requires jury trials for major crimes. But the court, strictly applying the precedents in the Puerto Rico and Hawaiian cases, ruled that the Filipino editor, as a resident of an overseas colony, was not entitled to relief under the Constitution absent a special designation by Congress. Chief Justice Fuller and Justices Peckham and Brewer—who had opposed similar rulings—threw in the towel this time, concurring in the judgment on the sole grounds that the court's unfavorable decision in *Mankichi v. Hawaii* was now legal precedent and thus should apply to the Philippines case.

John was unmoved. In a fiery dissent, he insisted that the constitutional right to a jury trial should apply to an overseas defendant: "As a Filipino committing the crime of murder in the Philippine Islands may be hung by the sovereign authority of the United States, and as the Philippine Islands are under a civil, not military, government, the suggestion that he may not, of right, appeal for his protection to the jury provisions of the Constitution, which constitutes the only source of the power that the government may exercise at any time or at any place, is utterly revolting to my mind and can never receive my sanction."[56]

He repeated his unyielding conviction that the law must be applied equally, to all, anywhere under the American flag: "In my opinion, guaranties for the protection of life, liberty, and property, as embodied in the Constitution, are for the benefit of all, of whatever race or nativity, in the states composing the union, or in any other territory, however acquired, over the inhabitants of which the government of the United States may exercise the powers conferred upon it by the Constitution."[57]

At the most contentious moment of the Insular Cases—after the Puerto Rico cases but before those of Hawaii and the Philippines—John celebrated his twenty-fifth anniversary on the court. Only Stephen Field, among recent justices, had achieved that milestone. The Bar of the Supreme Court, composed of the lawyers who appear before the tribunal, resolved to honor him with a testimonial dinner.

The dinner was an affirmation of John's continued good standing among his court colleagues and within the legal world despite his increasing disagreements with the state of the law. In just eight years, Justice Harlan had issued some of the most forthright rebuttals in the history of the court on some of its most consequential decisions: the *E.C. Knight* case on the government's power to go after trusts, the *Pollock* case on Congress's power to impose an income tax, the *Plessy* decision on legal segregation, and the *Downes* decision on the government's power to rule overseas colonies as it saw fit. People in the legal world understood how those decisions would shape the world of the twentieth century, and how Harlan's condemnations would linger as appeals to the greater wisdom of future generations. And yet, throughout the tumult of those decisions, Harlan retained the respect of his colleagues. His reverence for the Constitution touched a sentimental chord in their lawyerly souls; his ability to disagree ruthlessly with a colleague's ruling while sharing an apple with him on a streetcar appealed to their own desire for comity.[58] He was the ultimate court loyalist—a team player—who nonetheless considered it part of his oath to break with the team whenever his conscience dictated.

On December 9, 1902, just one day before the twenty-fifth anniversary of the day he was sworn in by Chief Justice Waite, with an excited Malvina and former First Lady Lucy Hayes in attendance, the sixty-nine-year-old John donned a tuxedo and joined much of official Washington at the New Willard Hotel, the capital's foremost showplace. Built on the foundations of the hotel whose lobby, filled throughout the nineteenth century with office seekers, gave its name to the term *lobbyist*, the New Willard stood just a stone's throw from the White House. Still unfinished, it was already considered the capital's most opulent setting.[59]

The stag dinner filled the ballroom with men from many chapters of John's career, from his Kentucky protégé Augustus Willson, to his judicial colleagues, to former attorneys general, including John W. Griggs and Richard Olney, who had argued some of their most famous cases before him. His sons Richard Davenport Harlan and John Maynard Harlan were there to represent the Harlan family; at the last minute, James, too, was summoned back from his post in Puerto Rico by the Justice Department, so that he could attend.[60] Though women were not official guests, Malvina and her daughters and daughters-in-law were invited to listen to the speeches from the balcony.[61] Among the most excited attendees was the court's newest member, Oliver Wendell Holmes Jr., the fabled Boston intellectual who had been confirmed by the Senate that very week.[62]

The event kicked off with a rousing speech by the ebullient new president, Theodore Roosevelt, who had taken office the previous year upon McKinley's assassination. Roosevelt's relentless drive had already quickened the pulse of the capital. The young president had every reason to look forward to John's support for his efforts to break up the trusts—a major initiative that seemed destined to end up on the Supreme Court docket—even as he bemoaned John's refusal to accede to his administration's heavy-handed control of overseas colonies.

Nonetheless, Roosevelt's speech deftly steered clear of any matters before the court; rather, the forty-four-year-old president chose to focus on Harlan's service in the Civil War, a way of flattering an older generation to whom he might appear something of an upstart.

"Mr. Justice Harlan came from Kentucky, a state in which the patriotism of the people was put to so peculiarly severe a test in the Civil War," Roosevelt began. "In the states of the farther North, it was easy for the man to make up his mind on which side he would unsheathe his sword. In the states of the farther South, it was equally easy."

Here, the president was shrewdly alluding to the hard-won wisdom that Harlan had gained about the dangers of division: war wasn't glorious for anyone in the border states; the damage to Kentucky's social fabric still hadn't been repaired.

But knowing that his audience included many of both Union and Confederate veterans, Roosevelt then stressed how in most places the dueling passions of the previous century had aligned into a spirited nationalism; he referenced his own southern roots—his mother being from Georgia, and his uncles having fought for the Confederacy: "And so I think I have the right to say that, knowing the southern people as I do, I would heartily advocate fighting twice as hard as you fought from 1861 to 1865 for the privilege of staying in the same union with them."[63]

The crowd of men, many in their fifties and sixties, responded heartily, with laughter and eager applause, according to the official proceedings of the evening.[64] This was the fellowship of reconciliation that so many policy makers had hoped to engender in 1877, when federal troops were pulled out of the South and, coincidentally, John joined the court. The plight of African Americans, whose interests were discarded in the eagerness to heal the national breach, was as distant as the jungle of the Philippines to this all-white crowd, gathered in the ballroom of their brand-new palace on Pennsylvania Avenue.

After the president, Chief Justice Fuller offered brief remarks, praising Harlan but also invoking a long-standing tradition of refraining from after-dinner speeches;[65] he deferred to Justice David Brewer, nephew of John's sometime-antagonist Stephen Field, to offer the court's tribute to its long-serving colleague.

Brewer averred that he had been tapped only that morning to deliver the address, but his remarks were trenchant and apt. He provided the quote of the evening, saying of Harlan: "He believes implicitly in the Constitution. He goes to bed every night with one hand on the Constitution and the other on the Bible, and so sleeps the sweet sleep of justice and righteousness."[66]

Brewer also addressed Harlan's tendency to disagree with the court's rulings. Perhaps because Brewer himself was a dissenter on the Insular Cases, he applauded Harlan's willingness to stand on principle, going so far as to suggest that his refusal to submit to the will of the court on equal rights for Black people would be remembered as an admirable, even prophetic stance.

"Some mistakes a man may never regret," said Brewer. "Brother Harlan made a mistake in holding that the Civil Rights Bill was constitutional. The court said so; in our governmental system, the Supreme Court, on constitutional questions, is infallible, though, as everyone knows, no one of its members comes within sight or sound of infallibility. But it was a mistake on the side of equal rights, and no act done or word said in behalf of liberty and equality ever fails to touch humanity with inspiring, prophetic thrill. John Brown of Osawatomie made a mistake and was hung for it. As our Kansas poet said: 'He dared begin. He lost, but losing won.' And although today his body is mouldering in the grave, his inspiring soul will march triumphantly on through all the coming ages."[67]

Other tributes followed, from the state of Kentucky, the US Senate, and even the Bar of Canada, whose representative, Sir Edward Blake, was a Harlan friend from Murray Bay, and fired off some good-natured quips about the justice's golf game.

John himself was warm and gracious, especially in thanking Roosevelt and paying tribute to men of the bar and his fellow veterans.

He mentioned his court colleagues, past and present, by name, and spoke movingly of the wisdom of the revolutionary generation that established the American system of government. He praised George Washington and his own namesake, John Marshall, by name.

Then, in the full warmth of his embrace by the nation's political and legal luminaries—and aware that he would have few chances to lecture them again—he couldn't resist proclaiming his creed of color-blind justice. This was the judicial philosophy that he had honed and refined and would carry with him for the rest of his tenure on the court, even though it wasn't shared by all, or even many, of the others in the room. But he was willing to sacrifice the bonhomie of this moment—the most gratifying of his career—to what he considered a higher truth.

"God bless our dear country!" he declared with evident passion. "God bless every effort to sustain and strengthen it in the hearts of the people of every race subject to its jurisdiction and authority!"[68]

Chapter 18

Freedom in the Workplace

As he passed his seventieth birthday, still enjoying the robust health that people had noticed since his youth, John could only look back on his astonishing journey, and how closely it reflected the struggles and triumphs of the nation. His one concession to age was to talk more about the past; war stories became a staple of his conversation and correspondence.[1] The conflict whose slowly advancing shadow had darkened his youth now figured as the pivot point of his adulthood. Defining the legacy of the Civil War and grappling with the changes it wrought was the great cause of his long career on the Supreme Court. The nation's crucible was his own.

The battle against racial discrimination was one product of the Civil War; another was the postwar industrial boom in the victorious North that attracted tens of millions of immigrants, the vast majority of them white Europeans, to live in often fetid conditions—the urban poverty equivalent of the sharecropper shacks of the South. In the seventy years after John's birth, the population of the United States exploded from 12.8 million people to 76.2 million—a sixfold increase.[2] The staggering growth wasn't distributed evenly but concentrated in urban areas. At John's birth, only 8.8 percent of Americans lived in cities; by his seventieth birthday, 39.6 percent made their homes there.[3]

The sheer magnitude of the growth put enormous strains on

health and safety. Families of eight or ten relatives crammed into tenements built for half that number. Public utilities couldn't keep up with the crowding; electric and gas fires consumed entire city blocks, while inadequate sanitation set off waves of typhoid fever. Meanwhile, the factories in which many urban immigrants worked were danger zones, equipped with new forms of machinery that could chop off a hand as smoothly and precisely as they cut a bolt of cloth. Those machines were powered by steam and electric engines that could—and frequently would—explode if overstressed. Between 1883 and 1907, close to seven thousand people were killed in boiler explosions alone.[4] These dangers were exacerbated by long hours and crowded conditions; tired, worn-out workers were more likely to have accidents, and employers took little responsibility for their victims: a maimed worker would be sent home to his family while another immigrant plugged his hole on the factory floor.

The endless influx of people reduced the demand for low-skilled workers, so salaries plunged to the equivalent of $15,000 per year in 2021 dollars. Skilled workers such as plumbers could, if fortunate, earn twice that amount.[5] Paychecks were even skimpier with the long hours figured in. Days on the line bled into nights, and Saturday shifts were part of a regular six-day work week.

Among the longest hours were at industrial bakeries, where shifts sometimes extended to sixteen hours. (In 1881, when bakers in New York City went on strike, they demanded that hours be *reduced* to twelve per day.)[6] With so many people jammed into cities, the demand for bread—the cheapest and least perishable food staple—soared. Bakeries often set up shop in the basements of large buildings, subterranean spaces veiled in "filth, cobwebs, and vermin," in the words of one New York City inspector of the era.[7] Enclosed in brick, with only narrow grates for ventilation, they were steaming hot in the winter and suffocating in the summer. Some were overrun by rats; others had sewage leaking from corroded channels made of brick, wood, or clay.[8]

Bakeshops had expanded at twice the pace of factories and were so notoriously ill-kept that progressives seized on them to establish standards that would protect both workers and the public.[9] Bakery regulation was an effective stalking horse for the workers'-rights movement; even wealthy New Yorkers with no special regard for immigrants or working people might pause at the thought of rat droppings in their breakfast toast.

Progressive Republicans in the mode of then–New York City Police Commissioner Theodore Roosevelt, who was awakened to the dire conditions of immigrant laborers by his friend the muckraking journalist Jacob Riis, made workman's reforms a leading cause of the day.[10] On February 12, 1895, the New York General Assembly passed the New York Bakeshop Act, modeled on a similar law in England that, among other provisions, applied minimum drainage and plumbing standards and banned live animals from places where breads and cakes were being made. It also cracked down on the pervasive practice of having workers in between long middle-of-the-night shifts sleep on the very tables where the dough was kneaded.[11] And it sought to limit the lengths of those shifts to no more than ten hours per day, up to a total of sixty hours per week.[12]

Within a year, four more states—New Jersey, Ohio, Maryland, and Massachusetts—followed suit in adopting their own bakeshop safety acts with similar provisions. Union leaders credited Henry Weismann, a labor activist and lobbyist, for spreading the word about the plight of the bakery workers.[13] Meanwhile, a series of inspections found that more than 100 of the 150 bakeries in New York City were in violation of at least some parts of the law.[14] Even though the clause limiting workers' hours received less attention than the more explicit public health provisions, the city's health commissioner, Cyrus Edson, declared that keeping workers fresh and alert was crucial to maintaining sanitary conditions.

"There is unmistakable evidence," Edson declared, "that these men are overworked and that, in consequence of this, they are sickly and unfit to handle an article of food."[15]

Joseph Lochner was a proud, willful, determined immigrant from Bavaria. He saw a chance for a better life in the United States and seized it, passing through New York Harbor in the early 1880s, in the last years before the Statue of Liberty extended her welcoming torch, and then journeying to the upstate city of Utica.[16] Perfectly located near two heavily trafficked canals and a railroad line, Utica was a burgeoning textile manufacturing hub. Thousands of immigrants made their way to the Utica mills every day, while others provided the services necessary for an American boomtown, replete with a row of Italianate mansions along leafy Rutger Park for the mill owners and managers. Burly and broad shouldered, with a walrus mustache,[17] Lochner worked for eight years in a local bakery,[18] with no apparent concern about long hours: he was saving up to open his own business. In 1894, the year before the General Assembly passed the New York Bakeshop Act, Lochner's Home Bakery opened its doors.

Proud to be living the American Dream, Lochner built what seemed to be a model business. Unlike the rat-filled basements of so many New York City establishments, his bakery occupied a trim two-story storefront. A picture of the interior from about a decade after the bakery opened shows a modern workroom for the time, with bakers attired in white aprons, a huge butcher-block worktable, sparkling metal vats and mixers, and shelves of trays to cool the freshly made breads and confections. Nonetheless, his labor practices drew the ire of the Journeyman's Union of Utica,[19] and he stubbornly tried to find ways around the law limiting his workers to a single ten-hour shift per day.

In 1896, the year after New York restricted the lengths of bakery shifts, one of Lochner's employees, Aman Schmitter, agreed to sign a contract in which Lochner promised to pay him 2 percent of the bakery's profits, making him appear to be a co-owner, rather than a worker, and thus eligible to work longer hours.[20] That bit of subterfuge didn't pass the smell test. In 1899 Lochner was indicted for knowingly and wrongfully allowing an employee—Schmitter—to work more than the legal maximum of sixty hours per week.

The precise circumstances of the indictment have been the subject of speculation for years. Did the Journeyman's Union, aware of Lochner's aversion to the law, demand that his bakery be inspected?[21]

Or did, perhaps, the Utica branch of the Association of Master Bakers, of which Lochner was a member, try to set up the case in order to challenge the constitutionality of the ten-hour work limit?[22] Likewise, the question of how much coordination—if any—existed between Lochner and Schmitter remains unresolved. The fact that the two men worked together for years before and after the indictment, with no apparent tensions, at least raises the suggestion that they were in cahoots.[23]

Whatever the swirl of motives surrounding the case, Lochner was convicted in a brief trial, and his conviction upheld by an appellate court. That put his fate in the lap of the state's top court, the New York Court of Appeals, overseen by Chief Judge Alton B. Parker. A supporter of labor reforms, Parker was about to quit his post to run for the Democratic nomination for president. Against the odds, he would win the nomination but go on to lose in a landslide to Theodore Roosevelt.[24]

At the time, however, Parker may have viewed the case as an opportunity to advertise his pro-labor bona fides. He cast the deciding vote and wrote the opinion upholding Joseph Lochner's conviction, declaring that the New York Bakeshop Act was "beyond question" a valid exercise of the state's police powers to protect public health.

"Many medical authorities classify workers in bakers' or confectioners' establishments with potters, stone cutters, file grinders, and other workers whose occupation necessitates the inhalation of dust particles, and hence predisposes its members to consumption," Parker wrote. "The published medical opinions and vital statistics bearing upon that subject standing alone fully justify the section under review as one to protect the health of the employees in such establishments."[25]

Though the name on the case may have been Joseph Lochner and the stakeholders the Journeyman's Union and Association of Master Bakers the fate of the New York Bakeshop Act captured the attention of some of the same Gilded Age forces who persuaded the

Supreme Court to thwart the income tax and antitrust laws. Here, too, was a major threat to the industrial order. Labor reforms masquerading as health laws would be a huge impediment to the factory economy, forcing costly modifications and safety adjustments while limiting work hours.

To many Gilded Age moguls and other opponents of government regulation, this was more than just interference in the operation of businesses; it affronted the whole American system of free enterprise. While it was easy to cry tears over Jacob Riis's depictions of immigrant toil, what, then, of the Joseph Lochners of the world? The stoutness of their hopes and dreams couldn't be contained in sixty-hour weeks. They would work every minute to better their lives—such was the relentlessness of their ambition.

Despite America's fulsome embrace of capitalism, there was nothing in the Constitution that specifically protected businesses. Congress had the power to regulate interstate commerce, and states could otherwise organize their economies as they saw fit. But after the passage of the post–Civil War amendments, and the coming of the postwar economic boom, those who feared an onslaught of government regulation began to look more closely at the Fourteenth Amendment—the same amendment that the Supreme Court had been reluctant to enforce in protection of African Americans. They even zeroed in on one of the clauses that had been invoked unsuccessfully by Black plaintiffs in both the *Civil Rights Cases of 1883* and *Plessy v. Ferguson*—the one guaranteeing "due process" of laws. What if "due process" meant more than just fair procedures, but a much more expansive protection of individual liberties? A hardworking immigrant, for example, should have the freedom to work as many hours as he wants—whether or not the state of New York thinks it is in his best interest to do so.

Putting aside, for the moment, the fact that most workers toiled long shifts not by choice but because the factory and bakery owners required them, the right to sell one's labor was the essence of American capitalism—or so thought most Gilded Age moguls and the laissez-faire lawyers who represented them.

As a legal concept, however, this "right to contract" was a recent invention. From its ratification in 1787, the Constitution had included a Fifth Amendment guarantee of "due process" under law, and it had been interpreted simply to mean that the federal government had to maintain fair procedures. The Fourteenth Amendment extended that mandate to state governments. The intention of the framers was clear: they meant to protect newly freed men and women from arbitrary treatment by hostile state governments. But proponents of laissez-faire economics saw an opportunity to broaden that protection to prevent states from infringing on business practices. That idea first appeared in a dissenting opinion by Justice Joseph Philo Bradley in an early Fourteenth Amendment case in 1873, but the court majority rejected the concept.[26] It popped up again in 1897, in the court's unanimous ruling against a Louisiana law that barred businesses from using out-of-state marine-insurance companies. Though the case was highly technical and attracted little attention, it advanced a jarringly broad interpretation of the Fourteenth Amendment:

> The "liberty" mentioned in that amendment means not only the right of the citizen to be free from the mere physical restraint of his person, as by incarceration, but the term is deemed to embrace the right of the citizen to be free in the enjoyment of his faculties, to be free to use them in all lawful ways, to live and work where he will, to earn his livelihood by any lawful calling, to pursue any livelihood or avocation, and for that purpose to enter into all contracts which may be proper, necessary, and essential.[27]

The author of that paean to individualism and free enterprise was a relatively new member of the court, Rufus W. Peckham Jr., who was himself an emblem of the Gilded Age elite. Like many of his brethren, he had entered the legal profession when it was considered the source of a healthy income, but no great riches, only to ride the railroad economy to wealth beyond his boyhood imagination.[28] Peckham hailed from a prominent Albany, New York, legal family, and, at the height of the Gilded Age, he represented banks, trusts, insurance companies, and the Albany and Susquehanna Railroad.[29] In the summers, he would repair to his mountain villa, Coolmore, famed for its commanding views of the Hudson River Valley.[30] Peckham maintained personal relationships with J. P. Morgan, John D. Rockefeller, Cornelius Vanderbilt, and other business elites.[31] Certainly, they had no greater friend on the Supreme Court.

Grover Cleveland had appointed Peckham to the high court in 1895, adding a far-right tilt to a bench already overcrowded with judicial conservatives. This was the product of the fact that from Ulysses Grant's arrival in the White House in 1869 until Teddy Roosevelt's ascension in 1901, the presidency was controlled by an unbroken string of pro-business conservatives; under Grant, the Republicans fully embraced the idea of unfettered industrial expansion, and the reign of Republican presidents was interrupted only by Cleveland, the "bourbon" Democrat from New York, who had a similar affinity for laissez-faire economics. Populism raged in the South and West, but in the North, both major parties were divided between conservative and progressive factions. When a true progressive, Democrat William Jennings Bryan, finally won a major-party presidential nomination, he was defeated in the pivotal 1896 election by conservative William McKinley. Only McKinley's assassination, which put the more progressive Roosevelt in the White House, broke the string.

Of the Supreme Court justices appointed during this period, John Marshall Harlan—the product of the extraordinary circumstances surrounding Rutherford Hayes's election, and Hayes's desire to appoint a southerner—was an exception. Northeastern railroad attorneys—or transplanted northeasterners such as Field, Fuller, and Brown, who built their fortunes representing corporate interests in other regions—were the rule. The court grew quite comfortable embracing ever more extreme theories to strike down laws that impeded business owners. The only area where the Fuller Court showed a reflexive restraint was the one for which the postwar amendments were explicitly intended: protection of freed men and women.

This was the constellation of jurists who would decide whether

Joseph Lochner should be fined $50 for allowing an employee to work more than sixty hours tending the ovens of his Utica bakery. His petition to the Supreme Court was reviewed by the justice assigned to oversee the circuit of New York, who decided quickly that it was worthy of reargument before the highest tribunal in the land. The justice was none other than Rufus W. Peckham Jr.[32]

Peckham wasn't the only larger-than-life character to have joined the court at the tail end of the Gilded Age. So, too, was Roosevelt's first appointee to the court, Oliver Wendell Holmes Jr. A man of surpassing urbanity, intimidating intellect, and a wit so caustic that it strafed anything in its path, Holmes was already eminent in the law when he joined the court in 1902. Two decades earlier, he'd challenged jurists everywhere with his treatise *The Common Law*, with its famous assertion that "The life of the law has not been logic; it has been experience."[33]

Just eight years younger than John, Holmes was born upon Boston's Beacon Hill, the citadel of American intellectual life of the time. His namesake father was a physician who was also known for his light philosophical essays proffering breakfast-table wisdom in the *Atlantic Monthly*; Holmes's mother, Amelia, was a devout abolitionist. As a thin, hatchet-faced youth with piercing eyes, Holmes put away his books and joined the Union army, seeing considerable combat and watching many friends die. As with John Harlan, Holmes saw the Civil War as the touchstone of his life; his one indelible experience. Nonetheless, it hardly dented his intellectual armor and may have hardened it in some ways. For Holmes, combat was a proving ground, and, as a much older man, he retained a soldierly affinity for others who had fought, including Harlan. But coming from the Boston social strata for which abolition was an almost religious cause, Holmes had little of Harlan's sense of the larger tragedy of the war, the way it divided families, corrupted institutions, and forced people to choose between state and national loyalty. If Oliver Wendell Holmes Jr. had a weakness, it was a lack of empathy for the struggles of those outside his discerning gaze.

Holmes's appointment to the Supreme Court, after a very distinguished two decades of teaching at Harvard and serving on the highest court in Massachusetts, marked a formidable break in the parade of corporate attorneys elevated by Roosevelt's predecessors; at sixty-one, Holmes was still whippet thin and loose limbed, with a full head of dark hair, and promised a fresh burst of intellectual vigor.

John Harlan, however, was more wary of Holmes than welcoming. In addition to sharing wartime service, there was much that the two men agreed upon. Harlan's ability to connect his life experiences to his jurisprudence would seem to validate Holmes's observations in *The Common Law*. But their personal styles and approaches to the law were vastly different. Harlan was blunt and unironic: he saw the law as the immovable foundation of a great society. Holmes, true to his professorial past, often stood outside of a dispute, mapping a path to what he considered the legally correct outcome. Holmes's observations about the judicial process were often beyond Harlan's scope of reference; at the same time, Harlan's ferocious, innate sense of fairness and justice exposed some of the bloodless thinking behind Holmes's delicate turns of phrase.

"Justice Harlan and Justice Holmes continued to be gentlemanly opponents," wrote their later colleague Justice Charles Evans Hughes, who observed the two men for a year. "Justice Harlan thought that Justice Holmes's constitutional views were 'unsound' and that his opinions had too many 'obscure phrases'; while Justice Holmes thought that Justice Harlan's opinions were verbose."[34]

Hughes also noted that Holmes, "always urbane," would refer to Harlan in judicial conferences as "my lion-hearted friend."[35] Holmes, whose letters to friends tended to include pithy observations about his colleagues, once confided that Harlan "although a man of real power, did not shine either in analysis or generalization." He compared John's mind to "a powerful vise the jaws of which couldn't be got nearer than two inches of each other"—suggesting that John's opinions lacked logic and subtlety.[36] He dubbed him "the last of the tobacco-spittin' judges."

Clearly, Holmes found Harlan's bluntness to be obtuse; Harlan found Holmes's archness to be supercilious. But underneath Harlan's suspicions and Holmes's condescension existed a baseline of respect. Holmes regarded Harlan as a formidable figure; he did not feel the same about all his judicial colleagues. And some of his observations may have been purely factual; the Kentucky-bred Harlan did extol the benefits of chewing tobacco and seemingly cared little whether it offended the sensibilities of his New England colleague, whom he otherwise treated with respect and, at times, a comradely fondness.[37]

On the day of Holmes's seventieth birthday, the justice arrived at court to find a bouquet of violets in his seat on the bench; they "alone indicated the nature of the occasion," according to the next day's *Washington Post*, which added, "The flowers were from Justice Harlan," his fellow septuagenarian.[38]

Rufus Peckham's decision to grant Joseph Lochner's petition to the Supreme Court excited the New York Association of Master Bakers, which promptly collected a dollar from each of its members to pay for better representation before the high court.[39] Peckham's decision had the opposite effect on the Journeyman's Union, which had already seized on the favorable ruling in the New York Court of Appeals to increase its demands to ban late-night shifts in bakeries and promote similar restrictions around the country.[40]

Lochner's choice of an attorney to handle his case before the high court was a stunner. Never before had such a curious character handled a major Supreme Court argument. Henry Weismann, like Lochner an immigrant from Germany, had been the public face of the Journeyman's Union and the figure most credited with pushing through the New York Bakeshop Act; two years later, however, the union ousted him from his position amid accusations that he'd been skimming money.[41] It wouldn't have been the first transgression in his career; he had earlier done jail time for the possession of explosives while a leader in the notorious anti-Chinese race-baiting Anti-Coolie League of California.[42]

Weismann responded to his ouster from the union by switching sides completely. He opened his own bakery and became a driving force against the very law he had pushed through the General Assembly. He also claimed to have studied the practice of law, which at that time did not require going to school. Nonetheless, as he prepared to argue before the Supreme Court in 1905, questions swirled about whether he had the requisite experience to earn a law license.[43] Lochner and his fellow bakers hedged their bets by hiring an experienced Brooklyn attorney to assist in the case. Though Weismann remained the engine propelling Lochner's defense, he sidestepped questions about his qualifications by ceding the title of lead counsel to the lawyer from Brooklyn, Frank Harvey Field.[44]

Weismann may have been more of an impetuous amateur than a legal professional, but he lucked out in his opposition. The job of defending the law fell not to the impassioned Journeyman's Union but to the state of New York, whose attorney general, John Cunneen, was defeated for reelection five months after the Supreme Court decided to take up the case. Feeling little stake in the matter, Cunneen unthinkingly agreed to an early hearing. This meant his successor, a man named Julius Marshuetz Mayer, would have to provide a written brief and personally argue the case in the first few months of his term; the team backing Joseph Lochner had been honing its arguments for the better part of a year before Mayer had a chance to acquaint himself with the facts.[45]

Mayer, however, appeared to be standing on the firmer legal ground. Seven years earlier, in a case involving most of the same justices as would hear Lochner's appeal, the court had voted 7 to 2 in favor of a Utah law that limited miners to eight-hour workdays.[46] Only Peckham and David Brewer, who once sweepingly decried all forms of economic regulation on behalf of workers as "paternal" and "odious," voted against the law.[47] The majority, however, declared that the state had the constitutional authority to protect health and safety, and that longer hours presented a health risk to miners. Therefore, all Mayer had to do was persuade the justices that long shifts in bakeries were injurious to workers' health and safety. Failing that, he could make a case that a state's police powers went well beyond regulating for health and safety—that other considerations, such as easing labor-management tensions, extending family time, or promoting civic engagement could justify a state limitation on work hours.

Mayer either didn't believe in government regulation or was so caught off guard by the early hearing date that he muffed the argument. His somewhat scanty eighteen-page brief appeared to concede that only health and safety could justify state intervention and, while he contended that long bakery hours were harmful to workers, he neglected to cite much of the considerable medical evidence supporting that claim.[48]

Weismann and Field, by contrast, contoured their arguments to appeal to the court's laissez-faire sympathies. In a nod to Peckham, they declared the New York Bakeshop Act to be a clear violation of the right to contract, as implied in the Fourteenth Amendment. More than that, they appealed to the court's antiunion sentiments by asserting that the law was passed only to appease a demanding labor constituency, the Journeyman's Union, under the guise of being a health and safety measure. That claim gained considerable credibility when coming from the mouth of the very person, Weismann, who had been the loud voice of that labor constituency.[49] Deeply uncomfortable with the growing political power of the labor movement, many of the justices seemed to welcome a chance to establish a clear limit to the amount of trouble unions could cause with the backing of sympathetic state legislatures.

Nonetheless, up until the minute the ruling was announced, the smart money among court observers was on upholding the law, not siding with Lochner; the precedents were too firmly in support of the New York Legislature's right to act. Within the court, however, there was only turmoil. Later evidence suggests the justices had initially lined up 5 to 4 behind the law, only to have one of their number—almost certainly Joseph McKenna—switch sides. McKenna, a politician with relatively slender legal credentials when he joined the court, acknowledged openly that he preferred to wait until he read his colleagues' written opinions to finalize his vote.[50]

This meant that when the crowd gathered at the court's chambers on April 17, 1905, a very pleased Rufus Peckham announced the court's ruling instead of a now-frustrated John Harlan.

No one could say that Peckham lacked confidence in his views. Speaking for himself, Brewer, McKenna, Chief Justice Fuller, and Henry Billings Brown, Peckham presented the right to contract, which had never been asserted so sweepingly, as a deeply engrained legal principle, and the state's police powers, which had been acknowledged for centuries, as a conditional grant of authority from the federal union.[51]

"The statute necessarily interferes with the right of contract between the employer and employees concerning the number of hours in which the latter may labor in the bakery of the employer," Peckham wrote, sidestepping the reality that the vast majority of workers didn't want to work longer than ten hours but were compelled by their employers to do so.

"The general right to make a contract in relation to his business is part of the liberty of the individual protected by the Fourteenth Amendment of the Federal Constitution," he continued. "Under that provision, no state can deprive any person of life, liberty, or property without due process of law. The right to purchase or sell labor is part of the liberty protected by this amendment unless there are circumstances which exclude the right. There are, however, certain powers, existing in the sovereignty of each state of the union, somewhat vaguely termed police powers, the exact description and limitation of which have not been attempted by the courts."[52]

Peckham proceeded to limit the police powers mainly to health and safety regulation. He rejected the idea that labor laws could be allowed on any grounds except the health of workers: "The question of whether this act is valid as a labor law, pure and simple, may be dismissed in a few words. There is no reasonable ground for interfering with the liberty of person or the right of free contract by determining the hours of labor in the occupation of a baker. There is no contention that bakers as a class are not equal in intelligence and capacity to men in other trades or manual occupations, or that they are [not] able to assert their rights and care for themselves without the protecting arm of the state, interfering with their independence of judgment and of action."[53]

As to the idea that long hours were inherently harmful to bakers, Peckham suggested that "it might be safely affirmed that almost all occupations more or less affect health. There must be more than the mere fact of the possible existence of some small amount of unhealthiness to warrant legislative interference with liberty."[54]

He then got to the core of his and his colleagues' complaint: "It is impossible for us to shut our eyes to the fact that many of the laws of this character, while passed under what is claimed to be the police power for the purpose of protecting the public health or welfare are, in reality, passed from other motives."[55]

Peckham never precisely characterized these other motives, but he was undeniably offended by government encroachment on business owners' ability to demand what they wanted of their workers. Against this onrush of opinion, John Marshall Harlan offered a counter-philosophy: judicial restraint. The Fourteenth Amendment does indeed constrain states, and he admitted that some violations of economic liberty could be justification for judicial intervention. But he insisted judges must defer to the wisdom of state legislatures as long as they had a reasonable basis for their action.

"The rule is universal that a legislative enactment, federal or state, is never to be disregarded or held invalid unless it be, beyond question, plainly and palpably in excess of legislative power," he wrote.[56]

Most likely, Harlan's opinion was originally written as the majority opinion, and it lacked—until the end—some of the brimming outrage of his most famous dissents. Still, one senses underneath his arguments the boiling irony that a court which had piously refused to interfere with the state legislature behind the Louisiana Separate Car Act did so with such alacrity and righteousness against the one that enacted the New York Bakeshop Act.

As he did in *Plessy v. Ferguson* and *Pollock v. Farmers' Loan & Trust Co.*, Harlan delved into the real-life implications of the case— its practical effects. Justice Peckham and the court's majority, in looking at the New York Bakeshop Act from the point of view of a worker who wanted extra hours, willfully ignored the problem the state of New York meant to address: the disproportionate clout of bakery owners, who demanded long hours of thousands of workers who had no desire for them and could be harmed by them. On that basis alone, Harlan insisted, New York's action passed the test of rationality—the state legislature was acting to correct a problem that was reasonably within its purview.

"It is plain that this statute was enacted in order to protect the physical well-being of those who work in bakery and confectionary establishments," he declared. "It may be that the statute had its origin, in part, in the belief that employers and employees in such establishments were not upon an equal footing, and that the necessities of the latter often compelled them to submit to such exactions as unduly taxed their strength. Be that as it may, the statute must be taken as expressing the belief of the people of New York that, as a general rule, and in the case of the average man, labor in excess of sixty hours a week in such establishments may endanger the health of those who thus labor. Whether or not this be wise legislation it is not the province of the court to inquire."[57]

Later, he elaborated on the ways in which the court should limit its inquiry:

I do not stop to consider whether any particular view of this economic question presents the sounder theory. What the precise facts are, it may be difficult to say. It is enough for the determination of this case, and it is enough for the court to know, that the question is one about which there is room for debate and for an honest difference of opinion. . . . If such reasons exist, that ought to be the end of this case, for the state is not amenable to the judiciary in respect of its legislative enactments unless such enactments are plainly, palpably, beyond all question, inconsistent with the Constitution of the United States.[58]

The lack of restraint showed by the court, Harlan warned, would hamstring the ability of legislatures to deal with pressing and even dangerous problems: "A decision that the New York statute is void under the Fourteenth Amendment will, in my opinion, involve consequences of a far-reaching and mischievous character; for such a decision would seriously cripple the inherent power of the states to care for the lives, health, and well-being of their citizens."[59]

Harlan's dissent was joined by justices Edward White and the court's newest member, William Rufus Day. But it wasn't the last word. Justice Holmes appended a short dissent examining the issues from his own lofty perspective. He suggested the court was invoking the social Darwinism of the British philosopher Herbert Spencer, whose "survival of the fittest" was a favorite doctrine of conservatives of the day.

"This case is decided upon an economic theory which a large part of the country does not entertain," Holmes wrote. "If it were a question whether I agreed with the theory, I should desire to study it further and long before making up my mind. But I do not conceive that to be my duty, because I strongly believe that my agreement or disagreement has nothing to do with the right of the majority to embody their opinions in the law."[60]

The announcement of the court's ruling was big news in New York and a subject of more modest coverage elsewhere. The labor movement understood that it had taken a massive hit. The *Baker's Journal*, the mouthpiece of the Journeyman's Union, reprinted an article that summarized the court's decision this way: "Everything that furthers the interests of the employers is constitutional," while whatever "may be undertaken for the welfare of the working people" is unconstitutional.[61]

The mainstream press was more divided. The *New York Evening Journal* reported on "A Sad Day for Labor Legislation," while the *Brooklyn Daily Eagle* promised, "The best minds will side with the United States Supreme Court on this matter. It makes for liberty, from no excess of which are men likely to suffer in constitutional land."[62]

Many papers reprinted substantial portions of Justice Peckham's opinion and Justice Harlan's dissent, reporting that when the decisions were announced, Harlan had, from the bench, "declared that no more important decision had been given in the last century."[63]

His assessment would prove prescient, as always, but even he could not foresee the turmoil the case would provoke in future decades, when the government's ability to respond to the Great Depression and a rising tide of social problems would be constrained, and the court's very structure would be thrust into the balance. *Lochner v. New York*, it turned out, would one day become so hated as a legal precedent that it almost brought down the Supreme Court.

Chapter 19

"I Am a Innocent Man"

The body of the young Black man hung over the Tennessee River while the eyes of hundreds of white people pierced the moonlit night. "That monster of a thousand feet and a thousand hands and heads," as a newspaper described the mob the following day, had invaded a lightly guarded jail in Chattanooga, Tennessee, the evening of March 19, 1906, and seized Ed Johnson from his cell.[1] His only floormate, a local bootlegger named Ellen Baker, had noticed something curious earlier in the evening: another prisoner had been moved to a cell on a lower floor. When she prodded the night jailer for an explanation, he confessed, "There is a mob coming in here tonight." When she heard noises, she began to scream, and the jailer and a second man rushed to quiet her. The second man assured her, "We ain't going to hurt you. It is that colored man we want."[2]

The vigilantes chose Chattanooga's most famous landmark—the 2,370-foot Walnut Street Bridge, a gleaming steel expanse built a decade and a half earlier—as the setting for their crime.[3] They wanted to make sure that everyone in the river port of more than thirty thousand people saw what they were doing. Ed Johnson had to die. The twenty-four-year-old carpenter, who did work for local churches, had been fingered in the crime of the century: the rape of a young white woman, Nevada Taylor. She had been seized in Forest Hills Cemetery, where her father was groundskeeper, in the neighborhood of St. Elmo near the base of Lookout Mountain.[4] Even though Taylor declined to make a definitive identification of Johnson, having already wavered on whether her assailant was even Black, and Johnson had been working at the Last Chance Saloon in view of numerous people at the time of the attack, he had been convicted in a bloodthirsty trial.[5]

Declaring that there was substantial reason to believe Johnson had been denied a fair process, a single justice of the US Supreme Court stepped in to spare him the gallows, ordering a review of the proceedings. The justice's decision set off an explosion of pent-up rage in a city that was home to thousands of diehard Confederates. "More unrest on the subject exists than was anticipated,"[6] the *Chattanooga Times* reported breathlessly, adding, almost invitingly, "Johnson is confined on the second floor of the jail and is yet not provided with a special guard."[7]

As the white mob strung a thick rope wrested from one of the city's trolley cars over the bridge's famed camelback beams, one of Johnson's attackers suggested they might spare him if he confessed. "I am not guilty," he insisted, "just like I've said all the time. I wasn't at St. Elmo that night, and I didn't have any strap. I was at the Last Chance Saloon all the time. I am not guilty, and I guess that's all I've got to say." He added, "I am ready to die, but I never done it."[8]

As the men placed the noose around his neck and began to pull, Johnson declared, "God bless you all. I am a innocent man." He hung, writhing and twitching, over the wide expanse of river for almost two minutes. People in the crowd pulled out pistols and shotguns and started peppering the body with holes, like a paper target in a gallery. The projectiles tore through the hangman's rope, and the pile of broken flesh thudded onto the bridge. A big, broad-shouldered man pressed his revolver into Johnson's lifeless body and fired five more times.[9]

The lynch mob then began chanting the names of two other people—that of Johnson's defense attorney, Noah Parden, and of the Supreme Court justice who'd intervened on Johnson's behalf: John Marshall Harlan. Amid the cacophony of cries for "Harlan! Harlan!" a man stepped forward to append a note to what remained of Ed Johnson. It was signed "the committee" and it read: "To Chief Harlan. Here is your Negro. Thanks for your kind consideration of him. You can find him at the morgue."[10]

Three days earlier, John Marshall Harlan had been at his home on Washington's Euclid Place. On this drizzly Saturday in late winter, the seventy-two-year-old was performing one of the more wearisome tasks associated with his job: sifting through last-minute petitions to the high court. The circuit overseen by Harlan covered Ohio, Kentucky, and Tennessee.[11]

There was a knock on the door, and two well-dressed Black men entered. The younger of them, in his late thirties, showed some of the fatigue of a hasty, seven-hundred-mile journey from Chattanooga. He had made the desperate mission because there was simply no time: Ed Johnson was sentenced to be hanged in only three days hence.

The man, Noah Parden, was renowned throughout Tennessee as a courtroom lawyer, hailed for his silver-tongued ability to woo a jury.[12] That was especially impressive since Parden was Black and juries in Chattanooga were white. Parden had not represented Johnson during his trial but picked up the case after state appeals were exhausted. He was determined to bring it all the way to the Supreme Court, even though he told the justice he'd been offered $5,000 to drop the matter and threatened with disbarment if he went through with his plan. Realizing there was no time to waste, Parden had roped in one of the better-known Black lawyers in Washington, fifty-five-year-old Emanuel Hewlett, to be his partner in what both saw as a last-ditch effort, almost certainly destined to failure.[13]

But Parden knew he'd been lucky in one respect. Like every Black person acquainted with the legal system, the renowned Tennessee lawyer knew that John Marshall Harlan had been the only justice to vote to uphold the Civil Rights Act and against legal segregation. If any member of the court could recognize the unfairness of the case against Ed Johnson, it would be Harlan.

And Parden had a story to tell. There had been no Black people in the jury pool for Ed Johnson's trial, a seemingly deliberate omission. The case should have been moved out of Chattanooga, where feelings were at such a fever pitch that lynch mobs had gathered outside the jail multiple times in the two weeks before the trial began. In the middle of the proceedings, a juror directed threatening exclamations at the defendant without being removed by the state judge.

Those were among the errors of law that combined to condemn Ed Johnson. The Supreme Court, in deciding whether to review a case, may concern itself only with mistakes of law, not facts. As Parden knew, the factual case against Johnson was flawed as well.

When the local sheriff—a sixty-one-year-old Confederate veteran named Joseph Shipp—had questioned a traumatized Nevada Taylor about the man who assaulted her, she at first suggested she had not seen the man, and recalled only his soothing voice. The assailant, she explained, had come up behind her on a moonless night and pulled a strap around her neck, which soon rendered her unconscious. She initially indicated she couldn't tell if he was Black or white. After being pressed by Shipp, though, the frightened twenty-one-year-old allowed that her assailant was Black and added, "He told me in a kind, gentle voice that if I screamed again, he would cut my throat."[14]

Chattanooga's two newspapers, the News and the Times, went wild with the news. "Brutal Crime of Negro Fiend,"[15] read the headline in the News. "Black Brute Managed to Cover Up Tracks Well and No Trace of Him Has Yet Been Found,"[16] reported the Times. It was, the News concluded, "A Crime Without Parallel in Criminal Annals of Hamilton County."[17]

The fury provoked by the news reports placed intense pressure on Sheriff Shipp, whose only evidence was the leather strap found at the crime scene. Amid all the turmoil, the sheriff was running for reelection and took pains to advertise his sense of urgency: "There is not a man in Hamilton County who is more anxious for the capture of the brute who committed this crime than is Sheriff Shipp," assured a News columnist. "I talked with him about the matter Wednesday, and his anxiety that the foul fiend should be brought to justice is simply intense."[18]

With Shipp's encouragement, local businesses chipped in to offer a

$375 reward to anyone who could provide information.[19] The following morning, Shipp received a phone call from a white man named Will Hixson, who worked at a medicine plant across from the cemetery where Nevada Taylor had been attacked. He said he had seen a Black man with a leather strap standing near the cemetery about a half hour before the time of the attack.[20]

The sheriff was so encouraged that he led Hixson on a search of the neighborhood. After that proved fruitless, Hixson called back to say he'd seen the man walking toward town. That person turned out to be Ed Johnson, who was later discovered on the back of a wagon, earning a few extra dollars delivering ice. When he found out that he was suspected of attacking Nevada Taylor, Johnson protested that it couldn't be so, because he was at the Last Chance Saloon, and volunteered the names of a dozen men who could confirm his alibi. But Black witnesses weren't likely to count for much, if anything, in an all-white courtroom.[21]

When word spread that an eyewitness had identified a suspect, both Shipp and Judge Samuel McReynolds, who was overseeing the case, sensed that passions were running out of control. On McReynolds's recommendation, the sheriff quietly moved the suspect to Nashville for safekeeping.[22]

The fears proved to be well founded. That Thursday evening, a mob of more than a thousand people, many of them armed with guns and carrying ropes, surrounded the jail. A mill worker with a double-barrel shotgun took the lead in demanding that Johnson be turned over. The terrified deputies informed him that the prisoner wasn't there. The man didn't believe him. The crowd responded by ransacking the building, cutting phone lines, smashing lightbulbs, shooting at the brick facing, and trying to bang their way through the locked steel door to where the prisoners were held.[23]

Chattanooga police tried to quell the violence, to no avail. National Guardsmen scrambled to the scene on a direct order from the governor but couldn't restore order.[24] At some point, Nevada Taylor's brother showed up and urged the mob not to take the law into its own hands.[25]

By the time that Judge McReynolds arrived, the steel door was almost busted through. At thirty-five, McReynolds was one of the state's youngest judges and an aggressive crime fighter. As a concession to the protesters, McReynolds promised that he would hold a special Saturday session—in just two days hence—and that Johnson's trial would be bumped ahead of all other cases.[26]

"I hope that before week's end, the rapist will be convicted, under sentence of death, and executed according to law before the setting of Saturday's sun," the judge promised.[27]

The following day, Sheriff Shipp brought Nevada Taylor to Nashville and showed her both Johnson and another prisoner, shining lights in their faces and asking them to talk and move around. Taylor pondered for fifteen minutes. She volunteered that she had never expected that her attacker would be captured. Finally, she responded that the man on the left—Johnson—had the same soft voice as the assailant. On further prompting from Shipp, she stated, "From that Negro's general figure, height, and weight, from his voice, as I can distinctly remember it, from his manner of movement and action, and from the clothing he wears, it is my best knowledge and belief that the man who stood on your left was the one who assaulted me."[28]

At the trial, which occurred a little more than a week later, Taylor was similarly circumspect when asked if she could identify her attacker, saying only, "I believe he is the man," and pointing to Ed Johnson.[29] Two days later, hoping for a firmer identification, the jury asked the victim to return to the stand.

"Miss Taylor, can you state positively that this Negro is the one that attacked you?" asked a juror.

Taylor responded, "I will not swear that he is the man, but I believe he is the Negro who assaulted me."

"Miss Taylor, as God sees you, can you say that is the Negro, the right Negro?" demanded another juror.

Visibly frightened and overwhelmed by the scene, she replied, "Listen to me, I would not take the life of an innocent man, but I believe that is the man." As she raised her right hand, as if to swear an oath, she broke down in sobs and was led, trembling, from the witness stand. One juror collapsed in emotion, while another shouted out, "If I could get him, I'd tear his heart out now!"

With the entire room in a frenzy, McReynolds quickly gaveled a recess, but then, shockingly, made no move to excuse the juror who had threatened Johnson.[30]

In his summation, Johnson's lead attorney, Lewis Shepherd, railed against the proceedings, stating that Will Hixson, the witness who first picked out Ed Johnson, couldn't possibly have made such a positive identification from his vantage point across from the cemetery. But he reserved his strongest condemnation for Judge McReynolds, whom he accused of overseeing a travesty of a trial. He quoted dramatically from English legal treatises about the role of a judge as an impartial arbiter—a standard that McReynolds had spectacularly failed to meet, in Shepherd's opinion.[31]

Sitting in his home on Euclid Place, listening to Parden and Hewlett describe the proceedings—the florid displays of emotion, the threats of violence, the biased exclamation by a juror who nonetheless was allowed to pass judgment on Johnson—John Harlan began to feel the same way about McReynolds's handling of the case. It would require extraordinary action for the Supreme Court to halt the runaway train that was carrying Ed Johnson to the gallows, but the Constitution demanded it.

John said nothing when Parden and Hewlett left for the day, letting the Chattanooga attorney make his way back to Tennessee in a state of uncertainty.[32] At a stop just north of his destination, a station agent warned Parden that a white mob was gathering at the rail terminal in the city; but when he arrived, he found an equal number of Black people prepared to protect him.[33]

He also learned of a telegram received with some consternation by the court authorities: "Have allowed appeal to accused in *habeas corpus* case of Ed Johnson. Transcript will be filed tomorrow and motion also made by Johnson's counsel for formal allowance of appeal of court."

It was from John Marshall Harlan.[34]

The Constitution guarantees due process of law to every citizen, and while other implications of the so-called due process clause had been hotly debated, no justice ever disputed that the document promised citizens a fair trial. And yet the shoddiness of the procedures used to try Black defendants in state courts of the former Confederacy was an open secret. For all the reasons that the Supreme Court had been reluctant to enforce the Fourteenth Amendment on behalf of substantive Black rights, so too was it eager to avoid a confrontation over procedural unfairness.

That did not deter Harlan. Perhaps he had been looking for such a case to puncture his colleagues' deference to state judicial proceedings. It was beyond debate that Ed Johnson's trial had been full of errors; he had been denied his constitutional rights as an American. In all probability, an innocent man would die for the crime of being Black in a country where trumped-up charges were all too conveniently applied to people of his race. The Supreme Court had been unaccountably reluctant to open the Pandora's box that was state-court procedures in the South, but simply because the problem was widespread didn't mean that a member of the nation's highest tribunal had to turn his back on an obvious injustice.

John's telegram had arrived in Chattanooga so late on Sunday that few people heard the news until Monday, the morning after a Black minister, Reverend W. B. Fleming of St. James Baptist Church, had come to the jail and baptized the prisoner on what was presumed to be the last Sunday of his life. Fleming brought with him a large number of followers, who were allowed into the premises. Outside, a fast-accumulating spillover crowd of Black supporters massed in a further show of solidarity.

Reverend Fleming asked Johnson to make a statement of faith, and the prisoner addressed his audience in what the *Times* called the "low, musical voice" that had factored into his trial. "I have had a change of heart, and I am ready to die," Johnson said. "The change came at me all at once, and I can't tell how it was. Before the change, I hated the people that were against me. I couldn't eat and could only think of the arrest and the trouble I was in. I didn't want to talk or eat and didn't want to see anyone. All at once, I said I was willing to give up my friends and folks and life itself if I had to, and then I felt different. I didn't hate the white people anymore, my appetite returned, and I am proud now to have anybody come to see me."

A bathtub at the end of the corridor served as a baptismal font, and Fleming blessed Johnson and guided him in immersion. When he emerged, he clapped his hands with joy and gazed upward in ecstasy. Others sang and prayed, and some of the women dropped to the floor in exultation. Johnson reiterated his innocence, and the crowd echoed its approval. At the peak of the frenzy, a church deacon expressed his belief that a miracle would happen and spare Johnson the gallows.

The following morning brought reports of Harlan's telegram.[35]

The news that struck the Black community as a message from God stunned the white officials of Chattanooga. They viewed the Supreme Court's interference as a direct challenge to their ability to keep their streets safe. More ominously, Harlan's decision set off an explosion of outrage among the many whites who had stood before the jailhouse and extracted Judge McReynolds's promise of a speedy trial. Mob justice was back in the air, and this time Chattanooga's civic leaders were prepared to blame Washington if something untoward happened.

"If by legal technicality the case is prolonged and the culprit finally escapes, there will be no use to plead with a mob here if another such crime is committed," reasoned the *Chattanooga News*. "Such delays are largely responsible for mob violence all over the country."[36]

While Parden began preparing in earnest for Johnson's appeal to the Supreme Court, the mob grew restless.[37]

At the Hamilton County Jail, Sheriff Shipp made a curious decision to give all his deputies the night off; Shipp told the jailer that "there wouldn't be any more danger," since Johnson was "a United States prisoner now."[38] Just one seventy-three-year-old night guard was left to protect the building that had nearly been ransacked a few weeks earlier.[39]

At eight o'clock in the evening, the elderly guard was upstairs when a group of white men carrying pistols and rifles broke in on the ground floor. The intruders flooded the public areas of the jail.

This time they wielded sledgehammers to pound their way through the steel door to the inmates. Hearing the ominous sound of hammer on steel, the terrified prisoners slowly began to realize what was happening. Soon the mob was racing through the halls and stairs of the jail. It took the marauders little time to reach the top floor, where only two prisoners were being held. Screaming his name, they grabbed Ed Johnson and carried him off to the Walnut Street Bridge and oblivion.[40]

The lynching of Ed Johnson was a shot across the bow of the Supreme Court. As the news ricocheted around the country, many commentators spoke of the need to strike back against vigilante justice. As the justice who set the forces in motion, Harlan was asked for his reaction. He was deliberately circumspect: "I cannot discuss the merits of the case, but an appeal was granted on the simple ground that the merits of the case should be gone into, and no other ground was considered," he said.[41]

Behind the scenes, wheels were turning. John felt a desire to rip the mask off the lynch mob and Ku Kluxism generally. It wasn't just a handful of degenerates who had killed Ed Johnson—the whole community of Chattanooga had killed him, by deliberately looking the other way.

This wasn't a problem peculiar to Chattanooga. In the forty years since the end of the Civil War, Black people had been murdered by vigilantes in frighteningly high numbers—from a high of 161 in 1892 to a still-striking 62 in 1906, the year of Johnson's death—and prosecutors in the South almost never brought the perpetrators to justice.[42] The usual explanation was that the murderers hid their identity behind sheets and masks. In fact, the authorities usually had no desire to bring charges. The Supreme Court had taken no official notice—until now. In response to Chattanooga's open defiance of the Supreme Court, John wanted to take action—not only against the mob but also against Sheriff Shipp and other officers who stood by and did nothing.

White Chattanoogans did little to discourage the notion that they backed the mob. The *News* proclaimed that the "lynching is a direct result of the ill-advised effort to save the Negro from the just penalty of the laws of Tennessee." The *News* went on to endorse Shipp's reelection, proclaiming, "His defeat would be entirely too much encouragement to defenders of such fiends as Johnson was. We repeat that we do not know how a white man can withhold support from Shipp under all the circumstances."[43]

Shipp was reelected by a vast margin.[44]

In Washington, John conferred with his colleagues at the home of Chief Justice Fuller, who shared his feeling that the authority of the Supreme Court was under assault. President Theodore Roosevelt condemned the "affront to the highest tribunal of the land."[45] Both John and Fuller consulted with Roosevelt's attorney general, William Moody, who agreed that the best course would be to bring federal contempt-of-court charges against the perpetrators.

That raised the question of who would investigate the case. In the pre-FBI era, there were so few federal law enforcement officers that two Secret Service agents had to be shifted from protecting the president to investigating Chattanooga. They came back with the names of some of the mob leaders and compelling evidence that public officials had failed to protect Johnson. Judge McReynolds, for instance, allegedly watched the attack from his courthouse without trying to stop it. Ultimately, however, the attorney general felt it better to focus on the far stronger case against Shipp. Leaving the jail so lightly guarded seemed an obvious dereliction of duty.

When the attorney general issued his indictments, targeting Shipp, his deputies, and the alleged leaders of the mob, it raised eyebrows in local communities throughout the nation. No one doubted that the US Constitution was clear in guaranteeing due process of law, but the job of enforcing that guarantee belonged to the state courts. If the Supreme Court disagreed with their rulings, it would send the case back to the states for retrials. The notion that the Supreme Court would conduct a trial on its own was unprecedented.

Eminent lawyers lined up to defend Shipp, both out of sympathy for him and a desire to keep the Supreme Court from meddling in state matters. Shipp chose Judson Harmon, an Ohioan who had been Grover Cleveland's attorney general and had his eyes on the Democratic nomination for president.[46] Harmon's arguments in the first phase of the case, seeking to determine the scope of the Supreme Court's authority to try Shipp and the others, prompted some stinging exchanges with Harlan but failed to carry the day. In the end, the justices, behind a sturdy opinion by Justice Holmes, decided they could indeed try whoever was responsible for defying the court's order.[47]

But even if the decision was constitutionally sound, it presented practical challenges. The nine justices would, for the first time in the court's history, be serving as a jury, charged with determining matters of fact, not law, against a range of defendants. Though others had been indicted, public attention focused on Shipp, the proud former rebel. In a pointed reminder of past battles, Shipp's defense team addressed the sheriff as "Captain Shipp," his Confederate military title.[48]

The case against him was substantial. There was the indisputable fact that he left the jail lightly guarded. Further, Ellen Baker, the only prisoner on the floor with Ed Johnson, testified that guards removed all the other prisoners from the floor that afternoon, appearing to clear the way for the mob.[49] In a dramatic piece of testimony, Shipp's Black cook stated that she overheard a dinner table conversation between him and his wife in which he predicted the lynching.[50] Then there were his own comments to a southern newspaper, blaming the Supreme Court for the lynching and stating that he did not attempt to harm any of the mob "and would not have made such an attempt if I could."[51]

Shipp, however, made a spirited defense. He testified that after learning from the local district attorney that the jail was under siege, he felt a sense of responsibility and rushed to the scene. He arrived before Johnson had been taken but was himself overwhelmed by the mob and held prisoner for a time in a side room.[52] Under cross-examination, however, these assertions seemed less credible. Shipp acknowledged that he wore his pistol during the time he was being held prisoner and never removed it from its holster. He also claimed, improbably, that he could not recognize any of the men who held him or any of the others ransacking the jail.

"You were sheriff of the county?" demanded the assistant attorney general who was cross-examining him.

"Yes, sir," Shipp replied.

"And you did not pull your gun?"

"No."

"You had strength enough to have pulled the trigger, I suppose?"

"Oh, I guess I could have pulled the trigger."[53]

When the Supreme Court retired to consider the case, the justices wrestled with the facts as a jury might, taking to heart the defense's contention that Shipp may have been guilty of poor judgment but did not conspire with anyone to have Johnson killed. After five days, though, they reached a verdict: six defendants, including Shipp, were convicted. The sheriff's sentence was ninety days in prison.[54]

The ex-Confederate returned to the South to a hero's welcome—more than five thousand people massed at the Chattanooga train station and a band playing "Dixie."[55] He took to wearing his old gray uniform around town; on his wedding anniversary, he used his Civil War sword to cut a cake decorated with the Stars and Bars.[56]

Though a national sensation when it occurred, the *Shipp* case quickly faded from memory. In the annals of Supreme Court history, it was the ultimate oddity: the one and only time that the high court served as an actual trial court. The proceedings are largely unremembered by legal scholars, though they set the stage for a more robust system of federal intervention in state matters, such as death penalty cases, later in the century. But as a historical turning point, the *Shipp* trial merits more attention. The long-running drama graphically laid out the horrors of lynching, forcing millions of Americans who had long averted their eyes to recognize its pervasive injustice. And, in fact, the number of lynchings per year dwindled in its aftermath.[57]

Perhaps more important, the case represented the first time that Black people saw the Supreme Court acting on their behalf—one of the intangible links in a chain of gestures by John Marshall Harlan that maintained Black people's faith in the Constitution. "Shipp was perhaps the first instance where the court demonstrated that the Fourteenth Amendment and the equal protection clause have any substantive meaning to people of the African American race," declared Justice Thurgood Marshall in 1991, pointing to Harlan's courage as the driving force behind the decision.[58]

Chapter 20

"Ever May His Name Be Said in Reverence"

The twentieth century didn't seem so new at all. In his eighth decade and the century's first, John kept getting drawn back into the causes and issues of his young adulthood, bringing his life full circle. Not enough had changed. The same divisions that had almost destroyed the country in his youth continued to haunt its future. Tragically, his own beloved judicial system was once again clearing the path to ruination.

Emboldened by the Supreme Court's acceptance of segregation, the states of the old Confederacy moved to choke off any remaining political power in the Black community by disenfranchising the very voters whom the Fifteenth Amendment had sought to protect. The weapons of choice were poll taxes, literacy tests, and, in some cases, empowering local officials to deny ballots to men deemed of poor character—in the opinion of the poll workers alone.[1]

No one was fooled as to the racial and—because some poor whites got swept up in the net—class dimensions of these assaults on suffrage. In 1901, Alabama enacted a new state constitution that granted permanent franchise to most white voters, partly by grandfathering in all Confederate veterans and their descendants, while subjecting Black voters to literacy tests and character assessments. Tens of thousands of Black voters were erased from the rolls; out of 184,471 eligible

Black voters before the new constitution, only about 3,000 survived its aftermath.[2]

Jackson Giles, a voting-rights activist who worked as a janitor, led a group of roughly 5,000 Black men in claiming that officials in Montgomery had arbitrarily violated their voting rights; Giles had paid his $1.50 poll tax and met the requirements laid out in the state constitution but had nonetheless been turned away from voting on account of his race. Booker T. Washington was the instigator and fundraiser behind the lawsuit. The plaintiffs' best chance—only chance, really—was to get their case heard in federal court. But the circuit court ruled that it lacked jurisdiction because of a law requiring that cases must involve sums greater than $2,000 to be justiciable in the federal system.[3]

That may have seemed like flimsy grounds, but it would have given the plaintiffs a chance to retool their case into a more robust claim that Alabama had violated the U.S. Constitution. Instead, when Giles appealed to the Supreme Court, a majority of six justices, led by Holmes, breezed past the jurisdictional question and ruled against the plaintiffs on the merits. In a suspiciously twisty argument, Holmes agreed that Alabama's new state constitution had been enacted to remove Black people from the voter rolls, but maintained that the plaintiff's requested remedy—being granted the right to vote—made no sense if the entire voting regime was unconstitutional. How, he asked, "can we make the court a party to the unlawful scheme by accepting it and adding another voter to its fraudulent lists?"[4] At the same time, Holmes claimed, simply declaring Alabama's constitution void would be meaningless, because the Supreme Court lacked any enforcement mechanism; it could not stand against "the great mass of the white population" that "intends to keep the blacks from voting."[5] Therefore, he concluded, the court was powerless to enforce "political rights"—and the plaintiffs' proper recourse was to the political branches of government. For Jackson Giles and millions like him, this was, of course, no recourse at all.

Justice David Brewer, joined by Henry Billings Brown, dissented.[6] Brewer argued that the court should have simply rejected the case on jurisdictional grounds. Harlan, going further in his own separate dissent, agreed. In brushing past the jurisdictional question, the court had betrayed its eagerness to cut off any hope that Black voters might someday achieve justice from the Supreme Court. Harlan averred: "As these are my views as to the jurisdiction of this Court, upon this record, I will not formulate and discuss my views upon the merits of this case. But to avoid misapprehension, I may add that my conviction is that, upon the facts alleged in the bill (if the record showed a sufficient value of the matter in dispute), the plaintiff is entitled to relief in respect of his right to be registered as a voter."[7]

The voting rights case showed how Harlan—known for his forceful rebuttals of court decisions that stripped away Black people's rights in the *Civil Rights Cases* and *Plessy*—was equally attuned to ways in which the court could disguise truly devastating rulings within a maze of dubious assertions and legalisms. His dissent in *Giles v. Harris* would not echo through the ages like his words in *Plessy*, but his simple assertion that the court could have denied jurisdiction without acceding to the plaintiffs' disenfranchisement was no less relevant to the preservation of Black people's rights.

Harlan had the backs of Black Americans when the spotlight was on him, and when it was not. Like *Plessy*, the *Giles* case got little popular attention at the time, partly because the public had come to anticipate the Supreme Court's capitulation to the Southern states. Unlike *Plessy*, which became infamous in later years, *Giles* remains little noticed, except in law-review articles. But its impact—the illegal disenfranchisement of millions of Black voters for six decades—was every bit as dire.[8] At the time, Black people greatly outnumbered whites in South Carolina and Mississippi, and amounted to 45 percent of Alabama's population.[9]

Fifty-eight years later, the Supreme Court would reverse itself on Holmes's contention that it was powerless to enforce "political rights."[10] Three years after that, Congress would pass the Voting Rights Act of 1965. But the negligence of the court in John's era, its submission to white resistance, had already established the South as a political bulwark of racism and conservatism, and choked off generations of potential African American senators, governors, and other public officials.

The recognition that the country was moving backward, not forward, on the issues of greatest importance to him infused John's judicial opinions and illuminated his speeches but didn't diminish his enjoyment of life. A religious man, he remained grateful for his personal blessings and eager to give back to his community. He raised his profile in the national Presbyterian Church, leading the push to build a cathedral in Washington—a project he embraced almost as a valedictory act.[11] He chaired the board and lobbied hard for generous congressional allotments for Garfield Memorial Hospital, a public hospital erected in the nation's capital in memory of the assassinated president, who had suffered for so long in his final illness.[12] It served patients regardless of their ability to pay, though Black people were usually diverted to the nearby Freedman's Hospital at Howard University. John also celebrated his Kentucky roots—a link that grew even stronger when his trusted protégé and law partner, Gus Willson, was elected governor.

The governor and his wife, who was as close to Malvina as John was to her husband, journeyed to Washington in December 1906 to help the Harlans commemorate their fiftieth wedding anniversary. The Willsons were there as honorary family members, joining the extended clan at a private celebratory supper.[13] The last of John's siblings, his sister Lizzie, whose home in Indiana he had visited with increasing frequency while courting Malvina, had passed away earlier that year at age seventy-eight. Of John's brothers who once seemed destined to constitute James's private law firm, only the oft-afflicted James had made it into his sixties, and he died in 1897, the same year as Robert, the only Harlan man other than John to achieve a national reputation.[14]

Neither John nor Malvina had slowed much at all. Their golden wedding reception at their home drew much of the cream of Washington, including President Theodore and First Lady Edith Roosevelt.[15] The following year, John was the guest of honor—with Malvina again hovering in the balcony—at another stag dinner celebrating his career, this one hosted by a group of fellow Kentuckians and staged at the brand-new Plaza Hotel in New York City.[16] In his speech, which was enshrined in the *Congressional Record*, John spoke warmly of his years in the Bluegrass State but also stayed true to his hard-earned belief that a strong national government should override merely sectional disputes and prejudices: "What would it mean to us to be Kentuckians if we were not also, or rather first of all, Americans, whose allegiance to the nation in matters of general concern is above allegiance to any state."[17] Two years after that, John made a pilgrimage to Transylvania University Law School, where the seventy-five-year-old justice offered a nostalgic tribute to his mentors, including George Robertson, who had nurtured his conservative unionist ideology.[18]

John's loyalty to the place of his birth and his pride in the election of his most trusted friend as governor masked a growing disappointment in Kentucky. The Civil War had obliterated the aristocratic landscape of his youth; in the decades after the war, segregation and vigilante justice turned his home state into a political and economic backwater. Like a boil that could never be lanced, white prejudice and insecurity still dominated Kentucky's domestic discourse. Hatred was increasing, not abating. The most flamboyant illustration of how race distorted Kentucky's politics was a new law that would eventually make its way to John's desk at the Supreme Court, inspiring one of his most anguished dissents.

It came about because of tiny, pastoral Berea College, about sixty miles from the Harlan home in Frankfort. An abolitionist preacher, John G. Fee, founded the college in 1855 with the financial backing and assistance of Cassius Marcellus Clay, Henry Clay's abolitionist cousin. Cassius Clay was well known to John from his youth, and it's likely that John crossed paths with Fee as well.

From its inception, Berea was intended to be an oasis in a sea of strife. Carved out of the wilderness on land donated by Clay, the fledgling settlement was named after the biblical town whose residents were "open minded and receptive to the gospel."[19] First came a thirteen-member church established by Fee and then a one-room schoolhouse. Fee declared that Berea College would not only educate men and women, but also Black and white people, side by side, in a biblical state of unity. Its charter declared that it "shall be under an influence strictly Christian, and opposed to sectarianism, slaveholding, caste, and every other wrong institution or practice."[20]

After the Civil War, the college grew in size and prestige. Even though it made some accommodations to the segregationist sentiments spreading like the plague around the rest of the state—such as maintaining separate dorms for Black and white students—it stayed true to its commitment to educate promising young people of both genders and races.

By the first decade of the twentieth century, however, its liberal attitudes were increasingly under siege. Legislators from other parts of the state, seeking to establish their segregationist bona fides, insisted that Berea College's comingling of Black and white students was a scandalous affront to the state's social norms. In 1904 a legislator from a county ninety miles away, Carl Day, submitted a bill prohibiting Black and white students from attending the same institution, public or private.

The so-called Day Bill was recognized, even in the South, as an extreme measure. Previous segregation laws proceeded on the assumption that states should not oblige unwilling whites to interact with Black people—in railroad cars or public school classrooms, for instance—but this law banned purely voluntary interactions between the races. Professors and students at Berea College understood the college's values and embraced them; now the state was saying that they couldn't associate with one another even if they wanted to.

Despite the odd posture of attempting to solve a problem that didn't exist at Berea College, Day's bill attracted extremely broad support. "Any man who voted in opposition would have the 'n----r question' brought up against him in all his future career," explained the *New York Post*.[21] One legislator privately wrote the college's president to say, "We understand that this proposed law is an outrage. The state has never contributed to the support of Berea College, and it has no right to interfere in its affairs. I want you to understand that I have no sympathy with this law; but the facts are these: the law is going to pass. Now, for me to oppose it would make it necessary for me to discuss the N----r question in every political speech as long as I live."[22]

When the college challenged the law in local courts—arguing that its property rights and constitutional liberties had been trampled—a Kentucky judge defended the measure as a reasonable application of the state's police powers. He cited Kentucky's interest in preventing racial mixing, declaring that no "well-informed person in any section of the country would deny" that segregation was a "sound" and "laudable" goal.[23]

He was outdone, however, by the state court of appeals, whose majority opinion, with one justice dissenting—significantly, one who would become president of the University of Kentucky[24]—went out of its way to defend the law as divinely inspired and dedicated to preserving the "purity of blood." The court of appeals attempted to put a scientific gloss on its justification for segregation as well:

"There exists in each race a homogenesis by which it will perpetually reproduce itself, if unadulterated," the court declared. "Its instinct is gregarious. As a check, there is another, an antipathy to the races, which some call race prejudice. This is nature's guard to prevent amalgamation of the races. . . . In the lower animals, this quality may be more effective in the preservation of distinct breeds. But among men, conventional decrees in the form of government precepts are resorted to in aid of right conduct to preserve the purity of blood. . . . In less civilized society, the stronger would probably annihilate the weaker race."[25]

All this hokum made its way to the Supreme Court in 1908. There were plenty of reasons to believe that the court might not simply apply the *Plessy* precedent to Kentucky: in the twelve years between *Plessy v. Ferguson* and *Berea v. Kentucky*, the mind-set of the court had changed. The economic conservatives who embraced the logic behind *Lochner v. New York* had narrowed the state's police powers to health and safety alone. The court had rejected as anathema the idea that a state could pass laws to promote social good through labor peace. Now came Kentucky with a law predicated on the idea that it was promoting social good through racial separation, and it stood on an especially wobbly foundation. There had been no actual racial dispute at Berea College; no threat to the peace.

Nonetheless, in a return to their pre-*Shipp* hands-off posture on southern repression of Black people, a large majority of the justices found their way to endorsing Kentucky's law. As an extra disappointment, Oliver Wendell Holmes Jr., who had been John's ally in the prosecution of Sheriff Shipp, concurred in the court's decision, though he declined to join the majority opinion by Justice David Brewer.

Rufus Peckham and Chief Justice Fuller joined Brewer, along with White and McKenna. These economic conservatives found a novel way to avoid having to contend with their own precedent in the *Lochner* decision—the one that banned state regulations that interfered with personal liberty: they claimed that Kentucky's segregation law didn't interfere with the personal liberties of teachers and students— it merely restricted the actions of a corporation, Berea College, which was a creation of the state and thus subject to its preferences.[26]

"In creating a corporation, a state may withhold powers which may be exercised by and cannot be denied to an individual," Brewer wrote.[27] In backing the law, the court need not contend with the Fourteenth Amendment or any individual rights, of Black or white people, he declared. The law may be allowed merely "as coming within the power of a state over its own corporate creatures."[28]

Despite Brewer's attempt to sidestep the Constitution, ironies abounded. The New York bakeries that were subject to that state's sixty-hour work week in the *Lochner* case were also corporations, but the justices had gone out of their way to find that the law violated the rights of an individual who might choose to work there and want to work longer hours. How were the teachers and students at Berea College any different?

Also, in *Lochner*, Peckham, Brewer, and the rest of the court's majority had had no hesitation about sweeping aside the decision of Judge Parker and New York's top court declaring that the bakery law had been intended to promote health and safety; now, three years later, in his *Berea College* opinion, Brewer professed that "this court should hesitate before it holds that the supreme court of the state did not know what was the thought of the legislature in its enactment."[29]

A quarter century earlier, in the *Civil Rights Cases of 1883*, the court had rejected the notion that incorporated businesses that discriminated against Black men and women were arms of the state; now, in the Berea case, it held the college to be a "creature" of the state by virtue of its incorporation alone.

Plainly, in John's eyes, the law meant one thing when applied to powerful interests and another thing entirely when applied to Black people and low-income laborers. His dissent in the Berea case wasn't as groundbreaking as his long, thoughtful exposition on the *Civil Rights Cases*. Nor was it as commanding as his thunderbolt of indignation in *Plessy v. Ferguson*. Instead, it evoked a sense of weariness, at battles fought and lost over and over, and a growing suspicion of the majority's true motives.

The rights of the teachers and students of Berea College, John insisted, were not separable from those of the institution. Clearly, Kentucky had not meant to make any such separation; the law had been intended as a statewide ban on interracial education, not a revision to the charter of Berea College.

"It is absolutely certain that the legislature had in mind to prohibit the teaching of the two races in the same private institution at the same time," he wrote. ". . . It is a reflection upon the common sense of the legislators to suppose that they might have prohibited a private *corporation* from teaching by its agents, and yet left individuals and unincorporated associations entirely at liberty, by the same instructors, to teach the two races in the same institution at the same time. It was the teaching of the two races *together*, or in the same school, no matter by whom or under whose authority, which the legislature sought to prevent."[30]

Once again, the court seemed to be performing legal somersaults to accommodate racial prejudice. The assault on the rights of teachers to practice their craft and students to receive an education, was, in John's eyes, a clear violation of the Fourteenth Amendment. Sensing the extent of the discrimination—the rank hatred—behind the law, the elderly justice summoned some of his old righteous eloquence.

"The capacity to impart instruction to others is given by the Almighty for beneficent purposes, and its use may not be forbidden or interfered with by government. . . ." he declared. "The right to impart instruction, harmless in itself or beneficial to those who receive it, is a substantial right of property—especially where the services are rendered for compensation. But even if such right be not strictly a property right, it is beyond question part of one's liberty as guaranteed against hostile action by the Constitution of the United States."[31]

The *Berea College* case was John's last testament on racial discrimination and the Constitution. Never again would he weigh in on the issue that, while brushed aside by most of white society, so uniquely burdened his conscience. But the legal misfortunes of Black people only furthered his interest in their advancement—probably because they had been treated so unfairly by the courts.

On March 8, 1910, he joined President William Howard Taft as a speaker at an event honoring graduates of Wilberforce University, the Black college in Ohio, held in the towering, Gothic chambers of Washington's Metropolitan AME Church. This grand church—the gathering place of many of the most distinguished Black leaders of the era—had become something of a second home for John. It was the successor to the church at whose Bethel Industrial School his late daughter, Edith, had taught, and his special feeling for it was evident. Fifteen years earlier, he'd been among the few white officials to attend Frederick Douglass's funeral there. He was a recurrent guest at the church's Bethel Literary Society for more than two decades, and the society had feted him in honor of his seventieth birthday in 1903.[32]

On that March day when John and Taft headlined the Wilberforce alumni celebration, the crowd of three thousand—"one of the finest and most representative colored audiences ever assembled in this city,"[33] in the words of the *Washington Bee*—probably included Robert Harlan Jr., who had moved back to the capital after his father's death to serve as an official in the War Department and practice law.[34] Robert Jr. and Mamie had reclaimed their places among the city's African American elites. The event at Metropolitan AME, featuring a major address by the president on the state of Black life, would have

attracted the fifty-seven-year-old son of Robert Harlan not only because of his family's connection to Justice Harlan but also because
of his personal friendship with President Taft, dating to their time
as classmates at Cincinnati's Woodward High School. Robert Jr.'s life
was intertwined with those of both speakers.

John's remarks—which were not published—were mere warm-
ups for the president, who not only endorsed the concept of Black
higher education but also pledged to increase federal funding. "I went
over the figures once or twice, and instead of being enough to indicate waste, there is an indication there is not nearly enough money
to even educate the leaders of the race that the race must have if it is
going to progress as it is,"[35] declared Taft, who was not known for either his eloquence or his succinctness.

The message would surely have been pleasing to both the justice
and Robert Jr., and the occasion would have offered each a chance
to reflect on the long family journey from Harlan's Station to the nation's capital at the dawn of the twentieth century.

Three months later, with another Supreme Court term completed,
John made his annual pilgrimage to Murray Bay, where he golfed,
rambled along the rocky shore, and spent quiet afternoons on the
Braemead veranda with Malvina and other family members. President Taft, whose own extended clan had long gathered at Murray Bay,
spending many happy summer evenings with the Harlans, had made
the politically necessary decision to stay in the United States for the
summer; he located his Summer White House in a rented mansion in
Beverly, Massachusetts.[36]

In July came shocking news: Chief Justice Fuller was stricken with
a fatal heart attack on Independence Day. John was personally fond
of Fuller, despite their many disagreements, and believed that he had
administered the court fairly.[37] Until Taft named a replacement, John,
as the senior associate justice, would be expected to serve as acting
chief. While the title was something of an honorific, since each justice
still had only one vote, there were some substantive powers to serving as acting chief: for one, John would decide which justice wrote the
court's opinion in a case, a deceptively important task.

That he did for all the fall of 1910, and seemed to enjoy the job enough to imagine doing it permanently.[38] Though he was seventy-seven—the same age at which Fuller had succumbed to his heart attack—John apparently thought his friend Taft might do him the honor of giving him the chance to spend his final years on the court as its chief. But Taft rejected the notion of appointing a chief justice simply as reward for long service and friendship. John, he felt, was too old. Instead, he made the unpopular decision to elevate sixty-five-year-old Justice Edward Douglass White, a Democrat and Confederate veteran, to the post.[39] Over their many years serving together on the court, John had never been particularly close to White, despite having been companionable enough to walk home together after long days on the bench.[40] Moreover, White had expressed concern about dissenting opinions as tending "to engender want of confidence in" the court—a charge aimed directly at Harlan, the court's most prolific dissenter.[41]

There was nothing White could do about this, however. John was determined to have his own say, and he got another opportunity the following spring, in 1911, when the court took on one of the most consequential antitrust cases of the era, involving arguably the most famous amalgamation in business history, John D. Rockefeller's Standard Oil. Prodded by journalistic accounts of the company's monopolistic practices by journalist Ida Tarbell of *McClure's* magazine, the Justice Department had moved to order the breakup of the giant oil trust under the powers granted in the Sherman Antitrust Act.[42]

The fact that the Supreme Court was open to the action at all was vindication for John, who sixteen years earlier had been the only justice to support the breakup of the Sugar Trust. At the time, John had called the majority's claim that a purely manufacturing monopoly did not constitute a restraint on interstate commerce "an interpretation so rigid, technical, and narrow" that it would render Congress helpless against the trusts.[43] He was right, and the other justices seemed to agree with him. The Sugar Trust precedent quickly began to unravel. In a 1905 case called *Swift & Co. v. United States*,[44] the court unanimously changed course and declared that the Justice Department could indeed act against a manufacturing monopoly if it affected interstate commerce—just as John had argued in his lonely dissent in the *E. C. Knight* case. The justices' shift toward support of antitrust actions had begun the previous year with a 5-to-4 decision in the much-ballyhooed *Northern Securities* case (*Northern Securities Co. v. United States*),[45] a top priority of President Roosevelt. The case involved the breakup of a railroad trust that dominated transportation in the West. John wrote the opinion for the plurality.

Now, in the *Standard Oil* case, the court once again confronted a breakup of a company widely regarded as acting in restraint of trade—and one far more infamous than the Northern Securities Company. Chief Justice White wrote in his majority opinion that the government could take action against private businesses if their practices in restraining trade were unreasonable—a legal test that came to be known as "the rule of reason."[46] Standard Oil, White declared, had violated that rule.

The decision once again validated John's concerns of sixteen years earlier and showed how his view—not that of the majority in *E. C. Knight*—had proven correct. But White's rule of reason suggested that courts, not the Justice Department, would be the final arbiter of which trusts should be broken up and which should be shielded from government interference.

That didn't sit well with John, who suggested that White's rule may yet "prove to be mischievous."[47] Congress, he noted, had intended to give the Justice Department the discretion to break up *any* monopoly that restricts trade—not only those that the court considered especially egregious. Once again, the justices were taking on decision-making powers reserved for the legislative branch.

"In my judgment, the decree below should have been affirmed without qualification,"[48] he wrote.

With the announcement on May 11 of the *Standard Oil* decision—a huge blow to the Rockefellers, which dominated the news—another term on the court was nearly completed. The following month, John and Malvina returned to their beloved Braemead, once again to enjoy the bracing breezes of Murray Bay. They were joined, as always, by their daughters Laura and Ruth. The granddaughter they had raised from babyhood—their own Edith's daughter of the same name—had made a society marriage to Erastus Corning IV of the New York Cornings and presented her grandparents with two great-granddaughters.

The Cornings did not visit John and Malvina that summer of 1911, but their son John Maynard stayed near his parents and brought with him his three youngest children. His eldest, Lysbeth, was already twenty years old and taking the grand tour of Europe with her mother; they joined the rest of the family in Murray Bay later in the summer. To his joy, John got to spend weeks enjoying the company of his only grandson—his twelve-year-old namesake, John Marshall Harlan II—and the two youngest of John Maynard's children, nine-year-old Janet and two-year-old Edith.[49]

When the calendar turned to September, John Maynard traveled with his father to New York, where the two of them caught up with old friends in the worlds of law and politics. When John Maynard returned home to Chicago, Malvina joined her husband in New York. He had caught a bad cold but was well enough to pay his respects at Grant's Tomb, the classical white temple with military-style sarcophagi modeled on Napoléon's that contained the remains of the late president and his wife, Julia. Returning the following day to show Malvina the splendid monument and view, John found himself reminiscing about Grant and contemplating the afterlife, wondering aloud whether memories of earthly activities carried over into what he called "the Great Beyond."[50]

Soon after their pilgrimage to Grant's grave, John and Malvina headed home to Washington for the start of the court's business. On October 9 a seemingly hearty John joined his brethren on the bench. It was a typical first day of a new term, marked by the ceremonial swearing in of new members of the Supreme Court bar and the formal submission of motions.[51] The following day, after spending a long time in hearings, he felt ill and was escorted home by Justice McKenna. When John slumped into a chair, a fearful Malvina called a doctor. It turned out he had a dangerously high temperature of 103.[52]

Malvina and the doctors were concerned enough to call for two of the justice's sons, James and John Maynard, to come to their father's side. The eldest Harlan son, Richard, was traveling in Europe with his wife. John's court messenger, James Jackson, who had been born enslaved in Maryland and became so close to the Harlans that he vacationed with them in Murray Bay, joined the family group at the justice's bedside.[53]

"Father is seriously ill and has been so since the adjournment of court on Tuesday last," John Maynard reported to Gus Willson that Friday. "For some days, he has had a slight cold. The matter was aggravated on Tuesday. . . . His wonderful vitality has enabled him to hold his own surprisingly well, but I cannot say that he is as strong this morning as he was yesterday."[54]

The following morning, he awakened to tell the assembled group, including his sons and daughters and James Jackson, "I am sorry to have kept you waiting."[55]

After so much good health, he seemed almost impatient in the face of what he probably realized was his final illness. His years of devout Bible study had left him with little doubt or fear of the afterlife. He felt secure in the legacy he had built on earth, which gave him hope for posterity—his and the nation's.

He died later that morning. Some reports called his condition bronchitis; Malvina said it was pneumonia. Both were infections that would have spread and choked off John's ability to breathe; in just two decades hence, either one would likely have been cured with antibiotics. Nonetheless, Malvina felt the hand of God taking her husband, declaring "the great summons came, and he 'fell asleep' on Saturday, October 14. . . . His noble life on earth was finished, and the new life in 'the glad Homeland, not far away,' had begun."[56]

John's funeral featured his favorite hymns, including one written by the father of his colleague Oliver Wendell Holmes Jr.[57] Almost all of official Washington crowded into New York Avenue Presbyterian Church on Tuesday, October 17, for the solemn ritual. Supreme Court justices, senators, congressmen, and Civil War comrades paid their respects at the handsome redbrick edifice where John and his family had worshipped for three and a half decades, and John had taught Sunday school and served as a board member. His friend President Taft was traveling on the West Coast and sent his condolences to Malvina.[58] In John's honor, every court in the city waited for the final tolling of the bells on New York Avenue to begin their day's work.

"It is a great thing to have in this community in these days a man of his station and his record who was not ashamed of the gospel of Christ," preached the church's pastor, Reverend Dr. Wallace Radcliffe.[59]

The church service, however, was emblematic of only about half of the world of remembrances for John Marshall Harlan. In the white portion of that world, John was honored for his stature in the law and his fine deeds dating back to the Civil War. "The life of few men has been more intimately associated with the history of the nation than that of John Marshall Harlan," wrote the *Boston Globe*.[60] No mention was made of his support for civil rights. Entirely unseen by white mourners was an outpouring of emotion in another portion of the world, one shuttered behind the walls of segregation. In the hamlets and churches of Black America, John Marshall Harlan's death was an epic passage, an occasion for painful, humbling grief and fear for the future of the race.

The leading newspapers of white America all featured long obituaries of the dead justice, with some running additional stories assessing Harlan "the man."[61] The *Louisville Courier-Journal*, Kentucky's leading newspaper, placed him "on the short roll of dead giants of the Supreme Court which makes the tribunal immortal."

". . . A stalwart, both physically and mentally, with catholic tastes, a rugged integrity, he brought to his stern conception of duty a judicial temperament and a heroic capacity for hard work and wholesome play that made him in an eminent degree the great jurist and the great man," the paper editorialized. In a veiled acknowledgment that not everyone in Kentucky agreed with his judicial opinions, the *Courier-Journal* added, "It is no time now to attempt to weigh accurately his work and to fix the place that history will assign him. And if it were the time, perhaps Kentuckians would better leave the task to others. For we in Kentucky, ranking him among the noblest of the state's sons, proud of his career and of the luster he has reflected on the land of his nativity, and fond of him personally as we are proud of him professionally, may well at this time mourn the dead Kentuckian, leaving to others the colder study of the dead jurist."[62]

As if to reinforce its appreciation of the man himself, separate from what he stood for on the bench, the *Courier-Journal* highlighted a story told by a former Confederate general, Basil Duke, who credited John with saving his life by letting him escape when he was caught behind Union lines visiting his wife.[63]

Other newspapers, such as the *Baltimore Sun*, alluded to John's passion for dissent, writing, "Justice Harlan was never afraid to dissent from a decision with the rest of the court lined up against him," while remaining firm in his principles even as "other members of the court changed their views as time rolled by." As an example, however, the *Sun* cited not the flashpoint cases involving civil rights but the more remote, though still significant, Insular Cases.[64] Other papers cited his opinion in the recent *Standard Oil* case as emblematic of his willingness to forcefully stake out a position.[65]

Against all the boilerplate plaudits, the tribute from William Jennings Bryan, three times the Democratic presidential nominee, including in the most recent election of 1908, stood out. No doubt remembering John's bristling dissent in the *Pollock* case, in which he decried the court's rejection of the income tax as favoring the wealthy over the laborers of the land, Bryan declared that "his name will be more revered as the people learn of the fidelity he has shown to their rights and interests. His death is a great loss to the country."

That loss was being felt on an entirely different level among Black people of all backgrounds. News of the jurist's death provoked an immediate emotional outpouring.

"When the spirit of John Marshall Harlan left its temple of clay last Saturday morning, a great light went out," proclaimed the *Washington Bee*. ". . . An entire race, today, is weeping because he has been taken from the bench. An entire race is bowed in grief because a friend has been taken from us. . . . Now that he is gone, we cannot help but tremble, and fear that no one after him may dissent against decisions against our race. A great and good man has gone to his reward, and if the prayers of the race are answered, and if future reward is measured by the good one has done while yet in life, then great will be the reward of the late, lamented Justice Harlan."[66]

The *Cleveland Gazette* was more succinct: "Justice Harlan—Ever may his name be said in reverence."[67]

The justice's passing "was a sad blow to the ten million Negroes of the country, for upon every possible opportunity, he proved himself to be their friend," lamented the *Savannah Tribune*.[68]

"The American Negro feels that in death he loses a friend," added a letter writer in the *Lexington Leader*. "Not because Justice Harlan especially loved him because his face is black, but rather because he did not hate him because his face was black and was always ready and willing to give him a square deal. Too broad to be prejudiced; too brave to be turned from what he knew to be right by the carping bugaboo of public sentiment; too just to be unjust, this scholar, jurist, and Christian man, realizing the Fatherhood of God and the Brotherhood of Man, dared lift his voice always in behalf of civil rights and human liberty."[69]

The writer placed him alongside Abraham Lincoln, Wendell Phillips, Charles Sumner, and William Lloyd Garrison among men who "were sent, as it seems by Providence itself."[70]

In cities to which John had little personal connection, as well as those where he did, Black mourners filled churches to pray for his soul. "We owe it to the memory of the late Justice Harlan to turn out and hear those who will speak in praise of the many noble qualities he possessed to an eminent degree,"[71] declared the *Chicago Broad Ax*, touting a memorial at Quinn Chapel, just south of downtown, at which mourners were urged to contribute to build a monument to Harlan.[72] In Boston's Roxbury neighborhood, mourners crowded into Saint Mark's Congregational Church to hear tributes to the late justice amid songs and recitations of poems by the African American writer Paul Laurence Dunbar. Organizers, which included the New England Suffrage League, called Harlan "the greatest friend of freedom and equality of citizenship under the Constitution ever on the Supreme Court."[73]

In John's home state of Kentucky, Black churches in Lexington and Frankfort held spontaneous services in the immediate wake of his passing. The Frankfort commemoration declared that "no consideration save that of universal brotherhood ever moved him."[74]

At least three Black churches in Washington held memorial services after the justice's death, culminating in a special citywide service painstakingly organized by national Black leaders and held at Metropolitan AME. Mourners filed in to the strains of Beethoven's "Funeral March on the Death of a Hero" and received a twelve-page commemorative booklet with John's image on the cover. The long service included numerous speakers extolling Harlan's greatness, along with performances by musical groups and soloists. A prominent Black attorney offered an assessment of Harlan's legal legacy, quoting excerpts from his greatest opinions.[75]

The huge event received no notice or attention in the white community; such was the iron gate of segregation. Members of John's family chose not to attend. Neither did invited guests including President Taft, former President Theodore Roosevelt, justices of the Supreme Court, and several senators. All sent their regrets.[76]

"He was no condescending friend of the Negro," declared one of many resolutions in John's honor. "Never by word or manner did he exploit his humane sentiments, or claim a vested right to the gratitude and reverence of our race. He had both, but they were spontaneous, unaffected, and sincere. He was the friend of humankind and freely acknowledged the humanity of the Negro."[77]

The first law review article assessing John's career was published the following spring of 1912. It was written by none other than John's old sparring partner, Justice Henry Billings Brown, the author of the majority opinion in *Plessy v. Ferguson* and some of the most important of the Insular Cases. Now retired because of encroaching blindness, the seventy-six-year-old Brown offered an evenhanded assessment of John's dissents and warm references to John's engaging personality and strong mind.[78]

The article was divided into subchapters including "Interstate Commerce," "Police Powers," "The Income Tax," "Sherman Anti-Trust Law," and "The Three Amendments"—that is, the postwar amendments to the Constitution.

"Mr. Justice Harlan not only believed in the loyal enforcement of the three postbellum amendments to the Constitution, but firmly believed in the wisdom of their enactment, notwithstanding a growing sentiment in his own party that the qualification of voters had better been left to the people of each state," Brown opined.[79]

Referring to the *Civil Rights Cases of 1883*, he wrote, "Mr. Justice Harlan dissented in a vigorous opinion to the soundness of which he stood to the last day of his life. It is not too much to say that he took a special pride in it. . . . Twenty-eight years have elapsed since this decision was rendered, and while it has been met with the general approval of the country, there is still a lingering doubt whether the spirit of the amendments was sacrificed to the letter, and whether the Constitution was intended to secure the equality of the races in all places affected with a public interest."[80]

Still, Brown concluded, "While judging from the past, the dissents of Mr. Justice Harlan will probably share the general fate and will not result in many changes in the law."[81]

Book Three

Chapter 21

Self-inflicted Wounds

The vindication of John Marshall Harlan began in his last year of life. That's when the Supreme Court cemented its reversal on antitrust law and allowed the government to break up the conglomerates that had dominated whole industries, setting higher prices for consumers and driving down wages for workers. To do so, the court abandoned its holding in the *E. C. Knight* case that manufacturing monopolies—which, in fact, meant most monopolies—were beyond the scope of the Sherman Antitrust Act.[1] Harlan had stood defiantly alone in rejecting the majority's decision in that case, insisting that his judicial brethren were imposing their conservative economic views on the people and using a deliberately narrow reading of the Constitution to distort the law.[2] It had soon become clear that Harlan's interpretation was correct, and the court had started backing away from its earlier stance as soon as 1904.

The shift was too late to make much of a difference to the Sugar Trust and its antagonist-turned-collaborator, Claus Spreckels. The German-born magnate died the day after Christmas in 1908, comfortably ensconced in his San Francisco mansion.[3] The court's reversal on antitrust cases sounded the death knell for other monopolies, however. In addition to ruling against Standard Oil, the Supreme Court, in the last spring of John's life, in 1911, allowed the breakup of James Buchanan Duke's American Tobacco Company, which had absorbed 250 smaller competitors in a relentless sprint to dominate the cigarette market.[4]

Those favorable decisions inspired more antitrust actions after John's death. Just three days after his funeral, with President Taft still in the midst of a two-month tour of the West Coast, the Justice Department brought a case against U.S. Steel Corporation and its officers, including J. P. Morgan, John D. Rockefeller, Andrew Carnegie, and Henry Clay Frick.[5] This aggressive move not only cast a harsh spotlight on an array of secrecy-obsessed moguls but also brought fresh attention to one of the least popular decisions of Taft's predecessor, Theodore Roosevelt. Four years earlier, Roosevelt had cut a deal with Frick to allow U.S. Steel to purchase one of the few remaining producers outside its realm, the Tennessee Coal and Iron Company, in order to pump cash into a faltering New York brokerage that owned much of its stock.[6] Roosevelt believed the move, which prevented the brokerage's bankruptcy, was necessary to avoid a panic on Wall Street and tacitly agreed to shield U.S. Steel from antitrust actions. Many critics, however, felt he had been bamboozled by Frick. The charge only made the combative Roosevelt more defensive of the deal.[7] The Taft administration's willingness to expose him to ridicule exacerbated the growing breach between the two former friends. It helped to spur Roosevelt's challenge to Taft in 1912, which disastrously split the Republican Party and handed the White House to Democrat Woodrow Wilson.[8]

Wilson's Justice Department kept pursuing the case against U.S. Steel, which ended after nine years in a narrow, 4-to-3 rejection by a depleted Supreme Court.[9] The defeat did not, however, do much to foreclose future antitrust actions. The creation of the Federal Trade Commission in 1914 took some of the onus off the courts, but prosecutions for monopolistic behavior continued. The Sherman Act has remained in force, with periodic revisions, for thirteen decades, bearing on such recent-era behemoths as AT&T and Microsoft. The law has curbed numerous attempts to control the market while serving to promote innovation—none of which would have been possible had the Supreme Court stuck to its stubborn *E. C. Knight* reasoning.

The shift in antitrust law added fuel to speculation that the justices might be willing to reconsider an even more harshly disputed decision: the *Pollock* income tax ruling. Even before John's death, it had become clear that his prophecy in that case was increasingly apt—that the court's insistence, against all precedent, that an income tax was an unconstitutionally direct tax, would render the government unable to meet its obligations. As the population grew, approaching a hundred million, and the United States assumed the role of a global power, the need for ever-higher tariffs to fund the basic functions of government threatened to strangle the economy.

Nonetheless, in deference to the court, Congress gave up on an income tax in the decade after the *Pollock* decision, allowing the worst excesses of the Gilded Age to flourish. The utter unfairness of the situation—which had fueled John's angry gestures toward Fuller and Field when the court announced its ruling—rankled a talented young congressman named Cordell Hull. At thirty-six, Hull had a background with some similarities to John's. Raised a few miles from the Kentucky border in the hills of Tennessee, Hull was a lawyer who came from a reasonably well-off family in a state suffering under the dominance of northeastern monied elites. Elected to the US House in 1906, he quickly perceived that tariffs served not only to protect domestic business monopolies but also to throw the burden of financing the government onto consumers of basic goods: a poor family in need of foodstuffs paid the same premium as a rich man laying out his banquet spread.

"I had deeply pondered the adverse Supreme Court decision and the opinions written on both sides," Hull wrote later.[10] And, indeed, John's arguments in his *Pollock* dissent suffused Hull's speeches on the income tax. "It was inconceivable to me that we had a Constitution that would shelter the chief portion of the wealth of the country from the only effective method of reaching it for its fair share of taxes," Hull declared.[11]

His solution was to get Congress to approve a new income tax, modeled closely on the one that had been struck down in *Pollock*, and thereby force a new lineup of justices to reconsider the case; George

Shiras, who was widely perceived to have been the justice who switched his position to strike down the tax, had retired in 1903.[12] At first, Hull's strategy went nowhere. The House was under the near-dictatorial control of the legendary Republican Speaker, "Uncle Joe" Cannon, and his party was closely aligned with the nation's business elites. Then, in the face of mounting budget problems, leaders across the political spectrum began to shift their positions. The 1908 campaign saw the injection of more progressives such as Wisconsin senator Robert LaFollette and Nebraska representative George Norris into the Republican ranks. Even some business-oriented conservatives began to worry about the government's hands being tied by tariffs.

No less a legal thinker than William Howard Taft, in his 1908 presidential campaign, surprised conservatives by signaling his disagreement with the *Pollock* decision. "It is not free from debate," he commented in an otherwise timid campaign, "how the Supreme Court, with changed membership, would view a new tax law."[13] Following Taft's election, Democrats led by Hull began whipping up outrage against the *Pollock* precedent.

"No decision of any court of last resort has been so universally condemned or its soundness so generally questioned as has this one," Hull thundered from the well of the House. He again declared that Harlan and the three other dissenters had captured the true intent of the Constitution: "Mr. Chairman, the vigorous, not to say indignant, manner in which the four dissenting justices, in their unanswered and unanswerable opinions, controverted and resented the reasoning and conclusions of the majority of the court has excited the admiration and won the hearty approval of every true lover of constitutional government."[14]

Harlan, of course, had been the most vigorous and emphatic of those dissenters, and Hull read long portions of John's dissent to his fellow House members, including his depiction of the *Pollock* ruling as "a judicial revolution that may sow the seeds of hate and distrust among the people of different sections of the country."[15]

Hull's persuasiveness, along with Representative Norris's successful challenge to the rules that had given Speaker Cannon so much control, carried the day: the House passed an income tax based largely on the one rejected in the *Pollock* case. The bill faced an even more formidable obstacle than Cannon in the Senate: Nelson Aldrich, chairman of the Senate Finance Committee, who had amassed a rubber fortune from the Belgian Congo and whose daughter Abby was married to John D. Rockefeller Jr.[16] Aldrich had long advertised his disdain for the income tax, calling it "communistic."[17] Confronted with the House bill, the sixty-seven-year-old Aldrich maneuvered behind the scenes to block it. He finally submitted to a compromise agreement to seek a constitutional amendment overturning the *Pollock* decision.

It was, and is, notoriously difficult to amend the Constitution. Any amendment requires a two-thirds majority in both the House and Senate, followed by the ratification of three-quarters of the states. Aldrich felt this was almost impossible. By gearing up the cumbersome amendment process, he triumphantly believed he had delayed the advent of the income tax for decades, if not forever.

But from its inception, the ratification movement enjoyed tremendous popular support. That ignited the furies of none other than William Dameron Guthrie and Joseph Hodges Choate, the lawyers who had devised the arguments that had won the *Pollock* case a decade and a half earlier. From their mansions in Long Island, New York, and Stockbridge, Massachusetts, Guthrie and Choate coauthored a lengthy treatise declaring that "It is imperative that Congress should not be able to exercise any such power" to tax incomes.[18] In the popular sphere, rather than a courtroom full of wealthy justices, their arguments fell on deaf ears. On February 3, 1913, the legislatures of Delaware, Wyoming, and New Mexico ratified the Sixteenth Amendment, bringing to thirty-eight the number of the then-forty-six states to approve the measure—two more than necessary.

With Woodrow Wilson preparing to take office with Democratic majorities in the House and Senate, approval of an income tax was a foregone conclusion. Hull wrote the bill, which eventually included a 1 percent tax on incomes above $3,000 per year, and which exempted more than 90 percent of families. Wealthier taxpayers faced sur-charges of up to 6 percent for incomes above $500,000.[19]

"I myself felt that if I should live two lifetimes, I probably would not be able to render public service equal to my part in the long fight for enactment of our income tax system," wrote Hull in 1948, after having served twelve years as secretary of state and bringing about the creation of the United Nations.[20] Fortunately for the United States, the ratification of the Sixteenth Amendment in 1913 came just in time for World War I, when John's prediction that tariff income would dissipate in a time of war came true.

As for the legacy of the *Pollock* decision, it is widely held in disdain. More than a decade after the advent of the income tax, Chief Justice Charles Evans Hughes, who served two separate tenures on the court between 1910 and 1941, went so far as to rank *Pollock* alongside the Dred Scott case as "self-inflicted wounds" that damaged the Supreme Court's credibility.[21]

But even as Chief Justice Hughes was condemning *Pollock* to the judicial dustbin, his own court was, to his occasional consternation, applying the precedent of another sweeping ruling in favor of the industrial elites that rested on a dubious foundation: the *Lochner* case. The court's determination to quash minimum labor standards and other business regulations held sway in the laissez-faire 1920s but precipitated a political crisis during the exigencies of the Great Depression. Harlan's dissent in the *Lochner* case, in which he called out the court for preventing Congress and state legislatures from addressing real human needs, predicted just such a situation.

Franklin Delano Roosevelt entered the White House in 1933 determined to use all the levers of the government to create jobs and boost salaries in a Great Depression economy with unemployment approaching 25 percent.[22] He insisted he wasn't interested in an ideological revolution, simply in helping people out of disastrous circumstances. To that end, he firmly believed that employers had driven wages so low that even working families couldn't cope, and their nonexistent buying power was further depressing the economy: without any consumer spending, whole industries atrophied. By paying their workers so little, corporate executives were strangling their own businesses.

Roosevelt's answer was a raft of programs that funded government jobs, created boards to determine fair wages, and subsidized farmers to reduce their crops in order to sustain agricultural prices. State governments stepped in to apply minimum standards for child laborers and women workers such as hotel maids: the rampant poverty and homelessness of women and children was viewed as a national disgrace.

The Supreme Court's answer to people who benefited from these programs—tens of millions of Americans in all—was the same as to the workers in Joseph Lochner's bakery. Echoing Justice Peckham's majority opinion in *Lochner v. New York*, the court ruled against New Deal program after New Deal program, leaving workers stranded and policy makers fuming. The court's wrecking ball struck down the Agricultural Adjustment Administration,[23] the National Industrial Recovery Act,[24] minimum wage laws, and many other New Deal–era initiatives.[25]

Some of the court's decisions were by bare 5-to-4 majorities, which only added to the anger of Roosevelt partisans. Four elderly justices—Pierce Butler, James Clark McReynolds, Willis Van Devanter, and George Sutherland—anchored the court's pro-business wing. Liberals derisively nicknamed them the Four Horsemen, after the figures in the book of Revelation who represented the evils at the end of the world. They were usually joined by a younger justice, Owen Roberts, and sometimes even by Hughes himself.

Though the Four Horsemen invoked multiple theories and justifications for invalidating New Deal programs, Peckham's notion of a right to contract defined their philosophy to the extent that the years from 1905 to 1936 came to be known as the "*Lochner* era" in jurisprudence. At the same time, other jurists and scholars began to see the fallacy of Peckham's arguments, which were predicated on the false notion that workers and employers were negotiating terms of employment like businessmen hammering out a contract. This simply wasn't true in one-company towns or, indeed, for whole industries in a time of rampant unemployment: workers had to take what little they could get, no matter how onerous the demands, lest they be kicked out and someone else given their jobs. In his *Lochner* dissent, John Marshall Harlan had pointed squarely at this logical imbalance in Peckham's thinking, suggesting that "employers and employees in such [bakery] establishments were not upon an equal footing, and that the necessities of the latter often compelled them to submit to such exactions as unduly taxed their strength."[26]

In June 1936 the Four Horsemen and Justice Roberts invoked the *Lochner* principle to strike down a New York minimum wage despite especially egregious circumstances: a Brooklyn launderer named Joseph Tipaldo paid his women workers a flat $10 per week, even though the state minimum was $14.88. To make matters worse, he tried to disguise his wrongdoing by giving them the $14.88 and forcing them to remit $4.88.[27] He was convicted, but leaders of the local hotel industry, sensing a chance to overturn the law, bankrolled his appeal all the way to the Supreme Court. In an opinion by Justice Butler, the court declared that legal precedents "clearly show that the state is without power by any form of legislation to prohibit, change, or nullify contracts between employers and adult women workers as to the amount of wages to be paid."[28]

The coldness of the court's rebuke stung. One of the more progressive justices, the Roosevelt appointee Harlan Fiske Stone, wrote to his sister, "We finished the term of Court yesterday, and I think it in many ways one of the most disastrous in history."[29] In dissenting in the case of Joseph Tipaldo, Stone echoed John Marshall Harlan in decrying the "grim irony in speaking of the freedom of contract of those who, because of their economic necessities, give their service for less than is needful to keep body and soul together."[30]

The court's rejection of minimum wage laws for women was announced on May 31, 1936, angering many struggling workers. Five months later, Roosevelt won the greatest landslide in the history of the country, carrying forty-six of forty-eight states; even more impressive were the Democrats' congressional victories, giving them a

5-to-1 majority in the House, and 4-to-1 in the Senate. Rarely had an election been so sweepingly decisive.

Roosevelt interpreted his triumph, in part, as a repudiation of the Supreme Court and its stubborn, destructive adherence to the *Lochner* precedent. He resolved to fight back. On February 7, 1937, he announced a proposal so aggressive and transformative that it caught many of his fellow Democrats off their guard: the president demanded the power to appoint a new Supreme Court justice for every one over the age of seventy who refused to retire. This would give FDR six new appointments and control of the court for decades. He rationalized the move as necessary to speed up the process of justice, but also suggested the older justices were locked in an outdated mind-set: "Little by little, new facts become blurred through old glasses fitted, as it were, for the needs of another generation," he said.[31]

Taking his case to the people, he declared in one of his famed radio "fireside chats" that "The American people have learned from the Depression" and elected an activist government committed to addressing economic ills. However, "the court has more and more often and more and more boldly asserted a power to veto laws passed by Congress and state legislatures. . . . We want a Supreme Court which will do justice under the Constitution—not over it."[32]

For the president and Congress to use their powers to completely remake the court, in order to overturn decisions with which they disagreed, was a radical step—a defenestration of a supposedly coequal branch of government. It struck at the heart of the rule of law. Many Roosevelt loyalists expressed misgivings. But with the overwhelming Democratic majorities in Congress, so recently suffused with gratitude to their victorious chief, the smart money remained on the passage of the so-called court-packing scheme.

Then came a shocking reversal. On March 29, less than three weeks after Roosevelt's fiery fireside chat, the court changed its position on minimum wages for women in a case called *West Coast Hotel Co. v. Parrish*.[33] Just ten months after having declared that New York's wage law for women could never be sustained because it violated the freedom of contract, the court approved an almost identical law in the state of Washington. Both rulings were by 5-to-4 votes; the difference was that Justice Owen Roberts switched sides, leaving the Four Horsemen in the dust.[34]

The press became entranced by Roberts's flip-flop, with many outlets declaring that the court had retreated out of fear of Roosevelt. The court's defenders cited calendars indicating that the justices' deliberations in *West Coast Hotel* had taken place before Roosevelt's scheme had been announced, though many observers were unpersuaded; even if it were true that the case had been decided earlier, the justices may well have felt the rising winds of the hurricane that was soon to hit them.

"We are told that the Supreme Court's about-face was not due to outside clamor," a *New Yorker* writer commented wryly. "It seems the new building has a soundproof room, to which justices may retire to change their minds."[35]

Both Hughes and Roberts denied that FDR had forced their hand, though both also cited public opinion as a legitimate factor in consideration of cases, raising the possibility that the results of the 1936 election, if not Roosevelt's machinations, had caught their attention.[36] Whatever the motivation, the justices' about-face obviated the need for the court-packing scheme, which died a quiet death in Congress. Roosevelt had lost the battle but won the war. Roberts's "switch in time that saved nine," as his vote in *West Coast Hotel* came to be widely known, was a milestone in legal history. Within weeks, the court had approved the Social Security Act[37] and the National Labor Relations Act,[38] two of the most consequential New Deal programs that went on to shape American life for decades hence. Never again would a New Deal program be struck down by the court.[39]

The "*Lochner* era" quickly became synonymous with judicial overreach. Fueled by thousands of scholars who came of age in the New Deal era, the case of the Utica, New York, baker entered the popular canon as an oft-cited civics lesson in how not to approach constitutional decision-making. The nearly unanimous verdict of history hasn't wavered, even in later eras. Legal conservatives have been quick to note that the source of Peckham's "right to contract"—the language about personal liberty in the Fourteenth Amendment—has more recently been cited to defend abortion rights. Thus, nominees to the high court from across the political spectrum have seen fit to repudiate the *Lochner* decision and its legacy of injustice as almost a confirmation ritual.

"The post–*Lochner* era cases were correct," reassured Clarence Thomas at his 1991 confirmation hearing. "I think that the court determined correctly that it was the role of Congress, it was the role of the legislature, to make those very, very difficult decisions and complex decisions about health and safety and work standards, work hours, wage and hour decisions, and that the court did not serve the role as the superlegislature to second-guess the legislature."[40]

The fact that Thomas, who often presented himself as a laissez-faire conservative, felt obliged to dismiss the *Lochner* precedent attests to its near-universal repudiation; far more than just FDR enthusiasts disdain its very name. The entire judicial system, along with almost all of the rest of the legal world, has come into concert with the view offered by Harlan in his 1905 dissent, which accused the court's majority of "enlarging the scope of the [Fourteenth] Amendment far beyond its original purpose" while "bringing under the supervision of this court matters which have been supposed to belong exclusively to the legislative departments of the several States."[41]

In the academic world, the defeat of *Lochner* has been hailed as a judicial revolution[42]—often ranked as one of three great turning points in American law, along with the advent of the post–Civil War amendments and the civil rights movement of the 1960s. Of all of these three momentous turning points, John Marshall Harlan is the only point of connection.

Chapter 22

"A Vicarious Atonement"

At the age of sixty-three, Robert James Harlan watched his world crumble. Known as Robert Jr. during his father's lifetime, he had always strived to live up to the first Robert Harlan's ideal of an educated, erudite man of the world. Raised in London and Paris, renowned for his outstanding penmanship and fine singing voice, Robert Jr. was also a lawyer, business owner, and senior civil servant, having amassed a three-decade-long career in federal office, from the surgeon general's office, to the Post Office, to the US Treasury Department. Now his job, and his proud standing in the world of politics and Washington's Black aristocracy, were in jeopardy.

In 1917 President Woodrow Wilson's administration was celebrating the start of his second term by stepping up its purge of Black officials. Wilson's pince-nez and academic bearing hid a racist heart: born in Virginia in 1856, the future president had spent his early years in a proudly Confederate household, watching the cause his parents ardently embraced dissolve into a legacy of poverty and death. He emerged into adolescence during the bitter years of white resentment over Reconstruction and grew to become the strongest advocate of postwar segregation ever to occupy the White House. Requiring photographs of all federal job applicants, Wilson's administration segregated the Post Office and, soon after, Robert Jr.'s own Treasury Department. Suddenly Black officials, including Robert Jr., were cordoned off and forced to use separate bathrooms and eating areas.[1] Fully embracing the spirit of the Supreme Court's opinion in *Plessy v. Ferguson*, Wilson explained to Black leaders that such policies were needed to prevent "friction" between the races, which in practice amounted to whites refusing to work alongside Black colleagues.[2]

As a civil servant, Robert Jr. couldn't be summarily fired, but the administration had discretion over his salary. Starting when Wilson took office, Robert Jr. began writing in desperation to his old classmate, former president Taft, in hopes of staving off the reductions.[3] Robert Jr.'s friendship with Taft had extended well beyond boyhood. In 1908, when Taft was running for president, Robert Jr. had been his advocate among Black voters and kept him informed of their opinions through frank letters addressed to "My dear judge," to which Taft responded to "My dear Harlan." It was Robert Jr. who alerted Taft to the fact that outgoing President Theodore Roosevelt's refusal to support Black soldiers who were accused of murder on flimsy evidence in Brownsville, Texas, had left a residue of anger that extended to Taft himself. "I must confess I was surprised at the bitterness of feeling displayed," Robert Jr. wrote.[4]

As president, Taft rewarded his friend with plum appointments, and Robert Jr. didn't hesitate to escort other Black applicants seeking federal jobs to the Oval Office, relishing his access to power. In later years, he even related the tale of how one such office seeker reflexively gave up his seat in Taft's waiting room to a white southerner, and Robert Jr. scolded him by saying, "Sit down, you damn fool; you are in the White House, not Arkansas."[5]

Now, in Wilson's second term, the White House had long since ceased to be a bulwark against the segregated South, and Robert Jr. lacked any recourse against the racist purges in the Treasury Department. He reached out again to the former president, explaining that his annual pay was in danger of being chopped more than 10 percent, from $1,800 to $1,600, even though his colleagues were all getting raises and his job reviews were excellent.

"You can understand how hurtful it is to me to be reduced when on every side, salaries are being increased, and having a clean record, and a high rating for efficiency makes it more humiliating," he wrote in July 1917. Then he added a line that had coded meaning for Taft, a friend to both sides of the Harlan family: ". . . because of a moral lapse made by my Grandfather—Why should I pay a vicarious atonement?"[6]

Robert Jr.'s lament about his white grandfather—presumably James Harlan, for whom he was named—highlighted the depth of his pain and resentment. American society had turned him into an emblem of misdeeds both national and personal. Almost a half century earlier, the first Robert Harlan had weathered a backlash in his own Black community over his decision to send young Robert to a predominantly white school. The political cost had been worth it for the formerly enslaved man to see his son grow up on an equal academic footing with the progeny of the Tafts, Cincinnati's most enlightened white family.

The first Robert Harlan had believed that full equality was just around the corner, but that proved to be a mirage. Every year added a brick to the wall of segregation. Now Robert Jr. was just a sad supplicant, begging his famous friend for assistance. To the white world, all of Robert Jr.'s accomplishments—the dozen-plus government postings, the clothing store he opened, the law firm he established with another Black attorney,[7] the social prominence he and Mamie achieved in Washington and Cincinnati—were sealed off in a parallel universe of little notice or concern. And without access to white customers or clients, there was almost no way he could build or maintain a fortune. Robert Jr. and his family were at the pinnacle of Black America, but the rewards available to that upper crust were rapidly dwindling to nothing.

The sheer weight of segregation bore down even more heavily on Robert Jr.'s son, Robert Dorsey Harlan. It was Robert Dorsey who, as a teenaged boy, had suffered the indignity of being evicted from an orchestra seat at Cincinnati's Harris' Family Theater, prompting a lawsuit brought in his name by his father.[8] That ejection was a harbinger, a warning bell, that for all the advantages of Robert Dorsey's birth, he would confront greater headwinds for every year of the long life to come.

At the turn of the century, when Robert Dorsey Harlan was in his twenties, the Washington-based weekly the *Colored American* praised him as a "brilliant young man" whose coveted job in the US Census Bureau seemed only the first of many great accomplishments.[9] That sense of promise blossomed further when, after a brief first marriage ended in divorce, he became betrothed to Nettie Langston, the granddaughter of John Mercer Langston, the old friend of Robert Dorsey's grandfather. The uniting of the two famous families was proudly noted in Washington's Black press.[10]

The marriage prospered, but the couple's fortunes dwindled.

Just six years after his marriage to Nettie, in 1916, Robert Dorsey Harlan filed for bankruptcy, reporting liabilities of $2,802.25 against assets worth only $242.25.[11] This was the year Wilson was running for his second term, putting his father's federal job in jeopardy. At the time, Robert Dorsey was managing the clothing store owned by his father at 1848 Seventh Street;[12] just a year earlier, under the headline "Colored Businessmen Thriving," a Black newspaper had reported that the shop had moved to larger quarters from its original home in the U Street corridor, the jazz-inflected commercial center of the city's Black community.[13] The move didn't take. The Harlan men were drowning together.

In 1921 Robert Dorsey Harlan faced another financial threat when the driver of an oil wagon sued him for $10,000 stemming from a car accident.[14] Soon after, he moved his family to Philadelphia, his mother's childhood hometown. For the next two decades, he shuttled between there and Washington, driving a cab and overseeing taxi businesses but encountering financial impediments at every turn.[15] Like his grandfather, Robert Dorsey loved horse racing; unlike his grandfather, he lacked a seasoned trainer's eye, the first Robert's uncanny ability to size up a horse at the starting gate. A regular at the Laurel Park track near Washington, Robert Dorsey frequently flushed away his earnings at the betting window.[16]

Sad and embittered,[17] Robert Dorsey Harlan died in September 1953, leaving behind five children.[18] Nettie had passed away five months earlier.[19] Probate records show he had assets worth $3,438.48

in the form of a heavily mortgaged row house in northeast Washington and a 1948 Cadillac appraised at $986.[20] A century after Robert Harlan had returned from the gold rush in triumph, carrying up to $90,000 in cash, the grandson upon whom he once doted left behind only the tiniest fraction of that amount, especially when adjusted for ten decades of inflation. It wasn't that the Harlans had lost their ambition; the rug had been pulled out from under them. The separate-but-equal doctrine of *Plessy v. Ferguson* was the law of the land. Almost six decades had passed since the court handed down its decision—encompassing Robert Dorsey's entire adulthood—and segregation had fulfilled its insidious destiny, squeezing the Black community of its wealth and quelling its vitality. Now Black lawyers were turning to the courts, looking for ways to break down the walls. And they discovered a set of instructions in the dissenting opinion that was appended to the Supreme Court's devastating ruling.

The movement for equal rights under the law began not with a fiery assault on segregation but an attempt to enforce it under the rules of *Plessy v. Ferguson*. The 1896 Supreme Court decision was loathed by Black people everywhere but remained the disgraceful law of the land. In the 1930s, almost no one saw a path to overturn it. The legal branch of the National Association for the Advancement of Colored People (NAACP), headed by a Harvard-trained lawyer named Charles Hamilton Houston and assisted by an idealistic, gregarious former student named Thurgood Marshall, alighted on a strategy of forcing the Supreme Court to acknowledge that Black people weren't being given anything like equal services under the *Plessy* doctrine, despite the justices' promise of separate-but-equal treatment.

Both Houston and Marshall had grown up the sons of ambitious parents in the striving Black middle class. But like Robert Harlan's descendants, they struggled for money; their families' position in their communities kept improving, but there was no corresponding increase in opportunity, simply because there was no money in the community and no way to access the vast resources outside it. Despite those obstacles, Marshall's father and mother, a railroad waiter and a teacher, wanted young Thurgood to think big during his upbringing on Division Street in Baltimore's Upton neighborhood.[21] He became enamored of a legal career during dinner table discussions in which his father demanded that he present arguments about current events. The University of Maryland Law School was his first choice, but it wouldn't accept Black people.[22] He enrolled instead in the predominantly Black Howard University Law School in Washington. That proved to be a fortuitous decision because it connected him with Houston, a mentor thirteen years his senior. Houston had recently arrived at Howard as vice dean. He vowed to apply the same standards to young Black men at Howard as he had confronted among the white elites at Harvard, thereby training a generation of lawyers to fight for civil rights. Himself the grandson of people held in slavery, Houston took the view that Black people could never improve their lot unless they learned to make the legal fight themselves. Waiting until whites woke up would get them nowhere.[23]

Marshall became a favored pupil of Houston's and, after passing the bar exam, set up a practice in Baltimore; but almost no one in the city's Depression-wracked Black community could pay him, so he supported himself as a night clerk at a venereal disease clinic.[24] Two years later, Marshall received his big break when Houston, who had become a special counsel to the NAACP, drafted the young lawyer to help with the case of a young Amherst College graduate named Donald G. Murray who had been rejected from University of Maryland Law School solely because, as the school explained in a letter, "the University of Maryland does not admit Negro students."[25] The case had special resonance for Marshall, having once hoped to attend that school himself, and he and Houston argued that the state had violated Murray's Fourteenth Amendment rights by rejecting him without offering an equal alternative. Maryland courts agreed, ordering the University of Maryland to admit Murray immediately.[26]

It was an impressive victory, but the fact that Maryland's judges had acceded so quickly to the NAACP's demands deprived Houston and Marshall of a chance to take the case to the US Supreme Court.

That opportunity arrived three years later when a man named Lloyd Gaines confronted a similar situation at the University of Missouri Law School; the Missouri Supreme Court ruled, improbably, that Gaines's offer of a chance to apply to an all-Black law school outside the state satisfied the separate-but-equal doctrine. Seizing on the rejection, Houston and Marshall took the case to the US Supreme Court, where the justices sided with the NAACP, with Chief Justice Hughes writing that, under the strictures of *Plessy v. Ferguson*, "the State was bound to furnish him within its borders facilities for legal education substantially equal to those which the state afforded for persons of the white race."[27]

Hughes declined to order that Gaines be admitted to the University of Missouri, however, and the victory proved pyrrhic. The NAACP had hoped that simply creating paths for Black students to enter all-white institutions would send a powerful message—that barriers would gradually break down, and segregation would ease, even if *Plessy* remained the law of the land.[28] World War II put that strategy on hold. In a time of national emergency, the organization's interracial board worried about appearing unpatriotic.[29] Rather than initiate a divisive legal campaign, the organization lobbied the government to ensure that the million Black soldiers serving in segregated units received fair treatment—though, without opportunities for promotion or service in any of the white-dominated areas of the military, their status was anything but equal.[30]

The end of the war brought about a reassessment. By then, the NAACP's Legal Defense Fund had become fully independent, enabling it to raise tax-exempt funds outside the main lobbying organization. Houston had returned to private practice, and Marshall led the Legal Defense Fund on his own. He would soon gain a new key ally in Constance Baker Motley, a recent graduate of Columbia Law School and pioneering Black woman attorney. Together with a growing team of civil rights lawyers, they would draw in legal talent, Black and white, from every corner of the country.

The question remained of how best to attack segregation. Up to that point, the actions of the NAACP had arguably served to reinforce *Plessy v. Ferguson*, expanding the regime of rules and accommodations necessary for an orderly implementation of segregation. A few Black men had gained access to formerly all-white professional schools, but the wider community remained cut off. That reality had been brought home to Marshall during the war years, when he traversed the South taking on cases involving police brutality and corrupt legal procedures; the threat of violence lurked on every corner. The chance to break the back of the segregated system in one punishing blow loomed larger in his mind.

Marshall sent word through the South in search of people willing to serve as plaintiffs in cases attacking segregation. It was a life-threatening proposition. Plaintiffs and lawyers met in secret, hiding from the prying eyes of sheriffs and deputies, knowing that the Ku Klux Klan stood ready to exact revenge. "You caught us!" Marshall exclaimed, when a reporter journeyed fifty miles south of Baton Rouge, Louisiana, to a little shack called Ethel's Fish Fry. It was twilight on a July evening in 1950 and the NAACP Legal Defense Fund chief plotted with local leaders in a backroom to register Black students at Louisiana State University.[31] If the students were turned away the following morning, Marshall would file suit. For the courageous people, young and old, involved in this and other attempts to build cases against segregation, the question was always whether there was any hope at all, or if they were risking their lives in vain.

At crucial moments, Marshall turned to what he called his "Bible,"[32] the dissenting opinion of Justice Harlan in *Plessy v. Ferguson*. Standing at the table around which his legal team had gathered, he read aloud Harlan's words: "*Our Constitution is color blind, and neither knows nor tolerates classes among citizens. In respect of civil rights, all citizens are equal before the law. The humblest is the peer of the most powerful.*"[33] The path to equality—the kill shot that would end segregation forever—was embedded in that document.

Marshall ordered a change in strategy. From here on, the NAACP Legal Defense Fund would no longer argue around the edges of *Plessy v. Ferguson*. It would forthrightly proclaim that *Plessy* had been wrongly decided and that Harlan's views had been the right ones after all.

Marshall and Motley put the new strategy to work in the case of another law student, Heman Marion Sweatt, who sought entrance to the segregated University of Texas. Realizing that the state could be in legal jeopardy, Texas's legislature had hastily assembled a new law school in an Austin basement and declared it to be an equal facility for Black students. Using the obvious disparity in facilities as an example, the NAACP Legal Defense Fund's brief to the Supreme Court noted how Justice Harlan had predicted exactly this outcome—that the separate-but-equal doctrine would, by its very separation, relegate Black people to second-tier status.

"In *Plessy v. Ferguson* . . . this Court abandoned the original conception of equal protection, adopting instead the legal fiction that segregation (in this case, in transportation) is not discriminatory," declared the lawyers for Heman Sweatt. ". . . the results of its abdication have been disastrous. The dissenting views of Mr. Justice Harlan in the *Plessy* case were correct, and should be adopted now."[34]

The Supreme Court did not, at that moment, choose to replace the *Plessy* holding with Harlan's opinion. But it moved several steps closer to doing so. It ruled that Texas's Black law school was not equal to the University of Texas, and that Sweatt must be admitted to UT. Moreover, Chief Justice Fred M. Vinson, a Kentuckian and Centre College alumnus whom President Harry Truman had elevated to the high court in 1946, hinted that the justices might yet have an appetite for overruling the *Plessy* doctrine.

"We have frequently reiterated that this Court will decide constitutional questions only when necessary to the disposition of the case at hand, and that such decisions will be drawn as narrowly as possible," Vinson wrote, explaining why the court didn't go further in attacking segregation through the case of Heman Sweatt. "Because of this traditional reluctance to extend constitutional interpretations to situations or facts which are not before the Court, much of the excellent research and detailed argument presented in these cases is unnecessary to their disposition."[35]

Vinson's words signaled that if the NAACP lawyers made a more sweeping claim, they would garner a more sweeping result. Behind the scenes, the justices were restless for change. "If some say this undermines *Plessy*, then let it fall, as have many Nineteenth Century oracles," wrote Justice Tom Clark in a memo to his colleagues. He was referring, no doubt, to disgraced former precedents such as *Pollock*, *E. C. Knight*, and—though it had been handed down shortly after the turn of the century—*Lochner*.[36]

Thurgood Marshall and Constance Baker Motley took the Supreme Court's ruling in *Sweatt v. Painter* as an incitement to push harder. Motley, for whom *Sweatt* was her first major civil rights case, was open about the debt owed to Harlan. "Justice Harlan's dissent in *Plessy* formed the basis of our legal arguments to end segregation in education,"[37] she wrote in her autobiography. She also attested, "In Justice Harlan's lone dissent . . . we find the germination of our twentieth-century legal heritage."[38]

Just three years after the success of *Sweatt v. Painter*, Marshall and Motley again climbed the marble steps of the Supreme Court Building, the iconic, pillared temple of justice that had opened in 1935, giving the third branch of government the imposing home it deserved. The NAACP Legal Defense Fund had taken Vinson's hint and recruited plaintiffs who symbolized the plight of larger numbers of African Americans. One was Linda Brown, a schoolgirl from Topeka, Kansas, who was eight when the case began and ten when it went to the Supreme Court. Justice for Linda Brown wouldn't be as easily wrought as for Heman Sweatt. He was one aspiring lawyer knocking on the door of the University of Texas Law School; she was a third grader who, like others of her race, had been forced to attend an all-Black elementary school farther away from her home than the white school was. Her school was part of a network of segregated institutions that deprived Black children of connections to the wider community, with devastating effects on their economic futures and psychological well-being.

Marshall, Motley, and an illustrious team of colleagues produced painstaking research into the ways that being taught in separate facilities stigmatized Black children and, in many cases, limited their performance, proving that segregation is inherently unequal. But their constitutional argument rested upon a lengthy reference to Harlan's

appeal for color-blind justice as the best inoculation against racial hatred. Fifty-seven years after he put pen to paper, John Marshall Harlan's words were at the foundation of the most important case of the
twentieth century.

"While the majority opinion sought to rationalize its holding on
the basis of the state's judgment that separation of the races was con-
ducive to public peace and order, Justice Harlan knew all too well
that the seeds for continuing racial animosities had been planted. . . ,"
concluded the lawyers arguing on behalf of Linda Brown. "Our Constitution, said Justice Harlan, 'is color blind, and neither knows nor
tolerates classes among citizens.' It is the dissenting opinion of Justice
Harlan, rather than the majority opinion in *Plessy v. Ferguson*, that is
in keeping with the scope and meaning of the Fourteenth Amendment as consistently defined by this Court both before and after
Plessy v. Ferguson."[39]

The Supreme Court heard oral arguments on the case of *Brown v.
Board of Education of Topeka* in the spring of 1953, but then asked for
rearguments that fall—an unusual request that served to buy time for
the justices to align their positions. The court was shaken when Chief
Justice Vinson died of a sudden heart attack. President Dwight Eisenhower quickly replaced him with California governor Earl Warren,
whose political instincts helped to persuade his brethren that a unanimous ruling would promote confidence in the decision.[40]

The ruling came down on May 17, 1954, with Warren delivering
the opinion. He began inauspiciously, by stating that the evidence of
the historic intent of the framers of the Fourteenth Amendment—
the ostensible purpose of the reargument—had proven to be
"inconclusive."[41]

It soon became clear that, to achieve the desired unanimity, the
opinion had been shorn of passion, reduced to a dry syllabus of judicial findings and conclusions. But in the end, the argument that won
the day was the one that had been so obvious to Harlan fifty-eight
years previously: that separating Black people harmed them griev-
ously, depriving them of opportunities to succeed, while also sowing
the seeds of racial animosity.

"We come then to the question presented: Does segregation of children in public schools solely on the basis of race, even though the physical facilities and other 'tangible' factors may be equal, deprive the children of the minority group of equal educational opportunities?" Warren intoned. "We believe that it does."[42]

The chief justice continued: "To separate [young children] from others of similar age and qualifications solely because of their race generates a feeling of inferiority as to their status in the community that may affect their hearts and minds in a way unlikely ever to be undone.... Whatever may have been the extent of psychological knowledge at the time of *Plessy v. Ferguson*, this finding is amply supported by modern authority. Any language in *Plessy v. Ferguson* contrary to this finding is rejected.

"We conclude that, in the field of public education, the doctrine of 'separate but equal' has no place. Separate educational facilities are inherently unequal. Therefore, we hold that the plaintiffs and others similarly situated for whom the actions have been brought are, by reason of the segregation complained of, deprived of the equal protection of the laws guaranteed by the Fourteenth Amendment."[43]

Brown v. Board of Education didn't close the book on segregation, or even put a full stop to the segregation era. The court ordered that its ruling be enforced "with all deliberate speed"; it continues to be carried out almost seven decades hence. But it expanded opportunities for tens of millions of people, ushering in a fuller understanding of the term "equal protection." It also removed the legal stamp of approval from the most abject of discrimination, reigniting a candle of hope that had been kept flickering through Harlan's generous words alone.

Throughout the decades-long battle, the spirit of John Marshall Harlan was a constant, vivid presence in the lawyers' bunker of the NAACP Legal Defense Fund. His arguments helped to shape theirs. And, finally, when segregation began to break down, the white world took another look at the man whose views had so often been veiled in dissent.

Chapter 23

"Justice Harlan Concurring"

Forty-three years after his death, John Marshall Harlan was back in the news. "Justice Harlan Concurring," read the headline on the *New York Times* editorial on the ruling in *Brown v. Board of Education*.

"Last Monday's case dealt solely with segregation in schools, but there was not one word in Chief Justice Warren's opinion that was inconsistent with the earlier views of Justice Harlan," the paper's editorial board declared. "This is an instance in which the voice crying in the wilderness finally becomes the expression of a people's will and in which justice overtakes and thrusts aside a timorous expediency."[1]

In the four decades since his passing, John's advocacy for civil rights had been noted only lightly, if at all, within the white community. Entire histories of the Fuller Court had been written without addressing its record on race.[2] In the New Deal era, when his dissenting opinions helped build the case against *Lochner* and other precedents that deprived people of economic protections, his views were only occasionally credited. With *Brown v. Board of Education*, much of that changed.

From here on, he would be a hero to many in the civil rights world, even though his reputation would be buffeted by shifting political winds, waves of backlash against racial progress, the inexorable march of historical revisionism and the legal world's conflicted feelings about dissenters. He would gain a legion of adherents but also suffer the occasional slings of those who reject his constitutional ideas or, perhaps, feel he didn't go far enough.

One thing was apparent, though: for the first time, John Marshall Harlan's views were firmly in the mainstream of American law.

A harbinger of changing attitudes toward Harlan's legal views had come even before *Brown v. Board of Education* was decided, and it dealt with criminal prosecutions, not race. Much as John's Supreme Court colleagues had been reluctant to enforce the Fourteenth Amendment against racial injustice, they also had been hesitant to apply it fully to procedures in state courts, giving states broad latitude to police their streets as they saw fit. This meant that even though the Constitution promised all US citizens robust protections against searches and seizures and mistreatment in courtrooms, people in certain states were subject to much more spurious procedures. On this issue, as on others, Harlan staked out a principled position that differed from those of his colleagues: he believed that the Fourteenth Amendment's guarantee of due process encompassed "fundamental principles of liberty and justice,"[3] which specifically mirrored those in the federal Bill of Rights—meaning that the same provisions of fairness that prevailed in federal courts must be provided in state courts.

John's views were widely ignored in his time, but by the middle of the twentieth century, in the face of some abject acts of injustice, the Supreme Court was more willing to revisit the matter.

On January 1, 1953, a ninety-three-year-old retired juvenile-court judge and Minnesota civic leader named Edward F. Waite produced a law review article chastising the legal community for willfully discrediting Harlan's views.[4] Waite quoted a 1947 case in which Justice Felix Frankfurter snidely offered that in the first seventy years after the ratification of the Fourteenth Amendment, "the scope of that amendment was passed upon by forty-three judges. Of all these judges, only one, who may be respectfully called an eccentric exception, ever indicated the belief" that the amendment required state courts to adhere to the federal Bill of Rights.[5] That eccentric exception, of course, was Harlan, and the dismissiveness of Frankfurter's tone reflected the extent to which justices felt free to write Harlan out of the judicial canon. Waite chafed at the slight to Harlan's memory.

As a young and middle-aged man, Waite had looked up to Harlan, whom he called "the Kentucky giant," without having known him personally. Now, in the 1950s, Waite pointed out proudly, Harlan's views were anything but outmoded, as his long-forgotten *Plessy v. Ferguson* dissent "has become a classic in the literature of civil rights under the Constitution."

Waite went on to note that the case that occasioned Justice Frankfurter's snub, *Adamson v. California*, involved a major issue: whether a California man could be forced to testify against himself in state court, given that the federal Constitution granted him a protection against self-incrimination. A 5-to-4 majority ruled that the state could do so; six decades earlier, Harlan had argued otherwise. For that he was called an eccentric outlier, a label Waite saw as a devious means of dismissing the views of a man who was deeply in touch with the nation's foundational values.

Waite was on to something. The Earl Warren–led Supreme Court would go on to vastly expand the protections for defendants in state courts, until they closely reflected those in the federal Constitution. The application of the Bill of Rights to state actions would be one of the greatest expansions of liberty in US history. Even *Adamson v. California* would be overruled just twelve years after Judge Waite penned his law review article.[6]

The one justice proved to be more prescient than the other forty-two.

On November 8, 1954, just six months after the ruling in *Brown v. Board of Education*, President Eisenhower announced a new nominee for the Supreme Court. His name was John Marshall Harlan II.[7]

The choice of John's namesake grandson, in the midst of a Harlan revival, provoked some commentary. The nominee himself stoked it when he jovially told reporters, recalling Holmes's depiction of his grandfather as "the last of the tobacco-spittin' judges," that the old man could indeed "hit a spittoon dead center at thirty paces." The comment came with the self-deprecating acknowledgment that his own life "does sound awfully tame" in comparison.[8]

The quip carried a deeper admission: the younger Harlan was a very different man from his grandfather. A Princeton-educated Rhodes scholar, John II had gone on to become a pillar of the East Coast establishment, a corporate lawyer who was coveted by clients such as the du Pont family of chemical barons. His career more closely resembled those of John's Gilded Age colleagues than his own frugal practice.[9]

In that respect, John II also differed from his father, John Maynard Harlan, whose reformist impulses never did get him elected mayor of Chicago, but damaged his law practice.[10] Indeed, the rise of John II followed some serious misfortunes in the lives of John's family members in the decades after his death. Malvina and her two surviving daughters had been left so penniless that members of the Supreme Court bar association set up a collection for them, aiming to raise the daunting sum of $40,000—about $1 million in 2021 dollars.[11] John's three sons, meanwhile, collaborated on a scheme to cover up for some disastrous investments by Richard, the eldest, that had drained a trust set up by his late father-in-law. With his wife's relatives prepared to go public with their complaints, Richard persuaded his brothers to help replenish the funds. The brothers and Richard's wife ended up enmeshed in lawsuits, rupturing the family.[12]

John's daughter Laura fared better. She stepped out of the background role reserved for unmarried daughters and sisters and went to work, serving as White House social secretary to First Ladies Florence Harding and Grace Coolidge, and showing better financial instincts than her brothers in establishing Washington's first woman-owned real estate business.[13]

John II seemed to atone for his father's excesses by becoming the soul of probity. More conservative than his grandfather, he nonetheless had his confirmation delayed by opposition from Mississippi's staunch segregationist Senator James Eastland.[14] Taking office in 1955, the second Justice Harlan served with distinction for sixteen years, upholding civil rights protections while dissenting on some criminal procedural protections his grandfather would likely have supported.[15]

Even as he carved out a very different—but also widely admired— legacy for himself, John II's office was adorned with John's portrait. The younger Harlan loved to tell the story of how a Japanese visitor once exclaimed, "I did not realize, Justice Harlan, that the post was hereditary."[16]

Another piece of John's legacy fell into place in 1964 when Congress enacted a new Civil Rights Act that closely mirrored the 1875 version. President John F. Kennedy had been assassinated the previous fall and his brother Ted took to the Senate floor to declare that "my brother was the first president of the United States to state publicly that segregation was morally wrong. His heart and soul are in this bill."[17]

Within weeks of the passage of the act, which banned discrimination in public accommodations, the owner of the Heart of Atlanta Motel, a sleek, modern 216-room resort in Georgia replete with a high-rise diving board and decks full of lounge chairs, moved to defend its whites-only policy.[18] His primary weapon was the Supreme Court's 8-to-1 decision in the *Civil Rights Cases of 1883*, which had invalidated the Civil Rights Act of 1875, and also occasioned John's first major break with his colleagues.

This time a different-minded Supreme Court moved quickly to take care of its leftover business post–*Brown v. Board of Education*. Voting 9 to 0 to reject the motel owner's claims, the majority of the justices declared that the new civil rights law was justified under Congress's power to regulate interstate commerce, especially since most of the motel's customers were from out of state.[19] Two justices, in concurring opinions, insisted that the law would be valid as an enforcement of the Fourteenth Amendment's equal protection clause as well.[20]

"Our decision should be based on the Fourteenth Amendment, thereby putting an end to all obstructionist strategies and allowing every person—whatever his race, creed, or color—to patronize all places of public accommodation without discrimination whether he travels interstate or intrastate," declared Justice William O. Douglas.[21]

John would have agreed, though he himself, in his epic dissent in the *Civil Rights Cases of 1883,* had introduced the idea that, should the court be reluctant to sustain a civil rights law under the Fourteenth Amendment, it could do so under Congress's power to regulate interstate commerce. "I suggest, that it may become a pertinent inquiry whether Congress may, in the exertion of its power to regulate commerce among the states," insist that civil rights be respected in all businesses courting out-of-state customers, he wrote.[22]

After eighty-one years, Congress and the Supreme Court finally heeded his advice.

As John's views were enshrined into law, they also came under a closer microscope. When President Lyndon Johnson followed up the Civil Rights Act with two executive orders intended to "correct the effects of past and present discrimination,"[23] he inaugurated the regime of rules and legislation known as affirmative action. It was aimed at utilizing government resources to give African Americans a better shot at the kinds of jobs and education they had been denied during segregation. But when white plaintiffs turned around and claimed they were being discriminated against, their defenders were quick to pick up the Harlan assertion that "the Constitution is color blind," co-opting the language of the civil rights movement and using it to support their own ends.

In 1978 a white medical school applicant named Allan Bakke sued the regents of the University of California, claiming that by reserving sixteen of a hundred slots at the Davis campus for minority students, the state had violated his equal-protection rights.[24] A narrow 5-to-4 majority sided with him, declaring that "the guarantee of equal protection cannot mean one thing when applied to one individual and something else when applied to a person of color."[25] Four justices, in a joint opinion, detailed the deprivations of segregation, noting that "against that background, claims that law must be 'color blind' . . . must be seen as aspiration rather than a description of reality."[26]

The complicated *Bakke* ruling didn't end affirmative action. It merely established new rules under which it could be governed. But the principle of color blindness continued to be the rusty hinge on which the debate proceeded. In 1985 the NAACP leader Benjamin Hooks published an op-ed in the *New York Times* under the provocative headline "The US Constitution Was Never Color-Blind."[27]

A month later, William Bradford Reynolds, the assistant attorney general for civil rights under President Ronald Reagan, who was rolling back affirmative-action programs, submitted a *Times* op-ed of his own, rebutting Hooks.

"It was the NAACP brief in *Brown* that argued, correctly, that 'the Fourteenth Amendment compels the states to be color blind. . . .' That argument prevailed and in what may be the Supreme Court's finest hour, a unanimous court overturned the separate-but-equal doctrine of *Plessy v. Ferguson* and adopted the view of the lone dissenter in that case, the elder Justice Harlan," Reynolds wrote. "In any consideration of the Constitution, Justice Harlan's dissent in *Plessy* invariably emerges as the definitive statement of the proper construction of the Fourteenth Amendment."[28]

Four years later, when the Supreme Court again amended affirmative-action rules, this time for government contracting, Justice Antonin Scalia, the conservative titan, quoted Harlan in his concurring opinion: "At least where state or local action is an issue, only a social emergency . . . can justify an exception to the principle embodied in the Fourteenth Amendment that '[o]ur Constitution is color blind, and neither knows nor tolerates classes among citizens.'"[29]

Ironically, Thurgood Marshall, who had placed Harlan's words at the center of the fight for civil rights, was now serving on the very Supreme Court that curtailed some types of affirmative action in the name of color blindness. The setbacks didn't dim Marshall's admiration for Harlan or faith in his words; indeed, Marshall contended that had the court heeded Harlan in 1896, there would be no need for remedies such as affirmative action.

"Justice Harlan, as you remember, dissenting in *Plessy v. Ferguson*, gave the first expression to the judicial principle that our Constitution is color blind and neither knows nor tolerates classes among citizens," Marshall stated on August 15, 1987, in a speech to the judges and friends of the Second Circuit. "In principle of race neutrality, our situation now, nearly ninety years later, would be far different than it is. Affirmative action is an issue today because our Constitution was not color blind in the sixty years which intervened between *Plessy* and *Brown*."[30]

The mystical significance attributed to Harlan's words during the affirmative-action debate rankled a young scholar named Gabriel Chin, who believed the laws of the United States were neither equal nor color blind, especially given the vastly unfair treatment of Chinese workers during the decades that covered Harlan's time on the court.[31] In particular, Chin remembered a little-quoted passage in Harlan's *Plessy* dissent that practically leaped up and smacked him in the face: "There is a race so different from our own that we do not permit those belonging to it to become citizens of the United States. Persons belonging to it are, with few exceptions, absolutely excluded from our country. I allude to the Chinese race. But by the statute in question, a Chinaman can ride in the same passenger coach with white citizens of the United States, while citizens of the Black race [cannot]."[32]

To Chin, this suggested prejudice against the Chinese, a conclusion bolstered by, among other things, Harlan's decision to join a 9-to-0 majority in the Supreme Court case that validated the Chinese Exclusion Act[33] and, especially, his decision to join Chief Justice Fuller's dissent in *United States v. Wong Kim Ark*,[34] in which Fuller argued that despite having been born on US soil, a Chinese man should not be granted birthright citizenship because his parents didn't intend for him to become a citizen.

Chin's argument—laid out in a 1996 law review article entitled "The *Plessy* Myth: Justice Harlan and the Chinese Cases"—caught the attention of many legal academics and seemed to feed an urge to debunk the notion of Harlan as a truly exceptional civil rights visionary; it also prompted a rebuttal by a professor and Harlan scholar named James Gordon. Gordon wrote that, in context, the passage about the Chinese in Harlan's *Plessy* dissent was intended "to challenge the unequal treatment of African Americans, not to support discrimination against the Chinese."[35]

By pointing out that Chinese were not excluded from the white railroad car, Gordon contended, Harlan meant to show that Louisiana's separate-carriage law could not have been instituted simply to prevent friction among races, as the state claimed, but rather to stigmatize one race—African Americans—and perpetuate the legacy of slavery.[36]

Gordon also noted that the case validating the Chinese Exclusion Act turned not on the crucial issue of equal protection but on the mundane one of Congress's power to abrogate a treaty. In this case, the treaty in question allowed Chinese workers to enter the US under certain conditions. The court's ruling that Congress has the power to override such a treaty was and is relatively uncontroversial and remains in force today, even though, in that case, it supported a highly objectionable piece of legislation.[37]

Auguring against the idea that Harlan was prejudiced against Asians was the justice's extraordinary support in the Insular Cases for granting full constitutional rights to Filipinos and Hawaiians when their home countries came under US control. There was also his strongly worded dissent in the case in which the Supreme Court declared that civil rights laws didn't permit the prosecution of a gang of whites who terrorized Chinese workers in the town of Nicolaus, California.[38]

Even in the birthright citizenship case, there was the evidence of his lectures—published after Chin's law-review article—in which Harlan took pains to show that his objections were not based on race, emphasizing that he would feel the same way about Europeans.[39]

Though Chin himself asserts that he was not claiming that Harlan was more prejudiced against the Chinese than his judicial colleagues[40]—only that he wasn't the far-sighted hero for the Chinese that he was for African Americans—his article fueled an appetite for Harlan revisionism. Some scholars and writers, casting ever more critical light on the social attitudes of the post–Civil War years, felt compelled to dismiss Harlan as a man of his times, who largely accepted the prevailing assumptions about race, despite his precocious endorsement of civil rights.

In the 1950s and 1960s, when civil rights activists heaped praise on whites who bucked their communities and stood up for racial equality, Harlan had looked like an unambiguous hero. In later decades, with a focus on the deep-seated effects of historical discrimination, activists regarded such actions as praiseworthy but hardly heroic; even whites who preached for civil rights enjoyed the privileges of a society that valued people of their race above others.

The writer Richard Kluger, in his magisterial 823-page history of *Brown v. Board of Education*, titled *Simple Justice*, meticulously related how Harlan "cut through" the logic of the majority opinion in *Plessy v. Ferguson* and accurately predicted the consequences.[41] But Kluger quickly shifted gears to declare that "even Harlan was to prove capable of grievous pettifoggery on the racial issue."[42] He laid out the facts of the *Cumming* case involving the Georgia school board that shifted funding from a Black high school to Black grammar schools. He quoted the court's unanimous opinion that it "need not consider [segregation] in this case. . . . No such issue was made in the pleadings." Then, Kluger added, with a rhetorical drumroll, "There was no dissenting opinion. The opinion of the court was written by Justice John Marshall Harlan."[43]

Later, when PBS broadcast its prize-winning, multipart history of the Supreme Court, its accompanying website declared, "Throughout his judicial career, Justice Harlan remained dedicated to winning civil rights for Blacks, although he stopped well short of advocating social equality among the races."[44] That represented a distinctly ungenerous assessment of the career of a man who risked his reputation to affirm the Civil Rights Act of 1875, which mandated social equality in public accommodations; unflinchingly defended his own socializing with Frederick Douglass; was one of only two white public officials to attend Douglass's funeral; and regularly visited and spoke at Black churches.

Against these critical thrusts there would emerge, across the political spectrum, other voices who were impressed, even awed, by Harlan's willingness to stand against the wind. C. Ellen Connally, the first Black woman elected judge in Ohio, was moved to correct the record on Harlan's authorship of the *Cumming* case.[45] Far from engaging in racial "pettifoggery," Harlan was probably taking control of the case in order to protect Black interests, steering the opinion away from an endorsement of segregation; by jumping in to write the majority opinion and then refusing to decide the case based on the equal-protection clause, he had likely prevented another sweeping defeat like *Plessy v. Ferguson*. The court's holding in the case, Connally believed, has been "misread and misinterpreted" by many scholars and writers, including Kluger.[46]

Connally, whose grandmother's brother was among the plaintiffs in the case, was typical of the many African Americans who defended Harlan against revisionists. From Frederick Douglass to the thousands of Black admirers who stepped forward after Harlan's death, such as Thurgood Marshall, Black leaders maintained an unbroken chain of admiration, drawing a circle of protection around his reputation.

Meanwhile, new crises and world-shaking events continued to draw attention to Harlan's prescience. The advent of the war on terrorism and the use of the US military installation at Guantanamo Bay as an overseas prison, where inmates are not accorded full rights under the US Constitution, cast a fresh spotlight on John's dissents in the Insular Cases—the largest part of his legacy yet to be adopted into law.

Harlan's insistence that the Constitution follow the flag, and his view that there is no justification for a colonial system under the US Constitution, were approvingly noted by Judge Juan R. Torruella of the United States Court of Appeals for the First Circuit, in two blistering law review articles.[47]

After quoting Harlan's dissent in *Hawaii v. Mankichi*, Torruella wrote ruefully, "Although these are irrefutable arguments, they have remained unattended."[48]

A further testament to the uniqueness of Harlan's legacy is how it has been embraced by disparate figures on the Left and Right—such as by both Thurgood Marshall and his old antagonist, Antonin Scalia. This seeming contradiction stems from liberals' admiration for the sheer humanity of his jurisprudence—the way he cut through the doctrinal thicket to show how cases impacted real lives—while conservatives applaud his faithfulness to the original intent of the Constitution. In the eyes of many scholars, Harlan adhered to the plain meaning of the post–Civil War amendments when other justices either avoided it, as in the race cases, or stretched it to cover entirely unintended circumstances, as in the economic cases. Scalia, for one, claimed that Harlan's dissent in *Plessy* was "thoroughly originalist."[49]

At his own Supreme Court confirmation hearing in March 2017, the conservative Justice Neil Gorsuch repeatedly cited Harlan as a role model. "Justice Harlan got the original meaning of the Equal Protection Clause right the first time, and the court recognized that belatedly," he testified. "It is one of the great stains on the Supreme Court's history that it took so long to get to that conclusion."[50]

When Gorsuch moved into his chambers at the Supreme Court building at 1 First Street NE in Washington, he adorned his wall with a portrait of John Marshall Harlan.[51] It joined an even more prominent representation of Harlan from his last years on the court—his gray brows furrowed with concern as his eyes gazed out toward the future. That picture was moved from a hallway to the justices' inner sanctum—the conference room where they meet to decide cases—by another Harlan admirer, Chief Justice John Roberts.[52] Harlan's faith in the Constitution over politics, in righteousness over expediency, presides over the current court like a cherished, if not always attained, ideal.

If Harlan's legacy continues to play out in courtrooms across the country, so too is it felt in the communities that were the settings for his major decisions, such as Chattanooga, where Ed Johnson met his murderous end on the Walnut Street Bridge.

For decades, a ghost hovered over that long expanse over the Tennessee River. When a school principal and Black community activist named LaFrederick Thirkill was a child, he recalls, his grandmother would become visibly agitated whenever the family car rattled over the Walnut Street Bridge. "It just wasn't a good bridge," was all he could get out of her.[53] Many older Black people steered around the bridge entirely, even though it was the main thoroughfare between the city center and North Chattanooga.[54]

The grip of the past was less constricting for white people. In 1990, to commemorate the bridge's hundredth birthday, civic activists banded together to preserve the 2,370-foot span as a crossway for pedestrians and have it added to the National Register of Historic Places.[55] As an act of city planning, the decision was a masterstroke. With new wooden slats on the old riveted steel, the bridge became a symbol of revitalization, sandwiched between modernistic new structures for the Hunter Museum of American Art and the Tennessee Aquarium. Thousands of people crossed it every day.

But something remained amiss: the horrific event that occurred on those very beams in 1906 was more sensed than discussed. Like Thirkill's grandmother, older Black people were too protective of their children and grandchildren to relate what happened there, even as it darkened their memories of their hometown. Whites like Lee Ann Shipp, a descendant of Joseph Shipp, heard nothing from family members about the lynching of Ed Johnson and the Supreme Court trial that followed. Shipp recalled only how a great aunt once told her what a fabulous storyteller her Confederate ancestor had been.[56]

The national legal world largely forgot that the Supreme Court had ever stepped out of its role as interpreter of the law to serve as a makeshift jury. The case had little usefulness as a precedent—not in the usual sense of defining constitutional law. Thus, it wasn't much taught in law schools; few civil rights scholars have even heard of it.

In Chattanooga, however, the passage of time began to loosen lips.

Around 2000, the young LaFrederick Thirkill heard about an abandoned African American cemetery along a vine-strewn edge of the
city limits. Concerned for his community's heritage, Thirkill volunteered to help clear the expanse of debris and eventually came upon
a stone marked "Ed Johnson" and the epitaph etched on its surface:
"God bless you all. I am a innocent man."[57]

Deeply moved, Thirkill wrote a play about the lynching, featuring dozens of characters spanning all of Chattanooga.[58] He faced
down some blowback from his fellow African Americans, many of
whom preferred to let the case disappear into the mists of time.[59] But
the thread of memory was being pulled. White civic activists such
as Eleanor Cooper, descendant of a minister who preached against
lynching, felt the need for all of Chattanooga, people of all races, to
confront their city's painful legacy.[60]

In other cases when centuries-old racial history is unearthed, assembling the facts can be a monumental task. Ed Johnson's murder,
however, is one of the most documented lynchings in history, thanks
to the facts laid out in the Supreme Court. They indicted a broad
swath of the Chattanooga community. In other cases, lynchings
were deplored as the work of faceless Klansmen. Johnson's murder
happened in the open, on the city's most famous landmark, before
hundreds of eyes, with the implicit approval of the sheriff and other
public officials. Thanks to John Marshall Harlan and the Supreme
Court case, no one could escape the conclusion that many civic leaders, from law enforcement, to the press, to preachers, to business
owners in their limestone mansions, were implicated in the crime.
Chattanooga society was saturated with Ed Johnson's blood.

In 2016 Thirkill, Cooper, and other Chattanoogans banded together to form the Ed Johnson Project, dedicated to telling his story.
It includes educational outreach and a filmed documentary. The centerpiece, however, is a memorial statue and plaza at the base of the
Walnut Street Bridge. Ed Johnson's place of remembrance will be less
than a stone's throw away from "Headquarters Row," where Confederate and Union generals took turns ruling the city.

In planning the $1 million memorial, members of the Ed Johnson Project kept coming back to the role played by Harlan, whose story is highlighted alongside those of Johnson, Noah Parden, and the other people who tried to save Johnson's life. Cooper speaks of "the huge respect" felt by members of the project toward Harlan.[61] Thirkill puts it more bluntly: "If it wasn't for him, what would have happened? It was he who made it possible for the case to go to the Supreme Court. It was he who let Noah Parden tell his story, and he listened. You wouldn't have the *Shipp* case. You wouldn't have the history. It would have never been on record. If it wasn't for his decision to put it before the justices, there would never be a rest of the story. You know the rest of the story? It was all because of him."[62]

When the Ed Johnson Project staged a competition to design the memorial, one top contender planned a statue of Harlan, seated like Lincoln alongside the other figures in the case. But in the final analysis, the Project chose a different design, with Harlan's role in the drama subordinate to those of Johnson, Parden, and his local cocounsel Styles Hutchins, who will be represented in standing statues.

Still, the legal conscience of the Project belongs to former Chief Judge Curtis Lynn Collier of the U.S. District Court for the Eastern District of Tennessee. Like many African American lawyers of his generation, Collier describes Harlan as having always been his "legal hero," an admiration that only grew when he learned of the Ed Johnson case.

"I think we were fortunate as a nation that Justice Harlan was in the place he was," Collier says. "He was willing to listen to a Black lawyer—which had never happened."[63]

At that freighted moment in time, Harlan stood as the embodiment of the Constitution itself. The law and the man, the document and the judge who interpreted it, became one. For an instant, justice prevailed. Then it all fell apart. But now, as the old railroad town on the Tennessee River seeks to transcend its belligerent past, the hand of justice is on it again, making the task seem, at the very least, possible.

Epilogue

"Our Basic Legal Creed"

Did John Marshall Harlan live up to his father's prophecy and become the greatest justice since his namesake? The case for him is relatively simple. During his long tenure, the Supreme Court assumed far greater power and relevance to everyday life by virtue of the post–Civil War amendments. Thus, the court contended with a broad range of cases that set the boundaries of American life for generations. Though many of the cases were matters of first impression, given the recent remaking of the Constitution, Harlan staked out firm, powerful positions that were completely at odds with those of his fellow justices. After the settling of time, greater wisdom prevailed, and Harlan's views—rather than those of his contemporaries—molded the laws of the United States.

The passage of time has shown that the most famous cases in which Harlan dissented were not close calls upon which reasonable jurists might disagree: they were abominations that continue to drag on the reputation of the court like iron chains. *Plessy* and *Lochner* exist alongside the Dred Scott case as the most thoroughly wrong-headed, widely deplored decisions in Supreme Court history. *Pollock* is similarly bemoaned, for having jeopardized national financing at a potentially disastrous moment and forcing the nation through an unnecessary constitutional amendment process. The *Civil Rights Cases of 1883* and *Berea College* have their own brightly colored frames in the rogue's gallery of constitutional law.

A wealthy and cossetted Supreme Court's use of the Fourteenth Amendment to scuttle democratically enacted laws to protect workers, boost wages, and ensure fair competition extended the injustices of the Gilded Age for decades and caused incalculable suffering. Harlan spent a considerable portion of his career fighting this trend and calling attention to its brutal effects. His willingness to stand against his colleagues on many of those cases proved that his faith in his own values extended beyond the racial sphere. But in the final analysis, his views on economic cases—while praised in his lifetime and vindicated in future decisions—are a less singular part of his legacy. In the eyes of the legal world, John Marshall Harlan will forever be the man who recognized equal rights for African Americans at a time when the rest of the white establishment acceded to legal falsehoods to prevent freed men and women from joining the American family.

He was the first, and only, father of equal protection under the law. But history has a curious way of dealing with firsts and onlys. His rightness and prescience are readily acknowledged, but the full measure of credit eludes him. History isn't made by dissenters, at least in the eyes of many legal scholars. In the American system, the law doesn't become the law until a majority of the Supreme Court deems it to be so. Those are the moments to celebrate, no matter how many voices were out there preaching the gospel all along.

Harlan deserves further consideration. His place in the legal pantheon as the greatest justice of his generation has been blocked, to some extent, by his younger contemporary, Oliver Wendell Holmes Jr., as University of Texas professor Louise Weinberg has forcefully argued.[1] Though Harlan was the "far greater" judge, she contended,[2] Holmes dazzled the legal world with his larger-than-life persona. His charm and intellect bled down through the years and continue to inspire scholars, more because of his "glittering aphorisms"[3] than the actual outcomes of his decisions; he flatters legal thinkers with the notion that doctrinal brilliance supersedes mere righteousness. Harlan, the judge whom Holmes wittily compared to a set of iron jaws that never fully connected, brought a firmer sense of justice, a more instinctive fairness. The force of his convictions contrasted sharply with Holmes's scholarly observations. Holmes understood the nuanced application of common law; Harlan had a stronger grip on the Constitution. And the future—the rights-based jurisprudence that dominated the twentieth century—belonged to Harlan.

He built the legal foundation for the midcentury revolution that brought civil rights to millions. The conception of equality under the law that he advanced grew to become almost an ideology unto itself, extending into the political realm through Barack Obama's rise to the presidency.

Even so, the influence of his legal opinions on civil rights has been overshadowed by the romantic resonance of his image as a solitary dissenter, the one against the many. His condemnation of the court majority in *Plessy v. Ferguson* rings down through the centuries not because it was legally sound but because it was morally right. It translates less like an application of legal doctrine than an act of resistance.

And yet it was both of those things. In one of the darkest hours of American law, when the court cleared the way for six decades of segregation, Harlan was both prophet and scold. While his colleagues resorted to racism, he fought for the Constitution. The fact that one white man, rather than none, believed that the national charter could support a diverse nation built on equality under the law—in fact, demanded it—sustained the faith of Black people for generations. The magnitude of his achievement is visible well beyond the gates of the legal academy.

In the history of the Supreme Court, there is no parallel to Harlan's career. There have been other passionate dissenters and other famous dissents. But no one stood so consistently against his brethren, only to be vindicated in later times. That makes his career an important clue in the ongoing search for how best to undertake the task of interpreting the Constitution without falling prey to the fears or prejudices of the moment. There are many theoretical approaches, with high-sounding names such as originalism and textualism, and Harlan has been persuasively linked to some of them. But the evidence indicates that his crucial differences with his colleagues stemmed more from the sensitivities of his life than any strategic vision of the law. Unlike many later-generation justices, whose careers vaulted them from law school, to clerkship, to faculty position, to judgeship with no intervening stops in the neighborhood of real life, Harlan's legal views were shaped by what he saw with his own eyes and felt in his own heart.

First came his upbringing in the home of James Harlan, under the mentoring gaze of James's friend and hero Henry Clay. Who better than a Whig nationalist, tutored in the greatness of the American system from the cradle, to understand how to move the nation away from the states'-rights disaster of the 1860s? Most of John's colleagues practiced common law in the courtrooms of their youth; John's father preached the Constitution.

But that document didn't prove to be as durable as James Harlan believed; it was weakened by a flaw in its reasoning, a chink in its metal. The promise to preserve "the Blessings of Liberty"[4] secured the compact, but there would be no liberty for one-eighth of the population. The emotional consequence of that contradiction was brought home when he watched his home state be ripped apart by slavery. Theodore Roosevelt was wise to trace Harlan's views to the unique stresses of living in a border state. John preached on street corners, organized, schemed, cajoled, and put his life on the line to preserve Kentucky's neutrality, only to see his state become a battleground between South and North. He chose sides without hesitation, but it would take longer for him to figure out how the Constitution had failed the nation at that crucial moment.

Perhaps he would have shared most other white people's desire to patch up the union as quickly—and imperfectly—as necessary, had Kentucky emerged from the conflict as economically strengthened as the home states of his northern brethren; instead, he watched as racism replaced slavery in poisoning the Bluegrass State's politics and prospects. In later years, scholars would probe the mystery of how a man who grew up in a slaveholding family and resisted demands for abolition could emerge as the nation's leading defender of Black rights. But his footsteps followed an entirely logical progression. The biggest wonder is why more southerners and northerners didn't see matters as clearly as he did. There was a pernicious reason they didn't. The assertion of white supremacy as a historic and allegedly scientific certainty presented a fresh challenge to the notion that all men are created equal.

If there is a mystery to Harlan's story, its solution lies in the person of Robert Harlan, the prodigal brother who rose to national prominence despite having been born into slavery. As a little boy, John watched the physically imposing Robert ride home from the races, his precious winnings encased in a leather pouch—Robert with his unique and puzzling hold on John's all-powerful father and, by extension, the entire household.

Robert's life proceeded to be an all-encompassing refutation of the notion of white supremacy, banishing the idea that Black woes stemmed from anything other than lack of opportunities. Starting in Harlan's Station, Robert built a small business; matched wits with the shrewdest gamblers of the age; scythed his way through the jungle to the Pacific and gold rush riches; crossed the Atlantic to pioneer American horse racing against Old World aristocrats; and then, in a long final chapter, emerged as a civil-rights prophet and political boss in his own right.

Robert's amazing journey, alighting on riverboats and gold rush boomtowns and storied British racetracks, ranged farther than John's own improbable rise through war and Reconstruction. Yet Robert was there at many of the stations of John's life, dazzling guests with his gift of a handmade piano at Lizzie's wedding, organizing delegates for John's benefit at the fateful 1876 Republican convention, and using his contacts with Black leaders to quell an embarrassing incident that threatened John's ambitions for the Supreme Court. He was there, too, to extend a hand to John's addicted brother James.

To John's northern-born colleagues, acceptance of segregation was the price of peace in the South; the personal cost to the hopes and dreams of freed men and women seemed barely to register in their minds. Henry Billings Brown argued that keeping Black people separate was a badge of inferiority only because Black people chose to construe it that way. His opinion in *Plessy v. Ferguson*—like his later opinions in the Insular Cases—was rich with the assumption of white supremacy: He wrote as though relating unspoken truths that were so widely understood that they required no proof and no argument.

John carried no such assumptions. Robert Harlan, after all, had gained wealth after securing his freedom and rose to leadership in the Reconstruction era when the federal government enforced Black rights. His fortunes dwindled in proportion to the withdrawal of federal support. As segregation took hold, there would be no more grand speeches by Robert before mixed-race audiences; no more riches to be gained by investing in Black entrepreneurs, as most of them lacked any chance of attracting white customers.

The mere awareness of Robert's life story would have been enough to render the usual prejudices untenable. But John and Robert had regular contact early in their lives. Sadly, it's unknown whether they continued to interact during John's time on the court, because none of Robert's papers survive, and John's are incomplete. But Robert visited Washington frequently during John's early years on the court, and there was no evidence of a rupture between them. If such a breach had occurred, it would have been highly unlikely that Malvina would have written so approvingly of Robert in her memoir.

After Robert's death, John crossed paths with Black friends of Robert Jr.'s during his visits to Washington's Metropolitan AME Church, and the two men would surely have run into each other on many occasions. The easy confidence that led Robert Jr. to call repeatedly on his friend William Howard Taft at the White House would likely have led him to the justices' chambers in the Capitol or John's home on Euclid Place, eager to get to know the man who had grown up in the same home as his esteemed father. Nonetheless, any record of their relationship, if it existed, seems to have disappeared into that vast, silent void between the races that opened up during segregation.

Yet the relationship between John's family and Robert's extended through the generations. On March 27, 1957, Robert Jackson Harlan— great-grandson of Robert, grandson of Robert Jr., son of Robert Dorsey—was sworn into the bar of the Supreme Court, an honor for those deemed capable of arguing before that august body.[5] Standing before Robert Jackson Harlan was Justice John Marshall Harlan II, whose chambers Robert J. had visited just seventeen days earlier. The two men pored over a family scrapbook and discussed their common roots.[6] Drew Pearson, a syndicated columnist, wrote about what he called "An Interesting Harlan Reunion," but mentioned only that Robert J.'s great-grandfather had been enslaved in the home of John II's great-grandfather.[7] The two Harlan scions continued to exchange letters.[8]

When Robert J. came before the court for his swearing in, he was sponsored by one of the great civil rights lawyers of the time, James Nabrit Jr.,[9] who three years earlier had argued *Bolling v. Sharpe*,[10] a companion case to *Brown v. Board of Education*, and would go on to become president of Howard University. James Nabrit Jr. was close to Robert J. Harlan in another way: his brilliant son, James Nabrit III, had married Robert J.'s daughter, Roberta "Jackie" Harlan, a year earlier.[11] In attendance that day at the Supreme Court was also fourteen-year-old Robert Jackson Harlan Jr.—the fifth Robert Harlan in the line, also destined for law school.[12]

The Robert Harlan family had, indeed, played more than their part in fighting segregation, even as their fortunes waxed and waned. Robert Jackson Harlan spent much of his career in federal jobs at the General Services Administration, where he was civil rights program officer and acting director of the Federal Contract Compliance Programs, overseeing fair employment practices for construction laborers. He played a similar role at the Federal Highway Administration.[13] He often put himself on the line to expose biases, going to white neighborhoods to determine whether home sellers were receptive to Black buyers. He related numerous stories of realtors discouraging him from making purchases in a detailed letter that covered three columns in the *Washington Evening Star*.[14] Meanwhile, Robert

Jackson Harlan Jr. clerked for a pioneering Black judge, John Douglass Fauntleroy, in Washington, DC.[15] And James Nabrit III and Jackie Harlan Nabrit were civil rights royalty, with James having followed in his father's footsteps in handling some of the major cases of the day, until their deaths in 2013 and 2008, respectively.[16]

They never forgot their connection to the white side of the Harlan family. As the decades went by, relatives on both sides became more curious about the nature of the relationship between Robert and John Harlan. Each seemed to accept, and even welcome, the likelihood that Robert and John were brothers; each looked with pride on the other.

In 2000, after DNA tests proved the likelihood of Thomas Jefferson's long-rumored fathering of children with the enslaved Sally Hemings, a scholar of John Marshall Harlan named Linda Przybyszewski proposed a DNA test to descendants of John and Robert. The test prompted a *Louisville Courier-Journal* headline, "DNA May Link US Judge, Slave."[17] The Associated Press article that followed proclaimed, "Rumors through the years indicated the two men were half brothers. Now, with blood samples from descendants of both men, the families can know for certain."

It took several months before Przybyszewski announced that the results had indicated a family link was unlikely,[18] though any disruption in the bloodlines of either side of the family over the five subsequent generations would have rendered the test invalid. While neither family accepted the results as dispositive, and the lack of a full report cast an air of uncertainty around the test, both were quick to note that it didn't much matter to them.

Eve Dillingham, a Connecticut pianist who was the only child of John II, expressed disappointment. She "said she and other family members had hoped the rumors that the two men were related were true," the Associated Press reported. "Regardless, there was a great bond between the two, she said, and 'whether it was a blood bond or not doesn't matter so much.'"[19]

Over time, the DNA test came to rankle Robert Jackson Harlan Jr., who had contributed his own sample. Perhaps it was the juxtaposition with the Jefferson-Hemings scandal that suggested the public was eager to expose centuries-old sexual misconduct, or the idea that his own family would gain in stature by a blood link to the white Harlans. He now says almost defiantly that "I am not related to the Supreme Court justice," and that Robert's father was "probably just some southern son of a bitch with missing teeth."[20]

His point is larger, and one that both sides of the Harlan family share: the story of race in America isn't one that lends itself to tidy, happy endings. Look closely, and the layers of abuse and injustice come into sharper, more ironic focus. So too do the moments of courage and transcendence. The story of Robert Harlan includes many such moments. It is heroic enough to account for its own myth. Looking at Robert only in terms of his relationship to John or James Harlan diminishes him, suggesting that his experiences are important only in reference to his proximity to them.

Robert Jackson Harlan Jr. is the last in the line of Robert Harlans, living alone in his aging row house in Washington. He carries some scars from having grown up as a Black man under segregation and coming of age in the turbulence of the civil rights era. He says his father taught him there were good and bad people of every race, and he basically agrees, but the times often conspired to put him at odds with the white community.

The longer arc of his family history is on his mind as well: how a lineage suffused with the hopes and vision of Robert Harlan, Robert Jr., John Mercer Langston, Thomas Dorsey, Mamie Harlan, Nettie Harlan, and his own parents and sister was denied the lustrous success that those forebearers imagined. The irony that the first Robert may have enjoyed more satisfaction than the fifth seems a perfect benediction for a story about the tragic price of segregation.

"You know, I always liked the stories with happy endings," he says in his living room, amid newspaper cuttings and photos of his illustrious family. "On the other hand, it ends the way it's gonna end whether you like it or not. And that's about what happened here."[21]

Thurgood Marshall was dead, and the worlds of politics and law crowded into the giant National Cathedral to remember him as the greatest of civil rights champions. President Bill Clinton led the mourners, who spilled outside the sanctuary and onto the lawn beyond. In the cavernous chamber, under the blue stained-glass windows, sat Supreme Court justices past and present, and Marshall's fellow warriors from the early years in the trenches. Back then, equal protection under the law was a cause to be pursued, case by case, plaintiff by plaintiff, in the face of death threats by the Ku Klux Klan and the snarling dogs of local sheriffs.[22]

Constance Baker Motley sat in a place of honor, as both a family friend and the first Black woman appointed to the federal judiciary.[23] At seventy-one, Motley was an almost regal presence; a woman in whose stature and bearing all the pride and dignity of the fight for equal rights were reflected. A decade and half before, she had been first in line for the Supreme Court—she might well have beaten Sandra Day O'Connor to become the first woman justice, had President Jimmy Carter ever gotten to make a pick. Now that dream was behind her. Listening to the Howard University choir sing "Lift Every Voice and Sing," her mind drifted back even further to the very germination of the modern civil rights movement. She and Thurgood had come so far since then, and the Supreme Court under Earl Warren had rewarded them with victory after victory. By the time of Marshall's death in 1993, however, the conservative legal movement had taken hold, and many of those decisions were in jeopardy.

"Marshall never lost his faith in the American judicial system," she wrote in a powerful remembrance of that day in the National Cathedral. "When the Supreme Court lost its liberal majority as Presidents Reagan and Bush appointed more and more conservative judges, Marshall simply wrote more and more biting dissents. I believe I know what sustained Marshall during all of those heartbreaking years when the Warren Court decisions were being denuded. Marshall had a 'bible' to which I believe he must have turned during his most depressed episodes. The 'bible' would be known in the legal profession as the first Mr. Justice Harlan's dissent in *Plessy v. Ferguson*. I do not know of any opinion on which Marshall relied more in his pre-*Brown* days than the Harlan dissent, which has since become the law of the land. Even the most conservative justice would not say in 1993 that Mr. Justice Harlan was wrong.

"I remember the pre-*Brown* days when Marshall's legal staff would gather around him at a table in his office to discuss possible new theories for attacking segregation. Marshall would read aloud passages from Harlan's amazing dissent. I do not believe we ever filed a brief in the pre-*Brown* days in which a portion of that opinion was not quoted. Marshall's favorite quotation was 'Our Constitution is color blind.' It became our basic legal creed. Marshall admired the courage of Harlan more than any justice who has ever sat on the Supreme Court. Even Chief Justice Warren's forthright and moving decision for the Court in *Brown I* did not affect Marshall in the same way. Earl Warren was writing for a unanimous Supreme Court. Harlan was a solitary and lonely figure writing for posterity."[24]

The life of the law connects generations, and so Judge Motley felt her own sense of closeness to John Marshall Harlan: she had met him many times in her journey toward freedom and enlightenment. He had stood beside her in battle, a fellow soldier in a fight that spanned the better part of a century and would continue into the next. Now, under the eyes of God, he was beside her again, as she mourned the loss of her professional partner and looked ahead to a worrisome, unknowable future. His words had always bolstered her, bracing her up when the entire legal system seemed arrayed against her. He gave her a reason to keep pushing: her brother in arms, her equal under law.

Acknowledgments

This book is the product of years of effort by many people. Foremost among them is the outstanding young journalist Adam P. Willis, who spent three years chronicling the soul-inspiring story of Robert Harlan. Through news accounts—many of which have only been digitized in the last decade—Adam charted Robert Harlan's journey across the United States, South America, and Europe. He connected with dozens of historians from Cincinnati to Newmarket, England. I joined him in following Robert's path from Harlan's Station to Lexington to Cincinnati to Saratoga Springs to London. Adam also researched much of John Marshall Harlan's life—from his early years, political career, and wartime exploits to his involvement in the Chinese cases, *Plessy v. Ferguson*, *Lochner v. New York*, and the horrific lynching of Ed Johnson in Chattanooga. Adam was a daily thought partner and editor in the development of the book. His values and insights are reflected on every page.

Alec Ward spent a year capturing the arc of civil rights law from the Civil War through the conflicts that comprised the *Civil Rights Cases of 1883*. He also provided fresh, original research into the behind-the-scenes dramas over the income-tax case, the Insular Cases, and the role of dissent in American law. Alec contributed his own, well-developed views on Harlan's place in the legal canon, and then went on to the University of Virginia law school, after which he plans to draw on his knowledge of Harlan while working in the Civil Rights Division of the U.S. Justice Department. His trajectory is fur ther testament to the idea, central to this book, that the life of the law spans generations.

Much of the initial research into the book, as far back as 2009, was performed by Lee Fang—then a freshly minted college graduate and now a nationally prominent journalist. Lee's enthusiasm for this project, his drive and vision, were indispensable to its realization.

I am also deeply grateful to Jordan Miller, who researched the chapter on the Sugar Trust and anti-trust law, and Alec "Will" Frydman, who chronicled how Harlan's dissents were vindicated in later generations, from the advent of the income tax to the twentieth century civil rights movement. Nicole Pottinger contributed research from Kentucky archives. My *Politico* colleague Katie Ellsworth, a genius in telling stories through photography, shaped and edited the photo inserts.

Priscilla Painton, my editor at Simon & Schuster, is justly renowned for her sharp line edits and story judgment. She is also unfailingly supportive, upbeat, and confident in her vision—every interaction with her is an energizing experience. My agent, Wendy Strothman, won my admiration years ago with her fierce commitment to excellence and unyielding belief in "books that matter." Wendy's track record of generating meaningful works of literature as an editor, publisher, and agent speaks for itself.

Many outstanding Harlan scholars and experts in the period read arly drafts and offered valuable advice. James W. Gordon of Western ew England Law School, a Harlan expert and pioneer in probing the of Robert Harlan, was a vital collaborator whose views were deeply uential in the development of this book. Gabriel Jackson Chin of University of California, Davis, read the entire manuscript and d insights that are sprinkled throughout the final work. Jack's l perspective on Justice Harlan's role in the Chinese cases only to validate his admiration of other aspects of Harlan's career. I unate to have a prominent expert in African American history aw in my own family, Elizabeth Herbin-Triant of the University assachusetts, Lowell. Betsy's input and advice led to many ents. Other Harlan scholars' work informed this narrative, m grateful for the time and advice of Tinsley Yarbrough, whose outstanding 1995 work "Judicial Enigma: The First Justice Harlan," is cited in many places; Linda Przybyszewski, who shared her wise analysis of Justice Harlan's thoughts and motives; Brian Frye and Josh Blackman, for offering their perspectives on Justice Harlan's law lectures; and Nikki Taylor, who provided a peerless understanding of Cincinnati's history and racial politics. James C. Klotter, the state historian of Kentucky, was generous with his time and his excellent perspective. His works are reflected throughout the book. Elizabeth Dowling Taylor offered important advice on the class dynamics within the African American community, and how they changed through the years.

Members of each side of the Harlan family gave their help and encouragement. Amelia Newcomb, managing editor of the *Christian Science Monitor* and the great-great granddaughter of John and Malvina Harlan, offered both family details and shrewd editing suggestions. Robert Jackson Harlan Jr., the great-great grandson of Robert and Josephine Harlan, shared his own life story and those of his many heroic family members. I also thank the late James Nabrit III for an early phone interview.

In Newmarket, England, Adam Willis and I were treated to a master class in horse-racing history from David Oldrey and Timothy Cox, who also provided extensive editing advice and assistance. Their exertions and sharp interest in Robert Harlan brought light to an underappreciated chapter in transatlantic racing history. Michael Church provided historical insights and a wonderful tour of Epsom Downs, home to the Derby. In Richmond, home to Robert Harlan, Elizabeth Velluet gave us a walking tour and recreation of life along the Thames in the nineteenth century. In Chattanooga, LaFrederick Thirkill shared his own story and investigation into the horrific lynching of Ed Johnson. Filmmaker Linda Duvoisin and journalist Mariann Martin provided their copious research and invaluable advice. Eleanor Cooper, Professor Susan Eckelmann, and Judge Curtis Lynn Collier were tremendously helpful as well. In Saratoga Springs, Field Horne was generous with his time and painted a picture of the horseracing capital in its Gilded Age heyday, and Myra B. Armstead provided amazing details on the city's Black community. The staff of the Cincinnati Museum, with special thanks to Sandra "Mickey" DeVise and Anne Shepherd, were greatly helpful in uncovering the footsteps of Robert Harlan and even allowed Adam to work out of their office.

In Kentucky, Roda Ferraro of the Keeneland Library uncovered numerous records of Robert's racing career. Stephanie Lang of the Kentucky Historical Society helped dig out important facts and details. Beth Morgan, librarian at John Harlan's alma mater, Centre College, plumbed the archives for relevant documents. The acclaimed authors and historians Maryjean Wall, Aaron Astor, Katherine Mooney, Yvonne Giles, Marion B. Lucas, James M. Prichard, Gary O'Dell, and Bill Marshall all shared important aspects of their own research.

Thanks, as well, to Professor Rogers Smith and the late Judge Juan Torruella. At Simon & Schuster, my great appreciation to Philip Bashe and Phil Metcalf, for their copy editing and assistance on the notes, in particular, as well as Hana Park and CEO Jonathan Karp.

I am deeply grateful for the advice of friends who either read portions of the book or provided expert advice, particularly Neil Swidey, Jonathan Nathanson, Judge Victor Wolski, and Professor Gary Bass. Many others provided ongoing support and encouragement, including Ambassador Swanee Hunt, Charlie and Luiza Savage, Stefan Fatsis, Aviva Kempner, Sasha Issenberg, Aaron Zitner, Michael Grunwald, Jon Auerbach, Carlo Rotella, Scott Greenberger, Gareth Cook, Kevin Baron, Mark Muro, Nancy Barnes, Robert Manson, David Zraket, Phillip Argyris, Mark Caro, Judy Abel, Scott Heller, Wendy Davis, Maria Rudolph, Nicole Rabner, Dan Diamond, Bryan Bender, Michael Crowley, Katie Kingsbury, Joanna Weiss, Eric Moskowitz, Nick Tzitzon, Dante Ramos, Steve Heuser, Carrie Budoff Brown, Elizabeth Ralph, Margy Slattery, Toby Stock, John Harris, Matt Kaminski, Susan Glasser, Ellen Clegg, Carolyn Lee, Mark Neuffer, John Firestone, Diane Asadorian Masters, Thomas Medicus, Katharina Uppenbrink, Nikolas and Montse Jaspert, Kate Maguire, Andrew Blechman, Sabine Vollmer Von Falken, Lisa Vollmer, Richard Jay Nussbaum, Jessie Atkin, and Kimber Riddle.

Thanks, too, to my many other friends and colleagues at *Politico* and former colleagues at the *Boston Globe*—too many to single out—for their support and encouragement. This is true, too, of my family members, especially George Canellos and Pamela Brown, Clio Canellos, Andrew Canellos and Elizabeth Reluga, James and Diane Triant, Bill Triant, Jeanne Triant, and Craig Estes. And a special thanks to my parents, Jean and George Canellos, who encouraged me to go to law school and supported me in the years when I first read the many amazing dissents of John Marshall Harlan.

Notes

PROLOGUE: "ONE MAN WITH GOD IS A MAJORITY"

1. "The Color Prejudice; A Young Negro Refused Admission to the Grand Opera-house," *New-York Times*, November 25, 1879.
2. Ibid.
3. Geo. P. Rowell's & Co's American Newspaper Directory (New York: Geo. P. Rowell, 1877), 752; "The Color Prejudice"; John Hope Franklin, "The Enforcement of the Civil Rights Act of 1875," Prologue, *Journal of the National Archives* (fall, 1974).
4. "Law Reports: Working of the Civil Rights Bill; A Test Case in This District—A Colored Citizen Refused Parquet Tickets at Booth's Theater—Mr. Tillotson Arrested—Bail Fixed at $1000," *New-York Times*, April 22, 1875.
5. United States Senate website, Senate.gov, "Landmark Legislation: Civil Rights Act of 1875," https://www.senate.gov/artandhistory/history/common/generic/Civil RightsAct1875.htm.
6. L. E. Murphy, "The Civil Rights Law of 1875," *Journal of Negro History* 12, no. 2 (1927): 110–27.
7. "A Colored Man Interviews the President," *New Orleans Republican*, September 5, 1871; "Long Branch—A Colored Cincinnatian's Visit to the President," *Cincinnati Daily Gazette*, August 8, 1871; "The President and His Relatives: A Negro Interviews His Excellency at Long Branch—Mr. Grant Talks in His Own Defense," *World*, September 5, 1871.
8. "A Horse Racer and a Cock Fighter Who Prays Every Night," *Cincinnati Enquirer*, November 27, 1870.
9. Nikki M. Taylor, *America's First Black Socialist: The Radical Life of Peter H. Clark* (Lexington: University Press of Kentucky, 2012), 117–25.
10. Murphy, "Civil Rights Law of 1875," 110–27.
11. Robert Harlan to Benjamin F. Butler, March 15, 1875, Benjamin Butler Papers, Library of Congress.
12. "General Butler on the Civil Rights Bill," *New York Daily Herald*, March 20, 1875.
13. "A Civil-Rights Case Goes Untested," *New-York Times*, June 15, 1875, 9.
14. "A Question of Color; Involving the Hue of a Ticket and a Man; Thomas Maguire Says He Excluded Green Not on Account of His Color, but Because of the Shade of His Ticket," *San Francisco Chronicle*, January 19, 1876.
15. "Alleged Violation of the Civil Rights Law at Jefferson City—Work in the U.S. District Court—Claim Warrant Question—General News," *St. Louis Post-Dispatch*, September 14, 1876; "Circuit Court: Fourth Day," *State-Journal* (Jefferson City, MO), December 1, 1876.

16. Alan F. Westin, "Ride-In!," *American Heritage* 13, no. 5 (August 1962): american heritage.com/ride.

17. Untitled column, *Recorder-Tribune* (Holton, KS), April 13, 1876; untitled column, *Brown County World* (Hiawatha, KS), October 25, 1883.

18. John Anthony Scott, "Justice Bradley's Evolving Concept of the Fourteenth Amendment from the Slaughterhouse Cases to the Civil Rights Cases," *Rutgers Law Review (1970–1971)* 25 (1971): 552–69.

19. Paul Kens, *Justice Stephen Field: Shaping Liberty from the Gold Rush to the Gilded Age* (Lawrence: University of Kansas Press, 1997), 25–36

20. Robert T. Swaine, *The Cravath Firm and Its Predecessors, 1819–1947* (self-pub., Ad Press, 1948), 31.

21. E. Merton Coulter, *Civil War and Readjustment in Kentucky*, Chapel Hill: University of North Carolina Press, 1926, reprinted 2011), 259, 278–80.

22. William Brown to George F. Edmunds, November 19, 1877, Senate Records, as quoted in Tinsley E. Yarbrough, *Judicial Enigma: The First Justice Harlan* (New York: Oxford University Press, 1995), 110.

23. James Speed to George F. Edmunds, November 10, 1877, Senate Records, as quoted in Yarbrough, *Judicial Enigma*, 111.

24. Malvina Shanklin Harlan, *Some Memories of a Long Life, 1854–1911* (New York: Modern Library, 2003), 94–102.

25. John Marshall Harlan to James Harlan, November 25, 1882, Harlan Papers, Library.

26. "The Dead and Gone," *Chicago Tribune*, January 1, 1883.

27. *Strauder v. West Virginia*, 100 U.S. 305-310 (1880).

28. *Civil Rights Cases*, 109 U.S. 10 (1883).

29. S. F. Phillips, "Brief for the United States," the *Civil Rights Cases*, U.S. Supreme Court, October term, 1882, 25.

30. Charles Devens and Edwin B. Smith, Brief for the United States, *U.S. v. Stanley, U.S. v. Ryan, U.S. v. Nichols*, Supreme Court, October term, 1879, 9

31. Melvin Urofsky, *Dissent and the Supreme Court* (New York: Vintage Books, 2017), 49–54.

32. Karl M. ZoBell, "Division of Opinion in the Supreme Court: A History of Judicial Disintegration," *Cornell Law Review* 44, no. 2 (Winter 1959): 198.

33. *United States v. Harris*, 106 U.S. 629 (1883).

34. Malvina Shanklin Harlan, *Some Memories of a Long Life*, 116.

35. Ibid., 112–14.

36. *Civil Rights Cases of 1883*, 109 U.S. 26 (1883).

37. *Civil Rights Cases of 1883*, 109 U.S. 61-62 (1883).

38. Malvina Shanklin Harlan, *Some Memories of a Long Life*, 112–14.

39. "Civil Rights—The Supreme Court Declared the Bill to be Unconstitutional," *Atlanta Constitution*, October 16, 1883.

40. Frederick Douglass to John Marshall Harlan, November 27, 1883, Harlan Papers, Library of Congress, https://brandeiswatch.wordpress.com/2014/02/21/letter-from-frederick-douglass-to-john-marshall-harlan/.

41. Frederick Douglass, "Civil Rights and Judge Harlan," *American Reformer* (December 8, 1883): 388, https://brandeiswatch.files.wordpress.com/2014/02/f-douglassw-article.pdf, Harlan Papers, University of Louisville.

CHAPTER 1: A FATHER'S PROPHECY

1. James C. Klotter, interviewed by Adam Willis, August 6, 2018.

2. Marion B. Lucas, *A History of Blacks in Kentucky: From Slavery to Segregation, 1760–1891* (Frankfort, KY: Kentucky Historical Society, 1992), 2, 108–17, notes that slaveholders in Kentucky held an average of five slaves, a figure indicating that the Harlans, whose property fluctuated between twelve and fourteen slaves, were among the state's wealthier families. For more on the small farm slave system in Kentucky, see John B. Boles, *Religion in Antebellum Kentucky* (Lexington: University Press of Kentucky, 1995), 101.

3. David S. Heidler and Jeanne T. Heidler, *Henry Clay: The Essential American* (New York: Random House Trade Paperback, 2011), 449–51; author's visit to Ashland, the Henry Clay Estate, in Lexington, Kentucky, June 24, 2017. For more on Clay the slave owner, see Heidler and Heidler, 8, 21, 28.

4. James C. Klotter, "Central Kentucky's 'Athens of the West' Image in the Nation and in History," in *Bluegrass Renaissance: The History and Culture of Central Kentucky, 1792–1852*, ed. James C. Klotter and Daniel Rowland (Lexington: University Press of Kentucky, 2012), 11–36; author's visit to Ashland, the Henry Clay Estate, June 24, 2017.

5. For more on Kentucky's Nonimportation Act of 1833, see Lucas, *A History of Blacks in Kentucky*, 72, 88, and Tim Talbott, "Slavery Laws in Old Kentucky," Kentucky History, accessed Fall, 2018, https://explorekyhistory.ky.gov/items/show/180.

6. James Harlan kept company with the rest of Kentucky's elite political society and seems to have known well the chief members of each of the state's first families, the Breckinridges and Crittendens of Lexington and the famous Clays of Ashland among them.

7. J. Winston Coleman Jr., "The Kentucky Colonization Society," *Register of the Kentucky Historical Society* 39, no. 126 (1941): 2; "The African-American Mosaic: Colonization," Library of Congress online, accessed Winter, 2019, https://www.loc.gov/exhibits/african/afam002.html; Jeffrey Brooke Allen, "Did Southern Colonizationists Oppose Slavery? Kentucky 1816–1850 as a Test Case," *Register of the Kentucky Historical Society* 75, no. 2 (1977): 95.

8. Jeffrey Brooke Allen, "Did Southern Colonizationists Oppose Slavery?," 97–98; Coleman, "Kentucky Colonization Society," 4. See also Lowell H. Harrison, *The Antislavery Movement in Kentucky* (Lexington: University Press of Kentucky, 1978), 31–39.

9. "Colonization," *Christian Statesman*, June 1, 1838; "American Colonization Society," *New York Observer*, June 16, 1838.

10. "Appointments by the Governor," *Commentator*, January 25, 1831; Yarbrough, *Judicial Enigma*, 4.

11. Kurt X. Metzmeier and Peter Scott Campbell, "Nursery of a Supreme Court Justice: The Library of James Harlan of Kentucky, Father of John Marshall Harlan," *University of Louisville Law Library Journal* 100, no. 4 (2009): 639–46.

12. David G. Farrelly, "Harlan's Formative Period: The Years Before the War," *Kentucky Law Journal* 46, no. 3 (1958): 1. See also Undated Autobiographical Typescript, 6, Harlan Papers, Library of Congress. John's description of the Harlan family's Big Reds and Little Blacks comes from an undated transcript in the Harlan Papers at the Library of Congress, henceforth referred to as Autobiographical Typescript.

13. Joel Richard Paul, *Without Precedent: John Marshall and His Times* (New York: Riverhead Books, 2018), 1–4.

14. Autobiographical Typescript, 3, Harlan Papers, Library of Congress. John recalls that his uncle Silas Harlan was distinguished by his "Indian hunting coat and hat." For more on the clashes between the Harrodsburg settlers and the Shawnee, see Kathryn Harrod Mason, *James Harrod of Kentucky* (Baton Rouge: Louisiana State University Press, 1951).

15. Mason, *James Harrod of Kentucky*, 243.

16. Ibid. See also Willard Rouse Jillson, "The Founding of Harrodsburg," *Register of the Kentucky Historical Society* 27, no. 81 (September 1929): 562.

17. Jillson, "Founding of Harrodsburg," 559–62; Michael J. Denis and Kelli Weaver-Miner, "Dragging Fact from Fiction: Harlan's Station, 'the Old Stone House,' and the Elijah Harlan House," Kentucky Ancestors Online, last modified May 23, 2014, http://kentuckyancestors.org/dragging-fact-from-fiction-harlans-station-the-old -stone-house-and-the-elijah-harlan-house/.

18. James Graves, "Battle of Blue Licks," HistoryNet.com, accessed Winter, 2019, https://www.historynet.com/battle-of-blue-licks.htm. Originally published in *Military History*, August 2002.

19. Denis and Weaver-Miner, "Dragging Fact from Fiction"; Mason, *James Harrod of Kentucky*, 198; "The Battle of Blue Licks," National Guard eMuseum, accessed Winter, 2019, https://kynghistory.ky.gov/Our-History/History-of-the-Guard /Pages/The-Battle-of-Blue-Licks.aspx.

20. Autobiographical Typescript, 6, Harlan Papers, Library of Congress; Yarbrough, *Judicial Enigma*, 3; James W. Gordon, "Did the First Justice Harlan Have a Black Brother?," *Western New England Law Review* 15, no. 2 (1993): 214, https://digital commons.law.wne.edu/lawreview/vol15/iss2/1/.

21. Author's visit to the ruins of Harlan's Station, June 23, 2017; Denis and Weaver-Miner, "Dragging Fact from Fiction"; Carolyn Murray-Wooley, *Early Stone Houses of Kentucky* (Lexington: University Press of Kentucky, 2008) 98–99.

22. Ibid.

23. James C. Klotter, *Kentucky Justice, Southern Honor, and American Manhood: Understanding the Life of Richard Reid* (Baton Rouge: Louisiana State University Press, 2003), 46.

24. Klotter, "Central Kentucky's 'Athens of the West' Image," 26; J. Winston Coleman Jr., *The Springs of Kentucky; An Account of the Famed Watering-Places of the Bluegrass State, 1800–1935* (Lexington, KY: Winburn Press, 1955), 32–34.

25. Martha Stephenson, "Old Graham Springs: At Harrodsburg, Kentucky, Once the Most Fashionable Summer Resort in the State—Now Only a Memory of the Past," *Register of Kentucky State Historical Society* 12, no. 34 (1914): 26–35; Coleman, *Springs of Kentucky*, 72–73. For biographies of Christopher Columbus Graham, see "One Hundred Years Old," *Louisville* (KY) *Courier-Journal*, October 8, 1884, and Ron Bryant, "Christopher Columbus Graham: An Extraordinary Kentuckian," Commonwealth of Kentucky: Office of the Kentucky Secretary of State online, accessed Fall, 2018, https://www.sos.ky.gov/admin/land/resources/articles/Docu ments/Graham.pdf.

26. For extensive studies in the mixed-race elite of the nineteenth and early twentieth centuries, see William J. Simmons, *Men of Mark: Eminent, Progressive, and Rising* (Cleveland: Geo M. Rewell, 1887); Willard B. Gatewood, *Aristocrats of Color: The Black Elite 1880–1920* (Bloomington: Indiana University Press, 1990); Allyson

Hobbs, *A Chosen Exile: A History of Racial Passing in American Life* (Cambridge, MA: Harvard University Press, 2014); Elizabeth Dowling Taylor, *The Original Black Elite: Daniel Murray and the Story of a Forgotten Era* (New York: Amistad, 2017).

27. During Robert's life, some sources reported his birthplace as central Kentucky, which appears to have been a mistake. Most sources, including those provided by his family and those who knew him, state that he was born in Mecklenburg County, Virginia. See "Colonel Robert N. Harlan," *Cincinnati Commercial*, September 8, 1881; "Triplett Vs. Harlan," *Cleveland Gazette*, June 4, 1887; "Col. Robert Harlan: One of the Best Known and Most Widely Travelled Colored Men in the United States," *Appeal* (Saint Paul and Minneapolis), https://digitalcommons.law.wne.edu/cgi/viewcontent.cgi?article=1092&context=facschol, May 10, 1890; "Robert Harlan," *Turf, Field, and Farm*, October 1, 1897; "Eventful Life of Robert Harlan," *Cincinnati Enquirer*, September 22, 1897, 6; Simmons, *Men of Mark*, 613–16. For the most extensive litigation of Robert's parentage, see James Gordon, "Did the First Justice Harlan Have a Black Brother?," 159–38.

28. For more on racial passing in nineteenth century in America, and a study of Robert's case in particular, see Hobbs, *A Chosen Exile*, 105–12.

29. For sources that identify Robert as the son of James Harlan, or which insinuate a biological relationship to John Marshall Harlan, see "Mr. Harlan," *Spirit of the Times*, October 1, 1859; "City Matters," *Cincinnati Enquirer*, May 21, 1871; ibid., July 4, 1871. Although Robert tended to ignore or dismiss suggestions that he was related the white Harlan family, during one anomalous interview, he "claim[ed] to be a blood relation of Justice Harlan, of the United States Supreme Court." See "The Republicans," *New Orleans Times-Democrat*, January 24, 1888. For the most extensive litigation of Robert's parentage, see James Gordon, "Did the First Justice Harlan Have a Black Brother?," 159–238.

30. Simmons, *Men of Mark*, 613–16; "Robert Harlan"; *Turf, Field, and Farm*, October 1, 1897; "Eventful Life of Robert Harlan," 6. See also James Gordon, "Did the First Justice Harlan Have a Black Brother?," 171–74, esp. note 34.

31. Malvina Shanklin Harlan, *Some Memories of a Long Life*, 20–22.

32. Ibid., 37.

33. Peter Scott Campbell, "John Marshall Harlan's Political Memoir," *Journal of Supreme Court History* 33, no. 3 (November 2008): 306, https://onlinelibrary.wiley.com/toc/15405818/2008/33/3. See also Malvina Shanklin Harlan, *Some Memories of a Long Life*, 41–44.

34. Jon Meacham, *American Lion: Andrew Jackson in the White House* (New York: Random House, 2009), 56–57, 121, 255–73.

35. Ibid., 57.

36. Irving H. Bartlett, *John C. Calhoun: A Biography* (New York: W. W. Norton, 1994), 177–201; Meacham, *American Lion*, 56–57, 222–59.

37. Heidler and Heidler, *Henry Clay*, 266, 346; Campbell, "John Marshall Harlan's Political Memoir," 306. See also Malvina Shanklin Harlan, *Some Memories of a Long Life*, 41–44.

38. Heidler and Heidler, *Henry Clay*, 266, 313–16.

39. Malvina Shanklin Harlan, *Some Memories of a Long Life*, 41–44; "Harlan, James," History, Art & Archives: United States House of Representatives online, accessed Fall, 2018, https://history.house.gov/People/Listing/H/HARLAN,-James-(H000210)/.

40. Meacham, *American Lion*, 56–57, 121, 255–73; Heidler and Heidler, *Henry Clay*, 262–67.

41. Autobiographical Typescript, 3, John Marshall Harlan Papers, Library of Congress.

42. Ibid., 4.

43. Malvina Shanklin Harlan, *Some Memories of a Long Life*, 21; John Marshall Harlan Papers, Scrapbook, Container 27.

44. Yarbrough, *Judicial Enigma*, 8; James Harlan to D. Howard Smith, August 5, 1851, Harlan Papers, Library of Congress.

45. Ibid.

46. Yarbrough, *Judicial Enigma*, 9.

47. "Colonization"; "American Colonization Society."

48. "Eventful Life of Robert Harlan," 6; "Brief Biography Col. Rob't. Harlan," *Cincinnati Union*, December 3, 1934; Simmons, *Men of Mark*, 613–16.

49. "Colonel Robert N. Harlan," *Cincinnati Commercial*, September 8, 1881.

50. Kent Hollingsworth, *The Kentucky Thoroughbred* (Lexington: University Press of Kentucky, 2009), 13.

51. Ibid., 20, 56.

52. Gary A. O'Dell, "At the Starting Post: Racing Venues and the Origins of Thoroughbred Racing in Kentucky, 1783–1865," *Kentucky Historical Quarterly* 116, no. 1 (2018): 29–78.

53. Katherine C. Mooney, *Race Horse Men: How Slavery and Freedom Were Made at the Racetrack* (Boston: Harvard University Press, 2014), 33, 35, 45; "Racing in the West," *Spirit of the Times*, June 7, 1890. See also Maryjean Wall, *How Kentucky Became Southern: A Tale of Outlaws, Horse Thieves, Gamblers, and Breeders* (Lexington: University Press of Kentucky, 2010), 109–142, esp. 122.

54. Mooney, *Race Horse Men*, 36.

55. O'Dell, "At the Starting Post," 48, 53.

56. Ibid., 55.

57. Ibid., 53–54; Gary A. O'Dell, interviewed by Adam Willis, November 9, 2017.

58. Lucas, *A History of Blacks in Kentucky*, 29–31.

59. Ibid., 32–33.

60. W. W. Stephenson, "Historic Homes of Harrodsburg, Ky.," *Register of the Kentucky Historical Society* 10, no. 30 (1912): 11; Hollingsworth, *Kentucky Thoroughbred*, 14.

61. "Robert Harlan," *Turf, Field, and Farm*, October 1, 1897; O'Dell, "At the Starting Post," 55n23.

62. For a Harlan family tree, see Malvina Shanklin Harlan, *Some Memories of a Long Life*, 202–3.

63. James W. Gordon, "Religion and the First Justice Harlan: A Case Study in Late Nineteenth Century Presbyterian Constitutionalism," *Marquette Law Review* 85, no. 2 (2001): 328.

64. Ibid., 322; Calvin Morgan Fackler, *Early Days in Danville* (Danville, KY: Danville and Boyle Historical Society, 1965), 112.

65. Boles, *Religion in Antebellum Kentucky*, 9–11; James Gordon, "Religion and the First Justice Harlan," 322, 337–38.

66. Fackler, *Early Days in Danville*, 112–18; "History," Presbyterian Church of Danville online, accessed Fall 2017, https://www.presbydan.org/our-history. For the authoritative history of Danville's First Presbyterian Church, see Calvin Morgan Fackler, *A Chronicle of the Old First: 1784–1944* (Cincinnati: Standard, 1946). For more on the racial politics of Kentucky Presbyterians and the churchgoing prac-

tices of Blacks in Kentucky, see Boles, *Religion in Antebellum Kentucky*, 80–100, and Lucas, *A History of Blacks in Kentucky*, 118–45, esp. 130.

67. James Gordon, "Religion and the First Justice Harlan," 322, 337–38.

68. John C. Young, *Scriptural Duties of Masters—A Sermon* (Boston: American Tract Society, 1846), 1–42; Yarbrough, *Judicial Enigma*, 21–22.

69. Young, *Scriptural Duties of Masters*, 1–42.

70. For more on the relationship between John and Centre College president John C. Young, see Farrelly, "Harlan's Formative Period," 373–78. See also James Gordon, "Religion and the First Justice Harlan," 317–422.

71. Malvina Shanklin Harlan, *Some Memories of a Long Life*, 250. James Harlan was appointed Kentucky's secretary of state in 1841 by the Whig governor Robert P. Letcher, remaining in office until the end of Letcher's term in 1845.

CHAPTER 2: JOURNEY INTO THE HEART OF SLAVERY

1. "Robert Harlan," *Turf, Field, and Farm*, October 1, 1897.

2. Ibid. According to William J. Simmons's 1887 book *Men of Mark*, 421, Robert was trained as a barber in Louisville and later opened a barbershop in Harrodsburg. Also see James Gordon, "Did the First Justice Harlan Have a Black Brother?," 172n36.

3. "Colonel Robert N. Harlan," *Cincinnati Commercial*, September 8, 1881; Jack D. L. Holmes, "The Abortive Slave Revolt of Point Coupée, Louisiana, 1795," *Louisiana History: The Journal of the Louisiana Historical Association* 11, no. 4 (1970): 352; Brian C. Costello, *History of Pointe Coupée, Louisiana* (Donaldsonville, LA: Margaret Media, 2010).

4. For more on the rise of steamboats in the nineteenth century, see Philip D. Jordan, "The Mississippi River: Spillway of Sin," *Arizona and the West* 9, no. 4 (Winter 1967): 317–32; Technology 1787–1880: "Steamboats on America's Rivers," Illinois State Museum online, accessed Spring, 2020, http://www.museum.state.il.us/RiverWeb/landings/Ambot/TECH/TECH3.htm, and "Society 1820–1870: the Riverboat Life," Illinois State Museum online, accessed Spring, 2020, http://www.museum.state.il.us/RiverWeb/landings/Ambot/SOCIETY/SOC6.htm.

5. "Colonel Robert N. Harlan," *Cincinnati Commercial*, September 8, 1881.

6. Klotter, "Central Kentucky's 'Athens of the West' Image," 11–35.

7. Ibid., 11–12; "Population of Lexington-Fayette, KY," population.us, accessed Fall, 2017, https://population.us/ky/lexington-fayette/.

8. Klotter, "Central Kentucky's 'Athens of the West' Image," 14–21.

9. Lucas, *A History of Blacks in Kentucky*, 107–8.

10. Ibid., 13–14.

11. Ibid., 30, 111, 122.

12. *Fayette County, Kentucky Records*, vol. 3 (Evansville, IN: Cook Publications, 1985), 327. Accessed at the Lexington Public Library, Lexington, Kentucky. James Gordon, "Did the First Justice Harlan Have a Black Brother?," 173n37, 200, cites Lexington 1840s tax records indicating that Robert was living with a free woman "of color" at that time.

13. James Gordon, "Did the First Justice Harlan Have a Black Brother?," 174n34; "Deaths," *London Morning Post*, March 1, 1861.

14. Heidler and Heidler, *Henry Clay*, 361–93.

15. Autobiographical letter from John Marshall Harlan to Richard Davenport Harlan, July 1911, 3–4, Harlan Papers, Library of Congress. The most extensive account of

John's life that we have in his own words comes from a letter he wrote to his son Richard, dated to July 1911, three months before his death.

16. Eric Foner, "Expanding the Slaveocracy: An Interview with Matt Karp," *Jacobin* online, accessed Summer 2018, https://www.jacobinmag.com/2017/03/slavery-civil-war-us-south-dubois-foner-karp; Heidler and Heidler, *Henry Clay*, 428–29.

17. "1844 Presidential Election," 270toWin, accessed Summer, 2018. https://www.270towin.com/1844_Election. Polk won the presidency with 170 electoral votes to Clay's 105. An online source, "1844 Presidential General Election Results—New York," Dave Leip's Atlas of U.S. Presidential Elections, accessed Summer, 2018, https://uselectionatlas.org/RESULTS/state.php?year=1844&fips=36&f=1&off=0&elect=0, shows that in New York State, Polk edged out Clay by just over 1 percent, with Birney garnering 3.25 percent.

18. Autobiographical letter from John Marshall Harlan to Richard Davenport Harlan, July 1911, 4, Harlan Papers, Library of Congress.

19. John S. D. Eisenhower, *So Far from God* (New York: Random House, 1989), 17–39.

20. Heidler and Heidler, *Henry Clay*, 220–21, 412–13.

21. Ibid., 411.

22. Ibid., 412.

23. John S. D. Eisenhower, *Zachary Taylor* (New York: Times Books, 2008), 40–72; Eisenhower, *So Far from God*, 166–91.

24. Autobiographical letter from John Marshall Harlan to Richard Davenport Harlan, July 1911, 3–6, Harlan Papers, Library of Congress; Heidler and Heidler, *Henry Clay*, 410–14.

25. Autobiographical letter from John Marshall Harlan to Richard Davenport Harlan, July 1911, 4–5, Harlan Papers, Library of Congress; Richard C Brown, *History of Danville and Boyle County*, 204–5.

26. Heidler and Heidler, *Henry Clay*, 414.

27. Ibid., 413–14.

28. Ibid., 414–15.

29. Henry Clay, *Henry Clay's Advice to his Countrymen Relative to the War with Mexico* (New York: H. R. Robinson, 1847), available at the Universities of Texas at Arlington Libraries online, https://library.uta.edu/usmexicowar/collections/pdf/usmw-E404-C62.pdf. See also Heidler and Heidler, *Henry Clay*, 426–29.

30. Autobiographical letter from John Marshall Harlan to Richard Davenport Harlan, July 1911, 1–2, Harlan Papers, Library of Congress.

31. Heidler and Heidler, *Henry Clay*, 426–29.

32. Lucas, *A History of Blacks in Kentucky*, 116; "Black Indians," *Louisville* (KY) *Courier*, September 18, 1850, 2.

33. Lucas, *A History of Blacks in Kentucky*, 116.

34. "Colonel Robert N. Harlan," *Cincinnati Commercial*, September 8, 1881, credits the vigilante group with eventually chasing Robert and his grocery business out of Lexington ("n----r" is spelled out in the original document). See also "Brief Biography Col. Rob't. Harlan," *Union*, and Paul McStallworth, "Harlan, Robert James," *Dictionary of American Negro Biography*, ed. Rayford W. Logan and Michael R. Winston (New York: W. W. Norton, 1983), 287–88.

35. H. W. Brands, *The Age of Gold: The California Gold Rush and the New American Dream* (New York: Anchor Books, 2003), 1–19; Carl Nolte, "Ships Under San Francisco: Gold Rush by Sea," *San Francisco Chronicle* online, last modified Au-

gust 20, 2012, https://www.sfgate.com/news/article/SHIPS-UNDER-SAN-FRAN
CISCO-There-was-a-Gold-Rush-3774242.php.

36. "Brief Biography Col. Rob't. Harlan," *Union*, recounts that Robert departed for
California in 1848. The first ship with arrivals from the East Coast and other regions of the United States did not dock in San Francisco until February 28, 1849,
so if Robert did leave Kentucky in 1848, his ship would have been one of the first to
enter San Francisco's Golden Gate. See Nolte, "Ships Under San Francisco."

37. James Gordon, "Did the First Justice Harlan Have a Black Brother?," 159. See also
"Colonel Robert N. Harlan," *Cincinnati Commercial*, September 8, 1881.

38. Heidler and Heidler, *Henry Clay*, 438–40.

39. For more on Zachary Taylor's ascent in the Whig Party, see Heidler and Heidler,
Henry Clay, 413, 427, 438.

40. Heidler and Heidler, *Henry Clay*, 426–29, 431.

41. "Chinese Museum: Whig Convention of 1848, The Chinese Museum of Philadelphia," PhilaPlace, Historical Society of Philadelphia online, https://web.archive.org
/web/20190725183709/http://www.philaplace.org/story/1812/.

42. Heidler and Heidler, *Henry Clay*, 441.

43. Ibid., 435–36, 440–43.

44. "Whig National Convention," *Dollar Newspaper* (Philadelphia), June 14, 1848;
"Crittenden Dialogue," *Louisville* (KY) *Daily Democrat*, June 29, 1848.

45. "Crittenden Dialogue," *Louisville* (KY) *Daily Democrat*, June 29, 1848.

46. Heidler and Heidler, *Henry Clay*, 462–75; Rockwell D. Hunt, PhD, "How California Came to Be Admitted," *San Francisco Chronicle*, September 9, 1900, available
at Museum of the City of San Francisco online, http://www.sfmuseum.org/hist5
/caladmit.html.

47. Heidler and Heidler, *Henry Clay*, 423–25, 482–83, 487.

48. Autobiographical letter from John Marshall Harlan to Richard Davenport Harlan, July 1911, 3, Harlan Papers, Library of Congress. See also Heidler and Heidler,
Henry Clay, 481.

49. "Brief Biography Col. Rob't. Harlan." The best surviving source on Robert's journey to San Francisco comes in a 1934 biographical article published in Cincinnati's
Union newspaper. The publisher of the paper and probable author of the article
was Wendell Phillips Dabney, a chronicler of Black Cincinnati and close friend
of Robert's son. According to the *Union* account, Robert embarked for California
when he was thirty-two years old, linking up with a party of white Kentuckians
and setting sail for Panama. See also "Eventful Life of Robert Harlan," 6, and "Of
Race Interest," *Cleveland Gazette*, May 17, 1890.

50. Nolte, "Ships Under San Francisco."

51. "Brief Biography Col. Rob't. Harlan," *Union*; Brands, *Age of Gold*, 74–86.

52. Brands, *Age of Gold*, 85.

53. "Brief Biography Col. Rob't. Harlan" *Union*; Nolte, "Ships Under San Francisco."

54. Nolte, "Ships Under San Francisco."

55. Author's visit to San Francisco Maritime National Historic Park, San Francisco,
May 12, 2018.

56. Brands, *Age of Gold*, 254–60.

57. Ibid., 252–53.

58. Gary Kamiya, "What Was Gold Rush–Era S.F.'s Favorite Pastime? Place Bets," *San
Francisco Chronicle* online, February 13, 2015, https://www.sfchronicle.com/ba
yarea/article/What-was-Gold-Rush-era-S-F-s-favorite-pastime-6080109.php.

59. Brands, *Age of Gold*, 252–54; Kamiya, "Gold Rush San Francisco's Favorite Pastime?"

60. See also James Gordon, "Did the First Justice Harlan Have a Black Brother?," 176n50. Over a long career in public life, Robert offered scant testimony about his experience in the gold rush. But in one speech before black Republicans in Cincinnati, he responded to an allegation from his rival Peter Clark that he had been "running a faro bank in California" in the early 1850s by confessing that "it was not faro, but the more innocent game of monte." See "Colonel Harlan Visits the West End and Attends a Meeting," *Cincinnati Commercial*, September 4, 1871. At a Grant Club meeting a year later, Robert refuted accusations that he had ever managed a gambling house of any kind, leaning on the alibi that he was in Cincinnati in 1850 and attending London's World's Fair in 1851, but tactfully avoided mention of his whereabouts in 1848 and 1849. See "Meeting of the East End Colored Grant Club—Difficulty with the West End Club," *Cincinnati Commercial*, September 6, 1872.

61. "Eventful Life of Robert Harlan," 6. According to Robert's *Cincinnati Enquirer* obituary, he started a trading post in California with $2,000 earned from horse sales in Kentucky, and returned from the West Coast with $50,000. "Of Race Interest," *Cleveland Gazette*, May 17, 1890, includes a slightly different dollar figure, reporting that Robert left California with $45,000, a number that could easily have been inflated or rounded to get the number published in his obituary. "Brief Biography Col. Rob't. Harlan," *Union*, reports Robert's gold rush wealth as significantly higher than other figures, writing that he had "3,000.00 on arrival and after a year and a half had increased it to $90,000 in gold."

62. "Brief Biography Col. Rob't. Harlan," *Union*.

63. James Gordon, "Did the First Justice Harlan Have a Black Brother?," 220n208. Yvonne Giles, historian of Lexington's Black community, email correspondence with Adam Willis, September 20, 2018, and interviewed by Adam Willis, December 6, 2018. See also "Eight Acres of History: Lexington's African Cemetery No. 2," The Lexington Public Library, 2015, Vimeo.

64. Malvina Shanklin Harlan, *Some Memories of a Long Life*, 21–22.

CHAPTER 3: FAITH AND THE FOUNDING FATHERS

1. Brown, *History of Danville and Boyle County*, 11; Farrelly, "Harlan's Formative Period," 375; John Marshall Harlan to W. C. Young, "The Inauguration of President Young," October 9, 1889, 49. For more on John C. Young's political views, see *Scriptural Duties of Masters*. For an overview of John C. Young's presidency at Centre College, see "Centre History," Centre College online, accessed Spring, 2018, https://www.centre.edu/centre-facts/centre-history/. See also Yarbrough, *Judicial Enigma*, 21–22.

2. Autobiographical Typescript, 4, Harlan Papers, Library of Congress. As a student at Centre College between 1848 and 1850, John spent much of his time living with an unspecified uncle, one of James's brothers, in Danville. See also Yarbrough, *Judicial Enigma*, 22.

3. William Ellis Feldhaus, *Epsilon Chapter of Beta Theta Pi: 100 Years at Centre, 1848–1948* (1948), Special Collections, Grace Doherty Library, Centre College; "John Marshall Harlan (1833–1911), Centre 1850," *Beta Statesman*, 8–11.

4. Brown, *History of Danville and Boyle County*, 4; Yarbrough, *Judicial Enigma*, 22.

5. Yarbrough, *Judicial Enigma*, 22.

6. Loren P. Beth, *John Marshall Harlan: The Last Whig Justice* (Lexington: University Press of Kentucky, 1992), 15.

7. Ibid.; Steve Luxenberg, *Separate: The Story of Plessy v. Ferguson and America's Journey from Slavery to Segregation* (New York: W. W. Norton, 2019), 34, 516n34.

8. "Colonel Robert N. Harlan," *Cincinnati Commercial*, September 8, 1881.

9. Nikki M. Taylor, *Frontiers of Freedom: Cincinnati's Black Community, 1802–1869* (Athens: Ohio University Press, 2005), 19–21.

10. "Remember, Cincinnati: 'Porkopolis' Was Not a Compliment," *Cincinnati*, November 14, 2016, https://www.cincinnatimagazine.com/citywiseblog/remember-cincinnati-porkopolis-not-compliment/.

11. Nikki M. Taylor, *Frontiers of Freedom*, 13, 26.

12. For more on the Underground Railroad in Cincinnati, see ibid., 138–60. For more on economic opportunity in Cincinnati during the industrial revolution and rise of the steamboat, see ibid., 10–27.

13. "Colonel Robert N. Harlan," *Cincinnati Commercial*, September 8, 1881.

14. Nikki M. Taylor, *Frontiers of Freedom*, 19–21. In the early to mid-nineteenth century, the city's population ballooned from 10,283 in 1819, to 56,388 in 1840, to 115,434 in 1850, to 161,044 in 1860.

15. Ibid., 1.

16. Ibid., 63–64.

17. Ibid., 50.

18. Ibid., 103.

19. Ibid., 117–25.

20. Ibid., 98–99.

21. Ibid., 82.

22. Ibid., 138–60; "Underground Railroad," Ohio History Connection, accessed Fall, 2017, https://ohiohistorycentral.org/w/Underground_Railroad.

23. "Brief Biography Col. Rob't. Harlan," *Union*; "Colonel Robert N. Harlan," *Cincinnati Commercial*, September 8, 1881.

24. Henry Clay Harlan to Orlando Brown, August 14, 1849, Orlando Brown Papers, the Filson Club Historical Society, Louisville, KY. Cited by Yarbrough, *Judicial Enigma*, 24. For more on the 1849 cholera epidemic in Kentucky, see Walter J. Daley, "The Black Cholera Comes to the Central Valley of America in the 19th Century: 1832, 1849, and Later," *Trans American Clinical and Climatological Association* 119 (2008): 143–53.

25. Malvina Shanklin Harlan, *Some Memories of a Long Life*, 199.

26. "An Annual Commencement of Centre College: Danville, Ky.," June 27, 1850, Digital Archives, Grace Doherty Library, Centre College.

27. Yarbrough, *Judicial Enigma*, 6, 22; Malvina Shanklin Harlan, *Some Memories of a Long Life*, 31–32.

28. The roof of the Crystal Palace was such a spectacle unto itself that it inspired two poems by the British writer William Makepeace Thackeray, already a sensation for his 1847 novel *Vanity Fair*. See William Makepeace Thackeray, "May Day Ode" and "The Crystal Palace," *The Works of William Makepeace Thackeray*, vol. 18 (London: Smith, Elder, 1869), 41–43, 168–71.

29. "The Crystal Palace," Victoria and Albert Museum online, accessed Spring, 2018. https://web.archive.org/web/20180204160942/http://www.vam.ac.uk/content/articles/t/the-crystal-palace/.

30. "The Great Exhibition: Queen Victoria's Journal," Victoria and Albert Museum online, accessed Spring, 2018. https://web.archive.org/web/20171028092223/ and http://www.vam.ac.uk/content/articles/g/great-exhibition-queen-victorias-journal/.

31. Thackeray, "May Day Ode," 41–43.

32. Author's visit to the Fontayne and Porter daguerreotype at the Public Library of Cincinnati, October 5, 2017. "Panorama of Progress: Building a City in the Photographic Age," Public Library of Cincinnati and Hamilton County online, accessed Fall 2017, https://1848.cincinnatilibrary.org/. It is possible, if not likely, that Robert knew Fontayne and Porter personally, even before traveling to the Great Exhibition. Cincinnati property records indicate that in the late 1850s, Fontayne and Porter owned a daguerreotype shop at 100 West Fourth Street in Cincinnati, the same street where Robert's own photography shop was located. Amanda Meyers, Genealogy and Local History Public Desk at the Public Library of Cincinnati, email to Adam Willis, March 15, 2018.

33. William B. Allen, *A History of Kentucky* (Louisville, KY: Bradley & Gilbert, 1872), 61–64; "Robertson, George," History, Art, & Archives: United States House of Representatives online, accessed Spring, 2018, https://history.house.gov/People/Listing/R/ROBERTSON, George-(R000322)/.

34. Sanders, "Judge George Robertson," Kentucky History, accessed Spring 2018, https://explorekyhistory.ky.gov/items/show/40; Yarbrough, *Judicial Enigma*, 23–24.

35. Alan Westin, "John Marshall Harlan and the Constitutional Rights of Negroes: The Transformation of a Southerner," *Yale Journal* 66, no. 5 (1957): 639; George Robertson, "Lecture on the Powers of Congress and the Resolutions of '98,'" *Scrap Book on Law and Politics, Men and Times* (Lexington, KY: A. W. Elder, 1855), 245–56, https://www.google.com/books/edition/Scrap_Book_on_Law_and_Politics_Men_and_T/ZSsVAAAAYAAJ?hl=en&gbpv=1&dq=%22Scrap+Book+on+Law+and+Politics,+Men+and+Times%22&printsec=frontcover.

36. "The Kentucky Resolutions of 1798," the Papers of Thomas Jefferson, accessed Spring, 2018, https://jeffersonpapers.princeton.edu/selected-documents/kentucky-resolutions-1798.

37. Robertson, "Lecture on the Powers of Congress and the Resolutions of '98,'" 245–56.

38. Tyler Anbinder, *Nativism and Slavery: The Northern Know Nothings and the Politics of Slavery* (New York: Oxford University Press, 1992), 44–46.

39. Westin, "John Marshall Harlan and the Constitutional Rights of Negroes," 639. For further analysis of John's relationship to Robertson, see Farrelly, "Harlan's Formative Period," 376–78.

40. Autobiographical Typescript, 4–5, John Marshall Harlan Papers, Library of Congress.

41. "Brief Biography Col. Rob't. Harlan," *Union*; "Colonel Robert N. Harlan," *Cincinnati Commercial,* September 8, 1881.

42. James Gordon, "Did the First Justice Harlan Have a Black Brother?," 182n73.

43. Descriptions of the Oakland Racetrack and its clubhouse are extrapolated from Robert Brammer and Augustus A. Von Smith, Oakland House and Racecourse, Louisville. Robert Brammer and Augustus A. Von Smith, Oakland House and Racecourse, Louisville, 1840, The National Racing Museum, Saratoga Springs, New York.

44. *Spirit of the Times,* July 2, 1853; *American Turf Register, 1845–1853,* 18–19.

45. Wall, *How Kentucky Became Southern,* 93.

46. O'Dell, "The Starting Post," 39.

47. Ibid., 55.

48. *Spirit of the Times,* July 2, 1853; *American Turf Register, 1845–1853,* 18–19; author's visit to Ashland, the Henry Clay Estate, June 24, 2017.

49. "Brief Biography Col. Rob't. Harlan," *Union;* "Colonel Robert N. Harlan," *Cincinnati Commercial,* September 8, 1881. For more on the prophecy of John's name, see Malvina Shanklin Harlan, *Some Memories of a Long Life,* 91.

50. "Brief Biography Col. Rob't. Harlan," *Union;* "Colonel Robert N. Harlan," *Cincinnati Commercial,* September 8, 1881.

51. Heidler and Heidler, *Henry Clay,* 428–40; Anbinder, *Nativism and Slavery,* 15; Nicole Etcheson, *Bleeding Kansas: Contested Liberty in the Civil War Era* (Lawrence: University Press of Kansas, 2004), 20–23. For analysis of the Whig Party's collapse, see Michael F. Holt, *Political Parties and American Political Development from the Age of Jackson to the Age of Lincoln* (Baton Rouge: Louisiana State University Press, 1992), 114–16; Aaron Astor, interviewed by Adam Willis, August 15, 2018, and August 30, 2018.

52. Klotter, interviewed by Adam Willis, August 6, 2018; Astor, interviewed by Adam Willis, August 15, 2018, and August 30, 2018; Gil Troy, "How an Outsider President Killed a Political Party," *Politico* online, last modified June 2, 2016, https://www.politico.com/magazine/story/2016/06/history-campaign-politics-zachary-taylor-killed-whigs-political-party-213935.

53. Jack K. Bauer, *Zachary Taylor: Soldier, Planter, Statesman of the Old Southwest,* rev. ed. (Baton Rouge: Louisiana State University Press, 1993), 314–27; Eisenhower, *Zachary Taylor,* 130–40.

54. Eisenhower, *Zachary Taylor,* 139–40.

55. Heidler and Heidler, *Henry Clay,* xxii–xxiv, 485–86, 491–92.

56. Autobiographical letter from John Marshall Harlan to Richard Davenport Harlan, July 1911, 7, Harlan Papers, Library of Congress.

57. Astor, interviewed by Adam Willis, August 15, 2018, and August 30, 2018; Klotter, interviewed by Adam Willis, August 6, 2018.

58. "1852 Presidential Election," 270toWin, accessed Summer, 2018. https://www.270towin.com/1852_Election/; Astor, interviewed by Adam Willis, August 15, 2018, and August 30, 2018; Klotter, interviewed by Adam Willis, August 6, 2018; "Person: Winfield Scott," National Park Service online, last modified August 23, 2019, https://www.nps.gov/people/winfield-scott.htm.

59. Lourainne Boissoneault, "How the 19th-Century Know Nothing Party Reshaped American Politics," *Smithsonian* online, last modified January 26, 2017, https://www.smithsonianmag.com/history/immigrants-conspiracies-and-secret-society-launched-american-nativism-180961915/.

60. Anbinder, *Nativism and Slavery,* 18.

61. Aaron Astor, *Rebels on the Border: Civil War, Emancipation, and the Reconstruction of Kentucky and Missouri* (Baton Rouge: Louisiana State University Press, 2012), 29.

62. Campbell, "John Marshall Harlan's Political Memoir," 308.

63. Boissoneault, "How the 19th-Century Know Nothing Party Reshaped American Politics."

64. Campbell, "John Marshall Harlan's Political Memoir," 306–8.

65. Astor, interviewed by Adam Willis, August 15, 2018; Anbinder, *Nativism and Slavery,* 34–37.

66. Campbell, "John Marshall Harlan's Political Memoir," 306–8.

67. "Correspondence of the *Louisville Democrat,*" *Louisville* (KY) *Daily Democrat,* July 20, 1848; "Correspondence of the *Louisville Democrat,*" *Louisville* (KY) *Daily Democrat,* May 24, 1855.

68. Campbell, "John Marshall Harlan's Political Memoir," 308.

69. "Speech of John M. Harlan, Esq.," *Kentucky Tribune* (Danville, KY), July 13, 1855.

70. Campbell, "John Marshall Harlan's Political Memoir," 308–310.

71. "Special Notices," *Kentucky Tribune* (Danville, KY), July 6, 1855. Kentucky newspapers published schedules of John's rigorous speaking tour around the state, providing a valuable record of his movements traceable nearly to the day.

72. "From Anderson County," *Louisville* (KY) *Courier*, July 7, 1855; Campbell, "John Marshall Harlan's Political Memoir," 308–310.

73. Wallace S. Hutcheon, Jr., "The Louisville Riots of August, 1855," *Register of the Kentucky Historical Society* 69, no. 2 (April 1971): 150–72.

74. "Bloody Work," *Louisville* (KY) *Journal*, 1855.

75. "Are We to Have a Dictator?" *Louisville* (KY) *Courier*, August 6, 1855.

76. "Another Decision Against Mr. Harlan," *Louisville* (KY) *Courier*, August 6, 1855; "John M. Harlan Nominated for Congress in Ashland District," *Louisville* (KY) *Courier*, May 19, 1859. In an email to the Adam Willis, dated August 14, 2018, James C. Klotter suggested that the "Frankfort Clique" term was deployed as a blanket disparagement for "a small group of Whigs" that included John C. Crittenden, Robert P. Letcher, and Orlando Brown, in addition to the Harlans.

77. Boissoneault, "How the 19th-Century Know Nothing Party Reshaped American Politics."

78. Lowell H. Harrison, "Charles S. Morehead," in *The Kentucky Encyclopedia*, ed. John E. Kleber (Lexington: University Press of Kentucky, 1992), 648. See also Hutcheon, "Louisville Riots of August, 1855," 150–72.

79. Campbell, "John Marshall Harlan's Political Memoir," 306–7.

CHAPTER 4: DREAD AND DRED SCOTT

1. "Judge John Marshall Harlan, Supreme Court," 1877, Portrait, Brady-Handy photograph collection, Library of Congress, Washington, DC.

2. Malvina Shanklin Harlan, *Some Memories of a Long Life*, 3–7.

3. Farrelly, "Harlan's Formative Period," 378–79.

4. Malvina Shanklin Harlan, *Some Memories of a Long Life*, 7–8.

5. Ibid., 10.

6. Ibid., 15; Denis and Weaver-Miner, "Dragging Fact from Fiction."

7. Malvina Shanklin Harlan, *Some Memories of a Long Life*, 22–25, 28.

8. Ibid., 14–22.

9. Ibid., 14–15, 27.

10. Ibid., 26.

11. Ibid., 30.

12. "Can't Take Care of Themselves," *Independent Democrat* (Concord, NH), May 15, 1856.

13. Malvina Shanklin Harlan, *Some Memories of a Long Life*, 21–22, 244n9.

14. Etcheson, *Bleeding Kansas*, 113–15.

15. Ibid., 100–111.

16. Joanne Freeman, *The Field of Blood: Violence in Congress and the Road to Civil War* (New York: Farrar, Straus and Giroux, 2018), 217–34; Anbinder, *Nativism and Slavery*, 214.

17. "Stampede of Slaves," *Cincinnati Enquirer*, January 29, 1856.

18. Ron Gorman, "Lucy Stone and the Margaret Garner Tragedy," Oberlin Heritage Center online, last modified September 21, 2013, http://www.oberlinheritagecen ter.org/blog/2013/09/lucy-stone-and-the-margaret-garner-tragedy/.

19. "Reviving the Old Whig Party," *New York Herald*, April 22, 1856, 4, https://www .newspapers.com/image/329320962/?terms=%22Reviving%20the%20Old%20 Whig%20Party%22&match=1.

20. Anbinder, *Nativism and Slavery*, 167, 170–71.

21. Ibid., 219.

22. Robert J. Rayback, *Millard Fillmore: Biography of a President* (self-pub., 2017), 406–8.

23. "Another Big Fillmore Meeting!—Speech from John M. Harlan, Esq.," *Evansville (IN) Daily Journal*, April 3, 1856.

24. Astor, interviewed by Adam Willis, August 15, 2018, and August 30, 2018. For more on the Know-Nothing Party in the presidential election of 1856, see Anbinder, *Nativism and Slavery*, 220–45. For analysis of the Know-Nothings' rapid decline, see Anbinder, *Nativism and Slavery*, 218–19.

25. For more on Roger B. Taney's military career beneath Andrew Jackson, see Carl Brent Swisher, *Roger B. Taney* (New York: Macmillan, 1935), 119–31. For more on Taney's service in Jackson's cabinet, see Swisher, 132–59. For more on Taney's work as Treasury secretary, see Swisher, 160–305. For more on Taney's appointment to the Supreme Court, see Swisher, 306–25. For more on Taney's jurisprudence, see Charles W. Smith, *Roger B. Taney: Jacksonian Jurist* (Chapel Hill: University of North Carolina Press, 1936), 3–21.

26. "Dred Scott's Fight for Freedom," *PBS: Africans in America*, https://www.pbs.org /wgbh/aia/part4/4p2932.html.

27. *Dred Scott v. John F.A. Sandford*, 60 U.S. 393, 1857.

28. Ibid.

29. Ibid.

30. Benjamin Curtis, Dissenting Opinion, "Dred Scott v. John F.A. Sandford," 60 U.S. 393, 1857.

31. *Dred Scott v. John F. A. Sandford*, 60 U.S. 393, 1857.

32. Ibid.

33. "Benjamin R. Curtis," Oyez Project, accessed Winter, 2019, www.oyez.org/justices /benjamin_r_curtis.

34. Gilbert H. Muller, *William Cullen Bryant: Author of America* (Albany: State University of New York, 2008), 241.

35. *Dred Scott v. John F.A. Sandford*, 60 U.S. 393, 1857.

36. "Meeting of the East End Colored Grant Club," *Cincinnati Commercial*, September 6, 1872. Robert recalls his first meeting with political rival Peter Clark, when Clark was still a young man working as "a clerk at Mr. Wilcox's grocery," the shop below Robert's first Cincinnati home. Robert recounts that he "took a liking" to Clark, "believing him to be a young man of promise," and offered him a $500 loan, which Clark declined. But Clark would return years later to request a loan, which Robert gave him. For more examples of Robert's business patronage within Cincinnati's Black community, see his ownership of the photography studio with John Presley Ball, cited in notes 43 and 45, and his proprietorship of the Dumas House. See also Wendell Phillips Dabney, *Cincinnati's Colored Citizens* (Cincinnati: Dabney, 1926), 25, and "Old Residences Which Have Been

Replaced by Modern Business Structures," *Cincinnati Enquirer*, September 28, 1924.

37. For sources that name Robert as the landlord of the Dumas House, see Dabney, *Cincinnati's Colored Citizens*, 25; "Old Residences," *Cincinnati Enquirer*, September 28, 1924. For a deeper history of the Dumas House and those who associated there, see "Club Life Among the Colored Men," *Cincinnati Enquirer*, April 15, 1900.

38. "Club Life Among Colored Men," *Cincinnati Enquirer*, April 15, 1900.

39. Ibid.

40. Ibid. recounts that "a powerful section of the leaders in the Underground Railroad had its headquarters" at the Dumas and notes that the hotel's labyrinthine hallways, "many turns and twists, and out of the way nooks" made it an ideal hideaway for runaway slaves. "None that ever had the good fortune to find shelter in the Dumas House was ever taken back to bondage."

41. Greg Hand, "An Escaped Slave Returned to Cincinnati in Disguise and Fooled Even Levi Coffin," Cincinnati Curiosities, last modified February 9, 2015, https://handeaux.tumblr.com/post/110540034622/an-escaped-slave-returned-to-cincinnati-in.

42. "Club Life Among Colored Men," *Cincinnati Enquirer*, April 15, 1900.

43. "Local Notices," *Cincinnati Enquirer*, October 21, 1857.

44. "J. P. Ball, African American Photographer," Cincinnati Museum Center online, accessed Fall, 2017, http://library.cincymuseum.org/ball/jpball.htm.

45. "Local Notices," *Cincinnati Enquirer*, December 19, 1857. By late October 1857, Robert was no longer advertising with J. P. Ball. See "Local Notices," *Cincinnati Enquirer*, October 21, 1857; "Half-price Premium Photographs," *Cincinnati Commercial Tribune*, November 23, 1857; "Robert Harlan's Gallery of Art," *Cincinnati Enquirer*, April 4, 1858.

46. For prominent examples of Robert's political rivalries in Cincinnati's Black community, see "The Colored Battalion," *Cincinnati Gazette*, September 9, 1870; "The Meeting of the Colored Braves," *Cincinnati Enquirer*, September, 1872; "The Man and Brother," *Cincinnati Enquirer*, September 6, 1872; "Meeting of the East End Colored Grant Club," *Cincinnati Commercial*, September 6, 1872; "Hon. Robert Harlan," *Cleveland Gazette*, May 14, 1887; "Triplett vs. Harlan," *Cleveland Gazette*, June 4, 1887.

47. U. P. Hedrick, *Manual of American Grape-Growing* (New York: Macmillan, 1919), 8.

48. "On Abe's 200th Birthday, We Remember . . . Lincoln's Lousy Week," *Cincinnati Enquirer*, February 12, 2009, 2.

49. Nikki M. Taylor, *Frontiers of Freedom*, 45; Shepherd, interviewed by Adam Willis, February 14, 2018.

50. "Meeting with the East End Colored Grant Club," *Cincinnati Commercial*, September 6, 1872; "Colonel Robert N. Harlan," *Cincinnati Commercial*, September 8, 1881; "Col. Robert Harlan, Member of the Ohio Legislature," *Cleveland Gazette*, May 1, 1886. See also *Ninth Annual Report of the Board of Trustees for the Colored Public Schools of Cincinnati for the School Year Ending June 30, 1858*, Cincinnati History Museum. For more on the East Side Seventh Street School House and Nicholas Longworth's involvement in its construction, see L. D. Easton, "The Colored Schools of Cincinnati," in *History of Cincinnati Public Schools*, ed. Isaac M. Martin (Cincinnati: Board of Education, 1900), 185–87.

51. Autobiographical letter from John Marshall Harlan to Richard Davenport Harlan, July 1911, Harlan Papers, Library of Congress.

52. "Another Big Fillmore Meeting!—Speech from John M. Harlan, Esq.," *Evansville Daily Journal*, April 3, 1856.

53. Plessy v. Ferguson, 163 U.S. 537 (1896).

54. Owen, "Pre-Court Career of John Marshall Harlan," 11–22; Westin, "John Marshall Harlan and the Political Rights of Negroes," 642–44.

55. Yarbrough, *Judicial Enigma*, 28.

56. Anbinder, *Nativism and Slavery*, 146.

57. Campbell, "John Marshall Harlan's Political Memoir," 310–11; Yarbrough, *Judicial Enigma*, 31–34.

58. "The Discussion of Thursday," *Western Citizen* (Paris, KY), June 10, 1859; Yarbrough, *Judicial Enigma*, 33–34.

59. Westin, "John Marshall Harlan and the Constitutional Rights of Negroes," 643.

60. "Capt. Simms at Paris," *Louisville* (KY) *Courier*, June 7, 1859. For John's own account of his campaign against Simms, see Campbell, "John Marshall Harlan's Political Memoir," 310–12.

61. "A Misrepresentation Corrected," *Frankfort* (KY) *Tri-Weekly Commonwealth*, July 29, 1859 ("n----r" is spelled out in the original document). See also Yarbrough, *Judicial Enigma*, 34.

62. Westin, "John Marshall Harlan and the Constitutional Rights of Negroes," 642n16.

63. Yarbrough, *Judicial Enigma*, 35–36.

64. Ibid., 37.

65. "Turf Intelligence," *Memphis Daily Avalanche*, February 17, 1859; "Harlan and His Horses," *Cincinnati Commercial Tribune*, April 23, 1859; "Gone to Foreign Parts," *Cincinnati Commercial Tribune*, June 22, 1858; *New-York Times*, June 24, 1858; "List of Passengers," *Liverpool Daily Post* (UK), July 5, 1858. According to 1850s newspaper clips, Robert took scouting trips to Europe in each of the three years before his move across the Atlantic. See also "Brief Biography Col. Rob't. Harlan," *Union*. For reports of Robert's Thoroughbred purchases, see "Sale of Kentucky Race Horses," *Memphis Daily Avalanche*, November 23, 1858; "Kentucky Race Horses for England," *Ohio Farmer*, November 27, 1858; and *New Orleans Picayune*, November 25, 1858.

66. Interview with British racing historians Tim Cox and David Oldrey at Newmarket, March 9, 2018; "The History of the Palace House, the Kings Yard and Rothschild Yard," *Palace House, Newmarket*, https://www.palacehousenewmarket.co.uk/palace-house/history-of-the-site.

67. "Sale of Kentucky Race Horses," *Memphis Avalanche*, November 23, 1858. Republished from a report that first appeared in the *Louisville* (KY) *Daily Courier*.

68. *New Orleans Picayune*, November 25, 1858.

69. "More Horses for the British Turf," *Liberator* (Boston), January 7, 1859. See also Mooney, *Race Horse Men*, 103–4.

70. "Turf Intelligence," *Memphis Daily Avalanche*, February 17, 1859.

71. *American Turf Register, 1858*, 27–28. Robert likely attended Kentucky races in 1858 to scout his new stable. At October's Produce Stakes in Lexington, he would have had the chance to see two future purchases: Lincoln, entered by the famed horseman John Harper, and the filly Des Chiles, entered by Jason L. Bradley, the same owner from whom Robert would buy the horse. See "Concluded To-morrow," *Memphis Daily Avalanche*, November 23, 1858. Des Chiles won both heats of the three-year-old Produce Stake, while Lincoln beat a field of horses that included

entries by R. A. Alexander, author of the American studbook, and John M. Clay, son of Henry Clay.

72. Goodwin, *Team of Rivals: The Political Genius of Abraham Lincoln* (New York: Simon & Schuster, 2006), 237–56.

73. "Sporting on Dit," *Cincinnati Commercial Tribune*, February 14, 1859.

74. "Richard Ten Broeck Dead," *San Francisco Call*, August 2, 1892. For more on Ten Broeck's proprietorship of Metairie, see Hollingsworth, *Kentucky Thoroughbred*, 25, and Mooney, *Race Horse Men*, 90–94.

75. Hollingsworth, *Kentucky Thoroughbred*, 25–32; "Richard Ten Broeck Dead," *San Francisco Call*, August, 2, 1892; John K. Ward, "£10 and Guts," *The Thoroughbred of California*, vol. 76, 1985.

76. Longrigg, *The History of Horse Racing*, 216–19, courtesy of Tim Cox, email to Adam Willis, March 11, 2018.

77. John K. Ward, "£10 and Guts," *The Thoroughbred of California*, vol. 76, 1985. The article published in Ward's book draws on memoirs Ten Broeck wrote from his deathbed, in which he reflected on his life and career in the horse-racing world. See also "Prioress," *Thoroughbred Heritage*, http://www.tbheritage.com/Portraits /Prioress.html.

78. "Racing Intelligence," *Louisville Courier*, February 22, 1859, republished from the *Cincinnati Enquirer*; Jeff Suess, "Our History: Spirit of History Alive at Burnet House Site," *Cincinnati Enquirer* online, last modified November 15, 2017, https:// www.cincinnati.com/story/news/2017/11/15/our-history-spirit-history-alive-bur net-house-site/866470001/.

79. "Racing Intelligence," *Louisville Courier*, February 22, 1859.

80. "Brief Biography Col. Rob't. Harlan," *Union*; *New-York Times*, March 4, 1859, re-ports that Robert and Ten Broeck were scheduled to sail on the next departure of the *City of Manchester*.

81. For descriptions of the *City of Manchester*, see "S/S City of Manchester, Inman Line," *Norway-Heritage*, http://www.norwayheritage.com/p_ship.asp?sh=cimanl; "Inman Line," *The Ship List*, http://www.theshipslist.com/ships/lines/inman .shtml; "Ship Descriptions," *The Ship List*, http://www.theshipslist.com/ships/de scriptions/ShipsCC.shtml; William H. Flayhart, *The American Line (1871–1902)* (New York: W. W. Norton, 2000), 115, 126.

82. "Eventful Life of Robert Harlan," 6; "Brief Biography Col. Rob't. Harlan," *Union*; "Im-portation of Blood and Other First Class Horses from America," *Liverpool* (UK) *Daily Post*, March 24, 1859; "American Horses," *Waterford Mail* (UK), March 29, 1859.

83. "To Correspondents: Mr. Harlan," *Spirit of the Times*, October 1, 1859.

CHAPTER 5: THE SOUL OF KENTUCKY

1. Yarbrough, *Judicial Enigma*, 38.

2. Ibid., 40.

3. James M. Prichard, *Embattled Capital: Frankfort Kentucky in the Civil War* (Frankfort, KY: Frankfort Heritage Press, 2014), 11.

4. Ibid., 14. For more on the Secession Crisis in Kentucky, see "Abraham Lincoln and the Secession Crisis in Kentucky," the Filson Historical Society online, Fall, 2018, https://web.archive.org/web/20160721203830/https://filsonhistorical.org/abra ham-lincoln-and-the-secession-crisis-in-kentucky-2/.

5. Malvina Shanklin Harlan, *Some Memories of a Long Life*, 47–50.

6. Lowell H. Harrison, "Governor Magoffin and the Secession Crisis," *Register of the Kentucky Historical Society* 72, no. 2 (1974): 97.

7. Ibid., 91–94, 100.

8. Autobiographical letter from John Marshall Harlan to Richard Davenport Harlan, July 1911, 8, Harlan Papers, Library of Congress.

9. Harrison, "Governor Magoffin and the Secession Crisis," 91–110; Thomas Speed, *The Union Cause in Kentucky* (New York: G. P. Putnam's Sons, 1907), 117; Malvina Shanklin Harlan, *Some Memories of a Long Life*, 47–48.

10. Autobiographical letter from John Marshall Harlan to Richard Davenport Harlan, July 1911, 8–9, Harlan Papers, Library of Congress.

11. "First Inaugural Address of Abraham Lincoln," March 4, 1861, https://avalon.law .yale.edu/19th_century/lincoln1.asp.

12. Abraham Lincoln to Orville Browning, September 22, 1861, https://quod.lib .umich.edu/l/lincoln/lincoln4/1:1003.1?rgn=div2;view=fulltext.

13. James M. McPherson, *Battle Cry of Freedom: The Civil War Era* (New York: Oxford University Press, 1988), 264–74; "Fort Sumter," American Battlefield Trust online, accessed Fall, 2018, https://www.battlefields.org/learn/civil-war/battles/fort -sumter.

14. Ulrich Bonnell Phillips, *The Life of Robert Toombs* (New York: Macmillan, 1913), 234–35.

15. Ibid., 236–37.

16. Autobiographical letter from John Marshall Harlan to Richard Davenport Harlan, July 1911, 7–9, Harlan Papers, Library of Congress; Yarbrough, *Judicial Enigma*, 39–41.

17. "Farmington Historic Plantation," American Battlefield Trust online, accessed Fall, 2018, https://www.battlefields.org/visit/heritage-sites/farmington-historic-plan tation; "Slavery at Farmington"; *Farmington Historic Home*, https://www.historic farmington.org/slavery.html.

18. Goodwin, *Team of Rivals*, 57–59.

19. Joseph C. G. Kennedy, *Population of the United States in 1860: Compiled from the Original Returns of the Eighth Census* (Washington, DC: Government Printing Office, 1864), 182.

20. Autobiographical letter from John Marshall Harlan to Richard Davenport Harlan, July 1911, 8–9, Harlan Papers, Library of Congress. See also Speed, *Union Cause in Kentucky*, 116–21. Captain Thomas Speed's account of the Unionist movement in Kentucky on the brink of war contains John's written reflection on his own efforts, in collaboration with Joshua and James Speed, to hold Kentucky within the Union as other slaveholding states broke away into the Confederacy.

21. Speed, *Union Cause in Kentucky*, 116–21.

22. Glenn W. LaFantasie, "The Confederacy Comes for Kentucky," *Salon*, last modified May 18, 2011, https://www.salon.com/2011/05/18/jefferson_davis_kentucky/.

23. Speed, *Union Cause in Kentucky*, 116–21; Daniel Stevenson, "General Nelson, Kentucky, and Lincoln Guns," *Magazine of American History* 10, no. 2 (August 1883): 115–39.

24. Autobiographical letter from John Marshall Harlan to Richard Davenport Harlan, July 1911, 9, Harlan Papers, Library of Congress; Yarbrough, *Judicial Enigma*, 44–45. For more on the Civil War regiment Zouaves, see "Regiments of the Civil War,"

American Battlefield Trust online, accessed Fall, 2018, https://www.battlefields
.org/learn/articles/regiments-civil-war.

25. Beth, *John Marshall Harlan*, 46–47.

26. Carol Sutton, "George D. Prentice: Great Man or Great Villain?," *Louisville* (KY)
Courier-Journal, September 18, 1955, sec. 3, p. 1; David G. Farrelly, "John Marshall
Harlan and the Union Cause in Kentucky," *Filson Club History Quarterly* 37, no. 1
(1963): 11–12; Yarbrough, *Judicial Enigma*, 42.

27. Farrelly, "Harlan and the Union Cause in Kentucky," 11; Beth, *John Marshall Harlan*, 48.

28. Farrelly, "Harlan and the Union Cause in Kentucky," 11–12; Yarbrough, *Judicial
Enigma*, 42.

29. Ibid., 11–14; Sutton, "George D. Prentice," sec. 3, p. 10.

30. Farrelly, "Harlan and the Union Cause in Kentucky," 14.

31. Ibid.; Beth, *John Marshall Harlan*, 47.

32. Flayhart, *American Line*, 126, notes that the *City of Manchester* took as many as
forty days on its first Atlantic crossing in 1851, but that she had cut the time to
"well under two weeks" in 1852.

33. Ibid., 114; "American Horses," *Waterford Mail* (UK), March 29, 1859, courtesy of
Tim Cox and David Oldrey, email to Adam Willis, October 1, 2017.

34. "Church of Our Lady and Saint Nicholas," *Historic England*, https://historicen
gland.org.uk/listing/the-list/list-entry/1205993; "Panoramic views of Liverpool,
1860," *National Museums Liverpool*, https://www.liverpoolmuseums.org.uk/mar
itime/archive/highlights/liverpool-panoramic-photo.aspx.

35. "Importation of Blood and Other First Class Horses from America," *Liverpool
Daily Post* (UK), March 24, 1859, courtesy of Cox and Oldrey, email to Adam Willis, October 1, 2017.

36. Ibid. The *Liverpool Daily Post* provided the pedigrees of both Ten Broeck and Robert's stables: "The thoroughbreds belonging to Mr. Ten Broeck are:- Ch. c. Starke,
4 yrs, by Wagner, out of Reel; and ch.c. by Lexington, 2 yrs, dam by Glencoe. The
qualities of Starke have been well tested on the American turf, and the price given
for him by Mr. Ten Broeck, 7,500 dollars, speaks forcibly as to his past and present owner's estimation of what he is worth. The Lexington colt is a fine two-year-
old, and full of promise. The same class of animals brought by Mr. Harlan are Des
Chiles, a three-year-old filly, by Glencoe, out of Brown Kitty, by Imp. Birmingham;
Cincinnati, a two-year-old, by Star Davis (he by Glencoe) out of Waitress [The-
atress], by Muckle John, out of Old Lady Jackson. Of the trotters in each lot, we
need say no more than that they exhibit every indication of being able to sustain
the high character established by American trotting horses in this country."

37. "American Horses," *Waterford Mail* (UK), March 29, 1859, courtesy of Cox and
Oldrey, email to Adam Willis, October 1, 2017.

38. J. H. Walsh, *The Horse in the Stable and the Field* (London: G. Rutledge and Sons,
1907), 89–90; Tim Cox and David Oldrey, interviewed by author, March 9, 2018,
Newmarket, England.

39. *Bell's Life in London and Sporting Chronicle*, August 21, 1859.

40. Cox and Oldrey, interviewed by author, March 9, 2018.

41. Ibid.

42. Ibid. While there is little to suggest that Robert and Ten Broeck were unwelcome
in the British racing world, they broke into a stodgy and insular British racing
aristocracy, and animosity toward the influx of foreigners that followed on their

heels developed over the next half century. See also "The Jersey Act," *Sport Horse Breeder*, https://www.sport-horse-breeder.com/jersey-act.html.

43. Cox and Oldrey, interviewed by author, March 9, 2018.

44. William Day, *The Racehorse in Training* (London: Chapman and Hall, 1885), 110–12, courtesy of Cox, email to Adam Willis, March 11, 2018.

45. *The British Racing Calendar, 1859*, vol. 87, 80.

46. "Importation of Blood and Other First Class Horses from America," *Liverpool* (UK) *Daily Post*, March 24, 1859; *Belfast News-Letter*, August 18, 1859; *Ulster Gazette*, September 3, 1859. All courtesy of Cox and Oldrey, emailed to Adam Willis, October 1, 2017. See also Cox and Oldrey, interviewed by author, March 9, 2018.

47. "Trotting in England," *Sporting Life*, August 3, 1859; "The Great Trotting Match Against Time for 800 Sovs.," *Birmingham* (UK) *Daily Post*, August 15, 1859. All courtesy of Cox and Oldrey, email to Adam Willis, October 1, 2017.

48. *Bell's Life in London and Sporting Chronicle*, August 21, 1859.

49. *Belfast News-Letter*, August 18, 1859, courtesy of Cox and Oldrey, email to Adam Willis, October 1, 2017.

50. "The Great Trotting Races at Aintree," *Liverpool Mercury* (UK), August 26, 1859, courtesy of Cox and Oldrey, email to Adam Willis, October 1, 2017.

51. Ibid.

52. "Liverpool Grand Trotting Races," *Sporting Life*, August 27, 1859, courtesy of Cox and Oldrey, email to Adam Willis, October 1, 2017.

53. "The Great Trotting Races at Aintree," *Liverpool Mercury* (UK), August 26, 1859.

54. For reports on the sale of Jack Rossiter at Tattersall's, see *Bell's Life*, July 8, 1860, and *Belfast News-Letter*, August 8, 1860.

55. *The British Racing Calendar, 1859*, vol. 87, 197, 284–85. Robert did not own the horse Ochiltree when he set out for England. By the time of a July 19 meeting in Nottingham, he had acquired the new horse, seemingly from a Mr. Angell, who had most recently raced the horse. In the late summer of 1859, Ochiltree won several races for Robert, taking first place at the Derby Summer Meeting, against 7-to-4 odds, and the Selling Stakes, against 5 to 4 odds. See British *Racing Calendar, 1859*, vol. 87, 284–85, 286–87.

56. "Mr. Ten Broeck and Mr. Robert Harlan," *Louisville* (KY) *Daily Courier*, March 21, 1859. For reports on Ten Broeck's disappointing early performance in England, see *Liverpool Mercury* (UK), August 26, 1859; *Sporting Life*, August 27, 1859; *Ulster Gazette*, September 3, 1859. All courtesy of Cox and Oldrey, email to Adam Willis, October 1, 2017.

57. "Deaths," *London Morning Post*, March 1, 1861; author's visit to Canonbury Villas, London, March 11, 2018.

58. Malvina Shanklin Harlan, *Some Memories of a Long Life*, 52; "Gen. Polk's Invasion—Views of the Union Men of Kentucky," *New-York Times*, September 12, 1861.

59. Malvina Shanklin Harlan, *Some Memories of a Long Life*, 51, 59–60.

60. Ibid., 59–60.

61. Ibid., 52, 59–60.

62. Ibid., 60.

63. Ibid., 62.

64. Autobiographical letter from John Marshall Harlan to Richard Davenport Harlan, July 1911, 10–11, Harlan Papers, Library of Congress; "To the People of Kentucky!—Camp Crittenden," *Louisville Daily Democrat*, October 9, 1861.

65. "Kentuckians Won't Volunteer for Lincoln," *Louisville* (KY) *Daily Courier*, November 13, 1861.

66. "Affairs in the Interior of the State," *Louisville* (KY) *Daily Courier*, October 29, 1861.

67. Malvina Shanklin Harlan, *Some Memories of a Long Life*, 72. See also Campbell, "John Marshall Harlan's Political Memoir," 318.

68. Speed, *Union Cause in Kentucky*, 195–99; Yarbrough, *Judicial Enigma*, 53.

69. Champ Clark, *My Quarter Century of American Politics*, vol. 1 (New York: Harper & Brothers, 1920), 64–66.

70. Autobiographical letter from John Marshall Harlan to Richard Davenport Harlan, July 1911, 22–27, Harlan Papers, Library of Congress. See also Yarbrough, *Judicial Enigma*, 45–46. For John's account of his time with General Sherman at Lebanon Junction, see Peter Scott Campbell, "The Civil War Reminiscences of John Marshall Harlan," *Journal of Supreme Court History*, 32:3, 269–71.

71. Dennis W. Belcher, *The 10th Kentucky Volunteer Infantry in the Civil War: A History and Roster* (Jefferson, NC: MacFarland, 2009), 8; Yarbrough, *Judicial Enigma*, 47.

72. For more on life at Camp Crittenden, see Belcher, *The 10th Kentucky Volunteer Infantry in the Civil War*, 8–14.

73. Yarbrough, *Judicial Enigma*, 48.

74. "Battle of Somerset at Mill Spring," *Son of the South*, http://www.sonofthesouth.net/leefoundation/civil-war/1862/february/battle-mill-spring-somerset.htm; Currier & Ives, "Battle of Mill Spring, K.Y., January 19, 1862," Undated, *Damour Museum of Fine Arts*, https://springfieldmuseums.org/collections/item/battle-of-mill-spring-k-y-jan-19th-1862-currier-ives/.

75. Autobiographical letter from John Marshall Harlan to Richard Davenport Harlan, July 1911, 11–12, Harlan Papers, Library of Congress; Prichard, *Embattled Capital*, 41.

76. "Zollicoffer, Felix Kirk," Biographical Directory of the United States Congress, http://bioguide.congress.gov/scripts/biodisplay.pl?index=z000012; "Death of Felix K. Zollicoffer," *Experience Mill Springs Battlefield*, https://www.millsprings.net/index.php/2013-10-01-18-24-22/death-of-gen-felix-k-zollicoffer. For an overview of the battle at Mill Springs, see also "Battle of Mill Springs," *Experience Mill Springs Battlefield*, https://www.millsprings.net/index.php/2013-10-01-18-24-22/battle-of-mill-springs.

77. Autobiographical letter from John Marshall Harlan to Richard Davenport Harlan, July 1911, 13–17, Harlan Papers, Library of Congress.

78. McPherson, *Battle Cry of Freedom*, 405–16.

79. Autobiographical letter from John Marshall Harlan to Richard Davenport Harlan, July 1911, 16–17, Harlan Papers, Library of Congress.

80. "Battle of Shiloh: Shattering Myths," American Battlefield Trust online, accessed Fall, 2018, https://www.battlefields.org/learn/articles/battle-shiloh-shattering-myths. See also McPherson, *Battle Cry of Freedom*, 405–17.

81. Autobiographical letter from John Marshall Harlan to Richard Davenport Harlan, July 1911, 17–18, Harlan Papers, Library of Congress.

82. Ron Chernow, *Grant* (New York: Penguin Press, 2017), 193, 199–207, 211–12.

83. McPherson, *Battle Cry of Freedom*, 510.

84. "Epsom Summer Meeting," *The British Racing Calendar, 1859*, vol. 87, 108–9. In 1859 and 1860, the years Robert was most active in the British racing scene, the Derby was held on June 1, 1859, with a winners prize £6,600, and May 23, 1860,

with a winners prize £6,050. Another prestigious race, the Oaks, was also held annually at Epsom, on June 3, 1859, with a winners prize of £4,295, and on May 25, 1860, with a winners prize £3,995. Derby entry statistics courtesy of Michael Church, email to Adam Willis, April 5, 2018.

85. Michael Church, "Every Man's Derby Day Holiday," https://www.michael churchracingbooks.com/everymans-derby-day-holiday/; Tour of Epson Downs with Church, March 8, 2018.

86. "Epsom Summer Meeting," *The British Racing Calendar, 1859*, vol. 87, 108–9.

87. Analysis of the elite British horse racing community is based on the author's tour of Newmarket with Cox and Oldrey, March 9, 2018.

88. "Latest on Doncaster," *Sporting Life*, September 14, 1859; "English Classics," Encyclopedia Britannica, https://www.britannica.com/sports/English-Classics; "Classic Races," *Horseracing*, http://www.horseracing.co.uk/horse-racing/flat-racing/classic-races.html.

89. Day, *The Racehorse in Training*, 110–12; Day, *Turf Celebrities I Have Known*, 220–21. All courtesy of Cox, email to Adam Willis, March 11, 2018.

90. "The Doncaster Meeting—Yesterday," *Sporting Life*, September 14, 1859; "Wednesday—The Great St. Leger," *Sporting Life*, September 17, 1859.

91. "More Horses for the British Turf," *The Liberator*, January 7, 1859. For further evidence of Robert's judgment of horses, see "A Colored Man Interviews the President."

92. "Doncaster Meeting," *Illustrated London News*, September 17, 1859.

93. "Wednesday—The Great St. Leger," *Sporting Life*, September 17, 1859.

94. Ibid.

95. "Doncaster Meeting," *Illustrated London News*, September 17, 1859.

96. "Wednesday—The Great St. Leger," *Sporting Life*, September 17, 1859.

97. *Racing Times*, March 5, 1860.

98. Ibid.

99. Ibid.

100. "A Horse for Three," *New-York Times*, January 4, 1860.

101. Ibid.

102. "Horse for Three," *New-York Times*, January 4, 1860; *Racing Times*, March 5, 1860.

103. "Horse for Three," *New-York Times*, January 4, 1860.

104. Ibid.

105. "Bevins v. Harlan," *Spirit of the Times*, March 31, 1860.

106. "Horse for Three," *New-York Times*, January 4, 1860.

107. "Deaths," *London Morning Post*, March 1, 1861.

108. *Bell's Life*, July 8, 1860. Announced that Jack Rossiter was slated for auction, noting that "his owner has no further use for him." See also *Belfast News-Letter*, August 8, 1860. Reported that Robert finally sold Jack Rossiter for 90 guineas. All courtesy of Cox and Oldrey, email to Adam Willis, October 1, 2017. For more on Tattersalls, see "Houndbloggers Abroad: Tattersalls, home of the Fox," *Full Cry: A Hound Blog*, https://houndwelfare.wordpress.com/2009/10/10/houndbloggers-abroad-tattersalls-home-of-the-fox/. For more on the famous Fox of Tattersalls, see: http://www.drf.com/news/tattersalls-history-under-hammer.

CHAPTER 6: JOHN VS. JOHN

1. Autobiographical letter from John Marshall Harlan to Richard Davenport Harlan, July 1911, 18, Harlan Papers, Library of Congress.
2. Harry T. Williams, *Lincoln and His Generals* (New York: Vintage Civil War Library, 2011), 138, 147.
3. Autobiographical letter from John Marshall Harlan to Richard Davenport Harlan, July 1911, 18, Harlan Papers, Library of Congress.
4. Ibid., 18–19.
5. Campbell, "John Marshall Harlan's Political Memoir," 318–20.
6. *The War of the Rebellion*, Series I, vol. 16, part 2, p. 236.
7. Yarbrough, *Judicial Enigma*, 49.
8. Autobiographical letter from John Marshall Harlan to Richard Davenport Harlan, July 1911, 18–20, Harlan Papers, Library of Congress.
9. Astor, *Rebels on the Border*, 89–90. For more on the Confederate offensive in Kentucky, see Coulter, *Civil War and Readjustment in Kentucky*, 166–69.
10. Autobiographical letter from John Marshall Harlan to Richard Davenport Harlan, July 1911, 18–19, Harlan Papers, Library of Congress; Yarbrough, *Judicial Enigma*, 50.
11. Autobiographical letter from John Marshall Harlan to Richard Davenport Harlan, July 1911, 21, Harlan Papers, Library of Congress.
12. Autobiographical letter from John Marshall Harlan to Richard Davenport Harlan, July 1911, 21–24, Harlan Papers, Library of Congress; "Perryville," American Battlefield Trust online, accessed Fall, 2018, https://www.battlefields.org/learn/civil-war/battles/perryville; Yarbrough, *Judicial Enigma*, 50.
13. Autobiographical letter from John Marshall Harlan to Richard Davenport Harlan, July 1911, 28, Harlan Papers, Library of Congress; Yarbrough, *Judicial Enigma*, 50–51.
14. "John Hunt Morgan," *Ohio History Connection*, https://ohiohistorycentral.org/w/John_H._Morgan; "The Civil War—Confederate Kentucky Troops," *National Parks Service*, https://www.nps.gov/civilwar/search-battle-units-detail.htm?battleUnitCode=CKY0002RC01.
15. Autobiographical letter from John Marshall Harlan to Richard Davenport Harlan, July 1911, 25–26, Harlan Papers, Library of Congress; Yarbrough, *Judicial Enigma*, 51. For more on John Hunt Morgan's "Christmas Raid," see Prichard, *Embattled Capital*, 96.
16. Autobiographical letter from John Marshall Harlan to Richard Davenport Harlan, July 1911, 25–26, Harlan Papers, Library of Congress; Yarbrough, *Judicial Enigma*, 51–52. See also John's account of his clash with Morgan's Raiders in Speed, *Union Cause in Kentucky*, 230–33.
17. Autobiographical letter from John Marshall Harlan to Richard Davenport Harlan, July 1911, 25–29, Harlan Papers, Library of Congress; Yarbrough, *Judicial Enigma*, 53–54.
18. Ibid., 268.
19. Autobiographical letter from John Marshall Harlan to Richard Davenport Harlan, July 1911, 25–26, Harlan Papers, Library of Congress; Yarbrough, *Judicial Enigma*, 53–54. For an analysis of James Harlan's legal career, see Metzmeier and Campbell, "Nursery of a Supreme Court Justice," 639–48.
20. Autobiographical letter from John Marshall Harlan to Richard Davenport Harlan, July 1911, 25–27, Harlan Papers, Library of Congress. For more on the 1862 invasion of Frankfort, see Prichard, *Embattled Capital*, 107–8.

21. Autobiographical letter from John Marshall Harlan to Richard Davenport Harlan, July 1911, 25–27, Harlan Papers, Library of Congress. See also Malvina Shanklin Harlan, *Some Memories of a Long Life*, 63–67.

22. Autobiographical letter from John Marshall Harlan to Richard Davenport Harlan, July 1911, 25–26, Harlan Papers, Library of Congress. For an analysis of James Harlan's estate, see Metzmeier and Campbell, "Nursery of a Supreme Court Justice," 642–43.

23. Autobiographical letter from John Marshall Harlan to Richard Davenport Harlan, July 1911, 26–27, Harlan Papers, Library of Congress.

24. *Bell's Life*, July 8, 1860; *Belfast News-Letter*, August 8, 1860. All courtesy of Cox and Oldrey, email to Adam Willis, October 1, 2017. Jack Rossiter was sold at auction at Tattersall's a little less than a year after Robert ran him at Liverpool, *Bell's Life* noting that "his owner having no further use for him." "Sale of Bloodstock at Tattersall's on Monday Last," *Sporting Life*, December 7, 1859. "Only three animals were knocked down at Tattersall's on Monday, Lincoln, brought from America by Mr. Harlan, and which was supposed to be one of the fastest horses in America, being sold for 39 guineas!" For more on Tattersall's, see "Tattersall's," *Encyclopedia Britannica*, https://www.britannica.com/topic/Tattersalls.

25. "From Friday's Gazette, April 18—Bankrupts," *Blackburn Standard*, April 23, 1862; "Bankrupts," *London Evening Standard*, April 19, 1862; "Bankrupts," *Windsor and Eaton Express*, April 19, 1862; "Bankrupts to Surrender at the Bankrupts' Court, London," *Northampton Mercury*, April 26, 1862.

26. Elizabeth Velluet, honorary secretary of the Richmond Local History Society, email to Adam Willis, February 22, 2018, citing *Whibley's Richmond, Twickenham and Hampton Court Directory and Guide, 1865–1866*; "Royal Regt of Artillery," *Bell's Life in London and Sporting Chronicle*, April 20, 1862. Lists Robert as living at "The Vineyard," in Richmond, England. See also bankruptcy notices, *supra* note 25, which located Robert in Richmond.

27. Author's tour of Richmond, England, and visit to Robert's address, 16 Hermitage Villas, with Velluet, March 7, 2018.

28. Author's tour of Richmond, England, with Velluet, March 7, 2018; "Richmond: the Lost Palace," *The National Archives*, https://blog.nationalarchives.gov.uk/richmond-lost-palace/; "Royal Palaces of Queen Elizabeth I: Richmond Palace," *Elizabethi*, http://www.elizabethi.org/contents/palaces/richmondpalace.html.

29. Mary Kilbourne Matossian, "Death in London, 1750–1909," *Journal of Interdisciplinary History* 16, no. 2 (Autumn 1985): 183–97.

30. "The Question of Slavery," *North London Record*, March 18, 1859.

31. For more on the London Emancipation Committee and British antislavery sentiment, see Douglas A. Lorimer, "The Role of Anti-Slavery Sentiment in English Reactions to the American Civil War," *Historical Journal* 19, no. 2 (June 1976): 405–20, and John Oldfied, "British Anti-Slavery," *BBC*, http://www.bbc.co.uk/history/british/empire_seapower/antislavery_01.shtml.

32. Goodwin, *Team of Rivals*, 459–72.

33. Astor, *Rebels on the Border*, 119–20, 124–31, 144.

34. Ibid., 119–20, 174–75. See also Coulter, *Civil War and Readjustment in Kentucky*, 170–88.

35. Yarbrough, *Judicial Enigma*, 55–56.

36. Ibid.

37. Ibid.

38. Clark, *My Quarter Century of American Politics*, vol. 1, 63–64.

39. Yarbrough, *Judicial Enigma*, 55–56.

40. Malvina Shanklin Harlan, *Some Memories of a Long Life*, 67–68. See also Prichard, *Embattled Capital*, 144.

41. "Stephen G. Burbridge," *The Filson Historical Society*, https://filsonhistorical .org/stephen-g-burbridge/; See also "Abraham Lincoln and Military Policy in Kentucky," *Filson Historical Society*, https://filsonhistorical.org/abraham-lin coln-and-military-policy-in-kentucky-2/; Bryan S. Bush, "Major General Ste-phen Gano Burbridge: 'The Scourge of Kentucky,'" https://web.archive.org/web /20090131173943/http://bryansbush.com/hub.php?page=articles&layer=a0607.

42. Bryan S. Bush, *Butcher Burbridge: Union General Stephen Burbridge and His Reign of Terror over Kentucky* (Sikeston, MO: Acclaim Press, 2008), 11–12, 123–24.

43. Stephen W. Sears, *George B. McClellan: The Young Napoleon* (Boston: Ticknor & Fields, 1989), 338. See also Tom Wicker, "A Case of 'the Slows,'" *New York Times*, October 30, 1988.

44. Sears, *George B. McClellan*, 132.

45. Ibid., 337–43.

46. For more on McClellan's presidential campaign against Lincoln, see Sears, *George B. McClellan*, 371–86.

47. Matilda Gresham, *The Life of Walter Quintin Gresham, 1832–1895*, vol. 2 (Chicago: Rand McNally, 1919), 823–25; Yarbrough, *Judicial Enigma*, 56–58.

48. Yarbrough, *Judicial Enigma*, 56–58.

49. *Louisville* (KY) *Daily Journal*, November 1, 1864, quoted in Yarbrough, *Judicial Enigma*, 57–58 ("n----r" is spelled out in the original document).

50. "1864 Presidential Election," 270toWin, accessed Fall, 2018. https://www.270towin .com/1864_Election/.

51. "1864 Presidential General Election Results—Kentucky," *Atlas of U.S. Presidential Elections*, https://uselectionatlas.org/RESULTS/state.php?year=1864&fips=21&f= o&off=o&elect=o.

52. Coulter, *Civil War and Readjustment in Kentucky*, 212–14.

53. George Thomas Palmer, *A Conscientious Turncoat: The Story of John M. Palmer, 1817–1900* (New Haven, CT: Yale University Press, 1941), 1–12.

54. For an overview of Palmer's political relationship with Lincoln, see Mark E. Neely Jr., "Palmer, John McAuley (1817–1900)," *The Abraham Lincoln Encyclopedia* (New York: Da Capo Press, 1982), 231–32; George T. Palmer, John M. Palmer's son and biographer, dwells often on the friendship between his father and President Lin-coln. See in particular *A Conscientious Turncoat*, 12, 163–65.

55. Coulter, *Civil War and Readjustment in Kentucky*, 254.

56. Ibid., 213.

57. Ibid., 264–67.

58. Christopher Phillips, *The Rivers Ran Backward* (New York: Oxford University Press, 2016), 293; Christopher Phillips, "How Kentucky Became a Confederate State," *New York Times* online, May 22, 2015.

59. "Reaction to the Fall of Richmond," American Battlefield Trust online, accessed Fall, 2018, https://www.battlefields.org/learn/articles/reaction-fall-richmond.

60. McPherson, *Battle Cry of Freedom*, 848.

61. Goodwin, *Team of Rivals*, 739.

62. Goodwin, *Team of Rivals*, 686–90; Astor, *Rebels on the Border*, 135. For more on the response to the Thirteenth Amendment in Kentucky, see Astor, 135–45, and Coulter, *Civil War and Readjustment in Kentucky*, 258–61.

63. Coulter, *Civil War and Readjustment in Kentucky*, 296–300. For more on the consolidation of Democratic power in postwar Kentucky, see Astor, *Rebels on the Border*, 168–207.

64. Coulter, *Civil War and Readjustment in Kentucky*, 259, 278–80.

65. *Commonwealth v. John M. Palmer*, 65 Ky., 570–75 (1866), quoted in Yarbrough, *Judicial Enigma*, 61.

66. "To Richard Pindell, Esq.," *Democratic Thinker*, https://democraticthinker.word press.com/2014/06/30/clay-to-richard-pindell-february-17-1849/. For more on Clay's letter to Pindell, see Heidler and Heidler, *Henry Clay*, 449–51.

67. Klotter, "Central Kentucky's Athens of the West Image," 11–35.

68. Hambleton Tapp and James C. Klotter, *Kentucky: Decades of Discord, 1865–1900* (Lexington: University Press of Kentucky, 1977), 9. See also Wall, *How Kentucky Became Southern*.

69. Tapp and Klotter, *Kentucky: Decades of Discord*, 398.

70. Mark V. Wetherington, "Ku Klux Klan," in *Tennessee Encyclopedia* online, last modified March 1, 2018, https://tennesseeencyclopedia.net/entries/ku-klux-klan/.

71. George C. Wright, *Racial Violence in Kentucky, 1865–1940: Lynchings, Mob Rule, and "Legal Lynchings"* (Baton Rouge: Louisiana State University Press, 1990), 25; Astor, *Rebels on the Border*, 123, 230; Eric Foner, *Reconstruction, America's Unfinished Revolution, 1863–1877* (New York: Harper & Row, 1988), 428.

72. Coulter, *Civil War and Readjustment in Kentucky*, 282–84; L. F. Johnson, *A History of Franklin County* (Franklin, KY: Roberts, 1912), 163. See also Phillips, "How Kentucky Became a Confederate State."

73. Wright, *Racial Violence in Kentucky*, 25. For more on the voter intimidation and suppression tactics of the Ku Klux Klan, see Astor, *Rebels on the Border*, 229–31.

74. For more on the Kentucky press and its complicity in racial violence, see Astor, *Rebels on the Border*, 136–40, 189–94, 238–39. For a discussion of the influence of the *Louisville Journal* and the *Louisville Courier* in postwar Kentucky, see Tapp and Klotter, *Kentucky: Decades of Discord*, 278–82.

75. "Result of the Ku-Klux Klan Tomfoolery," *Louisville* (KY) *Daily Courier*, April 8, 1868.

76. "Death's Brigade," *Louisville* (KY) *Courier*, March, 22, 1868.

77. Tapp and Klotter, *Kentucky: Decades of Discord*, 379.

78. *Frankfort* (KY) *Weekly Commonwealth*, March 20, 1868, quoted in Yarbrough, *Judicial Enigma*, 65.

79. Astor, *Rebels on the Border*, 168–207; Tapp and Klotter, *Kentucky: Decades of Discord*, 1–36.

80. *Louisville* (KY) *Daily Democrat*, March 8, 1867, quoted in Yarbrough, *Judicial Enigma*, 63–64.

81. For more on John's involvement in the Union Democratic Party, see Thomas L. Owen, "The Pre-Court Career of John Marshall Harlan" (electronic dissertation, University of Louisville, May 1970), 45–49, 81–92, https://ir.library.louisville.edu /cgi/viewcontent.cgi?article=2087&context=etd. For an overview of the Union Democratic Party, see Astor, *Rebels on the Border*, 174–76.

82. W. H. Wadsworth to John Marshall Harlan, November 27, 1868, quoted in Yarbrough, *Judicial Enigma*, 65–66.

CHAPTER 7: "KNOWLEDGE IS POWER"

1. "Introduction," *Census of Population and Housing*, 1860, *ix*.

2. *Sporting Life*, January 22, 1868.

3. *Flake's Bulletin*, February 26, 1868.

4. Adam Willis interviews with British racing historians David Oldrey and Timothy Cox, March, 2018 and November, 2020.

5. Author's visit to the National Underground Railroad Freedom Center, Cincinnati, June 25, 2017. For more on the Underground Railroad in Cincinnati, see Nikki M. Taylor, *Frontiers of Freedom*, 138–160. For more on the effects of the Civil War on Cincinnati's economy, see Taylor, 175–202.

6. "Married," *The Elevator* (San Francisco), March 20, 1868. For an extensive study of Robert's property records in Cincinnati, see James Gordon, "Did the First Justice Harlan Have a Black Brother?," 182n73.

7. *Cleveland Leader*, March 1, 1871.

8. "Real Estate Transfers," *Cincinnati Enquirer*, April 28, 1869; "Real Estate Transfer," *Cincinnati Enquirer*, December 16, 1869.

9. O. S. Poston to John Marshall Harlan, July 9, 1868, quoted in Yarbrough, *Judicial Enigma*, 11.

10. "In Queer Company: 'Col.' Bob Harlan in the Graphic's Idiot Gallery," *Tennessean* (Nashville), January 23, 1873; "From the Queen City—The Exercises of the Whittier," *Cleveland Gazette*, June 20, 1885; "The Clark Literary Circle—A Novel Way of Ousting Colonel Robert Harlan," *Cincinnati Enquirer*, February 21, 1874.

11. Elizabeth Dowling Taylor, interviewed by Adam Willis, September 25, 2017. See also Elizabeth Dowling Taylor, *Original Black Elite*.

12. "Robert Harlan," *The Elevator* (San Francisco), June 10, 1870.

13. "Allen Temple A.M.E. Church," *Cincinnati History Library and Archives*, http://library.cincymuseum.org/aag/history/allentemple.html.

14. For a description of Robert's formal military dress, see "A Colored Cincinnatian's Visit to the President."

15. "Grand Jubilee of the Colored People," *Cincinnati Commercial Tribune*, January 10, 1871.

16. "Emancipation Celebration and Picnic at Inwood Park Yesterday," *Cincinnati Enquirer*, September 24, 1872.

17. *Cincinnati Commercial*, August 29, 1872.

18. "The Colored Battalion," *Cincinnati Daily Gazette*, September 9, 1870.

19. "Maj. Travis Comes to Grief," *Cincinnati Enquirer*, September 6, 1870.

20. "Compliments of Colonel Robert Harlan to Joseph S. Nesbit," *Cincinnati Enquirer*, July 30, 1879; "Hymeneal: Celebrated Wedding of Colored People," *Cincinnati Enquirer*, July 25, 1879. This dynamic is especially evident in Robert's relationship with Peter Clark. Though Clark was Robert's chief political rival in the Black community, the two men were social friends. In July 1879, Robert hosted a party with a live band and two hundred guests to honor the marriage of Clark's daughter Ernestine.

21. "The Meeting of the Colored Braves," *Cincinnati Enquirer*, September 2, 1872.

22. "Col. Robert Harlan, Member of the Ohio Legislature," *Cleveland Gazette*, May 1, 1886; "Mr. Robert Harlan," *Cincinnati Enquirer*, October 21, 1871; "Colonel Harlan—Answers Our Correspondent and States How he Secured the 'Colonel,'" *Cleveland Gazette*, May 28, 1887.

23. Elizabeth Dowling Taylor, interviewed by Adam Willis, September 25, 2017; "'Blue

Veins' Knocked Out—A Disgraceful Affair—Harlan vs. Triplett Squabble Con-clude," *Cleveland Gazette*, May 7, 1887; Gatewood, *Aristocrats of Color*, 164.

24. Elizabeth Dowling Taylor, *Original Black Elite*, 69–70; "The Colored Brethren," *Cincinnati Enquirer*, December 16, 1872.

25. White-owned newspapers, both local and national, often taunted Robert with ra-cial slurs and tried to pit him against other Black politicians. See "De Big Kunnel," *Cincinnati Commercial*, March 26, 1874; "Awl Right: A New Secret Organization by the Republicans," *Cincinnati Enquirer*, October 1, 1875; *Cincinnati Enquirer*, March 4, 1874; *Cincinnati Commercial*, August 29, 1872; "A Colored Mass Meeting: Grant Republicans at Saratoga Get Up a Ratification Gathering," *New York Herald*, August 3, 1872, 4. In a few cases, race-baiting came from the Black presses them-selves. See *Western Appeal*, September 24, 1887. See also Robert's back and forth with the *Cleveland Gazette* columnist called Triplett, *supra* Chapter 1, note, 27.

26. For reports of Robert hosting these prominent Black friends at his 39 Harrison Street home in Cincinnati, see "Notes and News," *Cincinnati Enquirer*, June 14, 1876; *Christian Recorder*, June 16, 1881. See also Elizabeth Dowling Taylor, *Original Black Elite*, 67. General impressions of the late-nineteenth- and early-twentieth-century Black aristocracy are influenced by *Original Black Elite*, as well as an in-terview with Taylor on September 25, 2017.

27. "Meeting with the East End Colored Grant Club—Difficulty with the West End Club," *Cincinnati Commercial*, September 6, 1872.

28. "Our Bob," *Cincinnati Enquirer*, August 21, 1887, 12.

29. "Democratic District and County Conventions," *Cincinnati Daily Gazette*, Sep-tember 5, 1870.

30. "Personal," *New-York Tribune*, May 1, 1871.

31. "De Big Kunnel," *Cincinnati Commercial*, March 26, 1874; "Colored Mass Meet-ing," *New York Herald*, August 3, 1872, 4.

32. "Something About Robert Harlan, Esq.," *Cincinnati Enquirer*, April 18, 1870.

33. "Colonel Robert Harlan—His Cock Fights and His Dog Fights," *Cincinnati En-quirer*, November 27, 1870.

34. Famous chroniclers of nineteenth-century social life Henry James and Nellie Bly both commented on the diverse social scene in Saratoga. See Field Horne, *The Saratoga Reader* (Syracuse, NY: Syracuse University Press, 2004), 209–10, and Hotaling, *They're Off!*, 150–56. See also Elizabeth Dowling Taylor, interviewed by Adam Willis, September 25, 2017.

35. For an overview of a Black-run boarding houses in Saratoga, see Armstead, *Lord, Please Don't Take Me In August*, 13, 56, and Hotaling, *They're Off!*, 78.

36. "The Ratification Meeting," *Saratogian*, July 26, 1876; "Saratoga Joys," *World*, July 28, 1873; author's visit to the Saratoga Club, now home to the Saratoga Springs History Museum, December 9, 2017.

37. Field Horne, interviewed by author, December 9, 2017; Horne, *Saratoga Reader*, 208. For a photograph of the Grand Union Hotel, see Hotaling, *They're Off!*, 91.

38. Horne, *Saratoga Reader*, 209.

39. *World*, July 28, 1873. For more on Saratoga's Black boarding houses, see Armstead, *Lord, Please Don't Take Me in August*, 13, 56. For more on O. C. Gilbert's boarding house, see interview with Horne, December 9, 2017.

40. Author's visit to the Saratoga Race Course, Saratoga Springs, New York, Decem-ber 9, 2017.

41. Background on Black aristocratic social life in Saratoga is drawn from Elizabeth

Dowling Taylor, interviewed by Adam Willis, September 25, 2017; Horne, *Saratoga Reader*, 209–10; Hotaling, *They're Off!*, 151. For more on Robert's political activity in Saratoga Springs, see "Colored Mass Meeting," *New York Herald*, August 3, 1872, 4, and "The Ratification Meeting," *Saratogian*, July 26, 1876.

42. Jerry Carino, "In Long Branch, a President Slept Here—A Lot," *Asbury Park Press* online (APP.), last modified August 29, 2016, https://www.app.com/story/news/history/2016/08/29/long-branch-president-slept-here----lot/89101086/.

43. "A Colored Man Interviews the President"; "Long Branch—A Colored Cincinnatian's Visit to the President," *Cincinnati Daily Gazette*, August 8, 1871; "The President and His Relatives," *World*, September 5, 1871.

44. "The President and His Relatives," *World*, September 5, 1871.

45. "A Colored Man Interviews the President."

46. "The President and His Relatives," *World*, September 5, 1871; "A Colored Cincinnatian's Visit to the President."

47. See Harlan family tree, Malvina Shanklin Harlan, *Some Memories of a Long Life*, 202–3. For more on James Harlan Jr.'s alcoholism, see James Harlan to John Marshall Harlan, April [no day printed], 1892; James Harlan to John Marshall Harlan, April 11, 1892; James Harlan to John Marshall Harlan, January 2, 1892; James Harlan to John Marshall Harlan, [illegible] 24, 1892; James Harlan to John Marshall Harlan, April [no day printed], 1892; James Harlan to John Marshall Harlan, August 4, 1892; James Harlan to John Marshall Harlan, telegram, January 1898. John also exchanged letter with his friend and law partner Augustus Willson about the health of his brother James; see John Marshall Harlan to Augustus E. Willson, telegram, May, 14, 1894; John Marshall Harlan to Augustus E. Willson, telegram, November 21, 1894; John Marshall Harlan to Augustus E. Willson, November 21, 1894. For more on the Harlan burial plot in Frankfort, Kentucky, see "Elizabeth Shannon 'Eliza' Davenport Harlan," Find a Grave, accessed Fall, 2018, https://www.findagrave.com/memorial/111927432/elizabeth-shannon-harlan, and "James Harlan," Find a Grave, accessed Fall, 2018, https://www.findagrave.com/memorial/126932402/james-harlan.

48. Malvina Shanklin Harlan, *Some Memories of a Long Life*, 99.

49. Wright, *Racial Violence in Kentucky*, 26, 52.

50. Yarbrough, *Judicial Enigma*, 67.

51. Wright, *Racial Violence in Kentucky*, 41–42. For more on racial violence in Kentucky, see Astor, *Rebels on the Border*, 133–45. For more on lawlessness and racial violence in Danville and Boyle County, Kentucky, see Tapp and Klotter, *Kentucky: Decades of Discord*, 379.

52. James Gordon, "Religion and the First Justice Harlan," 358–61, esp. 360n238; "Watson v. Jones," 80 U.S. 679 (1871).

53. Ross A. Webb, *Benjamin Helm Bristow: Border State Politician* (Lawrence: University Press of Kansas, 1969), 88–93.

54. Benjamin H. Bristow to John Marshall Harlan, November 20, 1866, quoted in Yarbrough, *Judicial Enigma*, 68.

55. Ibid., 70.

56. See John Marshall Harlan to Bristow, September 27, 1871; John Marshall Harlan to Bristow, September 29, 1871; S. W. Haney to John Marshall Harlan, November 21, 1871, Harlan Papers, Library of Congress; John Mason Brown to John Marshall Harlan, November 25, 1871, Harlan Papers, Library of Congress. All quoted in Yarbrough, *Judicial Enigma*, 71.

57. John Marshall Harlan to Benjamin H. Bristow, September 27, 1871, Bristow Papers, Library of Congress, quoted in Yarbrough, *Judicial Enigma*, 71.

58. *Louisville* (KY) *Daily Commercial*, May 18, 1871, quoted in Yarbrough, *Judicial Enigma*, 1871.

59. For a brief biography of Leslie, see Tim Talbott, "A Kentucky Governor," Kentucky History, accessed Fall, 2018, https://explorekyhistory.ky.gov/items/show/542. For a portrait of Leslie, see Thomas E. Grove, Governor Preston Leslie, 1909, painting, Kentucky Historical Society, Frankfort, Kentucky.

60. *Louisville* (KY) *Daily Commercial*, June 3, 1871, quoted in Yarbrough, *Judicial Enigma*, 76 ("n----r" is spelled out in the original document).

61. "Harlan at Hopkinsville—He Meets with a Big Reception, but Disappoints Everybody," *Louisville* (KY)*Courier-Journal*, July 28, 1871; "Out in the State—Governor Leslie at Hopkinsville," *Louisville* (KY) *Courier-Journal*, August 2, 1871.

62. *Louisville* (KY) *Courier Journal*, July 28, 1871, quoted in Yarbrough, *Judicial Enigma*, 76–77.

63. Wright, *Racial Violence in Kentucky*, 26; Klotter, interview by Adam Willis, October 10, 2018. See also "Fifteenth and Walnut—Mr. Carlisle's Speech," *Louisville* (KY) *Courier-Journal*, August 5, 1871.

64. "Harlan at Hopkinsville," *Louisville* (KY)*Courier-Journal*, July 28, 1871.

65. *Louisville* (KY) *Commercial*, November 1, 1877, quoted in Yarbrough, *Judicial Enigma*, 77.

66. Ibid.

67. Campbell, "John Marshall Harlan's Political Memoir," 319–20.

68. "The Official Count," *Advocate*, September 8, 1871.

69. Campbell, "John Marshall Harlan's Political Memoir," 316. See also *Louisville* (KY) *Commercial*, July 28, 1872; *Cincinnati Gazette*, August 9, 1871, quoted in Yarbrough, *Judicial Enigma*, 79–80.

70. Chernow, *Grant*, 751; "Presidential Election of 1872: A Resource Guide," *The Library of Congress Web Guides*, https://www.loc.gov/rr/program/bib/elections/election1872.html.

71. Chernow, *Grant*, 741–52.

72. "Colored Mass Meeting," *New York Herald*, August 3, 1872, 4; see also *Saratogian*, July 18, 1872.

73. "Colored Mass Meeting," *New York Herald*, August 3, 1872, 4.

74. Ibid.

75. "Riot—War of the Races Inaugurated," *Cincinnati Enquirer*, October 8, 1872.

76. "A Riot in Cincinnati—A Mob of Armed Negroes Attack Greeley Procession," *Irish American*, October 19, 1872. Republished from the *Cincinnati Commercial*, October 8, 1872.

77. "Riot—War of the Races Inaugurated," *Cincinnati Enquirer*, October 8, 1872.

78. Ibid.

79. Ibid.

80. "1872 Presidential General Election Results— Ohio," *U.S. Elections Atlas*, https://uselectionatlas.org/RESULTS/state.php?f=0&fips=39&year=1872.

81. Ibid.

82. "The Colored Battalion Redivivus: They Recover Their Lost Arms and Elect Officers—Melancholy Snubbing of Major Travis," *Cincinnati Enquirer*, November 26, 1872.

83. "Harlan Is Happy," *Cincinnati Commercial Tribune*, December 15, 1872.

84. "A Discussion," *Cincinnati Commercial Tribune*, December 15, 1872. For more of Robert's punditry on foreign affairs, see "Second Battalion Ohio Militia," *Cincinnati Enquirer*, November 15, 1870.

85. "Correspondence," *The Elevator* (San Francisco), March 29, 1873. For more on Grant's second inaugural ball, see "The Inauguration Ball—Arrival of the President's Party," *The United States Senate*, https://www.senate.gov/artandhistory/art/artifact/Ga_beyond/Ga_beyond_38_00061.htm, and Monica Hesse, "For Many Presidential Inaugurations, the Second Time Is Not the Charm," *Washington Post* online, January 15, 2013, https://www.washingtonpost.com/lifestyle/style/for-many-presidential-inaugurations-the-second-time-is-not-the-charm/2013/01/15/e7a8f456-5923-11e2-beee-6e38f5215402_story.html.

86. "Colonel Robert Harlan," *Cincinnati Enquirer*, December 17, 1872; *Cincinnati Enquirer*, December 22, 1872; *Cincinnati Commercial Tribune*, January 8, 1873; "Special Post Office Agent Removed," *Evening Star*, February 27, 1874.

87. "A Singular Lawsuit," *Daily Milwaukee News*, November 27, 1871; *Cleveland Leader*, March 1, 1871; "The Harlan Unpleasantness," *Cincinnati Enquirer*, January 12, 1871; *Cincinnati Enquirer*, October 27, 1871; "A Woman's Right to Recover Damages for the Enticing Away and Harboring of Her Husband," *Cincinnati Gazette*, October 27, 1871.

88. "Court Reports," *Cincinnati Daily Gazette*, February 13, 1871.

89. "Marriage Licenses," *Cincinnati Daily Star*, December 22, 1876; "The Will of Elliott H. Clark," *Cincinnati Enquirer*, June 23, 1881. See also James Gordon, "Did the First Justice Harlan Have a Black Brother?," 182n73.

CHAPTER 8: JOHN, ROBERT, AND BENJAMIN

1. Robert Harlan to John Marshall Harlan, October 4, 1873, Harlan Papers, Library of Congress. See also "The Kentucky Republicans," *Cincinnati Enquirer*, May 19, 1876.

2. Robert Harlan to John Marshall Harlan, October 4, 1873.

3. "The Republicans," *New Orleans Times-Democrat*, January 24, 1888. Although Robert tended to ignore or dismiss suggestions that he was related to the white Harlan family, during one anomalous interview with the *New Orleans Times-Democrat* he "claim[ed] to be a blood relation of Justice Harlan, of the United States Supreme Court." A series of letters that Robert wrote to John in the 1870s, ahead of the 1876 Republican National Convention, held in Cincinnati, and leading up to John's 1877 appointment to the Supreme Court, are an important window into their relationship during high-profile stretches in both of their political careers. See letters dated June 9, 1873; October 4, 1873; March 28, 1876; May 31, 1876; June 22, 1876; July 17, 1876; August 2, 1876; March 1, 1877; March 7, 1877; April 14, 1877; June 1, 1877; October 10, 1877; November 10, 1877, Harlan Papers, Library of Congress.

4. "Probable Homicide," *Daily Morning Chronicle*, June 15, 1871; "From Washington," *Cincinnati Daily Gazette*, June 15, 1871. For a short biography of Wall, see Daniel J. Sharfstein, "Orindatus Simon Bolivar Wall," Slate, last modified February 22, 2011, https://slate.com/news-and-politics/2011/02/the-great-migration-from-black-to-white-an-overlooked-chapter-in-the-history-of-african-americans.html. See also Yarbrough, *Judicial Enigma*, 17–18.

5. Sharfstein, "Orindatus Simon Bolivar Wall."

6. "Probable Homicide," *Daily Morning Chronicle*, June 15, 1871.

7. "Courts of the District of Columbia," *Federal Judicial Center*, https://www.fjc.gov/history/courts/courts-district-columbia.

8. "At Jail," *Daily Morning Chronicle*, June 16, 1871; "Rum's Doings," *Daily Morning Chronicle*, June 15, 1871; "Captain L. Davenport," *Daily Morning Chronicle*, June 16, 1871. See also Yarbrough, *Judicial Enigma*, 18–20.

9. Autobiographical letter from John Marshall Harlan to Richard Davenport Harlan, July 1911, 4–5, Harlan Papers, Library of Congress.

10. For more on James Harlan Jr.'s alcoholism, see John's correspondences with James Jr. and Augustus Willson, *supra* Chapter 7, note 46. For John's knowledge of Davenport's alcoholism, see Bristol to John Marshall Harlan, September 18, 1871, Harlan Papers, Library of Congress, quoted in Yarbrough, *Judicial Enigma*, 19.

11. Yarbrough, *Judicial Enigma*, 18–20.

12. "Captain Davenport," *Evening Star*, August 24, 1871.

13. Bristow to John Marshall Harlan, September 2, 1871, Harlan Papers, Library of Congress, quoted in Yarbrough, *Judicial Enigma*, 18. For further biography on Bristow, see "Solicitor General: Benjamin Bristow," *United States Department of Justice*, https://www.justice.gov/osg/bio/benjamin-h-bristow.

14. Yarbrough, *Judicial Enigma*, 20.

15. "Probable Homicide," *Daily Morning Chronicle*, June 15, 1871.

16. "Personal," *Daily Morning Republican*, June 28, 1871; "Wall," *Daily Morning Chronicle*, June 28, 1871; "Admitted to Bail," *Cincinnati Gazette*, July 30, 1871.

17. Robert Harlan to John Marshall Harlan, November 5, 1871, quoted in Yarbrough, *Judicial Enigma*, 19.

18. Sharfstein, "Orindatus Simon Bolivar Wall."

19. Robert Harlan to John Marshall Harlan, November 5, 1871.

20. "The Case of Davenport—He Plead 'Not Guilty,'" *Schenectady* (NY) *Evening Star*, June 17, 1871.

21. "Pardoned," *Daily Milwaukee News*, January 4, 1872.

22. Ellwood W. Lewis, "The Appointment of Mr. Justice Harlan," *Indiana Law Journal* 29, no. 1 (1953): 46–74.

23. "Maine.—What the Republicans Have Been and Are Doing," *New-York Times*, August 26, 1872.

24. "Maine.—Gathering of Veterans," *Boston Globe*, August 28, 1872.

25. "Maine.—The Great Soldier's Convention at Portland," *New-York Times*, August 28, 1872.

26. Ibid.; Campbell, "John Marshall Harlan's Political Memoir," 317–18.

27. *Minneapolis Daily Tribune*, February 27, 1874 ("n----r" is spelled out in the original document).

28. "The Man and Brother—The Sixth Ward Colored Grant Club," *Cincinnati Enquirer*, September 6, 1872. In which Robert speaks before the Cincinnati's Colored Grant Club, of which Peter Clark also seems to have been a member. See Nikki M. Taylor, *America's First Black Socialist*, 114–15.

29. For more on Clark's membership in the Democratic Party, see Nikki M. Taylor, *America's First Black Socialist*, 6–8. For more on the Chillicothe Convention, see 116–25.

30. "To the Colored Citizens of the State of Ohio," *Scioto Gazette* (Chillicothe, OH), August 20, 1873.

31. *Scioto Gazette*, August 27, 1873.

32. "Colored State Convention," August 27, 1873; *Scioto Gazette*, August 27, 1873.

33. Ibid.

34. Kelly Lewis, "Bicentennial Flashback: Parties Sought Black Vote," *Cincinnati Enquirer*, November 21, 1988.

35. "To the Colored Citizens of the State of Ohio," *Scioto Gazette*, August 20, 1873.

36. "The Color Convention at Chillicothe," *Cincinnati Commercial*, August 23, 1873.

37. Ibid.

38. "Colored State Convention," *Scioto Gazette*, August 27, 1873; Nikki M. Taylor, *America's First Black Socialist*, 120–23.

39. "Speech by John M. Langston at Chillicothe," *Cincinnati Commercial*, September 24, 1873.

40. "Fred. Douglass," *Scioto Gazette*, September 17, 1873; "Fred. Douglass Goes Back on Peter Clark," *Cincinnati Commercial*, September 17, 1873; *Scioto Gazette*, September 10, 1873. See also Nikki M. Taylor, *America's First Black Socialist*, 124–25.

41. "The Clark Literary Circle—A Novel Way of Ousting Colonel Harlan," *Cincinnati Enquirer*, February 21, 1874.

42. "Marriage Licenses," *Cincinnati Daily Star*, December 22, 1876; "The Will of Elliott H. Clark," *Cincinnati Enquirer*, June 23, 1881. See also James Gordon, "Did the First Justice Harlan Have a Black Brother?," 182n73.

43. "Compliments of Colonel Robert Harlan to Joseph S. Nesbit," *Cincinnati Enquirer*, July 30, 1879. For more on Ernestine Clark's wedding, which Robert attended, see "Hymeneal: Celebrated Wedding of Colored People—Marriage of Peter H. Clark's Daughter to Joseph S. Nesbit," *Cincinnati Enquirer*, July 25, 1879.

44. John Marshall Harlan, "John Marshall Harlan's Political Memoir," 316–17.

45. See "Judge John Marshall Harlan, Supreme Court Yarbrough," 1877, Portrait, Brady-Handy photograph collection, Library of Congress, Washington, DC.

46. Chernow, *Grant*, 782, 787–88.

47. See "Judge John Marshall Harlan, Supreme Court," 1877, Portrait, Brady-Handy photograph collection, Library of Congress, Washington, DC.

48. *Louisville* (KY) *Commercial*, June 29, 1875, quoted in Yarbrough, *Judicial Enigma*, 82–84.

49. Yarbrough, *Judicial Enigma*, 80–85. For more on the effects of the Panic of 1873 in Kentucky, see Tapp and Klotter, *Kentucky: Decades of Discord*, 141–71.

50. *Louisville* (KY) *Commercial*, June 19, 1875, quoted in Yarbrough, *Judicial Enigma*, 80–83.

51. *Louisville* (KY) *Commercial*, November 1, 1877, quoted in Yarbrough, *Judicial Enigma*, 83.

52. Campbell, "John Marshall Harlan's Political Memoir," 318.

53. "Frankfort," *Louisville* (KY) *Courier-Journal*, August 24, 1875.

54. For more about the relationship between Bristow and Grant, see Chernow, *Grant*, 798–803.

55. Jean Edward Smith, *Grant* (New York: Simon & Schuster, 2001), 583; Foner, *Reconstruction*, 566. For more on the Grant administration's return to the gold standard, see Chernow, *Grant*, 778–83, 802–9.

56. H. V. Boynton, "The Whiskey Ring," *North American Review* 123, no. 253 (1876): 280–327.

57. "Club Life Among Colored Men: Old Dumas House on McCalister Street Partially Restored," *Cincinnati Enquirer*, April 15, 1900. See also Dabney, *Cincinnati's Colored Citizens*, 31.

58. Robert Harlan to John Marshall Harlan, March 28, 1876, Harlan Papers, Library of Congress.

59. "The National Convention—How the Radicals Will Be Positioned Next Week," *Cincinnati Enquirer*, June 6, 1876; "Official Proceedings of the Republican National Convention, Held at Cincinnati, Ohio" *Republican Press Association*, 4.

60. "The Colored Element," *Daily Times*, April 6, 1876, republished the correspondence of the *Cleveland Plain Dealer*.

61. "Notes and News," *Cincinnati Enquirer*, June 14, 1876.

62. For more on the prerequisites of membership in the Black aristocracy, see Elizabeth Dowling Taylor, *Original Black Elite*, 66–68.

63. Wasniewski, *Black Americans in Congress, 1870–2007*, 134–36; "Charles Edmund Nash (1834–1917), *Black Past*, https://www.blackpast.org/african-american-history/nash-charles-edmund-1844-1913/; "Nash, Charles Edmund," *History, Art, & Archives: United States House of Representatives*, https://history.house.gov/People/Detail/18846.

64. "Spirit of History Alive at Burnet House Site," *Cincinnati Enquirer*, November 15, 2017.

65. "The Man of Impressive Manners," *Cincinnati Enquirer*, June 10, 1876.

66. "Kentucky Republicans," *Cincinnati Enquirer*, May 19, 1876. John was elected a delegate "for the state at large."

67. Robert Harlan to John Marshall Harlan, May 31, 1876, Harlan Papers, Library of Congress; "Tragedy of Pike's Opera House Recounted in New Book," *Cincinnati Enquirer*, June 22, 2015.

68. Robert Harlan to John Marshall Harlan, May 31, 1876.

69. "Opening of the National Republican Convention," *Cincinnati Gazette*, June 14, 1876.

70. Claney, *Proceedings of the National Republican Convention Held at Cincinnati, Ohio*, 68–70.

71. Foner, *Reconstruction*, 566; Lloyd Robinson, *The Stolen Election: Hayes Versus Tilden—1876* (New York: Forge, 2001), 54–55, 60.

72. Robinson, *Stolen Election*, 54–55.

73. Ibid., 53–63.

74. Ibid., 61.

75. See Claney, *Proceedings of the National Republican Convention Held at Cincinnati, Ohio*.

76. Ibid., 106.

77. Ibid., 107.

78. "Hayes & Wheeler—Ohio and New York Sure Now—Republicanism Saved," *Summit County Beacon*, June 21, 1876. For seventh round ballot results, see the subhead, "Scenes from the Fateful Seventh Ballot."

CHAPTER 9: "DO-DO TAKE CARE"

1. "Seventh Ballot," *Summit County Beacon*, June 21, 1876.

2. John Marshall Harlan to Bristow, June 19, 1876, Harlan Papers, Library of Congress, quoted in Yarbrough, *Judicial Enigma*, 95–96.

3. Ibid., 95.

4. For more on the strategic matchup between Hayes and Tilden, see Robinson, *Stolen Election*, 71–95, 97–114, 115–30; "1876 Presidential Election," *270 to Win*, https://www.270towin.com/1876_Election/.

5. Ari Hoogenboom, *Rutherford B. Hayes: Warrior and President* (Lawrence: University Press of Kansas, 1995), 307; Foner, *Reconstruction*, 575–87.

6. "1876 Presidential Election," *270 to Win*, https://www.270towin.com/1876 _Election/.

7. For an archive of resources on the contested election of 1876, "Finding Precedent: the Electoral College Controversy of 1876–1877," *HarpWeek*, https://elections .harpweek.com/Controversy.htm.

8. Foner, *Reconstruction*, 576.

9. Ibid., *Reconstruction*, 576; Robinson, *Stolen Election*, 133–35, 137–42, 201–3.

10. Chernow, *Grant*, 847

11. Robinson, *Stolen Election*, 201–3; Malvina Shanklin Harlan, *Some Memories of a Long Life*, 82.

12. For a portrait of Justice Davis late in his life, see "Judge David Davis, U.S.S. Court," *Library of Congress*, https://www.loc.gov/pictures/item/2017893443/; "Davis, David," *CQ Press: Supreme Court Collection*, https://library.cqpress.com/scc/doc ument.php?id=bioenc-427-18166-979186&v=227ccbb608148c47.

13. Foner, *Reconstruction*, 579–80.

14. Chernow, *Grant*, 847.

15. Foner, *Reconstruction*, 574–75.

16. Ibid., 575–87; Hoogenboom, *Rutherford B. Hayes*, 310–312.

17. Foner, *Reconstruction*, 580; Robinson, *Stolen Election*, 166–70, 183–87, 202–213.

18. Foner, *Reconstruction*, 581–82; Robinson, *Stolen Election*, 199–213. For more on the White House encounter between Hayes and Grant, see Chernow, *Grant*, 852–53.

19. For more on Hayes's temperance, see Hoogenboom, *Rutherford B. Hayes*, 92.

20. Rutherford B. Hayes to William Henry Smith, and Smith's reply, October 1877, quoted in Beth, *John Marshall Harlan*, 123–24; Robert Harlan to John Marshall Harlan, March 7, 1877; Malvina Shanklin Harlan, *Some Memories of a Long Life*, 87–90.

21. Oliver B. Morton to Rutherford B. Hayes, March 1877, Hayes Papers, quoted in Yarbrough, *Judicial Enigma*, 99.

22. Malvina Shanklin Harlan, *Some Memories of a Long Life*, 87.

23. Ibid., 84–86.

24. Foner, *Reconstruction*, 577; Malvina Shanklin Harlan, *Some Memories of Long Life*, 84–86.

25. Hoogenboom, *Rutherford B. Hayes*, 309.

26. Malvina Shanklin Harlan, *Some Memories of a Long Life*, 84.

27. Yarbrough, *Judicial Enigma*, 101; Liesbeth Ramirez and Kathryn O'Dwyer, "Boston Club," New Orleans Historical, accessed Winter, 2019, https://neworleanshistori cal.org/items/show/1212.

28. For more on Packard's governance from the St. Louis Hotel, see Philip D. Uzee, "The Beginnings of the Louisiana Republican Party," *Journal of the Louisiana Historical Association* 12, no. 3 (Summer 1971): 197–98.

29. For an overview of the Louisiana Commission, see Hoogenboom, *Rutherford B. Hayes*, 308–15. A roster of the commissioners is included on p. 310. See also Richard Harlan's summary of the Louisiana Commission, reprinted in Malvina Shanklin Harlan, *Some Memories of a Long Life*, 83–86.

30. "Assassination of D. A. Weber," *New Orleans Republican*, March 16, 1877; "Presidential Election Investigation," *Index to the Miscellaneous Documents of the House of Representatives for the Third Session of the Forty-Fifth Congress*, 1878–'79, 597.

31. Hoogenboom, *Rutherford B. Hayes*, 312.
32. Ibid., *Hayes*, 310–14. See also Richard Harlan's summary of the Louisiana Commission, Malvina Shanklin Harlan, *Some Memories of a Long Life*, 83–86.
33. Uzee, "The Beginnings of the Louisiana Republican Party," 197.
34. Ibid., 198.
35. Malvina Shanklin Harlan, *Some Memories of a Long Life*, 86.
36. Ibid., 87–89.
37. David G. Farrelly, "John M. Harlan's One-Day Diary, August 21, 1877," *Filson Club Historical Quarterly* 24 (1950): 158–68, quoted in Yarbrough, *Judicial Enigma*, 103–4.
38. Yarbrough, *Judicial Enigma*, 102–6.
39. Ibid., 106.
40. Malvina Shanklin Harlan, *Some Memories of a Long Life*, 88–89.
41. Ibid., 89.
42. Robert Harlan to John Marshall Harlan, March 7, 1877.
43. Ibid., April 14, 1877.
44. Ibid., June 1, 1877.
45. Ibid., October 10, 1877.
46. Ibid., November 10, 1877.
47. "Slings and Arrows," *Boston Globe*, October 17, 1877.
48. John Morrill to Rutherford B. Hayes, August 25, 1877, Hayes Papers, Library of Congress; George F. Edmunds to Benjamin H. Bristow, October 27, 1877, Bristow Papers, Library of Congress. Both quoted in Yarbrough, *Judicial Enigma*, 109. For documentation on Edmunds's legal representation of railroads, see *Report of the Joint Special Committee to Investigate the Vt. Central Railroad Management* (St. Albans, VT: Messenger Printing Establishment, 1873), 45, 73, 374.
49. "Senate Executive Business," *New-York Times*, November 27, 1877.
50. See, in particular, Melville W. Fuller to Hannibal Hamlin, October 29, 1877, Senate Records; John Ledwick to S. J. Kirkland, November 17, 1877; Brown to F. Edmunds, November 19, 1877; Speed S. Fry to William Brown, November [illegible date], 1877; W. H. Painter to George F. Edmunds, undated. All in the Senate judiciary committee records on John's nomination, National Archives, and quoted in Yarbrough, *Judicial Enigma*, 109–12.
51. Speed S. Fry to William Brown, November [illegible date], 1877, Senate Records, quoted in Yarbrough, *Judicial Enigma*, 110–11.
52. James Speed to George F. Edmunds, November 1, 1877, Senate Records; Speed to Edmunds, November 10, 1877. Both quoted in Yarbrough, *Judicial Enigma*, 111.
53. Augustus E. Willson to Richard D. Harlan, April 11, 1930, Harlan Papers, Library of Congress; John W. Finnell to John Marshall Harlan, November 1877, Harlan Papers, Library of Congress. Both quoted in Yarbrough, *Judicial Enigma*, 112.
54. "The Latest News," *Weekly Davenport Democrat*, December 6, 1877. "The nomination of Harlan for judge of the Supreme Court will not be acted upon before the close of the special session. Mr. Edmunds, chair of the judiciary committee, which has charge of the matter, is away from Washington, and he is not expected to return in time to act upon the nomination. He does not like Harlan, and his dislike has affected his health so severely that he has gone to Virginia."
55. "Various Editorial Notes," *Argus and Patriot* (Montpelier, VT), December 5, 1877.
56. "Washington Letter," *Morning Herald* (Indianola, Iowa), December 13, 1877.
57. Malvina Shanklin Harlan, *Some Memories of a Long Life*, 91.

CHAPTER 10: DESTINY

1. Architect of the Capitol-Old Senate Chamber, chandelier is from Philadelphia's Cornelius and Company, https://www.aoc.gov/explore-capitol-campus/buildings-grounds/capitol-building/senate-wing/old-senate-chamber.

2. Ibid.

3. Supreme Court Historical Society, "Morrison R. Waite, 1874–1888," https://supremecourthistory.org/timeline_waite.html.

4. Malvina Shanklin Harlan, *Some Memories of a Long Life*, 91.

5. Vince Guerrieri, "Ohio Winter Fun: Sleigh Rides," *Ohio* online, last modified December 2019, https://www.ohiomagazine.com/travel/article/ohio-winter-fun-sleigh-rides, discusses Hayes's love of sleigh rides in Ohio and Washington. The 2004 White House Christmas ornament featured Hayes's sleigh.

6. Richard White, *The Republic for Which It Stands: The United States During Reconstruction and the Gilded Age, 1865–1896* (Oxford, MS: Oxford University Press, 2017), 346–47.

7. Ibid., 351.

8. Ibid., 349–50.

9. Ibid., 351.

10. Ibid., 352–53.

11. Beth, *John Marshall Harlan*, 134; Malvina Shanklin Harlan, *Some Memories of a Long Life*, 94–95, describes the social obligations attending the wife of a Supreme Court justice.

12. James Harlan to John Marshall Harlan, April [no day printed], 1892; James Harlan to John Marshall Harlan, April 11, 1892; James Harlan to John Marshall Harlan, January 2, 1892; James Harlan to John Marshall Harlan, [illegible] 24, 1892; James Harlan to John Marshall Harlan, April [no day printed], 1892; James Harlan to John Marshall Harlan, August 4, 1892; James Harlan telegram to John Marshall Harlan, January 1898. John also exchanged letters with his friend and law partner Augustus Willson about the health of his brother James. See John Marshall Harlan to Willson, telegram, May, 14, 1894; John Marshall Harlan to Willson, telegram, November 21, 1894; John Marshall Harlan to Willson, November 21, 1894; Yarbrough, *Judicial Enigma*, 165; John Marshall Harlan to Thomas W. Bullitt, October 17, 1880, Harlan Papers, University of Louisville.

13. Beth, *John Marshall Harlan*, 134.

14. Malvina Shanklin Harlan, *Some Memories of a Long Life*, 94–95.

15. Ibid., 101.

16. Ibid. 94.

17. Ibid., 95.

18. Callie Hopkins, "Lucy Hayes, Temperance, and the Politics of the White House Dinner Table," The White House Historical Association, October 25, 2018, https://www.whitehousehistory.org/lucy-hayes-temperance-and-the-politics-of-the-white-house-dinner-table#:~:text=Hayes%20was%20uncomfortable%20continuing%20to,served%20in%20the%20White%20House.

19. Malvina Shanklin Harlan, *Some Memories of a Long Life*, 96.

20. Ibid., 98.

21. Beth, *John Marshall Harlan*, 138.

22. Ibid., 139.

23. See Kens, *Justice Stephen Field,* for full account of Field's life and character.

24. Beth, *John Marshall Harlan*, 139.

25. Ibid., 134–35.

26. *Reynolds v. United States*, 98 U.S. 145 (1878); Quayle, *A Review of the Decision of the Supreme Court of the United States, in the case of Geo. Reynolds vs. The United States*, 52.

27. "Horrible Murder—A Colored Woman Tomahawked by Her Husband—He Brains Her With a Hatchet—The Murderer Escapes." Wheeling *Daily Intelligencer*, Wheeling, WV: April 19, 1872. Reproduced at http://www.wvculture.org/history /africanamericans/strauder01.html.

28. *Strauder v. West Virginia*, 100 U.S. 303 (1880).

29. Tom Perry, "Patrick County in the New York Times Ex Parte VA," The Free State of Patrick Blog, September 25, 2012, http://freestateofpatrick.blogspot.com/2012/09 /patrick-county-in-new-york-times-ex.html.

30. "Federal vs. State Authority." *Alexandria Gazette*, Alexandria VA. February 27, 1879.

31. "Federal vs. State Authority." *Alexandria Gazette*, Alexandria VA. February 28, 1879.

32. Ibid.

33. R. M. McKeithen, "Removal of Civil Rights Cases—Recent Developments," 44 N.C. L. Rev. 380 (1966).

34. *Strauder v. West Virginia*, 100 U.S. 303, at 306.

35. Ibid., at 307.

36. Ibid., at 308.

37. *Virginia v. Rives*, 100 U.S. 313 (1880).

38. Robert Harlan to John Marshall Harlan, June 1, 1877.

39. "The Nashville Convention—Colonel Harlan and Pastor Williams at Zion Church Last Night," *Cincinnati Enquirer*, April 20, 1876; *Cincinnati Commercial*, April 8, 1876.

40. Proceedings of the National Conference of Colored Men of the United States, Held at the State Capitol at Nashville Tennessee, May 6, 7, 8 and 9, 1879, http://col oredconventions.org/items/show/323.

41. David Blight, *Frederick Douglass: Prophet of Freedom* (New York: Simon & Schuster, 2018), 603.

42. Ibid.

43. Ibid.

44. *The Louisianian*, May 24, 1879.

45. Malvina Shanklin Harlan, *Some Memories of a Long Life*, 114.

46. Scott S. Greenberger, *The Unexpected President: The Life and Times of Chester A. Arthur* (Boston: Da Capo Press, 2017), 162.

47. Malvina Shanklin Harlan, *Some Memories of a Long Life*, 114.

48. Yarbrough, *Judicial Enigma*, 117.

49. Malvina Shanklin Harlan, *Some Memories of a Long Life*, 115.

50. Yarbrough, *Judicial Enigma*, 117.

51. Malvina Shanklin Harlan, *Some Memories of a Long Life*, 116.

52. John M. Harlan to James S. Harlan, November 25, 1882, Harlan Papers, Library of Congress

CHAPTER 11: STANDING ALONE

1. John R. Howard, *The Shifting Wind: The Supreme Court and Civil Rights from Reconstruction to Brown* (Albany: State University of New York Press, 1999), 125.

2. Proceedings of the National Conference of Colored Men of the United States, Held at the State Capitol at Nashville Tennessee, May 6, 7, 8, and 9, 1879, http://coloredconventions.org/items/show/323.

3. Howard, *Shifting Wind*, 125.

4. *Civil Rights Cases of 1883*, 109 U.S. 3 (1883).

5. *New Orleans Times-Picayune*, January 23, 1883, 1.

6. *Weekly Advertiser* (Montgomery, Alabama), April 7, 1883, 3.

7. John Marshall Harlan to James S. Harlan, November 25, 1882.

8. The four new justices were William Burnham Woods, 1881; Stanley Matthews, 1881; Horace Gray 1882; and Samuel Blatchford, 1882.

9. *Neal v. Delaware*, 103 U.S. 370 at 393–94 (1881).

10. Ibid., 397.

11. Peter Wallenstein, "Race, Marriage, and the Supreme Court from *Pace v. Alabama* (1883) to *Loving v. Virginia*," *Journal of Supreme Court History* 23, no. 2 (1967): 65–86.

12. *Pace v. Alabama*, 106 U.S. 583 (1883).

13. Wallenstein, "Race, Marriage, and the Supreme Court," 65–86.

14. *Civil Rights Cases of 1883*, 109 U.S. 3 at 26.

15. *Neal v. Delaware*, 103 U.S. 370, at 394.

16. Charles Lane, *The Day Freedom Died: The Colfax Massacre, the Supreme Court, and the Betrayal of Reconstruction* (New York: Henry Holt, 2008), 181.

17. *Civil Rights Cases of 1883*, 109 U.S. 3 at 19.

18. Architect of the Capitol-Old Senate Chamber, https://www.aoc.gov/explore-capitol-campus/buildings-grounds/capitol-building/senate-wing/old-senate-chamber, confirmed by photos of the Supreme Court chamber of that era.

19. Howard, *Shifting Wind*, 128.

20. Architect of the Capitol-Old Senate Chamber, https://www.aoc.gov/explore-capitol-campus/buildings-grounds/capitol-building/senate-wing/old-senate-chamber.

21. *Civil Rights Cases of 1883*, 109 U.S. 3 at 26.

22. Ibid., 35.

23. Ibid., 39–40.

24. Ibid., 53.

25. Ibid., 30, 53–57.

26. Ibid., 60.

27. Ibid., 60–61.

28. *Heart of Alabama Motel v. United States*, 379 U.S. 241 (1964).

29. *Civil Rights Cases of 1883*, 109 U.S. 3 at 51.

30. Ibid., 25.

31. Ibid., 61.

32. Howard, *Shifting Wind*, 131.

33. William S. McFeely, *Frederick Douglass* (New York: Simon & Schuster, 1991), 318, full text available at TeachingAmericanHistory.org, teachingamericanhistory.org.

34. Douglass to John Marshall Harlan, November 27, 1883.

35. Urofsky, *Dissent and the Supreme Court*, 111.

36. John Marshall Harlan to James S. Harlan and John Maynard Harlan, May 24, 1895, Harlan Papers, University of Louisville.

37. John Marshall Harlan to Joseph Philo Bradley, February 23, 1889, Harlan Papers, University of Louisville.

38. Josh Blackman, Brian L. Frye, and Michael McCloskey, "Justice John Marshall Harlan: Professor of Law," *George Washington Law Review* 81, no. 4 (July 2013): 1063, http://dx.doi.org/10.2139/ssrn.1403917.

39. Yarbrough, *Judicial Enigma*, 129.

40. Leon O. Hynson, "The Right of Private Judgment," *Asbury Theological Journal* 60, no. 1, (2005): 89.

41. Malvina Shanklin Harlan, *Some Memories of a Long Life*, 114.

42. Eulogy for Edith Harlan, New York Avenue Presbyterian Church.

CHAPTER 12: "THE COLONEL HAS INDEED SURPRISED US"

1. "Later News," *Richwood* (OH) *Gazette*, October 25, 1883, 1.

2. Nikki M. Taylor, *America's First Black Socialist*, 131, 136–37.

3. "Later News," *Richwood* (OH) *Gazette*, October 25, 1883, 1.

4. Howard, *Shifting Wind*, 131.

5. John Hope Franklin, *George Washington Williams: A Biography* (Chicago: University of Chicago Press, 1985; Durham, NC: Duke University Press, 1998), 60–64.

6. Ibid.

7. Ibid.

8. Ibid.

9. Ibid.

10. *Cincinnati Commercial*, June 27, 1879.

11. *Cincinnati Commercial*, June 29, 1879.

12. Kenny, *Illustrated Cincinnati: A Pictorial Hand-Book of the Queen City*, digitized by the Public Library of Cincinnati and Hamilton County.

13. *Cincinnati Commercial*, July 26, 1879.

14. Franklin, *George Washington Williams*, 63–64.

15. Ibid.

16. "Colonel Harlan Rises to Explain," *Cincinnati Enquirer*, July 23, 1879, 8.

17. Franklin, *George Washington Williams*, 76–78.

18. Ibid., 77–78.

19. Ibid.

20. "Philadelphia," *Indianapolis Leader*, June 24, 1882, 2.

21. James Gordon, "Did the First Justice Harlan Have a Black Brother?," 159.

22. "Philadelphia," *Indianapolis Leader*, June 24, 1882, 2.

23. Ibid.

24. Elizabeth Dowling Taylor, *Original Black Elite*, 76.

25. Ibid.

26. Ibid.

27. "Philadelphia," *Indianapolis Leader*, June 24, 1882, 2.

28. Elizabeth Dowling Taylor, *Original Black Elite*, 78.

29. "Grave-yard Legislation," *Cincinnati Enquirer*, April 12, 1880; *Cincinnati Commercial*, April 3, 1880; Franklin, *George Washington Williams*, 89–90.

30. Ibid.

31. *Cincinnati Commercial*, February 26, 1881.

32. *Washington Post*, October 26, 1881.

33. "The National Colored Committee," *Washington Bee*, December 22, 1883.

34. Ibid.

35. Robert Harlan to Butler, March 15, 1875.

36. "From the Queen City—Mrs. Mary E. Harlan's Will," *Cleveland Gazette*, June 27, 1885.
37. "Ousted from their Seats," *New-York Times*, January 13, 1886.
38. *Philadelphia Evening Bulletin*, October 24, 1885.
39. "Ousted from their Seats," *New York Times*, January 13, 1886, 1; "Harlan is Seated," *Cleveland Plain Dealer*, January 13, 1886.
40. "Out They Go," *Springfield Globe-Republic*, January 12, 1886.
41. "Nine Democrats," *Stark County* (OH) *Democrat*, January 21, 1886, 4.
42. "Another Wrong Righted," *Ohio State Journal*, March 25, 1886.
43. "Harlan Is Seated," *Cleveland Plain Dealer*, March 27, 1886.
44. "Harlan at Home," *Cincinnati Enquirer*, April 13, 1886.
45. "John Brown Memorial," *Cleveland Gazette*, February 5, 1887.
46. Ibid., April 16, 1887.
47. Ibid., April 23, 1887.
48. Ibid., October 1, 1887.
49. Iris Chang, *The Chinese in America: A Narrative History* (New York: Penguin, 2003), 117.
50. Ibid.
51. *Yick Wo v. Hopkins*, 118 U.S. 356 (1886).
52. Ibid.
53. *Baldwin v. Franks*, 120 U.S. 678 (1887) at 694 (Harlan dissent).
54. Ibid.
55. Gabriel J. Chin, "Chae Chan Ping and Fong Tue Ting: The Origins of Plenary Power," in *Immigration Law Stories*, ed. David Martin and Peter Schuck (St. Paul: Foundation Press, 2005), 2.
56. *Chae Chan Ping v. United States*, 130 U.S. 581 (1889).
57. Chin, "Chae Chan Ping and Fong Tue Ting," 13.
58. *Fong Yue Ting v. United States*, 149 U.S. 698 (1893).
59. The Judiciary Act of 1891 (26 Stat. 826), also known as the Evarts Act.
60. Malvina Shanklin Harlan, *Some Memories of a Long Life*, 127.
61. Ibid., 150.
62. Ibid.
63. Ibid.
64. Ibid.
65. Yarbrough, *Judicial Enigma*, 200–205.
66. Augustus Willson to John Marshall Harlan, July 5, 1880, Harlan Papers, University of Louisville; James made reference to vermin in a separate letter to John.
67. W. W. Acers to John Marshall Harlan, May 6, 1891, Harlan Papers, University of Louisville.
68. Willson to John Marshall Harlan, July 5, 1880.
69. John Marshall Harlan to Henry Harlan, July 10, 1889, Harlan Papers, University of Louisville.
70. John Marshall Harlan to John Maynard Harlan, February 7, 1894, Harlan Papers, University of Louisville.
71. Undated letter, James Harlan Jr. to John Marshall Harlan, Harlan Papers, University of Louisville, as quoted in Yarbrough, *Judicial Enigma*.
72. James Gordon, "Did the First Justice Harlan Have a Black Brother?," 229.
73. Ibid., 228–29.

74. Ibid., 229 .

75. Ibid., 228–29.

76. Ibid.

77. Malvina Shanklin Harlan, *Some Memories of a Long Life*, 128.

78. Ibid. 142.

79. Ibid., 150.

CHAPTER 13: IN TRUSTS WE TRUST

1. Uwe Spiekermann, "Claus Spreckels: A Biographical Study of Nineteenth Century American Immigrant Entrepreneurship," Business and Economic History On-Line, 3.

2. "The Sugar Magnate Claus Spreckels Testifies Before the Trust Investigation Committee," *Duluth* (MN) *Daily*, March 24, 1888.

3. Spiekermann, "Claus Spreckels," 5.

4. Ibid., 19.

5. Ibid.

6. "Sugar Magnate Claus Spreckels," March 24, 1888.

7. Ibid.

8. "The Sugar Trust's Foe," *New-York Times*, May 14, 1888.

9. "No Trust for Claus Spreckels," *New-York Times*. September 8, 1889.

10. "A Bitter Fight, Sugar Trust v. Claus Spreckels," *The Patriot*, August 05, 1891.

11. Ibid.

12. Spiekermann, "Claus Spreckels," 4.

13. Peter R. Dickson and Philippa K. Wells, "The Dubious Origins of the Sherman Antitrust Act: The Mouse That Roared," *Journal of Public Policy and Marketing* 20, no. 1 (Spring 2001): 5.

14. Foner, *Reconstruction*, 461.

15. "A Secret Out: Members of the State Board of Railway Assessors Have Annual Pullman Passes in Their Pockets," *Winona* (KS) *Clipper*, October 11, 1894.

16. Ibid.

17. Christopher Grandy, "New Jersey Corporate Chartermonering, 1875–1929," *Journal of Economic History* 49, no. 3 (September 1989): 678.

18. Dickson and Wells, "Dubious Origins of the Sherman Antitrust Act," 5.

19. James, *Richard Olney and His Public Service*, 108.

20. Ibid., 109.

21. Ibid., 97.

22. Ibid., 11.

23. Ibid., 1.

24. Ibid. 28.

25. Ibid., 29.

26. "The Domestic Sugar Industry and the Sugar Trust," *Times-Picayune* (New Orleans, LA), October 19, 1893.

27. *United States v. E.C. Knight Co.*, 156 U.S. 1 (1895).

28. Willard L. King, *Melville Weston Fuller: Chief Justice of the United States, 1888–1910* (New York: Macmillan, 1950), 3–10.

29. Ibid., 94.

30. Ibid., 36.

31. Daniel Hautzinger, "The Clash of Wealth and Labor in Chicago's Gilded Age," WTTW Chicago, last modified February 6, 2018, https://interactive.wttw.com /playlist/2018/02/06/clash-wealth-and-labor-chicagos-gilded-age.

32. Ibid.

33. Charles A. Kent, *Memoir of Henry Billings Brown: Late Justice of the Supreme Court of the United States Consisting of an Autobiographical Sketch with Additions to His Life* (New York: Duffield, 1915), 16.

34. George Shiras, 3rd, *Justice George Shiras, Jr. of Pittsburgh: A Chronicle of His Family, Life and Times*, ed. Winfield Shiras (Pittsburgh: University of Pittsburgh Press, 1953), 20–21.

35. Joe A. Fisher, "Knight Case Revisited," *Historian* 35, no. 1 (1972): 369.

36. Ibid.

37. Ibid.

38. Ibid., 371.

39. "Sugar Trust Case: Argument to Begin Today in the Supreme Court—Sketch of the Case," *Boston Journal*, October 24, 1894.

40. *United States v. E.C. Knight Company*, 156 U.S. 1 at 13.

41. Ibid., at 17.

42. Ibid., at 18 (Harlan's dissent).

43. *Gibbons v. Ogden*, 22 U.S. 1, 1824.

44. *United States v. E.C. Knight Company*, 156 U.S. 1 at 43.

45. Ibid.

46. Greg Timmons, "The Biggest Landslide in Midterm Election History," History Stories, October 23, 2018, https://www.history.com/news/midterm-elections-biggest -landslide-republicans-grover-cleveland.

47. Frank Latham, *The Great Dissenter: Supreme Court Justice John Marshall Harlan (1833–1911)* (Spokane, WA: Cowles Books, 1970), 134.

48. Ibid., 135.

49. "Inquiry into the Trusts: Joint Legislative Committee Begins Its Investigation," *New-York Tribune*, February 6, 1897.

50. "Steel Standing: U.S. Steel Celebrates 100 Years," *Pittsburgh Post-Gazette*, February 25, 2001.

51. U.S. Office of Management and Budget, "Federal Net Outlays," Federal Reserve Economic Data, October 16, 2018, accessed February 26, 2019, https://fred.stlouis fed.org/series/FYONET.

52. Thomas K. McCraw and Forest Reinhardt, "Losing to Win: U.S. Steel's Pricing, Investment Decisions, and Market Share, 1901–1938," *Journal of Economic History* 49, no. 3 (1989): 598, http://www.jstor.org/stable/2122506.

53. John Marshall Harlan to Gus Willson, December 1, 1905, Letter, From Filson Historical Society, Louisville, Kentucky, Willson Papers.

54. See *Swift and Company v. United States*, 196 U.S. 375 (1904).

CHAPTER 14: REQUIEM FOR THE GILDED AGE

1. William Jennings Bryan, *Speeches of William Jennings Bryan*, vol. 1 (New York: Funk & Wagnalls, 1913), 176–77, https://www.google.com/books/edition /Speeches_of_William_Jennings_Bryan/AJg5AQAAMAAJ?hl=en&gbpv=1.

2. Gary Richardson and Tim Sablik, "Banking Panics of the Gilded Age," federalre servehistory.org.

3. Ben Macri, "The 'Morgan Bonds,'" projects.vassar.edu, 2000.

4. King, *Melville Weston Fuller*, 193.

5. *Hylton v. United States*, 3 U.S. 171 (1796).

6. *Maier, Ratification*, 556.

7. *Hylton v. United States*, 3 U.S. 171.

8. *Springer v. United States*, 102 U.S. 586 at 602 (1881).

9. Swaine, *Cravath Firm and Predecessors*, 150.

10. John R. Vile, *Great American Lawyers: An Encyclopedia*, vol. 1 (Santa Barbara, CA: ABC-CLIO, 2001), 311–12.

11. Ibid., 312.

12. Ibid., 311.

13. "Income Tax Battle Is On," *New-York Times*, March 7, 1895.

14. Vile, *Great American Lawyers*, vol. 1, 315.

15. Swaine, *Cravath Firm and Predecessors*, 520.

16. "Joseph Hodges Choate Dies Suddenly," *New York Times*, May 15, 1917.

17. "Joseph Hodges Choate Facts," https://biography.yourdictionary.com/joseph-hodges-choate, quoting Strong, *Joseph H. Choate*.

18. "Income Tax Battle Is On," *New-York Times*, March 7, 1895.

19. Melvin Urofsky, *The Supreme Court Justices: A Biographical Dictionary* (Abingdon, UK: Routledge, 1994), 255.

20. Swaine, *Cravath Firm and Predecessors*, 522.

21. William Dameron Guthrie, written argument in *Pollock v. Farmers' Loan & Trust Co.*, 157 U.S. 429.

22. "Income Tax Cases: In the Supreme Court of the United States," Guthrie argument, pages 46–47.

23. Ibid., 47.

24. Swaine, *Cravath Firm and Predecessors*, 524.

25. Vermont General Assembly, "Report of the Joint Special Committee to Investigate the Vt. Central Railroad," 1873, 374.

26. Swaine, *Cravath Firm and Predecessors*, 524–25.

27. "Income tax cases: In the Supreme Court of the United States," Olney argument.

28. Ibid., Whitney argument.

29. Swaine, *Cravath Firm and Predecessors*, 526–27.

30. "Income tax cases: In the Supreme Court of the United States," Carter argument, 61.

31. "Income tax cases: In the Supreme Court of the United States," Choate argument, 2–3.

32. Ibid., 82.

33. *Pollock v. Farmer's Loan & Trust Co.*, 157 U.S. 429 at 581 (1895).

34. Ibid., at 596–97.

35. "Edward Douglass White," CQ Press Supreme Court Collection, https://library.cqpress.com/.

36. *Pollock v. Farmers' Loan & Trust Co.*, 157 U.S. 429 at 646.

37. Ibid., at 654.

38. King, *Melville Weston Fuller*, 207.

39. Swaine, *Cravath Firm and Predecessors*, 532–34.

40. King, *Melville Weston Fuller*, 214.

41. Yarbrough, *Judicial Enigma*, 171.

42. *Pollock v. Farmers' Loan & Trust*, 158 U.S. 601.

43. Swaine, *Cravath Firm and Predecessors*, 526–27.
44. *Pollock v. Farmer's Loan & Trust*, 158 U.S. 601 at 641.
45. Ibid., at 671.
46. Ibid., at 672–73.
47. David G. Farrelly, "Justice Harlan's Dissent in the Pollock Case," *Southern California Law Review* 24 (1951): 177.
48. "Justice Harlan Dissent: He Is Very Emphatic in the Expression of His Views," *New-York Times*, May 21, 1895.
49. "The Whole Law Invalid," *New-York Tribune*, May 21, 1895.
50. John Marshall Harlan to James and John Maynard Harlan, May 24, 1895, as quoted in Farrelly, "Justice Harlan's Dissent in the Pollock Case," 180.
51. Ibid., 178–81.
52. See Magliocca, *The Tragedy of William Jennings Bryan*.
53. Swaine, *Cravath Firm and Predecessors*, 520.
54. "'Meudon,' the William Dameron Guthrie Estate," https://halfpuddinghalfsauce.blogspot.com/, February 20, 2015.
55. "History of Federal Income Tax Rates, 1913–2020," Bradford Tax Institute, https://bradfordtaxinstitute.com/.
56. "History of Lattingtown Harbor," village of Lattingtown, https://www.villageoflattingtown.org/.

CHAPTER 15: THE HUMBLEST AND MOST POWERFUL

1. "Between Heaven and Hell," *Cleveland Gazette*, May 2, 1891.
2. Ibid.
3. Hamilton County court records, cases 89553, 89554, 89556.
4. Greg Hand, "The Jinx of Robinson's Opera House," *Cincinnati*, July 16, 2018.
5. "Between Heaven and Hell," *Cleveland Gazette*, May 2, 1891.
6. Hamilton County court records, cases 89553, 89554, 89556.
7. Elizabeth Dowling Taylor, *Original Black Elite*.
8. Tim McNeese, *Plessy v. Ferguson: Separate but Equal*, Great Supreme Court Decisions (New York: Chelsea House, 2007), 43.
9. Ibid., 56.
10. Ibid. 57.
11. Rodolphe Lucien Desdunes, *Our People and Our History: Fifty Creole Portraits*, trans. and ed. Sister Dorothea Ogla McCants (Baton Rouge: Louisiana State University Press, 1973), 140–41.
12. Ibid.
13. "A Wealthy Negro's Suicide," *New-York Times*, May 16, 1893.
14. Ibid.
15. Ibid.
16. Luxenberg, *Separate*, 435.
17. Ibid.
18. "Raised the Color Line," *Washington Post*, February 16, 1892.
19. Blight, *Frederick Douglass*, 647.
20. "Booker T. Washington's Atlanta Compromise," http://historymatters.gmu.edu/d/39/.
21. Luxenberg, *Separate*, 435.

22. Michael Kent Curtis, "Albion Tourgée: Remembering Plessy's Lawyer on the 100th Anniversary of *Plessy v. Ferguson*," *Constitutional Commentary* 13, no. 187 (Summer 1996): 192.

23. Mark Elliott, *Color-Blind Justice: Albion Tourgée and the Quest for Racial Equality from the Civil War to Plessy v. Ferguson* (New York: Oxford University Press, 2006), 70–72, 78–85, 97–98.

24. Curtis, "Albion Tourgée," 189. (Curtis credits it to Olsen, *Carpetbagger's Crusade*.)

25. Ibid., 189–91.

26. Ibid., 194–99.

27. Elliot, *Color-Blind Justice*, 301.

28. Ibid., 306.

29. McNeese, *Plessy v. Ferguson*, 64.

30. Elliott, *Color-Blind Justice*, 307.

31. McNeese, *Plessy v. Ferguson*, 63.

32. Ibid., 67.

33. *Weekly Pelican*, September 3, 1887.

34. Ibid., September 10, 1887.

35. McNeese, *Plessy v. Ferguson*, 74.

36. Ibid., 70.

37. Ibid., 71.

38. Ibid., 86.

39. Ibid., 89.

40. Elliott, *Color-Blind Justice*, 310.

41. McNeese, *Plessy v. Ferguson*, 105.

42. Albion Tourgée, brief of plaintiff in error, *Plessy v. Ferguson*, October term, 1895, page 26.

43. Ibid., 14.

44. Ibid., 24.

45. Ibid., 19.

46. Ibid., 3, 8–9.

47. Ibid., 31.

48. Elliott, *Color-Blind Justice*, 310. (Before the case was heard, Tourgée counted only Harlan in his camp; nothing changed after the arguments.)

49. *Plessy v. Ferguson*, 163 US 537 at 550.

50. Ibid., at 543.

51. Henry Billings Brown biography, Federal Judicial Center, https://www.fjc.gov/history/judges/brown-henry-billings.

52. Luxenberg, *Separate*, 149–50.

53. See *Downes v. Bidwell*, 182 U.S. 244 (1901), and *Hawaii v. Mankichi* 190 U.S. 197 (1903).

54. *Plessy v. Ferguson*, 163 US 537 at 551.

55. Ibid., at 554–55.

56. Ibid., at 562.

57. Ibid., at 557.

58. Ibid., at 559.

59. Ibid., at 560–61.

60. Ibid., at 550.

61. Ibid., at 559.

62. "Three Louisiana Cases Decided," *Times Picayune* (New Orleans), May 19, 1896, 8.

63. "Supreme Court Decision," *Omaha Enterprise*, May 30, 1896.

64. "Justice Harlan in Favor of Civil Rights," *Omaha Enterprise*, June 30, 1896.

65. C. Vann Woodward, *The Strange Career of Jim Crow* (New York: Oxford University Press, 1955), 85.

66. Ibid.

CHAPTER 16: THE WALLS OF SEGREGATION

1. "The Jim Crow Car Case," *Cincinnati Enquirer*, May 19, 1896.

2. *New York Age*, March 28, 1891.

3. T. Thomas Fortune, "Black & White: Land, Labour, and Politics in the South, 1884," http://www.Blacksandpresidency.com/grovercleveland.php.

4. James Elbert Cutler, *Lynch-Law: An Investigation into the History of Lynching in the United States* (London: Longmans, Green, 1905).

5. Caitlin Dickerson, "Overlooked—Ida B. Wells," *New York Times* online, March 9, 2018, https://www.nytimes.com/interactive/2018/obituaries/overlooked-ida-b-wells.html.

6. "The Wet at Washington," *Louisville* (KY) *Courier-Journal*, April 28, 1889.

7. "From the Queen City," *Cleveland Gazette*, December 11, 1886.

8. "Colonel Robert Harlan's Birthday Reception—An Affair of the Highest Order," *Cleveland Gazette*, December 25, 1886.

9. Ibid.

10. *Cincinnati Enquirer*, May 18, 1893.

11. "To the Colored Voters—An Appeal to Them to Assert Their Manhood," *Cincinnati Enquirer*, October 27, 1889.

12. Robert Harlan, "The Negro in Politics," *Cincinnati Enquirer*, March 3, 1891.

13. "Not Downed," *Cincinnati Post*, July 14, 1891.

14. *Historic Times* (Lawrence, KS), September 5, 1891.

15. "Raised the Color Line," *Washington Post*, February 16, 1992.

16. Ibid.

17. Ibid.

18. Ibid.

19. "Black Men Appeal," *St. Paul Globe*, July 5, 1892.

20. "Bob Harlan's English Racing Venture—Gossip About Plays and Players," *Cincinnati Enquirer*, January 20, 1895.

21. Douglass, Frederick, Decoration Day Speech, 1894, http://www.thiscruelwar.com/frederick-douglass-decoration-day-speech-1894/.

22. Blight, *Frederick Douglass*, 753.

23. "Douglass Memorial," *Cincinnati Enquirer*, March 9, 1895.

24. "Col. Bob Harlan," *Piqua* (OH) *Daily Call*, June 18, 1896.

25. "St. Louis—How Afro-Americans at the Convention Fared," *Cleveland Gazette*, June 20, 1896.

26. "Eventful Life of Robert Harlan," 6.

27. Ibid.

28. "Robert Harlan Dead," *Louisville* (KY) *Courier-Journal*, September 22, 1897.

29. "Eventful Life of Robert Harlan," 6.

30. Ibid.

31. "Harlan Buried," *Cincinnati Post*, September 24, 1897; *Cincinnati Enquirer*, September 25, 1897.

32. Ibid.

33. Blackman, Frye, and McCloskey, "Justice John Marshall Harlan," 1078.

34. Ibid., 1084.

35. Ibid., 1087.

36. Malvina Shanklin Harlan, *Some Memories of a Long Life*, 117.

37. Blackman, Frye, and McCloskey, "Justice John Marshall Harlan," 1077.

38. Ibid.

39. Yarbrough, *Judicial Enigma*, 118–19.

40. Ibid., 197.

41. John Marshall Harlan to James S. Harlan, October 8, 1881, Harlan Papers, Library of Congress.

42. Malvina Shanklin Harlan, *Some Memories of a Long Life*, page 153.

43. Ibid., 154.

44. C. Ellen Connally, "Justice Harlan's 'Great Betrayal'? A Reconsideration of *Cumming v. Richmond County Board of Education*," *Journal of Supreme Court History* 25, no. 1 (March 2000): 75.

45. *Cumming v. Richmond County Board of Education*, 175 U.S. 528 (1899).

46. Connally, "Justice Harlan's 'Great Betrayal'?," 73.

47. Ibid., 77.

48. Ibid., 79.

49. Ibid., 82.

50. Ibid., 84.

51. *Cumming v. Richmond County Board of Education*, 175 U.S. 528 at 545.

52. *Berea College v. Kentucky*, 211 U.S. 45 (1908).

53. Connally, "Justice Harlan's 'Great Betrayal'?," 72.

54. *United States v. Wong Kim Ark*, 169 U.S. 649 (1898).

55. Ibid. at 650.

56. U.S. Constitution, Fourteenth Amendment.

57. *United States v. Wong Kim Ark*, 169 U.S. 649.

58. Ibid., at 724.

59. *Elk v. Wilkins*, 112 U.S. 94 (1884).

60. Ibid., at 122–23.

61. Blackman, Frye, and McCloskey, "Justice John Marshall Harlan," 1104.

62. Ibid., 1108.

63. Ibid.

64. Ibid., 1109.

CHAPTER 17: THE CONSTITUTION FOLLOWS THE FLAG

1. "Kahuku: Survival of a Plantation Town," Victoria Keith Productions, 1988 (documentary on YouTube).

2. "President Cleveland's Message About Hawaii December 18, 1893," http://www.let.rug.nl/usa/documents/1876-1900/president-clevelands-message-about-hawaii-december-18-1893.php.

3. "Hawaii Reports: Cases Determined in the Supreme Court of the State of Hawaii," Volume 12, 1900, 193–228.

4. Ibid.

5. Ibid.

6. Ibid.

7. Ibid.

8. *Hawaii v. Mankichi* 190 U.S. 197 (1903).

9. "Hawaii Reports: Cases Determined in the Supreme Court of the State of Hawaii," Volume 12, 1900, 228.

10. Kinzer, *The True Flag: Theodore Roosevelt, Mark Twain, and the Birth of American Empire*, 6.

11. Nasaw, *The Chief*, 126.

12. Ibid.

13. Ibid., 132.

14. Kinzer, *The True Flag*, 9.

15. Ibid.

16. Nasaw, *The Chief*, 125–26.

17. Roger D. Cunningham, "The Black 'Immune' Regiments in the Spanish-American War," National Museum of the United States Army, https://armyhistory.org/the-black-immune-regiments-in-the-spanish-american-war/.

18. United States Census Bureau, "Census of the Philippine Islands: Taken Under the Direction of the Philippine Commission in 1903," 1905.

19. United States Census Bureau: "Report on the Census of Porto Rico—1899."

20. United States Census Bureau data through demographia.com, http://www.demographia.com/db-state1900.htm.

21. Wikipedia, "List of countries by population in 1900."

22. Kinzer, *The True Flag*, 6.

23. Ibid.

24. Ibid., 10.

25. Ibid., 9.

26. Smith, *Civic Ideals*.

27. John Marshall Harlan, "James Wilson and the Formation of the Constitution," *American Law Review* 31 (July/August 1900): 481–504.

28. *DeLima v. Bidwell*, 181 U.S. 1 (1901).

29. *New York Times*, January 28, 1900, 4.

30. Finley Peter Dunne, "Mr. Dooley," syndicated comic strip, 1901.

31. H.R. Con. Res. no. 72, fifty-sixth Congress, second session.

32. "Gov. John William Griggs," National Governor's Association, nga.org/governor/john-william-griggs/.

33. Published transcript of oral arguments of *Goetze v. United States*, December 18, 1900, and January 10, 1901, 286.

34. Ibid., 333.

35. U.S. Constitution, Article 1, Section 9, Clause 8.

36. Published transcript of oral arguments of the Porto Rican Cases, Oral Argument of John K. Richards, Solicitor-General of the United States, January 9, 1901, 693.

37. Ibid., 694.

38. *Loughborough v. Blake*, 18 U.S. 317 (1820).

39. *Downes v. Bidwell*, 182 U.S. 244 at 374.

40. Ibid., at 376.

41. Ibid., at 377.

42. Ibid., at 379.
43. Ibid., at 181.
44. Ibid., at 182.
45. *Mankichi v. Hawaii*, 190 U.S. 193 (1903).
46. Ibid., at 211.
47. Ibid., at 215.
48. Ibid., at 236.
49. Ibid.
50. Ibid., at 240.
51. "Offices for Justices' Sons," *New York Times*, January 12, 1901.
52. "Harlan's Confirmation Blocked," *New York Times*, January 16, 1901.
53. Yarbrough, *Judicial Enigma*, 197.
54. James Shanklin Harlan to John Marshall Harlan, June 3, 1902, Harlan Papers, University of Louisville.
55. *Dorr v. United States*, 195 U.S. 138 (1904).
56. Ibid., at 155–56.
57. Ibid., at 154.
58. Yarbrough, *Judicial Enigma*, 129. (Harlan shares an apple on a streetcar with Justice McKenna.)
59. "Washington History," National Park Service, nps.gov, www.nps.gov/nr/travel/wash/dc36.htm.
60. Malvina Shanklin Harlan, *Some Memories of a Long Life*, 168.
61. Ibid.
62. "Dinner Given by the Bar of the Supreme Court of the United States to Mr. Justice John Marshall Harlan," publication of the Supreme Court, 1904, 81.
63. Ibid., 10–12.
64. Ibid.
65. Ibid., 31.
66. Ibid., 35.
67. Ibid.
68. Ibid., 30.

CHAPTER 18: FREEDOM IN THE WORKPLACE

1. Yarbrough, *Judicial Enigma*, 129.
2. U.S. Census Bureau https://www.census.gov/programs-surveys/decennial-census/decade.1830.html.
3. U.S. Census Bureau https://en.wikipedia.org/wiki/Urbanization_in_the_United_States.
4. Millhiser, *Injustices*, 84.
5. Ibid.
6. Ibid.
7. Ibid., 16.
8. Paul Kens, Lochner v. New York: *Economic Regulation on Trial* (Lawrence: University Press of Kansas, 1998), 9.
9. John Schudel, "Bakers and Their Struggles," *American Federationalist* 3–4, no. 7 (1896): 135.
10. Kens, Lochner v. New York, 28.

11. Ibid., 13.
12. *Lochner v. New York*, 198 U.S. 45 (1905).
13. Schudel, "Bakers," 135.
14. Kens, Lochner v. New York, 90.
15. David Bernstein, *Rehabilitating Lochner: Defending Individual Rights Against Progressive Reform* (Chicago: University of Chicago Press, 2011), 26.
16. "Lochner v. New York," Landmark Cases, C-SPAN, http://landmarkcases.c-span .org/Case/4/Lochner-v-New-York.
17. Ibid. (Lochner family photo.)
18. David E. Bernstein, "Lochner v. New York, *A Centennial Retrospective*," *Washington University Law Review* 83, no, 5 (2008): 1487 https://core.ac.uk/download/pdf /233178567.pdf.
19. Ibid., 90 http://landmarkcases.c-span.org/Case/4/Lochner-v-New-York (contract from 1896).
20. "Lochner v. New York," Landmark Cases, C-SPAN, http://landmarkcases.c-span .org/Case/4/Lochner-v-New-York (contract from 1896).
21. Kens, "Lochner v. New York," 90.
22. Bernstein, *Rehabilitating Lochner*, 29.
23. Ibid.
24. "United States Presidential Election of 1904," Britannica.com, https://www.britan nica.com/event/United-States-presidential-election-of-1904.
25. *People v. Lochner*, 177 N.Y. 145 at 165 (1904).
26. *The Slaughter-house Cases* 83 U.S. 36 (1873).
27. *Allgeyer v. Louisiana*, 165 U.S. 578 (1897) at 589.
28. Megan W. Benett, *The Judges of the New York Court of Appeals: A Biographical History* (New York: Fordham University Press, 2007).
29. Ibid.
30. Mary Ellen Johnson, "Altamont Nearly Became the Namesake of a Wealthy Supreme Court Justice," *Altamont* (NY) *Enterprise* online, last modified December 13, 2018, https://altamontenterprise.com/opinion/columns/glimpse-guilderland -history/12132018/altamont-nearly-became-namesake-wealthy-supreme.
31. Benett, *Judges of the New York Court of Appeals.*
32. *New-York Tribune*, May 1904.
33. Oliver Wendell Holmes Jr., *The Common Law* (Boston: Little, Brown, 1881).
34. Charles Evans Hughes, *The Autobiographical Notes of Charles Evans Hughes*, ed. David J. Danelski and Joseph S. Tulchin (Boston: Harvard University Press, 1973), 170–72.
35. Yarbrough, *Judicial Enigma*, 127.
36. Ibid., 126.
37. Ibid., 129.
38. Brad Snyder, "The House That Built Holmes," *Law and History Review* 30, no. 3 (August 2012): 667.
39. Bernstein, *Rehabilitating Lochner*, 30.
40. *The Labor Champion*, January 22, 1904.
41. Kens, "Lochner v. New York," 111–12.
42. Ibid., 53.
43. Ibid., 114.
44. Ibid., 115–16.

45. Ibid., 122.
46. *Holden v. Hardy*, 169 U.S. 366 (1898).
47. Ibid., at 398.
48. Kens, "Lochner v. New York," 127.
49. Ibid., 125.
50. Interview with University of Kentucky law professor Brian L. Frye, November 3, 2017, and draft of his working paper and research on the last-minute switch.
51. *Lochner v. New York*, 198 U.S. 45 (1905).
52. Ibid., at 53.
53. Ibid., at 57.
54. Ibid., at 59.
55. Ibid., at 64.
56. Ibid., at 68.
57. Ibid., at 69.
58. Ibid., at 72–73.
59. Ibid., at 73.
60. Ibid., at 75.
61. Kens, "Lochner v. New York," 144.
62. *Brooklyn Daily Eagle*, April 18, 1905.
63. "Court Kills Ten-Hour Law," *Buffalo Morning Express*, April 18, 1905, 2.

CHAPTER 19: "I AM A INNOCENT MAN"

1. "Johnson Hanged On Bridge With Rope From Trolley Car," *Chattanooga News*, March 20, 1906. For the Supreme Court's detailed accounting of the Johnson lynching, see Justice Melville Fuller's opinion in the 1909 decision holding Sheriff Ship and Chattanooga law enforcement officers in contempt of court for the murder. *United States v. Shipp*, 214 U.S. 386 (1909).
2. Testimony of Ellen Baker, Transcript of Record in *United States v. Shipp*, Docket No. Original No. 5, 252–254. National Archives, Washington, DC. Courtesy of Linda Duvoisin and Mariann Martin. In a newspaper account of her testimony in Chattanooga, Baker also recalls a member of the mob poking his gun through her cell bars and telling her to shut up. See "Moonshiner A Witness," *Chattanooga Times*, February 14, 1907.
3. "Johnson Hanged On Bridge With Rope From Trolley Car," *Chattanooga News*, March 20, 1906; "Walnut Street Bridge," *Historic Bridges*, https://historicbridges.org/bridges/browser/?bridgebrowser=tennessee/walnut/.
4. "Wheels of Justice Turn Fast in St. Elmo Assault Case," *Chattanooga Times*, January 28, 1906; "Johnson Says He's Innocent," *Nashville Banner*, February 1, 1906.
5. Noah W. Parden, "The Case of Ed Johnson," *Voice of the Negro* 3, no. 5 (1906): 361–63; "Wheels of Justice Turn Fast in St. Elmo Assault Case," *Chattanooga Times*, January 28, 1906; "Ed Johnsons Jury Stands 8 to 4 for Conviction," *Chattanooga News*, February 9, 1906.
6. "Now Up to Last Court," *Chattanooga Times*, March 16, 1906.
7. "Johnson Granted a Reprieve," *Chattanooga Times*, March 13, 1906.
8. "The Organization and How It Carried Out Its Purpose," *Chattanooga News*, March 20, 1906; "God Bless You All—I Am Innocent," *Chattanooga Times*, March 20, 1906.

9. "Johnson Hanged on Bridge With Rope From Trolley Car," *Chattanooga News*, March 10, 1906; "The Organization and How It Carried Out Its Purpose," *Chattanooga News*, March 20, 1906; "God Bless You All—I Am Innocent," *Chattanooga Times*, March 20, 1906; *United States v. Shipp*, 214 U.S. 386 (1909); Testimony of R. E. Prichard, Transcript of Record in *United States v. Shipp*, Docket No. Original No. 5, 779-783. National Archives, Washington, DC. Courtesy of Linda Duvoisin.

10. "Saucy Note for Justice Harlan," *Knoxville Sentinel*, March 26, 1906; "Negro Lynched by Chattanooga Mob," *Birmingham News*, March 20, 1906; Parden, "Case of Ed Johnson," 361–63.

11. Malvina Shanklin Harlan, *Some Memories of a Long Life*, 158.

12. Monk, Herbert L., "Only One of Noah W. Parden's 224 Murder Clients Has Been Put to Death," *St. Louis Globe-Democrat*, February 26, 1928, 3.

13. "The Chattanooga Case," *Boston Herald*, March 28, 1906. Contains a short letter from Hewlett attesting to his presence alongside Parden during the meeting with Justice Harlan. "A Colored Home-Coming," *Chattanooga Times*, October 16, 1906; Monk, "Only One of Noah W. Parden's 224 Murder Clients Has Been Put to Death," 3; "Career of Negro Lawyer Chosen Prosecutor's Aid," *St. Louis Post-Dispatch*, January 8, 1935.

14. "Awful Crime at St. Elmo," *Chattanooga Daily Times*, January 24, 1906; "Johnson's Trial is Progressing Rapidly," *Chattanooga News*, February 6, 1906. Contains lengthy testimony from Nevada Taylor about the night of her assault and her work with Sheriff Shipp afterward to find the culprit. Noah W. Parden, "The Case of Ed Johnson," *Voice of the Negro* 3:5 (1906): 361–363. For a brief biography of Shipp, see "The Sheriffs of Hamilton County: Sheriff Joseph F. Shipp, 1904–1908." Hamilton County Sheriff's Office, http://www.hcsheriff.gov/gen_info/past_sheriffs/joseph_shipp.asp.

15. "Brutal Crime of Negro Fiend," *Chattanooga News*, January 24, 1906.

16. "Black Brute Managed to Cover Up Tracks Well and No Trace of Him Has Yet Been Found," *Chattanooga Times*, January 25, 1906.

17. "Brutal Crime of Negro Fiend," *Chattanooga News*, January 24, 1906.

18. "J. F. Shipp Seeks an Indorsement for Sheriff," *Chattanooga Times*, January 26, 1906; H. M. Wiltse, "Stories of the Town," *Chattanooga News*, January 26, 1906.

19. "Negro Now in County Jail; Suspect of St. Elmo Crime," *Chattanooga News*, January 25, 1906.

20. "Johnson's Trial Is Progressing Rapidly," *Chattanooga News*, February 6, 1906.

21. "Wheels of Justice Turn Fast in St. Elmo Assault Case," *Chattanooga Times*, January 28, 1906; "Johnson's Trial Is Progressing Rapidly," *Chattanooga News*, February 6, 1906.

22. "Law and Order Victorious over Overwhelming Odds," *Chattanooga Times*, January 26, 1906; "Wheels of Justice Turn Fast in St. Elmo Assault Case," *Chattanooga Times*, January 28, 1906. Though McReynolds announced to the mob at the Chattanooga jailhouse that Johnson had been secreted to Knoxville, the prisoner was in fact imprisoned in Nashville. See *United States v. Shipp*, 214 U.S. 386 (1909).

23. "Law and Order Victorious," *Chattanooga Times*, January 26, 1906.

24. "Mob Foiled in Its Efforts," *Nashville Banner*, January 26, 1906; "The Part Played by Local Militia," *Chattanooga News*, January 26, 1906.

25. "A Fierce and Frenzied Mob Foiled by Brave and Determined Officers," *Chattanooga News*, January 26, 1906; "Wheels of Justice Turn Fast," *Chattanooga Times*, January 28, 1906.

26. "Law and Order Victorious," *Chattanooga Times*, January 26, 1906; *United States v. Shipp*, 214 U.S. 386 (1909). For more on Justice McReynolds, see "Biographies of Key Figures in Shipp Case: Judge Samuel McReynolds," *Famous Trials*, http://law2 .umkc.edu/faculty/projects/ftrials/shipp/mcreynolds.html.

27. "Suspect Arrested and Rushed to Knoxville," *Chattanooga Times*, January 26, 1906.

28. "Wheels of Justice Turn Fast," *Chattanooga Times*, January 28, 1906.

29. "Grasping at Last Straw," *Chattanooga Times*, March 7, 1906.

30. "Dramatic Incidents at Johnson's Trial," *Chattanooga News*, February 8, 1906; "Ed Johnson Jury Stands 8 to 4 for Conviction—Jurors Unable to Stand Terrible Nervous Strain," *Chattanooga Times*, February 9, 1906; "Supreme Court Shocked," *Chattanooga Times*, March 21, 1906; Parden, "Case of Ed Johnson," 361–63.

31. "Ed Johnson Jury Stands 8 to 4 for Conviction," *Chattanooga Times*, February 9, 1906; "The Jury Finds Ed Johnson Guilty; He Will Hang for His Fiendish Crime," *Chattanooga News*, February 9, 1906.

32. "Career of Negro Lawyer Chosen as Prosecutor's Aid," *St. Louis Dispatch*, January 8, 1935.

33. Monk, "Only One of Noah W. Parden's 224 Murder Clients Has Been Put to Death," 3.

34. "Justice Harlan Allows Appeal of Ed Johnson," *Chattanooga Times*, March 19, 1906; *United States v. Shipp*, 214 U.S. 386 (1909).

35. "Justice Harlan Allows Appeal of Ed Johnson," *Chattanooga Times*, March 19, 1906.

36. "The Johnson Case Again," *Chattanooga News*, March 19, 1906.

37. "Day of Doom Is Very Near," *Chattanooga Times*, March 18, 1906; "Justice Harlan Allows Appeal of Ed Johnson," *Chattanooga Times*, March 19, 1906.

38. Testimony of Joe Franklin, Transcript of Record in *United States v. Shipp*, Docket No. Original No. 5, 443-447. National Archives, Washington, DC. Courtesy of Linda Duvoisin.

39. *United States v. Shipp*, 214 U.S. 386 (1909).

40. "Johnson Hanged on Bridge With Rope From Trolley Car," *Chattanooga News*, March 20, 1906; "The Organization and How It Carried Out Its Purpose," *Chattanooga News*, March 20, 1906; "God Bless You All—I Am Innocent" *Chattanooga Times*, March 20, 1906; *United States v. Shipp*, 214 U.S. 386 (1909).

41. "Outraged Majesty of the Supreme Court Calls for Action," *Washington Times*, March 20, 1906; "Supreme Court Debates Steps Against Lynchers," *New York Times*, March 22, 1906; "Justice Harlan—Informed of Lynching of Ed Johnson and Comments on Action Taken By Supreme Court," *Chattanooga News*, March 20, 1906.

42. "Lynchings: By Year and Race," *Famous American Trials: The Trial of Joseph Shipp et al.*, http://law2.umkc.edu/faculty/projects/ftrials/shipp/lynchingyear.html. Statistics are drawn from the lynching archives of the Tuskegee Institute.

43. "The Sheriff's Race," *Chattanooga News*, July 18, 1906.

44. "Why Victory Was Gained," *Chattanooga Times*, August 7, 1906.

45. "To Arrest Lynchers," *Washington Post*, March 22, 1906.

46. "Washington Will Soon Be the Mecca for Chattanoogans," *Chattanooga News*, September 5, 1906; "May Employ Judge Harmon," *Chattanooga News*, September 14, 1906. For a brief biography of Judson Harmon, see "Judson Harmon," *Ohio History Connection*, https://ohiohistorycentral.org/w/Judson_Harmon.

47. *United States v. Shipp*, 203 U.S. 563 (1906).

48. Testimony of Joseph F. Shipp, Transcript of Record in *United States v. Shipp*, Docket No. Original No. 5, 1094-1109. National Archives, Washington, DC. Courtesy of Linda Duvoisin.

49. "Testimony of Ellen Baker," Famous American Trials: The Trial of Joseph Shipp, et al., http://law2.umkc.edu/faculty/projects/ftrials/shipp/bakertestimony.html.

50. "Testimony of Julia Wofford," Famous American Trials: The Trial of Joseph Shipp, et al., http://law2.umkc.edu/faculty/projects/ftrials/shipp/woffordtestimony.html. "I heard him say one day at the dinner table that if the execution would be stayed, Ed Johnson would be mobbed," Wofford said in her testimony.

51. *United States v. Shipp*, 214 U.S. 386 (1909); "Federal Intervention," *Chattanooga News*, May 29, 1906; "That Famous Interview," *Chattanooga Times*, February 14, 1907.

52. "Johnson Hanged on Bridge with Rope from Trolley Car," *Chattanooga News*, March 20, 1906. Contempt of Court page 313–14.

53. Testimony of Joseph F. Shipp, Transcript of Record in *United States v. Shipp*, Docket No. Original No. 5, 1120-1121. National Archives, Washington, DC. Courtesy of Linda Duvoisin.

54. *United States v. Shipp*, 214 U.S. 386 (1909); "The United States Supreme Court Will Punish the Lynchers of Chattanooga, Tenn.," *Broad Ax*, May 29, 1909; "Former Sheriff Shipp to Serve 90 Days in Prison," *Nashville Banner*, November 15, 1909.

55. "Trio of Prisoners Back Home Again," *Chattanooga News*, January 31, 1910.

56. "Honor Captain and Mrs. Shipp," *Chattanooga Times*, August 13, 1922.

57. "Lynching in America: Statistics, Information, Images: Lynching Statistics, by Year," *Famous Trials*, http://law2.umkc.edu/faculty/projects/ftrials/shipp/lynchingyear.html.

58. Mark Curriden and Leroy Phillips, *Contempt of Court: The Turn-of-the-Century Lynching That Launched 100 Years of Federalism* (New York: Faber and Faber, 1999), xvii.

CHAPTER 20: "EVER MAY HIS NAME BE SAID IN REVERENCE"

1. Richard H. Pildes, "Democracy, Anti-Democracy, and the Canon" (2000), University of Minnesota Law School, Minneapolis, MN, Constitutional Commentary 893: 301–2.

2. Ibid., at 303.

3. Ibid., 304; *Giles v. Harris*, 189 U.S. 475 at 485 (1903).

4. Ibid., at 486.

5. Ibid., at 488.

6. Ibid., at 488.

7. Ibid., at 504.

8. Samuel Brenner, "'Airbrushed Out of the Constitutional Canon': The Evolving Understanding of Giles v. Harris, 1903–1925," *Michigan Law Review*, 107: 853.

9. US Census Bureau, https://www.census.gov/content/dam/Census/library/working-papers/2002/demo/POP-twps0056.pdf; see also, Gabriel J. Chin and Randy Wagner, "The Tyranny of the Minority: Jim Crow and the Counter-Majoritarian Difficulty," Cambridge, MA, Harvard Civil Rights-Civil Liberties Law Review, Vol. 43, p. 65.

10. Baker v. Carr, 369 U.S. 186 (1962).

11. Malvina Shanklin Harlan, *Some Memories of a Long Life*, 174–75.

12. Ibid., 195–96.
13. Ibid., 183–85.
14. Ibid., family tree.
15. Ibid., 175.
16. Ibid., 189.
17. Yarbrough, *Judicial Enigma*, 212 (also in Harlan papers and Congressional record).
18. Yarbrough, *Judicial Enigma*, 213.
19. "Berea Early History," Berea College website, https://www.berea.edu/about/history/.
20. David E. Bernstein, "Plessy vs. Lochner: The Berea College Case" (working paper, George Mason University School of Law, Arlington, VA, January 2000), 4.
21. Ibid., 7 ("n----r" is spelled out in the original document).
22. Ibid., 8 ("n----r" is spelled out in the original document).
23. Ibid., 10.
24. *Berea v. Commonwealth* 123 Ky. 209, 94 S. W. 623 (1906), dissenting justice Henry Stites Barker.
25. Ibid.
26. *Berea College v. Kentucky*, 211 U.S. 45 (1908).
27. Ibid., at 53.
28. Ibid., at 58.
29. Ibid., at 56.
30. Ibid., at 61–62.
31. Ibid., at 67.
32. "Large Audience Attends Memorial Meeting in Church: Justice Harlan Called (Colored) People's Friend," Metropolitan A.M.E, article published by the church, 1995.
33. "Taft's Wilberforce," *Washington Bee*, March 19, 1910.
34. "Men of the Hour," *Colored American*, March 28, 1903. Notes that Robert James Harlan has opened a real estate law practice with a business partner, another Black man named R. R. Horner. Also notes that Robert Jr. is "well qualified, being a member of the bar in the State of Ohio and the District of Columbia."
35. "Taft's Great Speech," *Washington Bee*, March 19, 1910.
36. Doris Kearns Goodwin, *The Bully Pulpit: Theodore Roosevelt, William Howard Taft and the Golden Age of Journalism* (New York: Simon & Schuster, 2013), 582.
37. John's letter to his sons following the Pollock decision.
38. Beth, *John Marshall Harlan*, 180–81.
39. Ibid., 181.
40. Ibid., 182.
41. "Glimpses of Harlan, the Man," *Baltimore Sun*, October 14, 1911.
42. Goodwin, *The Bully Pulpit*, 442.
43. *United States v. E.C. Knight*, 156 U.S. 19 (1895).
44. *Swift & Co. v. United States*, 196 U.S. 375 (1905).
45. *Northern Securities Co. v. United States*, 193 U.S. 197 (1904).
46. *Standard Oil Co. of New Jersey v. United States*, 221 U.S. 1 at 2 (1911).
47. Ibid., at 82.
48. Ibid.
49. Malvina Shanklin Harlan, *Some Memories of a Long Life*, 197.
50. Ibid., 199.
51. Beth, *John Marshall Harlan*, 189, quoting an October 11, 1911, letter from J. E.

Hoover, the secretary of James Harlan, to Richard Harlan, detailing the justice's condition.

52. Ibid.

53. Malvina Shanklin Harlan, *Some Memories of a Long Life*, 163.

54. Ibid., 189, quoting letter from John Maynard Harlan to Augustus "Gus" Willson, October 13, 1911.

55. Ibid., 190.

56. Ibid., 200.

57. Ibid.

58. "Justice J. M. Harlan Dead," *Boston Globe*, October 14, 1911, 1, https://www.newspapers.com/image/431130955/?terms=%22Justice%2BJ.M.%2BHarlan%2BDead%22.

59. "Large Audience Attends Memorial Meeting in Church," Metropolitan AME Church, published 1995.

60. "Justice J. M. Harlan Dead," 1.

61. "Glimpses of Harlan, The Man," *Baltimore Sun*, October 14, 1911.

62. "John M. Harlan," *Louisville Courier-Journal*, October 15, 1911.

63. "Stories of Justice Harlan Related by Louisville Men," *Louisville Courier-Journal*, October 15, 1911.

64. "Glimpses of Harlan, The Man," *The Baltimore Sun*, October 14, 1911.

65. "Justice J. M. Harlan Dead," 1.

66. "Justice Harlan," *Washington Bee*, October 21, 1911.

67. *Cleveland Gazette*, October 21, 1911.

68. *Savannah* (GA) *Tribune*, October 21, 1911.

69. J. M. McInham, "Negro on Harlan—Colored Man Pays Tribute to Dead Justice Who Dealt Justly with His Race," *Lexington* (KY) *Leader*, October 17, 1911.

70. Ibid.

71. "Memorial Services in the Memory of the Late Justice John M. Harlan," *Chicago Broad Ax*, November 28, 1911.

72. "Negroes Honor Harlan," *Belleville News Democrat*, November 29, 1911.

73. "Boston Memorial to Harlan Projected by Boston Literary," *Iowa State Bystander*, November 17, 1911.

74. "Tribute to Harlan," *Lexington* (KY) *Leader*, October 19, 1911.

75. "Large Audience Attends Memorial Meeting in Church," Metropolitan AME, published in 1995.

76. Ibid.

77. Ibid.

78. Henry B. Brown, "The Dissenting Opinions of Mr. Justice Harlan," *American Law Review* 46 (May–June 1912), 321–52

79. Ibid., 15.

80. Ibid., 15–16.

81. Ibid., 32.

CHAPTER 21: SELF-INFLICTED WOUNDS

1. *United States v. E.C. Knight Co.*, 156 U.S. 1 (1895).

2. Ibid., at 18.

3. John Hibble, "Claus Spreckels in Aptos," *Aptos Life*, post September 1, 2017.

4. *United States v. American Tobacco*, 221 U.S. 106 (1911).

5. Goodwin, *The Bully Pulpit*, 667.

6. Ibid., 529.

7. Ibid.

8. Ibid., 667–68.

9. *United States v. United States Steel Corp.*, 251 U.S. 417 (1920).

10. Cordell Hull, *The Memoirs of Cordell Hull*, vol. 1 (New York: Macmillan, 1948), 48.

11. Ibid., 49.

12. Ibid.

13. John D. Buenker, *The Income Tax and the Progressive Era* (New York: Taylor & Francis, 1985), 54.

14. Cordell Hull, Speech to Congress March 29, 1909, Box 130, Reel 80, Cordell Hull Papers, Library of Congress.

15. *Pollock v. Farmers' Loan & Trust*, 158 U.S. 601 at 665 (1895).

16. Buenker, *Income Tax and the Progressive Era*, 63.

17. Ibid.

18. Joseph H. Choate, William D. Guthrie, et al., "Memorandum submitted to the Legislature of New York in opposition to the Amendment," April 11, 1910.

19. Internal Revenue Service, "Historical Highlights of the IRS," Revenue Act of 1913, Irs.gov.

20. Hull, *Memoirs of Cordell Hull*, vol. 1, 71.

21. Charles Evans Hughes, *The Supreme Court of the United States: Its Foundation, Methods and Achievements* (New York: Columbia University Press, 1928), 50

22. U.S. Bureau of Labor Statistics, 1933, average unemployment was 24.9 percent, as quoted in https://www.thebalance.com/unemployment-rate-by-year-3305506.

23. *United States v. Butler*, 297 U.S. 1 (1936).

24. *Schechter Poultry Corp. v. United States*, 295 U.S. 495 (1935).

25. Ibid. and *Adkins v. Children's Hospital*, 261 U.S. 525 (1923).

26. *Lochner v. New York*, 198 U.S. 45 at 69 (Harlan dissent).

27. Colin Gordon, "Growing Apart: A Political History of American Inequality," University of Southern California, http://scalar.usc.edu/works/growing-apart-a-political-history-of-american-inequality/sidebar-new-deal-minimum-wage-cases.

28. *Morehead v. New York ex rel. Tipaldo*, 298 U.S. 587 (1936).

29. Leuchtenberg, *The Supreme Court Reborn*, 168.

30. *Morehead v. New York ex rel. Tipaldo*, 298 U.S. 587 at 632.

31. Leuchtenburg, *The Supreme Court Reborn*, 134.

32. Roosevelt, Franklin Delano, Fireside Chat, March 9, 1937.

33. *West Coast Hotel Co. v. Parrish*, 300 U.S. 379 (1937).

34. Ibid.

35. Barry Friedman, *The Will of the People: How Public Opinion Has Influenced the Supreme Court and Shaped the Meaning of the Constitution* (New York: Farrar, Straus, and Giroux, 2009), 233.

36. Neal Devins, "Government Lawyers and the New Deal," *Columbia Law Review* 96, no. 1 (January 1996): 254.

37. *Steward Machine Co. v. Davis*, 301 U.S. 548 (1937).

38. *NLRB v. Jones & Loughlin Steel Corp.*, 301 U.S. 1 (1937)

39. Leuchtenburg, *The Supreme Court Reborn*, 230.

40. Clarence Thomas, Senate Confirmation Hearing Transcript, 1991, from R Street Senate Confirmation Hearing Database.

41. *Lochner v. New York*, 198 U.S. 45 at 73 (1905).

42. See Ackerman, *We the People*, and many others.

CHAPTER 22: "A VICARIOUS ATONEMENT"

1. Dick Lehr, "The Racist Legacy of Woodrow Wilson," *Atlantic*, November 27, 2015.

2. Elizabeth Dowling Taylor, *Original Black Elite*, 334–35.

3. Robert James Harlan to William Howard Taft, July 1, 1913, Taft Papers, Library of Congress.

4. Ibid., August 1, 1908.

5. "Give Them Hell!," *Cleveland Gazette*, June 1, 1935.

6. Robert James Harlan to William Howard Taft, July 3, 1917.

7. "Men of the Hour," *The Colored American*, March 28, 1903.

8. Hamilton County court records, cases 89553, 89554, 89556.

9. "Young Harlan Promoted," *The Colored American*, June 9, 1900.

10. "The Week in Society," *Washington Bee*, June 25, 1910.

11. "District Court News," *Washington Post*, December 16, 1916, 4.

12. Ibid.

13. "Colored Businessmen Thriving," *The Indianapolis Freeman*, June 19, 1915.

14. "Wagoner Sues Autoist," *Washington Herald*, March 3, 1921, 3; *Washington Post*, "Driver, Hurt, Asks $10,000," March 3, 1921, 2.

15. Robert Jackson Harlan Jr., interviewed by author, October 30, 2017, at his Washington home.

16. Robert Jackson Harlan Jr., interviewed by Adam Willis, February 2019, at his Washington home.

17. Ibid.

18. *Washington Evening Star*, September 26, 1953.

19. Ibid., May 2, 1953.

20. U.S. District Court for the District of Columbia, Probate record number 81,719, filed August 17, 1954.

21. Charles L. Zelden, *Thurgood Marshall: Race, Rights, and the Struggle for a More Perfect Union* (New York: Routledge, 2013), 14.

22. Mark Tushnet, *Making Civil Rights Law: Thurgood Marshall and the Supreme Court, 1956–1961* (New York: Oxford University Press, 1996), 415.

23. Ibid.

24. Zelden, *Thurgood Marshall*, 26.

25. Kofi Lomotey, "Murray v. Pearson," from Encyclopedia of African American Education, Volume 1, page 649.

26. Ibid. See also Zelden, *Thurgood Marshall*, 45.

27. *Missouri ex rel. Gaines v. Canada*, 305 U.S. 337 at 351 (1938).

28. Zelden, *Thurgood Marshall*, 14.

29. Constance Baker Motley, *Equal Justice Under Law: An Autobiography* (New York: Macmillan, 1965), 62.

30. Ibid.

31. Richard Kluger, *Simple Justice: The History of* Brown v. Board Education *and Black America's Struggle for Equality* (New York: Alfred A. Knopf, 1975), 287–88.

32. Constance Baker Motley, "Remembering Thurgood Marshall," *New York University Law Review* 68 (1993): 210.

33. Ibid.

34. Brief filed for *Sweatt v. Painter*, Library of Congress, NAACP Legal Defense and Education Fund Papers.
35. *Sweatt v. Painter*, 339 U.S. 631 (1950).
36. Tom C. Clark, memorandum in *Sweatt v. Painter*, as quoted in Tushnet, *Making Civil Rights Law*, 145.
37. Motley, *Equal Justice Under Law*, 102.
38. Ibid., 91.
39. Brief filed for *Brown v. Board of Education*, Library of Congress, NAACP Legal Defense and Education Fund. Papers.
40. Kluger, *Simple Justice*, 679.
41. *Brown v. Board of Education*, 347 U.S. 483 at 489.
42. Ibid., 493.
43. Ibid., 494–95.

CHAPTER 23: "JUSTICE HARLAN CONCURRING"

1. "Justice Harlan Concurring," *New York Times*, May 24, 1954, 10E.
2. See King, *Melville Weston Fuller*.
3. *Hurtado v. California*, 110 U.S. 516 at 557-558 (1884).
4. Edward F. Waite, "How 'Eccentric' Was Mr. Justice Harlan?," *Minnesota Law Review* 37 (1953): 173.
5. *Adamson v. California*, 332 U.S. 46 at 62 (1947).
6. *Pointer v. Texas*, 380 U.S. 400 (1965).
7. Tinsley E. Yarbrough, *John Marshall Harlan: Great Dissenter of the Warren Court* (New York: Oxford University Press, 1992), 87.
8. "Family Job," *New Yorker*, December 4, 1954, 40–41, as quoted in Yarbrough, "John Marshall Harlan," 88.
9. See Yarbrough, *John Marshall Harlan*, 63–69.
10. Ibid. 35.
11. "Aid for Harlan Family," *New York Times*, August 9, 1912.
12. Yarbrough, *John Marshall Harlan*, 36–40.
13. "Miss Laura Harlan," unsigned obituary, *New York Times*, January 18, 1949.
14. Yarbrough, *John Marshall Harlan*, 91–113.
15. See *Escobedo v. Illinois*, 378 U.S. 478 (1964) and *Miranda v. Arizona*, 384 U.S. 436 (1966).
16. Yarbrough, *John Marshall Harlan*, vii.
17. Canellos, *Last Lion*, 98.
18. *Heart of Atlanta Motel, Inc. v. United States*, 379 U.S. 241 (1964).
19. Ibid.
20. Ibid., 278 (Justice Douglas concurring) and 291 (Justice Goldberg concurring).
21. Ibid., 286.
22. *Civil Rights Cases of 1883*, 109 U.S. 3 at 61.
23. Thomsen, Global Issues: Women's Rights, 63.
24. *Regents of the University of California v. Bakke*, 438 U.S. 265 (1978).
25. Ibid., at 289–290.
26. Ibid., at 327.
27. Benjamin Hooks, "The U.S. Constitution Was Never Color-Blind," *New York Times*, November 27, 1985.
28. William Bradford Reynolds, "Racial Quotas Hurt Blacks and the Constitution," *New York Times*, December 9, 1985.

29. *City of Richmond v. J. A. Croson Co.*, 488 U.S. 469 (1989), Scalia opinion (page not available).

30. Thurgood Marshall, "A Colorblind Society Remains an Aspiration," speech delivered August 15, 1987, blackfacts.com.

31. Gabriel J. Chin, "The Plessy Myth: Justice Harlan and the Chinese Cases," *Iowa Law Review* 82 (1996): 151.

32. *Plessy v. Ferguson*, 163 U.S. 537 at 560.

33. *Chae Chan Ping v. United States*, 130 U.S. 581 (1889).

34. *United States v. Wong Kim Ark*, 169 U.S. 649 (1898).

35. James W. Gordon, "Was the First Justice Harlan Anti-Chinese?," *Western New England Law Review* 36, no. 3 (2014): 287, at p. 297.

36. Ibid.

37. Ibid., 322.

38. *Baldwin v. Franks*, 120 U.S. 678 (1887).

39. Blackman, Frye, and McCloskey, "Justice John Marshall Harlan," 1108.

40. Gabriel J. Chin, interviewed by author, June 2019, at University of California, Davis.

41. Kluger, *Simple Justice*, 81–83.

42. Ibid., 83.

43. Ibid.

44. "Biographies of the Robes," *The Supreme Court: The First Hundred Years*, thirteen .org/supremecourt/index.html.

45. Connally, "Justice Harlan's 'Great Betrayal'?," 72.

46. Ibid., 73 and 86.

47. See Juan R. Torruella, "The Insular Cases: The Establishment of a Regime of American Apartheid," *University of Pennsylvania Journal of International Law* 29, no. 2 (2014): 283, and Juan R. Torruella, "Ruling America's Colonies: The Insular Cases," *Yale Law and Policy Review* 32, no. 1 (2013): 56.

48. Torruella, "The Insular Cases," 315.

49. Antonin Scalia and Brian A. Garner, *Reading Law: The Interpretation of Legal Texts* (Saint Paul: Thompson/West, 2012), 191.

50. Hearing on the Nomination of the Hon. Neil M. Gorsuch to be an Associate Justice on the Supreme Court of the United States, Senate Judiciary Committee.

51. Neil Gorsuch, *A Republic, If You Can Keep It* (New York: Crown, 2019), 23–24.

52. Author interview with Amelia Newcomb, November 2020.

53. LaFrederick Thirkill, interviewed by author, February 8, 2020, in Chattanooga, Tennessee.

54. Ibid.; also interviews with Eleanor Cooper, Linda Duvoisin, Mariann Martin, and Susan Eckelmann, February 8–9, 2020.

55. U.S. National Park Service, National Register of Historic Places, npgallery.nps.gov.

56. Linda Duvoisin, interview with LeAnn Shipp, as related on February 9, 2020, in Chattanooga.

57. Thirkill, interviewed by author, February 8, 2020.

58. Ibid. The play is called *Dead Innocent: The Ed Johnson Story*.

59. Ibid.

60. Eleanor Cooper, interviewed by author on February 8, 2020, in Chattanooga.

61. Ibid.

62. Thirkill, interviewed by author, February 8, 2020.

63. Curtis L. Collier, interviewed by author, February 10, 2020, by telephone.

EPILOGUE: "OUR BASIC LEGAL CREED"

1. Louise Weinberg, "Holmes' Failure," *Michigan Law Review* 96, no. 3 (1997): 691–723.
2. Ibid., 722.
3. Ibid., 720.
4. U.S. Constitution, preamble.
5. Supreme Court record, provided by Robert Jackson Harlan Jr. on February 6, 2020.
6. Drew Pearson, "An Interesting Harlan Reunion," *Washington Post*, March 10, 1957.
7. Ibid.
8. John Marshall Harlan II to Robert Jackson Harlan, June 25, 1957. It notes returning the family scrapbook and discusses RJH's application to the United States Attorney's office.
9. Supreme Court records, provided by Robert Jackson Harlan Jr., February 6, 2020.
10. *Bolling v. Sharpe*, 347 U.S. 497 (1954).
11. Matt Schudel, "James M. Nabrit III, Civil Rights Lawyer, Dies at 80," *Washington Post*, March 26, 2013.
12. Robert Jackson Harlan Jr., interviewed by Adam Willis, February 2019.
13. "Harlan Retires from Post with FHWA Rights Office," *Washington Post*, October 16, 1976.
14. "House Hunter Encounters Racial Obstacles," *Washington Evening Star*, September 28, 1961.
15. Robert Jackson Harlan Jr., interviewed by author, February 2019.
16. Schudel, "James M. Nabrit III."
17. "DNA May Link U.S. Judge, Slave," *Louisville* (KY) *Courier-Journal*, March 19, 2000.
18. Associated Press, "DNA Tests Show No Link Between Justice, Ex-Slave," *Louisville* (KY) *Courier-Journal*, September 3, 2001.
19. Ibid.
20. Robert Jackson Harlan Jr., interviewed by Adam Willis, February 2019.
21. Ibid.
22. Michael Kranish, "Marshall Eulogized as 'Rock of Justice,'" *Boston Globe*, January 29, 1993.
23. Motley, "Thurgood Marshall Reminiscence," 208.
24. Ibid., at 210–11.

Bibliography

Ackerman, Bruce. *We the People.* Vol. 1, *Foundations.* Cambridge, MA: Harvard University Press, reprint edition, 1993.

Allen, William B. *A History of Kentucky.* Louisville, KY: Bradley & Gilbert, 1872.

Anbinder, Tyler. *Nativism and Slavery: The Northern Know Nothings and the Politics of Slavery.* New York: Oxford University Press, 1992.

Armstead, Myra B. Young. *Lord, Please Don't Take Me in August: African Americans in Newport and Saratoga Springs.* Champaign: University of Illinois Press, 1999.

Astor, Aaron. *Rebels on the Border: Civil War, Emancipation, and the Reconstruction of Kentucky and Missouri.* Baton Rouge: Louisiana State University Press, 2012.

Bartlett, Irving H. *John C. Calhoun: A Biography.* New York: W. W. Norton, 1994.

Bauer, K. Jack. *Zachary Taylor: Soldier, Planter, Statesman of the Old Southwest.* Rev. ed. Baton Rouge: Louisiana State University Press, 1993.

Belcher, Dennis W. *The 10th Kentucky Volunteer Infantry in the Civil War: A History and Roster.* Jefferson, NC: MacFarland, 2009.

Benett, Megan W. *The Judges of the New York Court of Appeals: A Biographical History.* New York: Fordham University Press, 2007.

Bernstein, David. *Rehabilitating Lochner: Defending Individual Rights Against Progressive Reform.* Chicago: University of Chicago Press, 2011.

Beth, Loren P. *John Marshall Harlan: The Last Whig Justice.* Lexington: University Press of Kentucky, 1992.

Blight, David. *Frederick Douglass: Prophet of Freedom.* New York: Simon & Schuster, 2018.

Boles, John B. *Religion in Antebellum Kentucky.* Lexington: University Press of Kentucky, 1995.

Brands, H. W. *The Age of Gold: The California Gold Rush and the New American Dream.* New York: Anchor Books, 2003.

Brown, Richard C. *A History of Danville and Boyle County Kentucky 1774–1992.* Danville, KY: Bicentennial Books, 1992.

Buenker, John D. *The Income Tax and the Progressive Era.* New York: Taylor & Francis, 1985.

Bush, Bryan S. *Butcher Burbridge: Union General Stephen Burbridge and His Reign of Terror over Kentucky.* Morley, MO: Acclaim Press, 2008.

Canellos, Peter S., ed. *Last Lion: The Fall and Rise of Ted Kennedy.* New York: Simon & Schuster, 2009.

Cannon, George Q. *A Review of the Decision of the Supreme Court of the United States, in the Case of Geo. Reynolds Vs. the United States.* Salt Lake City: Deseret News, 1879.

Chang, Iris. *The Chinese in America: A Narrative History.* New York: Penguin, 2003.

Chernow, Ron, *Grant*. New York: Penguin Press, 2017.

Claney, M. A. *Proceedings of the National Republican Convention Held at Cincinnati, Ohio*. Concord, NH: Republican Press Association, 1876.

Clark, Champ. *My Quarter Century of American Politics*. Vol. 1. New York: Harper & Brothers, 1920.

Coleman, J. Winston, Jr. *The Springs of Kentucky: An Account of the Famed Watering-Places of the Bluegrass State, 1800–1935*. Lexington, KY: Winburn Press, 1955.

Costello, Brian C. *History of Pointe Coupée, Louisiana*. Donaldsonville, LA: Margaret Media, 2010.

Coulter, E. Merton. *Civil War and Readjustment in Kentucky*. Chapel Hill: University of North Carolina Press, 2011. First published by Chapel Hill: University of North Carolina Press, 1926.

Curriden, Mark, and Leroy Phillips, *Contempt of Court: The Turn-of-the-Century Lynching That Launched 100 Years of Federalism*, New York: Faber and Faber, 1999.

Cutler, James Elbert. *Lynch-Law: An Investigation into the History of Lynching in the United States*. London: Longmans, Green, 1905.

Dabney, Wendell Phillips. *Cincinnati's Colored Citizens*. Cincinnati: Dabney, 1926.

Day, William. *The Racehorse in Training*. London: Chapman and Hall, 1885.

———. *Turf Celebrities I Have Known*. London: F. V. White, 1891.

Eisenhower, John S. D. *So Far from God*. New York: Random House, 1989.

———.*Zachary Taylor*, New York: Times Books, 2008.

Elliott, Mark *Color-Blind Justice: Albion Tourgée and the Quest for Racial Equality from the Civil War to Plessy v. Ferguson*. New York: Oxford University Press, 2006.

Etcheson, Nicole. *Bleeding Kansas: Contested Liberty in the Civil War Era*. Lawrence: University Press of Kansas, 2004.

Fackler, Calvin Morgan. *A Chronicle of the Old First: 1784–1944*. Cincinnati: Standard, 1946.

———. *Early Days in Danville*. Danville, KY: Danville and Boyle Historical Society, 1965.

Flayhart, William H., *The American Line (1871–1902)*, New York: W. W. Norton, 2000.

Foner, Eric. *Reconstruction: America's Unfinished Revolution, 1863–1877*. New York: Harper & Row, 1988.

Franklin, John Hope. *George Washington Williams: A Biography*. Durham, NC: Duke University Press, 1998. First published 1985 by University of Chicago Press (Chicago).

Freeman, Joanne. *The Field of Blood: Violence in Congress and the Road to Civil War*. New York: Farrar, Straus and Giroux, 2018.

Friedman, Barry. *The Will of the People: How Public Opinion Has Influenced the Supreme Court and Shaped the Meaning of the Constitution*. New York: Farrar, Straus, and Giroux, 2009.

Gatewood, Willard B. *Aristocrats of Color: The Black Elite, 1880–1920*. Bloomington: Indiana University Press, 1990.

Goodwin, Doris Kearns. *The Bully Pulpit: Theodore Roosevelt, William Howard Taft and the Golden Age of Journalism*. New York: Simon & Schuster, 2013.

———. *Team of Rivals: The Political Genius of Abraham Lincoln*. New York: Simon & Schuster, 2006.

Gorsuch, Neil. *A Republic, If You Can Keep It*. New York: Crown, 2019.

Greenberger, Scott S. *The Unexpected President: The Life and Times of Chester A. Arthur*. Boston: Da Capo Press, 2017.

Gresham, Matilda. *The Life of Walter Quintin Gresham, 1832–1895*. Vol. 2. Chicago: Rand McNally, 1919.

Harlan, Malvina Shanklin. *Some Memories of a Long Life: 1854–1911*. New York: Modern Library, 2003.

Harrison, Lowell H. *The Antislavery Movement in Kentucky*. Lexington: University Press of Kentucky, 1978.

Hedrick, U. P. *Manual of American Grape-Growing*. New York: Macmillan, 1919.

Heidler, David S., and Jeanne T. Heidler. *Henry Clay: The Essential American*. New York: Random House Trade Paperback, 2011.

Hobbs, Allyson. *A Chosen Exile: A History of Racial Passing in American Life*. Cambridge, MA: Harvard University Press, 2014.

Hollingsworth, Kent. *The Kentucky Thoroughbred*. Lexington: University Press of Kentucky, 2009.

Holmes, Oliver Wendell, Jr. *The Common Law*. Boston: Little, Brown, 1881.

Holt, Michael F. *Political Parties and American Political Development from the Age of Jackson to the Age of Lincoln*. Baton Rouge: Louisiana State University Press, 1992.

Hoogenboom, Ari. *Rutherford B. Hayes: Warrior and President*. Lawrence: University Press of Kansas, 1995.

Horne, Field. *The Saratoga Reader*. Syracuse, NY: Syracuse University Press, 2004.

Hotaling, Ed. *They're Off! Horse Racing at Saratoga*. Syracuse, NY: Syracuse University Press, 1995.

Howard, John R. *The Shifting Wind: The Supreme Court and Civil Rights from Reconstruction to Brown*. Albany: State University of New York Press, 1999.

Hughes, Charles Evans. *The Autobiographical Notes of Charles Evans Hughes*. Edited by David J. Danelski and Joseph S. Tulchin. Boston: Harvard University Press, 1973.

———. *The Supreme Court of the United States: Its Foundation, Methods and Achievements*. New York: Columbia University Press, 1928.

Hull, Cordell. *The Memoirs of Cordell Hull*. Vol. 1. New York: Macmillan, 1948.

James, Henry. *Richard Olney and His Public Service*. Boston: Houghton Mifflin, 1923.

Johnson, L. F. *A History of Franklin County*. Franklin, KY: Roberts, 1912.

Kenny, D. J. *Illustrated Cincinnati: A Pictorial Hand-Book of the Queen City*. Cincinnati: Robert Clarke, 1875.

Kens, Paul. *Justice Stephen Field: Shaping Liberty from the Gold Rush to the Gilded Age*. Lawrence: University of Kansas Press, 1997.

———. *Lochner v. New York: Economic Regulation on Trial*. Lawrence: University Press of Kansas, 1998.

Kent, Charles A. *Memoir of Henry Billings Brown: Late Justice of the Supreme Court of the United States Consisting of an Autobiographical Sketch with Additions to His Life*. New York: Duffield, 1915.

King, Willard L. *Melville Weston Fuller: Chief Justice of the United States, 1888–1910*. New York: Macmillan, 1950.

Kinzer, Stephen. *The True Flag: Theodore Roosevelt, Mark Twain, and the Birth of American Empire*. New York: Henry Holt, 2017.

Klotter, James C. *Kentucky Justice, Southern Honor, and American Manhood: Understanding the Life of Richard Reid*. Baton Rouge: Louisiana State University Press, 2003.

Klotter, James C., and Daniel Rowland, eds. *Bluegrass Renaissance: The History and Culture of Central Kentucky, 1792–1852*. Lexington: University Press of Kentucky, 2012.

Kluger, Richard. *Simple Justice: The History of Brown v. Board Education and Black America's Struggle for Equality*. New York: Alfred A. Knopf, 1975.

Lane, Charles. *The Day Freedom Died: The Colfax Massacre, the Supreme Court, and the Betrayal of Reconstruction*. New York: Henry Holt, 2008.

Latham, Frank. *The Great Dissenter: Supreme Court Justice John Marshall Harlan (1833–1911)*. Spokane, WA: Cowles Books, 1970.

Leuchtenberg, William E. *The Supreme Court Reborn: The Constitutional Revolution in the Age of Roosevelt*. New York: Oxford University Press, 1995.

Longrigg, Roger. *The History of Horse Racing*. New York: Stein and Day, 1972.

Lucas, Marion B. *A History of Blacks in Kentucky: From Slavery to Segregation, 1760–1891*. Frankfort, KY: Kentucky Historical Society, 1992.

Luxenberg, Steve, *Separate: The Story of* Plessy v. Ferguson, *and America's Journey from Slavery to Segregation*. New York: W. W. Norton, 2019.

Mason, Kathryn Harrod. *James Harrod of Kentucky*. Baton Rouge: Louisiana State University Press, 1951.

McFeely, William S. *Frederick Douglass*. New York: Simon & Schuster, 1991.

McPherson, James M. *Battle Cry of Freedom: The Civil War Era*. New York: Oxford University Press, 1988.

Meacham, Jon. *American Lion: Andrew Jackson in the White House*. New York: Random House, 2009.

Millhiser, Ian. *Injustices: The Supreme Court's History of Comforting the Comfortable and Afflicting the Afflicted*. New York: Nation Books, 2015.

Mooney, Katherine C. *Race Horse Men: How Slavery and Freedom Were Made at the Racetrack*. Boston: Harvard University Press, 2014.

Motley, Constance Baker. *Equal Justice Under Law: An Autobiography*. New York: Macmillan, 1965.

Muller, Gilbert H. *William Cullen Bryant: Author of America*. Albany: State University of New York, 2008.

Murray-Wooley, Carolyn. *Early Stone Houses of Kentucky*. Lexington: University Press of Kentucky, 2008.

Nasaw, David. *The Chief: The Life of William Randolph Hearst*. New York: Mariner Books, 2001.

Palmer, George Thomas. *A Conscientious Turncoat: The Story of John M. Palmer, 1817–1900*. New Haven, CT: Yale University Press, 1941.

Phillips, Christopher. *The Rivers Ran Backward*. New York: Oxford University Press, 2016.

Paul, Joel Richard. *Without Precedent: John Marshall and His Times*. New York: Riverhead Books, 2018.

Prichard, James M. *Embattled Capital: Frankfort Kentucky in the Civil War*. Frankfort, KY: Frankfort Heritage Press, 2014.

Przybyszewski, Linda. *The Republic According to John Marshall Harlan*. Chapel Hill: University of North Carolina Press, 1999.

Rayback, Robert J. *Millard Fillmore: Biography of a President*. Self-published, 2017.

Robinson, Lloyd. *The Stolen Election: Hayes Versus Tilden—1876*. New York: Forge, 2001.

Scalia, Antonin, and Brian A. Garner. *Reading Law: The Interpretation of Legal Texts*. Saint Paul: Thompson/West, 2012.

Sears, Stephen W. *George B. McClellan: The Young Napoleon*. Boston: Ticknor & Fields, 1989.

Simmons, William J. *Men of Mark: Eminent, Progressive, and Rising*. Cleveland: Geo M. Rewell, 1887.

Smith, Charles W. *Roger B. Taney: Jacksonian Jurist*. Chapel Hill: University of North Carolina Press, 1936.

Smith, Jean Edward. *Grant*. New York: Simon & Schuster, 2001.

Smith, Rogers M. *Civic Ideals: Conflicting Visions of Citizenship in US History*. New Haven, CT: Yale University Press, 1997.

Speed, Thomas. *The Union Cause in Kentucky*. New York: G. P. Putnam's Sons, 1907.

Swaine, Robert T. *The Cravath Firm and Its Predecessors: 1819–1947*. Self-published. New York: Ad Press, 1948.

Swisher, Carl Brent. *Roger B. Taney*. New York: Macmillan, 1935.

Tapp, Hambleton, and James C. Klotter. *Kentucky: Decades of Discord, 1865–1900*. Lexington: University Press of Kentucky, 1977.

Taylor, Elizabeth Dowling. *The Original Black Elite: Daniel Murray and the Story of a Forgotten Era*. New York: Amistad, 2017.

Taylor, Nikki M. *America's First Black Socialist: The Radical Life of Peter H. Clark*. Lexington: University Press of Kentucky, 2012.

———. *Frontiers of Freedom: Cincinnati's Black Community, 1802–1869*. Athens: Ohio University Press, 2005.

Thomsen, Natasha. *Global Issues: Women's Rights*. New York: Infobase, 2010.

Tushnet, Mark. *Making Civil Rights Law: Thurgood Marshall and the Supreme Court, 1956–1961*. New York: Oxford University Press, 1996.

Urofsky, Melvin. (editor) *The Supreme Court Justices: A Biographical Dictionary*, Abingdon, U.K., Routledge, 1994.

———. *Dissent and the Supreme Court*. New York: Vintage Books, 2017.

Wall, Maryjean. *How Kentucky Became Southern: A Tale of Outlaws, Horse Thieves, Gamblers, and Breeders*. Lexington: University Press of Kentucky, 2010.

Walsh, J. H. *The Horse in the Stable and the Field*. London: G. Rutledge and Sons, 1907.

Wasniewski, Matthew. *Black Americans in Congress, 1870–2007*. Washington, DC: US House of Representatives, 2008.

Webb, Ross A. *Benjamin Helm Bristow: Border State Politician*. Lawrence: University Press of Kansas, 1969.

White, Richard. *The Republic for Which It Stands: The United States During Reconstruction and the Gilded Age, 1865–1896*. Oxford, MS: Oxford University Press, 2017.

Williams, T. Harry. *Lincoln and His Generals*. New York: Vintage Civil War Library, 2011.

Woodward, C. Vann, *The Strange Career of Jim Crow*, New York: Oxford University Press, 1955.

Wright, George C. *Racial Violence in Kentucky, 1865–1940: Lynchings, Mob Rule, and "Legal Lynchings."* Baton Rouge: Louisiana State University Press, 1990.

Yarbrough, Tinsley E. *John Marshall Harlan: Great Dissenter of the Warren Court*. New York: Oxford University Press, 1992.

———. *Judicial Engima: The First Justice Harlan*. New York: Oxford University Press, 1995.

Young, John C. *Scriptural Duties of Masters—A Sermon*. Boston: American Tract Society, 1846.

Zelden, Charles L. *Thurgood Marshall: Race, Rights, and the Struggle for a More Perfect Union*. New York: Routledge, 2013.

Index

Page numbers beginning with 503 refer to notes.

Photo Credits

INSERT 1

1. Library of Congress
2. Kentucky Historical Society
3. Kentucky Historical Society
4. Library of Congress
5. New York Public Library
6. Courtesy Harlan Family
7. Portrait by Matthew Harris Jouett, 1818 (credit: Wikimedia Commons)
8. Library of Congress
9. Library of Congress
10. Wikimedia Commons Public Domain
11. Wikimedia Commons Public Domain
12. New York Public Library Digital Collections
13. Courtesy of Gina Ruffin Moore
14. Speed Art Museum
15. Old Newmarket
16. Adam Willis
17. Library of Congress
18. O. S. B. Wall in Joseph T. Wilson's *The Black Phalanx: A History of the Negro*
19. Creative Commons
20. Library of Congress
21. US Supreme Court

INSERT 2

1. Museum of the City of New York
2. Library of Congress
3. New York Public Library Digital Collections
4. Wikimedia Commons Public Domain
5. Library of Congress
6. California State Library
7. Wikimedia Commons Public Domain
8. Newspapers.com
9. Wikimedia Commons Public Domain
10. Josh Blackman
11. Courtesy Robert Jackson Harlan Jr.
12. Library of Congress, Manuscript Division, the Frederick Douglass Papers at the Library of Congress
13. Newspapers.com
14. Library of Congress
15. Library of Congress
16. Library of Congress
17. National Archives
18. Library of Congress
19. *New York World-Telegram and Sun* Photograph Collection—Library of Congress
20. Collection of the Supreme Court of the United States
21. Collection of the Supreme Court of the United States

About the Author

Peter S. Canellos is a longtime senior editor for *Politico* and formerly the *Boston Globe*, where he served as Washington Bureau Chief and Editorial Page Editor and oversaw two Pulitzer Prize–winning projects and seven Pulitzer finalists. At *Politico*, he is currently Managing Editor for Enterprise, responsible for all investigative and magazine coverage. He is also an award-winning writer and editor of *Last Lion: The Fall and Rise of Ted Kennedy*, which was a top-ten *New York Times* bestseller.

A graduate of the University of Pennsylvania and Columbia Law School, he has spent much of his career furthering the development of young writers. He is a lead organizer of the IWMF/Elizabeth Neuffer fellowship program at the International Women's Media Foundation.

He lives in Washington, D.C., and Great Barrington, Massachusetts. Visit www.peterscanellos.com.